DATE DUE

FORTRESS
CALIFORNIA
1910–1961

FORTRESS CALIFORNIA 1910–1961

························

From Warfare to Welfare

ROGER W. LOTCHIN

New York   Oxford
OXFORD UNIVERSITY PRESS
1992

ersity Press

ork   Toronto
tta   Madras   Karachi
Petaling Jaya   Singapore   Hong Kong   Tokyo
Nairobi   Dar es Salaam   Cape Town
Melbourne   Auckland

and associated companies in
Berlin   Ibadan

Copyright © 1992 by Oxford University Press, Inc.

Published by Oxford University Press, Inc.,
200 Madison Avenue, New York, New York 10016

Oxford is a registered trademark of Oxford University Press

Library of Congress Cataloging-in-Publication Data
Lotchin, Roger W.
Fortress California, 1910–1961 : from warfare to welfare /
Roger W. Lotchin.
p.   cm.   Includes bibliographical references and index.
ISBM 0-19-504779-6
1. Defense industries—California—History—20th century.
2. United States—Armed Forces—California—History—20th century.
3. Military bases—Economic aspects—California—History—20th
century.   4. Military-industrial complex—California—History—20th
century.   5. Cities and towns—California—Growth—History—20th
century.   6. California—Economic conditions.   I. Title.
HD9743.U7C25   1992   338.4'76233'09796—dc20   91-21408

2 4 6 8 9 7 5 3 1

Printed in the United States of America
on acid-free paper

This book is dedicated with appreciation to Shelbyville, the prettiest town in the Illinois country, and to my teachers and friends at Shelby Unit District Number Four: Dave Anderson, Norman Arnold, G. W. Bedell, Prentice Cole, Ralph Cox, Lucile Dintelman, May Douthit, Carroll "Red" Endsley, U. L. Evans, Carl and Cleora Finley, Clarissa Flenniken, Clara Fox, Miriam Herron, Lucille Kelley, Beulah Knecht, Howard Lester, Joe McAdam, O. H. McNelly, Ray V. Manessier, Arthur Muns, Leon Poynter, Virginia Price, Harold Redicks, Fred Reed, Bob Rowe, Nellie Row, Ned Schrom, June Sporleder, and Ruth Thomas. By any measure, their service to education has been outstanding.

Preface

I have written this book with one special end in view—to diversify the approach of urban and other historians to their subject matter. The field of urban history has always been a lively one, punctuated by various controversies. In large measure these arguments have centered on questions of methodology and interpretation. The recent Chicago Historical Society Conference on "Modes of Inquiry for American City History" serves as a typical example. I have no quarrel with either of these approaches. Yet I remain convinced that most of the progress in the discipline of urban history in the last three decades has been achieved through topical diversification into new or relatively uncharted areas, regardless of methodological or conceptual-theoretical orientation. In addition, I regard nearly all of these methods and theories as eminently legitimate; and so I have little interest in joining in the controversies about them. Although I have proposed a new interpretation of urban history, I have not tried to give it "interpretive hegemony" beyond the field of my own inquiry. For those who believe that a new interpretive paradigm is the panacea for the discontents of urban historians, I have no argument. Let us have the paradigms, and we will see if they can be substantiated through testing. I have been more interested in creating a new topical frontier for the field than in finding a methodological or theoretical orientation that would dominate the thinking of urban historians in the manner that the frontier thesis or the consensus school once dominated the field of American history.

Rather, I have insisted in this book on the importance of the relationship of war and defense on the one hand and urbanization and urbanism on the other. For several thousand years, war and urbanization have been outstanding features of civilized societies. And in the twentieth century, they are even more so, since both are hyperdeveloped. Moreover, war and urbanization have been consistently more important than many of the other influences that historians often stress. Industrialism was once the great panacea for city boosters and later for historians in search of interpretive lift. Still, the era of industrialism is long gone and we are now supposedly in an epoch of post-industrialism. Likewise labor has waxed and waned over the years, peaking in the years between 1933 and 1960 and now declining. Even Marxist historians write of the decline of class consciousness since the Great Depression. Racial, religious, sexual, and ethnocultural bias have gone the way of industry and unions, although not into such pronounced decline. The United States has long since lost its frontier character, and to give but one more example, there is reason to hope that the Cold War is over. All these supposedly constant influences on American society have come and gone, substantially declined, or fluctuated wildly. Yet cities and war have not. Throughout the twentieth century cities have grown (as metropolitan areas more recently rather than center cities), wars have recurred, and defense, with the exception of the period 1919–33, has continued to exert an extraordinary influence.

In short, the importance of war and urbanization have been much more unchanging than *many* of the current or past emphases in the field of American history. Yet historians have paid scant attention to these two consistently crucial facts of historical evolution in relationship to each other. My purpose in writing this book was to end this neglect and to encourage others to take up the idea as well. If I succeed in this effort, there will be ample room for methodological and theoretical approaches once the subject has been legitimized. In fact, I have tried in a modest way to suggest some of the theoretical approaches in the course of attempting to fill this crucial gap in the literature. As in any pioneering work, most of these theories are still hypotheses, but many of them are substantially documented. There are plenty of historians out there who will be happy to test them further.

Chapel Hill, North Carolina　　　　　　　　　　　　　　　　　　R.W.L.
May 1991

Acknowledgments

Like all scholars, I owe debts of gratitude to many more persons than I can acknowledge. That is especially true of the many men and women who have preceded me in the field of history and whose works I have endlessly drawn upon. I am also especially indebted to my colleagues in the field who read all or parts of the manuscript: Terrence McDonald, David Johnson, and Jim Leloudis. I owe an an equal debt to many research libraries. The Huntington Library granted me a fellowship and several trips to their priceless holdings; the Bancroft Library, as usual, was wonderfully helpful. Although it is somewhat off the beaten path of historians, the Library of the Institute for Governmental Studies at the University of California also has an exceptionally rich urban history collection and a remarkably generous and graceful staff.

I received help from the Southern Historical Collection at UNC, from many other branches of the Davis Graduate Library there, especially the microform reading room, the general circulation desk, the Map Collection, the Humanities Reference Department, and above all the Business and Social Sciences Department. Ridley Kessler and his staff at BASS not only preside over an outstanding collection, but went way out of their way to make even the most obscure materials available to me. The Institute for Research in the Social Sciences was equally constructive.

All told, I worked many months at the National Archives, the Library of Congress, the San Diego Historical Society, the Archives Department at San Diego State University, the Special Collections Department and the Library for Intergovernmental Studies at UCLA, the Special Collections Department of the Claremont Colleges Library, the Stanford University Special Collections Department, the Special Collections Department of the Occidental College Library, and the University of San Francisco Library. All were more than helpful, and Murny Gerlach of San Diego State and Rick Crawford of the San Diego Historical Society were especially so. I owe an equal debt to the many urban historians who have suffered through this project with me. Their names would fill an entire chapter. Larry Stillman, David Long, and Maria Karres drew the indispensable maps, without which the idea of the metropolitan-military complex could not have been rendered visible. In addition, the manuscript was expertly typed and edited by my secretary Eunice Hernandez, with help from Mattie Hackney and Pamela Fesmire. Without their assistance the project would have collapsed. Several graduate or undergraduate research assistants were equally constructive, including Dana Leder, Annette Cox, and Bill Moye. As usual, Sheldon Meyer of Oxford University Press has been extremely patient, sensitive, and thoughtful in handling an author's dilemmas, and manuscript editors Stephanie Sakson-Ford and Scott Lenz have been most helpful. Special thanks are due to my classmates Carol Beam Smith and Barbara Walk Tice, who managed to straighten out the dedication for me, and to Michael Crane of I.R.S.S., who helped computerize the index. Finally, I owe my greatest debt to my wife, who helped me on every phase of the book and shared my research trips and ideas, and to my son, who let himself be dragged all over the country as though these scholarly journeys were as important as tennis, girls, piano, and French II.

Contents

·······························

Introduction

The city and the sword have been partners from time immemorial, for as long as there have been cities and war. Yet until recently, few have tried to narrate and analyze their essential relationship. Perhaps there is none. Given the magnitude of change over a span of several millennia, the association of the city and the sword may have been ad hoc and ephemeral and therefore incapable of codification. Possibly each era of warfare and urbanization-urbanism[2] featured a different connection between the two. Perhaps not. In any case, it is high time that we attempt to find out. Urbanization and militarization have been central features of all civilized life in the Western world. Sometimes they have been more important and sometimes less, but both have always been significant. Many authors have written about one or the other, especially warfare. We have learned treatises on the principles of warfare; on land, sea, and air war; on military conflict in different epochs; on civil-military relations; on militarism; on martial technology; on the great captains; on the science of supply; in short, on almost every conceivable aspect of armed conflict.[3]

Although the literature of urban history is not as complete as that about war, it too covers most topics, eras, and nations. American urban history has been especially rich, and each edition of the *Urban History Review* reminds us of how completely we have encompassed the field.[4] Some of these studies treat military matters, but none makes the association of the city and the sword over a long period of time a central feature of its analysis. This is a curious omission, since wars have had such a dramatic impact on American cities. Whether one is looking at the racial and ethnic riots of the Civil and First World wars, the strategy of the American Revolution, the prosperity of the Second World War, or the polarization of the Vietnam War, the phenomenon of armed conflict has obviously influenced urbanization and urbanism.[5]

There is also an extensive "war and" category which includes books about battles in cities, but virtually nothing about the generic subject of war and cities. One can read of sexual theories of war causation; the thoughts of Voltaire, George Washington, Thomas Jefferson, Benjamin Franklin, Clausewitz, Sigmund Freud, Bertrand Russell, and Jean-Paul Sartre on war; war as a social, anthropological, psychological, philosophical, and historical phenomenon; war and children; war and women; war and capitalism; war and socialism; war in primitive and modern societies; war and agriculture; how to fight wars or end them; war, sadism, and pacifism; war poetry; war literature; war correspondents' literature; war and disease; war and generations; war and Darwinian evolution; and so forth. Niccolo Machiavelli has explained the art of war, Albert Einstein has theorized about its causation, and Ernest Hemingway has compiled the best stories about it. There is a Guinness book of land warfare, though hopefully not a book of World War records, and even books on war and animals. There is an absolutely staggering, mind-boggling literature of this sort, yet astonishingly little about war and the cities, where most *humans* in Western civilization live.[6]

Yet cities have been crucial to war. In the Second World War, for example, American soldiers bombed Berlin in planes manufactured in Los Angeles, attacked the Pacific islands in landing craft curiously enough fabricated in Denver, fought Rommel in tanks produced in Detroit, crossed the oceans in Liberty ships constructed on San Francisco Bay, loaded their ships from a Norfolk dock, threw their farewell parties in a Charleston bar, fought for housing in a San Diego neighborhood, saw their first exotic person in San Francisco's Chinatown, kissed their wives and sweethearts goodbye from a New York City pier, slept in their cars on a Brooklyn street, sampled the night spots and sometimes the jails of Jacksonville, eternally rumbled over and under the streets on the trolleys and subways and pavements of scores of towns, and rioted with the San Francisco police to celebrate the ending of their ordeal. From a strategic perspective, the city was at least equally important. Military efforts against cities created several turning points in the conflict. The Blitz of London in 1940 crippled the German effort to reduce British air power, and the Battle of Stalingrad provided the turning point on the eastern front. Most of the air war was waged against cities; and although that effort did not produce a decisive effect in Europe, it certainly did in the Far East.[7] In short, the war touched the city at every turn, and the city in turn touched the warriors back. It was the same in most American conflicts and in every one since the Civil War. Thus, there is a gap in the literature of both war and urbanization and above all at the linkage point between the two.

With certain exceptions such as Neil Wynn, American historians have even failed to follow the lead of Europeanists in investigating the related but different topic of war and society. And despite the fact that cities are increasingly becoming synonymous with "society," even the European students of war and society seldom analyze this subject from an urban perspective. Yet this topic fairly cries out for analysis because of the central place of cities in war and the dominant place of martial strife in the twentieth century. The city should long ago have become an important category of thought on war and society. At this moment, the hiatuses in these otherwise remarkably well-researched fields cannot be explained, but it is not impossible to begin to fill them. It is the purpose of this book to discuss this urban and military relationship.[8]

The Golden State is an ideal place to begin the investigation. California is one of the most completely urbanized units in the United States. In 1980, 91 percent of the population was classified as urban, so that the city and "society," the analytical category preferred by the war and society literature, are virtually coterminous. At the same time, it is one of the states most heavily dependent upon military spending. This has been the case for many years, not just since the Second World War. California is usually considered the most important American example of the interface between business, government, the military, politicians, and scientists. Much has been written about the more recent history of this military-industrial alliance, but as yet its origins have not been carefully explored. With the exception of the work of Benjamin F. Cooling, Peter Hall, Paul Koistinen, and Ann Markusen, American historians in general have also slighted the historic origins of the broad phenomenon known as the "military-industrial complex." This book will attempt both of these tasks and in the process try to provide a fresh perspective.

In his farewell address in 1961, President Dwight Eisenhower called attention to the ominous partnership between civilian, government, and military elements, which he termed the "military-industrial complex." This was not the first time the President had warned of this menace, but this was the warning that stuck in the minds of press and public and the one that has come to characterize this civil-military relationship. However apt the phrase might have been as a way to educate the public, it oversimplified the matter in several important ways. Ike described a monolith, whereas the nature of the military-industrial complex was much more pluralistic. He stressed the military partnership with industry, thus neglecting everything else. He conveyed a sense of "we" and "they," which has characterized discourse about the relationship ever since. The President also implied that the origins of the military-industrial complex were relatively recent, and he gave the impression that the complex was made up only of the rich and powerful, as opposed to the common people. Ike was correct that a relatively powerful alliance had grown up between the civil and military sectors in the United States, but the term and its accompanying explanation implied a number of fundamental misapprehensions.

In California, where war and urban society are both hyperextended, the connection between these two entities did not originate through the World War II or Cold War actions of bureaucrats of the modern nation-state or through defense giants such as Boeing, Rockwell International, Lockheed, General Electric, McDonnell-Douglas, or Bethlehem Steel. It grew out of the efforts of World War I and interwar city builders to find an economic niche for their rapidly growing and dynamic but unstable cities and military men hoping to arrest the decline of their services. Initially, industry played hardly any part in this drama. Of the two most prominent actors, the city boosters played the leading role, a task that this book seeks to explore.

Simultaneously, this book aspires to encourage the field of urban history to move beyond several of its traditional or recently acquired interpretive emphases. Theories of Marxism, modernization, industrialization, power structures, bosses and reform, and social history all have made significant contributions to urban history. These interpretive approaches are by no means irrelevant to the future of mainstream urban history or history written about cities by non-urban historians. The recent luminous study of European cities by Lynn Lees and Paul Hohenberg,

The Making of Urban Europe, 1000–1950, reminds us again, despite our denials, how enduring is the modernization theme. That is particularly true of the book's stress on the human consequences of urbanization. Nonetheless, modernization, Marxism, social history, and industrialization have been pored over endlessly by urbanists and others; and it seems time to look past these topics to fresh approaches.

Terrence McDonald has argued that social history has taken over a disproportionate segment of the field of urban history and, one might add, other subdisciplines as well. Without in any way denigrating such work, one can easily agree with Professor McDonald's assessment that political history and other approaches need to be revived or devised in order to illuminate further the topic of urban history. The military is a literally enormous reality in California cities; yet its presence cannot fruitfully be explored as a consequence of industrialism, the transition from *Gemeinschaft* to *Gesellschaft,* social evolution, minority history, or the workings of a Marxist model of historical development. Nor can it be explored by asking who governs. The presence of the military in California has more to do with the workings of the modern nation-state than with the demands of industrialism; more to do with the New Federalism and intergovernmental relations than with the problems of uneven capitalist development; more to do with the way in which influence was expended than with the question of whether aristocrats, bosses, reformers, or professional politicians governed; more to do with political outcomes than with political culture; and more to do with the process of urbanization than with history from the bottom up.[9] Modern Western historians have called for a "new Western history," based on a fuller exposition of the theme of conquest and its attendant effects on blacks, women, Native Americans, and Asians.[10] However appropriate this approach might be for general Western history, it too is only marginally germane to the study of the militarization of twentieth-century Urban California.

This book proposes a different interpretive model from that which often prevails in urban history or in allied disciplines. Despite what is currently popular to say about urban history, its progress has been enormous in the years since Richard Wade published the *Urban Frontier* and Sam Bass Warner produced *Streetcar Suburbs.* For example, there are many good histories on the subjects that those two men pioneered (nearly a dozen on suburbs alone).[11] Recent studies have added greatly to this corpus of materials. Whereas in 1959 the literature was spotty in nearly all areas, today one can find books on every aspect of politics, urban renewal, city fires, women, Hispanics, blacks, ethnic relations, the auto, transit, housing, suburbs, real estate development, police, collective violence, violent death, health, technology, government, cities and regions, comparative urbanism, neighborhood, the Sunbelt, city planning, architecture, the South, the idea of the city, and just about everything else. This remarkable topical proliferation has been the principal force driving the intellectual progress of the discipline. In line with that diversification, this book on the metropolitan-military complex aspires to move that process one step further.[12]

This body of new literature has been impressive, but it has left some room for further interpretive progress, especially in determining the urban dimension or variable. Some historians actually deny its existence. In explaining urban history, others present litanies, strive for interpretive hegemony, or employ bipolar models. Either urban development is explained by a list of vast, impersonal influences or it is accounted for by the elimination of one of two opposites—race or caste, class or caste, gender or demography, ethnicity or economics, ethnicity or class, democracy or order, school professionals or democracy, and so forth. Comparable examples in national history would be the debates over class versus ethnocultural influences in politics, the disagreement over ritualism versus pietism, or the controversy over markets between Adam Smithians and Marxists. These approaches have not been without result. The isolation of the main influences on urban history through listing, bipolar analysis, or interpretive hegemony has produced considerable progress.[13]

In this study, I would suggest a different approach. Anyone who has lived with the complexities of urban historical analysis for twenty-five years will recognize the impossibility of interpretive hegemony. History is just too complicated to allow for an assessment that seeks interpretive hegemony for some single set of actors like the power elite, race, industrialism, the bourgeoisie, political pluralism, or whatever. Listing usually presents a more complex analysis, but such litanies also fall short because they do not produce a functional description of the catalogs. And the depersonalization of history through a preoccupation with enormous, faceless influences is equally unsatisfactory. As Terrence McDonald and Eric Monkkonen have emphasized, political and governmental events occur in cities because some *person or persons* take political decisions to facilitate their occurrence.[14]

In this study, I would propose a tripartite approach, based on a division of labor. The principal influences driving the story in this book are the modern nation-state, the reality of the city, and city boosterism. The primary human agency in the story is to be found in the boosters, and the two vast impersonal forces are represented by the former two. This study will also argue that each of these influences, although distinct in many respects, interpenetrate. For example, it is impossible to separate the influences of class and race in black history because the two often coincide. By the same token, it is impossible to seal off hermetically the categories of gender and class in women's history or class and ethnocultural influences in political history. This is especially true when talking about matters as elusive as consciousness. Similarly, one cannot perfectly isolate the fact of the city from the boosters, who promoted its interests, nor from the nation-state, which provided resources for it. There is an irreducible overlap in each of these dualities and even among all three. Yet the three are distinct as well. This book will seek to understand the importance of the urban variable by demonstrating the interplay and interpenetration of these three crucial influences in developing the most significant civil-military partnership in twentieth-century American history.

California city builders set out to construct a series of great metropolises; and, more than anything else, that effort is what created the close ties between the city and military in the Golden State. In the process of developing this intimate association, California city builders were among the architects of the second phase of the history of cities and war. Perhaps more than any other set of people, these city builders furthered the process of converting warfare into welfare. Clifford Cummings, an engineer at the Jet Propulsion Laboratory in Pasadena, captured the essence of this process in speaking of the aircraft industry crisis in the late 1950s.

He noted that the aircraft firms "argue that our country is plagued with being too efficient in its production for its own economic good, and hence that inefficient production such [as] is generated by making planes and missiles that will in all probability never be used is essential to economic stability." His comment could not be more to the point. This book is about the fifty-year struggle by the boosters of Fortress California to help the businessmen do exactly that, to create a close relationship between war and society, to transform warfare into welfare.[15]

FORTRESS
CALIFORNIA
1910–1961

PART I

THE CITY AND THE SWORD: THE RISE OF THE METROPOLITAN-MILITARY COMPLEX

Although cities and war have coexisted in an uneasy partnership for forty-odd centuries, scholars have by and large neglected this connection between the city and the sword. However, military officers never did. They planned their campaigns to capture, flank, starve, or destroy cities, and urban dwellers planned their cities so as to resist these attentions. The connection between war and urbanization did not escape city boosters either, when this species appeared. Exactly when California cities first recognized the importance of war to the city-building process is unknown, but it must have been early. The Spanish themselves established military garrisons for many of the California settlements, including the famous Presidio of San Francisco. As early as 1854, the United States government created the Navy Yard at Vallejo, and from at least that time onward, American Urban California was aware of the uses of military patronage for city boosting. The Philippine Insurrection at the turn of the century and the visit of the Great White Fleet in 1908 further whetted urban appetites for military installations. The preparedness campaign of World War I sharpened them again. James D. Phelan, who led California in so many matters—some good and some not—also captained this charge. As soon as it was decided to build up the American fleet in response to the holocaust raging in Europe, the California senator demanded that the West Coast get a substantial piece of this new fighting unit. In 1919 it did, and California cities immediately set about feuding vigorously over who got what. The interwar years to 1933 quieted but did not end the rivalry, and the prospect of new defense spending under the Roosevelt administration quickened the conflict again. Cities battled for aircraft industries, flying fields, naval bases, and headquarters.

By the time of the bombing of Pearl Harbor, California cities had created a well-entrenched pattern of pursuing military wealth in order to create urban greatness. San Diego had already acquired the foundation for its present status as one of the two largest American naval bases. Its assets included the Eleventh District Naval Headquarters, a naval training station, a marine base at nearby Camp Pendleton, the Naval Radio Station, North Island Naval Air Station, the destroyer fleet, and assorted repair facilities. San Francisco Bay had procured about as much—Sunnyvale Naval Air Base, Hamilton Field Air Force Base, the Oakland Supply Depot, Alameda Naval Air Station, and the Ames Aeronautical Laboratory, to go with the Presidio, Twelfth District Naval Headquarters, and other sundry assets that it

1

already possessed. Los Angeles had won and lost the fleet anchorage, had gained Reeves Field, had garnered March Air Force Base in outlying Riverside County, and had created a base for the aircraft/aerospace boom that would begin with the outbreak of hostilities.

Thus, each city had become a metropolitan-military complex by the time the Japanese attacked Pearl Harbor. Each had longstanding political ties between civilian and military sectors as well as a huge military or potentially military economic investment to protect. Each had institutionalized its union with the military through political institutions like the naval and military affairs committees of the chambers of commerce, city governments, and educational devices and had invented pageants to link the emotional life of the metropolis to the fate of the military. And they had developed a cadre of experts in administrative and political fields accustomed to dealing with each other and expert in urban and military affairs. Ed Izak of San Diego, Richard J. Welch of San Francisco, and Charles F. Curry of the North Bay were not the least of them. The war vastly increased the resources of these competing cities, but the pattern of acquiring them had already been set. Thus conflict heightened rather than created this habit. These metropolitan-based entities were not part of any overall national grouping on behalf of either urban or military interests, nor were they a military-industrial complex. They were vigorously metropolitan rather than national and they competed with each other impetuously for the spoils of war.

CHAPTER 1

••••••••••••••••••••••••••••••

The Metropolitan-Military Complex:
A Mutual Dilemma of Relative Decline

Happy is the city that thinks of war in time of peace.
SENATOR JAMES D. PHELAN,
1920

We do not need the [United States] fleet to protect us from anybody. We feel sure that the nations on this sunny side of the globe will all let us alone if we will let them alone. . . . What we want of the fleet is to sell it supplies, do the necessary repair work, and enjoy the company of the uniforms at our society hops. That, of course, is all the East wants of the Navy in time of peace, and hitherto they have hogged it all.

San Francisco Chronicle
May 29, 1919

Today San Diego boasts a total capital investment of $28,000,000 in naval establishments, with an annual naval payroll of $30,000,000 [of an "annual naval appropriation" of $300,000,000]. We should protect this great investment and keep this vital payroll. . . .

San Diego Union
November 6, 1934

The kind of prosperity which comes from warship building is like the wild dance of some savage before casting himself into the flames. It is the prelude to a catastrophe.

Los Angeles Times
December 24, 1937

The President's announcement of plans for immediate upbuilding of the Navy must be approved by thinking Americans.

Los Angeles Times
December 30, 1937

The American city has always had many images, often contradictory. On the one hand, it is pictured as the center and even the source of the extraordinary dynamism of America: the place where power is centered, where ideas clash, compete, and congeal, and where wealth collects. Yet on the other hand, Urban America is often seen as victimized and helpless, the product of massive outside forces over which it has little or no control. Historians, social scientists, city planners, and politicians all have contributed to this portrait of urban impotence and dependency.[1]

Any number of mayors, often looking for federal funding of their enterprises, have echoed the point.[2] In some respects these witnesses have been correct, but in many others their testimony vastly distorts the reality of American urban civilization. Cities have frequently been responsible for their own destinies in large part, and California cities have perhaps been more responsible than most.

The interplay of the city and the sword reveals this independence quite clearly and provides us with some indispensable insights into the rise of the Sunbelt, the advance of twentieth-century California, the development of the New Federalism, and the evolution of what we have come to call the "military-industrial complex" as well. By 1980, American military spending had come to be an extraordinarily important economic stimulus to the process of urbanization. A study of the Los Angeles Area conducted in the 1970s concluded that defense spending underlay a staggering proportion of that megalopolis's economy. Some 500,000 Southern Californians worked in aerospace alone in 1967; and by 1974, a whopping total of 3,618,000 persons labored in defense work in the state of California.[3] It would not be difficult to produce similar evidence for San Diego; Norfolk, Virginia; Jacksonville, Fayetteville, and Goldsboro, North Carolina; Phoenix; Albuquerque; San Antonio, and many other settlements, large and small. As early as 1930, military spending contributed 30 percent to San Diego's annual payroll.[4] Yet this economic input was hardly some outside force over which cities had no control. Defense is obviously a function of the national government, but it is and was significantly influenced by local factors, including urban political power. Metropolitan representatives helped shape military spending legislation; and, more important for our purposes, cities had *almost absolute control* over the impact of that money. When the American fleet sailed through the Panama Canal in 1919 on its way to the Pacific coast of the United States, it carried with it a multi-million-dollar contribution to the process of urbanization wherever the ships and men settled. Invariably, they settled where they were welcome.

Undoubtedly the militarization of the West Coast would have produced or sustained the process of urbanization wherever it touched down. Moreover, particularly during and after the Second World War, cities could not avoid their marriage to the defense industry. Even in the early years, the services possessed some properties in urban areas, and these they were technically free to develop or neglect. Between 1919 and 1939, however, the California cities largely determined how closely they associated with the military. Particularly in the 1920s no city was under compulsion to become a garrison town. Before the pre-World War II crisis temporarily eliminated its choice in the matter, Urban California decided whether to receive or reject the military filip to the process of urbanization. Generally speaking, the cities freely chose to accept this new military contribution to the economic development of urbanism, to enhance that contribution whenever possible, and to defend it vigorously whenever necessary. The presence of military resources in California in 1919 was obviously a function of what Oscar Handlin has called "the centralized national state,"[5] but the urban targeting of those resources was largely a function of urbanization. The marriage of the city and the sword in California was a voluntary rather than a shotgun affair.

It was also an ardent and very fruitful alliance, contributing to the acceleration of American governmental structures, encouraging the westward reorientation of American culture, and aiding the legitimization of the military in American society.

Though the New Federalism is usually attributed to the New Deal period and to civilian and reform impulses, the drive in California antedated these developments. It featured all of the crucial attributes of the supposedly new federal-urban ties and did so long before the New Deal. These, in turn, helped to make good the West's claim to prominence. What is now termed the Sunbelt was in the making long before World War II, and this evolution drew crucial resources from California's civic-military match from the Progressive Era onward. Any attempt to understand the New Federalism, the rise of the Sunbelt, and the military-industrial complex must come to grips with California urban history from 1917 onward. In California, the three were, in large part, products of special patterns of urbanization.

These patterns were both dynamic and highly competitive. The cities of the Golden State had grown rapidly since the year 1900. The first decade of this century produced what was to become the second most rapid rate of urban growth in twentieth-century California history. Though the decade from 1910 to 1920 did not prosper as much, its rate of growth was still impressive. That of the 1920s would top any decade from 1900 to 1970. Yet this extraordinary achievement did not produce a sense of calm and well-being among major California cities. In part, the insecurity arose from the uneven distribution of urban progress. Southern California cities grew much more rapidly than the others, but within both the major California metropolitan areas—San Francisco Bay Area in the north and San Diego and Los Angeles in the south—the rate of urban growth differed markedly. The imbalance heightened the insecurity of all these cities and quickened the competition both between Northern and Southern California and within them.

Strangely enough, even the big winners in this war among cities did not gain the satisfaction and security that their victories should have generated. By 1920 Los Angeles was clearly winning this conflict, but it had not attained peace of mind in the process. Neither Los Angeles nor San Francisco had achieved what they considered a satisfactory manufacturing base although both were in the process of doing so. Like American cities throughout the West, California urban areas carried within themselves a cultural notion, a sense of what a city should be, based upon eastern cities.[6] And though they did not call it that, almost all city boosters believed in what might be called the "doctrine of industrial advantages."[7] The architects of Urban California in particular fervently believed that industrialization held the key to urban stability, continued prosperity, economic diversification, and sectional independence. Therefore, the relative urban decline of San Francisco, San Diego, Oakland, Vallejo, and other big towns combined with the relative insecurity of Los Angeles to produce cities that were simultaneously growing yet more than a little unsure about the future.

The First World War did not ease these anxieties. On the one hand, the war produced a considerable economic boom in the Golden State and throughout the West.[8] Extractive industries like fishing, mining, lumbering, and agriculture boomed along with shipbuilding. These activities brought marked prosperity to California cities and to new migrants like the Mexicans as well. However, the boom collapsed after the war, leaving a trail of economic dislocation behind it. The newly founded aircraft industry folded, shipbuilding declined dramatically, and the extractive industries fell off significantly as well. The war also produced serious inflation, profiteering, and social tension. Labor unrest was a serious problem from at least 1916 to the census year, and both radicalism and antiradicalism flared up along with it. The economy did not fully right itself until 1921.[9] As Paul Kennedy has noted, this adverse economic impact was worldwide and struck a blow to some portions of the world's economic structure from which they did not recover until after World War II.[10]

Thus, if the conflict generated a boom, it also produced a severe bust after the armistice. Moreover, the martial prosperity can easily be exaggerated. Historians and other analysts who have linked the affluence of California so closely to war have sometimes forgotten that the least war-related decades in twentieth-century California history have been the most prosperous, at least in terms of growth. By contrast, the rate of population increase in both the First World War decade of 1910 to 1920 and the period 1940 to the present fall considerably below that of the peacetime decades of 1900 to 1910 and 1920 to 1930. Therefore, it is quite possible that the stimulating aspects of the war boom have been exaggerated.[11] In any case, whatever the long-term effect of World War I, its short-term legacy of conflict, inflation, anti-radicalism, and economic collapse stood out more vividly to contemporaries in 1919.

In this context, the Great War and its aftermath served to heighten further the metropolitan rivalries and economic insecurities endemic to the Golden State and to give enormous significance to a little remarked event of the same year. In 1919, the United States Navy divided its recently modernized and enlarged fleet and sent half of it to the Pacific coast. Strategically speaking, the scuttling of the German fleet in the wake of the war, the improbability of combat with Great Britain in the Atlantic, and the persisting tensions between the United States and Japan in the Pacific underlay this decision to divide American naval strength between the two coasts. However, West Coast representatives had demanded such a division for years, particularly since the naval preparedness program of 1916.

From 1916 to 1919 interest mounted as Congress considered the future of the Navy, and Urban California sought to assess the impact of naval rearmament on the future of urban development. A consensus favorable to the acquisition of naval installations quickly appeared, and when the Navy did likewise in 1919, the cities of the Golden State outdid themselves to welcome it. Intended, at least in part, to keep the peace between the United States and Japan, this naval realignment triggered economic war up and down the West Coast, as San Diego, Los Angeles, Seattle, Vallejo, and San Francisco battled furiously for possession of the sailors.

It would be a rather severe mistake to consider this competition simply a matter of local history, a major event in a minor arena. The dispatch of the American fleet to the Pacific coast was a critical event in the development of California and the West Coast and a crucial stage in the evolution of the Sunbelt as well. The emergence of the Sunbelt was essentially a reorientation of the American patterns of urbanization, and the resources of the United States Navy provided a critical lever with which to enhance that realignment. Most dramatically the presence of that service promised a strikingly important population increase to the city that could capture all or part of this maritime complement. During the late teens and early twenties the fleet and its shore personnel were estimated variously at 45,000 to

60,000 people, not counting dependents, camp followers, and related personnel.[12] Even if we accept the lower estimate of population as the correct one and exclude dependents, the figure represented a significant addition to the residents of *any* California city and a staggering addition to the population of several.

In 1920, Los Angeles contained 576,000 people and San Francisco embraced another 506,000.[13] Therefore, the flotilla could conceivably have added nearly 10 percent to the urban population. Had the fleet's numbers been added to San Diego, at 74,000, or Vallejo, at 21,000, it would have amounted to a 60 percent increase in the case of the former and more than a 200 percent increase for the latter.[14] Looked at in terms of metropolitan growth, the gains would have been significant even for Los Angeles County at 936,000 or for the comparable Northern California area of San Francisco, Alameda, and Contra Costa counties at 903,000.[15] San Diego County's 112,000 residents would have risen by 40 percent, and Solano County's (Vallejo) 40,000 by more than 100 percent.[16] Naturally, these men and their dependents also would have created an enormous military payroll for the urban area lucky enough to capture it.

But this brief outline represented only the beginning. The main naval home base on the West Coast would cost from $60 million to $100 million and would be complemented by many other capital investments in California cities, not to mention the regular expenditure of large sums for supplies.[17] Beyond these obvious contributions to the economies of Urban California, city builders visualized a whole series of economic developments that would benefit the economy of cities. The presence of the Navy would improve California harbors, particularly those of San Diego, Los Angeles, and Vallejo. The latter two each had rather defective natural harbors that required constant dredging and seawalling, and the presence of the Navy would insure them of a preference in federal harbor spending. San Diego's harbor also needed much dredging, and its boosters hoped to benefit from the same connection. Better harbors would facilitate commerce, and the greater volume of commercial traffic would complete the cycle by providing a rationale for still further federal spending on the harbors.

These improvements, in turn, were linked to a revival of the United States merchant marine on the West Coast. For a time, the First World War had promoted a recovery in the merchant marine, but the high costs of operation and foreign competition soon brought a reversal and with it a demand for government operating subsidies for the ailing American carriers. The presence of the fleet gave civilian boosters a perfect rationale for this federal aid. If the Pacific coast needed defending, and the fleet seemed to answer that question, then the fleet needed auxiliary vessels to use in time of emergency. The First World War had revealed the American deficiency in this respect and forced the Navy into dependence on foreign auxiliary vessels. As urban navalists frequently pointed out, even the voyage of the Great White Fleet, the first great display of modern American sea power, had been compromised and sullied by the Navy's reliance on foreign auxiliaries.[18]

The multiplication of merchant shipping would in turn necessitate the revival of the shipbuilding industry in California. The West Coast had once been prominent in shipbuilding, but when iron and steel replaced wood as the principal building material, the business declined.[19] The First World War temporarily revived coastal shipbuilding and more than rekindled California urban interest in this pursuit. The conflict created a great shipbuilding boom; then the peace smashed it, and city interests spent the next twenty years trying to recapture the euphoria of 1917–18. Here again, an alliance with the Navy could prove useful. New Navy yards, especially those proposed for the San Francisco Bay and Puget Sound areas, would multiply the repair and construction facilities for civilian and military ships, employ the many idled wartime ship workers, and provide a multiplier effect for the entire economies of the shipbuilding cities. The latter was considered crucial. An unusually large part of shipbuilding expenditures stayed within the community in the form of wages, and this industry also spread the military booster to a disproportionately large number of firms.[20] As a business organ put it in anticipation, "The decision of the Senate Navy Committee to establish a great naval base on San Francisco Bay marks the beginning of a period of great industrial development here."[21]

Ship construction, repair, and reconditioning were peculiarly well suited to produce the urban revival by bolstering the local economy through diversification, the city builders' traditional panacea.[22] Industrialization stood very high on the California city builders' list of measures that might overcome that section's colonial dependence on the Eastern United States. In one respect, World War I had exacerbated this condition, and military spending in California represented a way to alleviate the problem. The Liberty bond drives had raised large sums in California, which in turn had been shipped off to the East, aggravating the metropolitan and sectional balance-of-payments problem. Military spending represented a means of recapturing these monies, and if defense dollars also produced industrialization, they might eliminate other outflows of money for industrial products as well.[23]

Just as important, the flow of federal funds into California cities could potentially work in a countercyclical direction. American cities had long employed public works expenditures to counter the effects of the economic cycle, and California cities hoped to build on this tradition by substituting permanent government spending on military projects and payrolls that would be relatively immune from the economic cycles. Stable federal spending might help the state's cities avoid another bust like the one that had overtaken Southern California in the 1880s, while still allowing the cities to enjoy the boom.

To a degree that most cities in the United States would find difficult to comprehend, California cities depended upon advertising to ensure their economic wellbeing. Before the development of a more stable economic base, Southern California in particular relied upon the very large transfer of capital that accompanied the migration of home builders, retirees, health-seekers, and tourists to the Southland. Here again, the service connection could be very helpful. The naval trainees at Treasure Island or San Diego often numbered several thousands, and the periodic visits of the fleet totaled many more. In the early twenties, the fleet visits brought 35,000 strangers to a city; and by the time of the San Diego, California Pacific Exposition of 1935, the advent of the fleet produced nearly 60,000. "One thing that San Diegans should realize is that the officers and men of the fleet represent virtually every city and hamlet in the nation," wrote a booster in 1935. "These 4,000 officers and 55,000 men will write home about San Diego and the Exposition, one of the greatest and most effective forms of advertising that any city or Exposition ever enjoyed." As the West Coast learned in World War II, many of these servicemen and their visiting relatives came back to stay.

All of these matters were vital to Urban California, but they do not exhaust the list of hoped-for benefits. As the metropolitan-military partnerships grew and matured, the cities of the Golden State found an increasing number of urban interests that could be linked to the crucial matter of "national defense." By 1941, therefore, Urban California regularly employed the lever of national defense for a host of projects often dimly or even unrelated to it.

If the cities of the Golden State suffered from a sense of relative decline and relative insecurity, the American military endured even more adversity. In fact, the services experienced both relative and absolute decline, and cataclysmic decline at that. At the end of World War I, the Army and Navy claimed several million men; but by the early twenties both branches found themselves fighting to defend a force level in the one hundred thousands. Moreover, the slippage was both qualitative and quantitative. With the excitement of war behind them, the Army and Navy found that their postwar recruits were inferior both mentally and physically to those who had joined or been drafted during the conflagration itself.

These predicaments would get worse before they got better. Though an army of 115,000 spread over a vast continent did not exactly amount to Prussian-style militarism, pacifist agitation convinced many Americans of the sinister character of its warriors and helped keep them on short rations. This starvation diet, in turn, together with a barrage of peace propaganda questioning the legitimacy and, indeed, often the humanity of the military, encouraged a sense of isolation and alienation reminiscent of the Army's frontier days. Simultaneously "the Washington Naval Limitaton Treaty froze the Navy's strength; government neglect and hostile public opinion kept it below treaty tonnage; and air power advocates such as Billy Mitchell raised serious doubts about its role as the country's first line of defense."[24] The Navy either had to give up this assignment to, or share it with, the advocates of air power, or it had to incorporate this new weapons system into its own arsenal and therefore exercise at least partial control over it. That meant either cutting out some other cherished naval armament such as the battleship or requesting an economy- and pacifist-minded Congress for larger appropriations to develop naval air power. The Army had somewhat the same tasks. Air power had to be either freed from Army control or merged into its system.

The flyers, in turn, though they could embarrass and vex the older services by charging that the Army and Navy kept aviation under wraps because it threatened their primacy within the military system, faced very real dilemmas of their own. The aviators were not represented by a separate government department and therefore had to fight with the vested interests of the other two services for funds and authority to develop Army and Navy air strength. Moreover, the "birdmen," as contemporaries called them, lacked strong economic and political constituencies outside the confines of the miltary. Postwar contract cancellations devastated many pioneer American airplane manufacturers, and the postwar glut of secondhand plans had the same depressing effect on the airplane market as analogous surpluses were having on its automobile counterpart. Throughout the twenties, the aviation manufacturing business struggled to recover. Moreover, though the public thrilled to the feats of First World War aviation heroes and their barnstorming successors in the twenties, this enthusiasm did not easily translate into the material and nonmaterial resources needed for aviation progress. The United States lacked landing fields, marked air routes, aviation markets, and governmental regulation of the business. In truth, there was not much business to supervise. From the twenties well into the thirties, passenger mileage grew; but during the early period especially it did not provide an easily exploited mass market for the aviators comparable either to today's air travel market or to the auto market of the 1920s. The public admired the barnstormers, but they loved their automobiles more and remained skeptical of the desirability of air travel or freight possibilities.

In a sense, then, each of the branches lost a mission when the guns fell silent on November 11, 1918, and each had to regain a place for itself in the civilian and increasingly urban world. The cities of the Golden State could assist this quest in crucial ways, and the services recognized this potential as quickly and as fully as their civilian counterparts noted the possibility of mobilizing military resources to aid in their own schemes of urban defense and development. Thus the services needed civilian friends to protect themselves against further decline just as California cities needed military allies to halt their own displacement or to stabilize their gains. This "mutual dilemma of relative decline" and relative insecurity created a series of novel political coalitions—or "metropolitan-military complexes"—to enhance California's martial investment.[25]

American urban history has always been an interplay of the unique and the general experience of cities, and, so far as the twentieth century is concerned, it is the unique rather than the common phenomena that need to be emphasized. We are constantly reminded that we live in an "urban nation," that we partake of an "urban-industrial" culture, or that we are perennially passing through and beyond the "process" of modernization, of which urbanization is a constituent part.[26] Each of these statements has its usefulness, to be sure, but the approaches they are rooted in all tend to subordinate the individual experience of urban areas to some broader purpose. By stressing the commonalities of urban experience, historians have frequently lost sight of the other side of the coin: that urbanization "proceeds at various rates, produces diverse outcomes for specific times and places, and encourages vastly different allocations of resources, population, money, culture, and power."[27] New York City and Chico, California, have doubtless shared many experiences. Both have had urban problems, have been shaped by their internal and external transportation facilities, have developed class structures, have produced specialization of occupation, land use, and other matters, have undergone suburbanization, and have served as central places. However, that tells us little about what is most crucial to the comparison—their relative success.

Historians of an earlier America understood that metropolitanism, or urban rivalry, was a critical factor in shaping both local and national history and, as this book will argue, this proposition holds true for twentieth-century California urban history as well. Metropolitanism held the key to much local political history, but it was also of decisive importance in the development of the New Federalism, the evolution of the military-industrial complex, the development of American military policy on the West Coast, and the growth of the Sunbelt and the distribution of resources within that region and the West. Urbanization, modernization, class, and so forth do not per se tell us much about these major topics.

Although corporate America grew markedly during these years, compromising regional, metropolitan, state, and urban loyalties in California, the period from 1920 to 1950 promoted strong counter-tendencies as well. By creating either new opportunities for California cities or threats to their current vested interests, these trends encouraged urban competition. In fact, despite the discontinuities and breaks in California and American history since the year 1900, the metropolitan rivalries of California have remained a constant. On a more regional level, the rapid economic exploitation of the West, the westward drift of population, the supposed new opportunities for investment and trade in Asia, and the First World War all created new visions of wealth. The opening of the Panama Canal and the transfer of the fleet to the Pacific further heightened the urban sense of opportunity and therefore the urge to compete for it. In the end, several of these devleopments would prove chimerical or ephemeral or both, but their influence held on nevertheless.

On the local level, the literally staggering redistribution of power, influence, and prosperity amongst California cities heightened the combat again. For example, San Francisco County grew from 342,000 to 634,000 between 1900 and 1940, only to be overtaken by Los Angeles County, which exploded from 170,000 to 2,700,000 in the same period of time. Yet not only was "The City" threatened by the Southland metropolis, it was besieged by its own suburbs as well, as cross-bay Alameda County marched from 130,000 to 513,000 between the Spanish-American and the Second World wars.

Even Los Angeles found itself under attack from its endlessly multiplying suburbs and unincorporated areas. As the City of the Angels surrendered its power to annex its surrounding areas, it too began to lose vis-à-vis both its own individual suburbs and the rapidly burgeoning county government, which ruled an empire larger than some American states.[28] To the South, despite its remarkable growth, San Diego County rapidly declined proportionately in comparison with Los Angeles County. In 1900, San Diego County contained 35,000 residents, and Los Angeles County held 170,000.[29] On the eve of World War II, the comparable figures were 289,000 and 2,785,000. In other words, a near tenfold increase in the Border City had not narrowed, but rather widened, the absolute gap between it and Los Angeles from 135,000 to 2,496,000. As a percentage of its powerful neighbor, San Diego County fell from 20 to 10 percent.[30]

Perhaps more important still, in the 1910s, when the decision to post part of the fleet to the Pacific was under consideration, San Diego County doubled in population from 61,000 to 112,000 and still fell farther behind in absolute terms, as Los Angeles County exploded from 504,000 to 936,000. Los Angeles city had slipped less dramatically compared with its suburbs, but its population had nevertheless declined from 63 percent to 54 percent of the county total between 1910 and 1940. The slide had begun in the decade of the 1910s. The same period witnessed the eclipse of San Francisco city and county, as the "Cool Gray Lady" registered only a modest growth of 20 percent and fell behind Los Angeles city, 506,000 to 576,000.

San Francisco's immediate trans-bay competitor outdistanced "The City" by 31 to 20 percent in the First World War decade, and Oakland outgrew its neighbor even more dramatically in the 1900s, thrusting forward over 100 percent while San Francisco lagged well behind at eighteen.[31] Even Long Beach, often belittled for its ethnocultural character as the principal seaport of Iowa, shot up from 17,000 to 55,000 in the second decade of the twentieth century. And although it would seem farfetched to suppose that Long Beach could match the population of Los Angeles city, it did possess a potentially good harbor that could, and eventually did, come to rival that of its gigantic neighbor.

Technological development added to both insecurity and the sense of opportunity. The rapid adoption of the automobile in California, especially in the Southland, jeopardized the interests of every urban core by vastly decentralizing the metropolis away from its central business district and therefore promoting competitive places outside the control of the center city and often outside the center city itself. New sprawling plant construction and the rapid adoption of electrical power allowed for a decentralization of economic units to match that of the population. Rapid highway building, particularly in the Los Angeles area, intensified the outward flow of people and economic institutions; and these in turn came to concentrate more and more around these new transportation arteries. The telephone and, in the twenties, the radio provided the necessary communications to hold the California metropolises together, reducing the need for face-to-face contact in the social and business worlds and again increasing the potential for urban sprawl.

Water, flood control, and harbor technology boosted the process along. Flood control measures made an increasingly large part of the Southland, in both the mountains and the Los Angeles Basin and San Fernando Valley, available for housing. Artesian wells and enormous aqueducts to the Owens River, the Mono Basin, and the Colorado River made up for the water deficit of the arid Southland, without which neither the remarkable urban nor the agricultural development of the area could have proceeded for long. Similarly impressive public works connected San Francisco and the East Bay to the waters of the Tuolumne and Mokelumne rivers, hundreds of miles distant. Suburbs sprouted up under the impetus of this resource. The East Bay Region in the north was able to escape the control of San Francisco in part because it had completed its own water utility district before San Francisco and therefore was not beholden to the metropolis for this precious commodity.

Unlike the Los Angeles area in the Progressive era, the thirst of the San Francisco suburbs did not become the means for satisfying the land hunger of the center city. Finally, harbor technology added to the process of urbanization by eliminating yet another geographic restraint. In an earlier era, the natural advantages of big-city harbors had been very important. However, as the nineteenth century progressed, technology became more and more able to create artificial harbors that served as well as the natural ones. This technology multiplied the potential urban sites and therefore the competitors for metropolitan empire, and Los Angeles pioneered the way. Beginning in the 1880s, both municipal and federal monies poured into the harbor; and by 1920, the City of the Angels possessed a first-class port that it continued to improve thereafter. Neighboring Long Beach followed suit. San Francisco's first-rate natural harbor, and San Diego's very good one, could no longer be counted upon to guarantee victory in the race for urban empire.

In this fluid and dynamic situation no city felt secure, and all shared a vast metropolitan anxiety. In 1880, Los Angles contained a mere 11,000 residents to San Francisco's 233,000. The future Southland capital did not even equal Oakland, Sacramento, or San Jose in population. By 1920, the City of the Angels had outgrown them all, including San Francisco, which itself had doubled in size during that time. The advantages of geography, which San Francisco possessed in abundance and San Diego, to a lesser extent, did not guarantee against relative or even absolute urban decline. Nor did the tremendous headstart which San Francisco had long enjoyed, the established patterns of population migration, or the presence of a vast agricultural hinterland like the Central Valley. New technology could create land or water where there was none, spread out population in suburbs or congest it in skyscrapers downtown, produce an oasis in the absence of local water supplies, destroy geographic distance by transportation or communications innovations, find new resources such as oil, develop new industries like the movies overnight, produce new crops in endless variety, and, in short, provide limitless potential for the development of cities.

Hollywood has often been described as a dream factory, specializing in the manufacture of unreality. In a sense, California itself has always been a vast dream factory where argonauts, businessmen, health seekers, retirees, cultists, radicals, Hindus, fundamentalists, and humanistic psychologists contended for public attention and personal affluence or salvation. However, the visions of the city builders were just as numerous and equally grandiose, and they were not illusions. Both dreams and nightmares came true for them with a sometimes frightening, edge-of-the-seat regularity that Hollywood would have been hard-pressed to duplicate.

In order to make their dreams realizable (and hold their nightmares at bay), all the major California cities and many minor ones mobilized for combat. Colbert Coldwell, the new president of the San Francisco Chamber of Commerce, put the matter in its proper perspective in 1923:

> San Francisco must capitalize its natural advantages and step up its voltage for the competitive tournament among world cities. . . . The law of selection—survival of the fittest—applies to business as well as to organic forms. The highly successful business institution is a product of evolution. The highly successful city is the same.[32]

Appropriately enough, it was an Italian-American, James Bacigalupi, president of the Bank of Italy, who later elaborated this notion into a kind of city-state nationalism:

> When I speak of San Francisco—mark you—I do not allude alone to the [City] of St. Francis; but rather to that great economic, social, and cultural area of a budding empire which stretches from the sun-scorched Tehachapi Mountains to the snow-capped peak of Mt. Shasta; from the sentinel Sierras to . . . an awakening Orient.
>
> Our greatest need of the moment is to stress this metropolitan conception: to think in terms of a metropolitan area, rather than of a distinct and isolated political subdivision: and to plan and to work together toward making it as mighty, if not mightier, than any the world has ever known.[33]

Spokesmen for Los Angeles understood this language perfectly.

> Southern California has become known to the United States as almost as much of
> an economic unit as we think of New England. But is there not something bigger than
> southern California, tributary to this port? Consider the territory bounded by Fresno
> on the north, then skirting Salt Lake City, Butte, the San Juan Basin in southeastern
> Colorado, Phoenix, Tucson, New Mexico, El Paso, on across the Rio Grande, down
> to the states of Sinora [sic] and Sinoloa [sic] and lower California. All this section,
> drained by the Colorado River, is one vast entity, and just as Seattle has been called
> the entrepot of the Northwest, may we not rightly call Los Angles the entreport of
> the Pacific Southwest, and is not Los Angeles the harbor through which this entire
> section will receive and discharge its commerce?[34]

To a much greater extent than either city's representative realized, these explanations were unnecessary. The "metropolitan conception" had already captured the
consciousness of Urban California and given it a sense of urgency as well.[35] "San
Francisco is now at the turning point," stated an editorial in the *Journal of Commerce* in 1920. "There is . . . a tide in the life of all communities, which if taken at
the flood, leads on to victory," San Francisco Supervisor Edward Wolfe contended
that same year.[36]

In each case, the community tide led to a flood of public works and other city-
building activities. Los Angeles threw its life-giving aqueducts out ever farther, to
the Mono Basin and then the Colorado River; it constructed an area-wide highway
network designed specifically to create an auto-age city; it simultaneously dredged
its harbor deeper and surrounded it with an ever-lengthening seawall; it enlarged its
municipal power plant; it initiated countywide urban planning; and it hustled up
and down the coast, out to sea, and into the interior drumming up business. One
month, the Chamber of Commerce sailed forth to Hawaii aboard the *City of Los
Angeles* to bring "the commercial relations of Hawaii closer to Los Angeles."[37]
Another month, the Chamber arrived in Mexico City to sing the praises of the
Southland, then cast longing glances to the Orient and the elusive China trade, then
toured the California coast in a chartered train, euphemistically labeled the "Los
Angeles Chamber of Commerce Golden Rule Sociability Tour," trying all the while
to seduce and divert San Francisco's trading partners. Thereafter, the booster train
would be off to the wilds of deepest, darkest Oregon, where every whistle-stop audience was treated to a serenade from the Chamber of Commerce glee club.[38]

San Francisco sang its own praises equally well, hiring a publicity agent to direct
its own campaign, matching Los Angeles tour for tour, and dispatching its own
superb municipal band to enrapture the no doubt skeptical Oregonians. Civil projects multiplied almost in proportion to the urban drummer's mileage. From about
1910 till the end of the Second World War, San Francisco underwent a renaissance
worthy of Paris's Baron Haussmann, one that produced many of the city's most
important contemporary landmarks. The Hetch Hetchy water system, the Civic
Center (one of the finest in the world), the Sunset and Twin Peaks tunnels, the Palace of the Legion of Honor, Coit Tower, the Cow Palace, the Municipal Railway,
much of the highway system, the picturesque Marina District, the Islais industrial
district, the city airport, and several parks were completed in this period, and the

Palace of the Fine Arts was rescued form the wrecker's ball.[39] By 1936–37 San Francisco had thrown its splendid Golden Gate and Bay bridges across the bay. Metropolitanism was the single most important political issue in the city from one world war through the next, and these great public works were, in large part, the product of the keen inter-urban rivalry of the time.

City-building issues had an even higher priority in San Diego. The city fought for railroad connections to Arizona and the East, politicked for the Boulder Dam project, lured tourists and residents with a world's fair, steadily improved its "harbor of the sun," employed the most prestigious city planners to order its growth, continually improved its magnificent Balboa Park, and matched the mountains of booster literature emanating from its northern neighbors ream for ream. And each of the cities made a major effort to add military installations to its bridges, aqueducts, parks, and ceremonial buildings. It would be incorrect to imagine that the military resources were the main goal of all the cities, but they were a major goal of all of them and the pre-eminent goal of some.

In each city, political alliances, or metropolitan-military complexes, grew up to achieve the defense component of the booster program. These included both civilian and service elements and, at least initially, were based upon a single city. Early in the period, however, these political coalitions merged to represent single metropolitan districts, or large parts of them. Historians and other analysts have made much of the contemporary ties between the military and civilian sectors of society, but they have certainly misunderstood an important part of their origins and nature as well. The "military-industrial complex," as the alliance is called, is usually attributed to either the Second World War or the Cold War period and, as its label implies, is linked to industrialism. Recent studies have tentatively pushed back the origins of the military-industrial complex into the interwar period.[40] These latter studies are correct in stressing the earlier origins of civilian-military cooperation in economics and politics, but they share the tendency to view the phenomenon from the center of the problem rather than from the periphery. It is not likely that there is, or ever has been, a single entity centered in Washington which comprehends most of the elements involved in defense spending. Even those analysts who describe the military-industrial complex as sprawling and decentralized continue to employ the single term to describe it and to cling to a Washington-centered view.

The term "iron triangle," used to describe the ties between Congress, the Pentagon, and the defense contractors, is likewise deficient in this respect. American politics have never been that simple and have always been much more local than the terms "military-industrial complex" or "iron triangle" imply. Political parties, as Franklin D. Roosevelt learned to his dismay in the 1938 purge of the Democratic party or Ronald Reagan learned in the 1986 congressional elections, have very tenacious local roots. That would seem to be equally true of military-civilian relationships as well. Therefore, historians and other analysts of the topic should either discard such terms altogether as too unitary and abstract or re-examine the military-industrial complex from the bottom up in order to understand its sources of support.

First and foremost, in California, what is called the military-industrial complex, *initially involved cities more than industries.* The coalitions mobilized to promote military growth in Urban California were organized on urban rather than industrial bases, and, indeed, military investment was specifically designed to compensate for the Western industrial lag. By 1939, much of this manufacturing deficit had been made up; but even then, at the halfway point of this study, some military industries like aircraft were still quite modest. In other words, Urban California initially chose defense investment as a growth strategy precisely because it had not captured enough industry, civilian or military. Thus, the term "metropolitan-military complex" would seem more appropriate than military-industrial complex. *Its origins stemmed from metropolitan anxiety rather than from industrial necessity.* But if the alliances contained only a small industrial component, unlike the overgrown and subsidized defense industries of today, they contained a very impressive cross-section of most other urban social, political, governmental, and economic elements. What is perhaps just as striking is that these military booster projects, like other works of metropolitanism, drew very little criticism, even in the pacifist decades of the twenties and thirties. Pacifists may have worried about militarism, but that fear did not translate into opposition to military and naval bases in *their* home towns.[41]

Accordingly, the issue of urban defense development cut across many of the political lines that would be prominent in American politics from the twenties to the sixties, at both the local level and above. Competition between city and city or alliances of cities provided the principal political cleavage on defense-related issues. The career of William Kettner, known fondly to his San Diego constituents as the "million dollar congressman," illustrates the principle perfectly. Where military investment was concerned, this fantastically successful public servant cared not a snap for the usual matters that agitated politics, including his Democratic party allegiance. As he put it, his "partisanship was entirely subordinate to his citizenship," which he defined almost exclusively as the acquisition of every conceivable military installation that the San Diego part of his district could hold.[42] Neither in San Diego nor in the other California cities did the issues traditionally stressed in urban or national history significantly embarrass that quest. What is more, traditional political antagonists who fought each other on diverse matters cooperated lovingly on this one. Liberals and conservatives; Democrats and Republicans; labor and capital; cities and suburbs; center and periphery; natives and foreigners; Jews, Catholics, and Protestants; California Progressives and stand patters, even cities and their often critical hinterlands usually fought shoulder to shoulder for more defense resources. A sense of community and the pursuit of defense investment went hand in hand. The militarization of the West Coast may have disturbed and alarmed the Japanese, but it had a wondrously pacific effect on California city politics.[43]

Although urban and labor historians have lately emphasized the importance of class cleavages in American history, in California both ends of society enthusiastically supported the militarization of California cities.[44] Of this there can be little doubt, since the urban electorate repeatedly ratified the coupling of militarization and urbanization. Nearly every major California city and many minor ones donated immensely valuable land, waterfront, or other assets to the American services; and almost invariably the voters passed these referenda by impressive margins. These elections, like most special ones in California cities, usually drew a smaller turnout than regular municipal elections, much less national ones. However, given the overwhelming support, one must assume that if an opposition existed, it was either not numerous or not motivated enough to vote. Los Angeles, Vallejo, San Diego, Oakland, Alameda, and Marin County gave and gave, until their attitudes could no longer be in doubt. Alameda provided perhaps the most impressive and expensive proof of its willingness to join its fate to that of the military by donating 5400 acres of prime waterfront land to the Navy in 1920 by a 30-to-1 margin.[45] Tiny Vallejo, a town of only 21,000 in 1920, demonstrated almost equal enthusiasm. In the words of Frank R. Devlin, longtime Bay Area resident, Vallejo advocate, and local expert on naval affairs,

> . . . the people of Vallejo, in some instances the third generation, have been building up the community; bonding themselves up to the very eyes meeting the needs of a Navy Yard town; . . . streets were paved and a big industrial Y.M.C.A. constructed largely by the people of the town under the special urging of Secretary [of the Navy] Daniels; and generally the people there have been meeting every demand of the government to improve the town materially and the moral atmosphere and to make it what I think it has become, an ideal naval town.[46]

In every California city competing for service largesse, the mass of the electorate found imposing institutional allies in impressive numbers. Though the picture varied somewhat with the degree of preoccupation with defense, every city government took an active role in promoting the metropolitan-military complex. In San Diego and Vallejo, urban governments literally organized and led the charge. Even in the major cities of Los Angeles, San Francisco, and Oakland, where the complexity of urbanization produced many more economic opportunities and therefore a less single-minded pursuit of service patronage, that quest was nevertheless quite important. For example, the urban legislatures in both San Francisco and Los Angeles featured military affairs committees exclusively dedicated to enhancing the military investment of their respective metropolitan area. In San Diego and Vallejo, the interface between the civilian and military sectors was so important that the municipal governments per se were sometimes overshadowed by their military affairs committees.

Other powerhouse political and economic organizations followed where the city fathers led. Chambers of commerce played an especially active role, invariably in close association with the municipal or county governments or both. In some cases, the chamber of commerce functioned almost as a branch of the city government. For example, for years the San Francisco Chamber actually received a municipal operating subsidy for its normal expenses and an extra one for its promotional activities. Elsewhere, chamber-government ties were equally close and their collaboration in military matters equally thick. Both the San Diego and Vallejo chambers operated almost as lower houses of the urban legislatures and sometimes as upper houses and executives as well. Like their city government partners, the chambers' courtship of the soldiers and sailors was institutionalized rather than improvisational.[47] Although the chambers featured military affairs committees, by the Second World War the Los Angeles Chamber of Commerce had a committee for both military (Army and Air Force) and naval affairs and, in addition, published a weekly newsletter devoted solely to civil and military aviation.

The urban chamber of commerce supposedly spoke for the interest of the city as a whole, but the specialized business organizations held the same opinions on the metroplitan-military alliances. For example, the Central Business District Association of Los Angeles supported the alliance as fervently as did outlying groups like the Long Beach Chamber of Commerce. In San Francisco, the Downtown Association of the central business district marched side by side with its competitors, the Mission Street Merchants Association, the Polk-Van Ness and Larkin District Association, and the North Beach Merchants Association. Other San Francisco business supporters of the urban-military alliance included the Commercial Club, the Foreign Trade Club, the San Francisco Retail Merchants Association, the Central Bureau of San Francisco Organizations, the San Francisco Junior Chamber of Commerce, the *Daily Commercial News,* and the *San Francisco Journal of Commerce.*[48]

Labor leaders traditionally suspected the soldiery as an instrument of class oppression, but they did not oppose the developmental aspects of the militarization of Urban California. In fact, the regular labor organizations enthusiastically supported the local defense buildups because of their job-producing potential and also because much of the interwar militarization of California cities benefitted the sailors and aviators, who, unlike the soldiers, could not get at striking workingmen. Therefore, it was not unusual to find such unlikely allies as conservative ex-Congressman Joseph Knowland of Oakland, publisher of the *Oakland Tribune* and chamber of commerce leader, working hand in glove with George S. Hollis, president of the San Francisco Labor Council, for the acquisition of the main home base of the Pacific Fleet, while outside their conference room the Bay Area was rent by bitter labor conflict.[49] As Hollis's followers put it in a 1921 resolution, "Be it Resolved, by the San Francisco Labour Council, . . . that the hearty support of this organization . . . is hereby pledged to the movement for a main naval base at Alameda."[50] That statement represented Labor's enthusiasm for urban defense spending in 1941 or 1953 or 1961 as accurately as it did in 1921.

The attitudes of radical labor organizations are somewhat more difficult to get at, but they too at least acquiesced in the local defense buildup. For example, San Francisco Socialist Supervisor Margaret Mary Morgan served on the base-boosting organizations, and her later radical counterpart, Harry Bridges, raised no objections to the military development of the San Francisco Bay Area.[51] Bridges and his waterfront allies often professed their desire to stay out of the Second World War; but during the 1930s his newspaper made little mention of, much less opposition to, the snowballing defense investment in the San Francisco Bay Area. Los Angeles radicals made a similar distinction. Until the Nazi attack on Russia, they opposed war in the abstract, or American entry into the Second World War, but not the defense orders flowing to the aircraft factories whose workingmen the Communists sought to organize.[52]

Supposedly neutral civil organizations shared the views of their more "committed" leftist neighbors. In San Francisco the Public Spirit Club, the powerful Civic League of Improvement Clubs, and the very prestigious Commonwealth

Club all upheld the militarization of the City of St. Francis and its hinterland. So did the media all over California. The *Oakland Tribune,* the *San Francisco Chronicle,* the *San Francisco Examiner,* the *Los Angeles Times,* the *Los Angeles Examiner,* the *San Diego Union,* and the *San Diego Evening Tribune* each backed its respective city's campaign. Even the *San Francisco Examiner* supported the Bay Area's drive despite the fact that the Hearst chain of newspapers had Southland entries like the *Los Angeles Examiner* in communities competing with the Bay Area for military favors.[53]

Somewhat more surprising, religious organizations of all persuasions did their bit, too. The San Francisco Federation of Churches might hold mass meetings in support of the Washington Naval Limitation Agreements, but they just as enthusiastically welcomed the fleet to town or took a leading role in Navy Day, specifically designed to promote the fortunes of that service. For example, in 1925 the Rev. Dr. James L. Gordon, pastor of the First Congregational Church in downtown San Francisco, cooperated with the Navy League of the United States in putting on a "monster Navy Day sermon."[54]

The ethnic position on urban militarization reflected the religious one. Since the publication of Nathan Glazer and Daniel Moynihan's *Beyond the Melting Pot,* a whole school of ethnocultural historiography has grown up around the thesis that the American melting pot did "not happen"; that is, that the various nationality and religious groups have maintained a relatively high degree of behavioral and structural distinction.[55] That proposition would gain little support from the story of the metropolitan-military complexes. With regard to the military development of the areas, the ethnocultural groups behaved in the same manner as the so-called Anglo-Americans. When the Great White Fleet appeared off the coast of California in 1919, that state did not possess the cultural diversity that it eventually would. However, the substantial ethnocultural distinctions that were present did not create marked ethnic differences on the issue of the metropolitan-military complex.

In 1919, for example, San Francisco contained the most ethnic diversity in California, and there the evidence of ethnocultural unanimity on the recruitment of local military resources existed in abundance. The 1920 census listed the Irish, Jews, Germans, Italians, and White Anglo Saxon Protestants in the Bay City, and each contributed substantially to the local defense and development coalition. Among the Irish, Thornwell Mullaly, Robert N. Lynch, John I. Nolan, Richard J. Welch, Joseph J. Tynan, John A. O'Connell, Patrick H. McCarthy, Michael M. O'Shaughnessey, Daniel Ryan, James D. Phelan, Eustace Cullinan, and John Francis Neylan stood out. So did Julius Kahn and his wife Florence, Herbert and Mortimer Fleishhacker, Ralph Stern, Milton Nathan, Jesse Colman, Milton Sapiro, Milton H. Esberg, Barney Hirschberg, and William P. Roth, amongst San Francisco's Jews. Italian Americans James Bacigalupi, Angelo Rossi, Ralph Belgrano, and Stephen Malatestas represented their ethnic group; and Frank Havenner, Frederick J. Koster, ex-Mayor Schmitz, and Fred Dorhmann, Jr., led the German contingent. The Anglo-Americans were similarly numerous: James Rolph, Atholl McBean, David Barrows, William H. Crocker, John S. Drumm, George T. Cameron, Colbert Coldwell, Andrew Lawrence, Frederick Ainsworth, Wallace Alexander, Charles Stanton, C. E. Capwell, George Hollis, George Hearst, Hiram Johnson, and Robert

Dollar were some of the most notable. M. H. DeYoung and W. J. Citron represented the French.[56]

Though this list is not comprehensive, it is typical. To say that it comprised much of the elite of "The City" would be a classic understatement. For example, the group of men mentioned above included four mayors (Schmitz, McCarthy, Rolph, and Rossi), five members of the House of Representatives (the Kahns, Havenner, Welch, and Nolan), two United States Senators (Phelan and Johnson), four presidents or secretaries of the Chamber of Commerce (McBean, Coldwell, Alexander, and Lynch), county and national commanders of the American Legion (Stern and Belgrano), several top labor leaders (O'Connell, McCarthy, and Hollis), an heir, an editor, and a commander-in-chief of the California Hearst empire (Hearst, Stanton, and Neylan, respectively), publishers of the *Chronicle* and *San Francisco Journal* (Cameron, DeYoung, and Lawrence), five influential bankers (Drum, the Fleishhackers, Crocker, and Bacigalupi), two nationally famous retailers (Capwell and Dohrmann, who was also the leading light of regional planning in San Francisco), and a miscellany of other prominent figures.[57] Ryan was head of the State of California Harbor Board, which ruled the Port of San Francisco; O'Shaughnessy was the most important city bureaucrat in town; Cullinan was the chief legal defender of Pacific Gas and Electric; Roth was vice president and general manager of Matson Navigation; and Dollar was the head of Dollar Navigation Company. The leaderships of the metropolitan-military complexes in Los Angeles, the East Bay, and San Diego were equally impressive, although not quite as culturally diverse.[58]

Impressive documentation has recently been offered testifying to the fact that intramural ethnic discord, as distinguished from nativism, reigned supreme in contemporaneous eastern cities like New York, Chicago, and Boston. In particular, the frictions generated by upthrusting Jews, blacks, Slavs, and Italians trying to displace the politically dominant Irish provided city politicians with endless ammunition, as did later ones between Jews, Germans, and Italians on the eve of World War II. The City of St. Francis shared some of the strains of the "tribal twenties" and "troubled thirties," especially the latter; but when it came to bases, bombers, and barracks, the local tribes spoke a language befitting San Francisco's patron saint.[59]

In view of the foregoing, it is perhaps superfluous to mention that the local congressmen and senators played a leading role in bringing California cities into alliance with the services. Every California senator between the administrations of Woodrow Wilson and Dwight Eisenhower supported the coupling of the military and civilian sectors in the Golden State. Hiram Johnson, Samuel Shortridge, James D. Phelan, John D. Works, William Gibbs McAdoo, Sheridan Downey, William Knowland, and Thomas Kuchel each contributed importantly to the proliferating Sunbelt alliances between the cities and the sword, though Johnson dropped out during the isolationist struggles preceding the Second World War. Because of their more specific geographic ties to urban constituencies of metropolitan areas, members of the more popular branch of government outdid the senators. Practically without exception, urban congressmen led the campaigns for greater military investments. Amongst this crowd of supplicants, Charles Forrest Currey, Richard J. Welch, William Kettner, Julius Kahn, Chet Holifeld, Carl Hinshaw, Gordon

McDonough, Sam Yorty, Ed Izak, and Bob Wilson stand out, but many others distinguished themselves in the same pursuit. Quite a few of this group served on the War, Navy, and Armed Forces committees of one or another branch of the legislature, while Kahn headed the Military Affairs Committee and Hinshaw served as second-in-command on the post-World War II Armed Services Committee. Many of the rest held similarly important posts on other committees which had a dramatically positive effect on the militarization of California, especially the Rivers and Harbors Committee, the Joint Committee on Atomic Energy, and the appropriations committees of both houses.

Eventually these political ties expanded to ever greater areas. Early on, San Francisco Bay cities formed a special pressure group, the Bay Cities Naval Affairs Committee, to coordinate the metropolitan efforts to acquire the Navy's main West Coast home base. Until 1933, Vallejo did not join its sister cities in this common endeavor; but long before the Carquinez town came into it, the alliance had stretched much farther afield. The Bay Area drew solid support from as far east as Fresno and Stockton in the Central Valley and as far north as Santa Rosa. In fact, Congressman Homer Lea of Santa Rosa often spearheaded the Bay Area battles in the 1930s. The other metropolitan areas shared the same experience. The Imperial Valley behind San Diego backed that port outlet, and Los Angeles drew sustenance from as far away as Riverside and San Bernadino counties. Thus the courtship of the services tended to narrow the traditional hostility both between city and country and between center cities and their suburbs. In that sense, the experience of Urban California with the services flew very much in the face of that of the other America. Back east, city and country conflict flared almost continuously in incidents great and small, from the 1928 presidential election or Scopes trial to the everyday relations of farm, town, and city.[60]

These civilian elements found willing allies in both the ranks of the regular military services and their civilian auxiliaries. In San Francisco, for example, the American Legion, particularly the C. C. Thomas [Naval] Post, the Association of the Army of the United States of America, the Military Order of the Loyal Legion, the Military Order of the World War, and the Navy League, of which the City of St. Francis was the western section headquarters, cooperated consistently to enhance the Bay Area's partnership with the soldiers. Or, to give just one more example, in San Diego the civic supports system included the Fleet Reserve Association, the Military Order of the World Wars, the Navy League, the Navy Civilian Administrators Association, the North Island Association, the American Federation of Government Employees, and the Admiral Kidd Club. In certain respects, these civilian auxiliaries (most of whose members worked for the military) proved crucial assets, especially in the periods of heightened pacifist activity, for veterans could speak out forthrightly on military policy without fear of reprisals, something that greatly concerned their regular service brethren.

The very reticence of the servicemen to speak out publicly makes a tracing of military-civilian allegiances more difficult, as does their commitment to a national institution. Still, the military men often found themselves quite entangled with their urban-civilian counterparts in a given geographic area. The organizational arrangements of the Navy encouraged this involvement more than did those of the

Army. The Ninth Army Corps area headquarters in San Francisco commanded an immense empire that took in the entire Pacific Coast, including rival metropolitan areas to the north and south. Naval organization differed considerably, being more specifically targeted on individual urban areas, and therefore promoted a closer interface between local representatives of that service and its civilian opposite numbers. San Diego, San Francisco, and Seattle each possessed a naval district headquarters (the eleventh, twelfth, and thirteenth respectively); and, due to local peculiarities, the Mare Island Navy Yard at Vallejo had its own command, separate from the Eleventh Naval District in San Francisco.[61]

The political ramifications of this organizational division of labor were predictable. For example, in the great battle over possession of the Navy's main West Coast home base, the naval personnel at Mare Island sided with Vallejo, while the headquarters contingent in San Francisco backed the mid-bay civilian coalition competing for the base. The Eleventh Naval District in San Diego consistently supported the claims of the two chief cities in the Southland. To everyone's confusion, the Navy Department in Washington backed first one side and then another.

If the New Federalism is defined as a direct, continuing, and close working relationship between the cities and the federal government, largely bypassing the state government, then the evolution of the federal-urban "partnership" in California must be closely linked to the development of the metropolitan-military complex in every Golden State city. As usual, tiny Vallejo led the way. From the early Wilsonian years, that navy town supported a regular Chamber of Commerce observer and lobbyist in Washington, beginning with the enormously effective Dr. J. J. Hogan. The San Diego Chamber of Commerce worked as closely with its municipal government as did that of Vallejo; and, also like Vallejo, the southern city maintained close ties with the nation's capital. The Dieguenos did not post a permanent representative to Washington as soon as the Carquinez Straits town did, but its representatives shuttled to and from the Potomac so frequently as to be almost permanently lodged on the Southern Pacific or Santa Fe railroads. From the early twenties, the San Francisco Chamber of Commerce supported a permanent representative in Washington, but obviously the federal-urban partnership, though often portrayed as largely a big-city alliance with Washington, was at least as important for the smaller towns of Urban California. Thus, although it would be mistaken to posit an exclusively military causation for the rise of the federal-urban partnership, the New Federalism did, in part, have a martial origin.

CHAPTER 2

....

Capturing the Navy: San Diego

Although California today is noted for its vast aerospace and electronics industries, it was Navy rather than Air Force spending that created what has mistakenly been called the "military-industrial" complex in the Golden Land. The taste for defense investment and the concomitant political alliances that those expenditures involved came to the state with sailors, not aviators. In fact, at that point in time, there was no Air Force. Perhaps two direct quotations from participants in this saga, the first from the famous Admiral George Dewey of Spanish-American War fame and the second from a classical civilian military booster organ, will illustrate the importance of the "metropolitan-military" complexes in the distribution of defense installations on the West Coast. As will become obvious from the two statements, the United States Navy did not initially foresee a major role for the border city of San Diego.

> In its letter . . . of March 18, 1909, the General Board [of the Navy] adheres to its "opinion, heretofore expressed, that it is not good policy, economical, or desirable, from a naval standpoint, to establish a naval station on the coast of California south of San Francisco." The expressions above regarding the desirability of having the inner harbor of San Diego available for capital ships of the Navy are not to be taken as a reversal of opinion of this respect.
>
> > Admiral George Dewey,
> > President of the General
> > Board to the Secretary of the Navy
> > December 19, 1912

> Today San Diego boasts a total capital investment of $28,000,000 in naval establishments, with an annual naval payroll of $30,000,000 [out of an "annual naval appropriation" of $300,000,000]. We should protect this great investment and keep this vital payroll.
>
> > San Diego Union
> > November 8, 1934

Despite the opinion of the hero of Manila Bay, San Diego became what that officer thought it could not, a major naval base.

The spirited competition among California cities for maritime facilities revealed in dramatic fashion the military beginnings of the federal urban partnership—as well as the genesis of what has come to be called the military-industrial complex. Moreover, contrary to expectations, it was the smaller cities like San Diego and Vallejo (74,000 and 21,000 respectively in 1920) who most successfully practiced the "New Martial Federalism" in the early years. The immediate precipitant of this rivalry was the appearance off the shores of California of half of the American fleet in 1919.

Actually, that year brought a revival of interest in the fleet rather than a completely new beginning. The visit of Theodore Roosevelt's Great White Fleet in 1908 had whetted West Coast appetites for military investment fully a decade earlier.[1] All along the coast of California the fleet received a rapturous welcome, and everywhere local boosters noted the lack of facilities to service the fleet once it had arrived in the Golden State. Visions of drydocks, marine bases, Corps of Engineer dredges, fuel depots, training stations, arsenals, naval academies, and other war-related paraphernalia competed in the city builders' minds with the inflated real estate values, population increases, industrial growth, and economic independence that these naval assets could be expected to produce. The naval preparedness program of 1916 rekindled interest in seafaring matters and led to congressional efforts to secure both a West Coast Navy and a U.S. Naval Academy.

These efforts were spearheaded by senators James D. Phelan of San Francisco and John D. Works of Los Angeles, especially the former. Phelan mounted a campaign to gain a United States naval academy for the West Coast and when that venture failed, plunged into a second contest over naval spoils. According to participants in the ensuing congressional debate, Congress had been persuaded that whenever the new Navy got large enough, it would be divided between the two coasts. The navy had already reached this decision, setting the number of battleships at around thirty.[2] In the opinion of Phelan and Works, the 1916 naval preparedness building program would allow the Navy to reach the requisite size for division. In July 1916, Works introduced an amendment to the famous naval appropriations bill that would have mandated that a certain number of the new ships contemplated in the act would be stationed on the Pacific coast. Although this modification failed of adoption, it united the West Coast behind the measure. Not a single state vote was cast against the amendment from a seven-state region of the Pacific Coast, including California, Oregon, Washington, Idaho, Nevada, Utah, and Arizona. The votes included that of Works, a Civil War veteran who knew the horror of war and who actually opposed American entry into the First World War itself.[3]

Although most of the country was mesmerized by the Great War raging in Europe, senators Phelan and Works argued forcefully that the real danger did not exist on the Atlantic side of the country which shared an ocean with the European belligerents. To them, Japan, the "Yellow Peril," constituted the more immediate threat, although for decidedly implausible reasons. The senators argued that Japan might assault the West Coast in the fashion of their sneak attack on Port Arthur in the Russo-Japanese War, and that Japanese immigrants were attacking it in advance as fifth columnists. They held that the Japanese were not assimilable because of color, that they were a threat to democracy, and that the United States needed a West Coast fleet to end American subservience to the Island Empire. Congress refused to accept this logic, but a message from seven states has to be heard by those in authority, and in 1919 the fleet was divided and sent westward. Secretary Josephus Daniels made the decision to divide the fleet, against the advice of many of his most prestigious advisors, including Admiral William S. Sims, commander of the American fleet in World War I.[4]

The division of the fleet emphasizes again the convergence and cooperation of the three influences stressed in this book. The Navy required transportation and housing and social, recreational, and other assets that existed only in urban areas. Without cities, the fleet could not have been divided. Clearly, however, the policy of the nation-state dictated the division of the ships between the Atlantic and the Pacific. A series of American-Japanese disputes going back to the San Francisco school crisis of 1906, and including the California anti-Japanese alien land legislation, Japan's Twenty-one Demands on China, the competing interests of the two powers in Manchuria and Siberia, the Open Door, and immigration restriction all fueled the competition between the two major Pacific powers. A naval building race resulted from this rivalry and from a fear by the navy that it would not be able to defend American "interests" in the Pacific if that necessity arose. The war anxiety of 1916 certainly helped pass the 1916 bill which would have given the United States a navy second to none. Nonetheless, the great naval program of 1916 *was not really designed for World War I.* All parties realized that the new ships would not be part of a newly created two-ocean fleet that would protect against or participate in a postwar, two-ocean military conflict. West Coast urban boosters had to have the buildup in order to justify dividing the larger fleet so that they could secure half of it for the Pacific states. Only the nation-state could take this action.

Yet as the San Francisco school crisis of 1906 had indicated, Pacific Coast urban interests helped materially to conjure up the "Yellow Peril" that a two-ocean navy would be needed to confront. The authoritative history of the Pacific Navy describes the "Japanese Menace" as just as much myth as reality, a judgment that this book endorses.[5] Although Japan's ambitions might jeopardize Russia and certainly did threaten China, the Island Empire did not menace American security or any substantial American economic interest. Even the seamen recognized that no modern Navy possessed the logistical or other resources to mount a cross-ocean attack on this country. So, in large measure, the "Yellow Peril" did not exist, except in the minds of navalists, publicists, and politicians. Urban politicians like John D. Works and James D. Phelan helped to create the notion of the "Yellow Peril"; they wanted the Navy divided so that the Pacific Coast could benefit from its presence. The division of the fleet was therefore as much a political matter as a strategic one, and the city builders and their representatives possessed considerable political influence in these affairs. No President and no military service, especially one as politically savvy as the American Navy, could afford to ignore the concerns represented by seven states. In fact, the Navy and the Pacific Coast had identical interests in the matter. The Navy saw the war and Japan as a way to augment its strength vis-à-vis the naval forces of other powers. And the Pacific cities saw the rise of the Navy as a way to enhance their own power in relation to other American metropolitan areas. For both, the 1916 naval bill and the 1919 division of the fleet represented a coming of age.

To put it mildly, the postwar reappearance of the sailors added to the ambition of the boosters. If the original visit of the Great White Fleet sparked enthusiasm, the coming of an even greater one in 1919 turned an interest into an obsession. Yet by the time the other cities had become fascinated with the possibilities of friendship with the services, San Diego, one of the smallest but most successful urban competitors, had long been busy recruiting naval patronage. From 1913 onward that city had waged an almost textbook campaign to secure military resources; and by the year of Versailles, it had succeeded well enough to change the plans of the Navy and lay the foundations for its eventual elevation to a first-class city. More than any other California city, San Diego's experience exemplifies the way in which a city, even a modest one, could mold its own future.

The Navy brought with it enormous potential for the urbanization of California, but local opinion, support, and aid would determine where the sailors settled. San Diego was under no compulsion to accept the Navy's contribution. Its growth had been substantial, rising from 17,000 to 74,000 between 1900 and 1920, while the county had surged from 35,000 to 112,000 in the same twenty years.[6] Moreover, a large productive and growing hinterland, including the aptly named Imperial County, surrounded the city; and San Diego made up a part of a seven-county congressional district which included Orange, Imperial, Riverside, San Bernadino, Mono, Inyo, and San Diego counties. The district literally constituted an empire the size of the state of Ohio; and although San Diego had to share much of this territory with its fundamentally aggressive neighbor to the north, the area provided ample opportunity for the southern city as well.[7] Obviously, San Diego did not face stagnation, much less extinction. It could easily have taken a qualitative stand on further growth, accepting only that which would have enhanced its already picturesque and charming life-style.

The options of no-growth or qualitative-growth strategies were seriously considered, but as Greg Hennessey has demonstrated, San Diego opted for the standard American version of boosterism.[8] Local city builders, like their counterparts across the land, wanted to compete with their neighbors for urban greatness and real estate profits. Therefore, they chose to court the Navy rather than let it go without a fight to Los Angeles, Santa Barbara, Monterey, Santa Cruz, San Luis Obispo, San Francisco Bay, or any of the other potentially competitive ports that might have laid claim to it. The idea of the city, in this case, proved decisive over a concern for urbanism qualitatively defined, over the traditional anti-urban view of Americans, or even over the longstanding American suspicion of the military and militarism.[9] From the very beginning, San Diego leaders had a precise notion of what a city should be and an equally exact idea of how the Navy could be used to help them create it. The partnership of the city and the sword was a very comfortable one, in part because the Navy provided a means to achieve industrial development while not sacrificing the famous quality of life in the city.

That alliance eventually focused vast forces of military development on the San Diego area, thereby tying the fate of urbanization to defense. Nonetheless, the Border City was not simply a product of the exigencies of the modern nation state. In the future, the city would become ever more reliant upon such outside influences and would never again possess the kind of freedom it had enjoyed in 1913. Nor would the Navy. Neither the city nor the outside force that accelerated its urbanization was a free agent, or independent variable. San Diego certainly became dependent upon defense spending, but the navy became dependent upon, and hostage to, the political influence of the metropolis. The Navy needed civilian, political, and economic constituencies as badly as the city needed defense spending.

This mutual dependence had initially unfolded in the Progressive years. The waning of this era in California found San Diego bursting with energy and ambition and simultaneously plagued by doubts of its permanence. Population growth had been impressive, and city builders busied themselves with undergirding that progress with solid public works. John D. Spreckels sought to give the city a railroad outlet to the East with his San Diego and Arizona Railroad, for which city voters provided several subsidies. Other boosters fought to make the city the southern terminus of a great transcontinental highway, and nearly everyone helped to develop the harbor at the end of both routes. Tidelands fell to the march of improvement and piers jutted out into the bay as the city campaigned against San Francisco for the right to hold an international exposition celebrating the opening of the Panama Canal. John Nolen had provided a city Beautiful Plan to direct and thus civilize urban growth.[10]

Yet this impressive evidence of progress did not bring peace of mind. In fact, every mayoral election in the teens reflected the insecurity of this booming town. Growth seemed to be the only major issue in these municipal elections. The Socialists mustered 3,000 votes out of a total of 14,600 in the 1913 mayoral primary, but otherwise the decade reverberated to the sounds of development politics. However, not all parties agreed on how the progress should be achieved. Though the lines of demarcation did not always show distinctly amidst the political fogs of election day, the principal cleavage seemed to be between those backers of the "City Beautiful Movement," who would lure new residents by stressing the city's climate and beauty, and those who wanted to attract population by industrialization. This argument came to a head in the 1917 mayorality campaign, in which smokestacks and geraniums came to symbolize the two sides. The chimney candidate won the election by 12,000 to 9,000, and thereafter the rift healed. Nonetheless, the anxiety did not abate.[11]

In fact, several events of the 1910s added to this uncertainty. A terrific flood in 1916 extensively damaged public and private property. The First World War deranged business conditions, and every slight downturn in the economy brought fresh doubts even while the city's population doubled in a single decade. Worse yet, San Diego's rival cities gave no quarter. Los Angeles fought to secure the transcontinental highway terminus and simultaneously invaded the San Diego back country with its own road and rail system. The Southern Pacific Railroad sabotaged construction of the San Diego and Arizona Railroad to protect its own investments in Los Angeles. San Francisco downgraded the rival San Diego exposition by getting President Taft to refuse to invite foreign participation in that ostensibly international event. As the city's historian points out, "There was no doubt that San Diego was lacking in political influence and it was time to do something about it."[12]

What it did was deft. The normally Republican San Diego congressional district became temporarily Democratic. When a candidate from Riverside won the Republican nomination for congressman from the Eleventh District, the San Diego Chamber of Commerce prevailed on one of its own, Democrat William Kettner, a chamber director, to make the race, and he won. California went for Theodore Roosevelt, but generally Republican San Diego returned a Democratic congressman. Tokens of Democratic gratitude were not long in coming and were military in character. In a sense, as Richard Pourade has noted, the party of the geraniums had won.

Service patronage gave the city an industry but without the offending smokestacks. Or, to put the matter more ironically, the militarization of San Diego became the ultimate savior of its City Beautiful.[13]

William Kettner practiced the New Martial Federalism with a virtuosity equaled only by Charles Forrest Curry and a few other California metropolitan-military politicians. Learning perhaps from San Diego's unsuccessful competition with San Francisco for the government's blessing on its 1915 exposition, Kettner kept much of his campaign low-keyed. During his tenure in the House of Representatives and for many years thereafter, the greatest available naval prize was the main home base of the Pacific Fleet. The Navy defined a main home base as one capable of holding, servicing, and supplying the entire fleet—literally a mammoth enterprise. As Admiral Charles J. Badger defined it to a congressional committee, "A main home base is one within the continental territory of the country, from which the fleet can operate at all times and which is designed to maintain the fleet in all respects both in peace and war."[14] Kettner did not openly aim for this trophy, though he probably worked to get it from an early period. Instead, the San Diego congressman concentrated publicly upon smaller, less dramatic and newsworthy projects. As any Navy man knew, enough of these modest installations could eventually become a very major one, but the other competitive cities did not seem to take note of this crucial fact. Moreover, Kettner seldom asked the Congress to appropriate very much money at one time. The main home base, which San Francisco sought, would cost an estimated $60 million to $150 million. That figure readily caught the eye of the media, rival cities, congressional economizers, political pacifists in the Congress, disarmament advocates, and politicians running for reelection. By contrast, San Diego's requested installations were mom-and-pop affairs with commensurate price tags.[15]

And invariably, Kettner could make a plausible case to the Congress or the Navy Department that it was getting something for almost nothing. Like the potlatch givers of the Pacific Northwest, the San Diegans always offered some impressive gift to their guests. These usually took the form of a choice morsel of urban real estate, often potentially valuable waterfront or tideland. On important occasions, the land donations could be combined with some otherwise unused piece of government property to appear to be a three-for-one package. If the federal government would just contribute another modest sum, cajoled the superbooster, it would acquire an entirely new asset and save an existing one from obsolescence or desuetude.

In all of these dealings, the San Diego representative understood the importance of reciprocity, stake driving, and legislative camouflage. From the beginning of his term in 1913, Kettner cultivated legislative alliances and was particularly successful in courting Sunbelt congressmen from the historic South.[16] Moreover, he knew well the rules of stake driving. As defined by Robert Caro, the biographer of Robert Moses, this art presumed that if a public endeavor got to the survey stage or possibly a little farther, it would never be abandoned by the government agency sponsoring it. In other words, once the surveyor's stakes had been driven, legislators, executives, bureaucrats, and other interested parties would not want to explain why public monies had been wasted on a project that would not be pushed to completion.[17]

Kettner played this game superbly well, and his small appropriations were ideally suited to rope the Congress into something it did not want to incur the embarrassment of later abandoning.

In numerous instances, the Congress, or most of it, did not even know that it had made the original investment. The Navy might own a piece of property here, the United States Shipping Board one there, the Army one here, or the Department of Commerce one there. Much of the money for these properties lay buried in annual appropriations measures for diverse departments and did not come to light until Kettner offered them in one of his package deals.

If these measures appeared a bit subterranean, the "million dollar congressman" had underwater ones to match, usually in partnership with the United States Army Corps of Engineers. Despite its magnificent bay, San Diego's harbor required much improvement in order to be able to accommodate even a portion of the United States fleet. By dredging the bottom, literally thousands of acres of anchorage could be created or several feet could be taken off the bottom of the entrance to the harbor, facilitating the berthing of ever larger naval vessels or commercial ships. The money for this sort of submarine boosterism might come out of the regular Corps of Engineers' budget, which allocated expenditures according to the volume of harbor traffic, which of course, their appropriations inevitably increased. Alternatively, the expenditures might originate in the naval affairs committees, the military affairs committees, the rivers and harbors committees, the commerce committees, the House Ways and Means Committee, or the Senate Finance Committee. Moreover, the Southland Democrat understood thoroughly the Navy's requirements, and he knew how the Navy thought about its problems. Accordingly, his proposals were tailored to the Navy's needs, presented in technical, bureaucratic language that the servicemen might have written themselves, and subordinated to the realities of Navy, congressional, and metropolitan politics.

Kettner brilliantly orchestrated these measures behind the scenes, seldom orating in the House and behaving modestly and speaking factually when he did. The Southland congressman also moved quickly to cultivate Southern congressmen, chairmen of the House Naval Affairs and Appropriations committees, bureaucrats in the Army Corps of Engineers, Navy officers, and civilian officials of the Navy Department. It is no wonder that he won the admiration of his congressional colleagues. As Illinois Congressman Fred Britten of the House Military Affairs Committee put it in 1920, "He [Kettner] has hypnotized not only the committee but Congress, and that is the reason that he does so well for San Diego."[18]

Yet his charming the Congress was not the only reason for the San Diegan's success. He captivated bureaucratic politicians as well. From the beginning of William Kettner's first term (and Woodrow Wilson's) in 1913, the New Freedom and the new Martial Federalism proved to be natural allies. Secretary of the Navy Josephus Daniels and his Assistant Secretary, Franklin D. Roosevelt, were among the earliest of the powerful men to succumb to the lure of the Harbor of the Sun, and Kettner soon added many others to the list. He constantly bombarded Washington officials with the virtues of the Border City; and when this barrage did not prevail, he paraded congressmen, bureaucrats, and admirals to Southern California to see for themselves.[19]

Daniels marched on his own account as well. Upon ascending to the secretaryship in 1913, the North Carolina editor decided to visit the shore installations of the country. President Taft's Secretary of the Navy, George V. L. Meyer, had slated many of these for closure and Daniels wanted to inspect for himself. In the South, Wilson's appointee saved the Charleston and Key West navy yards and reopened the Pensacola one as a new air station. In New England, the North Carolinian saved other bases from termination. However, his trip to the Pacific outweighed even these actions in importance because both expert and political opinion demanded a two-ocean navy, and a whole congeries of shore installations must be built to accommodate the Pacific branch of the fleet. That program was an enormous opportunity for both the Navy and the cities in which it would base. It also represented a considerable opening for Wilsonian Democracy, since each set of urban installations promised considerable monetary and other patronage. In inspecting the Pacific Coast, Daniels never lost sight of either the military or political implications of his visit.[20]

Not that he could easily have forgotten. Every city unlimbered its biggest civic guns to force or lure the Navy to their shores. Long Beach even offered the secretary the Pacific Ocean! And Daniels soon began to change the plans of his naval experts. For example, he prevented the demotion of the Mare Island Navy Yard against the better judgment of his advisors, and he halted planning for installations on Puget Sound. Next, he journeyed to San Francisco, damned its advantages with faint praise, and made a mental note to remove its naval training station (subsequently relocated to San Diego). However, the Secretary was impressed with the efforts of San Francisco city builders to capture the fleet from a skeptical official. "Better boosters I never saw or heard," Daniels concluded. However, he soon met superior ones in San Diego. At the Harbor of the Sun he decided to upgrade materially the heretofore neglected naval establishment, again contravening the Navy's plans for a main base in San Francisco Bay. Of course Kettner, using information from the San Diego Chamber of Commerce, had carefully prepared the Secretary while both were in Washington. As Daniels put it, "It was not difficult to convince me of the advantages of San Diego." The Border City enjoyed proximity to the Panama Canal, a mild climate, and the "whole population was united to convince the new Secretary that San Diego was by far the best site for Naval bases on the Pacific." The Border City was indeed grateful. At the end of his tenure Daniels confided to his diary that "Bill Kettner called and said San Diego would never forget what I had done there." To prove it, "when my term of office expired, friends in that city offered to give me a house if I would spend my last years in San Diego."[21]

The military dividends from this federal-urban partnership appeared on both the San Diego cityscape and the Navy's plans for the development of shore stations on the East Coast.[22] In 1913, San Diego possessed one coaling station, dating from 1898, and little else. More discouraging still, from the Diegueno point of view, official naval planners intended to keep the Border City's naval presence limited. The 1909 General Board opinion envisioned a small naval establishment for San Diego, and the famous 1916 Helm Board investigation of shore installations did not concede much more. However, the Helm Report modestly began the process of planning ever greater facilities for the Bay of San Diego. By 1920, what had been merely a coaling station and torpedo training ground had been conceded the status of operating base.[23] Progress on the ground matched the theoretical conceptions of the Navy's planners.

Like many other crucial developments in the history of Southern California, these advances were frequently attributed to the natural advantages of the area. The movies, the aircraft industry, the great population migrations, and the Navy supposedly were irresistibly attracted by the climate and geography of the Southland, giving that megalopolis an air of inevitability. In thinking this way, Southern Californians have carried forward into the twentieth century a very popular nineteenth-century booster idea which Charles Glaab and Theodore Brown have termed the "doctrine of natural advantages." According to this notion, the fate of a great city would be determined by its natural and therefore God-given assets, such as a productive hinterland, a good harbor, and a good climate.[24] Perhaps no other American urban area has been as enamored of this idea as the Southland megalopolis. At the same time, it is doubtful if any other American metropolitan area has done more to circumvent, alter, ignore, or obliterate its natural surroundings. For example, Los Angeles built a great harbor where God had intended none, brought water from hundreds of miles away to offset its local water deficit, rearranged its geography to control flooding, drilled artesian wells hundreds of feet into the ground, filled underwater catch basins with imported water when the water table fell and pulled in salt water, carried housing development up what are almost sheer cliffs in its neighboring mountains, and, in the absence of coal deposits nearby, generated electricity from the water coursing south through its Owens Valley Aqueduct.[25] As a further indication of its attitude toward geography, the city partially destroyed three of its main natural assets—sunshine, pure air, and scenery— through the creation of pollution, and it has still continued to grow. So much for the rigor of its geographic imperatives. San Diego did not alter its God-given situation quite as much, but it operated on the same principle.

The Border City's willingness to do so explains more than geography does about its success in attracting the Navy. San Diego's two main natural attractions for the Navy were its weather and its harbor. The mild, dry climate provided more training days for ships and later planes, reduced heating costs in winter, and allowed a pleasant, outdoor all-year-round life-style for officers, men, and civilian support personnel. It required only a short steaming time to get from the harbor to the nearby fleet training grounds, which were conveniently located off of the heavily trafficked commercial sea lanes. Finally, the city rested near the Mexican border and Latin America, where in the past it had been frequently deemed necessary to dispatch marines and soldiers aboard Navy vessels.[26] Obviously, San Diego enjoyed very definite natural advantages.

However, Los Angeles possessed virtually the same ones. And the City of Angels had made up for its comparative disadvantage by building an impressive and what seemed to be an endlessly growing artificial harbor. In fact, despite having been created by the dredge rather than by the Deity, the Los Angeles harbor served as the main fleet anchorage from 1922 until the Navy split that force in 1938 and sent one part back to the Atlantic (over the protests of Southern California spokesmen) and, in 1940, one to Pearl Harbor.[27] In most respects, San Francisco possessed more geographic advantages still, particularly its harbor, which literally dwarfed even the beautiful and useful San Diego Bay in both a quantitative and qualitative sense. In terms of man-made assets, the adversity of the comparison between San Diego and its larger rivals was downright severe. Like any other business, the Navy looked for certain urban resources upon which it could draw once it took up residence in a metropolitan area. Among others, San Diego lacked a shipbuilding capacity; a large volume of commerce to defend or draw sustenance from; a sizable, skilled, and trained labor supply; and good rail links.[28]

San Diego's efforts to rectify these defects rapidly paid off, initially in the form of federal aid for San Diego Bay, secured through the good offices of Admiral George Dewey. Since the largest ships of the Navy could not pass comfortably into the bay in its unimproved state, harbor dredging seemed to be the logical first step. Kettner, Senator John D. Works of San Diego and Los Angeles, and Rufus Choate of the Chamber of Commerce moved to get the Corps of Engineers to dredge the entrance to the harbor. The Corps proved willing, but needed congressional authorization in the form of an appropriation. To get that, Kettner had to approach Dewey, currently president of the General Board, the chief policy-making body of the Navy. Dewey did not concede much, but he did authorize the dredging of San Diego Harbor to a depth of thirty-five feet over the middle ground and forty feet over the bar. That meant that the new ships of the fleet could enter the harbor; without that capacity, it would have been next to impossible for San Diego to demonstrate fully its potential usefulness to the fleet.[29] At that point, however, there was not much of a fleet in the Pacific, and many of the ships for which the deepened harbor entrance was designed had not yet been built. But San Diego was determined to be useful anyway.

Thereafter, the effectiveness of Kettner, the Navy's re-evaluation of the utility of Southern California, and the First World War produced an impressive number of ways in which the Border City could help in strengthening the country's first line of defense. The coaling station had to be completed and a "fuel oil" station added to it if the fleet were to be serviced properly, and the Congress funded these improvements in 1914. A $300,000 appropriation followed to build the largest radio station in the world. As usual, the New Federalism, the new military buildup, and the omnipresent California metropolitan anxiety were intimately intertwined. Kettner discovered in 1914 that the Navy Department desired a radio station site in Southern California and had inspected a location in San Diego. When the San Diego forces learned that Whittier, California, had already tendered a site for the station, the Chamber of Commerce countered with an offer of four different locations. The Navy liked one of these, but found that the owner lived in New Jersey and wanted more than the service could afford. Kettner not only found the owner but bargained down his price to something that the Navy could pay.[30] For the time being, Whittier would have to wait for national recognition.

Nothing could better illustrate the comprehensive and mutually reinforcing nature of these California urban-navalist conspiracies than the military improvements made in San Diego from 1913 to 1923, by which time San Diegans had constructed a major military base in their metropolitan area. The Border City secured an advance marine base (the nucleus of Camp Pendleton) in 1917 which was commissioned in 1921; procured a naval air station for North Island in the same year: deftly pilfered a naval training station from San Francisco in 1917; added a Navy hospital in 1919; gained the designation of a Naval Operating Base in 1920; and in 1921 tacked on a naval supply depot, a submarine repair base, and the Eleventh Naval District Headquarters.[31] Simultaneously, Kettner and his booster allies landed their 1915 exposition and secured further appropriations for Fort Rosecrans at the entry to the harbor.

Kettner received much better federal treatment for the exposition from the Democrats than from the Republicans. The former endorsed the fair and helped in other ways. Naturally a regional fair, even in a city of less than 75,000 people, had to have a visit from the fleet. The dredging of the harbor allowed the fleet to settle comfortably into the berths provided for it. That in turn enabled San Diego to prove the utility and large capacity of its harbor. The officers and men could then be introduced to the area, its climate, its fleshpots, its more genteel hospitality, and its liberality with its waterfront. The presence of the Navy required a marine detachment, and its commandant, Joseph Pendleton, just happened to fall in love with San Diego and recommend a permanent marine base for the area. So did many of the Washington dignitaries whom Kettner escorted in and out, ostensibly to see the fair, but in reality to reconnoiter the naval possibilities of the Border City as well. Franklin D. Roosevelt was not the least of these converts, nor was he the last.

The continuing federal dredging program produced ever more berthing spaces and anchorage area. These artificial improvements allowed San Diego to lay claim to the large American destroyer fleet once the First World War ended and the ships needed to be mothballed. Fitting perfectly into the urban developmental puzzle, the mud and sand derived from dredging this site went into a five-hundred-acre parcel for the marine base. Incidentally, in filling in the mudflat, San Diegans also pursued their dream of the City Beautiful, since a marine base was considered a much more sightly urban asset than a mudflat. Across the bay, the Navy established an air station in 1917, building on the work of pioneer aviator Glenn Curtiss.

Geopolitical factors, as one excellent analysis has termed them, strengthened the urban navalists' hand considerably.[32] American entry into the First World War made the marine base seem more urgent, necessitated more and better training facilities, highlighted the dawning importance of air power, demanded greater shipbuilding facilities, created a larger Navy, and offered a chance for a city to become a convalescent point for wounded sailors. San Diego cashed in on each of these opportunities. The Marine Corps initiated what was to become Camp Pendleton, and the Zimmerman Note, with its implied "Mexican Peril," added to the urgency of this project. The war gave further impetus to the development of naval aeronautics on North Island as well. As usual, Congressman Kettner facilitated this progress, brokering the dispute between the Navy and John D. Spreckels's interests over the Navy's use of North Island. Finally, the First World War produced a shipbuilding plant on San Diego Bay designed to construct cement ships.

If anything, the end of the conflict created more opportunities than its beginning had. The transfer of 1919 brought the larger part of the fleet to Pacific waters, where it promptly overtaxed the limited facilities available to service it and therefore set off fresh cries for improvements. And since the war had required the rapid buildup of the destroyer force to counteract the German submarine menace, the postwar Navy found itself with excess destroyers that needed storing. San Diego eventually got this mothball fleet and ultimately parlayed that acquisition into another, a ship repair facility. Again, First World War surplus proved useful. Kettner urged the Congress and the United States Shipping Board to grant the cement shipbuilding facility to the Navy to be reconverted into a repair plant. By 1921 this otherwise irrelevant facility would become a submarine repair base and subsequently would be enlarged into a destroyer repair plant.

The "augmented fleet" required the mending of personnel as well as materiel, a fact that Captain H. C. Curl, a doctor at the temporary hospital at the Naval Training Station, brought to William Kettner's notice. A city councilman pointed out a potential medical site in Balboa park and, as Kettner put it, "knowing the handsome way in which the Navy takes care of its unfortunates," he went after and received authorization for a hospital that became a reality in 1919.[33] It is no wonder that the Navy designated San Diego an operating base in 1920 and made it the headquarters for the Eleventh Naval District in April 1921.[34]

The Bay Area's Southland counterparts, especially those in San Diego, had known this truth all along, having practiced it expertly themselves over the same period of time. The long years of deadlock at the Golden Gate aided the Southland efforts considerably. Originally slated for a very minor role in the Navy's plans, San Diego consistently gained from this delay. As in the Bay Area, each new installation strengthened the case for the next and made the whole complex less susceptible to abandonment.

Yet threat of desertion was a very sobering one for the city of San Diego. Despite its best efforts, the Border City had not achieved a diversified economy by the advent of the Great Depression; and therefore its naval investment continued to loom large in importance. All in all, the Navy, tourism, retirement, and in-migration produced impressive capital transfers to San Diego; but beyond these things, there was not much else. Until the coming of Consolidated Aircraft Corporation in 1935 to join the Ryan Company, aircraft manufacturing remained small and, even if added to the fish, agricultural, and lumber processing industries, did not amount to a significant factory base. San Diego's commerce was larger, but not much more promising to city boosters. As in Gold Rush San Francisco, a huge amount of cargo came across the docks into the city, but hardly anything went out in return. Even incoming goods consisted mostly of building materials and fuel, which would not be needed if the growth of the city happened to stagnate. Although the Harbor of the Sun claimed a vast tributary area, including the productive Imperial Valley to the east, most of it paid no tribute. The larger portion of the seven-county empire that made up the Eleventh Congressional District, of which San Diego was the principal population center, was bound to Los Angeles.

That fearsomely energetic city even extended its commercial dominance into the Imperial Valley directly east of San Diego, which according to the geographic determinism of the boosters should have been the natural back country of the Border City. The Southern Pacific Railroad and the highway system leading to Los Angeles made the reality somewhat different. At great cost, John D. Spreckels extended the San Diego and Arizona Railway to the Imperial Valley and beyond, but this line did not overcome the Southern Pacific lead into this Colorado River delta country. Nor did Spreckels find a way to surmount the costs and other difficulties of operation imposed by the mountainous terrain the railway had to traverse.

By the twenties, 70 percent of the automobile traffic to Southern California went to Los Angeles, and San Diego fared no better in diverting this stream than it did in turning aside the flow of commerce from the Imperial Valley. Numerous highway-building schemes attracted the support of local promoters, but few miles of hard road materialized. Moreover, most of the transcontinental routes to the borders of the state, boosted by San Diego, funneled traffic westward toward Los Angeles as well as toward San Diego, and these autos were usually diverted to the Southland metropolis at places like Tucson or Yuma. Besides, at any time some Angeleno road-building scheme might channel still more travelers and retirees into the City of the Angels, depriving San Diego of the modest but life-giving stream of people that chose it over its neighbor. Each city also competed for the equally precious flow of water from the Colorado River. Both cities yearned for the waters of the Colorado to compensate for their own geographic disadvantages, and competition between them remained sharp until the Boulder Dam Project was assured. Once again, Los Angeles won hands down. It built the quarter-billion-dollar aqueduct to the Colorado and thereby gained control of the Southland's future water supply without which urbanization could not proceed. Since San Diego possessed no such resources, it remained dependent upon its neighbor for its future water supply. Although the Great Depression did not strike San Diego as hard as it did many other American cities, it worsened most of that city's long-standing economic difficulties. With one-third of the economy based on federal and largely naval spending, San Diego was in no position to re-examine its relationship with the federal government.

Nor did it. Instead, San Diego sought to broaden its federal-urban partnership, which led to an ever-increasing interface between urbanism, the New Federalism, and the New Navalism, as San Diego quickly won a well-deserved reputation for cooperation with the services. As in the earlier period, a massive public consensus supported the New Martial Federalism. The press, city government, Harbor Commission, civic clubs, labor unions, political parties, and public stood solidly behind the courting of the Navy. The old civic debate over industrialization, water rights, the power of the Spreckels interests, the city manager form of government, land use regulations, and corruption perennially waxed and waned; but seldom did civilian San Diego seriously question the outsized presence of the Navy in their community. The Navy pushed especially hard to get the harbor improvements and land donations which a generous community bestowed upon it, almost ritually threatening to decamp if it were turned down. San Diego was bombarded with these threats, although it is difficult to see how that city could have been more cooperative short of electing an admiral to the mayoralty.

The Harbor Commission typified the Border City's uncritical support and its astounding success. Reorganized in 1928 to remove "politics" from decisions affecting the port, the Harbor Commission was composed of appointed members with a budget largely free from city council or mayoral influence. In 1931 the electorate approved a further reorganization, which guaranteed the commission $150,000 per year and control of all revenues generated by the port. Since aviation, commerce, railroads, highways, passenger shipping, recreation, tourism, industry, civic beautification, fishing, military, and other important interests centered in large part on the Harbor of the Sun, the Harbor Commission possessed tremendous power. It could plan and to an extent regulate development of the heart of the city and thereby exact concessions in return for privileges granted, especially to the military. It is thus not surprising that the multiplication of Navy piers, anchorage grounds, base sites, and turning basins in one part of the harbor was echoed in the proliferation of parks, yacht harbors, industrial sites, harbor drives, and airport runways in another.

These tradeoffs took place in an open and unabashed manner. Joe Brennan, port director, explained that the city had spent $3.5 million by 1931. "Because the city improves its port, so does the war department and so does the navy," he continued.

> For example, the city builds a pier, steamship lines start making calls and gain cargo likely to drag bottom—and the war department, being charged with the care for water commerce as a side line, digs a deeper channel to it, and at the same time creates valuable operative lands. The federal government has spent upwards of $2.5 million deepening channels. . . . The city by its own dredging fills in tideland which the navy sees as good locations for a supply depot and purchasing department. Given the land, the navy erects the building, adds a pier, brings in more ships—and gives wholesalers a new market and retailers more customers.
>
> A very good illustration of the interlocking nature of San Diego port development is in progress just now. The war department is dredging a turning basin for the Navy's big airplane carriers and with the dredged material filling in a second unit of the city's airport, Lindbergh Field. The basin, of course, is also a deepwater expansion of the commercial port.
>
> Hence, the "making" of new land where shallow tide flows and extension of shore to somewhat constricted water area is held to be economically advisable. . . . This real estate, a strip miles in length with trackage of two transcontinental railroad systems on the shore side and harbor waters on the other must be deemed a highly advantageous municipal asset. . . . By reclamation of tidelands through its own and federal dredging, San Diego has upwards of 100 acres for lease to industries seeking waterfrontage or requiring water transportation.[35]

Brennan might have added that the new land was also slated for the long-awaited waterfront civic center and the scenic harbor drive recommended by the second John Nolen Plan for San Diego.[36] The Navy's perennial threats to go somewhere else must have promoted a sense of political subservience amongst San Diego officialdom, but sometimes it was impossible to determine who was exploiting whom.

And since the Harbor Commission was largely immune from electoral review, it was free, within the limitations of its own resources and those of the Navy, to continue in a business-like manner the coupling of the city and the sword. As it did, the ambition of the city grew apace. Slated for a very minor role in 1916, then accorded the status of a secondary operating and training base in 1921, the city claimed to be the second largest naval base in the country by the end of the twenties. By the advent of the Roosevelt administration in 1933, San Diego aspired to the role of main West Coast home base—assigned to San Francisco Bay by naval planners. In the mid-twenties the Navy transferred its submarine base from Los Angeles to San Diego, and in 1933 a part of the cruiser forces followed the subs. That allowed San Diego to claim that it needed a new graving or dry dock to repair and service ships of the cruiser class and below and new piers to accommodate them. These materialized in 1941.[37] Meanwhile, a turning basin between the naval air station on North Island and the Broadway Pier on the mainland was dredged out, and a total of five square miles of thirty-five-foot anchorage was created by 1931. The turning basin enabled San Diego harbor to handle the newly created aircraft carriers of the *Saratoga* and *Lexington* class and at the same time enlarged Lindbergh Field, its commercial airport, assuring the city a foothold in the fields of both naval and civilian aviation thereafter. The new anchorages allowed the Harbor of the Sun to prove its military utility in 1935 by sheltering the entire Battle Fleet during its visit to the San Diego World's Fair.

Obviously, the growing threat of war influenced these events, but San Diego's cooperation continued to be important. For example, in 1933, a terrific storm so overwhelmed the anchorage of the fleet in the artificial harbor of Los Angeles that the Navy decided to remove a part of it to San Diego. In response, the Harbor Commission immediately began dredging the berths necessary to accommodate this new acquisition. When the commander of the cruiser division called the Commission about recreational facilities for the sailors, the response was lightning fast. As one account put it, "The next day the bulldozers began building ball fields and tennis courts on made land that the city had created in 1928—just in case." The city's response to the 1935 proposal to bridge the Bay from San Diego to Coronado was equally prompt and more dramatic. The Navy strenuously opposed this idea. As usual, it threatened to withdraw from the area and requested covering fire from the city. Unlike San Francisco, which had built two bridges across its bay, and over serious Navy misgivings as well, San Diego stopped this project dead in its tracks. Not until many years later did the Border City dare to build the San Diego-Coronado Bridge, as much an architectural masterpiece and emotional landmark as the Golden Gate Bridge is for San Francisco. In short, the Border City tried its best to keep the climate of defense investment congenial to a service that not only warned that it would take its business to other ports, like San Francisco or Los Angeles, but could easily have done so.[38]

The City of the Angels, though by far the most dynamic of the California cities, ultimately gained least from the Navy. It would be impossible to ascribe this outcome to geography, to strategic considerations, or to the imperative necessities of the Navy's training schedule. Los Angeles was far more strategic than San Diego, as a possible target for enemy action against it, as a base of support for operations in distant Pacific places like Hawaii, and as a valued source of supplies, services, and personnel. Moreover, its weather and geography were very similar to its neighbor to the south. Los Angeles had originally been accorded a minor role in the California urban naval drama. The Helm Board of 1916 had recommended a submarine base for the Southland metropolis, largely on geographic grounds, but had not been impressed with its general suitability for the Navy's purposes. Although the southern city claimed the fleet anchorage in 1922, the navy never completely changed its mind about the limited utility of Los Angeles. However, the extraordinary growth of the City of the Angels in the 1920s, from 576,000 to 1,238,000, induced the Navy to reconsider its original denigration of this active metropolis. That municipality built an enormous breakwater to enclose its artificial port, and its almost terrifyingly rapid development provided many of the labor, industrial, commercial, transportation, and other requirements lacking when the Navy planners made their original location decisions. For a time, naval planners looked longingly to the south as an alternative main home base site, but the newfound Bay Area unity of 1933 brought them back to their initial support of San Francisco Bay.

The lack of enthusiasm was mutual. Los Angeles had produced quite a number of booster miracles by 1941, but these did not include any in the realm of urban navalism. The Navy certainly did not occupy the central place in the City of the Angels that it did in San Francisco, San Diego, or Vallejo. In 1934, the *San Diego Union* could, with considerable truthfulness, boast that "the Navy is integrated into this community more completely here than in any other American port."[39] As late as 1940, the Los Angeles Chamber of Commerce had to remind its readers that although the "fleet is based at Los Angeles for strategic reasons, [it is] in our own interest as well as the Navy's that this community should exert itself to make Los Angeles the place where the Fleet personnel *prefers* to be based." "Closer social relations between Angelenos and Navy residents are also in order," admitted *Southern California Business,* "and we might well take a tip from other cities which honor the Fleet with gala social affairs."[40]

Throughout the period, Los Angeles's naval acquisitions reflected its lack of zeal. Because of the inadequate depths of the Main and Bonita channels into the Golden Gate and because of its proximity to superior training grounds, the Navy decided in 1922 to make Los Angeles, rather than San Francisco, the main fleet anchorage. At least that was their public rationale for this decision. However, in the succeeding years of the interim period the Navy did not invest in the shore installations that would have made the anchorage into a main or even secondary base. The port of Los Angeles-Long Beach received its submarine base, a naval dispensary, and some warehouses and supply functions. In the 1930s, the Navy turned offshore San Clemente Island into a secret training base, but Los Angeles did not secure the supply depots, ordnance facilities, dry docks, and other naval infrastructure that would have made the harbor into a permanent naval base. The harbor even lost some of its meager resources during the period, as San Diego claimed the submarine base in the twenties and a part of the fleet cruiser forces in 1933.

Despite its earlier lethargy, in 1933 Los Angeles began a base drive of its own. For years the city had gradually built up its breakwater to give protection to its artificial and largely open, starkly unprotected harbor. In that year it began a massive addition to this great public work. Finished in 1938, it was designed to allow the entire fleet to lie within it at anchor. In 1933 the city also began agitating for the acquisition of a Navy dry dock and supply depot, which would have been the nucleus of a main home base. In 1938, the Los Angeles electorate voted to donate an air station site to the Navy. This soon became Reeves Field on Terminal Island, and before the war broke out, it had achieved the status of a fleet air base. However, in 1937 Los Angeles discovered that San Francisco Bay had already been chosen as the site for the main home base, and in 1938 it began to lose the fleet itself, at the very moment when the breakwater would have allowed an adequate anchorage. Beginning in the early thirties, the Atlantic and Pacific fleets had been consolidated in the Pacific Ocean, but in 1938, the Atlantic Fleet was reconstituted in response to the increasingly menacing situation in Europe. Then in 1940, the government withdrew another 35,000 men when the Pacific Fleet departed for Pearl Harbor. Unlike the case in San Diego and San Francisco, they did not leave behind a highly developed naval infrastructure to guarantee the community's boast that the absence would be only a temporary one.[41]

The remarkable outcome in San Diego derived from an extraordinary community effort. Urban historians have frequently been criticized for anthropomorphizing their subjects, making diverse cities seem to have human characteristics and to move in a united way as an individual would. Whatever the general validity of this criticism, it has little relevance to the navalist campaigns of early- and mid-twentieth-century San Diego. That city would eventually regret at least the wartime complexities of its association with the military, although it never seriously regretted its partnership. However, in the earlier years it had few such second thoughts, and a literally singular unanimity prevailed. Congressman Kettner and the Chamber of Commerce led these battles, but, as the naval referenda document, the general populace backed their leaders to the hilt. For example, the donation of the hospital site in Balboa Park carried by a ten-to-one majority, and the same electorate voted 40,288 to 305 to donate 500 acres of tidelands for the marine base.[42] By 1929, San Diego had given away one-third of its waterfront to the Navy, a figure that reached 3,000 acres by 1955.[43] However much the industrializers and naturalizers may have disagreed over the necessity of smokestacks, their quarrel did not extend to four-stack destroyers. If it is true that Americans harbored a traditional fear of the military and militarism until well into the twentieth century, it was not in evidence in the Border City.

Less unanimity has prevailed among scholars and other city watchers about the effectiveness of this kind of campaign, or, to put it differently, about the significance of the city in creating this defense empire. Contemporary urban builders naturally thought that their own contributions were decisive, and their successors have continued to stress the importance of local efforts to enhance the forces of urbanization by this naval association. Curiously enough, many social science interpretations, even Marxist ones, have partially accepted this booster vision of the process of city creation.[44] However, many other analysts, local and cosmopolitan, have tended to lapse into the language of modern social science determinism or nineteenth-century urban geographical determinism with special emphasis upon the critical influence of climate. Sometimes this argument emphasizes the amenities of "pleasant living conditions," defined as the natural advantages of the area in general. Naval spokesmen stressed the importance of geography while emphasizing the overall needs of the Navy as the crucial factor in the placement of its shore installations.

Navy personnel were openly grateful for the "generosity" of San Diego and were frequently astonished at its extent, but they always insisted publicly that the strategic, material, and personnel requirements of the Great White Fleet, rather than those of a Greater San Diego, dictated its actions. Each of these latter arguments rejects the booster explanation of local growth and agrees with Kenneth Boulding's argument. As he put it, "We have passed from the stage where the cities nurtured civilization to a world in which the city is simply a victim or beneficiary of forces far beyond its own control."[45]

If that contention is true of any modern cities, those inhabiting the Sunbelt are not among them. In their case, the interpretation of the boosters and the advice of Oscar Handlin is much more appropriate. Though himself a believer in the crucial role of outside forces in shaping the city in history, Handlin offered these qualifiers:

> However useful a general theory of the city may be, only the detailed tracing of an immense range of variables, in context, will illuminate the dynamics of the processes [of urbanization] here outlined. We can readily enough associate such gross phenomena as the growth of population and the rise of the centralized state, as technological change and the development of modern industry, as the disruption of the traditional household and the decline of corporate life. But *how* these developments unfolded, and what was the causal nexus among them, we shall only learn when we make out the interplay among them by focusing upon *a* city specifically in all its uniqueness.[46]

The modern state with its ever-greater defense requirements certainly created one of the cardinal opportunities for the Sunbelt, and the amenities of that region surely helped it to exploit these possibilities dramatically. Yet the cities themselves constituted an important, even crucial variable. If they did not create the opportunities, they greatly influenced how "these developments unfolded," especially the timing and geographic distribution of military resources.

In one respect, local option was the decisive causal nexus, to employ Handlin's phraseology. San Diego did not have to become a Navy town, at least before the Second World War, and it did not have to remain one after that conflict. The most important reason for the placement of what became the main home base in San Diego was that the city let the nation-state put it there. For the most part, the city held veto power over the initial coming of that service simply by virtue of its control over its own waterfront, which was almost entirely municipal property. Even the imperatives of the First World War did not substantially change this situation.[47] Almost everything the services got in San Diego came from enthusiastic city offers and much local brokerage of crucial matters. Moreover, many, if not most, of these military resources could have been put somewhere else. Los Angeles or San Jose had substantially the same amenities as San Diego and therefore possessed as much claim to facilities like the North Island Naval Air Station, the naval training station, Camp Kearny, Camp Pendleton, the operating base, or the Eleventh Naval District Headquarters. Moreover, the Border City had much less strategic significance than Los Angeles, San Francisco, Portland, or Seattle. All these cities were closer to the expected scenes of action in a hypothetical Pacific War; during the interwar years, the Navy repeatedly stressed the primary strategic importance of San Francisco Bay and Puget Sound. Of course, when the Red Menace replaced the Yellow Peril, San Diego was even farther from Russian borders than those of Japan. Nor did its proximity to the Mexican border provide a strategic rationale that its distance from the Red and Yellow perils denied. Naval planners stressed the vulnerability of San Diego to incursions from south of the border and therefore argued against its use as the main home base of the Pacific Fleet, though that is precisely what it became.[48] It may have made military sense to station marines and soldiers close to the border for interventions abroad or as defense against Pancho Villa–style raids on American territory. However, given the mobility of the Mexican cavalry, the placement of the only American naval air station and naval training station on the Pacific Coast within ten miles of that supposed threat is indeed a strategic enigma. Military strategies seem to have been no more compelling than natural amenities in determining the distribution of military bases. If we add that San Diego lacked sufficient rail and air connections, a large labor force, plentiful supplies, warehouse facilities, industrial capacity, commercial traffic, and fuel supplies, all of which Los Angeles possessed, it is even more of a mystery why the chief operating base in Southern California and ultimately the main home base on the Coast were developed one hundred miles south of the resources it depended upon and, in case of war, would have had to protect.

However compelling the phrase, the experience of San Diego refutes Eisenhower's notion of a military-industrial complex. The city had no armaments industry, like Vichers, Armstrong-Whitworth, or Bethlehem Steel, when the Navy arrived.[49] No merchant of death dictated the placement of the Navy in San Diego. Nor did any supposed military figure. The city got the prize of the fleet because of the brokerage of an urban congressman, the drive of its boosters, and the political and military calculations of a civilian politician, the Secretary of the Navy. The military-industrial elements were simply lacking. The nation-state was divided in its counsels between the service experts, who favored a main home base in San Francisco Bay, and the civilian Secretary. The San Diego boosters were influential in their activities, and the fact of the city was overwhelmingly compelling. The Navy had to locate in some city; that part of the case was open and shut. Which city they picked was determined by the interplay of San Diego and the nation-state, if a civilian Secretary of the Navy intent on building the Democratic party can be said to represent the nation-state.

CHAPTER 3

Creating the American Singapore:
The San Francisco Bay Area
and the Quest for Naval Riches

In the long run, the piecemeal, accretional naval development of San Diego led to the most important concentration of Navy resources on the Pacific coast. Contemporaneously, the spirited competition for the Navy's main West Coast home base overshadowed the opportunistic and almost haphazard militarization of the Border City. That controversy centered on the San Francisco Bay Area, and it demonstrates even more forcefully than the experience of San Diego the decisiveness of the urban veto power. In contrast to the Southland, metropolitan rivalry postponed rather than promoted the militarization of the Bay Area. The delay lasted from 1916 to 1933 and, as a consequence, denied the San Francisco metropolitan area a greater military stimulus than it otherwise would have had and ultimately diverted the major California naval investment to Southern California. This outcome again contravened the logical imperatives of both military strategy and natural amenity and demonstrated once more the extraordinary powers of political mobilization in a small city. In the south, San Diego with its 1920 population of 74,000 had captured more naval resources than its giant neighbor, with 576,000. In Northern California, Vallejo with 21,000 would defeat "The City" and its population of 506,000 plus Oakland with nearly a quarter of a million more.

In the Bay Area, the entanglement of the city and the sword dates from the foundation of the Presidio in 1776, the year of San Francisco's birth. The American occupation of 1846 produced a military construction program that lasted well into the 1850s, and the Civil, Spanish-American, and First World wars triggered others. By 1920 the San Francisco metropolitan area had acquired impressive martial assets and had felt the stimulating effects of heavy military spending upon metropolitan development. World War I prosperity came at a peculiarly significant moment for San Francisco.

Perhaps no other political issue was so influential in San Francisco between the wars as the loss, revealed in the 1920 census, of its West Coast pre-eminence to Los Angeles. This relative decline dramatically links the militarization of the Bay Area to urbanization/urbanism. The "Entrepôt of the Pacific" desperately needed new assets and resources to stem its slide. Though thinly disguised in the rhetoric of "national defense," San Francisco openly sought a military multiplier to stimulate its own faltering pace of urbanization. San Francisco's maritime dependence and the Navy's greater potential bounty led the city, in its interwar pursuit of military resources, to concentrate on that service.

Other Bay Area cities felt the same insecurity. The Navy had founded the Mare Island Navy Yard in 1954, and for a time it had served its purposes well. However, by the twentieth century the vagaries of Bay Area water currents together with the advance of military technology threatened to limit or possibly end its utility. The operation of the waters tended to silt up the channel into Mare Island, and the increasing gigantism of Navy construction combined with this natural defect to make it increasingly difficult for Navy vessels to pass to and from the yard. As early as 1909, the General Board had questioned the utility of further developing Mare Island, and various other Navy spokesmen would make even more menacing remarks thereafter. For Vallejo, across the river from the yard, these comments threatened sudden death. Even with the presence of the Navy, that city had grown only very modestly, especially by California standards. Without that service, the Carquinez Straits town could easily have become the anomaly of a no-growth town in an exploding metropolitan area. Despite its origins in the Gold Rush era, Vallejo had never developed a diverse urban economy. As late as the post-World War II era, it possessed only two "industries"—the United States Navy and one flour mill. Naturally, any threat to the former brought forth a spirited response from a united city.

The East Bay cities of Alameda, Oakland, Berkeley, and their suburbs did not face stagnation from an adverse naval decision, but they did stand to lose or gain a great deal from the rapid metropolitan development of the state. Each presented a threat to the potential of the others, and all faced eclipse by the cities and towns of the more dynamically growing urban Southland. In addition, the East Bay cities feared the loss of their independence and identity in a "Greater San Francisco," a scheme of consolidation put forth with rising enthusiasm as the smaller core city of San Francisco became more acutely aware of its relative decline vis-à-vis its own suburbs as well as Los Angeles.

The transfer of the fleet to the Pacific in 1919 seemed at least a partial answer to this pervasive metropolitan anxiety. Although strategic factors have not generally been considered important to the process of urbanization, they were crucial to the development of Urban California—and long before the onset of World War II. Western city builders had long lobbied for a more equal division of the Navy between the two coasts, and the First World War strengthened their hand. From the 1916 debates over naval preparedness, Pacific Coast urban navalists insisted ever more stridently that a greater part of the enlarged Navy be posted to western waters to "protect" them. Though the fleet was initially dispatched to Europe instead of to the Pacific, the world war and the buildup provided the leverage that the West Coast needed. The postwar sinking of the German fleet removed the chief threat to the peace in the Atlantic, but the continuing Japanese and American rivalry to the west seemed to substitute one peril with another. The great increase of the Navy during the war made it feasible to divide the fleet, and the scrapping of Admiral Mahan's One-Fleet Theory of strategy made it easier for the Navy to take that action. In doing so, it is probable that the Navy hoped to build up a series of new political constituencies on the Pacific Coast, comparable with the Charlestons and Norfolks on the Atlantic, in order to support the Navy's own conception of national defense.

Even before the Navy steamed to the West, that service had worked out plans for the allocation of its resources on the Pacific Coast. Secretary of the Navy Josephus Daniels announced in 1919 that the Mahan One-Fleet Theory was dead and that, after a decent burial, half of the Navy would be stationed in Pacific waters. To accommodate the fleet, the Navy planned a series of shore installations. These were distributed both strategically and politically. The Navy had learned in World War I that an emergency would require many shore facilities not always needed in time of peace, and they made certain that these would be placed in or, in the case of Portland, near the major West Coast metropolitan areas. The two most desirable plums were to be given to Puget Sound and San Francisco Bay respectively, and the Bay Area was to have the main West Coast home base of the Pacific fleet. This facility would cost $60 million to $100 million and would bring with it an estimated 45,000 naval personnel. It was grandiosely referred to in Northern California as the "American Singapore."

These allocations had been made by the naval experts, and the various urban spokesmen never tired of commending an arrangement so obviously in the interest of national defense. Such an argument appealed to a generation of businessmen and politicians undergoing "Taylorization" in the economic world and experiencing the more specifically urban version of this idea in the realm of government: the "Goo Goo doctrine of expertise" frequently employed in American cities on behalf of charter and structural reform.* In fact, the doctrine of expertise formed the basis of the political strategies worked out by coast cities to get and hold the fleet and to distribute naval resources among the Pacific urban areas. For instance, all the cities united in demanding the fleet for Pacific waters, citing the naval experts and their various strategic theories to back up this claim. Once the sailors had been secured, the cities again publicly deferred to the experts' judgment in placing their facilities around the coast and even within specific parts of the various metropolitan areas. In the San Francisco Bay Area, for example, the two leading contenders for the operating base site, Alameda and Hunter's Point in San Francisco, each fought vigorously for that prize but agreed to let the naval experts decide ultimately. Just as city finances and other crucial matters should be turned over to experts, so should the distribution of maritime resources, argued the Bay Area boosters. This was at the same time a validation of their Taylorist philosophy, which some interpreters have termed the most important ideology invented in the United States since the Founding Fathers, and a shrewd political strategy. The experts, after all, agreed with the Bay Area boosters that the main base should be located in the San Francisco Area.

This logical formula should have contained the political infighting for naval personnel and materiel, but in practice numerous influences undermined the doctrine of expertise. For one thing, the successive fleet commanders had considerable discretion as to where they would station the Pacific Navy, and each time they moved it around, they whetted local appetites for permanent possession. At the same time, technological development rendered obsolete or obsolescent the decisions of earlier

---

*"Taylorization refers to a method created in the late nineteenth century by Frederick Winslow Taylor to improve industrial efficiency. Urban reformers, derisively named "Goo Goos" by their enemies, tried to apply Taylor's methods to urban government.

experts. For example, the dawning importance of air power called into question the choice of San Francisco Bay as a main home base, and the use of carriers and larger battleships made certain Bay Area sites, such as Mare Island, obsolescent at the very least. Simultaneously, the multiplying urban advantages of the rapidly developing metropolitan Southland increased that area's ability to handle the entire fleet, and military improvements to the installations there strengthened southern claims anew. Moreover, the naval experts themselves frequently disagreed. The future role of the Mare Island Navy Yard, the location of the main base, the site of the West Coast dirigible base, the strategic defense perimeter of the fleet, the future of the battleship, and even the supposedly moribund issue of the One-Fleet Theory aroused enormous controversy within the Navy itself. These discords, in turn, sabotaged the Navy's claim to expertise and encouraged civilian defense boosters to take sides based on metropolitan interests rather than on national defense grounds. This recrudescense of metropolitanism further undermined the doctrine of expertise and encouraged the Navy, in self-defense, to play off one city against another.

These controversies surfaced rapidly and just as quickly centered on the issue of the main West Coast home base. Some of the Navy's placements were readily accepted, and shore installations grew up from them. By 1923, Congress had approved an impressive list of facilities for San Diego; its Southland neighbor, Los Angeles, got a submarine base. The two shared the fleet anchorage, and Southern California remained the fleet training ground. San Francisco Bay representatives agreed to most of these decisions, thinking their own portion would be forthcoming soon. And, according to naval plans, their share should have been.

Serious and comprehensive naval investigations of the possibilities of the West Coast date from the Preparedness Debate of 1916. As a spinoff of the decision of that year to increase the Navy greatly in case of American involvement in World War I, the Navy authorized a study of shore installation potential on the West Coast. The resultant Helm Investigating Commission of 1916 produced a series of findings that were all that the San Francisco navalists could have hoped for. The Helm Board definitely viewed the problem of coastal defense as one which began at and continued north from San Francisco. The naval experts recommended an aviation base for San Diego and a submarine base for Los Angeles. Aside from these facilities, the Helm development program offered little to the Southland. The board designated San Francisco Bay and Puget Sound as the most strategic areas on the coast, and both were slated to receive main home bases (the General Board of the Navy had recommended a "new naval base in the San Francisco Bay Area" in 1910). Subsequent naval plans altered the emphasis of the Helm Board somewhat, usually by according the San Francisco base the first priority of the two, but down to the early thirties, the Navy insisted that the Bay Area and the Seattle Area constituted the most important strategic points on the Pacific coast.

Not only did the Helm Board de-emphasize the naval significance of the metropolitan Southland, it also cast doubt on the future of Mare Island Navy Yard and therefore on the future of Vallejo. The report recommended that the Navy choose a mid-bay site. After eliminating the bid of the Olympian city of Berkeley, in conjunction with Albany and Richmond, for the San Francisco main home base, the choices eventually narrowed down to the city of Alameda in the East Bay and Hunter's Point in San Francisco. The Navy eventually decided in favor of Alameda, largely because that city offered the entire site free of charge, and San Francisco accepted the decision. Almost to a man and woman, the residents of Vallejo rejected it. That city—its unions, its press, its chamber of commerce, its government, and the naval officers of its Navy Yard—all fancied Mare Island as the proper place for the American Singapore.

In fact, the Carquinez Straits site was about the worst possible location for the main West Coast home base. In some respects it was downright absurd. Over the years, the Navy had expended over $20 million to maintain and build up the Mare Island facility, but by 1916 had come to the conclusion that the installation had reached the limits of its utility—or even the point at which the yard should be phased out. Under no circumstance did the Department believe that Mare Island should be built up into the main home base. Vallejo and its naval meal ticket nestled on the very modest Napa River, near Carquinez Straits. This location was thirty miles from the fleet anchorage in San Francisco Bay, a situation which wasted fuel in transit and which was remote from the Golden Gate entrance and exit from the Bay Area. The Navy valued highly its ability to get the entire fleet in motion quickly and out of its anchorage to the scene of action. Stationed at Mare Island, the fleet would have taken longer moving out to sea and would have been unable to disperse and line up for action.

What is more, the channel to the island silted up badly from the action of the tides moving the river-borne debris about. Only continual dredging had kept the passage open, but by 1916, the machines were losing the battle to keep up with the mud and the ever-growing size of Navy ships. Already, in that preparedness year, the Navy could not get its largest vessels to the Mare Island yard, and with the introduction of carriers, the problem became worse. On one occasion ships actually waited five weeks for a dredge to dig a channel into the mud-besieged facility. Smaller and older vessels could still reach the installation, but once they did, their situation was none too good. The area had little berthing space, many of the ships required special dredging of a berth before they could settle in, and the Napa River channel was so narrow that new or repaired ships launched from Mare Island ran a serious risk of plunging across the river into the Vallejo waterfront. Nearby San Pablo Bay and the Straits of Carquinez contained a limited amount of deep water anchorage for the fleet, but that area lay astride the main path of river and bay traffic. An anchorage at that point would have jammed the entrance to both the navy yard and the straits and would have crowded the ships together (in the manner of the current mothball fleet anchored there) into a perfect target for attack.

The Vallejo site was as short of land as it was of water. Considerable new ground could have been created by dredging, which would have only added to the expense of the constant dredging already required. Mare Island did not have good land transportation connections, lacked an adequate labor supply, and in general did not possess the industry and commerce necessary to provide for 45,000 new residents and their civilian and military needs. Vallejo boasted about its milder climate which promoted year-round shipbuilding, but outside of this asset and its current investment, it had little to recommend it as a major naval base.

Alameda, situated on a mid-bay island across from San Francisco, possessed almost every advantage that Vallejo lacked. This included an enormous anchorage where the entire Pacific Fleet might lie at anchor, lots of land (part of it dredged into being), easy access to the bay exit through the Golden Gate Straits, adjacency to the great port facilities of the area, and a location in the middle of the Bay Area metropolitan district with its huge labor supply, housing stock, well-developed industrial base, commercial facilities, warehouses, central rail and road links to the rest of Northern California, and mature urban infrastructure in general. Without a doubt, Alameda enjoyed enormous geographic and man-made advantages unmatched by any area on the West Coast. The beautiful bay of San Diego, the Harbor in the Sun, possessed in 1928 a total of five square miles of sheltered berthage with a thirty-five-foot depth. Fully a decade earlier, the San Francisco Bay harbor, of which Alameda sat astride, possessed at least ten times that much.[1] Theoretically, the mid-bay alliance which sought the base for their own cities had at least that much more political power. Through the middle of the twenties, this included the solid backing of the Navy Department itself.

How, then, did the city of Vallejo and its Mare Island local naval allies overcome this mighty coalition and stalemate the Bay Area base issue for seventeen years? In part, the explanation lies in a series of unique and/or transient events that combined at a critical moment in time to undermine the legitimate claims of San Francisco, Alameda, Oakland, and their partners. The base project became a live issue in 1916, but soon thereafter American entry into the First World War demanded a military orientation toward Europe rather than the Pacific. This meant that money needed to prosecute the sea war against Germany could not be spent for a great western base. Then peace brought the usual demands for disarmament and economy, and the pacifism and arms limitation activities of the twenties made new naval appropriations unpopular.

However, these were peripheral rather than central problems. The Alameda base could have been initiated with an extremely modest appropriation, entirely insignificant in the total Navy Department budget and utterly invisible in the larger federal budget itself. By 1928, the federal government had provided about two and a-half million dollars to dredge and improve the San Diego harbor and a considerable sum to dredge the impossible channels leading to Mare Island. As small a sum as $10,000 to $20,000 would have been enough to initiate the Alameda base. At a time when San Diego was offering one-third of its waterfront to the Navy, Congress would not even accept a 5,400-acre *gift* of land from the city of Alameda.

Economy was more a political slogan than a real cause of the stalemate. So was the issue of disarmament. The naval base at San Francisco would merely have provided operating facilities for the ships already allowed under the Washington Naval Limitation Treaty and, therefore, would have constituted no threat of an arms race. If any American installation in the Pacific could have been considered a menace to Japan, it was Pearl Harbor; and the stalemate in the Bay Area actually led to the more rapid buildup of that base because of the failure to get a base at San Francisco on the mainland.

This acceleration of the development of Pearl Harbor truly violated the Navy's sense of priorities. In the early 1920s the Department thought that the construction of the San Francisco main home base was more important than the continued buildup of Pearl Harbor into an American forward operating base. In spite of these preferences, the Navy was partly responsible for the outcome. For some strange reason, that service insisted upon a more centralized base for San Francisco Bay than if it had built elsewhere, though that idea made progressively less sense in an age of air power. The notion possessed just as little political logic. With a centralized base, most of the naval patronage would have gone to the Alameda area rather than being spread out around the bay to avoid either airplane bombs or political flak. Although a large number of cities went along with the Navy Department proposal, many found themselves empty-handed. Vallejo, though not without a share of the spoils, feared it would soon lose them. From at least 1910, various Navy spokesmen had cast doubt on the utility of Mare Island, urging either a ceiling on its development, a reduction, or an abandonment of the naval investment there. The proposed centralized naval base seemed designed to make these nightmares come true. The proposal base would have included a dry dock and repair facility, supposedly for large ships, and also a supply depot. Vallejo owned the principal West Coast supply depot at that time, so that city would have lost part of its economic base to the new centralized facility. More importantly, it feared the loss of the remainder, since it was felt that the Navy would not permanently tolerate the expense of separate overhead on two naval construction and repair plants within thirty miles of each other. Vallejo's desire for the base, therefore, was born of both hope and fear.

The Navy's own organization allowed the Straits city to fight more effectively on behalf of its interest and, incidentally, against the wishes of its parent branch. San Francisco's Twelfth Naval District was one of four in the country which did not have control over the navy yard within its district. As Secretary of the Navy Daniels explained it, "The work of the commandants [of these four districts] is of such nature and so vast and so important that it would be impracticable for the commandants of the navy yard either from different localities or otherwise to handle the combined duties satisfactorily."[2] That left the naval complement at Mare Island free to organize and fight on behalf of its own interest instead of being subject to the command of the Twelfth Naval District Commandant at hostile San Francisco. Accordingly, the Vallejo Chamber of Commerce, newspapers, and politicians could draw on the seafaring expertise of Mare Island to buttress their city's claims before the naval and congressional investigating committees, in the congressional hearings, and in public debate.

Vallejo's ability to exploit these advantages was, in large part, determined by another extraordinary congressional figure, a Northern California analogue of William Kettner. Although less is known of his methods, Charles Forrest Curry may have been even more remarkable than his Southland colleague. Unlike the case of Kettner, we know more about why rather than how it was done in Vallejo, but it was universally agreed that however the triumph was achieved, Curry was the organizer of victory. He benefited from a coincidence of political and necrological developments within a short and critical span of time. When the base fight began in 1916, San Francisco had two senators, Hiram Johnson and James D. Phelan, both residents of San Francisco interested in locating the facility in the mid-Bay Area. Of the two, Phelan was the leader of the battle and also the first to fall, in the 1920 election, to Samuel Shortridge of Los Angeles, who took over in 1921. That replaced a San Franciscan with a Southern Californian who had a different set of interests. Phelan had come very close to gaining his point by 1921, while Shortridge would sit idly by while the Bay Area was deprived of its naval training station, which was given to San Diego.

At about the same moment, the mid-bay alliance lost three veteran congressmen. J. Albert Elston of Berkeley died in late 1921. The press speculated that this was a suicide over an early setback in the base campaign. Both San Francisco congressmen soon followed him in death by natural causes. The loss of Julius Kahn in late 1924 was particularly serious, since he headed the House Military Affairs Committee. John I. Nolan, a labor congressman who died in late 1922, was ultimately replaced by Richard Joseph Welch, another Kettner/Curry-style figure. However, he came onto the scene only in 1926, too late to deface the artistry of his North Bay competitor. These unfortunate occurrences deprived "The City" of seasoned leadership at the exact moment of decision. No such problem plagued Vallejo. Curry maneuvered in both the House and Senate to line up coalitions, and these openly championed the cause of Mare Island. On occasion, westerners, Southlanders, southerners, and midwesterners lent a hand against Alameda; and this coalition ultimately prevailed.

However, the process of urbanization itself and the nature of urbanism in the area proved even more decisive. San Francisco Bay was a mature and complex urban area in 1916, one which was both fragmented and sprawling. The three major bays of San Francisco, San Pablo, and Suisun, in addition to Richardson's Bay and many inlets, plus the historical development of the Bay Area had left it even more disjointed than the classic "Fragmented Metropolis" of Los Angeles. In particular, San Francisco and Vallejo were miles apart and did not have an obvious identity of interest at that moment in history. Charles Curry's congressional achievements were a direct expression of this divergent interest. For all his legislative brilliance, the congressman's career merely reflected the patterns of urbanization that he represented.

Such urban complexities were much more simple in Vallejo and in San Diego than in the more advanced urban area at mid-bay. Both these modest cities could concentrate more single-mindedly upon military resources because they lacked other interests. The Carquinez city had literally nothing else to bank on in 1916 and had accordingly organized its political power around its one pre-eminent interest, a navy yard. Though San Diego outranked Vallejo in size, it did not possess much more economic diversity in 1916 and therefore not much more political diversity. San Francisco and its East Bay neighbors contained more complications of every kind, especially economic and political. Though the leaders of these areas backed the drive for militarization, they also had to devote much time to other political problems—the clash between labor and capital, freight rates, merchant marine subsidies, the protection and promotion of a significant industrial base, the tensions between center city and peripheral development, the defense of the city against some of its own resident businesses like the Southern Pacific Railroad, and the development of internal transportation facilities including bridges to hold the metropolis together. Vallejo and San Diego suffered much less from these complexities.

Simplicity characterized their cityscapes as well. In 1928, San Diego possessed a grand total of four major piers marring the tabula rasa of its bay, at a time when the historic waterfront of San Francisco was literally studded with them. San Diego and the Navy would grow up together on the Pacific Coast rather than sequentially. San Francisco arose around its waterfront, which was heavily invested with commercial and industrial ventures of all kinds, and it did not contain very many eligible sites by the time the Navy needed them. The Helm Board of 1916 designated a southeastern San Francisco location as a potential base site; but it needed extensive improvement and eventually the deficiencies of this Hunter's Point site forced "The City" to accept the choice of cross-bay Alameda for the main home base. In the fifteen years after William Kettner's advent to Congress in 1913, San Diego alienated about one-third of its waterfront to the Navy and a total of 6000 acres to "Army, Navy and Marine use."[3] In San Francisco, that sort of generosity was simply out of the question, and it was coming to be less and less possible in the East Bay as well. The magnificent Alameda locality included 5400 acres, but much of it would have to be reclaimed from the waters of the bay; and as the twenties progressed, urbanization eliminated other potential locales. Urbanization rapidly encroached upon the Alameda site itself once politics forced the Navy to forgo building a base there, and the full area was no longer available in 1929. Like San Diego, Vallejo's development did not impede the coupling of urbanization and militarization. San Francisco, with its greater variety, diversity, and complexity, proved as willing, but not as able, to enter this partnership. In the Bay Area, especially in its center city, the process or urbanization worked to cramp rather than to facilitate the marriage of militarization and urbanization.

Despite its manifest political, geographic, and economic advantages, the central bay location did not become the main home base. Although at first glance this outcome might appear to be of merely local significance, it had major consequences for the patterns of urbanization in California. The stalemate in San Francisco Bay deflected naval development to the Southland, mostly to San Diego. By 1928, the Border City, to which the General Board of the Navy had accorded such a minor role in its earlier opinions and to which official naval policy had consigned the status of secondary operating base as recently as 1920, had become the second largest naval base in the United States.[4] That meant that the Navy would supply one of the anchors of the remarkable explosion of urbanization in the Southland from that time hence. Just as the general patterns of American urbanization have shifted from the Northeast and Midwest to the South and West, or Sunbelt, those within California have gone through an equally momentous reorientation from north to south. San Diegans, like the good Southern California boosters that they are, usually attribute the Navy's arrival to the weather. In reality, the decision had more to do with the political climate.

Neither atmospheric conditions nor the city of San Diego entered publicly into the initial controversy. The Bay Area was not rent by discord about whether to locate the main home base in San Diego or Alameda, but rather whether it should go to Mare Island or Alameda. This controversy began in earnest one month before American entry into World War II. With Senator James D. Phelan spearheading the drive, the San Francisco forces secured Senate agreement to the appropriation of $10 million toward "the acquisition and development of the East Bay locale as a navy yard."[5] The accompanying congressional debate revealed the principal actors, arguments, and hidden agendas that were to characterize the struggle until 1925.

From the beginning, both sides based their strategy upon the doctrine of expertise. Although this idea was familiar to the world of business and government as a means of promoting efficiency, modernization, rationalization and so forth, in the struggle between cities it became a more specific political rationale. The idea fit in very comfortably with metropolitanism, or the "politics of urbanization," and could be put to diverse uses on its behalf. San Francisco employed most of them, both in its more civilian endeavors and in its efforts to lure military assets. In the base battle, the doctrine of expertise was deployed in a very clever fashion. Instead of being used as a tactic to rationalize or modernize business or government, it was employed as a political formula to counteract the fragmentation of the Bay metropolis. Since several cities wanted to capture the naval base and had plausible claims to back their ambitions, the doctrine of expertise could be used to settle the question almost by neutral arbitration. As negotiated by the San Francisco and Oakland activists in the struggle, the formula allowed each of the competing cities to put forward their favored base sites, but each agreed that the Navy experts would ultimately decide the location.

Following the Navy's lead enabled the Bay Area urban navalists to claim they acted in the name of "national defense" and to argue that they were interested in the welfare of the entire Bay Area, or metropolitan "family," as the *San Francisco Examiner* would put it. Since four different investigating committees—three naval and one congressional—in seven years agreed that the mid-bay site, rather than one at Vallejo, San Diego, or Los Angeles, was the proper situation for the main home base, the San Francisco strategy was a sound one. National defense and metropolitan geopolitics could be comfortably and, in truth, scientifically meshed.

In pressing this claim, the mid-bay alliance continually reiterated the pledge that the site there would not jeopardize the interest of Vallejo. But although San Franciscans and Oaklanders repeatedly stressed that the Mare Island Yard would always be an integral part of the new Bay Area naval establishment, they never convinced the Carquinez town of their sincerity. Bad management in part explains that failure. Initially the Navy preferred to phase out the Vallejo installation, and unfortunately one of the Senate spokesmen for the mid-bay coalition, Senator Claude Swanson of the Senate Naval Affairs Committee, made the mistake of admitting on the Senate floor that "for some time the Government has realized that the location of the yard ought to be changed to a point lower down the bay, where there is deep water."[6] In the very act of reassuring Vallejo of its continuing role despite Swanson's blunder, Senator Phelan compounded the slip by admitting that "it may have been originally a mistake to have located the navy yard at Mare Island," but "it is preposterous to propose to abandon that yard."[7] Vallejans immediately seized upon the expressions of doubt and ignored the reassurances.

Even San Francisco's willingness to accept the naval experts' decision to pass over Hunter's Point in favor of an Alameda site did not reassure their northern neighbors. Vallejo adamantly refused to abandon its claims as a quid pro quo for San Francisco's renunciation of its own. Neither were the Straits boosters and their allies persuaded by the threat that if Alameda lost the base, the entire Bay Area would lose the facility completely, since no other city would be picked over Alameda. In their angrier moods, the San Franciscans tried to red-bait the shipworkers' town, but fared no better with that tactic. The charge of disloyalty in blocking the base did not seem too convincing when leveled at a city of shipbuilders who had shattered records for performance and productivity during the recent world war.

Congressman Curry set some records himself in combatively defending the interest of his district. He too could call on the expertise of Navy men, though only those from Mare Island, and, more important, he was able to stress the economic aspect of that argument in the process. Vallejo spokesmen refused to accept the assurance that the two repair and construction facilities of the area would be complementary rather than competitive. No one, they argued, would build a pair of yards that close together and accept two overhead charges rather than one. Eventually, they held, the facilities would be merged and that would mean a loss of $25 million naval investment in Mare Island. It would be an unnecessary waste, too, it was argued, because the Mare Island Yard was perfectly capable of serving as the home base. That way the government could add twenty to forty million to its present investment in the Bay Area, preserve Mare Island, still get a main home base, and do so for $60 million instead of $150 million. While the Vallejans and their military allies trumpeted these arguments to the public, Representative Curry circulated about the congressional corridors, lining up support from Southlanders, New Englanders, Midwesterners, and legislators from the historic South.

From the beginning, both sides sought outside allies, and in this competition, San Francisco gained the first round. In the Senate appropriations test, "the City" won by a 46 to 26 margin, with Southern senators voting en bloc for the Bay City and providing more than a third of the aye votes. This Sunbelt connection could not prevent the loss of the appropriation in the House, however; instead of the $1 million they wanted, Congress authorized a series of compromises which took the form of further investigations to firm up and flesh out the specifics of the favorable Helm Report of 1916. The first of these provided their findings in 1919; but in the meantime, San Francisco suffered a serious blow, apparently without noticing it. The Navy had decided in 1917 to transfer the Bay Area naval training station to San Diego in order to take advantage of the climate. Instead of fighting for this installation or delaying its departure until the main home base was assured, San Franciscans and their Bay Area allies let the facility slip and did not wake to the importance of their loss until 1919. That was a crucial matter because San Diego would buttress its claims to further naval consideration by its superiority as a training area. In the short run, it would get an installation designed to train 6,000 to 12,000 men at a time. The former figure represented nearly one-tenth of the city's 1920 census population. Of course, the presence of both the extra men and the new installation could then be advanced to rationalize the general utility of San Diego to the Navy and to request further additions of both.

In the meantime, the Navy promised more but delivered less to San Francisco and its mid-bay allies. In 1919, the investigation chaired by Rear Admirals W. Parks and J. S. McKean reaffirmed the Helm Board's preference for a mid-bay home base site. However, this inquiry also dragged the process out by mandating further soil borings before recommending a final choice between the competing mid-bay sites. The Navy quickly made these tests, and in 1921, a Special Joint Committee of Congress on Pacific Naval Bases gave Alameda the nod. The same year the United States Senate, by a vote of 40 to 30, gave that city the gate.[8] For the most part, the desertion of its Sunbelt allies from the historic South produced this reversal of San Francisco's fortunes. In the 1917 Senate vote, the South had been overwhelmingly in favor of the mid-bay site, while the midwestern states had been equally opposed. New England agreed with the latter, but not by such an impressive margin. In 1921, the midwestern opposition deepened slightly, while the Atlantic support declined somewhat, and the South and New England changed sides. Most dramatically, sixteen Southern votes for Alameda in 1917 became fifteen negative ones in 1921. That represented approximately 35 percent of the winning yea vote in 1917 and 37 percent of the victorious nay tally in 1921.

The next year brought fresh reverses. The United States government signed the Washington accords, which limited the tonnage of the Navy. The treaty still left a tremendous amount of naval shipping to be accommodated on the Pacific coast, but it gave the opposition a better talking point in the economy-pacifist argument. A more momentous decision accompanied the tonnage limitation. In 1922, Los Angeles, despite its artificial and grossly inferior harbor, was designated the official West Coast fleet anchorage of the Pacific squadron. The Navy emphasized the proximity of the southern metropolis to the Navy's training grounds in Southern California, and also stressed the defects of the three channels leading into San Francisco Bay, especially the northern Bonita Channel. In the Bay Area, these problems were considered the crucial factor that threw the anchorage to the City of the Angels. The Navy's decision meant that the Bay Area would see less of the fleet and the Southland, more.

The Golden Gate coalition gained some compensation in 1923 when the Navy designated San Francisco and its Twelfth Naval District Headquarters as an operating base, even though Congress had not appropriated anything for the home base. And in that same year, yet another naval investigating team urged the Congress to take that step. The Rodman Board again recommended the Alameda site to the government, but the legislators once more refused to accept the experts' decision. Despite an intensive campaign by Bay Area interests such as the chambers of commerce, the Knowland family, and the Bay Cities Naval Affairs Committee, Congress remained unpersuaded. The Navy Department itself even dispatched an officer to the Pacific Northwest to rally chambers of commerce and the media around the Alameda choice. The Portland and Spokane chambers and media responded enthusiastically, but the Congress remained recalcitrant. Worse still for the mid-bay alliance, Representative Curry picked that moment to bring off perhaps his greatest coup. The congressman won Calvin Coolidge over to the side of Vallejo. As the *San Francisco Chronicle* sadly noted, " Proposals for the new naval base at Alameda, California, are regarded by President Coolidge as likely to involve unwarranted expenditures in view of the defensive power of the present base at Mare Island." The chief executive admitted that he had "not conferred with Navy Department officials about details," but added that the United States must not violate the spirit of the recent arms limitation agreement, especially if it cost money, "except for those [projects] of the most necessary nature."[9] Of course the Navy Department, with whom the President had not consulted, would have described the base in exactly that manner.

"The City" and its allies made one more concerted attempt to get the base in the 1920s when San Francisco partisan Admiral C. J. Peoples advanced the idea of a supply base at India Basin south of Market Street. As later events were to prove, the Navy considered a major supply base to be the critical installation in a main home base, so the suggestion really portended greater things to come. It was essentially an entering wedge. However, Congress also refused to fund this idea; the base issue sputtered out in 1925, and for the next several years remained quiescent.

This outcome left the Navy in a curious position, with its main battle fleet in the Pacific, but without an adequate West Coast main home base for this flotilla. Unfortunately the base at Alameda had not yet received its first stake by 1920. The construction of this facility, considered indispensable by the Navy, remained stalled, while the minor installations at San Diego, Vallejo, and elsewhere went on abuilding. Instead of concentrating its resources in one facility, California urban politics forced the Navy to scatter its facilities up and down the coast. The fleet anchorage was in the south, but the main West Coast supply depot remained in Vallejo; and Mare Island and Bremerton, Washington, held onto their dry docks. This forced the sailors to steam hundreds of miles to pick up their coffee rations or get repairs and then travel back south to train. Although the Navy designated San Francisco an operating base in 1923, the disposition of naval resources on the West Coast during the remainder of the 1920s continued to reflect the pattern of Bay Area and Southland urbanization rather than the designs of its strategic operations planners. Thus the rivalry among Golden State cities—the California metropolitan anxiety—had fragmented the Navy about as badly as the cities themselves.[10]

Indeed, the intramural struggles of Bay Area cities not only postponed base appropriations, they also jeopardized the interests of all local urban areas involved. By 1930, the Navy considered Mare Island an obsolete facility, and its retention was an unsuccessful attempt by that service to win political support from Vallejo for the Alameda-Bay Area base. Since Vallejo refused to consent to the quid pro quo of an Alameda installation, the Navy now considered scrapping the north-bay yard, and for a time the base's appropriations were cut pending the outcome of the struggle. Worse yet, the Navy simultaneously considered entirely abandoning the Bay Area as a base site for some place like San Diego or Los Angeles, where local rivalries did not intrude so forcibly into military policy. Both the political infighting of the Bay Area and the growing importance of the southern metropolitan areas led the Navy to cast longing glances southward. As the harbors in the Southland improved, as its metropolitan infrastructure supplied more of what the Navy needed, and as its cooperation increased, the Navy wavered in its commitment to San Francisco Bay.[11]

While Los Angeles drove stakes and built away on its perennially expanding breakwater and San Diego burrowed ever deeper into its harbor floor, San Francisco and its Bay allies took several stop-gap measures. "The City" mobilized to improve the Main and Bonita channels into the mouth of the Golden Gate. The lack of a suitable entrance to the Bay had supposedly caused the Navy to designate Los Angeles the main fleet anchorage in 1922. If so, the dredging seemed to have paid off. Even before the base stalemate developed, the Golden Gate metropolitan-military complex began a supplementary campaign to get the fleet to visit the Bay of St. Francis more often. The harbor improvements would, of course, facilitate these more frequent sojourns, and fleet calls did become frequent. According to the prestigious Admiral Joseph Mason Reeves, testifying at the Navy's 1929-30 Sunnyvale dirigible base hearings, the fleet in 1929 had spent about 60 percent of its time "in and around San Francisco." To confuse matters, in the same year the equally august General Board of the Navy asserted that the "fleet operates in [Los Angeles] a greater part of the year." Whatever the exact division of visits between the two regions, San Francisco apparently claimed a large share of fleet calls.

Unable in 1924 to get Congress to accept the offered Alameda site for the new base, the Navy Department made other provisions that secured something of what it wanted. In order to repair and service the larger Navy vessels which Mare Island could not handle, the Navy Department leased the Hunter's Point dry docks of the Bethlehem Steel Company at an annual expense of $137,000. That arrangement lasted at least from 1924 to 1929.[12] In that year, the Navy sought to expand on its Hunter's Point accommodation by initiating the long-sought main home base at that location. After all, the Navy boards of inquiry had designated that spot as the second most desirable one for the base, and, by 1929, the process of urbanization further jeopardized the hoped-for Alameda site. Much of that area had been leased to private parties for a landing field and to the War Department for an airport supply depot. Currently proposed bay bridge projects threatened to pre-empt some of the remainder. As the Navy's secret correspondence dolefully put it, "In connection with the question of constructing a bridge across the lower part of San Francisco Bay, practically all of the locations south of Goat Island are predicated upon crossing this site [Alameda] at one place or another, thus greatly reducing its potential value for Naval activities."[13] The government eventually bought the Hunter's Point dry dock, but did not place the main home base there.

The Navy did not think it could build the base at all as long as Charles Curry lived and took an interest in the matter. However, this stricture did not necessarily benefit Vallejo and its Navy yard. Mare Island's construction contracts were cut drastically in 1922, apparently in response to the naval limitations agreements of that year. More ominous, the regular maintenance and upkeep appropriations of the Vallejo facility suffered as well. Since the Navy did not know where its main home base would ultimately be, it refused to invest further in Mare Island pending a clarification of its role in West Coast defense.[14] The north-bay Navy town did manage to secure further congressional appropriations for dredging its silting channels and secured a submarine base as well. But essentially the deadlock damaged the interests of all Bay Area parties. The Navy was forced to improvise facilities; Mare Island suffered from neglect; the main operating base at Alameda did not receive its first stake in the 1920s; and naval progress in the Bay Area did not match that in the metropolitan Southland, especially in San Diego.

This stalemate endured until the late 1920s, when a combination of circumstances revived the chances of the Bay Area. Movement began at the local level and then was strengthened by developments in the national and international spheres. In 1930 the precociously successful, obstructionist Congressman Curry died; and in 1932, his son and successor failed to be re-elected. Thus metropolitan politics no longer blocked the deployment of naval resources. Then in 1933, the Navy opened a new dirigible installation. Although it did not amount to much militarily, it was politically strategic. In 1929 the House Naval Affairs Committee's investigation of a West Coast dirigible facility revealed that the Navy was split several ways over the main home base question as well as over the more immediate issue of the dirigible station. As a consequence, an amusing parade of expert military witnesses, backed by their metropolitan-civilian allies and armed with strategic theories tailor-made for each city, marched before the committee, asserting the superiority of their own West Coast localities. Carl Vinson joined in the spirit of things by asserting the claims of the historic South; and Congressman McClintock of Oklahoma even put forward the name of that Great Plains state as a compromise dirigible station site, though he did muster the self-restraint not to ask for a naval base.

Sunnyvale, situated at the southern end of San Francisco Bay, finally got the nod, but not before the Bay Area metropolitan-military complex had been badly shaken. Los Angeles and San Diego combined to fight for this particular installation and, for a time, seemed to be winning the battle. Initially the Navy Department favored a lighter-than-air base site at Camp Kearny in the San Diego area, and, in truth, it probably should have gone there. At that point, the Navy viewed the dirigible as a long-range reconnaisance vehicle which would serve as the eyes and ears of the fleet. *If* it made sense to train fleet personnel at San Diego and to anchor the fleet at Los Angeles, then it must have made equally good sense to post its eyes and ears close by. Once again, however, metropolitan anxieties seemed to be more decisive than military logic, and the base for the ill-starred dirigibles went to the Bay Area.

It did so because after its initial rebuff, "The City" organized for sustained action. Facing the loss of still another naval installation and possibly the last at that, the San Francisco city government and its Chamber of Commerce put up a tremendous fight for the dirigible station. Eventually the Bay City mobilized an impressive coalition of Bay Area cities, including Vallejo, in the fight for the south-bay Sunnyvale base. The Sunnyvale battle also initiated a reconciliation with Vallejo, since that city eventually came to support the claims of the southern bay dirigible site and thereby joined the Bay Area base coalition. And although it amounted to only a $5,000,000 commitment, the establishment of a base at Sunnyvale broke a long dry spell for the Bay Area. More important, as many from the Southland recognized, the minor airship station was really the entering wedge for the main home base, since dirigibles were supposed to operate with the fleet.

By 1933, an ever-more-threatening world situation, plus a President and Congress anxious to end unemployment and rebuild the Navy, brought fresh naval resources into the West Coast contest. But money had never really been the problem; the "politics of urbanization" had, and, fortunately for the Bay Area, its own stalemate broke in these same years. Congressman Curry died in 1930, making an accommodation easier, and in 1933 the metropolitan-military complex at Los

Angeles moved openly to secure the coveted main West Coast home base. The City of the Angels began agitating for a Navy yard and supply depot which would have been competitive with those in Vallejo and would obviously have been the nucleus of a main home base as well. Admiral Thomas J. Senn, commandant of the Eleventh Naval District in San Diego, and the commandant of the Pacific Fleet both supported these Angeleno demands, and the Navy Department allowed them to investigate the idea. These moves toward the duplication of the Mare Island facilities threatened Vallejo and solidified the adherence of that town and its service allies to the San Francisco coalition and galvanized that group into redoubled efforts.

The Commandant of the Twelfth Naval District in San Francisco, G. W. Laws, noted gleefully that "the recent publication in the news columns that interests in southern California, with favorable endorsement by the Commander in Chief, U.S. Fleet, were proposing to establish a Supply Base [the germ of a main home base] in San Pedro, acted like an electric shock. The more so as the first accounts indicated that a depot adequate for war purposes was in mind." Laws slyly added that "although the Commandant [Laws] has given assurance as to the real extent of the Depot, he could not opportunely do so until after counteractive measures on the part of the communities composing the San Francisco Bay Area had received great impetus."[15] Obviously the commandants of each naval district backed the political ambitions of their own home cities.

Slightly earlier, by 1931, the Navy Department, as opposed to its fleet and district commanders, had already retreated back into San Francisco's camp. That service hit upon—or rather, was driven into—a base strategy that matched military decentralization to the urban decentralization of the Bay Area. Vallejo had correctly feared a centralized base. Despite its denials, the Navy planned to dismantle Mare Island Navy Yard and to remove its shipbuilding and repair functions to a site near the proposed main home base facility across from San Francisco. In the late 1920s and early 1930s the process of urbanization forced the Navy to redesign the main home base concept so as to quiet the fears of Vallejo and satisfy the developmental aspirations of other cities around the Bay. Strangely enough, military considerations were not decisive. For at least a decade, the Navy had speculated upon the implications of air power to its own role, and its 1923 maneuvers had demonstrated the shocking vulnerability of the Panama Canal to carrier-based air attack. Yet the crucial factor in the Navy's decision was the perception of Twelfth Naval District Commandant Admiral C. C. Cole that the Alameda site was being converted to business uses and that the process of urbanization was rapidly consuming other potential sites. This realization brought a turnaround in naval policy. Unless the Navy wished to abandon the Bay Area altogether, a decentralized base was the only kind possible.

By 1931, a civilian airfield took up part of the land previously offered for the Alameda base; an Army airport and supply depot stood on another; the Bay Bridge threatened to undermine the utility of the Yerba Buena Island to the Navy; and the land that would have been used for the alternative site at Hunter's Point in San Francisco had fallen to the march of urban progress. The Bay Bridge encroachment on Yerba Buena Island, in the middle of the bay between Oakland and "The City," provided the final stimulus. As the Chief of Naval Operations put it to the Secretary of the Navy.

> The condition which brings this general situation acutely to attention at the present time, and which renders a reconsideration of the general policy in regard to this area essential, is a probability, in view of the early construction of this bridge across Yerba Buena, that political influence will be sufficient, in the absence of any definite plans, to dislodge the Navy therefrom with no other suitable site for its personnel depot, supply depot, or piers for submarines, destroyers and supply vessels.
>
> The question which appears pertinent at the present time is whether the main home base desired in San Francisco Bay must contain, in *one* geographical area, all facilities required by the base development project or whether it would satisfactorily meet requirements to provide these facilities in locations within that area where they would be available to a fleet anchored there. It is believed that a scrutiny of the requirements above enumerated will show the impossibility of assembling these facilities within the limits of one definite area. Furthermore, it is feared that we may defeat our own purposes by adhering even approximately to this requirement on account of the large amount of money which would be required therefore; whereas if we utilize the facilities now available, prepare definite plans, and gradually work toward them it would seem that the Navy would be better prepared on the outbreak of hostilities.[16]

Upon reconsideration, the Navy realized that it had already quietly slipped enough improvements into the Bay Area to constitute the foundations for a main home base. These included a new submarine base at Mare Island, the Sunnyvale base, the Pinole Shoal Dike to protect the entrance to Mare Island from serious silting, the nucleus of a supply base at India Basin in San Francisco, a marine detachment headquarters, the Twelfth Naval District Headquarters in San Francisco, and an ordnance depot at Mare Island. A main home base still required a new heavier-than-air station, a new supply depot, and a new construction and repair yard to accommodate the larger ships that could not use the Vallejo plant. The Navy thereupon set about building up its current assets and looking for the three installations that it lacked. Unless the Navy wished to abandon the Bay Area altogether, a decentralized base was the only kind possible. Therefore, although military considerations did enter into the decision, the politics and process of urbanization, rather than the threat of an air raid to a centralized facility, dictated the timing and the design of the West Coast main home base.

The Navy then worked out a clever political strategy to implement its policy. To quiet the suspicions of Southern California, the Navy began in 1933 to reiterate that it needed no new main west Coast base at present; instead, it would invest the new federal monies in the "floating Navy" and existing installations. The department had already decided to build the new decentralized main home base secretly and step by step instead of a centralized one in one dramatic push. This ploy satisfied a number of interests. It solidified Vallejo's ties to the urban navalist coalition by its promise to improve and maintain Mare Island; it gave a plum to each of the Bay Area cities involved in base politics; and it finally initiated the construction of the American Singapore.

While the Navy completed its secret plans, Congress redeemed the Navy's promise to concentrate upon the "floating Navy" and existing installations. That allowed the Navy to point to the overtaxed shore facilities which needed more money to handle the expanded fleet. The Navy then followed a strategy of overload with the Congress and the President. It built up the "floating Navy" and then stationed the biggest part in the Pacific, where it swamped the available facilities. That act, in turn, justified more ample shore installations, which demanded more expenditures still. A main home base required planes to defend it, repair shops to mend its ships and planes, depots to supply it, and marine detachments to patrol it. These necessitated laboratories to improve the planes, reserve outfits to supplement the regulars, bridges and roads to connect the whole complex, and shore batteries to protect the lot. This strategy of overload worked to the distinct advantage of San Francisco, which had been denied so much for so long that its overloading was more dramatic when the ships and planes finally came.

Ashore in the Bay Area, civilians worked feverishly to hasten that day. Under the leadership of Mayor Angelo Rossi, Supervisor Carl Miles, and the *San Francisco Chronicle,* a formal pressure group—the second Bay Cities Naval Affairs Committee, a subcommittee of the Bay Area Industrial Development Committee—was established. Twelfth Naval District Commandant G. W. Laws played an equally prominent role. In September 1932, he called a peace conference to bring together the warring Bay Area factions in a renewed effort to secure the naval base. Fittingly enough, the meeting was held on Navy property on Yerba Buena Island. This time, the Bay Area responded nearly unanimously. Laws, the mayors of San Francisco and Vallejo, and the Commandant of Mare Island publicly announced the new alignment and its program in 1933.

These developments encouraged and broadened the program of the Bay Area metropolitan-military complex. Civilian San Francisco and its allies had consistently championed higher levels of naval spending and, after 1933, escalated their demands. The multifaceted base issue remained the central focus of the agitation, but now the defense coalition added significant new requests. Ironically, on the very eve of the Nye Committee's investigation of the munitions makers in the last war, the San Francisco Bay Area coalition embarked on a full-fledged naval rearmament drive for the next, one in which the so-called "Merchants of Death" were allocated a key role.

Thereafter, the struggle quickened. The leading papers and the Bay Cities Naval Affairs Committee mounted campaigns for the base; retired and active military men spoke through the media for greater defense spending; a son of the President was hired as aviation editor of the *San Francisco Examiner;* and Bay Area congressmen sponsored so many projects in the House of Representatives that its Naval Affairs Committee became "the most important committee, from the standpoint of local interest." Simultaneously the Navy began flexing its muscles in a political way. Suspiciously timed West Coast naval maneuvers, described by the press as the "most significant" war games in naval history—an attack on coastal cities to test their defenses—occurred just before the advent of the Roosevelt administration in 1933. Even more suspect, given the Navy's longstanding demand for a base and greater naval spending, the admirals made San Francisco a chief target of this mock attack on the California coast. Predictably, the city was destroyed in the assault, after which the press quickly drew the appropriate conclusions that the coast needed more bases and naval rearmament. The incoming Roosevelt administration, from which the Navy and its urban navalist allies expected great things, came to power just as the West Coast papers broadcast the news that the mock attack had proven the coastal cities defenseless. These efforts soon produced "a methodical development of the San Francisco Area" that turned it by 1940 into "one of the most important centers of national-defense activity in America."

The expansion of the public shipbuilding industry and the revival of its near-extinct private counterparts stood high on the Navy's wish list for the new decentralized base. With the San Francisco alliance again leading a Bay Area campaign, the Navy moved to modernize Mare Island and to grant Vallejo its fair share of contracts from the revived naval construction program. Thereafter, in 1939, Representative Richard J. Welch secured legislation to purchase and expand the Bethlehem dry dock at Hunter's Point. For a time, this installation had the distinction of being "the largest repair yard in the country." Bay Area congressmen also helped secure a differential for private shipbuilding yards on the West Coast which was designed to help them compete with eastern shipbuilders. The Maritime Act of 1938 granted this subsidy to the West, though only on merchant as opposed to Navy construction. Together with the Hunter's Point purchase, this differential brought about the shipbuilding revival the Bay Area had fought so long to achieve.

This was a particularly significant victory for both the Bay Area and the Navy. The latter wanted a West Coast shipbuilding renaissance as a precaution against enemy attack on Atlantic shipbuilders, and urban navalists counted on the industry to provide a crucial multiplier effect to the process of urbanization. An unusually large part of shipbuilding expenditures stayed within the community in the form of wages, and this industry also spread the military booster effect to a disproportionately large number of other concerns. Ship construction, repair, and reconditioning were peculiarly well suited to produce the hoped-for urban revival by bolstering the local economy through diversification, the city builders' traditional panacea. Yet this aim brought the Bay Area into conflict with the East Coast shipbuilding monopoly, which had denied private West Coast yards a single government shipbuilding contract from World War I until the Maritime Act of 1938. Understandably the Navy hedged on this fight, supporting the revival of West Coast private builders but not the differential that their Atlantic suppliers opposed. In the end, however, the Bay Area secured both, but failed to break the corner on Navy, as opposed to civilian, contracts held by Atlantic coast shipbuilders.

Since both the naval buildup and the new main base required air power as well as surface vessels, the defense and development coalition also pushed for a dirigible base and then a research laboratory at Sunnyvale; the Alameda Naval Air Station; and naval reserve air bases. In addition, civilian San Francisco and its partners supported a dynamic aircraft industry that could provide another economic multiplier. They also backed air-mail subsidies, a fleet of merchant airplane auxiliaries that could be pressed into service in case of war, and a trained reserve of pilots.

Opened in mid-1933, the Sunnyvale installation represented the first large-scale augmentation of air power in the Bay Area. Unfortunately, a series of disasters led the Navy to de-emphasize development of lighter-than-air weapons systems until the outbreak of World War II, and the Navy transferred the Sunnyvale naval contingent to San Diego in 1935. As part of its systematic buildup of the new operating base, however, the Navy had already committed itself to the construction of the "largest naval aviation base on the Pacific Coast." Like the railroads of the nineteenth century, the Navy usually demanded and received immensely valuable Bay Area land in return for its installations, and Sunnyvale and Alameda air stations were no exceptions. The Alameda voters again gave the land; and, as it sometimes did, the Navy intervened in the election by threatening to go elsewhere if the contest turned out adversely. In addition, by 1939 the agitation for an aviation research laboratory had gained Franklin Roosevelt's support, and by 1940 it was opened. Eventually the Ames Aeronautical Laboratory grew up at the Sunnyvale base, subsequently renamed Moffett Field. So the struggle for the Sunnyvale base had not been in vain. The land dedicated to it by the Navy would be used to house this far more important research and development laboratory. In the long run, a foothold in the research realm was much more important to the Bay Area than a dirigible base.

These were highly significant national defense measures, but as urban defense and promotional ventures they were even more impressive. The coast aircraft industry had largely bypassed San Francisco Bay in favor of Southern California and the Seattle area. Even Lockheed, which grew up in the Bay Area at Sunnyvale, had deserted that locale for the Southland. But through its acquisition of the Alameda and Sunnyvale-Moffett Field installations and the Army's Hamilton Field, the Bay Area secured the significant foothold in the research and repair sections of the industry that it had not been able to acquire through the free working of the market. Coupled with the revival of shipbuilding, these represented outstanding achievements in the drive to industrialize the Bay Area and the West.

In return for these air installations and in order to keep them operating with modern weapons and trained personnel, civilian defense boosters supported certain weapons systems, subsidies to aircraft manufacturers, and an air reserve. As usual, national defense supplied the rationalization for these political positions, and economics provided the rationale. Civilian defense boosters hoped the airplane would provide yet another American "transportation revolution" that would lead to a "new industrial era," particularly in California. Enlightened government subsidies, like those earlier given to railroads, could produce this manufacturing renaissance, Elliott Roosevelt constantly reminded his father through the pages of the *San Francisco Examiner*. In turn, an extensive aviation business might train as many as 50,000 commercial pilots, who would contribute to the national defense by their membership in an air reserve and who would not likely be in unions (that notion proved somewhat farfetched).

An improved supply depot, the final feature of the base program, soon materialized. After the usual land-donation election and after the customary urban intramural rivalries—this time among San Francisco, San Mateo County, and Oakland—had delayed the project for two full years, the Navy developed a site on the Oakland middle harbor. By 1941, the government had poured $20 million into this development.[17]

Still other plums fell just prior to the war. The city of San Francisco had reclaimed—partly with federal funds—the Yerba Buena Shoals for the World's Fair site of Treasure Island, which the Navy then obtained for a training and patrol station. As "compensation" for the "loss" of a potential airport site, which the city probably could not have developed into a modern airport anyway, San Francisco received $10 million worth of improvements to its existing landing field. Then, just as the war broke out, the city proposed a major environmental restructuring—the Reber Plan. Among other things, this proposal would have transformed San Francisco and San Pablo bays into a military-industrial park. Nothing else in the twenty years under review shows so clearly the priorities of some of the civilians in the metropolitan-military complex. Among other things, this plan—through reclamation, dredging, and damming—would have created two land crossings of the bays; large amounts of military, industrial, and agricultural land; a new naval base; monstrous causeways into the city; an entirely new East Bay waterfront; a union transportation terminal beyond the wildest dreams of most cities; and the long-coveted direct transcontinental railroad link for San Francisco. In the process, such Bay Area landmarks as Strawberry Point, much of the Tiburon and Sausalito water fronts, Richardson's Bay, an enormous portion of San Pablo Bay between Point Molate in Richmond and Pinole Point, and the even larger section of San Francisco Bay east of a straight line drawn from the Port of Richmond to a point west of the Emeryville approach to the Bay Bridge would have been transformed from picturesque scenery into new land. And all at federal expense!

For civilian purposes, this plan had very decided advantages. According to the Reber Plan expert David Long, the proposal was the single most extensive and comprehensive city plan in American history and would have conferred many developmental, water, and environmental benefits on the Bay Area. However, by creating numerous bottlenecks in the unobstructed bay and by radically reducing the water area in which the fleet could operate or anchor, the Reber Plan would have somewhat reduced the naval utility of San Francisco Bay. The proposed earth-and-rock dam south of Yerba Buena Island would have severed the main fleet anchorage from the Bay exit at the Golden Gate. This obstruction would have made the anchorage less useful to a fleet that had to pass rapidly through that strait and out into the Pacific for military action. Overall the plan would have sacrificed some of the geographic defensive advantages of the Bay Area, leaving the Navy more constrained and cramped than it had been before the redesigning of the bay. Yet its proponents argued that the attack at Pearl Harbor gave the project more rather than less military urgency, and the San Francisco Board of Supervisors endorsed it as a means to win the war. Under questioning, the sponsor of the resolution admitted that the Reber Plan could not be completed in time for this conflict, "but he was thoroughly convinced . . . that this will not be the last war."[18]

The other interests in the Bay Area metropolitan-military complex were less impressed with this long-range view of national defense than with the immediate threat of the Reber Plan to their own metropolitan programs. The plan would have given San Francisco direct transcontinental railway connections with the rest of the continent (it had sought these since the 1850s) while cutting its waterfront in two; however, it would have denied Oakland the direct access to the sea that it presently enjoyed, cramped the Navy, cut off Mare Island from direct access to the ocean, blocked the south-bay cities in the same way, and redesigned the entire East Bay waterfront. This realization brought vetoes from Oakland, San Mateo County, Vallejo, the Navy Department, the State of California, and even San Francisco itself.

Nevertheless, by World War II, San Francisco led the Bay Area in securing a staggering naval commitment. The fleet anchorage eluded the city's grasp because of its transfer to Pearl Harbor and the Atlantic, but the new West Coast home base had been acquired and largely developed when the Japanese attacked Hawaii. By that calamitous moment, the Bay Area had finally gained the position that the Navy had assigned it over twenty years earlier. Military historians such as Walter Millis have minimized the nation's war preparedness before 1941, but the impact of defense spending in the Bay Area alone was astonishing. Six months before the conflict, the Navy had already invested one billion dollars in the metropolitan area, including $650 million in shipbuilding. Interestingly enough, Los Angeles, which still claimed the main fleet anchorage, apparently did not learn of the secret base buildup in the Bay Area until mid-1937, when it was too late to prevent the completion of the American Singapore.

Once the decision had been made to bring the fleet west and to regard Japan as the enemy, the logic of the militarization of the Bay Area appeared both inescapable and cumulative, although military experts recognized that these needed to have very definite limits. The endless militarization of the Bay Area did not seem desirable. Nor did military logic completely rule the implementation of the militarization of the Bay Area. It required the elimination of local metropolitan vetos *in order to begin* military stake driving in the Bay Area. When that point had been reached, rapid progress ensued.

Richard J. Welch, probably the most successful member of the Bay Area metropolitan-military complex, gave voice to this classic logic in a 1941 congressional resolution favoring still another bridge over San Francisco Bay, this time from Hunter's Point to Bay Farm Island. The ostensible rationale for this scheme was to evacuate the city's population in case Japanese sea or air attacks destroyed the other bridges and land escape routes. Noting the many martial establishments recently developed, he argued that "the lessons of modern warfare have demonstrated the necessity of adequate highways between national defense activities." Chairman Carl Vinson of the House Naval Affairs Committee, whose knowledge of things military was legendary, put the matter in much better perspective in his reply: "Of course, the lessons of modern warfare have demonstrated also the danger of concentrating so many of the things you have enumerated in the San Francisco Bay Area and it would seem to me that the lessons of modern warfare would justify us taking away a great many of those things and putting them somewhere else." Therefore, as a defense proposition the militarization of the Bay Area had a certain logic. As a strategy for city building, it was brilliant.

CHAPTER 4

•••••••••••••••••••••••••••••••

Dive Bombers in the Land of Oz:
Los Angeles and the Aircraft Industry

There is going to be a Detroit of the aircraft industry. It ought to be here in Los
Angeles.

EDWIN CLAPP
Los Angeles Examiner
June 18, 1926

The strategic military importance of cities has waxed and waned over the centuries.
In some eras armies have keyed upon urban areas and at other times they ignored
them. With notable exceptions, like the American Civil War, navies usually passed
cities by. Air forces followed that lead at first, but by the Second World War the
strategic and tactical importance of cities had become overwhelming to that service.
The California urban-military configuration developed entirely in keeping with this
latter pattern. For compelling economic and political reasons, the aerial sectors of
the military grew up in close proximity to and dependent upon cities in the Golden
State. Again, these cities were not shaped by large outside forces over which they
had no control; in fact, the military was the dependent variable initially, and the
cities, the independent ones. Like nineteenth-century railroads, which needed
entrée into a political and economic backing from a pre-existing urban network,
twentieth-century California Army installations, Navy bases, marine stations, Air
Force bases, and aircraft and other defense factories faced the same requirements.
These considerations will be discussed in some detail below, but suffice it to say here
that the patterns of militarization largely reinforced rather than altered the urban
network that already existed when the services arrived in California. Or, to focus
the matter more sharply, the patterns of urbanization in California greatly dictated
the patterns of militarization that the in-migrant services created. California was
already disproportionately urban, its southern sector was rapidly outpacing its
northern counterpart, and its suburbs were everywhere mushrooming. The military
occupation of the largest state on the Pacific Slope did not alter these fundamental
relationships.[1]

The development of the aircraft industry, symbiotically related to the aerial
arms of the Army and Navy, illustrates this pattern perfectly. This business had
existed in California from the Progressive era. For a time, aircraft manufacturing
pioneer Glenn Curtiss built planes in San Diego in 1911, and the equally famous
Glenn L. Martin founded his firm in Los Angeles in 1912. Martin produced planes
in Los Angeles until he was shut down by the government in 1917, but by the First
World War Curtiss had concentrated his operations in Buffalo. The European con-

flagration vastly stimulated aircraft manufacturing. However, upon the conclusion of that conflict, the government abruptly and without notice canceled its aircraft contracts en masse. As mentioned previously, the termination of First World War contracts, plus the flooding of the aerial market with surplus military airplanes and Liberty engines, badly mauled the entire American aircraft industry. Yet by the end of the twenties the industry had come back solidly. Together the civilian and military divisions of the airplane business provided a strong further stimulus to the development of California cities, particularly Los Angeles and later San Diego as well.[2]

In certain key respects, the advent of the airplane industry in Southern California closely approximates the story of an earlier military technological innovation, the firearm, and its impact upon the population of Europe. According to John S. Pettengill, the invention and diffusion of the firearm in Early Modern Europe enabled the nobility of that continent to dominate the peasantry more fully. That predominance was reflected in a decline in real peasant incomes from 1500 to 1650 as European nobles succeeded in exploiting their monopoly on firearms to wring greater exactions from their peasants. In twentieth-century California, the technologically triggered reallocation of incomes did not flow from one class to another, but rather from one section of the United States to another. In the later case, the weapon was the airplane rather than the firearm, but the resulting income redistribution was profoundly important. It significantly accelerated the relative decline of the urbanized Northeast, the Middle Atlantic, and the Midwest and at the same time markedly hastened the rise of California and the West.[3]

In addition, this new weapon greatly encouraged the liaison between the city and the sword. By the 1970s, Los Angeles and its surrounding region had come to rely to an extraordinary degree upon the related industries of defense aircraft, space, and electronics. According to a study by the Community Analysis Bureau of the City of the Angels, Los Angeles County was overwhelmingly dependent upon aerospace and defense industries for its economic well-being. In 1962, 43 percent "of all manufacturing employment in the two county area [Los Angeles and Orange] was found to depend on government aerospace contracts either directly or indirectly." Earlier, in the mid-fifties, the ratio had been 55 percent in Los Angeles County; and, as late as 1960, aerospace alone accounted for fully 75 percent of the manufacturing jobs in neighboring San Diego County. Obviously, by the 1970s the economic foundations of the nation's second largest metropolitan area and its nearby urban rival rested heavily upon what in 1914 had been a new technology of war.[4]

In the period under review, roughly 1910 to 1961, two developments proved decisive to the evolution of the aircraft industry in Southern California. The first was the initial concentration of the industry in the Southland. Between 1908 and 1938, a number of firms located in Southern California or settled in permanently there if they were of local origin. By the latter date, about 60 percent of the airframe manufacturers in the United States resided in this "island on the land," to borrow the apt phrase of Carey McWilliams. When the second decisive development, World War II, occurred, that section was in an ideal position to benefit from it. The Second World War covered the industry with gold, vastly accelerated the coupling of the city and the sword, and created the close interdependence of the region upon this complex range of defense economic stimuli.[5]

This much is well documented, but the influence of California cities upon the concentration of the aircraft industry in the Southland is less perfectly understood. Local patriots and boosters have long known better, but scholars generally neglect the significance of the process of urbanization, the quality and character of urbanism, and the leadership of urban promoters in bringing about the localization of the aircraft industry in Southern California. Some observers describe the industry as nearly footloose; others stress the supply of skilled labor, the availability of capital, the geographic advantages, and the combination of favorable climatic and geographic conditions, or, as Edward Ullman put it, amenities.[6]

This former argument is one of the most popular explanations of the location of the aircraft industry in the Southland. Yet this interpretation is no more satisfactory than its less well-known competitors. To say that an industry is footloose explains only its lack of a necessary connection with any locality, not its eventual settlement in Southern California. Or to put the matter another way, if the industry was footloose, why did it come to be so heavily concentrated in one single metropolitan area? Or indeed, to highlight the urban variable, why did it need to be in any city at all? Why would an industry that apparently had a virtually unlimited range of locational choice exercise such a narrow preference for cities, especially those of one section of the United States?

Certainly the availability of capital, educational facilities, and skilled labor do not answer this question, since many metropolitan regions could have matched, or exceeded, the Southland's financial and labor resources, especially in 1920. And since the modern aircraft industry grew up in a number of climatic and geographic areas running the gamut of American regions from Long Island to eastern Missouri to eastern Kansas to Georgia to Connecticut to Puget Sound to Texas and back to Southern California, we cannot take much comfort from the "natural advantages" explanation of our problem. Moreover, San Diego, which enjoyed a somewhat better climate and an equally advantageous physical situation for aircraft manufacturing, claimed only a minor portion of the Southland industry, while its imperious neighbor grasped by far the larger portion, despite its inferior weather.

If climate and geography did not guarantee a city a share of the aviation booty, neither did it secure a Southland aircraft producer against failure. Several early Southern California aircraft manufacturing companies, failed to make the cut that narrowed the team down to seven major companies by the end of the thirties. Nor did these advantages suffice to keep the leaders of the industry in the area once they had invested there. For a time, Boeing dispersed a significant share of its activities to the island on the land, but did not find its natural advantages sufficiently compelling to remain there. Neither did Glen Curtiss nor Glenn Martin, two other early industry leaders, who once built planes in the Southland and also formed part of the exodus from the area.[7]

As a postmortem to the amenities explanation, the example of Boeing might be pointed out. By 1989, the Washington State firm, located in a very different natural setting, had become the General Motors of the aerospace industry, threatening to eliminate entirely its southern California competitors from the civilian airplane market, and holding ninth place in the military market as well. Indeed, despite the heavy rainfall and perennial wetness of the Puget Sound area, the Seattle firm generally prospered and always held its own from the early years of the industry right down to the present.[8]

If these traditional explanations do not clear up the mystery of the industrial location of the aircraft business, what does? Part of the explanation lies in the extreme vulnerability of the civilian aircraft industry and, to a lesser extent, its service counterparts during the interwar years. The present-mindedness of modern civilization makes it easy to believe in the inevitability of both the civilian branch of the industry and its military counterparts. Perhaps that is true, but it did not appear so to aviation pioneers who struggled against the tides of adversity and public and official ignorance to make a success of the airplane. The Armistice caused much more damage to the aircraft manufacturing industry than the planes themselves had previously inflicted upon Germany. Without a commercial aviation business to return to, as the auto industry could fall back upon civilian demand for cars, and with federal funds "limited," the aircraft industry faced hard times. The Great Crash of 1929 inflicted another crippling defeat, as commercial firms folded and the military services sustained spending cuts and then political damage from the "merchants of death" uproar. As late as 1938, according to the definitive history of the aircraft industry, that business was still on shaky foundations despite the onset of orders for war material.[9]

Equally hard times had befallen the Army Air Force. Perhaps the depth of these difficulties can be seen from the extreme position of Henry Arnold, commanding officer at March Field in Riverside, California, during the years 1931-35. The future World War II celebrity found himself in far different circumstances, beset by both political and financial problems. Not only did the Air Corps fear pacifist and budget-cutting political pressures, but it also worried over its very existence as an independent entity. Some members of the services, ostensibly on economy grounds, were pushing for a merger of the military branches into one department of defense in which the Army Air Corps might lose ground, especially to the Navy. Even without such a consolidation, the Navy seemed to be outshining the Army flyers throughout Southern California.[10]

Arnold, who was no unseasoned observer, thought that his service, his command, and his own career hung in the balance, and his actions did not belie this conviction. To cope, he tried desperately to win the favor of civil society. So anxious was the commanding officer of March Field to please the surrounding political constituency that he was available as a speaker to almost any organization in the area, large or small, influential or not. At any given time the head of one of the two most important Army air commands in the entire United States might be talking to the Los Angeles Chamber of Commerce, to a junior college class on aeronautics, to the students of a high school class in Riverside, to the women's clubs of Riverside, to a Los Angeles breakfast club, or to a small veterans' organization. On another day he might be staging a private air show for a *Los Angeles Times* wheelhorse, a celebrity like Will Rogers, or a Pomona horse breeder. The next day might find him and his aviators entertaining the spectators at the 1932 Olympics, the massed crowds of "Iowa Immigrants" at Long Beach, or the members of the movie colony. Between civic appearances he might dash off to catch up on service politics in Washington or to the Ninth Corps Headquarters in San Francisco. Nearly any given day would find the tireless March Field officer struggling to get the Army Air Force before the public and the media—press, radio, and movies.

Budget problems were dismal. His planes were literally falling apart, and when they did so with pilots in them, political *and* media problems arose. Meanwhile he did not have enough money to make ends meet at his post in Riverside. On one notable occasion when the commander needed machinery, Arnold was reduced to begging for the right to bid on equipment confiscated by the government from Prohibition bootleggers! At another time, Arnold found himself without maps for a West Coast Army air maneuver. In order to put on the "games," the commanding officer was forced to borrow the appropriate cartographic charts from the Automobile Club of Southern California!

These conditions created the final component of an important metropolitan-military alliance as a hyperactive but insecure metropolis sought stability; two fledgling air services struggled to hold and enlarge their foothold in the American defense structure; and a blighted, nascent industry fought to survive. Their mutual apprehensions of decline created the basis for a partnership that would transform the urban landscape inside the great wall of California.[11]

In sum, throughout the period the military aviation business was noticeably vulnerable. Therefore, they needed any help they could get. This made the resources of city boosters an important element in building military aviation. Even if the flyers and manufacturers had not been so severely strapped, these urban contributions would have been impressive. They included control of publicity to popularize a new means of transportation, air power propaganda, political support for a host of projects, landing fields which grew into airports, support for the procurement of military air installations, research facilities for scientific testing of aircraft, leadership in the institutionalization of aviation activities, manufacturing sites in close proximity to military testing and training grounds, financial backing, labor supplies, a promising civilian market, air races and demonstrations, and, for the service aviators, a raison d'être. Together these constituted an extraordinarily "air-minded" urban culture, congenial to the development of nearly every aspect of a new technology of war, transportation, and communication.

Two additional factors seem much more relevant than the footloose, ameneties, natural advantages, or other popular explanations of the localization of the aircraft industry. One, which will be treated later, is the differential performance of various aircraft companies. In the interwar years, the largest concentration of the most competitive airframe manufacturers was in Southern California, and as they increased their portion of the market at the expense of their eastern competitors, they expanded the urban Southern California share as well. Business efficiency produced this outcome, not amenities or geography. A second critical factor in the seduction of the aircraft industry was the character and process of southern California urbanization and the efforts of its promoters to build a great city. From the beginning, Los Angeles, as a city, had certain advantages over its real or its potential competitors. One of the most important of these artificial advantages was a leadership devoted, perhaps even fanatically, to building a great city where the encouragements of nature were, at best, ambiguous.[12]

Perhaps more than any other American city, Los Angeles was the product of a development conspiracy by its leadership. From the founding of the Los Angeles Chamber of Commerce in the late 1880s until the end of the First World War, those efforts had combined with certain natural advantages to produce an extraordinary success. At the time of the historic census of 1920, the city contained 576,000 people and had gained that impressive total from an 1880 base of 11,000. Natural advantages, whether defined as climate, geography, or amenities—pleasant natural living conditions—played a significant role in this growth drama. The climate attracted many, if not most, of the early residents; the discovery of oil in the nineties fleshed out a very narrow economic base; amenities attracted an ever larger stream of tourists; and rich soil and congenial weather encouraged an impressive agricultural development. More by luck than sense, the area also gained the movie industry in these years, and it too was somewhat influenced by climatic and geographic factors.[13]

However, much of the success of the area came in spite of rather than because of its natural advantages. Los Angeles and San Diego had no known iron ore deposits nearby and would not discover any until the intense search for minerals prompted by the Second World War. No great stream of immigration flowed naturally to its doors at that time, as was the case of contemporaneous New York City, or even the Southland today. Nor did it possess an advantageous geographic location for trading with either the awakening Orient or the already wide-awake national domestic markets of the United States. Southern California lay in the extreme southwest corner of the country, about as remote as it could be and still remain within the United States. Unlike nearly all of the great cities east of the ninety-eighth parallel, the future megalopolis did not lie on any great or even significant waterway or lake. The Southland also lacked the central geographic position of northern California and therefore did not acquire major railroad links until after the Bay Area and the Central Valley. It might have waited longer still had not the voters of Los Angeles agreed to subsidize the Southern Pacific Railroad to build into town when that company threatened to bypass them. The connection was made in 1876 and allowed the Angelenos to capitalize upon their climate and scenery by extensive advertising throughout the country.[14]

As tourists and new residents poured in, the promoters turned to filling out the infrastructure of a future metropolis. To overcome the imposing distances of this great island on the land, real estate developers built one of the finest electric trolley systems in the country. As the limited port facilities of Wilmington, Long Beach, and San Pedro became less and less able to handle the growing volume of traffic, the city government and its booster supporters commenced a campaign to wrest control of the harbor from the Southern Pacific Railroad. Simultaneously, they began to improve the port. The first of these victories had been achieved by 1900 and the second had been launched with vigor. By the same year, the population, at 102,000, threatened or seemed to threaten to outrun the water supply needed to build a large city amidst an arid but productive agricultural hinterland. This feat would not have taken much effort, since the cities of the area lay in a region of extremely low rainfall. At the turn of the century, the precipitation at Los Angeles varied between five and eight inches per annum, somewhat below normal, but still illustrative of the near desert character of most of the Southland. The City of Los

Angeles built the Owens Aqueduct and later several others to overcome that geographic deficiency, and in the process began to cope with still another—the lack of fuel sources nearby.

In 1880, the closest known coal deposits to Los Angeles were some five hundred miles distant in Coahuila, Mexico, and Utah. The Owens project produced electrical power as well as water. Both the municipal water and power system and the harbor were put under public control to insure cheap water, electricity, and port charges, an edge that a lively city would find useful in its competition. To the south, San Diego completed similar, although far less impressive, improvements. Thus, if Donald Douglas, the Lockheed brothers, Robert Gross, Jake Kindelberger, Gerald Vultee, Reuben Fleet, Claude Ryan, and the other founders of the aircraft industry were able to consider the value of the Urban Southland amenities or natural advantages to their businesses, it was only because the promoters the City of the Angels and the Harbor of the Sun had already provided a basic urban infrastructure. They had done so in large part by surmounting geographic deficiencies—great distances, an out-of-the-way location, lack of fuel sources, limited water supplies, and, in the case of Los Angeles, a poor harbor—that threatened to constrain and limit the process of urbanization. Initially, geography was definitely more of a hindrance to growth rather than an amenity producing automatic urban development.

The post-World War I response of Angelenos and San Diegans to the airplane confirms this point. The residents of these cities became "air-minded," to use their phrase for the idea, for the same reason that they earlier had become harbor-minded, water-minded, transit-minded, and electric-power-minded. The airplane, like the other technologies that had been employed to solve developmental and economic problems, was a means to evade the discipline of nature upon the process of urbanization rather than a way to capitalize upon the natural advantages of area. Southland boosters touted the plane as a way to cope with the greater distances of the West, and later historians have echoed this point, stressing the fact that western spaces forced the adoption of the airplane. Air travel could link together the vast reaches of the West much more rapidly than railroad travel and thereby save money for the businessman and the community. More important, the natural disadvantages of the West in general, and southern California in particular, made the nascent aircraft industry unusually attractive. Los Angeles, San Diego, and San Francisco all shared the nineteenth-century American urban booster illusion that industrialization was the indispensable prerequisite to major urbanization. Western remoteness from markets and freight rates, which Westerners considered discriminatory, made the realization of this dream difficult if not impossible. For example, without contiguous deposits of coal and iron ore Los Angeles could not develop a large-scale steel industry because the cost of transporting the necessary tons of raw materials from Utah or even more distant points and the cost of shipping them to faraway consumers would have priced the finished product out of the market.

Not until the post-World War II invention of a more efficient means of steel making—one which required less fuel—was Southern California able to found a modern steel industry. Before that time, any manufacturing industry that could withstand the adverse freight rates of the area was especially welcome to the developers of this most important urban oasis, to employ Gerald Nash's happy phrase.[15]

Motion-picture products suited these requirements wonderfully well, since they represented a high value in extremely low bulk. In a somewhat different way, airframe products provided an additional means of overcoming the geographical disadvantages of the Southland. Planes did not generate large transportation costs because they flew away on their own rather than being carried by some other means of conveyance. Moreover, they did not require the transportation of great quantities of resources over vast distances. Initially the manufacturers built them out of wood, which the West possessed in quantities that could be shipped cheaply over long distances by water. This product joined tourism, federal investment, population migration, movies, oil, and technological expertise amongst the few southern California "exports" capable of surmounting or circumventing the mountains, deserts, and distances that separated the area within "the great wall of California" from the remainder of the country.

In 1920, this barrier seemed even more formidable. In fact, as late as 1976, a study by the Los Angeles city government concluded that the Southland did not yet have a stable economy, though by that time the area had acquired aircraft, space, electronics, shipbuilding, garment, and other industries mostly lacking in 1920. Small wonder that their predecessors in 1920 felt the pressures of the metropolitan anxiety that much more acutely. The island oasis felt that it could not compete with the industrial power of its more remote American sister cities, and it was continually menaced, or thought it was so by the Bay Area to the north. Moreover, it was increasingly fragmented within by the endlessly self-generating process of suburbanization which threatened to subvert the interests already built up in the major cities of the region. Although Southern California, even then, was a Christian community, its cities had an extremely Darwinian character.[16]

Just as in the case of these fiercely competitive cities, the floating Navy, and the air arm of both services, the aircraft industry endured the same unease. Like the floating Navy, this industry suffered from both relative and absolute decline, and like the aerial branches did not have a long tradition of service to the country to protect itself from the postwar measures of demobilization. Therefore the airmen were more vulnerable than the sailors, and the infant civilian aircraft industry was practically defenseless. After the armistice, the federal government canceled contracts wholesale, flooded the market with surplus World War I planes and Liberty engines, and drastically reduced the military demand for either. Perhaps 90 percent of the business was destroyed at the stroke of a pen. Unlike the auto factories, which had a large civilian market to return to after the war, the commercial aircraft business had no such cushion to fall back upon. With defense spending "limited," in addition to all its other woes, the aircraft industry faced hard times. These conditions created the final component of an important metropolitan-military alliance. At the same time that a hyperactive but insecure metropolitan area sought stability, two fledgling air services struggled to enlarge their foothold in the American defense structure and a blighted, nascent manufacturing business fought to survive. Mutual apprehensions of decline created the basis for a partnership that would transform the urban landscape inside the great wall of California.[17]

The civilian partners in this alliance moved quite consciously to create conditions that would be most congenial to the development of aviation. Their reasoning was familiar. "Commercial aviation is today making long strides in America—advancing much faster than the layman realizes," noted San Diego aircraft industry pioneer George H. Prudden in 1927. "The city that is not alert to this development in providing an airport will simply be left behind." "Successive civilizations have prospered and spread their contemporary influences only to the degree that they have improved their transportation facilities," agreed Harris M. Hanshue, president and general manager of Western Air Express.

> Cities have grown great and nations, powerful because of their dominance of trade routes and world commerce. Each advance in the science of transportation has seen prestige shift from communities and countries schooled in the passing method to those who have sensed the importance of and seized the opportunity afforded by the new practice. . . . The phenomenal growth of Southern California would have been impossible except for automotive facilities and the comprehensive system of highways centering in the City of Los Angeles.
>
> Each period in transportation history has seen communities penalized under existing systems seizing upon the new agency as a means for advancing their interests. But the automobile and the airplane coming upon the scene almost simultaneously and—to a certain degree—each complementing the other, have appealed most strongly to the same areas. In this connection, it is interesting to note that the most significant developments in aerial passenger service have centered in Los Angeles and Detroit.[18]

To contemporary observers, the airplane seemed perfect to help the urban area realize these hopes because it was ideally suited to overcome the Southland's geographic disadvantages. "Los Angeles has become the metropolis of the West, despite the fact that she has been separated by thousands of miles from the great industrial, commercial, and financial centers of the East," boasted the editor of *Southern California Business*. "It is natural that she would grasp at improvements in transportation that would hasten the transfer of mail and goods." More important still, civil aviation would provide demand for a kind of factory product which could withstand the transportation charges that the remoteness of California and freight rate discrimination imposed on its manufacturers. Therefore, flying could help increase and diversify the manufacturing base that the Southland and other California cities were so concerned about. This factor was critical, because California urban boosters, especially those in the Southland, considered industrialization crucial to the stability of their urban region. No city could be great without manufacturing, and an industry which evaded both geography and rate discrimination would be doubly welcome to an aspiring metropolis.[19]

Aircraft production promised both industrialization and diversification. With the airframe industry must come allied industries, thought the boosters. The manufacturers of airplane motors must be attracted to the plane makers and so must the makers of other airplane parts, the subcontractors. Where motors led, mufflers would follow, together with parachute makers, research and development facilities, and flying schools. As these economic linkages developed, further multiplier effects would inevitably ripple out to increase the local wage and salary pools and then the business of service industries where the money would be spent.

Commerce seemed destined to benefit too. Some Southland and California products could move faster via the air, and businessmen could increase the speed of metropolitan business transactions via air mail or personal business trips. By the same means, cities could modify their dependence on the railroad, whose rate discrimination so vexed them. Moreover, the reach of urban empire could be expanded considerably with the new means of travel. The plane traveled an "ocean of air," or an "unseen ocean," as it was sometimes called, and these aerial seas led literally everywhere. Regardless of railroad or highway connections or mountain obstacles, a city with airways could always get to any other that had an airport. This flexibility attracted Americans in general and Southern Californians in particular in much the same manner as the automobile appealed to Americans, who were sick and tired of the constraints of earlier forms of transportation. Americans had always prized personal freedom of movement, and the airplane seemed to enlarge this realm vastly, even more than the auto had. Also, to get anywhere meant to enlarge the potential area of the urban hinterland; speed and flexibility would see to that.[20]

Predictably, in a section of the country whose history closely resembled an endless land-speculation bonanza, the air boosters considered real estate as well. Airports stood at the center of the promoters' vision. With uncanny accuracy, the city builders predicted that landing fields would undoubtedly attract airframe manufacturing enterprises, then airplane motor makers and the like, flying schools, and finally hotels and cafes. "There will undoubtedly be little community centers around the fields where airplanes land and take off. Each field will produce a community of no small importance." Private residences would then gravitate to the other activities and all would stand on increasingly valuable realty.[21]

Other less general visions complemented these. Airplanes and airports possessed a national defense relevance, so they might attract federal subsidies, and these federal monies in turn could help cities escape the domination of the state government. From early on, American cities have complained of the heavy hand of their state government rulers (sometimes the criticism had validity and sometimes it did not), and a federal airport program might stimulate a new, lucrative enterprise from which the direct federal-urban partnership might exclude the legislators and administrators at Sacramento. For San Diego, this possibility was both general and specific to the drive for naval resources. The dredging of the Harbor of the Sun cemented the Navy to the Border City, both by improving the naval anchorage and extending the landing areas at North Island Naval Air Station and at the civil landing strip at Lindbergh Field as well. The harbor would thereafter be able to accommodate the new carriers being built by the Navy, and Lindbergh Field and North Island could better oblige the aviators when in port.[22]

The boosters did not forget the issue of national defense. However, by a happy coincidence of interest, that important problem fit right into the scheme for urban development. The Army and Navy could only benefit from the training of pilots (who would be available for national emergencies, especially wars), the construction of airports, the concentration of manufacturing enterprises, the aggregation of technical expertise, and the inculcation of "air-mindedness." Besides, argued air ace Eddie Rickenbacker, the wings of air power would protect the California cities, hovering over them as an "angel of peace or as the most deadly weapon that man ever created."[23]

Once the advantages of airplane manufacture, travel, and defense had been surmised, California urbanites, particularly those south of the Tehachapis, moved to harness this new technology to urban development. At first these booster efforts seemed uncoordinated and even desultory, but by the 1930s, the air booster activities had begun to overlap significantly. Much of the campaign fell under the all-encompassing wing of the Los Angeles Chamber of Commerce, especially its Aviation Department, together with a few other institutions like the *Los Angeles Times,* which harbored similar developmental ambitions for Southern California. Although the influence of these two institutions was pervasive, the airplane story in California is considerably more complex than that of the Navy. No single issue, like that of the American Singapore, provided focus to the effort to develop the aviation business and aircraft manufacturing. Instead a complex mosaic of causation developed around the attempt to link the fate of the urban form and the new technology. Most of these efforts took place in the Southland, but Northern California was represented as well. The two sections created a series of advantages, an air-minded urban *culture,* which could not be duplicated elsewhere. Together with the greater efficiency of the California airframe industrial firms, these booster activities explain the alliance between the birdmen and the island on the land.

It could perhaps be argued that urban historians have frequently exaggerated the influence of city boosters on urban development in general and that to explain the location of a great aeronautical complex in Southern California would be to repeat that mistake. However, the first assumption still remains to be proven and the second can perhaps be tested as a part of that process. In making this examination, it must be stressed that the traditional interpretations of the location of the airframe industry in California are simply inadequate. The potential of the airplane did not burst forth on the Urban California scene immediately after World War I, but by the mid-twenties, the idea had captured the imagination of the elite, and they moved to implant the concept in the mass mind as well. "Air-mindedness," especially in Southern California, seemed the necessary first step. Since the public did not understand the importance of the new means of transportation and warfare, the leaders of Urban California sought to dispel their ignorance. Despite the fact that air power was not exactly a specialty of the chambers of commerce and their non-military allies, the effort to sell the airplane had both a civilian and defense dimension. Although each side had its own reasons for popularizing the birdmen of Southern California, soldier and civilian cooperated in this task throughout the interwar period. As in the case of the floating Navy, this alliance covered a broad range of activities. Air races, dirigible spectaculars, record-setting distance flights, media coverage of aerial activities, and ringing testimonials to the efficacy of air power kept up the pressure for air-mindedness. So did regular mock air attacks on supposedly vulnerable California cities, followed by equally well-publicized genuine assaults on the federal budget for more coastal, aeronautical, and naval defense spending to protect the coast.

Although the media of Urban California was not obsessed with the progress of the aircraft industry from 1919 to 1941, the newspapers and periodicals did provide consistent coverage of aviation advances and prospects. This attention gave boosters, leaders in the field of aviation, and military figures regular opportunities to put their case before the California public. The missionaries of a new technology needed little urging to accept this assistance. "We are in step with the main parade of air progress," contended the *San Francisco Examiner.* "Let's advertise the fact to the world by the best and most dramatic method." *Southern California Business* enthused that "almost as soon as a few figures become available they are lost in the wake of the industry's meteoric growth. . . . The progress of commercial aviation in California, as elsewhere, will be limited in the future only by man's historic desire to be transported from place to place as rapidly as possible." The Border City's "industrial future undoubtedly is aviation," argued Phil Swing, a prime mover in the Boulder Dam and the All-American Canal projects.[24]

Although the late twentieth century may take the airplane for granted, earlier generations had to labor long and hard to gain acceptance for this new technology. Cities aided this process enormously. Either through the boosterism of their leaders, the crowds they could easily gather, their financing, publicity media, markets, mechanical lore, concentration of machine shops, collections of allied technologies like motors, or strategic placement at the center of the established transportation routes, cities provided a series of crucial external economies for an embattled technology. However, unlike the auto, plane ownership did not become universalized. Even today, planes carry masses of passengers or freight, wealthy persons who own their own, or military personnel. This novel means of conveyance never developed a mass constituency with the public as the auto did; although the car and the plane came onto the scene at virtually the same historical moment, the former gained acceptance very quickly and the airplane did not. Therefore, the flyers needed all the help they could get, from urban leaders, military services, legislators, and other influential persons. Publicizing the plane became a major urban effort.

"I am morally obligated to generations yet unborn for the unique position that I was granted and the service rendered during the World War from an instrument . . . created by our genius, known as the airplane," wrote aviation war hero Captain Eddie Rickenbacker in 1925. "Then there came the time of the bird men," he continued. "I have seen and heard them criticized and complimented to such an extent that they were supermen and some of us unfortunately believed it and one of these days we are going to wake up and find that we are all supermen—that everybody can fly an airplane, that there is nothing much to it."[25]

In order to make everyone a superman in his or her own plane, the air boosters had to gain the media spotlight. This they did by a series of aerial spectaculars, as they raced before delighted and awed urban gatherings or wearily fought their way toward new distance records over vast expanses of the North American continent. On other occasions they ploughed toward Asia through the "unseen oceans" of air over the visibly menacing waters below. The danger was not at all imaginary: in the Dole Race from Oakland to Hawaii, nine aircraft started but only two arrived. The military often provided planes and pilots for these events, while their urban partners supplied landing fields, sponsorship, pilots, prizes, and publicity. These cities, of course, also mobilized their own crowds, the indispensable requirement for popularizing the new means of transportation and destruction.

As early as 1919 both Bay Area and Southland boosters sponsored air races, but the activity seemed more important to the South. Among the earlier efforts was the first round-the-world flight—made by Douglas Aircraft Army planes taking off in 1924 from Clover Field in Santa Monica. Southern California aircraft products received further advertisement from the 1928 National Air Races and Aeronautical Exposition. "Los Angeles obtained the national event in competition with a half dozen other cities" and gave away $200,000 to civilian as well as to Army, Navy and National Guard flyers. Fifteen hundred planes took part. Other spectaculars followed in the 1930s. In 1932, Henry H. Arnold, the commander of March Field at Riverside, volunteered to add an aeronautical dimension to the Olympic proceedings at Los Angeles and was promptly accepted.[26]

The Army Air Force gained further exposure to large urban crowds later the same year at an air meet at Long Beach. Even allowing for exaggeration, the reported spectator totals are impressive. "Hap" Arnold's March Field command staged the demonstration itself to a paid attendance of 20,000, some of whom waited from 8 a.m. until 1:30 p.m. to see the planes pass in review. An estimated 70,000 more witnessed the event from the sidelines. A large throng also turned out to greet the dirigible *Macon,* which arrived at its post at Sunnyvale in 1933. Several thousand crowded the field and thousands jammed the roadways leading into the landing area. In 1933, Los Angeles again hosted a national air races meet. Even earlier, the governor of California gave institutional form to the air shows by proclaiming "Aviation Week," and, as one of the organizers of the meet put it, "The majority of the activities, of course, will be in and around Los Angeles." Toward the end of the decade more long-distance endurance flights supplemented these local affairs, which occurred frequently in Los Angeles in the thirties. March Field alone put on demonstrations regularly.[27]

Even more spectacular displays were staged by the services during annual or special military maneuvers. American cities had not necessarily figured in nineteenth-century American military maneuvers, but the advent of air power put urban areas squarely onto the target. First World War air raids on cities suggested one future use of air power, and that fact was followed by postwar theoretical justification to match. Giulio Douhet of Italy and contemporary air power strategists around the Western World devised military theories of air power that would have given an independent role to the air force, allowing them to provide a decisive blow to enemy forces well behind the lines of infantry combat. These, it was argued, would neutralize a nation's will or ability to fight by demoralizing civilian populations, destroying communications lines, and knocking out strategic resources like dams, railway networks, bridges, supply centers, and manufacturing works. Of course, many of these resources were located in urban centers, and thus from the beginning the concept of air power had a disturbingly urban implication. It should be emphasized that these theories were simply that and had received precious little verification in combat experience in the First World War. Moreover, air power doctrines were blatantly self-interested. In the aftermath of the Great War, the fledgling air services of different armies needed a continuing role in military matters; and however much they may have believed their own ideas, Douhet, William Mitchell, and the other air-power advocates' interpretations served to justify the existence and expanded role of their own air services. So the idea of aerial warfare was both a military strategy and a bureaucratic power play.

Once again, the historical context of this effort must be emphasized. To a later age, inured to the dangers of nuclear war and familiar with the conventional destructiveness of air forces, the significance of air power may seem a given. However, in 1919 and, indeed, for years thereafter a very different situation prevailed. Not until the sinking of the *Repulse* and the *Prince of Wales* in the early stages of World War II did an air force demonstrate its capacity to sink a battleship in actual combat. Moreover, the claims of air power to a decisive role in conflict only received their final ghastly confirmation in the incendiary and atomic raids of the war's latter months. Even commercial aviation transportation did not prove consistently profitable until the advent of the Douglas DC-3 in 1935. For most of the period under review, the airplane was a technology in search of both a commercial and military mission. Therefore, every display of the utility of aviation was highly valued.

These exhibitions were not long in coming. From the early twenties on, California cities were targeted for the demonstration of air power. "Enemy warships could approach the California coast and turn loose 600 or 700 airplanes to destroy San Francisco and spread ruin through the state," noted the *San Francisco Examiner,* paraphrasing a speech by Admiral William Sims to University of California alumni at Oakland. A practical test, "theoretically" designed to reduce San Francisco to a "heap of ashes," followed two months later. As usual, this event carefully exploited the urban crowd by combining instruction in air power with entertainment. "The gates will be open at 1 o'clock," invited the *Examiner,* "and there won't be a dull minute until the strains of 'Home Sweet Home' after the final dance in the evening." A number of other moments during the twenties proved to be equally lively. In 1925 a lone Army aviator ranged over San Francisco in another test and found the city totally vulnerable. "We have almost no defense from the air," lamented the *San Francisco Chronicle* some months later.[28]

By the end of the twenties this effort had become institutionalized into a kind of urban "air power theater," designed both to "educate" and to entertain a frightened metropolitan public. The flash of "brilliant flares in the night sky, the booming of anti-aircraft guns and the whirl of airplane propellers last night apprised the city of the holding of the annual benefit of the Army Relief Association at the Presidio," explained the *San Francisco Examiner* in 1923. The brilliance, boom, and whirl grew still more familiar in the 1930's. In late January 1933, Pacific coast newspapers announced that an "enemy force" of naval planes "would drone in large numbers some dawn around February 15 [shortly before the inauguration of FDR] over one or two of the Pacific Slope's three great population centers, Los Angeles, San Francisco, and Seattle." In a sneak preview of the outcome, "Navy men" noted that the exercise would "prove . . . that the west coast is inadequately protected from overseas attack. The "problem is declared by naval authorities to be the most significant to security of the United States of any yet devised or executed," concluded the *San*

Diego Union. By some strange coincidence, the "Navy men" turned out to be well informed, as the *San Francisco Examiner* reported that its home city "was theoretically blown to bits."[29]

The carnage mounted as the years passed. In 1935 the Army, Navy, and National Guard airmen "raided" the San Diego Exposition on successive nights amidst the roar of sirens and anti-aircraft guns, while Expo visitors peered skyward to see their attackers illuminated by powerful spotlights. Two years later, the Navy returned to the attack just as the Washington and London Naval Limitation Treaties expired, "destroying" Hilo, Hawaii, and mounting another assault on California coast cities. Meanwhile, the Army Air Corps rained "destruction" over much of Southern California. For starters, the Corps mock-gassed Bakersfield on April 4, 1937, and then moved back south for several days of maneuvers at its Antelope Valley bombing range north of Los Angeles. Reversing the usual pattern, the Air Corps this time employed live bombs against an imaginary city, marked out with lime on the Muroc Dry Lake to resemble the real City of Angels. "In three blistering weeks of mimic warfare in the clouds," Muroc Los Angeles, in succession, lost its "largest aircraft factory," part of the San Pedro docks, the railroad yards and rail connections to Salt Lake City, and the remainder of the aircraft factories, and was, like its transmontane sister city, gassed in the bargain. An Air Corps spokesman claimed that these results "have taught . . . that America today stands more vulnerable to an attack from the air than ever before in modern history."[30]

Various service units demonstrated this vulnerability in the following years. As usual, the urban masses and media played a large role. "A spirit of gaiety, intermingled with the grim atmosphere of war, will hover over the Los Angeles-Long Beach harbor district tomorrow when the annual Harbor Day celebration is presented as the curtain raiser to the 1938 Foreign Trade Week observance," promised the *Los Angeles Times* in 1938. The National Guard would provide the grimness with the usual attack on the harbor, complete with air-raid sirens, searchlights, anti-aircraft guns, and even a blackout of the San Pedro area. In September, 10,000 American Legionnaires saw Navy fliers pass in review over San Pedro Bay, while an estimated 100,000 "saw the review from the coastline, eastward from Point Fermin, through the Palos Verdes Hills to Long Beach." Though neither civilian nor military spokesmen dwelt publicly on the political purposes of these exhibitions, they sometimes let slip some of the non-military motivations for their activities. "INVADING ENEMY FOUGHT BY ARMY NAVY AIR FORCES," screamed a *San Diego Union* headline in 1938. The article went on to explain that "while Congress mulled over the needs for National defense this week, army and navy airmen went through the grim routine of battling a theoretical enemy invading the American shores." That western comment on eastern affairs, of course, revealed one of the things that the airmen were about. Congress apparently got the message (though obviously the necessity of rearmament was stressed by other influentials besides city boosters), since 1938 witnessed the beginning of serious American preparations for World War II. Metropolitan leaders had long ago been converted to this necessity.[31]

Of course, California cities did not put on the major military maneuvers, though they doubtless played a role in the minor ones staged by National Guard or reserve units. However, the urban fabric lent itself to the credibility of the air power thesis. When urban politicians, boosters, educators, clubmen, scientists, media men, and even local air-power theoreticians took up the cudgels to persuade those who remained unconvinced by the droning planes, screaming sirens, piercing searchlights, or simulated explosions, these spokesmen enjoyed easy access to numerous forums to do so. Each of the cities was honeycombed with a series of communications networks, educational channels, and propaganda outlets which could be used by those with an air-power or aviation message to transmit.

Urban service organizations provided one such outlet. From the Kiwanis Club of Riverside to the prestigious Commonwealth Club of California, San Francisco invitations flowed out to military aviators to explain the virtues of their means of transportation and destruction. Chambers of commerce, realty boards, tourist hotels, and veterans' organizations offered other forums for the enlightenment of the public.

The radio and newspaper media provided an even better one and, what is more, one that was hardly neutral. Newspapers in particular covered the military events in depth with news stories, guest contributions by military men, and considerable photographic material. And when this data ran short, the media carried stories about the bombings of Ethiopia, Guernica, and Nanking to compensate for the temporary cessation of simulated mayhem. Live radio braodcasts of the home-grown spectaculars heightened their impact.

However, from early in the period newspapers became the most active advocates for the aviators. The omnipresence of William Randolph Hearst interests dictated this sympathetic press attitude, at least in part. The Hearst chain dominated the *San Francisco Examiner,* the *San Francisco Call and Post* and the *Bulletin* by the end of the twenties and owned the *Los Angeles Examiner* as well. Though posturing on occasion for the common soldiers by denouncing the prejudices of military castes, Hearst supported the kind of military preparedness, particularly naval and aeronautical, which would have maximized the influence of such elites. In this case, it is difficult to sort out the local and extra-local influences, since Hearst remained politically involved in "The City" where his journalistic career began. Moreover, his son George, who lived there for much of the interwar period, was active in the local affairs of the press chain and, predictably enough, shared his father's convictions about air and naval preparedness. However, discounting the influence of either Hearst, the other newspapers of Urban California would have been sympathetic to the message of air power.[32]

Of course, not every metropolitan spokesman defined that idea in the same way. There was both an Army Air Corps and a Navy definition of air power, although the two were not mutually exclusive. Army air power was designed to strike behind enemy ground forces and disable strategic targets, terrorize civilian populations, or destroy a water-borne invasion fleet. Navy air power was carrier-based and destined to attack other naval forces. Whether or not the American Navy actually anticipated attacking enemy cities, they believed in the theoretical possibility of an enemy air attack on West Coast cities. Otherwise they would not have been able to claim that naval forces constituted America's first line of defense. However, at this point the two ideas competed, as both the Navy and the Army Air Corps competed for the right to provide shore-line and long-range defense of the coastline. The Navy wanted to defend the coast by carrier-based planes, which would intercept the aerial attackers far out at sea; and the Air Corps wanted to perform the same duty via the services of the Flying Fortresses, which could supposedly disrupt the assault on West Coast cities by sinking the attacking carriers long before they could launch their own planes.

There was also some dissent on the deadliness of air power, perhaps reflecting the dependence of various cities on one or another of the services. In the Navy town of San Diego, where battleship admirals still upheld the importance of that weapon, one might find occasional skepticism of the Army Air Corps doctrines that "the next war will wipe out whole cities and populations, employing newly devised explosives, and amazing aircraft." Three years later, in 1938, the same paper could insist that "in spite of their growing importance, planes still do not form the back-bone of national protection." American security, argued the *San Diego Union,* "must still depend upon ships of various types, and shore batteries placed in advan-tageous positions." The same year, Congressman Ed Izac of San Diego defended the battleship in a debate with Maury Maverick, his counterpart from San Antonio, Texas—itself a major Army Air Corps center. However, these reservations implied a qualification rather than a rejection of the doctrine of air power. As the *San Diego Union* admitted in August 1941, "Definite battlefields no longer exist. Each city, town, hamlet, farm or home is a potential scene of death and destruction. Bombing planes know no barriers and their crews, apparently, abide by no codes of ethics." Perhaps the Border City had too many airplane factories by that date to reject the notion of air power entirely.[33]

San Diego even had its own air-power theorist, as did other cities. Warren Jef-ferson Davis, an attorney in the Border City and air-power enthusiast, added his own local twist to the theories of air power. Active in setting up chapters of the National Aeronautical Association and sensitive to both the supposed threat of Japan to Pacific cities and the very real menace of metropolitan rivalry, Davis pounded home the threat of air attack. "The next war will come at the drop of a bomb, and our cities, without an adequate protecting air force, will be ruthlessly wiped out," predicted Davis in 1927. "The airplane can fly almost at will over a battle fleet and drop bombs with deadly precision," added Davis, and only other airplanes could prevent these things from happening. These views were shared by former Senator James D. Phelan of San Francisco, who wrote the introduction to Davis's book and to whom it was dedicated.[34]

As American entry into World War II approached, these views received official sanction in Los Angeles, where large-scale production of aircraft was rapidly trans-forming that place into an arsenal of democracy. With a "large, modernized Navy, a well-trained and equipped Army, and, most important of all, a large and well-trained Air Force with the latest and best equipment available," argued Mayor Fletcher Bowron, "we will know the peace and security that we cannot otherwise realize." The mayor's conviction that air power was the most important element of national defense was entirely in keeping with the primacy of aircraft production in that city. As the conflagration approached and the area's aviation manufacturing rose, the mayor's estimation of air power went up with it. Speaking in April 1941 of the need to protect the city's "stores and shops and factories" from "the enemy within," Bowron contended that "from this locality will go forth the bombers and Flying Fortresses and the fighting planes that will mean the turning of the tide of fortune of the World War." This statement exactly reflected the opinion of air-power theorists, who insisted that aviation could provide the decisive difference in modern welfare. The supposed capacities of the as yet unproven Flying Fortresses received even more dramatic confirmation in both the media and the public schools. In September 1941, the *Los Angeles Daily News* published the claim that a new bomb sight provided the Army Air Force with the ability to hit a miniscule target from very high altitudes. That extraordinary testimony to the effectiveness of precision bombing was then picked up by the first issue of the *Defense Digest* of the Secondary Division of the Los Angeles County school system, designed for guidance activities and English, social studies, and industrial arts classes. "The school as an influential agency in modern democratic society is recognizing its responsibility for helping young people to meet the problems of this age," noted the *Digest* in a foreword pointing out the overriding importance of national defense. Then the educators explained to those high schoolers who had not aleady read it in the *Daily News*, "It is said on good authority that in tests on Muroc Dry Lake, a flying fortress dropped FIVE of EIGHT dummy bombs inside a 30 INCH circle" from an altitude of 16,000 feet. The *Digest* then came perilously close to arguing that the Flying Fortresses were the country's first line of defense, a point vigorously disputed by the Navy. This claim came at a time when the inaccuracy of British night bombing had forced that country to switch from precision to area bombing because of their inability to hit a factory or even a good-sized town, much less a thirty-inch circle. All of this air-power publicity was, of course, advertisement for the products of a crucial local industry as well. Throughout the interwar years, the largest portion of the aircraft market was military, and by 1938 it was even more so. This meant that the market was both a political and economic one.[35]

Besides favoring the use of local manufactures in warfare, civilian boosters provided other political services that would help ensure the continuation and expansion of both their civil and military markets. These services were both general and specific. As noted previously, the California metropolitan areas provided frequent opportunities for either the civilian or military air boosters to vent their views about the importance of aircraft. This barrage of information and opinion helped to create a favorable public image of the aviation industry in its broadest sense. However, these political pressures could be and were brought to bear on specific issues of importance to any of the three principal branches of the industry in California—military flying, aircraft manufacturing, and civilian aviation. Regretting the proposed cut in the budget of the National Advisory Committee for Aeronautics, the headquarters of the California Department of the American Legion tried to find ways to help fend off the blow. "We do not know just how this bill will affect your status at March Field," wrote Commander Van Hogan to Henry Arnold. "[We] would, therefore, greatly appreciate receiving your valued views on the matter, to intelligently appeal to our National representatives at Washington to assist you in the splendid work you are so ably carrying out for the good of the service and the protection of our American ideals."[36]

On occasion, the civilians performed some splendid work of their own. When Henry H. Arnold arrived in 1931 to assume control of the Army Air Corps base at March Field, he soon discovered a rather striking gap in the facilities at his disposal. Despite the fact that the First Wing, one of only three wings in the entire Army Air Corps, had its headquarters there, Arnold found that he had no bombing and machine-gun range. The Navy would not share the Pacific because "it was duck-boarded for their operations. Understandably, an advocate of air power might find the lack of a bombing range somewhat cramping to his service's mission and ambitions, and Arnold did. Muroc Dry Lake in the Mojave Desert over the mountains to the north seemed the ideal solution to this fundamental problem. However, that area was criss-crossed with railroad land, contained some school land, and would certainly be beset by hundreds of claims if word leaked out that the Air Corps wanted possession. To help secure guidance to the most advantageous site, Arnold called on "friends in the Automobile Club of Southern California," who took the airmen to the right spot. Having singled out the potential dimensions of the range, the airmen started the procedure of getting the public land withdrawn from sale so that the Army could use it. Though the land acquisition looked simple enough, it took until 1939 to secure a clear title. In the meantime, the Air Corps was rebuffed by several government agencies, including the Department of the Interior office in Los Angeles. Arnold then turned to the Los Angeles Chamber of Commerce in an effort to mobilize quietly metropolitan political support. They in turn helped to interest local congressmen in the problem.[37]

Whether the Air Corps would have obtained the bombing range without the aid of the civilian allies is impossible to determine. The fact is, they were aided in acquiring the facility, and, more important, the Muroc bombing range was an important air power asset. Not only could it be used for maneuvers, which generated political publicity in the metropolitan press, but it also allowed the testing of aircraft on a large scale. According to Hap Arnold, commander of the Army Air Corps in World War II, "The classes at the Air Corps Tactical School at Maxwell Field, Alabama, were just then beginning to develop strategic and tactical doctrines that would later guide our air campaigns in World War II" during the time that he commanded the First Wing at March Field. "We felt that out in the 1st Wing, that we were doing much to furnish the practical tests for, and proofs of, the Maxwell Field theories," Arnold noted in his autobiography. "A very different attitude from Douhet's toward bomber escort and a very different view of precision bombing resulted." Obviously these maneuvers provided both advertising (local spokesmen usually pointed out the manufacturing site of the military planes) and testing for metropolitan manufactures. So the Muroc Air Force Base, opened in 1933, not only advertised and tested local products along with the air-power theories that would be used in the coming world war, it also provided the basis for the creation of what evolved into the huge aerospace complex located there, now under the new name of Edwards Air Force Base.[38]

Other political assistance influenced civilian flying more than military aviation, but bore importantly on both. Without airports the industry could not develop, and considerable civilian and military effort went into securing these assets. As early as 1925, the Ninth Army Corps in San Francisco, with jurisdiction over the entire

West Coast, participated heavily in this endeavor. "Several important steps have been taken during the past year as definite efforts to assist commercial aviation and stimulate interest in its development," the Corps' Annual Report recorded. "The Air Officer has conducted what might be termed a landing field 'campaign' urging the establishment of municipal airports, one of the greatest needs of commercial aviation," the same source continued. "Landing field specifications and data have been assembled and sent, with appropriate letters and accompanying information (noteworthy among the latter, a comparative time chart showing the advantage of the airplane over other means of transportation in the matter of speed) to forty-one cities along the principal airways of the Ninth Corps Area. Nineteen percent of these cities have as a result of this work, expressed their interest in establishing airports and working toward that end." What the railroad industry thought of this movement to create alternatives to its own travel services can only be imagined.[39]

Before long, the municipal governments of San Francisco, Oakland, San Diego, and Los Angeles joined the number of cities who had responded positively. They too identified the landing fields as a critical factor in the development of aviation and aircraft industries. In other transportation matters, California cities did not necessarily consider themselves bound to provide terminals or stations. Urban California usually owned its own port facilities, or, as in the case of San Francisco, the state government did, but public ownership did not automatically extend to other areas.

Throughout the period, San Francisco had both public and private transit while mass transportation in Los Angeles remained in private hands. Public and private power companies shared the electricity market in both places as well, although in the Bay Area, private concerns enjoyed the lion's share. Obviously, cities did not supply terminals for the railroad companies nor bus depots for auto transport. Despite the inconsistency of providing municipal transportation stations in one field and not another, and regardless of the vaunted laissez-faire reputation of the twenties in America, California municipalities cheerfully shouldered the burden of providing municipal airports, air terminal buildings, and even public sites for aircraft manufacturing. By 1930, each of the principal cities had brushed aside the arguments of laissez-faire and established municipal airports. The Los Angeles area, in fact, teemed with both public and private fields. Urban dominance of this area continued throughout this period, but by 1940 the cities had turned to the federal government for aid to airports, and by war's end they had received a considerable amount. Both the earlier municipal dominance and the later turn to the federal government seems related to investment capital. The historian of Los Angeles Municipal Airport has noted, "As private capital did not always move fast enough or far enough to satisfy the public, a drive began to supplement private airports with municipal installations." Rapid technological development demanded even greater investment in these facilities to accommodate night flying, greater speeds, and heavier aircraft. With the cities strapped financially and given the interstate nature of air commerce and an ever more compelling national defense rationale for federal funding, California cities naturally turned to Washington for monetary aid.[40]

In providing these facilities, municipal officals and their supporters outside the field of government fully agreed with their military counterparts about the national defense relevance of airports. This concern appeared in the twenties, long before any credible military threat to the West Coast had materialized, and remained vital to civilian air boosters throughout the period. Neither urban nor military authorities fully spelled out the ways in which civilian airports would benefit the national defense in time of emergency, but they assumed that wartime conditions would necessitate more flying than service airports could handle. Airports gained popularity more frequently because civilians conceived of them as urban defense measures.[41]

Private interests supplemented the efforts of the public authorities. The Los Angeles area in particular was honeycombed with airports, public and private. The most impressive of these latter was the United Airport at Burbank next to Los Angeles proper. Built by United Aircraft, it eventually passed into the hands of Lockheed Aircraft and then, just before the outbreak of World War II, under control of the city of Los Angeles. For many years, Clover Field in Santa Monica served the Douglas Company. Between the public and private efforts of the Southland aviation interests, a large number of usable airfields had materialized, and by 1929, these efforts had paid large dividends, especially in the Los Angeles area. According to Fred B. Rentschler, president of United, a conglomerate that had an interest in Boeing, Stearman, Northrup, and Pratt-Whitney, no other American city "would compare with Los Angeles either in activity or in the number of available centers [airports]."[42]

Time and again urban spokesmen voiced the metropolitan anxiety that underlay so many important public ventures in Urban California. "The inauguration of this terminal [Mills Field, San Francisco's municipal airport] for aerial traffic is an event of vital importance to San Francisco's participation in the next great commercial development, the commerce of the air," enthused the *Chronicle* in 1927. A city's "future commercial greatness lies in the air, and the commonwealths and communities that fail to prepare for air development will find themselves terribly in the background when the hour of the airplane strikes," warned the same source. The reason was obvious. "Nobody is going to operate aircraft to or from a city which has no airport any more than he would inaugurate steamship service to a community which lacked landing facilities," explained the *San Diego Magazine.*

But the airports had other potential critical advantages as well. In planning and developing their airports, Metropolitan California really intended to develop entire aviation industrial parks, since aviation boosters always assumed that the landing fields would inevitably attract both the aviation operating companies and aircraft manufacturing industries. "With this city a great terminal for air commerce it should also become a center for industries allied to air commerce," the *Chronicle* explained in 1927. "All of these [aircraft] industries are making their plans for expansion upon the supposition that this airport will be built," cautioned the *San Diego Union* the same year, in urging the construction of what would become Lindbergh Field. The landing fields could be used for both manufacturing and testing sites. The latter problem became ever more important as the airplane evolved from a curiosity to a highly sophisticated piece of technology dependent upon large capital investment and scientific knowledge.[43]

Military airfields complemented the civilian airdromes and added yet another favorable element in the mix of Southland and California aviation advantages. Like the aircraft industry itself, the Southern California location of military flying installations was often explained by the doctrine of natural advantages. As usual, a more complex reality underlay this Southland rationalization. In the long run, the patterns of urbanization determined the California distribution of military aviation, particularly Army Air Corps installations. Aviation theorists correctly foresaw that cities were vulnerable to air attack and that other planes were needed to help fend off these assaults. That meant that the patterns of militarization would reinforce rather than alter the patterns of urbanization, since the defending planes had to be posted near the site of the most important enemy targets. Bombardment groups would engage the enemy far out over the Pacific rather than in the skies over metropolitan California, so they did not have to be located exactly at the scene of defense. Flying schools, on the other hand, could be more widely dispersed.[44]

By the outbreak of World War II, the distribution of military aviation in California had come to approximate these strategic and tactical requirements, but for most of the interwar years it did not. Until the activation of Hamilton Field in Marin County in 1930, the Bay Area had negligible military aviation, aside from the unimportant Crissey Field in San Francisco, and its second important installation, Alameda Naval Air Station, barely opened in time for the beginning of the war. For most of the period, therefore, the military aviation of the state mirrored the patterns of urbanization with the most rapidly growing area claiming all or most of the service flyers in the Army Air Corps fields at March Field in Riverside, near Los Angeles, and Rockwell Field and North Island Naval Air Station in San Diego. Or to put the matter a different way, San Francisco, which the Navy considered the military key to the West Coast, continued largely undefended by air power throughout the period, and Seattle and Portland, much closer to the assumed Japanese enemy, remained even more vulnerable and for a longer period of time.[45]

Civilian and military air boosters often attributed this maldistribution of martial resources to the Southern California climate and geography, which allowed for year-round flying, wide open spaces for military maneuvers and testing, low fuel costs for buildings, and so forth. These variables may have been influential in the placement of aviation facilities, but besides ignoring the strategic aspect of the problem, this argument overlooks other factors as well. Military planes would have to fly in many kinds of climatic and geographic conditions and therefore should have been tested and perfected in the kinds of natural surroundings in which they would have to perform combat missions. If the West Coast was really vulnerable to air assault, as the service spokesmen so frequently asserted, then Seattle and San Francisco were more defenseless than so remote an area as the Southland, and the planes that would be needed to defend these cities required realistic testing conditions.

Moreover, the climatic advantages of Southern California did not impress all observers as equally deterministic. In particular, it did not truly possess good, year-round flying weather. Dudley Steel, a Southern California booster, aviation pioneer, Richfield official who sold gasoline to the Army Air Corps, and aviation activist, noted frequent fogs and soupy flying days in his memoirs. Hap Arnold, commander at March Field, stated the problem even more emphatically. "Rockwell

[Field in San Diego] is far from satisfactory on account of prevalent fogs," noted Arnold to General Oscar Westover in discussing the need for a new bombing range. "[In] view of the fog conditions prevalent during this season of the year," Arnold informed Harry Carr of the *Los Angeles Times,* Carr would have to find his own way over to March Field. As Dudley Steele put it in another context, "Because of fog and very little knowledge about how to get down through fog with passenger planes safely, there were no airlines using Mines Field" in the early days before it became Los Angeles International Airport. No less an authority than Charles A. Lindbergh echoed this skepticism of Mines Field and its fogs when investigating a West Coast terminal for what became Trans-World Airlines.[46] These conditions continued, of course, and in 1948 led to "the first commercial installation of FIDO, the army's label for an [$800,000] airport fog-dispersal unit," designed for "greatest use" during the months of November through February, when fog conditions are most prevalent." This device was pioneered by the Army Air Corps in Great Britain during the Second World War, and was further tested and perfected at another California location before its installation at Los Angeles International Airport. Although the president of the Long Beach Chamber of Commerce could claim twenty years earlier that there "are only about fifteen day in the year when climatic conditions are not suitable for flying here," the Los Angeles Department of Airports of a later era found the situation more complex. The Southland may have had relatively good aeronautical conditions, but "ideal, year round flying weather" it did not possess.[47]

Once again, the importance of the political climate outweighed the influence of the natural one. The weather did play some role in the establishment of the first service aviation installations in Southern California. The first Navy man came to North Island, San Diego, in 1911 to enroll in the primitive flying school which pioneer aviator Glenn Curtiss had opened in 1911. Curtiss himself had been attracted to the spot by local initiative. The Aero Club of San Diego, established in 1910 by D. C. Collier, knew of Curtiss's desire to establish an aviation school in San Diego, and in February 1911 the club requested the owners of North Island, the Coronado Beach Company, to provide Curtiss some land. This Spreckels subsidiary agreed to let Curtiss use the land and erect the "necessary plant" upon it for a period of two years, free of charge. Shortly thereafter both the Army and Navy established flying schools on the island. The Army became a tenant of the Coronado Land Company in 1912, and the Navy flyers joined them in 1916. Though the Navy's official history did not explain the exact role of climatic conditions in motivating the two services' initial decision to come to North Island, that factor eventually influenced the nature of the aviation activities put there. Both services decided to place training schools there and both did so, at least in part, because of the natural advantages of the area. However, other influences soon came into play.[48]

J. B. Lippincott, a Los Angeles resident, lobbyist, and government worker during World War I, approached San Diego Congressman William Kettner to try to devise means of securing for Southern California some of the military cantonments built to train men for that conflict. Whenever the two confronted federal officials, however, they were met with the "objection that so much time and expense was consumed in transportation of men and supplies to our Pacific southwest." To counter these arguments, Kettner and Lippincott presented a series of rebuttals based on the advantages of climate in fuel savings, allowing more flying and training time, and so forth. "Partly because of these arguments, military camps, especially flying fields, were put on our southwest Pacific coast," noted Lippincott in recounting the decisions. The qualification is appropriate, because many climatic advantages could have been secured in several other southwestern states situated closer to the Atlantic embarkation points. Moreover, despite the balmy weather, for a time the Southland stood on the verge of losing all First World War military installations as a result of the competition between cities, both nearby and remote from the scene. "Because of the efforts of various other sections of the United States to obtain these military establishments," wrote Lippincott to Kettner, "quite naturally the War Department was disinclined to locate cantonments in areas showing such bitter rivalry. This resulted in the temporary elimination of Southern California from the construction program." Learning of this veto, the San Diego lobbyists persuaded the Los Angeles Chamber of Commerce to cooperate with the Border City rather than compete. Once this urban political infighting ceased, the military authorities came to appreciate much more fully the advantages of the Southland climate.[49]

The government certainly should have enjoyed the climate of North Island, where it had both Army and Navy aviation schools, since the federal authorities had been allowed use of the land at absolutely no cost. During the First World War, the two services decided that they wanted permanent possession of the property, but they could not get the Coronado Beach Company to agree to a price. After a court challenge which upheld the company's title, Kettner moved in to arrange a compromise. San Diego's "Million Dollar Congressman" got the services to agree to an award for the land based on the opinion of a San Diego jury and then persuaded the Congress to ratify this agreement with appropriate legislation. Despite service threats to pull out, a check for $6,098,333.33 went from the federal government to John D. Spreckels on December 30, 1921, and the North Island aviation land passed into government hands in return.[50]

This decision would have enormous consequences over time, since it added considerably to the momentum linking the city and the sword in the Southland in general and in metropolitan San Diego in particular. And in doing so, Kettner and the San Diegans helped to alleviate a considerable naval aviation problem. Congress had limited the Navy by law to the possession of only six shore naval airfields; therefore, every good one meant a great deal to a service that needed these installations. When the aircraft carriers came into port, they often had business other than aviation to take care of, such as repairs, maintenance, and training. These did not necessarily involve the naval aviators, who had their own training to pursue. If only carrier bases had been available to them without an adjacent site for the planes to park and train, either the carriers would have had to spend more time than necessary at sea or the aviators would have spent more on the ground and could not have devoted enough time to their own training. By playing the honest broker, Kettner retained naval aviation for San Diego and guaranteed a reasonable training schedule for the Navy. Of course, the Army benefitted from its own continued possession of adjacent Rockwell Field.

It profited from another Kettner acquisition as well. During the First World War, the Army Signal Corps established what became March Field near Riverside, California. "The selection of this flying field I know was largely due to your efforts," wrote J. B. Lippincott gratefully in 1918 to William Kettner. As Lippincott went on to explain, for six months after the outbreak of World War I, the federal government invested hardly any money in Pacific coast war production, especially when compared with "the enormous outlay in the east."[51]

> Coincident with these conditions we had the most intensive bond drives throughout the country, including our Pacific Coast. This resulted in the gradual drift of our financial resources from the Pacific coast to the East and the unbalancing of our western trade, finance, and labor. These conditions were particularly acute in your city of San Diego. Business was depressed and it was a severe struggle for us to bear our quota in the bond subscriptions which our patriotic citizens assumed. Very largely because of these general conditions here it was urged that a cantonment might be placed in the southwest. There immediately arose a vigorous competition, if not strife, between the cities of Los Angeles, San Francisco, and San Diego.

It was this conflict that Kettner and his allies helped to quell, and it was this outcome that brought the geographically counter-cyclical military investments to Southern California to balance the outflow of dollars to the East. March Field Air Station floated in upon this golden tide of federal dollars.[52]

These various decisions would make the participants in them look like prophets and visionaries to a later generation unfamiliar with the circumstances. At the time, however, no one really understood the consequences for any of the branches of aviation. "I was a member of the board that agreed upon the selection of North Island at that time and agreed upon the division of the island," testified Commander John Towers, chief of the Navy's Bureau of Aeronautics and a former commander of North Island Naval Air Station. "I think I am safe in saying that none of us at that time realized what the growth of the aircraft was going to be, particularly the growth of the aircraft of the fleet." Obviously the Navy did not completely know what it was giving, and San Diego could not fully comprehend what it was getting. The boosters nonetheless had the nerve and drive to go after an asset that they knew would complement the rest of their naval establishment. Needless to say, the development of aviation was impressive and tended to strengthen greatly the Southland metropolitan-military status quo.[53]

Subsequent political and military decisions reinforced these initial allocations of aviation units to California cities. A significant portion of the rationale for military aviation placement stemmed from the earlier decision to station the fleet in Southern California and to postpone the construction of the Alameda main home base. No one planned this outcome at the time, but the naval planes had to be stationed with the fleet itself; and as the aircraft carriers became more and more important, this necessity grew and, with it, the significance of the Southland's monopolization of the fleet. The Navy found itself unable to build facilities in the Bay Area for the floating Navy, or the flying Navy. A similar imbalance affected the Army Air Corps. With the Bay Area and Seattle unable to claim facilities capable of handling aviation, and the Navy Department unable to break the veto of Vallejo over the same matter, the Southland could go ahead strengthening its own ties to the military services. It was at considerable pains to do so. The San Diego Harbor Commission early dredged out larger berths in its harbor to accommodate the new aircraft carriers that took up stations there in the early thirties. These carrier planes had to operate from shore bases as well as from the carriers, so the importance of North Island Naval Station grew apace. The City of Los Angeles took advantage of the situation to buttress its own connection with both the Navy and aviation by donating the land in 1939 for the construction of Reeves Field, another Navy flying installation. If the military necessity of this decision seems obvious, it might be pointed out that the fleet, with which the Reeves Field flyers was supposed to operate, was dispatched in 1938 back to the East Coast and, in 1940, out into the Pacific to Pearl Harbor.[54]

In any case, these Navy decisions helped to produce similar Army Air Corps moves. In 1931, the Army Air Corps "assumed responsibility for Coastal defense around the U.S. mainland, a task which had previously been the U.S. Navy's cherished prerogative." The Air Corps had some responsibility for this assignment even earlier. This meant that the Air Corps had to protect the naval bases as well as other potential coastal targets. As the Navy's official history of North Island Naval Air Station explained it, "The greatest use of aircraft by the Army in the defense of the Naval Base at San Diego may occur at a time when the fleet is elsewhere. . . ." This mission reinforced and stabilized the placement of Rockwell Field, which shared North Island with the naval aviators, as well as March Field at Riverside. Although the creation of a great naval base at San Diego was not a part of the Navy's original plans, once this installation began to develop there it gradually made sense to provide the planes to defend the ships and others to defend the base. Simply put, the Army fliers had to protect the Navy aviators and the sailors as well. Therefore the original booster victories in acquiring the Navy led inevitably to further ones, this time with the Army Air Corps.[55]

Unfortunately, that left no one to defend the San Francisco Bay Area. This oversight might not have been so important had not both the Navy and the Army Air Corps considered that northern California metropolis to be the strategic key to the entire Pacific coast. As the earlier discussion indicated, the Navy, though it wavered once from its opinion, consistently considered the San Francisco Bay Area to be the ideal site for its greatest West Coast naval base. The Navy's history of North Island, which cited testimony to congressional committees, letters, and official documents, produced a number of unimpeachable witnesses to the Bay Area's importance.

MRS. [FLORENCE] KAHN: Now what is the reason for desiring to abandon Rockwell Field [in favor of San Francisco Bay]?

GENERAL FECHET: *The principal reason is due to the fact that the conditions at Rockwell Field are very crowded and it is also badly located strategically.* [Emphasis in the original] It is very near the southwest corner of the United States and it is also right on the sea with no protecting barrier.

Testifying at the same hearing on this problem of moving part of the Air Corps from the Southland to the Bay Area at the same hearing, the Acting Secretary of War noted that "it would be most advantageous for the national defense as a whole to have the Army [Air corps units from Rockwell Field] move up into the San Francisco Bay area. I say that," continued F. Trubee Davison, "from the standpoint of strategy and from the standpoint of training and from the standpoint of economics." The House Military Affairs Committee provided dramatic confirmation. "The San Francisco Bay area is recognized as the central and strategic point in the defense of our west continental coast," argued the legislators. "At the present time this area is without any substantial provision for its air defense, the only military field being a small one without accommodations and advantages necessary for a fighting air defense."[56]

Naturally, both the services and the civilian military boosters in the Bay Area had noticed this considerable anomaly of concentrating American military power four to five hundred miles distant from the recognized strategic center of the coast. When the next round of military air power investment occurred, both boosters and servicemen moved to use that opportunity to redistribute the advantages of air power to the San Francisco region. What became the Alameda Naval Air Station materialized across the bay from "The City" by the end of the 1930s, but it had been a part of the Navy's maneuverings for a great naval base in the Bay Area since the late twenties. As noted earlier, when the Navy sought to locate a lighter-than-air base on the West Coast, it triggered an intense competition for this asset between the cities of the San Francisco Bay region, including even the naval-yard town of Vallejo and the allied forces of Los Angeles and San Diego. Led by the San Francisco Chamber of Commerce, Northern California won this round in 1930. With the Alameda Naval Air Station on the drawing boards, the dirigible base at Sunnyvale represented a considerable Navy commitment to rectify the imbalance of air power in metropolitan California.

At about the same time, the Army Air Corps began to compensate for its own neglect of the northern metropolis. This, too, involved the Navy, which had long wanted to acquire all of North Island and had tried to persuade the Army to move its Rockwell Field contingent elsewhere. The Navy claimed that military flying conditions were too congested in the San Diego area and that the Army could do its job from other bases. The Navy planes, on the other hand, had to be placed with the fleet, and thus no site other than North Island would do. By 1930, this argument had persuaded the Army, and it planned to use this opportunity to relieve the aeronautical poverty of the north. The Air Corps' Rockwell Field force could vacate North Island, thereby pleasing the navy, and re-establish itself near San Francisco. Two roadblocks immediately appeared. With budget matters very tight, the Army did not think it was getting enough in return for its transfer and the reversion of its field and improvements on North Island to the Navy. As the Acting Secretary of War put it, "the financial end" of the transfer did not satisfy his department.

Shortly thereafter, "apparently the financial part became satisfactory to the War Department," noted the Navy's history of North Island laconically, "after the citizens of California had agreed to donate approximately 1100 acres of land in the Country of Alameda California and approximately 917 acres of land in Marin County, California for aviation and other military purposes." It should be emphasized that the citizens of California did not donate this land; rather, the citizens of the urbanized Bay Area did. They were led by the San Francisco Chamber of Commerce (although the territory in question rested in adjacent counties and not in San Francisco) and the governments of the principal cities and counties which raised the money for the land or helped to push through referenda agreeing to its donation. These actions helped to satisfy the Army and to quiet the objections of the Bureau of the Budget, which did not want to spend any money in a Depression year. In effect, the civilian, urban real estate donations avoided that unpleasant political necessity by compensating the Army Air Corps for the loss of Rockwell Field to the Navy. In the process they facilitated the acquisition of an important martial asset of their own. To put the matter another way, the needs of the modern nation state had to be brokered into existence by the deeds of one of the competing urban areas.

The Army first agreed to this transfer and compensation, but then reneged. As General Douglas MacArthur explained it, his branch felt that it had received no quid pro quo from the Navy. As the general noted in May 1932, "At one time the Army was sympathetic, to the extent that it considered a negotiation which would involve the Navy transferring a commensurate field to the Army. . . . [The] Navy, however, had no such commensurate field and the negotiation ceased." The negotiations recommenced and finally came to fruition in 1935 when the Navy decided to cut back on its dirigible development program in the wake of the *Akron* and *Macon* disasters. This left the Bay Area Sunnyvale Field without a mission. In a complex trade and redistribution of military air power, the Navy exchanged Sunnyvale to the Army in return for which that service vacated Rockwell Field on North Island. Part of the Air Corps group went to March Field, Riverside; the bombardment group had gone even earlier to the newly opened Hamilton Air Force Base located on the land donated by Marin and Bay Area boosters; and the supply functions went to Benton Field in Alameda, donated by urban civilians again. Of course, the Sunnyvale site itself, the indispensable quid pro quo, had been donated by Bay Area citizens in their earlier efforts to gain a share of the military aeronautical services.

Together these opportunities provided more to the Air Corps than the competitive offer from the "citizens of San Diego" of "769 acres of ground near Chula Vista near San Diego Bay and the sum of $100,000 to be used in the development of this site as a substitute for Rockwell Field." Despite the objection of Congressman Phil Swing, who tried to prevent the transfer, the Army preferred to move. One cannot doubt the importance of the imperatives of the modern nation state in these high-stakes negotiations, nor the frequency with which their game was being played with urban chips.[57]

Together these developments concentrated a tremendous portion of American military aviation in California and further enriched the mixture of aerial activities in that state. However, it should be emphasized that until the war broke out, Southern California possessed most of this activity. With the exception of Hamilton Field, which opened its doors as Marin Meadows Field in 1930, the other aviation additions commenced operations after the middle of the decade and sometimes later, not in time to help create a San Francisco branch of the civilian aircraft industry before World War II. These developments also came too late to influence the decisions of the Consolidated and North American aircraft companies, both of which came to the Southland in 1935. Between civilian and military aviation, Southern California benefitted from an extraordinary concentration of aviation activities. The *San Diego Union* revealed that by 1935 the entire Navy would have 1000 planes in operation, of which fully 500 would operate from the Border City. Six months later the same source stated that San Diego had become "America's greatest air center." March Field and civilian aviation at either San Diego or Los Angeles were not included in this count, so the total Southland flying stock was even more impressive than the *Union's* boast.[58]

Put differently, these figures meant that Southern California possessed easily the best airplane market in the United States. Some authorities have discounted the importance of the market to airplane manufacturers. One customer, the United States government, purchased the vast majority of the output, and its "flying operations" were "so widespread [that] . . .any attempt to 'locate' the market is futile." In addition, as William G. Cunningham wrote in his classic study of aircraft industrial location, "Industries whose products are in themselves [a] means of transportation . . . obviously will be little affected by a pull toward the market. Indeed, the market for such mobile items is practically impossible to define or locate." That argument is dubious, to say the least, particularly in view of the rapid technological evolution of aircraft in the 1930s. The testing of aircraft by the manufacturers was extensive, but still minor compared with that of the military. On any given day, hundreds of service planes flocked into the air and provided an excellent means of measuring performance in all areas. For example, the Douglas Navy planes were routinely tested at the Naval Air Station in nearby San Diego. Not only did Southern California have a large number of planes, but they were remarkably diverse: carrier, land, and sea planes; fighters and bombers; observation and combat planes; and heavier- and lighter-than-air craft on and above the island on the land. It would be hard to imagine a more varied market, with planes of all sorts under various and rigorous tests.[59]

The development of air strategy and tactics progressed concurrently with the technical evolution of military aircraft. As noted earlier, the tactics and strategy eventually employed in World War II were hammered out in or near the Southland and to a lesser extent in California in general in both Army and Navy maneuvers. Sustained technical and tactical change made proximity an important consideration for the aircraft manufacturers, since they required timely information to keep up with the dynamic mechanical evolution of aircraft and air-power doctrines and tactics. These two aspects of air power were inextricably intertwined. In order to conceptualize the strategy and tactics, one had to understand their technical possibilities. Not too surprisingly, the dissemination of this information reinforced the importance of the Southern California location for the aircraft manufacturers. These patterns can be seen through the correspondence of the commander of March Field, Henry H. Arnold. Three points of origin and destination overwhelmingly dominated Arnold's correspondence—Army Air Corps Headquarters in Washington, D.C., Ninth Corps Headquarters in San Francisco, and Southern California in general. Perhaps half the correspondence passed back and forth within this latter realm, and not very many letters to non-military personnel were

exchanged outside Southern California, even to the area around Ninth Corps headquarters in San Francisco. Moreover, the personal contacts of the March Field commander were even more locally oriented, so that word-of-mouth information cir-
culated via face-to-face contact in the same geographic area as written
correspondence.[60]

Certainly Arnold did communicate directly with Southland aircraft manufacturers for the purpose of helping them to compete in the military market. On
November 9, 1932, Claude Ryan wrote to Arnold, stating his intention to get back
into the aircraft manufacturing business and asking the commander's advice about
what the Army Air Corps required in certain flying craft. After outlining the deficiencies of "the present pursuit plane in use in the service" and "the new low-wing
Boeing pursuit" craft, Arnold gave the builder of the *Spirit of St. Louis* some general
counsel. My "advice in this regard would be for you to have a talk with some one
who knows the whole Air Corps picture," suggested Arnold. "From that get your
own ideas as to which type of airplane you think you could best produce for Army
purposes. I will be glad to do that myself any time that I see you."[61]

Arnold had an even closer relationship with the manufacturers close by, especially the Douglas Aircraft Corporation. On June 6, 1932, Arnold wrote to thank
Donald Douglas "a thousand times" for giving him several tickets for the movie
Grand Hotel which he and his wife had enjoyed, and to "accept your invitation for
the trip on your yacht." Later in the same year Arnold again accepted a social invitation from Douglas. Other correspondence reveals that the commander knew that
"times are hard" at the Douglas plant in early 1933. As he noted, "There is but little
business, and the Douglas Company is not taking on anybody at all. As a matter of
fact, they have but recently discharged quite a few men." By year's end Arnold had
moved to do something about the firm's plight. In letters to Major Carl Spaatz, at
the Office of the Chief of Air Corps, Washington, D.C., Arnold argued the case of
Air Corps adoption of a new "Douglas Northrop" aircraft. More important, he
revealed that a research interface had developed between the March Field command and the Douglas Aircraft Corporation. "Herewith are plans covering the
Douglas Northrop high speed bomber," Arnold informed Spaatz. "The planes con-
form to the ideas of the officers of this post as the plane into which the future pursuit
plane will develop," he continued. "It is to be noted that the performance of this
plane compares very favorably with the latest Boeing pursuit, . . . [and] it has these
advantages over any pursuit designed so far. . . ."[62]

In a postscript, the commander gave Spaatz instructions on how to help
"Dutch" Kindelberger (a Douglas employee and future president of North American Aircraft) get through the maze of negotiations in Washington. "I think it would
be a good idea to tell Dutch just what he should do next after coming in to see you."
When Spaatz responded by questioning the utility of the Douglas plane, Arnold
went back to the attack and in the process of urging the Douglas Northup machine,
revealed the existence of a research interface between the aircraft manufacturers
and the Air Corps men who had to use the machines.[63]

One of the main reasons for sending in the drawings and being insistent that such a
plane be developed was to get something with which we could work along these lines.

It is not feasible to take the Northrop attack [plane] as is for it does not fill the bill. We realized that here was a plane that would carry a considerably greater load than the single seaters now being developed, and at the same time have a much greater cruising range, higher high speed, and lower landing speed. As far as we knew, no attempts were being made to produce such a plane. Until such a plane is produced, any ideas as to their employment and possible effectiveness must be theoretical. Accordingly, if there is any money available, we should proceed at once to buy enough of these planes to equip at least one squadron. . . .

From the above, [omitted discussion of airplane performances] I am convinced that there is a very distinct place in the Army Air Corps for such an airplane and not only a distinct place for such a plane, but unless we start developing it without delay, we are laying ourselves wide open in that we have not utilized all means at our disposal to improve the airplanes with which we are equipped.[64]

Obviously the aircraft industry had worked closely with the March Field flyers in developing this aircraft; and just as evidently, the airmen needed to do so in order to ensure their chances of getting what they needed. John B. Rae has pointed out that the aircraft business is not like the automobile industry in that it does not exactly mass-produce its output. Airplanes are constantly modified as they go along the production cycle, responding in the manufacturing process to new information, experience, changed demands on the aircraft, and other new developments. As Rae put it, "Aeronautical science and technology have changed too fast to permit very much standardization." This type of rapid evolution surrounded the Southland aircraft industry on every side, and it benefited from the proximity. By the same token, the presence of the manufacturers helped the military aviation men as well.[65]

Despite the academic denials of the importance of proximity to markets in the aircraft industry, no less a business authority than *Fortune Magazine* clearly recognized its significance:

Furthermore, this [early aircraft] industry was sleeping in the same bedroom, if not in the same bed, with the U.S. Army and Navy. The army had one of its principal training centers and repair depots at Rockwell Field near San Diego during the early twenties, and one of the first men to fly the original Douglas plane was the commanding officer, Major Henry Arnold—now major general and Deputy Chief of Staff. And up the coast at San Francisco there was Crissey Field, where the army's observation squadron was commanded by Major George H. Brett—now also a major general and acting chief of the air corps. The navy kept the bulk of its fleet in California waters and its only West Coast air base at San Diego. On army and navy orders Donald Douglas built his business; more of the same kind of orders built the aircraft boom of 1941.[66]

This, of course, specifically credits both the importance of the personal tie to Arnold and the proximity of the aircraft pioneers to the military services.

The manufacturers were also sleeping close to their civilian clients. A recent economist's analysis documents the importance of the civilian market. According to Paul Rhode, civilian markets in the twenties and early thirties were local and regional rather than national. So the plane makers, who produced only about 6000 vehicles at the height of the Lindbergh boom, did not have the same sales opportunities as the auto makers with their millions of new models. Contrary to the claims of William Cunningham on aircraft location, the local civilian market was crucial to the planemakers. Fortunately, in part because of the stimulated activity on behalf of flying, the Southern California local market was the best in the United States.[67]

The bedroom analogy had an even greater relevance than *Fortune* might have suspected because the ties between Arnold and Donald Douglas took on a more personal dimension with the marriage of Bruce Arnold to Barbara Douglas. According to President Reuben Fleet of Consolidated Aircraft Corporation, this "dynastic alliance" markedly affected his own business. Fleet noted that General Arnold "told me that he wouldn't stand for us to manufacture any commercial aircraft as that would be cutting into Don Douglas' domain upon which he was principally dependent for transports. We were restricted by Hap's wish that we not produce commercial aircraft." The crusty old aircraft buccaneer went on to explain that "kinship exceeded friendship in this case. Naturally we agreed to this restriction." We need not accept this story in toto, nor deny the importance of young love, but in the context of metropolitan-military business relations, it would be hard not to regard this nuptial as a dynastic alliance.[68]

The importance of metropolitan-military friendships can be assessed in a different light through the practice of military rotation. Military officers came through and passed out of the portals of Urban California as their career fortunes waxed and waned. City boosters singled out the promising men, cultivated them, and hoped that they would be subsequently posted to a position with significant decision-making power. As luck would have it, that is exactly what happened to two old Southern California hands, Henry H. Arnold and John H. Towers, who moved to the capital to head the Army Air Corps and the Navy's Bureau of Aeronautics, respectively. Moreover, they did so in the latter half of the 1930's, when the deepening world crisis remarkably increased the resources of those two agencies.

It would not be possible to document a direct cause and effect relationship between the advent of these career officers in Washington and the mounting prosperity of Urban Southland airframe firms. However, given the business practices of the era, it is possible to suggest that these personal ties did nothing to hurt their chances. The close deepening relations of such military men as Hap Arnold on the one hand and metropolitan leaders like Robert Millikan, Theodore von Karman, Reuben Fleet, and Donald Douglas on the other indicate clearly that their business relationships grew with their friendships. And in the case of Arnold and Towers, these personal ties gave the Urban Southland good friends in Washington at a time when that friendship could crucially affect the future of the aircraft industry and therefore its home cities.

Another element of the Southern California metropolitan environment illustrates this proposition perfectly. California Institute of Technology would become a foremost aeronautical research center which, by the time of the bombing of Pearl Harbor, had joined the interface between the city and the sword. This affiliation was no more coincidental than the placement of the Navy and the service air installations within the island on the land, nor was it the outcome of ivory-tower, pure academic research, divorced from the pervasive metropolitan anxiety of the Southland. The upgrading of Cal Tech into a great research institution was a result of that urban rivalry. Much of this story centers around two personalities—Robert Andrews Millikan and Theodore von Karman.

Robert Millikan came onto the Southern California scene in stages. From the late teens to 1921, when Millikan made his definitive break with the University of Chicago, the trustees, patrons, and faculty of the California Institute of Technology had wooed the physicist to come west. Cal Tech (until 1920 Throop Institute) at that time was not a great scientific center, but it harbored considerable ambitions to become one, and that goal brought Millikan into the picture. Dr. Arthur A. Noyes, formerly of MIT, had himself been lured there earlier, and Noyes hoped that the recruitment of Millikan would turn the Pasadena school into a first-rate academic establishment. Noyes did not deceive Millikan about the present condition of Cal Tech. According to Millikan's reconstruction of the conversation, "The Institute was indeed a very weak institution, with practically no endowment, with but three permanent buildings on the campus." Nonetheless, it did have a few impressive assets. Despite its failings, "the president of its board, Mr. Arthur Fleming, was tremendously interested in the Institute's development and each year he made up its deficit from his personal fortune." Noyes went on to explain that "the Institute was ideally located in the most rapidly growing area in the United States, an area that had terrific need for science and its applications but with no possibility of satisfying that need save as the California Institute of Technology could qualify for such a role."

Noyes pointed out some of the area's assets, such as the Huntington Library, Mt. Wilson Observatory, and the "world's first 220,000 electrical transmission line." However, in Millikan's mind, "the biggest asset that C.I.T. had, in addition to the remarkable board of trustees, was Dr. Noyes himself." The professor nicely laid out the academic aspirations he had for Cal Tech. "If the latter could become outstanding primarily in physics and chemistry, the basis of all enginering and of all biology—[it] would constitute . . .a research center in Pasadena of no mean proportions." Noyes even promised to subordinate his own field of chemistry to Millikan's field of physics since he felt that greater developments would be forthcoming in the future from Millikan's area. Finally, Board of Trustee president Fleming promised "to transfer his fortune in trust to the Institute" if Millikan would make the switch. That would have put $4,200,000 at the service of Cal Tech and about $100,000 per annum at the service of the physics department. To use a cliché, this was an offer the scientist could not refuse.[69]

These academic aspirations dovetailed perfectly with the metropolitan ones that pervaded the Southern California urban environment. Noyes, of course, had referred specifically to the advantages of operating in an "exploding metropolis," but the composition of the Cal Tech board of trustees made the connection all the more explicit. From Fleming on down, the membership of the Board of Trustees that recruited Millikan reads like an honor roll of Southern California city boosterism. The 1928-29 edition of *Who's Who in California* described Arthur Fleming as a lumber manufacturer who had once practiced law and engaged in many lumber and land businesses as well as being a director of the Southern California Edison

Company and president of the Board of Trustees of Cal Tech. Henry William O'Melveny was also a lawyer and vice president of the Los Angeles Trust and Savings Bank as well as a director of the Farmers and Merchants National Bank and Security First National Bank. Another lawyer, George S. Patton, was a former manager of the Huntington Land and Improvement Company and chairman of the Board of Trustees of the Henry E. Huntington Library in addition to his trusteeship at Cal Tech. The other board member represented the *Los Angeles Times,* an enormously influential urban development corporation by itself. He was Harry Chandler himself, head of the *Times* empire, director "in 35 corporations, including banking, land, transportation companies and oil, irrigation and manufacturing enterprises," and clubman par excellence. It would have been hard to find anyone more closely associated with the booster impulse in Southern California, if for no other reason than that he owned a huge portion of it. The *Times's* head, together with the other board members, represented businesses intimately connected to urban growth.[70]

Nor had Chandler, Fleming, Noyes, Norman Bridge, and their fellow urban influentials recruited the wrong man. Robert Millikan gloried in the opportunity to link science and research to the growth of metropolitan Southern California in order to improve the fortunes of both. To Millikan, science held the key to the problem of metropolitan anxiety. The physicist understood the insecurity of Southern California, but whereas the ordinary booster would have responded to the problem by attracting yet another industry or tempting another mass of Iowans to the Golden State, Millikan moved to create a metropolitan research and development infrastructure and to lure or train the elite technical personnel who would staff these institutions. In his later years Millikan would remember this effort in Toynbeesque terms. "This author," wrote the physicist of the British historian,

> finds the stimulus to the development of the earliest civilizations (found in the latitude belt which includes North Africa, Asia Minor, Babylonia and Northwest India) in the gradual progressive desiccation of these areas and the consequent forcing of man to get his food not from the unaided bounty of nature, such as was at his disposal when these same regions were covered, as Toynbee assumes, by very luxurious vegetation, but from the development of food crops through artificial irrigation and husbandry enforced by the threat of starvation. In other words, according to Toynbee, it was the response of early men to difficult, challenging conditions that started off the development of the earliest known civilizations in this world.
>
> Southern California has faced and still faces a somewhat similar challenge. Thus, she has no coal, which has in general been considered the basis of great industrial developments. In her semiarid climate she has not the natural hinterland commonly considered essential for the support of such a huge population as wants to live here. In order to meet the challenge of these handicaps she must of necessity use more resourcefulness, more intelligence, more scientific and engineering brains than she would otherwise be called upon to use.[71]

Millikan saw this response developing before and after he arrived to meet the challenge. Again, the physicist designated science as the critical element. In one of his earliest speeches at Cal Tech, Millikan argued that "the distinctive opportunity of the Institute began to appear when the Mount Wilson Observatory was founded, and when a world center of creative work, first in a single science, began to develop here. As I read values," he continued, "the Mount Wilson Observatory has already been the greatest asset possessed by Southern California." He continued that this would be "not excluding the Los Angeles Chamber of Commerce, for it began to demonstrate the possibility of making this climatically favored Southwest region a center for the development of great scientific, intellectual, and cultural activities and values."

It is only because of the existence here of the Mount Wilson Observatory that it became possible for Southern California to take the next step and to bring together creative influences and productive men in the fields closely allied to those already cultivated at the observatory, namely, the fields of physics, chemistry, mathematics, and their application in engineering. A few of the far-visioned men of Southern California saw these possibilities and set about taking the first steps toward their realization in the development of the Institute.[72]

Besides Mount Wilson to encourage the scientist, Southern California had brought water from miles away to overcome its water deficit. Cal Tech helped with that problem by raising the efficiency of the pumps in the aqueduct system, thereby effecting "a savings of millions to the residents of Southern California." The Southland also "met the challenge of having no coal by developing the world's first 220,000 volt electrical transmission line," which imported power from 400 miles away. "In a word, if Southern California is to continue to meet the challenge of her environment in the foregoing and in other fields," cautioned the physicist-promoter, "her supreme need, which transcends all others in this scientific age in which we live, is for the development here of men of resourcefulness, of scientific and engineering background and understanding—able, creative, highly endowed, highly trained men in science and its applications."[73]

Given the preference of Millikan and his board of trustees and colleagues, those applications were predictable. The Nobel Laureate, who sat on the committee of academics and trustees who ran Cal Tech, proceeded systematically to build up that institution and simultaneously to break down the barriers between metropolitan business, government, and academic research and to create the kind of interface between these sectors that later came to characterize the arms industry in Southern California. According to Theodore von Karman himself, Millikan pioneered in establishing this kind of close relationship between business and the university world at a time when "such industry-university tie-ups were quite rare in the United States." He added, "Universities in any case never stooped to go to industry; they insisted industry come to them." By contrast, Millikan intended to stoop whenever possible.[74]

His "first move immediately upon coming" to Cal Tech was to entice Southern California Edison to build its "one million volt laboratory for solving their problems of long-distance transmission of electric power" on the Cal Tech campus in order to facilitate the exchange of academic and business research contributions. "The next project has [had] to do with the rise of the aviation industry in Southern

California," noted Millikan. Like the transmission line and the power dams, this industry created a product which could withstand the transportation costs imposed by the out-of-the-way geography of the island on the land. In 1926, the Guggenheim Fund granted generous "subsidies to four universities that would use the money to pursue the science of aeronautics," but entirely overlooked Southern California, an ironic omission in view of later events. Millikan promptly caught the train to New York to rectify that oversight and, after a trip to the Southland by fund officials, succeeded in persuading Guggenheim officials to include Cal Tech in the grant. However, the Pasadena scientist's account of this episode is entirely too modest concerning the degree of his success. Not only did the physicist redirect a part of the award to Cal Tech, but he also secured a seat on the foundation board for himself. Whether because of or in spite of this fact, Cal Tech received the largest amount of money given by the Guggenheim Fund to any university. The Fund made large grants ranging from $15,000 to the Harvard Graduate School of Business to $350,000 to CIT. By contrast, Stanford University, the potential San Francisco Bay Area competitor of Cal Tech in aeronautics, received only $195,000. Prior to "the organization of the Fund, Mr. Daniel Guggenheim had established the Daniel Guggenheim School for Aeronautics at New York University with an endowment of $500,000." However, at that time New York was a well-established center of the aircraft industry in its own right and was right next door to the headquarters of the Fund itself.[75]

Even allowing for this grant previous to the establishment of the Fund, Cal Tech fared well, for it received another $250,000 jointly with the city of Akron for the creation of an "Airship Institute," to be dedicated to the development of lighter-than-air ships. This project was to be "supervised by the California Institute of Technology," and together with the heavier-than-air monies from Guggenheim, this allocation gave Cal Tech the largest single portion of the money distributed by the New York group. For the record, the Pasadena school secured more than twice the appropriations of such established schools as MIT, the University of Washington, and Georgia Tech; three times as much as Stanford; and about eight times the amount secured by the University of Michigan. In 1926, when the Fund began distributing its monies, Cal Tech was not the well-established academic instition that it would become, so its monetary acquisitions are all the more remarkable. However, the New York Fund attached the condition that Millikan would have to recruit a top European aerodynamicist to head the Cal Tech program.[76]

Millikan agreed to this condition and shortly initiated a campaign to hire Theodore von Karman, then working in Germany. It is interesting to note that Stanford University also received one of the Guggenheim grants for aerodynamic research and, like the Pasadena physicist, simultaneously pursued von Karman. One can only speculate on what would have happened to aeronautics in the Bay Area had that worthy accepted Stanford instead of Cal Tech. Given the Hungarian German's proclivity for scientific entrepreneurship, the San Francisco Area might well have acquired a much larger foothold in the aerospace industry than it ultimately secured. In any case, the Bay Area institution lost the competition, and von Karman signed with the Pasadena school. The aerodynamicist had turned down both institutions in 1928, but by the next year von Karman, who was Jewish, had grown increasingly uneasy about developments in Germany; and his disquiet coincided with another letter from Pasadena in July 1929. On this occasion, Millikan asked for the name of a top substitute candidate, in case von Karman still refused, but this time the Hungarian-born scientist responded positively.[77]

In inviting von Karman to Pasadena, Millikan was quite explicit about how the aggrandizement of von Karman's branch of physics would promote the joint tasks of building Cal Tech and Urban Southern California. "We do not have the funds to develop all the engineering sciences here," Millikan explained to von Karman in their first interview. "But I am convinced the aircraft industry will be attracted to Southern California. So with your help and the Guggenheim Foundation I think we can make Cal Tech the nation's center of aeronautics." Since at least 1926, Southern California interests had been mobilized to make Los Angeles and vicinity the "Detroit of the aircraft industry," and von Karman's role in this drama was unmistakably clear. He was to play Henry Ford.[78]

The completion of a wind tunnel for testing stood high on von Karman's list of improvements at the Institute, and this facility was completed in 1928 and opened in 1930. This project had been initiated in 1926 by Millikan's son Clark and Arthur L. Klein, a Cal Tech Ph.D. "known on the campus as 'Maj' because of his rank in the student military training organization." Von Karman had consulted on this program even before coming to Pasadena full time, and he felt strongly that his own version of the tunnel was much superior to that which the younger Millikan and Klein had proposed. Von Karman's version was adopted only because of the backing of von Karman by Millikan Sr. In any case the wind tunnel became the centerpiece of the new aeronautics laboratory, fittingly named the Guggenheim Aeronautical Laboratory of the California Institute of Technology (GALCIT); it helped to transform the Institute. "In 1926 Cal Tech had only a minor interest in aeronautics," noted von Karman, but the Hungarian scientist and the new facilities changed all of that.[79]

Von Karman himself, like Millikan Sr., was a great enthusiast for creating interfaces—between mathematics and engineering, between society and the universities, between academe and industry, and between the college cloister and the soldiers' barracks. He continually sought ways to apply the science of physics to the problems of an urban society. Like Millikan, he was particularly interested in demonstrating the utility of academic science to the practical world of business and military science. Once in Pasadena, his opportunity was not long in coming. Some "students from the military services started to attend my classes beginning in 1932, largely as a result of the recommendation of a friend of mine who was the head of the Navy's lighter-than-air department," noted von Karman in his autobiography. First the Navy invaded the cloister, but "the Army liked the results and sent some of their own men. These young men later became the generals who were to play an important role in my subsequent work for the Air Force." As the aerodynamicist put it, with modest understatement, in another context, "Small things exert great influence on men's lives."[80]

So did bigger ones. Millikan hoped for great things from lighter-than-air craft, as did the Navy, the Goodyear Company, and Harry Guggenheim. Guggenheim wanted to make Akron, Ohio, the dirigible center of the world and enlisted CIT in the project. To realize this hope, the New York philanthropist created "a four-story airship research institute" at Akron Airport which was guided and operated from Pasadena under von Karman's direction, although it was attached to the University of Akron. "This was actually part of Millikan's grand plan," noted von Karman, "which he indicated he would put into effect when he first asked me to head the Guggenheim Laboratory." This project did not come to technological perfection, however, due to a series of airship disasters which caused the Navy to cut back on its airship development program in the mid-thirties. However, the episode was important in a further context, aside from giving von Karman another set of contacts amongst the military men in Dayton, Ohio, the home of the Army Air Corps' Materiel Division. The investigation of the problems of airships led to a further emphasis upon research into the weather, which was thought to have contributed to the mishaps of the airship. Von Karman believed, therefore, that the study of the weather should be upgraded, despite the fact that "very few academicians accepted meteorology because it was regarded as a guessing science." Millikan agreed with the aerodynamicist again "and added the study of weather to the curriculum." This concentration provided another resource that could mutually benefit the Air Corps, the city, and CIT. "General M. H. (Map) Arnold, Chief of the Army AirCorps, was attracted to the new course and sent some of his officers to enroll in the classes." Cal Tech's weather experts went on to supply vital information to the American armies at the Normandy Invasion, the Battle of the Bulge, and the crossing of the Rhine during World War II.[81]

Another group of CIT experts cemented its ties to the Southern California aircraft industry and in turn helped that business to enlarge greatly its share of the national airplane market, building on the foundations that Millikan and von Karman had laid. The Guggenheim Aeronautical Laboratory at California Institute of Technology (GALCIT) opened its doors in 1929 and promptly moved to accomplish Millikan's "grand plan." The official history of the Guggenheim Laboratory summed up the thrust of this scheme. "The GALCIT has, from the beginning, maintained a close contact with the aircraft industry. There have also been continuing and intimate relations with the military and other government agencies since the early days of the laboratory," noted the historians in honor of its twenty-fifth anniversary. "Furthermore, members of the laboratory staff have been instrumental in creating and developing organizations and facilities which have later become independent of the GALCIT, but with which close association continues to be maintained."[82]

The Cal Tech emphasis upon "fundamental research but also an interest in the current problems of the airframe companies" appeared early. Upon completion, Cal Tech's wind tunnel "was one of the highest performance wind tunnels in existence," noted the GALCIT official history. "It was originally expected that about half of its time would be occupied with research problems pursued by members of the staff and students, while the other half would be available for the testing of models of aircraft under development by industry and government." With the collapse of the Douglas military market in the early thirties, that firm turned to the manufacture of commercial aircraft and looked to Cal Tech for help in solving its engineering problems. This coincidental convergence of Cal Tech's hopes and Douglas's necessities resulted in their collaboration on the famous DC series discussed below.[83]

Even before the advent of the DC series, CIT had moved to create the kind of interface that Millikan Sr. and von Karman desired. From the beginning Douglas's personnel helped to teach courses in aeronautics. Arthur Raymond, son of the operator of the famous Raymond Hotel in Pasadena, came over from Douglas to offer courses in airplane design, and when Raymond quit to succeed Dutch Kindelberger as Chief Engineer at Douglas, he passed the job on to others at Douglas. Aircraft industry personnel and, beginning in 1933, military personnel as well enrolled in Cal Tech courses. As Arthur Raymond noted of his interface, "It was quite useful because it helped keep me abreast of things. Also it was helpful as a means of recruiting good people to the company." This training went on from the very beginning. Of the first two holders of Guggenheim Graduate School of Aeronautics degrees, one ended up back at Cal Tech and the other as "Scientific Advisor in the Directorate of Research and Development, Headquarters U.S.A.F." The line of graduates grew longer. "In its relations with industry as with the government, probably the GALCIT's greatest contribution has been the students it has trained and sent out," noted the GALCIT history. "Of these the greatest percentage has entered the engineering departments of aircraft conpanies." The reciprocity of the relationship was affirmed by the same source. "Much of the GALCIT's history of the past twenty-five years could not have been written had it not been for its close association with these agencies of the government"; that is, the Army, Navy, Air Force, and NACA (National Advisory Committee on Aeronautics).[84]

This development was in line with a long-range trend noted in the early sixties by one of the designers of the DC-3. "The engineering and research parts of the aircraft organizations are gradually becoming larger relative to the size of the organization as a whole," noted Arthur Raymond in 1964. In the thirties, as this trend was just beginning to get under way, Cal Tech's value to the aircraft industry, both civilian and military, grew as the necessity of research become ever more imperative. As the thirties ended, the aircraft companies came to the realization that the 1929 CIT wind tunnel would no longer suffice for the greater speeds of the planes of the future, and Consolidated, Douglas, Lockheed, and North American decided to build a replacement that would accommodate speeds up to 750 miles per hour. "A design group was set up at the GALCIT under Clark Millikan's leadership, and the project was started." Neither this nor the Jet Propulsion Laboratory, conceived during the war, opened their doors till after the Second World War. However, the initiation of each and their ultimate management by Cal Tech indicates how far the "grand plan" of Millikan Sr. had been implemented. It indicates as well the extraordinary success of the Southland urban conspiracy which had backed Throop Institute, Robert Millikan, Donald Douglas, and Theodore von Karman to begin with.

The DC-3 provided the most spectacular early coup of the scientists and soldiers. In the early thirties, Millikan's son, Clark, and "Maj" Klein, who had worked with von Karman in building the Cal Tech wind tunnel, established ties to the Douglas Aircraft Corporation, where Klein "worked part time." The two men had labored on the Alpha plane of Douglas designer John Northrop, who had recently returned to that firm. One day Klein "reported" to von Karman "that his company would like to use the Cal Tech laboratories to explore some problems in the DC-1, the predecessor of the great DC-3 airplane which introduced the era of commercial aviation." Needless to say, the CIT scientists were enthusiastic. Of course, "this was the thing that Millikan [senior] had been waiting for—an opportunity to provide facilities for the airplane industry and to see Cal Tech grow as it helped the new industry grow," explained von Karman. He added, "Some of the first tests were actually paid for by the Guggenheim Foundation because the industry had not yet clearly seen its role in sponsoring research."[85]

It would not be so hesitant in the future. Klein and Clark Millikan together with von Karmon smoothed out several problems of the DC-1 having to do with turbulence and eddies, and they also helped the company design a metal frame for the DC series instead of employing wood design. The entire aircraft industry was moving from wood to metal frames at this time and, of course, it was crucial for the Douglas company to hurdle this barrier smoothly and efficiently. Any firm that did not make this cut faced a declining future in an increasingly metal frame industry.

CIT continued to work on the DC planes, and "the first plane that went through tests for nine months in our Guggenheim Laboratory was Douglas's DC-3," noted Robert Millikan. He proudly observed, "When the Douglas DC-3 came out of its tests and corrections made in our new wind tunnel, it had a cruising speed of 185 miles per hour, and Mr. Douglas publicly gave credit to CIT aerodynamicists for the extra 35 miles of speed without increase in power." In von Karman's "opinion our work at Cal Tech with the basic DC (Douglas Commercial) design, and the ideas we proposed to Douglas, made the DC-3 a truly great airplane."

Of course, the DC-3 went on to become a famous and useful airplane, possibly the most famous American aircraft ever built. This strategic importance was not lost on the scientists who helped build it. The DC-3 beat out the Boeing 247 as the workhorse of the commercial air fleets in the Depression decade, and thereafter Douglas was inundated with orders that might well have gone to build up Boeing and Seattle instead. This success aided both the scientists and their Southern California urban hinterland. As von Karman modestly observed, "I am sure that our efforts and the assistance of our wind tunnel advanced Cal Tech's importance in the minds of the new airplane manufacturers." Harry Guggenheim was equally convinced. "I wish I had put all my money into the long-haired men," he told Millikan after the Second World War, speaking of the creators of the CIT aerodynamics laboratory. Millikan exposed the other, or urban, side of the coin when he stated that "in no small degree because of the spectacular success of the DC-3, Southern California captured the larger share of the airplane business of the country and has held it to date [1950]."[86]

Just before and immediately after the outbreak of World War II, von Karman and his "long-haired" friends paid added dividends upon metropolitan Southern California's investment in them. Von Karman reminisced that "one day in 1936 three young men appeared in my office at Cal Tech with an unusual proposal." Frank J. Malina, John W. Parsons, and Edward S. Forman requested that the physicist allow them to conduct rocket experiments at Cal Tech. Although rocketry had generated a modest literature up to that point, it had not produced much else and was still considered a hare-brained idea. Von Karman welcomed such proposals and immediately embraced this one. Consequently the three men began rocket work at the GALCIT.

At first the results were dangerously comic. An early experiment literally fizzled, leaving everything in the lab covered with a fine coat of rust. Another blew up and could easily have killed Malina. These incidents earned the experimentors the nickname of the "Suicide Club." However, in time the rocket became feasible mechanically and then financially. The latter grew out of the Army's sudden interest. General Hap Arnold, by now Commander in Chief of the United States Army Air Corps and an old metropolitan Southern California hand who was an intimate of both Millikan and von Karman, convened a meeting of scientists in Washington to consider two Air Corps problems. One arose from reduced visibility caused by the icing of airplane windows. The other was rocketry. The Massachusetts Institute of Technology representative at the meeting laughingly volunteered for the icing problem and said that "Karman can take the Buck Rogers job." The professor did, and Buck Rogers turned out to be a very good bet. The Army Air Corps produced $10,000 in research funds, which guaranteed a return on Cal Tech and von Karman's decision to make Cal Tech "the first American university to treat rockets seriously." This would not be the last time that the Sourthern California metropolitan-military complex would benefit from the curiosity of one of its own university scientists or the ignorance of someone else's. Nor would it be the last time the area would be critically influenced by the character of its academic and scientific resources and preferences.[87]

In 1939 Cal Tech established GALCIT Project No. 1, which von Karman called "the first U.S. Army Air Corps rocket research project." Prophetically, the dangerous business of rocket experimentation was undertaken on land in the Arroyo Seco, where the Malina, Parsons, and Forman group had begun its work in 1937 and where the famous Jet Propulsion Laboratory would soon arise to carry it even further. Between 1939 and 1941, Jack Parsons and the other rocketeers worked out the "method of making large rocket charges . . . that has made possible such outstanding rockets as the Polaris and the Minuteman and has helped give the United States its excellence in large solid rocket engines," argued von Karman years after. As usual, Cal Tech could draw upon the resources of the Urban Southland to support the project. When the time came for airplane testing of the rockets, March Field at Riverside supplied the test site, and Lieutenant Homer Boushey, one of von Karman's students, served as test pilot. When this test succeeded, another occurred, again using a von Karman alumnus, Major Paul H. Dane, as pilot, the Muroc Dry Lake testing range as the test site, and an A-20 Douglas Havoc Bomber, manufactured in nearby Santa Monica. This was the "first aircraft takeoff in America with a permanently installed rocket power plant, and, as it turned out, the beginning of practical rocketry in the United States."[88]

The fortunes of the metropolitan Southland took off along with the plane. Not only did this series of events produce a coup for science, Cal Tech, and the Air Corps, it led directly to the addition of another promising aeronautical manufacturer to the defenders inside the Great Wall of California. Just as Admiral Yamamoto's carrier-based planes brought the interwar period to a close amidst the flames of Pearl Harbor, von Karman, Malina, Parsons, and their associates launched Aerojet General, which was to loom large in the coming war and larger still in the aerospace picture after the war.

Like so many metropolitan Southern California projects, this one developed out of the carefully nurtured relationships between the city and the sword. Cal Tech's "JATO [jet-assisted takeoff] rockets had been so promising that one day just before the A-20 test, Frank Malina came up with an interesting proposal," von Karman recalled. "Why not set up a business to sell JATO units to the armed services?" General Hap Arnold advised the group that an academic institution should not get into munitions manufacturing and that a private business apart from Cal Tech would be more suitable. After weeks of debate, the group secured its incorporation papers on March 19, 1942. Of the founders, only Andrew G. Haley, a Washington, D.C., lawyer, had prior business experience. Shortly thereafter, this critical figure was "called to active duty as a major" stationed in the capital. After a phone call from von Karman to General Arnold, Haley again became a civilian, "with a letter in his pocket stating that his release from active duty was in the best interests of the armed services in the development of jet propulsion." At the time of the appearance of von Karman's memoirs in 1967, the firm employed 34,000 people who handled $700 million worth of business yearly.

The beginnings were much more modest. With $1200 in capital, a Colorado street address, and considerable hope, the firm moved to Azusa in the Pomona Valley in January 1943, in time to accept a quarter-million-dollar contract from the Air Force. To fulfill the contract Aerojet needed a new factory, but the Defense Plant Corporation turned down its request. As usual, von Karman found an earlier personal tie decisive. Colonel Leslie Skinner, "developer of the proximity fuse and then head of bazooka development, whom I had visited earlier in the year at Aberdeen–Army Weapons Testing Range, where the two had consulted on the aerodynamics of weaponry–"suddenly became my champion," wrote von Karman later. Skinner's advocacy brought a reversal of the Defense Plant Corporation's decision and a grant of $149,000 for Aerojet's plant. The physicist explained that "this decision actually put Aerojet on its feet. It is interesting how again and again a human relationship can create history."[90]

In the case of Aerojet, these human relationships can be traced directly back to the original decision of the Cal Tech trustees to use that school literally to engineer the development of the Urban Southland and their subsequent recruitment of Millikan and von Karman. This tie is not so overwhelming in the case of all the other aircraft companies that located in Southern California, but it is impressive nevertheless. Each company had a different experience with its development-minded metropolitan hinterland, but all received substantial, and in some cases critical, assistance from the booster cabal that manipulated the Los Angeles area.

Much of this story centers on the career of Douglas Aircraft, both because of its own success in the field and because of its role in spawning other successful Southern California aircraft companies. By the time of the advent of the DC (Douglas Commercial) series and especially the DC-3, the Douglas firm had become the foremost airframe company in the United States, and this status threw much of the assembly business into the lap of Southern California. That triumph fueled the growth of the Southland as an urban area at a time when its economic woes had mounted considerably. Much of the success of the Douglas Aircraft Company derived from its own internal strengths and cannot be credited to its booster-infested hinterland. A part of this strength can be seen in the extraordinary role of the firm in spinning off other companies started by its own former employees.[91]

Arthur Raymond, one of the Douglas engineers on the DC series, observed in retrospect:

> I'm sure that the fact that Douglas was here had quite a bit to do with other companies being formed here. In some cases, such as North American, it actually came about through Dutch [Jack] Kindelberger transferring over [to North American Aviation, Inc., which moved to Southern California when Kindelberger became president]. I guess the same thing is true of Jerry Vultee of Vultee. In the case of Lockheed, it was started independently of Douglas, but Douglas people joined it later. The effect was that this area became an aircraft center, and Douglas was the seed corn.[92]

Raymond did not mention John Northrop, who also worked with Douglas and later established another Southland aircraft firm, Northrop Aircraft Incorporated.

Douglas himself came into the Southern California picture in 1920 while working for aviation pioneer Glenn L. Martin in Cleveland, who had earlier left the Southland despite its supposed natural advantages for aircraft manufacture. The official history of the then fledgling Douglas company as well as more recent scholarly analyses argue that the Southern California climate prompted this decision, and in subsequent years Douglas and his spokesmen frequently cited the natural superiority of the region. Most of the other airframe companies also mentioned this factor at one time or another, although they did not always give it first priority. Neither did Douglas, but he did so publicly and frequently enough to boost the fortunes of the doctrine of natural advantages in explaining the industrialization and urbanization of the metropolitan Southland. Had Douglas and the company historians stuck consistently to the theory, they might have settled the case, but unfortunately for the historical record, the corporate explanation varied from time to time and place to place. For example, in 1938 Douglas himself accorded priority to climate and geography in a magazine article, only to claim the same precedence on a later occasion for the favorable labor conditions in the Los Angeles area. In contrast, in 1920, Douglas explained to Jerome Hunsaker, his former MIT mentor, that his move to California was prompted by "personal reasons, but [also] because I have felt that if there is to be any civilian aeronautics it will be there that it will first attain real success." The 1943 company history offered a different version. According to Frank Cunningham, Douglas's wife decided in January 1920 to move back to Southern California because the weather would be easier on their children. When Douglas subsequently joined her and wrote to Martin submitting his resignation, he advanced four other reasons. He argued that "factories on the coast were easier to construct as heating was a minor problem and much of the work could be done in the open air"; flying was normally year-round; labor conditions were better; and, save Boeing, "there was no major producer on the coast." On other occasions, the firm or Douglas also stressed the importance of better access to financing in Southern California. To confuse the issue more, when the company moved a part of its operation to Tucson after the Second World War, it cited the natural advantages of that city as the principal reason for moving. Obviously, the move to Arizona, whose climate hardly resembles that of Southern California, and indeed the increasing decentralization of the industry after the Second World War, confirms the suspicion that several alternative geographic and climatic locales could have sustained the aircraft industry in the period when Los Angeles and Southern California came largely to monopolize it. Pluralism was obviously quite possible, so other matters were clearly more important.[93]

No single factor will suffice to explain either Douglas's preference for the Urban Southland or that of the industry in general. Each company had a somewhat different experience, but all shared certain man-made advantages inside the Great Wall of California that did not exist or could not be easily secured elsewhere. Most of these artificial advantages were created by Southern California boosters anxious to retain and expand their share of the aircraft industry. And, as Professor Luckingham has noted, the climate was just as attractive all over the Southwest.

The migration of Douglas himself illustrates this principle perfectly and further exemplifies the omnipresent influence of the *Los Angeles Times*-Chandler interests. At first glance, the motivations for Douglas's move are somewhat controversial. On closer examination, the problem is less complex. The explanation of climate cannot be taken seriously because several hundred miles of California coastline have virtually the same climate as Los Angeles. In fact, San Diego has a marginally superior one. Any number of places in the West, from San Jose to San Diego, had wide-open spaces for testing and the high aridity that allowed much plane construction outside the factory walls. Again San Diego is drier than Los Angeles and had more open space than it felt comfortable with. Thus climate tells us nothing about the specific choice of Los Angeles from among a number of alternative western spots. The absence of a competing aircraft firm, a second reason contained in one of the Douglas histories, carries the same deficit. Vast stretches of territory had no competing aircraft makers.

Douglas's belief that California would be the place where civil aviation would first succeed tells us more about his motivation but less about his initial success. The civilian market was of little importance to the airframe pioneer because, after the Cloudster, 90 percent of his business up to the 1932 DC-3 contract came from the military. Yet despite his ill-starred prophecy that the civilian business would help his own firm, Southern California aviation did prosper, as Paul Rhode has noted. Therefore, Douglas could well have been motivated by this trend, even though he misjudged how much he would initially profit from it. Finally there is the potential influence of his wife. After all, Charlotte Marguerite Ogg Douglas packed up and moved the kids to L.A. in January 1920 before Douglas took a leave from Martin to join her. The histories of the firm do not explain why Mrs. Douglas left without her husband or whether they planned in advance that the move to Los Angeles would be permanent. Given her dislike of the Cleveland weather and housing shortages, Charlotte might conceivably have made the decision to move and left it up to Donald to react. If so, she would have been responsible for the most important industrial location decision of the twentieth century. Douglas's move created the hub of the rising aerospace industry that has done so much to reorient the economic history of the late twentieth century. Ironically, this explanation would confound all of us who have tried to account for the concentration of the aircraft business. Still, this conjecture seems unlikely. Douglas was close to an old-fashioned industrial buccaneer and it is not likely that he would brook that kind of independence from his wife. The histories of the company make it plain that Donald Douglas was the dominant partner in the marriage and that his wife often had to accept neglect while the industrialist pursued his other love, making airplanes. So although possible, the Charlotte Douglas thesis seems unlikely and in any case undocumented by solid source material.[94]

Although it has recently been called a "fiction," the booster explanation is both more plausible and better documented than any of the alternatives. The booster account of Douglas's move is based on the correspondence between Bill Henry and Douglas and other letters rather than a corporate history. Robert Gottlieb and Irene Wolt, historians of the *Los Angeles Times,* note that during 1919 Harry Chandler had dispatched Henry, one of his reporters, to the East to investigate the future possibilities of the aircraft industry. This action was part of a campaign by Chandler and other Los Angeles boosters to develop a manufacturing base for the City of Angels. This drive captured a number of corporations for Los Angeles and landed Henry in Cleveland at the Glenn L. Martin Company. Chandler gave his star reporter a year off to look over the nascent airframe industry to see if it would be appropriate for Southern California. During that time Henry worked for the Martin firm, where he met Donald Douglas, and the two "decided to try to set Douglas up on his own in Los Angeles." Henry first persuaded Chandler that the aircraft industry and Douglas were a good bet and then wrote to Douglas assuring him that Chandler's support would be decisive with Los Angeles money men. As Gottlieb and Wolt put it, "Now, I'm convinced that the thing will go,' Henry wrote to Douglas, urging him to come west immediately." Douglas promptly did.[95]

Nor did the courtship end there. When Douglas came to Southern California, he had few resources and no airplane orders. His initial overtures to men of capital left that situation unchanged, until Bill Henry intervened again. This time the Chandler emissary introduced the aircrafter to a "well-to-do young man named David R. Davis who would finance an airplane which could fly coast-to-coast nonstop." That brought a $40,000 order to Douglas who produced the Cloudster with it, a plane which took to the air in February 1921. A 1941 *Fortune Magazine* article confirms this booster interpretation of the Douglas move to the Los Angeles area, although in a slightly different version. As *Fortune* put it, "Douglas did not choose Los Angeles primarily either for its climate or because its labor market was favorable. He hoped for financing, and he first found it in a young man named David R. Davis, who had wealth and a machine shop and liked the Douglas ambition to build a plane that would span the continent nonstop." Douglas then turned to the military market and won an order for three planes from the Navy. Once again, Henry intervened, this time to provide the new capital needed to finance the Douglas entrée into the largest contemporary airplane market, that is, the military services. Chandler underwrote $1500 of a $15,000 loan and gave Douglas a list of nine names of other prominent Angelenos to contact for the rest of what he needed. All nine contributed to the stake, which put Douglas into the military market where he prospered ever afterward. Although the importance of this loan has been discounted, Douglas "urgently" needed capital, and even his biographers and firm historians admit that the bankers were reluctant to provide it until Chandler underwrote the loan.[96]

The loan was a relatively modest sum, but it was the one that got Douglas started in the business. Doubtless to a man who had brought only $600 to Southern California with him, the funds did not seem so meager. Douglas had no firm at all at the time of the partnership with Davis and a very small operation at the time of the loan. In the midst of a depression and failing to get the loan, he might have packed up and left. Other early California operators, including Glenn L. Martin, did just that. At the time of the loan, Donald Douglas was working out of the back room of a barber shop, in attics, and in rented dirigible hangars. Unlike a later era when the planemaker had an enormous capital investment in Southern California, in 1922 he had little stake to keep him in Los Angeles. In addition, the booster story of the Henry-Chandler influence on Douglas was the one that was believed in Southern California by contemporaries familiar with the history of airplane manufacturing. As Don Thomas of the L.A. All-Year Club wrote to John Oliver La Gorce of the *National Geographic* magazine in 1944, "Bill Henry is widely known and highly regarded hereabouts. He is so modest that you may not have known he made the initial contacts which 'made' Donald Douglas in the early days when Douglas had an idea but no capital." Nor did Chandler lose interest or Henry end his responsibilities when the Scottish-American got his partner or his money. The Early Birds of Aviation was an organization made up of the pioneers, men and women who had soloed before December 17, 1916. In other words, they knew the early aviation field backward and forward. Early Birds former president and trustee Waldo Waterman was also chairman of the Smithsonian Liaison and Plaque Committee, which had the task of authenticating historically the feats of the aviation and aircraft industries. "I well remember the days of your being 'watch dog' for Harry Chandler, when Doug was building the Cloudster," Waterman recalled to Bill Henry.[97]

The critical nature of this money can be seen from the condition of the aircraft "industry" in 1922, the year that Douglas secured his Navy contract. In that year, the airframe business hit its postwar low with a total production of 263 planes, down from 14,000 in 1918. Outside of the military demand, there was hardly any market at all. *Southern California Business* appreciated completely the timing of this loan to Douglas. "Douglas got his real start by proving his designing abilities to the Navy," noted the official Chamber of Commerce organ in 1936. However, "Douglas needed a grub-stakes of $15,000 to build the first three planes for the Navy that were to launch him on his real career." Soon after providing Douglas with this money, Chandler and two other real estate operators and boosters, William May Garland and Moses Sherman, leased land to Douglas for his "new factory." To the importance of the Douglas invasion of the military market, it should be added that the firm produced hardly anything but martial aircraft until the advent of the DC series in the early 1930s.[98]

So the elimination of Mrs. Douglas and climate leaves us with the booster, labor, financial, and aviation culture explanations. In reality, the problem is much simpler than this quadrupartite division of labor appears because all four of these explanations derive from the influence of the boosters. As will be seen below, from the 1880s until World War II, the boosters, led by the *Los Angeles Times,* systematically destroyed the power of labor in order to give the area an edge over competing cities. The financial advantages derived from the same Chandler influence, and the favorable aviation culture was methodically built into Southern California by the same parties. In other words, Chandler's emissary picked an aircraft winner for Southern California and then the boosters made that place as congenial for him as possible.

The experience of the premier Southland aircraft firm reflected that of the industry as a whole. The early pioneers secured their capital from local sources and with few exceptions did not have access to the big-money markets of the country. However, the local support that Douglas received allowed him to make that transition when conditions proved favorable. This switch came in the late 1920s when the Morrow Board Report led to changes in the industry. The Congress responded to the Board's recommendations by passing the air Commerce Act of 1926 to promote and regulate "civil aviation" and legislation to reorganize "both Army and Navy air forces to improve their status within the services, along with an orderly five-year procurement program to give the Army a first-line strength of 1,600 planes and the Navy 1,000."

These events, together with Lindbergh's near simultaneous flight, boosted the industry out of its "speculative" phase to a position "approaching financial respectability just in time to benefit from the Great Bull Market." Douglas literally capitalized on this new development, securing expansion money by "incorporating the Douglas Aircraft Company in Delaware in 1928." Yet even after the big money became available for a short period before the crash, the metropolitan Southland continued to provide crucial local support, in this case by providing the new company with "the first revolving credit given to an aircraft manufacturing company in the United States." Predictably, a booster organization, the Security First National Bank, headed by Joseph Sartori, "arranged" the matter. The Sartoris were to Southern California what the Gianninis and the Bank of Italy-Bank of America were to the San Francisco Bay Area. Moreover, Security First National also was "one of the principals offering the stock" from the Douglas Incorporation, so some of the big money actually came from the metropolitan Southland.[99]

The California Institute of Technology dramatically nurtured the tie between Douglas and his company's metropolitan hinterland which the publishers, real estate tycoons, and bankers had created. Like the earlier loans from Davis and Chandler's Big Ten, this new assistance allowed Douglas to break into the other end of the aircraft industry at a time when he badly needed to do so. The Great Depression hit all of the aircraft industry hard, but it brought special burdens for a company that depended almost entirely upon military contracts. The orderly five-year development program of 1926 faded away under the impact of the economic crisis, so Douglas suffered from a drastic shrinkage of his market at the same time that capital sources dried up. Between 1931 and 1934, government aircraft spending declined from $31,000,000 to $13,000,000. It is then not surprising that when

Douglas received a request from TWA in 1932 to produce a better plane than the Boeing 247 being produced for United Airlines, the firm took up the challenge, both to produce a great airplane and to make up for the loss of military business. The need to create a superb aircraft brought the ambitious Pasadena school into the picture with the hopeful, yet harassed, aircraft company.[100]

Actually, the placement of the momentous DC-3 order itself owed something to Southern California boosters. Transcontinental and Western Airways, which became Trans World Airways, the name by which it is still known, was half-owned in Los Angeles and half in the east. Its eastern wing contained both Pennsylvania Railroad and General Motors money, but its western wing was based on three Los Angeles airlines. Harris "Pop" Hanshue operated Western Air Express (WAE), the most important of the L.A. firms. According to the *Times* historians, Robert Gottlieb and Irene Wolt, WAE was "another [Harry] Chandler syndicate" in which "banker Henry Robinson and realtor [William May] Garland" also joined. Western was the most important of the companies that merged to form TWA because of its profitability and experience and its possession of routes from Los Angeles to Salt Lake City, Kansas City, and Dallas. The merger needed a West Coast terminus, and Los Angeles was the most important city on the coast when the government in 1930 muscled the several firms to consolidate into one.[101]

Shortly thereafter, United Airlines, which had been founded by Boeing, placed an order for sixty Boeing 247s. The Seattle firm had designed a revolutionary airplane, representing an important step in the "airframe" revolution," a machine which would make those of United Airlines' competitors obsolete in comfort, safety, and speed. The Seattle firm and United had agreed that no other company would get any 247s until United had a fleet of sixty, an enormous number for the time. Thus United would get a tremendous headstart from Boeing. This arrangement between United and its Seattle parent company created a crisis for the rest of the aviation business. Either the other carriers had to wait two years while United cut deeply into their traffic or they had to commission a plane competitive with the Boeing 247. They chose the latter course which led eventually to the order with Douglas.

However, at the time, Douglas was not the logical choice for the contract. Jack Frye, the de facto head of TWA, devised specifications for the aircraft that his firm hankered after and invited five manufacturers to meet them. Douglas was the smallest and least likely of the group to succeed. He had produced at least six planes used by WAE in the past, but he mainly manufactured military machines and had no experience in constructing large civilian planes. Yet he did have some acquaintances inside TWA. Jack Frye had founded one of the companies that formed TWA, Standard Airlines, which flew routes east from Los Angeles and later merged with WAE. In these days, the airmen were a small and tight-knit group and Douglas and Frye had shared the Angeleno environment for more than ten years before the crucial TWA order. Upon receipt of the invitation from his fellow Angeleno, Douglas and his staff went into almost round-the-clock deliberations and came up with a revolutionary design within two weeks. When the smallest and least experienced of the competitors explained their concept to the TWA judges in New York, Jack Frye said,, "I like it. What do you think, Slim?" Charles A. Lindbergh answered that he liked the craft too, but insisted that it be able to take off anywhere on its route with one engine. Lindbergh was concerned with safety, but also with overcoming one of the natural disadvantages of flying in the West. The Western TWA routes led over high-altitude country and the thin air forced the motors to work much harder. The Douglas staff of future superstars said they would try. With the help of Cal Tech they succeeded.

In the early thirties, Robert Millikan's son Clark and "Maj" Klein established ties to the Douglas Aircraft Company, where Klein worked part time. The two men had already collaborated on the Alpha plane of Douglas designer John Northrop, who had recently joined the company. One day Klein reported to von Karman "that his company would like to use the Cal Tech laboratories to explore some problems in the DC-1 airplane," the predecessor of the great DC-3 which introduced the era of commercial aviation. Needless to say, the CIT scientists enthusiastically agreed. Von Karman explained that "this was the thing that Millikan senior had been waiting for—an opportunity to provide facilities for the airplane industry and to see Cal Tech grow as it helped the new industry grow." He went on to observe that "some of the first tests were actually paid for by the Guggenheim Foundation because the industry had not yet clearly seen its role in sponsoring research."[102]

It would not be so hesitant in the future. Klein and Clark Millikan, together with von Karman, worked out several problems of the DC-1 regarding turbulence and eddies, and they also helped the company create a metal frame for the DC series to replace the heretofore predominant wood design. The entire aircraft industry was moving from wood to metal at this time and, of course, it was crucial for the Douglas company to hurdle this barrier smoothly and efficiently.[103]

The long-haired academics helped them over, and they would aid in the next jump as well. The CIT scientists continued to work on the DC planes, and "the first plane that went through tests for nine months in our Guggenheim Laboratory was Douglas's DC-3," noted a proud Robert Millikan. Its flight testing took place at Mines Field, Los Angeles' municipal airport. When the "DC-3 came out of its tests and corrections made in our new wind tunnel, it had a cruising speed of 185 miles per hour and Mr. Douglas publicly gave credit to CIT aerodynamicists for the extra 35 miles of speed without increase in power." In von Karman's opinion, "Our work at Cal Tech with the basic DC design, and the ideas we proposed to Douglas, made the DC-3 a truly great airplane." Even before the DC-3 succeeded, the firm and the university had already created the kind of interface typical of today's industry. Bailey Oswald, Douglas's head of aerodynamics for the DC-3 project who later became chief of aerodynamics for the firm, was a 1932 CIT Ph.D. in aeronautical engineering. The DC-3 went on to become a famous and useful airplane, possibly the most famous American aircraft ever built. It is always characterized as the first plane to support itself both aerodynamically and financially. As such, it ushered in the age of commercial air transportation and, as noted earlier, it also beat out the Boeing 247, which that firm discontinued after the appearance of the DC-3. The importance of that victory was not lost on the scientists who helped to achieve it. When the DC-3 squeezed out the Boeing 247 as the workhorse of the commercial air fleets, Douglas was thereafter inundated with orders that might well have gone to build up Seattle. This success aided both the scientists and their Southern California urban hinterland. As von Karman modestly asserted, "I am sure that our efforts and the assistance of our wind tunnel, advanced Cal Tech's importance in the minds of the new airplane manufacturers." Harry Guggenheim agreed. "I wish I had put all my money into the long-haired men," he told Millikan after the Second World War, speaking of the creators of the CIT aerodynamics laboratory. Millikan noted the other, that is, the urban, side of the coin when he stated that "in no small degree because of the spectacular success of the DC-3, Southern California captured the larger share of the airplane business of the country and has held it to date [1950]."[104]

Donald Douglas did not stop at wishing. As previously noted, his people continued to teach at Cal Tech; he continued to employ CIT graduates; and he built and maintained a tight research interface with the "long-haired" academicians. When Frank P. Goss, city editor of the *Long Beach Sun/Long Beach Press Telegram,* wrote to the Douglas firm in August 1941 requesting material for a story to commemorate the dedication of a new Douglas plant, he found out exactly how much of Robert Millikan's grand design had been implemented. Goss explained to von Karman, "I am informed by the Douglas management that all of the scientific aerodynamical research for their product is conducted by the California Institute of Technology." He continued, "They suggested that I write and ask you if you would be good enough to furnish us with a story written in the language of the layman, describing some features of this important branch of airplane construction.[105]

In general, the press portrayed the nascent aircraft industry in a favorable light, and in 1926 in particular used its columns to spotlight the growing and potential contribution of the business to the development of the metropolis. The press continued to boom the industry's progress right up to World War II. Although these encomiums were merely expressions of excitement and sympathy, moral support often touched upon material advantage.[106]

It did so rather forcefully in the labor climate of Southern California. Organized labor found the area south of the Tehachapis to be peculiarly uncongenial territory. This antagonism went back to the days of Harrison Gray Otis. The *Times* patriarch was both a builder of cities and a destroyer of labor organizations and, in the publisher's mind, these two acts were intimately connected. Otis's animus grew out of his own difficulties with the printer's union and culminated in the historic bombing of the *Times* building in 1910. Throughout his career and that of his successor up to the Second World War, the foremost Los Angeles newspaper and the huge material empire attached to it remained staunchly anti-labor. Together with the Chamber of Commerce, the Merchants and Manufacturer's Association, the city and county governments and especially the Red Squad of the latter, large sections of the business community, and the middle classes as well, the *Times* turned the City of the Angels into the American open-shop town par excellence. They did so in the name of urban progress, for they assumed that the lack of unions provided Los Angeles with a crucial advantage in its deadly warfare with San Francisco, itself a good union town even in the twenties. Fewer unions meant lower wages, and that in turn meant higher rates of industrialization and general economic growth.[107]

The labor leaders at the Golden Gate fully recognized the potential danger of allowing Los Angeles this wage differential and tried on occasion to eliminate it by unionizing their California neighbor. These campaigns generally failed, and one of the most appreciative beneficiaries of this "economic freedom" was none other than Donald Douglas. The Southland aircrafter was peculiarly anti-union, more so than some of his colleagues in the airframe industry. Aided by his local Los Angeles friends and such unlikely allies as Sydney Hillman and Phillip Murray of the Congress of Industrial Organizations (CIO), Douglas stood out against the organizing drives that badly damaged the open-shop fortress in the 1930s and forced some of his fellow airplane builders to the bargaining table. Douglas outdid even his more celebrated holdout colleague, Henry Ford, succumbing only in 1943 and then only under duress from the government.[108]

Labor costs did indeed constitute a large factor in airframe production. As Edwin Clapp noted in 1926, at a time when the Douglas firm employed about 500 men, "the labor advantage is the big thing, since labor cost represents 75 per cent of producing an airplane." In the same article he argued that skilled labor earned as much in the industry as they did in the East, but he did not try to reconcile these two statements. Labor sources in the 1930s argued that the men received only a pittance, even after the wartime emergency brought sustained prosperity to the builders. William G. Cunningham's study of industrial location in the aircraft industry bears out the opinion of the union men as to the level of wages and also confirms that the industry had unusually high labor costs. However, Cunningham's estimate is considerably lower than Clapp's, 46 percent to 75 percent. Still, that lower figure is enough to qualify airframe manufacturing as "a high-labor-cost, low-materials-cost industry." In any case, the *Los Angeles Times* consistently upheld the open shop in Southern California and for Douglas. This stand helped to retain the competitive advantages of low-wage labor in a high-labor-cost industry for Southland metropolitanism.[109]

Aside from cheapness and docility, Douglas and his airframe colleagues required a supply of labor that was skilled and adequate in numbers. Any large city could have afforded the latter advantage, although as Consolidated Aircraft Corporation's 1935 location in San Diego demonstrated, a city of at least 100,000 was required. However, both San Diego and Los Angeles benefitted increasingly from the fact that they were already airframe manufacturing centers where a large body of laborers skilled specifically in aircraft production could be found. This fact, of course, owed something to the prior work of the boosters in seducing Douglas, successfully fighting to retain Lockheed, and wooing Consolidated. However, a part of the skilled pool derived from other sources, namely the service flying fields concentrated in the area in defiance of military logic. As one booster organ noted, proximity to North Ireland Naval Air Station, Rockwell Field, and March Field provided a group of skilled aircraft mechanics who often moved into the civilian fields. Together with all of the other advantages that airframe builders enjoyed, the open shop, the lower wages, and the supply of skilled workers helped to make Southern California an extremely congenial place for aircraft manufacture.[110]

Although Lockheed often languished in the shadow of the Douglas Aircraft Company, it did not escape the boosters' notice, and the Southland metropolis proved a very agreeable place for that firm as well. The facts of Lockheed history up to the point that it became inseparably linked to the Los Angeles area are available only in bare outline. This is especially true of the information explaining the location decisions of the company, but a pattern consistent with the Douglas experience still emerges, particularly for the three crucial decisions that made a success of Lockheed.

Unlike some of the other California pioneer aviators, Lockheed did not desert the state of its corporate birth. The Loughead (later changed to Lockheed) brothers grew up on a ranch in the San Francisco Bay Area, ten miles from Sunnyvale, where the Lockheed Missile Systems Division would later be located. Malcolm and Allan became interested in flying at an early age, but according to the official history of Lockheed Aircraft Corporation, "there was little aviation activity in San Francisco"; and in 1910, Allan went off to Chicago to work for an air-minded auto distributor. After varied success there, Allan returned to the Bay Area because of the distributor's withdrawal of his patronage. Allan and Malcolm remained in San Francisco until 1915, experimenting with various types of airplanes, including flying boats. During their stay there the brothers drew on local resources to maintain their airplane habit. This included a local cab company and the Panama-Pacific Exposition of 1915, which allowed them to earn money flying visitors about the Bay Area.[111]

When the fair closed, the Lockheed family moved to Santa Barbara. The official history does not explain the rationale for this decision, which would be crucial for both the development of the corporation and the process of urbanization in the Southland. In any case, the brothers established an aircraft company in Santa Barbara that soon folded. The company ventured after the cross-channel trade to the islands, bid on World War I Navy contracts, tried its hand at barnstorming, learned much from its design experiments, and still went broke in 1921. By this time Malcolm Lockheed had left the corporation and another Californian from Santa Barbara had joined it. John Northrop proved to be the guiding design genius of the corporation, but not for long; the oversupply of planes and engines after World War I drove the company into its first bankruptcy. Allan Lockheed secured Northrop a job at Douglas. This first Lockheed firm seems to have had no lasting technical or organizational significance for the Southland, but it did link the fortunes of Lockheed to Southern California urbanization.[112]

For the next few years Allan Lockheed "sold real estate in Los Angeles during its spectacular postwar growth" as well as hydraulic auto brakes for his inventor brother Malcolm. Then in 1926, Allan and Northrop joined forces again to revive the Lockheed company. As in the Bay Area, they found financing from local sources, this time a brick and tile manufacturer named Fred S. Keeler. This backing, plus good design, successfully launched the company into the airplane market. However, as the great bull market heated up, outside investors grew interested in the Hollywood firm. Against the wishes of Allan Lockheed, the directors decided to sell to Detroit Aircraft, an eastern corporation that aspired to become the General Motors of the aircraft industry. Instead, it became the drag on the firm's progress that eventually brought it to the ground for a second time and on two occasions nearly eliminated this promising addition to the Southland's process of urbanization.[113]

The first instance occurred in 1928 when the new parent firm tried to move

Lockheed to Detroit. Carl Squier, who now headed Lockheed, traveled to Burbank, where the firm had relocated from Hollywood, to arrange the departure. He personally preferred to stay in the San Fernando Valley, but he needed help to dissuade the Detroit company from moving. "I went to the Chamber of Commerce in Burbank and said, 'Give me all the help you can if you want to save the company," Squier recalled. Whereupon "the Chamber of Commerce went to work—the bankers helped, everybody helped [Squier to] compile a brochure of facts" that enabled him to change the company's mind.

In his presentation Squier stressed the climatic advantages for testing and for heating reductions as well as the cheaper electricity and rent available in Burbank. Obviously climate played a role, but as usual, it took the support of the boosters even to bring the climatic arguments to bear. Moreover, Squier did not state that the climatic advantages outweighed the others. In any case, the Detroit firm desisted, but according to Squier, the margin was hair's breadth: "We came back to re-set some of the machinery that had been torn up [for shipment to Detroit]." Thus the actions of the local boosters retrieved a situation that outside forces had almost ruined. Put another way, the outside influences upon which urbanization is supposedly dependent would have concentrated this branch of the airframe industry elsewhere, decentralizing it before it reached a critical mass in Los Angeles. Only the strength of urban influences prevented Detroit Aircraft from moving and thereby added to the momentum of this species of industrial urban growth within the Great Wall of California.[114]

They nearly left once again in the early thirties. Allan Lockheed had noted at the time of the liaison with Detroit Aircraft that his own company was the only money-earning component in that large merger. The Great Depression demonstrated the consequences of this state of affairs as Detroit Aircraft lost money, its stock value, and everything else. Lockheed did not immediately go into receivership, but the Detroit failure caused the Army to cancel its contract with Lockheed, thus depriving it of a potential market when it badly needed one. It would take several years and considerable effort to restore Lockheed's position with its service buyers. In the meantime, the Burbank firm itself fell into receivership in October 1931. In June 1932, the company was sold to a group of investors for $40,000 by the U.S. District Court. Robert Ellsworth Gross headed this group, which also included Carl Squier, and nearly all of the modest purchase price was raised from San Francisco and Los Angeles sources rather than from outside financial circles. However, in mid-1932, the firm faced bleak prospects. The Great Depression was nearing its worst point, and capital had dried up just at the moment when the new Lockheed Aircraft Corporation most desperately required money. The industry was just then undergoing what John B. Rae has called the "airframe revolution," which increasingly substituted metal for wood frames. This change necessitated access to large amounts of capital to produce a plane that would be competitive with the industry leaders who had made the transition.[115]

The ultimate capital acquisition proved to be the fourth and decisive turning point which helped to entrench Lockheed permanently in California. Fully one year after Gross and his associates purchased the bankrupt company, it still did not have enough capital to finance the Electra airplane, the product that would put the company back on its feet with both the investing public and the aviation companies and carry it through the airframe revolution. Up to that time, Gross had canvassed both the New York and San Francisco money markets without success. As Courtlandt Gross reported to his brother on a conversation with "Freddie" Warburg, "I told him . . . that any overtures which we had made to him and to any other of our New York banking friends had been received with no enthusiasm and no cooperation." A subsequent attempt to invade the San Francisco money market produced a similar repulse. The partners of the relevant firm could not decide how to list the stock, and Robert Gross, in frustration, finally turned to the local market in Los Angeles. Even in his own tropical back yard, Gross could not count on getting the funds from the major Los Angeles brokers and ultimately resorted to G. Brashears and Company, a modest but respectable house.[116]

Success followed immediately. Brashears took the stock issue, sold it to the public, and then took on a second offering. Gross observed, "This stock has been placed in Southern California. Over 80 percent of the public stock is parked right here in Los Angeles." This money tided the company over the first year of the Electra development, but, as in the earlier instance of the Detroit Aircraft Corporation, it was close. In this case, Robert E. Gross actually spent much of his own time covering the Los Angeles financial district in his private automobile, selling stock.[117]

Even with the help of Brashears and the battered coupe, Lockheed experienced financial difficulties for several more years. Brashears continued to help, selling "some $1.5 million worth of Lockheed stock, chiefly in the Los Angeles area," between 1933 and 1937. In 1935 the firm took a directorship on the Lockheed board. Once this base of monetary support had been established by local investors, Lockheed successfully invaded the San Francisco and New York City money markets. The firm also obtained a $200,000 loan from the Reconstruction Finance Corporation in 1934. In the meantime, Lockheed benefitted from the renaissance of the airplane market both at home and abroad. However, even with these favorable developments and the continuing technical achievements of Lockheed, which permitted the corporation to introduce several successful entries into the airlines market, especially to the feeder lines, the company suffered financial stringencies up to the end of 1936. The Burbank firm's own corporate history admits that until this point, the company still played in the "minor leagues."[118]

Part of the problem was the major-league competition of the great DC-3 and its successors which co-opted much of the commercial airplane market and left room only for the smaller scale business of the feeder lines. The Lockheed Electra and its successors did well here, but this business did not produce a large volume trade. From 1932 to 1936 Lockheed failed to regain a significant position in the military market; this failure also limited the company's growth. In those years, the Burbank company sold "only five Lockheed planes" to the services. Gross concluded that the company must make a successful large-scale entry into the military market; and as early as the beginning of 1935, he began trying to do so. In 1937, the Army Air Force requested a Lockheed bid on a fighter plane, and from that point on, the corporation profited greatly from its military connection. This new beachhead, together with orders from the British government, for whom the San Fernando Valley firm produced the Hudson bomber, led to an unparalleled improvement in the company's fortunes. By the end of 1936, 1200 Lockheed employees had produced planes that sold for $4,000,000. On the eve of Pearl Harbor, 53,000 workers constructed $145,000,000 worth of planes. In the process the company struggled from fifth to first leading producer in the industry. Despite the repeated statements by Gross that the commercial market was the most important one, the sales soon proved it not to be.

It is almost certain that Lockheed would have gained greatly from military demand once war seemed imminent. Every possible producer had to be used to meet the emergency, and the major ones were in a position in which they could not lose. Yet in the meantime, the airplane industry benefitted from its local connections—this time military—to keep itself going. Just as Donald Douglas drew on the defense resources concentrated in the Southland metropolitan area, so did the Lockheed Aircraft Corporation.

A "barbecue held in Mr. Walter Wallace's garden in San Marino was the scene last week of quite a gathering of airplane people who were invited to honor General [Henry] Arnold and the high aviation officers," Gross informed one of his financial contacts in 1937.

> I feel I learned a great deal about our relative position and standing in Army circles, and I am of the opinion that as time goes on we are going to be offered more and more service business, it being merely a question of whether we have the courage to hold out for our prices and conditions, or whether, swept off our feet by the prospect of big volume, we will be tempted to do a lot of business just for the sake of doing a lot of business.[119]

Lockheed's interest in government contracts reveals clearly the mutual metropolitan-military anxiety that drove the soldiers and civilians into each other's arms. Gross wrote to his brother Courtlandt in mid-1934, "I have been loath to go into the military thing at all, feeling that it was a lot nicer not to have to depend on the light and shadow of politics." However, "the job of putting out the Electra has proved such an undertaking that some way or other we have got to scare up a lot of business to support it . . . I want to plan a careful, methodical effort and advance it relentlessly move by move until we get a good contract." The political situation at home seemed opportune. Moreover, "the outlook for the export of aircraft is excellent, there being little question but that a major conflict is in the making in the Balkan States and probably the Orient." In effect, wars and defense spending represented a way to stabilize Lockheed's position in the industry, and the company set about getting a foothold.[120]

The Burbank company had experienced difficulty seizing a place in the market in its other attempt in 1931. The "old ring of military contractors and politicians [was] then in power," noted Gross, and "the Lockheed company and Detroit Aircraft, whose fortunes were already beginning to wane, had great difficulty in getting a good audience for the machine" it had submitted for government approval. The situation seemed more promising after the advent of the New Deal, but that government generated uncertainties of its own by canceling mail contracts, forcing the breakup of aviation-aircraft combines, and raising production costs through Section 7-A of the National Industrial Recovery Act. Other politicians created disquiet by their denunciations of the industry as "merchants of death." Nevertheless, Lockheed made its overture to the military in a letter to the Army Air Force in early 1935.[121]

Initially the corporation was unsure how to proceed. Early advice held that the approach should be made through the Material Division at Dayton and that "a contractor who tries to bring outside pressure on Wright Field [Dayton] by getting the Service groups [March Field, San Diego, etc.] rooting for him is apt to hurt his case." Within the year that latter opinion had been revised. As in the case of Douglas, March Field personnel helped to advise the Burbank company on what kind of plane to build. "Strictly confidentially," Gross informed his brother, "Carl [Squier] . . . went over to March Field last week and got some information on the latest thoughts in the Air Corps."[122]

> Dutch Kindelberger and I spent about two hours here one afternoon discussing the same thing, and as a result of these discussions, I have decided that we must revise our aspirations to build a light bomber for the Army and switch our tactics to a long-distance reconnaissance or twin-engined observation rather than the Electra converted.[123]

By this point, Lockheed representatives had dispersed to spread the word on their product to the West Coast air stations, Shreveport, Louisiana, and Dayton, Ohio. Observing the outcome back in Washington, Courtlandt Gross, the firm's eastern representative, reported to his brother, "Apparently, the missionary work which Carl [Squier] and you and Hall have been doing on the coast, at Shreveport, and at Dayton has begun to take effect. There has been a good deal of talk in G.H.Q. [General Headquarters] Air Force on the subject of twin-motor multi-place fighters." Courtlandt continued, "The result is that information is now being prepared in Washington on the subject which will be sent back to the various fields for discussion and comment and which will in all probability lead to the ultimate issuance from Dayton of specifications and design competition data for airplanes of this kind." The corporation was working for a "K" contract, or "an outright purchase under the Extraordinary Military Secrets Section K." The "much-coveted section K . . . is of course the apple of the aircraft manufacturers' eye and everybody tries to get a contract under this section," Robert informed Courtlandt. Obviously, Lockheed and the other plane manufacturers needed every bit of information they could obtain from whatever source they could get it—Army, Navy, Kindelberger, Douglas. Proximity to these firms or service branches with information was critical.

While that battle hung in the balance, the company moved forward on another front. Lockheed had proposed a bomber plane to the government based on the Electra. The Czechoslovak government needed airplanes, and Lockheed proposed to sell the Electra bomber to them. Gross had expected the Army and Navy to veto the sale because of their own interest in the plane. When those two services approved the purchase, the Lockheed president feared that "the United States Army considers the plane a flop." This made the foreign possibility more tempting. Gross noted, "If we are going to be flat on our backs around here as a result of getting no contract from our own Government . . . it might be decidedly interesting to be building a military airplane for somebody and getting $125,000." On the other hand, he concluded, "if we are going to get a crack at the Army and right quick, I would be in favor of telling Avia [the Czech purchasing corporation] nothing doing at any price."[124]

The uncertainty cleared up in 1936–37. Lockheed began selling Electras to the Army Air Force despite the fact that General Arnold himself informed Gross's brother that "the chances were better than even that the Army didn't know how to operate the airplanes" it had purchased. The firm also secured a contract to build a stratospheric plane for the Army Air Force, which it delivered in 1937. In the same year Lockheed obtained a contract for the plane that would become the famous P-38 of World War II. The firm reckoned the planes at $200,000 each.[125]

Consolidated Aircraft Corporation came to Southern California two years after the Lockheed firm had been refinanced and therefore retained by Southlanders. That firm, which ultimately became the core property from which the General Dynamics defense conglomerate was built, did not come to Southern California under the identical circumstances that Donald Douglas did, nor did it originate in California as Lockheed had. However, to an equal or greater degree, the story of Consolidated proves the hollowness of the doctrine of natural advantages when applied to the aircraft industry. It also discounts the amenities or strategic location interpretations, not to mention any based on economic determinism. San Diego, just as its larger neighbor, had taken an early interest in aviation. Like Los Angeles, San Diego developed impressively in the twentieth century, but did not feel secure in its growth. And with better reason, because San Diego's economic base was even narrower than that of Los Angeles, and the depth of its insecurity matched its economic problems. The Border City was a perfect example of the metropolitan malaise plaguing California cities. Given San Diego's precocious campaign to capture the Navy, it should be no surprise, therefore, that its efforts to grasp a part of the aircraft industry were also strenuous. As in the case of the other California metropolises, San Diego visualized the aircraft industry as the answer to both its metropolitan anxiety and its industrial lag.

The coming of Consolidated represented the biggest victory for the Harbor of the Sun since its initial success with the Navy Department during the First World War years. Unlike the Douglas or Lockheed cases, in which the motivation for the corporation's move is not entirely clear, the rationale for Consolidated's migration was explicitly and forcefully stated by the corporation president at the dedication of its first San Diego plant in October 1935. Predictably, the booster-oriented *San Diego Union* emphasized the ideal flying conditions of the area in its first-page story, but the fifth-page speech of president and general manager Reuben Fleet stated the case in a more complex manner. Near the end of his list of particulars, and without emphasis, "Major" Fleet explained that the corporation sought "a southern climate unhampered by snow and ice and yet not unbearably hot, with all-year-round flying weather for test flying and flight deliveries." It is incontestable that San Diego possessed these advantages, especially as compared with arctic Buffalo, where Consolidated had been for the previous twelve years. However, so did a number of other cities, including both Los Angeles and Long Beach, which the

Border City had successfully defeated in the competition for the possession of Consolidated.[126] For that matter, so did the San Francisco Bay and Monterey.

Aside from the climatic advantages over the wintry shores of Lake Erie, every other prerequisite on the Major's list was a man-made advantage created by the people of San Diego and frequently by the city government itself in its official corporate capacity. The Major headed his list of locational advantages with the requirement for "a sizable city," an informed decision on his part that again emphasizes the advantages of cities for the development of aircraft manufacture. "For more than five years," Fleet explained, "we carefully surveyed all cities in the United States having more than 100,000 population. We decided finally upon Southern California. In this choice we were aided by the chamber of commerce of Los Angeles which prepared data for our examination." He informed his audience that "this great commercial body sent its assistant manager of industrial relations, E. P. Querl, east periodically to keep us posted on the growth of Southern California," and "twice each year I flew around the country examining localities and municipal airports." Fleet "wanted a site on a publicly-owned and operated airport having a publicly-owned waterfront on a good but not congested harbor, with a seaplane base and ramp adjacent to protected water, in a city large enough to furnish a reasonable supply of labor and materials, in a Southern climate unhampered by snow and ice. . . ."[127]

Several other Border City assets impressed the Consolidated leader. One was the efficiency and expeditious conduct of the San Diego Harbor Board. As explained earlier, San Diegans established this nonpartisan institution in the late 1920s to expedite the development of the city and the harbor by divorcing harbor matters from politics. Basically, the board was a standard progressive device. The businesslike efficiency of the Harbor Board must have assured Fleet that he was dealing with a public body with great power over the area in which he was interested. As a matter of fact, Fleet credited Emil Klicka, "San Diego banker and chairman of the Harbor Commission," with persuading the Consolidated Board of Directors to make the move to the Port of the Palms. It might be pointed out in passing that Klicka operated out of Bank of America headquarters in San Diego, so he was not simply another banker.[128]

Fleet expressed almost equal admiration for the San Diego Chamber of Commerce, which waged a seven-year war to lure Consolidated to the Harbor of the Sun. The Border City Chamber tipped the scale in favor of San Diego after the Los Angeles Chamber had persuaded the aircrafter to come to Southern California. Moreover, Fleet had all but signed with the representatives of the Long Beach-Los Angeles Harbor when the San Diegans intervened with information that changed the corporate mind. The Chamber had something to do with creating other favorable conditions also—in this case the open-shop tenor of Southern California in general and San Diego in particular. Fleet did not mention this asset in his list, but there is little doubt of its importance. Although Consolidated initially decided to move in 1933, it did not do so until 1935; the delay was occasioned in part by the counteroffers made by a furiously competing Buffalo Chamber of Commerce. Moreover, without pointing out cause and effect, the official biography of Reuben Fleet notes that the Major moved the firm to San Diego at a time when labor problems in the

East were becoming worse. In 1934, Consolidated was hit by a strike in Buffalo, and as Fleet described his move, "I picked up 311 selected employees and brought them out to San Diego, paying their moving expenses. Another hundred, having been promised work when they got there, paid their own way. We left all the bad Radicals back there in Buffalo." Obviously, the Major had delayed in order to receive the Buffalo counter-offer and had been finally motivated by the nature of that bid plus the character of the labor difficulties he confronted in that city.[129]

Nor was this the first time he had had these problems. Fleet harbored a long-time dislike of radicals, beginning with his early life in the Puget Sound region. The Major got his nickname from his education at Culver-Stockton Military Academy in Missouri as well as his First World War and National Guard service. The latter had brought him into contact with the Industrial Workers of the World in 1911 in Aberdeen, Washington. There Fleet had been commanded by the governor to mobilize his National Guard unit to counter the supposed menace of the Wobblies. Instead, Fleet asked the sheriff in question to deputize Fleet and his men and let them handle the IWW as civilians. They quite literally did this in classic Pacific Northwest fashion, rounding up IWW members and running them out of town through a gauntlet of men well armed with barrel staves. Shortly thereafter, the National Guard ordered Major Fleet to San Diego for border duty during the upheavals of the Mexican Revolution. That trip whetted Fleet's appetite for the San Diego region, but did nothing to change his mind about Wobblies or radicals, whom he encountered once again in the then quite embittered San Diego area.[130]

The union drive in the aircraft industry hardened the Major's attitudes again. If the manufacturer had left some "bad radicals" in Buffalo, he soon found some more in supposedly union-free San Diego. Like Donald Douglas, the Consolidated president resisted union organization and signed in 1937 only under intense pressure from the government. However, labor problems troubled Fleet sufficiently thereafter to help motivate him to leave the industry. Along with government taxes, which wiped out most of his profits, and the fear that the auto industry was using the war emergency to move into control of aircraft manufacturing, Fleet's dislike for unions convinced him to sell out just before the attack on Pearl Harbor. Obviously, San Diego eventually turned out to have union problems of a rather formidable nature, but no one could quarrel with the open-shop reputation of Southern California at the time when Fleet made the decision to defect from Buffalo.[131]

The proximity of the Naval Air Station complemented the originally favorable labor climate. Consolidated sold its product almost exclusively to the Army and Navy; and in 1933, when that corporation decided to move West, North Island in San Diego possessed both Army and Navy air stations. March Field in Riverside was also relatively close by. Contiguity with the North Island Naval Air Station was especially beneficial because at the time of the transfer, Consolidated specialized in making the famous flying boats. As Fleet, Robert Gross of Lockheed, and others learned to their sorrow, the military services repeatedly changed their minds about aircraft requirements. These decisions required delays, extra expenditures to comply with the alterations, new tests, and other burdensome modifications of the original plans. Thus, a plant location close to military testing and training sites and, therefore, close to the frontiers of rapidly advancing and changing military aeronautical technology and science, was particularly useful to the aircraft manufacturers. In this case, proximity to the corporation's only significant airplane market made a considerable difference.

Although Major Fleet merely mentioned the municipally owned and operated airport as one asset amongst many, San Diegans always attributed crucial significance to this landing field. In fact, they designed their aircraft industry campaign around Lindbergh Field, located in downtown San Diego. Facing the military flying installation across the Harbor of the Sun and the aircraft-carrier turning basin inside it, and flanked on both sides by other service institutions, Lindbergh Field symbolized exactly the San Diego boast that "the navy is integrated into the community more completely here than in any other American port." Lindbergh Field was one of the most important means toward this end of creating a civil-military interface and one of the most significant assets that helped to lure Consolidated to the Mexican border.[132] According to Jack B. Lyman of the San Diego Chamber of Commerce in mid-1927, "Practically every city of any size in the United States is considering the construction of a municipal airport as the paramount issue of the hour." San Diego authorities agreed and launched the project that would eventually materialize into Lindbergh Field. As the *San Diego Magazine* argued, "Nobody is going to build planes where he cannot fly them any more than anybody is going to build ships where he cannot launch them." Unlike other cities "aghast at the cost involved," who "dared" not plan a "complete harbor for air commerce," San Diego went all out, with "preparation, study, and careful planning," initially by no less a person than John Nolen himself. Nolen had put an airport into the 1925 city plan at the insistence of the aviation committee of the Chamber of Commerce.[133]

Thereafter the city raised $650,000 through a bond issue and hired Major T. C. Macaulay, subsequently designated the "Father of San Diego Aviation," to operate the airport. It is perhaps worth noting that the seven-year campaign to lure another major, Reuben Fleet, to the Mexican border began about the same time; and, as majors often do, these two officers knew each other very well. At the dedication of Consolidated's new plant in 1935, Fleet described the other major as "my old friend, Maj. T. C. Macaulay, who was instructing at North Island [Army Air Station] when I learned to fly there in 1917." By another stroke of good fortune, Macaulay was now the general manager of the San Diego Chamber of Commerce; and he and Thomas F. Bomar, head of the Chamber's aviation department, actually handled the final negotiations that brought Consolidated to San Diego instead of to the Los Angeles-Long Beach harbor area. Needless to say, the Major's arrival at the Border City was no simple outcome of geography, economic determinism, climate, or culture. San Diego worked hard to acquire Consolidated and did so by providing everything that the manufacturer would need, right down to an old-boy Army Air Corps pal, who as Chamber of Commerce president could make the offer.[134]

Before the arrival of Consolidated, San Diego had enjoyed some success in attracting other aircrafters or encouraging the ones already there, but compared with the triumphs of Los Angeles, the Border City progress had been slight. In 1928, for example, the promise of the construction of Lindbergh Field had lured Ryan Aeronautical and Prudden-San Diego, but the Depression damaged the industry.

Ryan himself withdrew for a time, and by 1935, San Diego had achieved only modest success. Perhaps that record can be explained by the city's slowness in completing Lindbergh Field. Orville McPherson, executive manager of the Chamber of Commerce, had explained the problem a few years earlier. He noted in 1928 that "San Diego had unrivaled opportunities for the development of the aircraft industry, and for aerial transportation." The city "lacked the big essential, however: a municipal airport. Before we could make a bid for aircraft industries, we had to build an airport." It would appear that McPherson knew exactly what he was talking about. The city did not succeed with Consolidated until Lindbergh Field was "pretty well complete" in 1933. When the Consolidated plant opened in October 1935, the corporation's president could "note with pleasure this week's federal allotment of $583,619 to enlarge and improve Lindbergh field, thus insuring its holding its A-1 rating." The city had made a major commitment to the field and, through its political influence, had acquired federal funds to guarantee the continued development of that facility.[135]

The airport provided a large space for the Consolidated factory, which was the customary arrangement between Southern California cities and their aircraft partners. It was also typical of other aircraft cities such as St. Louis. In that midwestern city, both the Robertson-Curtiss and McDonnell firms had built their planes on municipal land at Lambert Airport. By the same token, almost every airframe factory in the Southland rested on publicly or privately owned airport land. In addition, Consolidated enjoyed access to the seaplane ramp, the municipal harbor, and the airport for testing purposes.[136]

Consolidated also benefited from the services of Cal Tech. As in the case of Douglas Aircraft, these proved crucial. Perhaps two examples will suffice. Fleet's version of the development of JATO (jet assisted takeoff) and therefore of aeronautical jet propulsion differed from that of von Karman. According to the Major, JATO grew out of Consolidated's need to find a method of lifting his flying boats out of the water more efficiently. The takeoff of the flying boats consumed a disproportionately large amount of the plane's fuel and thereby reduced its range. Fleet remembered that he contacted Robert Millikan, who called in von Karman, who in turn summoned his young rocket whiz kids to solve the problem. The resultant disposable rockets provided one solution, and the GALCIT wind tunnel furnished another. Similarly interested in improving the efficiency of his planes, Fleet approved a project by former Douglas partner David R. Davis to develop a more efficient airfoil. Davis worked out the idea mathematically, and the tunnel, at a cost of $40,000, proved to the astonishment of all that the airfoil was 20 percent more efficient. Consolidated exploited this literal windfall in developing its line of airplanes, which eventually fought in the Second World War. Reuben Fleet thought so highly of the GALCIT wind tunnel that relations between Consolidated and Cal Tech became definitely strained when Fleet concluded that Cal Tech discriminated against his company in the distribution of wind tunnel data. In fact, Fleet argued that Cal Tech invariably provided wind tunnel data to his Los Angeles competitors before Consolidated saw the data. Whether this is true is difficult to document, but there is no question that Fleet believed it to be. Nor is there any doubt of the high value placed on the services of CIT scientists by the aircraft pioneers. The boosters had built up that university in order to apply science beneficially to its economic life, and it had certainly done so.[137]

Obviously, Consolidated derived marked man-made advantages in its Southland metropolitan location. The National Advisory Committee for Aeronautics (forerunner of the present National Aeronautics and Space Administration) sought some of the same ones in choosing the San Francisco Bay Area for the location of another important institution. This was the Ames Research Center, the second NACA research laboratory in the United States. As the Second World War approached, members of the National Advisory Committee became increasingly apprehensive that American aeronautical research and development would not keep pace with that of the rapidly rearming powers of the world, especially Germany. The NACA research facilities at Langley, Virginia, could not be expanded sufficiently to accommodate the needs of the immediate bleak future, and the advisory committee began to search for a second site. As might have been expected, this decision generated a considerable amount of interest. It came both from the Virginia congressmen and senators who feared the loss of a part of their local resources and from the other parties who hoped to gain them. For two years the necessity of this new research facility was debated, investigated, promoted, and resisted. Two different commissions of inquiry, which contained such ex-West Coast hands as Admiral John H. Towers, Chief of the Navy's Bureau of Aeronautics, and General H. H. Arnold, head of the Army Air Corps, reported in favor of a West Coast site; and one of them specifically recommended the former dirigible base near Sunnyvale, California, since renamed Moffett Field. This installation had passed to the Army via the complicated deal previously described giving the Navy full possession of North Island, San Diego. Arnold now offered the site to NACA, and the committee of inquiry, of which he was a member, accepted.[138]

The site selection process quickly became political, as cities like San Francisco (which actually sent a retired military officer east to lobby its claims), Los Angeles, San Diego, Sacramento, Chicago, Fort Worth, Indianapolis, Buffalo, Spokane, and even Dismal Swamp, Virginia, battled furiously for the nomination. In addition, eastern aircraft manufacturers and congressmen opposed the selection of the West Coast site, although many eastern newspapers, such as the *New York Times,* favored the West. Eventually, a compromise was worked out that allowed an appropriation for a new NACA research center without specifying a site, provided a large increase for the Langley Field facilities, and left the choice of a site up to a committee. The committee included Charles Lindbergh as chair (who already favored Sunnyvale), Robert H. Hinckley, head of the Civil Aeronautics Administration, Towers, and Arnold. Needless to say, Sunnyvale and its Bay Area backers got the nod.[139]

It seems certain that the final placement of this facility was as political as the process leading up to it, and thus largely fits the pattern of Urban California boosterism. NACA based its decision on a scientific-looking set of six criteria and denied any political motivation in its placement despite the political flap that the selection triggered. However, in the longer run, the location of the Ames Center was determined, not merely influenced, by the prior location of so much of the aircraft industry on the West Coast. In the same negotiations, NACA opted for an eastern airplane-engine research center, eventually placed in Cleveland, for precisely the same reasons: proximity to the rest of the industry. Point four of the negotiations specified that "the site be readily accessible to the aircraft industry on the West Coast." NACA wanted to be "near the big western aircraft companies but not so near that it would be under pressure from industry to divert its attention from basic research to routine test work." Two of the remaining criteria were location on a military base and proximity to a flying field, both of which had been produced by the earlier Bay Area drive to secure the Sunnyvale base. The other three provisions involved assets that many big cities would possess—adequate electrical power, an industrial "center capable of providing labor, supplies, communications and transportation facilities, and other logistical support," and attractive living conditions for employees, with proximity to a university of "recognized standing." In other words, of the three criteria that were unique to the Bay Area and which gave it preference, all were built into the area by its boosters—the aircraft industry, Hamilton Field, Alameda Naval Air Station, and Moffet Field. If one leaves out of consideration one of the criteria (the defensibility against carrier-based air attack by the very kind of instruments Ames was designed to test), then these specifications would seem to have been written for the San Francisco Bay Area, located midway between the airframe centers in Seattle and Los Angeles-San Diego. In the bargaining, the congressmen and senators stalked the halls rounding up votes. Eventually the Langley, Virginia, facility was significantly expanded in what was obviously part of a political bargain.[140]

The official history of the Ames Center affirms the sensitivity of the site selection committee to the problems of national defense and notes that Salt Lake City, a spot obviously less vulnerable to carrier attack, came in second in the site competition. The rejection of this Great Basin locale underscores again the frequent divergence between national defense and city-booster criteria. The Mormon capital possessed all of the qualifications that gave San Francisco Bay the nod, plus that of relative invulnerability to attack from naval air power.[141]

Understandably, such a contingency worried defense planners, concerned for the safety of the plane industry, as the world moved toward a war in which air power was already reaching its apogee. The concentration of 60 percent of the capacity of a critical defense industry in three West Coast sites susceptible to carrier attack and, in the case of San Diego and Los Angeles, to conventional naval shellfire, did not escape the notice of envious cities buried comfortably safe in the nation's heartland. As early as 1938, representatives of interior urban areas began a campaign for what they euphemistically called "decentralization." Obviously Chicago and other cities wanted to capture a piece of the aircraft industry themselves, but just as evidently, their strategic theory did not suffer from the same burden of geographic illogic that their West Coast brethren labored under. For once, in the Midwest the imperatives of geography, city building, and national defense marched in lockstep and required no elaborate rationalization.

This situation was not without its irony. The air power advocates of the Army and Navy had spent considerable energy demonstrating the potency of the air weapon by running off numerous mock air attacks in the Los Angeles and San Francisco areas. The metropolitan media duly registered these "victories." For example, on May 11, 1937, the *Los Angeles Times* noted the results of "the most extensive air maneuvers in history," by quoting "high-ranking Air Corps officers" who maintained "that Los Angeles is extremely vulnerable to attack from the air." The paper went on to relate that "three squadrons of bombardment aircraft took off from three points within 180 miles of Los Angeles and within a half hour had theoretically destroyed the city's largest aircraft factory." The same paper had spent a good part of April and May bombarding its urban readers with similar warnings. The next year the Army Air Force sallied forth to drive the point home to the cities of the East Coast. By 1938, even the *San Diego Union* admitted that "virtually every major airplane factory now supplying combat planes to the army and navy is located on the Atlantic and Pacific coasts, where they are highly vulnerable to destruction by bombers unleashed by hostile aircraft carriers." The Border City booster medium went on to inform its readers that the "army and navy war plans divisions have perfected secret plans for concentrating airplane factories in the Midwest where they would be safe from aerial bombardment." Therefore, it should not have been surprising that interior cities volunteered to strengthen the national defense by relieving Los Angeles and San Diego of a part of the aircraft industry under this proposed deconcentration away from exposed coastal sites.[142]

Congressman Ralph E. Church of Chicago led the charge. He contended that "the fact that we in Illinois may benefit by the location of airplane factories in our state is only incidental to the all-important fact in my mind that the country as a whole will benefit by having a stronger national defense." As part of his campaign, Church argued for the location of a research laboratory (a reference to the argument over the placement of what became the Ames Center) in the "interior" in order to facilitate the migration of the airframe manufacturers away from their vulnerable coastal sites. In a statement that revealed his thorough understanding of the drive of Urban California for the Ames Aeronautical Laboratory, Church argued that "the mere location of reserach facilities inland would itself give encouragement to the development of aviation industries in the interior." The *Chicago Tribune* and its isolationist publisher, Colonel Robert McCormick, came to the congressman's aid, as did the Chicago Association of Commerce and the automotive industry. For a time, as Consolidated president Reuben Fleet had foreseen, the automotive industry seemed poised to move into the manufacture of both airframes and airplane parts. This threatened the manufacturers of both these products and therefore jeopardized both the airframe manufacturers and subcontracting firms which had grown up around the airframe business.[143]

Urban Southland spokesmen fought back with refutations of the charge that the airplane industry was primitive and would have to be taken over by the automotive industry. They also hardened their climatic determinism to justify the "expansion of these [airframe] plants where they are" instead of moving them to the interior, which the Los Angeles Chamber of Commerce said "gives recognition of the incomparable natural advantages of the area for that industry." Airframe manufacturing did greatly expand in the Southland; but in the long run, the Chicago congressmen proved correct, as the outbreak of hostilities brought exactly the kind of decentralization for which the competitors of Urban Southern California had contended.[144]

Both to minimize the possibility of attack and to escape the labor and housing shortages that the defense buildup created in the existing aircraft production centers, government planners dispersed the industry to Wichita, Chicago, Louisville, Oklahoma City, Columbus (Ohio), Dallas, Omaha, Kansas City, and Tulsa. At war's end, many of these plants closed down, but eventually the interior cities had their way and gained a greater share in the industry.[145]

Finally, as if to add insult to injury, the Ames Research Center, which NACA had insisted on putting on a Bay Area site close to the San Andreas Fault and resting upon slowly subsiding land, ended up housing research that could have been done better in a Southland location. Despite the approach of a war that had forced the creation of the Ames Center, its founders insisted that it would be devoted to pure research and not be immersed in the everyday practical research of the aircraft companies. Thus it was located between Los Angeles and Seattle. However, the coming of the war reoriented the priorities of the laboratory from basic research to the "short-range airplane-development problems" of the airframe industry from which NACA had deliberately sought remoteness. Moreover, once the war commenced, the Ames Research Center shared the vulnerability to air attack of the airframe industry itself. Therefore, we are entitled to doubt the original non-political definition of the lab's rationale.[146]

Many years ago, geographer William C. Cunningham wrote the definitive study of the location of manufacturing in the aircraft industry. This social scientist's study concluded with what was essentially an historian's conclusion: namely, that the concentration of this industry occurred through a very complex process. No deterministic forces—economic, cultural, climatic, geographic, or modernizing—determined this outcome.

> In summary, the location of the aircraft industry is not the product of a single factor nor a group of a few locating factors. A complex of elements, scientific and otherwise, accounts for its present distribution [1951]. The element of chance, such nonscientific items as the home town of the inventor or promoter, the availability of early financial backing or suitable buildings, has determined the location of many companies. Industrial inertia proves effective in maintaining the original pattern. On the other hand, large units of the industry, ostensibly, have consciously sought and scientifically selected the sites considered best for the production of airframes, engines, or propellers; the elements considered have necessarily been different for each.[147]

Cunningham might have mentioned in conclusion, as he did earlier in his book, that "new and rapidly growing cities such as Detroit and Los Angeles which welcomed the new industry more heartily than did older conservative cities, became aircraft centers."[148]

Basically, this model investigation concludes that any number of influences or combinations of factors determined the location of the aircraft industry, including airframes, which came to concentrate so heavily on the West Coast. None of the traditional factors that determined industrial location in other businesses stood out in molding the configuration of the aircraft industry. Everything from research facilities, to government orders, labor costs, materials, capital, climate, and geography is mentioned, but none is given definite priority. The corporate histories and other sources of the industry provide equally pluralistic interpretations. However, this multiplicity still does not explain how an industry that had a very high degree of locational choice and which moved about with less restraint than other businesses came to concentrate so heavily in Southern California. To repeat an earlier question of this inquiry, why did an industry that had seemingly maximum choice in location fail to exercise it?

One part of the answer to that query is that the Southern California firms turned out to be better competitors and aggregated a major portion of the industry in the Urban Southland. A second part of the answer lies in the greater diversity of Southern California assets. If no one aspect of the economics of aircraft production can explain the victory of the Angelenos and San Diegans, then the answer must lie in the mix of advantages that those towns possessed. Various other metropolises claimed one or even several of the superiorities needed to gain the edge, but none possessed the variety of assets that the metropolitan Southland did. For example, both the New York and San Francisco metropolitan areas held large reservoirs of capital and labor, skilled and unskilled. However, neither place could boast of as good a climate as Los Angeles and San Diego, though the degree of difference between the Urban Southland and "The City" is often exaggerated. Phoenix, Tucson, Albuquerque, and El Paso enjoyed climatic and geographic advantages, but did not have the capital, labor, or scientific resources of Southern California. Boston could boast of a great technological institution in MIT, but not about its climate nor even its receptivity to new economic activity. Many cities could, perhaps, have mobilized public opinion behind a novel economic entity, but could not have supplied the open spaces for testing that the industry required. Buffalo might have a skilled labor force and even an aviation tradition, but it also had active unions (as did San Francisco, New York, and Chicago), a Siberian winter, and a procrastinating business leadership. San Antonio enjoyed proximity to Army flying fields, as Pensacola did to Navy ones, but neither could point to the kind of labor, financial, or other resources that the Southland claimed. Finally, the kind of leadership that the City of the Angels and San Diego benefitted from was probably their most important advantage.

Not every American city could boast of that quality. By 1920, many American urban centers had lost the drive that had formerly characterized them, and as Frostbelt urban energy waned, that of the Sunbelt metropolises waxed. For example, one southwestern city after another launched development campaigns from the 1920s on. None, however, fought more consistently for growth than did Los Angeles and San Diego; and it was this battle that, more than any other single factor, determined the location of the aircraft industry in Southern California. These twentieth-century city builders may not be as famous as Robert Moses of New York, or Baron Haussmann, who rebuilt Paris, or the planners of the Vienna Ringstrasse. Still, they molded their own cities just as fatefully, if not as majestically, and, almost certainly, with even greater long-term effect. For years before and after the aircraft industry became a part of the massive fortress within the Great Wall of California, the boosters had been rather systematically laying the foundation for further growth in general and for the development of the airframe industry in particular.

If the industry required a labor force, the boosters brought a large population to the South and underwrote its permanence and aggrandizement with their water engineering. If the industry needed airports, Long Beach, San Diego, Santa Monica, and Los Angeles accommodated them. If the plane makers desperately lacked capital, Security Pacific, Brashears, or some private Southland investor provided it when San Francisco or New York City would not. If the industry profited from its proximity to several of the foremost centers of military aviation technology, the boosters had earlier secured these assets. If Douglas, Lockheed, North American, Consolidated, Vultee, and Ryan wanted a cheap and docile labor force, their booster friends did their best to develop and prolong its presence. If the airframe producers needed wide-open spaces for testing, amenities to secure their executives, and a dry climate for open-air assembly, it was the representatives of the Los Angeles, San Diego, and Burbank chambers of commerce who camped on their doorstep, persistently advertising their own section over all the others that might have qualified. If the increasingly technological character of the aeronautical industry demanded easy and ever-growing access to both the material and intellectual resources of the scientific community, the Southland Haussmanns would create Throop Institute de novo into a scientific wonder, as they would later construct the University of California at San Diego. CIT would eventually provide its own testing facilities and then be called upon to manage both the Southern California Cooperative Wind Tunnel and the Jet Propulsion Laboratory, and the boosters would also supply a public counterpart in the form of the Ames Research Center in Northern California. If a relatively new technology of transportation needed an air-minded public, that too could be provided. Finally, if an industry largely dependent upon the government for a market cried out for political influence (and who can doubt that it did?), urban politicians from the stature of United States senators down to the city planning commissions stood ready to mobilize it.

It takes no stretch of the imagination to convince American historians that the megamilitary structure around a city like Charleston, South Carolina, derives from the city-building ambitions of that area and the political influence of their servants like Pitchfork Ben Tillman and Mendel Rivers. It should take no greater intellectual gymnastics to understand that a defense industry like aircraft could share the same fate. After all, in 1926 Angelenos had fatefully advertised their conviction that "there is going to be a Detroit of the aircraft industry. It ought to be here in Los Angeles." In 1941, it was.[149]

CHAPTER 5

"Mars Has a Hand in Your Pocket": Urban California in the Second Great War

The Japanese assault on Pearl Harbor brought a temporary cessation of the Darwinian competition amongst California cities. Public officials, media representatives, civic personnel, labor leaders, and politicians nearly unanimously called for a community effort on behalf of national defense. The time for petty bickering over the spoils of urban imperialism had passed and the time for unity had come. California civic leaders reiterated this theme frequently in the next four years and, to an extent, they acted upon it. Immediately after December 7, 1941, the war crowded other matters off the front page. First came the staggering and disheartening news of repeated Allied defeats in the Pacific, followed by a series of regulations which called upon citizens to give up everything from the Rose Bowl to street lighting to fast driving, and, finally, came the furor over Japanese relocation.

These events sufficed to keep down the urban competition through the first half of 1942, but thereafter the old habits of the Imperial City reappeared, especially in the most successful of the breed, Los Angeles. As late as August 1944, Mayor Fletcher Bowron continued to call for unity, either in the face of Axis resistance or against the many eastern urban competitors for military wealth. At a conference of mayors in Los Angeles, the civic reformer claimed that the "Barrier of the Tehachapi in California" had "been lowered perceptibly" and called for coast-wide solidarity in the face of eastern aggression:

> If we are to help with the war . . . and if we are to help win the peace, and if we on the Pacific Coast are to gather to ourselves any of the particular advantages that are to accrue, we must stand together. . . . We must not worry, if a contract comes to the coast, whether it goes to Seattle or Portland or San Francisco or San Diego. If we had a little more of that spirit of the idea that this coast must be considered as [one] against the concentration of political interests in the East Coast, and those Texas politicians, who are just about running the country, we would get a little bit farther along.[1]

San Francisco's Angelo Rossi answered in the same manner, although perhaps a bit more disingenuously, that "so far as San Francisco is concerned there never was any rivalry, nor was there any Tehachapi barrier, and I am glad to hear Mayor Bowron say that they have buried the hatchet down here."[2] He followed that mixed metaphor by noting that "since Mayor Bowron became mayor of Los Angeles, there has been a closer spirit of friendship than prevailed before that."[3] Perhaps this was true, but the new condition of amity still left a lot of room for friendly competition and some not so friendly. It also allowed lots of opportunities for using the national emergency on behalf of local improvements. John Anson Ford, Los Angeles County supervisor and possibly the most knowledgeable person in that area on the subject of government and politics, informed a radio audience of this fact well before the outbreak of hostilities. After explaining the difficulty in drawing the line between public and private interests, he noted that "the accident of a national defense emergency is being employed, in the opinion of at least one of my colleagues, to unjustifiably enrich the property values of private interests." And, as he ruefully admitted, this was probably only the beginning. "It may be that here and there throughout the county, private interests will get away with murder . . . in securing federal funds for projects that really cannot justly qualify."[4] However, city leaders had an incurable habit of thinking that quite a few matters qualified.

The imperial flame burned especially brightly in Los Angeles. Both San Francisco and San Diego looked out for their interests, but they seemed bent to the pavements beneath the storm of change brought on by the conflict. The City of the Angels flew comfortably above it and on toward its long-term goals. Bowron summed up the Los Angeles attitude in a Memorial Day ceremony in 1944. Looking at the mechanized wilderness of modern warfare where "distance and space are annihilated, death rains from the skies and comes up out of the seas and breathes upon the air," the mayor found the westering spirit still alive and well. "Our young men" who faced the awesome weaponry of twentieth-century combat "prove a thousand fold that the courage and daring and ingenuity and gay pioneer spirit that founded these United States is very much alive today."[5] This description was a fairly exact metaphor for Los Angeles itself, which, like its frontier ancestors, fought tooth and nail for its share of the wealth and yet called in the government to aid its urban individualism whenever necessary.

Contract allocation was one such area and one that documents most thoroughly the Darwinian continuities between the prewar and war periods. Although the City of the Angels abounded with economic theorists who distrusted the influence and power of the national government in general and that of social planners in particular, the Los Angeles Chamber of Commerce moved swiftly to exploit the government's martial buildup. From mid-1940 onward, while the skies poured death onto Europe, Africa, and Asia, it rained war contracts in the United States; and Los Angeles leaders insured that much of this downpour would irrigate the arid metropolitan Southland.

American cities have not always responded with the same alacrity to the opportunities of government programs, even in the era of big government. For example, with the passage of the National Housing Act of 1949, cities like Detroit and New Haven swiftly took advantage of government subsidies, while many others, like Dallas, did not.[6] World War II proved no exception. San Diego did not establish a Washington office to help its businessmen bid on contracts until April 1943.[7] Los Angeles, by contrast, had a man in Washington from early on, but expanded its constituency service in June 1943 to establish a special branch for dealing with defense contracts.[8] In a series of articles reprinted in 1941 in *Southern California Business,* Dr. Wilford J. King of New York University argued for financing the war by taxes instead of by loans or inflation and for taxes on spending and consumption rather than on investment, corporate incomes, and excess profits. The Southern California journal entitled the article "Mars Has a Hand in Your Pocket." With the opening of Los Angeles's new war contract service several weeks later, the condition became mutual.[9]

There were many other city hands in the martial pocket at this time, but those of Los Angeles must have been among the most active. Although Angeleno spokesmen habitually complained of federal neglect during the war, to the historical observer it would appear that the metropolitan hand was indeed quicker than the martial eye. "The Los Angeles Plan," as that aid came to be called, consisted of a record-keeping service that informed the Chamber of Commerce of the plants among the 6000 Los Angeles factories that could be converted to war production; it maintained contact with the Defense Distribution Service to keep that government agency informed of potential defense contractors in the area; it provided Chamber of Commerce liaison with other government agencies in Washington to keep abreast of military needs their constituents might meet; and it supplied Chamber of Commerce representation for Southland manufacturers in their dealings with Washington. As would be the case again, this program turned out to be a model for other metropolitan communities battling for defense work.[10] At that point, the government was publicizing its defense opportunities by running "defense exhibit" trains to "several cities" to demonstrate the same opportunities that Los Angeles had won under its own plan. The Angeleno plan put the idea on a permanent basis and eliminated the need for a railroad trip there.

Long Beach soon followed suit. The Chamber of Commerce there called a mass meeting of businessmen that "resulted in the incorporation of the Associated Defense Industries of Long Beach" (ADI), which required 3 percent of all contract monies secured by their services. They also moved to establish a second association, the Long Beach Manufacturers, Inc., limited to members of the ADI, to gain prime contracts, which would then be distributed among its adherents.[11]

San Diego created its own comparable organization in April of 1943, again by Chamber of Commerce initiative, with a budget of $240,000 to finance offices in both the national and state capitals. In a frank admission of the attempt to exploit the needs of national defense on behalf of urban industrial development, the booster *San Diego Union* wrote that the program was designed to "speed the city's war effort and launch a comprehensive program of economic and industrial development." Acutely aware that its northern rival had maintained such liaison "for many years," San Diegans hoped to catch Los Angeles by imitating it.[12]

The plans succeeded very well; in fact, too well. By the end of 1942 Los Angeles had been designated the "No. 1 critical labor shortage area" in the country by the War Manpower Commission, and local leaders began to worry about a loss of contracts due to the inadequate work force.[13]

This fear did not materialize for another year, but by the end of 1943 the problem had become real. Both Los Angeles and San Diego spokesmen felt that their areas stood to lose contracts due to labor shortages, and, as usual, Los Angeles took the offensive. In late November, a Hollywood-style sham battle complete with maneuvers took place in the Los Angeles Coliseum. Resounding with "blazing gun fire and detonations of ground mines," its purpose was to kick off the crusade for more war workers. Outside, ringing the stadium, would be "static displays of planes, tanks, big guns and other equipment," some of it made in L.A. After this flamboyant simulation, volunteers coordinated by city, county, Chamber of Commerce, U.S., and civil defense authorities would hit the streets for a house-to-house campaign for war workers. In addition, the unemployment rolls would be checked for idle hands; schools would be urged to allow released time for student workers (this was widely done) and to produce war goods in school shops; the government was petitioned to release key supervisorial personnel for war production; non-defense industries were given manpower caps which they could not exceed; absenteeism was to be investigated; moonlighting and overtime were to be encouraged; and the forty-eight-hour week was to be suspended for those helping to increase the defense worker pool. By April 1944, the effort to recruit more workers had apparently failed because Los Angeles had been again designated a "No. 1 Critical Labor Shortage Area," and within such areas "the further letting of contracts has been greatly curtailed."

This policy fell especially hard on small businesses of the Southland, and there were a large number of these, many of whom had been heavily pressured by the government to enter war production in the first place.[14] San Diego also lost contracts due to the manpower situation.[15] As the war entered its final year, W. C. Mullendore, Los Angeles Chamber of Commerce president, was launching a campaign to defend these small business interests in their defense work.[16]

Yet despite the losses to small firms, large concerns in Southern California continued to enjoy the miracles of defense spending. In March 1945, the area had so many contracts that it could not find enough workers to fulfill them. Consolidated alone lacked 4000 men to keep up its pace of production, and both jet production at Ryan Aeronautical Company and in Los Angeles and rocket production around Pasadena suffered from the labor shortage. Despite the labor shortfall, the government did not make good on its threat to redirect the contracts to competing cities and regions. Quite literally, the Southland metropolis had more defense contracts than it knew what to do with.[17]

The martial metropolises also hoped to perfect their transportation networks by linking them to the war. San Diego and San Francisco had more interest in highways than did Los Angeles, but all three looked to the defense emergency to aid their airport schemes. San Francisco had long been interested in good roads to the Redwood Empire, a resort area to the north, and joined with other members of the Redwood Empire Association to get "defense" highways built to this tourist area. It was not clear whether these roads would help repel a Japanese invasion or allow supplies and reinforcements to relieve the beleaguered defenders of a possible siege of Portland or Seattle, but Bay Area members of the association wanted the roads just the same. In fact, this tourist organization even sponsored a Western States Defense Highway Conference to be held at the Palace Hotel in San Francisco in January 1941.[18] On another occasion San Francisco supervisor Adolphe Uhl suggested that the currently unprofitable Golden Gate Bridge be unloaded on the federal government as "part of the Defense Highway System." Upon being informed that this shift would be illegal, Uhl tried to persuade the government to maintain the bridge, and

The Urban Martial Carpet: World War II

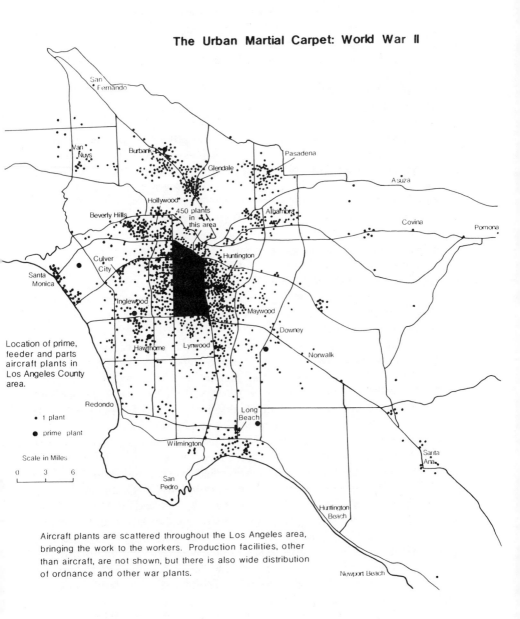

450 plants in this area

Location of prime, feeder and parts aircraft plants in Los Angeles County area.

- 1 plant
- prime plant

Scale in Miles

0   3   6

Aircraft plants are scattered throughout the Los Angeles area, bringing the work to the workers. Production facilities, other than aircraft, are not shown, but there is also wide distribution of ordnance and other war plants.

finally the Board of Supervisors opened a campaign to get the national government to pay tolls for using it.[19]

In the meantime "The City" moved to refresh its ties with Salt Lake City. In September 1943, the Downtown Association presented a check for $150,000 to the secretary of the Salt Lake City Chamber of Commerce as California's contribution to the "Victory Highway," which would run from Salt Lake City to San Francisco. The secretary said precious little about defense, but he did stress the fact that San Francisco had lost out in the competition for Salt Lake City business in the last fifteen years. That loss was largely because it had not been as energetic in courting the Mormon capital as had Los Angeles, whose Chamber of Commerce actually maintained a branch office in Salt Lake City! Guy P. Blackman spoke of defense against the loss of the spoils of war, rather than of protection from the Japanese. "We are in a position where we must cooperate in preserving what the war has forced upon us," noted the Utah spokesman a full two years before the war ended. "Utah will provide the raw materials. She looks to the Pacific Coast to process those materials into the finished product."[20]

Bay Area spokesmen, like the *San Francisco Chronicle,* argued for federal improvement of one-fifth of the state's bridges, better access roads "to military reservations like the Benicia arsenal, Fort Ord, Hamilton Field, the Sacramento air depot, and the San Francisco forts," and for the reconstruction of sub-par state roads that were needed for defense.[21] Why the state had not maintained proper access roads to military installations as it would have for other businesses is unknown, but there was at least a certain national interest rationale for such projects, along with the booster one.

There was much less rationale, if any, for two other rather idiosyncratic San Francisco projects, a second Bay crossing and the Reber Plan. For years, San Francisco had tried to overcome its geographic isolation on the San Francisco Peninsula by bridges, railroad schemes, and other means; and the looming war emergency presented another means to do so, in this case by a third bridge. Even before the war broke out, San Franciscans tried to tie the possibility of air attack to a third bay crossing. Illustrative of the masterful way in which these development projects were intertwined and reciprocally reinforcing, the Board of Supervisors urged Congress to construct the bridge because San Francisco had so many military facilities that it would undoubtedly be a likely target of enemy attack by air. (Of course, Bay Area builders had helped put the installations there in the first place.) Since the city possessed only two bridges leading out of the city that could be used to evacuate after an enemy onslaught, and those structures might have been disabled by air attack, the city needed another avenue of escape. With the bridges out, refugees had only the highways down the peninsula on which to flee, and supposedly those roads would not be enough. A third bay crossing from Hunter's Point to Bay Farm Island South of Alameda would alleviate this threat.

In proposing the bridge, Congressman Richard J. Welch emphasized the "great importance of the proposed bridge to the security and development of San Francisco."[22] This scheme had more to do with development than security, since a new bridge would be as vulnerable to air attack as the Golden Gate and Bay bridges and, what is worse, might be hit while refugees were actually escaping on it. The peninsula represented an altogether superior route, which could not be destroyed or closed by any military technology available in the Second World War.[23]

This idea would resurface after the war. However, in the meantime it seems to have been subsumed under the more comprehensive Reber Plan, or the San Francisco Bay Project. The proposed low-level bridge was apparently a part of the Reber Plan introduced to the Board of Supervisors in 1941. It would have transformed San Francisco and San Pablo bays into a kind of military-industrial park. Among other things, this environmental reorganization would have created, through reclamation, dredging, and damming, two land crossings of the bays; large amounts of military, industrial, and agricultural land; a new naval base; monstrous freeway causeways into the city; an entirely new East Bay waterfront; and the long-coveted direct transcontinental railroad link for San Francisco. And all at federal expense! Not only would this plan provide these assets, but it would supply an escape route invulnerable to bombing in case the city had to be evacuated. As the *Western Construction News,* an organ of the San Francisco Junior Chamber of Commerce, described the project, it would "immeasurably strengthen the military defense of the Bay Region and provide facilities which would make the area the industrial center of the Pacific Coast." The *News* maintained that the "co-creator," John Reber of San Francisco, conceived the project "as a means of providing better military and naval and air force facilities." Still, they admitted that the scheme opened "wide possibilities for future industrial, agricultural, residential, and recreational development, as well as possible solutions to current water supply, flood control and transportation problems."[24]

San Franciscans would return to this massive $120 million plan after the war, although they failed to implement it. Nonetheless, as a project of urban transformation it was breathtaking, fully justifying the remarks of Supervisor Jesse Colman that it "was the most fascinating thing to which he had ever listened."[25] It was also unique in American urban experience and that of western Europe as well. Metropolitan in scope, it encompassed both urban and rural landscapes and contained something for everyone, or nearly everyone. The Navy would get a new naval base, a modern submarine base, and a torpedo boat base. The Army Corps would receive new flying fields with underground hangars. San Francisco would acquire its escape route and, not incidentally, train tracks across the bay. Marin County would gain fresh land for development; the East Bay would secure new harbors; and the cities would get an inexhaustible water supply in the two freshwater lakes. Agricultural interests would profit from the creation of new irrigable land from the marshes bordering the bays and water for irrigation upstream. Residential areas would open to prospective home owners, who could play in the waters of the freshwater lakes as well. Flood control would ensue inevitably from all of this redevelopment by providing a huge reservoir for mountain water runoff. Several of the hills in the area would disappear into the various fill schemes and so would much of Richardson's Bay and smaller inlets, but the engineers thought the whole idea feasible, whatever the effect on the beauty of the Bay Area.

Perhaps the most astonishing part of this proposal was the new Grand Central Terminal, which would have been in what is now the bay between Yerba Buena Island and the Oakland shore. Several cities around the nation possessed central stations, but nothing compared with that proposed for the middle of San Francisco Bay. It would have brought together in one place not only the railroads but also the local surface transit, ship terminals, and overland bus lines, with a commercial airport adjacent, capable of "handling both land planes and sea planes."[26] This station would be truly grand, as was the project proposal in which it came. Perhaps the cumulative effect of the career of Robert Moses transformed an American city more than this one would have, but no other single scheme in American planning history can compare with the Reber Plan in scope and imagination. It clearly dwarfs the better known but equally abortive Burnham Plan for San Francisco of 1906.[27] It also dwarfs some of the better known European grand plans of renovation, including the Haussmann reconstruction of central Paris and the Vienna Ringstrasse.

Unfortunately for the Bay Area city builders, the plan was too broad and imaginative, particularly for San Francisco's neighbors. Although the media reported that the plan was gaining adherents into the first half of 1942, Oakland, Vallejo, and the United States Navy were not among them. The Board of Supervisors passed a resolution and began discussing the matter in April, but opposition surfaced almost immediately. When an Oakland representative suggested to the Board of Supervisors that the massive works could not be completed in time to contribute to the present war, Supervisor and Labor spokesman Dewey Mead answered that it was true that "the proposed project could not have any material effect on the present war, but he was thoroughly convinced, although he hoped he was wrong, 'that this will not be the last war.'"[28] The Board of Supervisors admitted that this project would be considered a "local improvement," but that the war made the military facilities of the plan imperative and therefore gave the project national importance. That was why the sponsors thought the federal government should pick up the tab.

Regardless of who paid, interests and communities down the peninsula, such as Redwood City, South San Francisco, and San Mateo County, and those east and north, such as Oakland, the East Bay salt gatherers, the commandant at Mare Island, and the Navy itself, objected. The southern communities feared the "improvement" would ruin their beaches by preventing the flow of sand from the Central Valley rivers and feared the blocking of access for south bay shipping, the loss of the tidal scouring action of the Sloughs, and so forth. Oakland and Vallejo would have to detour their shipping through locks, and Mare Island would possibly have to tolerate the creation of the south bay naval base and Navy yard they had long opposed. Collectively, this opposition influenced members of the Board of Supervisors as well.[29] Jesse Colman opted out when the Navy opposed the plan; Supervisor Gerald O'Gara cautioned that "The City" should move only in concert with its East Bay neighbors; and two other supervisors refused to join their colleagues in recommending a congressional investigation of the project. The Board adopted the recommendation anyway by a vote of seven to four, but the war, like the earthquake before it, postponed a comprehensive replanning scheme of great magnitude.[30]

If San Francisco thought that the road to victory led through the Redwood Empire or across the bay and over to Salt Lake City, San Diego believed that it ran to Riverside and to the Imperial Valley. San Diego builders had worked away at this latter scheme for many years, first promoting its own railway to the valley and then turning to highways when the railroad proved inadequate. The motor road over the mountains to the Imperial Valley needed considerable work to eliminate curves and grades, and in 1943 the Chamber of Commerce revived the project as a "low elevation highway" now "badly needed by the military."[31] The improvement of the highway to Riverside, U.S. Route 395, which ran from the Canadian to the Mexican border, was needed as a backup highway in case flooding washed out the more heavily used Route 101. "This would present a serious situation in case of a military emergency," noted highway booster Frank G. Forward of the Chamber of Commerce.[32] While these ideas awaited the passage of federal highway acts, San Diego gained numerous highway windfalls by virtue of its role as a defense center. "Because of the strategic importance of local establishments, the [federal] government has spent huge sums in access highways here," explained Arthur Hayler, California district traffic engineer, "giving San Diego a major part of new construction in the state at a time when only the most essential projects are being undertaken."[33] The San Diego founders of the metropolitan-military complex had certainly laid its foundations well. Once the bases and factories were acquired, the government had to build the infrastructure to service them.

Highways and railroads were crucial to development, but each city looked to the future. The war taught them that the airplane would be equal to even the hyperbole of the boosters. Aircraft spread havoc in enemy cities, shipped the sick and wounded home in record time, shuttled servicemen and goods across continents, and bore hurried bureaucrats to Washington to hear the latest government excuse or to the West to listen to the civic leaders' most recent grievance. Urban California had placed airport modernization on the development agenda long before these demonstrations of the practicality of air transportation, but the war brought the item to the top of the list. Each of the cities sensed that a new era in transportation would open up in the wake of the war, and each looked back to the myriad stimulating influences that had accompanied previous American transportation revolutions. Not Los Angeles, San Francisco, nor San Diego intended to miss out on any of them.

Notwithstanding these good intentions, Los Angeles lagged behind its Darwinian competitors. Both San Francisco and San Diego gained from military construction that added significantly to their airports during the war. Lindbergh Field in San Diego was largely rebuilt in 1944, and San Francisco's airport received similar treatment. The Bay City did not get this aid without a struggle, however. San Francisco had created a large addition to Yerba Buena Island, called Treasure Island, in the late 1930s, using Bay fill dredged from Yerba Buena Shoals next to the island. This new land was developed to house the World's Fair of 1939; and after its close, the city intended to put an airport on the site, or at least a downtown air terminal. The government had helped to build the island by providing $5,587,830 in Works Progress Administration monies; and when war loomed ahead, the Navy asked to use the island for a naval station. In early 1941, the Navy and city entered into an agreement that bound the Navy to improve the island for an airport in return for using it "under the National Defense program." By this agreement the Navy sponsored a Works Progress Administration project of $1,680,000, of which $400,000 was spent to "improve the field."[34]

Thereafter, the Navy informed the city that it could not "develop the island, with permanent improvements for its own purposes unless it held title." The city still wanted to get an airport from the transaction and refused to grant title, whereupon the Navy brought condemnation proceedings in April of 1942. San Francisco officials refused to grant title unless compensated by several millions to be expended by the services in the improvement of its other airport, Mills Field [today's San Francisco International Airport] in San Mateo. Although this has generally been portrayed as a painless proceeding, the Navy refused point-blank to provide either the money or its equivalent in services to the San Francisco landing field, claiming that the government had paid the city by the PWA and WPA funds already invested in the island. Mayor Angelo Rossi answered that the government could, by that logic, claim title to any of the hundreds of public works built by these two agencies all over the country.

Eventually San Francisco prevailed, in this case scoring a double victory. The Navy built a naval station on Treasure Island, which could not have been used for a modern airport anyway, and, as compensation for the city's $7,874,000 investment in the island, pumped several millions of dollars into the airport in San Mateo County.[35] Although the island could have been used for purposes other than airport development, it is completely isolated from San Francisco proper by a large expanse of water and probably would not have been very useful to it. "The City" drove a hard bargain.

Los Angeles did not exploit the war so adroitly. Before the outbreak of that conflict, its electorate voted $3.5 million to improve Mines Field. Although this sum would have sufficed at 1941 prices, the city could not "secure a sufficiently high priority rating during the period of the emergency long before the entry of this country into the war." The Civil Aeronautics Administration "advised" Mayor Bowron in early 1943 that it had "ample funds" to extend the runways of the airport if "we could get the nod from either the Army or Navy indicating that our airport would be valuable for their operations during the war." Despite technical data from Pan American Airways showing that the city's eighty-mile greater distance to Honolulu was more than made up for by other favorable flying conditions, the services would not reroute military traffic through the Southland metropolis in order to give the City of the Angels fresh leverage to secure government funds to build this booster project.[36]

Unable to spend its own monies, get fresh funds from the federal government, or divert the flow of military traffic away from San Francisco, Mayor Bowron accused the services of bias against his area. The city's bad luck had been due "to the attitude of key Army and Navy and other governmental officials," lamented the mayor. "I understand that many millions of dollars have been expended by the government for the lengthening of runways and other improvements to municipally owned airfields in Washington and Oregon and much improvement work has been done in the vicinity of the San Francisco Bay region," he stormed.[37]

The uproar did not move Washington, where that condition was hardly in short supply anyway, so Bowron and other Angelenos continued to feel aggrieved. This supposed snub made them doubly determined to protect any military installations that they already possessed or to gain what someone else did. San Diego and San Francisco seemed less vigilant in this regard, perhaps because they already had an ample supply of bases, barracks, headquarters, and factories. Well into the postwar period, however, Los Angeles leaders sounded the note of persecution. Nowhere did the San Francisco "advantage" in federal patronage seem more galling than in the procurement of federal offices. Angelenos felt outraged that they had to travel up to San Francisco to carry on business with the federal government. As a premier arsenal of democracy, Los Angeles residents wished to transact their defense business at home instead of having to make a demeaning trip to the rival Bay Area to do so. "I respectfully submit," wrote Mayor Bowron to the chairman of the War Production Board, "that on the basis of war industry production, Southern California is entitled to the regional office of the War Production Board and that such offices should be located in Los Angeles, rather than in San Francisco." "The City" was not centrally located and produced fewer war products, he argued.[38]

The mayor did not explain why he thought that isolated Los Angeles was more centrally located to do bureaucratic defense work for the West. Nor did San Diego's virtually identical location prevent him from seeking some of that city's martial assets. Like the Light Brigade, the mayor saw enemies to both the right and left of him; and a month after his unsuccessful assault on the City of St. Francis, he charged into action against San Diego. "You are authorized to represent the City of Los Angeles," Bowron instructed Morgan Adams, the Los Angeles representative in the District of Columbia, "urging the Secretary of the Navy to move the headquarters of the Commandant of the Eleventh Naval District from San Diego to Los Angeles." "Remind him that Los Angeles is the center of the third largest metropolitan area in America," he fumed, "and that we feel that the importance of this immediate area has not been fully appreciated at Washington."[39]

The Port of the Palms would undoubtedly have considered this outburst a sneak attack. It certainly came at a curious time because the mayor was simultaneously complaining about the vulnerability of the area to attack from the Japanese, as opposed to his California rivals. "We may expect an enemy assault at any time in the Los Angeles metropolitan area," he informed the City Council in June 1942. Worse still, he noted in August, "representatives of the aircraft industry particularly feel that their plants are not fully and adequately protected." The plants were vulnerable to both attack and sabotage. Unfortunately, "there are so many war industries in this locality" that putting the Army to guard them would spread out its personnel so much that they would not be able to "defend against possible invasion."[40] The Angeleno chief executive could not protect his military resources (from the Japanese et al.) unless he had fewer of them, and he could not have fewer of them as long as he kept trying to acquire more.

Faced with this unpleasant choice, the getting of more naturally prevailed. In August 1942, the Southland again succeeded, this time in securing a branch office of the National Advisory Committee for Aeronautics, located in Santa Monica. The NACA research and testing agency on the West Coast was Ames Laboratory, located at Moffett Field in the Bay Area, and Los Angeles aircraft and civic leaders felt that their area suffered from not having a NACA office in the midst of their own plane-manufacturing sea. "The new office in Southern California is part of a national program to expand facilities for coordination of scientific work in support of the war effort," President Carleton B. Tibbetts of the Los Angeles Chamber announced, and it gave the aircraft industry a direct contact with NACA, an arrangement sadly lacking in the past.[41]

Military traffic through the port of Los Angeles showed the same woeful appearance. Until August of 1943, the Army classified Los Angeles as a subport of the San Francisco port of embarkation, through which most of the sinews of war flowed to the Pacific theater. On the face of it, this designation was degrading to the defenders inside the Great Wall and unprofitable as well. In August 1943, the Los Angeles Harbor Department succeeded in eliminating both the psychological and financial liabilities. This new military dispensation elevated Los Angeles to a full port of embarkation status and called for numerous improvements in the Southland apparatus for supporting the war, including an enlargement of the Camp Anza staging area near Riverside from a capacity of 8,000 to 25,000.[42]

Mayor Bowron credited the Harbor Department, especially board member Morgan Adams (formerly the city's man in Washington) and the president, George H. Moore, with this victory. "Many good local citizens were moved to protest because of the shock to the civic pride of this great metropolitan area when our harbor had previously been designated a subport of San Francisco by the Army Transport Service," Bowron wrote in congratulation to the Board of Harbor Commissioners for eliminating this outrage. The eradication of this military sin, explained the chief executive, meant "not merely proper recognition, but also increased shipping of war materials to the South Pacific theatre of war through our local facilities." Moreover, this increased shipping "will undoubtedly establish shipping lanes that will mean trade relationship and greatly increased commerce with the Dutch East Indies, Australia, China, the Malay States, and India, after the successful termination of the war."[43]

It will be recalled that all this came almost exactly one year after Mayor Bowron had declared that the rivalry between his city and San Francisco was over and called upon the West to stand together against the urban East. Perhaps the chief executive was even sincere then when he declared the "barrier of the Tehachapis in California" to have been "perceptibly lowered." However, the barrier looked real enough to embattled San Franciscans as they tried to protect yet another military asset that the Los Angeles mayor fancied.

Local politicians habitually voiced support for the kind of armament policies that would support a big defense establishment, from which rhetoric both they and their service partners would benefit. Mayor Bowron of Los Angeles did so in an especially revealing manner in early 1945 as the war subsided and the question of the size of the peacetime Navy arose. The chief executive praised the Navy's Bureau of Supplies and Docks for its role in the war and noted its local expansion from 195 to 3000 people in the area, which the Navy assured him would grow even more. "This will be no mushroom growth," the mayor promised his listeners. "After this war we must, we will, maintain a great Navy, fully prepared for any emergency to keep the peace, and we should and undoubtedly will, have a permanent supply depot here in San Pedro" (an asset which would justify greater Navy use of Los Angeles's artificial harbor).[44] The Navy soon established one in the Southland.

"You may be assured that the City will be reasonable in the matter of acquirement by the Navy of the additional land required, now owned by and under the control of the City's Harbor Department," the mayor wrote to a Navy official as the war drew to a close.[45] And the Navy, too, proved "reasonable," authorizing the base in early 1945. However, the Los Angeles Chamber of Commerce, competing with the city and its harbor department to claim credit for the new acquisition, almost ruined the deal by prematurely announcing it in *Southern California Business*. The arrangement required quiet diplomacy because the Army would have to cede real estate to the Navy, and publicity would jeopardize that process. "When the Navy gets something from the Army or vice versa, the negotiations must be carried on with all the tact of international diplomacy," the chief executive scolded Leroy M. Edwards, president of the Chamber of Commerce. Further Darwinian complexities were involved as well. "Quietly, we have been endeavoring to offset an effort to build a larger Naval Supply Base at Alameda or a new one elsewhere on San Francisco Bay," Bowron lectured his booster ally at the chamber. "And locally we have a very delicate situation because the City of Long Beach has offered several sites to the Navy and is still endeavoring to exert influence at Washington to have the Supply Base located in the Long Beach area."[46]

The struggle for wartime housing revealed the outlines of this urban "war within a war" once again. Each of the cities recognized the importance of wartime population migration, both for a booming future and for the embattled present, which required that the cities have a work force adequate to their roles as arsenals of democracy. Without sufficient workers, the martial metropolises would lose military contracts. Yet new residents also required added housing, and the war put a severe limitation on that industry because of scarce materials and labor. Therefore, each of the martial metropolises had to struggle to keep their workers housed. Once again, the conflict brought numerous benefits to California cities. In early 1942, at a time when other cities found it difficult even to procure building materials, San Diego had the largest public housing program in the nation and Los Angeles, the second. Upon completion of Ramona Gardens, the City of Angels would have 33,000 units of public housing, three times the entire urban population of 1880.[47] San Francisco and its neighbors prospered as well.

However, "The City" thought that its neighbors gained more than it did. By mid-1943 the global conflict had created an acute housing shortage in the Bay Metropolis which was causing it to lose potential residents to its own suburbs because the government was granting materials for construction of housing in Oakland, Alameda, and Richmond while virtually ignoring San Francisco. To alleviate its wartime shortage and to retain these workers for the future, the San Francisco Board of Supervisors petitioned the National Housing Agency to allow the building of 5000 war houses in the city.[48] This request touched off a fight among San Francisco neighborhoods. Much as they wanted to aid the war effort, the Board of Supervisors did not want the Laurel Hill Cemetery and the Calvary Cemetery lands turned over to public housing. Temporary shelters would be inappropriate to such a "high-class" residential area; besides, the city wanted to build streets to connect to the Richmond District on the same land and feared that the war homes would contribute to traffic congestion.[49] They wanted housing, but somewhere else in the city. The same problem arose in other neighborhoods, but it eventually proved susceptible to compromise. The civic and improvement clubs of the neighborhoods agreed to take more public housing, but they were assured that no single district would be overloaded with them. This agreement kept more housing out of the Park-side and Sunset districts, but allowed it into southern districts in measured amounts.[50] Still, the end of 1942 saw no letup in the housing crisis in the city.[51]

The struggle for shelter continued right up to the final months of the global conflict. Although Los Angeles and San Diego had complained a year earlier about the loss of contracts occasioned by their designation as a Number One Critical Labor Shortage Area, by March of 1945 they still had more contracts than they could find the workers to fulfill. Without more public housing, protested Ed Izak of San Diego, Carl Hinshaw of Pasadena, and Gordon McDonough of Los Angeles, the defense effort of the West Coast would be crippled for lack of working people just at the time that the Pacific War was coming to dominate American military activities. The new jets and rockets could not be accommodated in the Pasadena area without housing, said the conservative Hinshaw; nor could Consolidated produce its Super Liberators nor Ryan its new jets, agreed Izak. The fact that these areas were already stuffed with defense contracts mattered little, these spokesmen maintained. The contracts had already been let to these West Coast congested areas, and the war effort depended upon their getting enough labor and therefore housing to fulfill the contracts.

In these arguments, the usual circularity prevailed. The city builders had lured the aircraft industries in the first place; these in turn brought the contracts which created congestion; and instead of bringing a decentralization of these defense industries, the congestion provided instead more leverage for these metropolitans to rationalize the need for still more government spending in the Southland. Of course, if 4000 more workers miraculously appeared in San Diego, the number Izak claimed were needed to overcome Consolidated's deficit, further federal spending would be required for the urban infrastructure that must come with housing; and the new housing would provide an additional rationale for more defense contracts; and so on.[52]

The exemptions from housing construction limits were part of a larger picture of urban competition to ease the restrictions of war for the benefit of urban areas. Just as each of the areas fought to evade construction ceilings or to get federal public housing, they sought to ease Office of Price Administration regulations to allow extra charges for additional tenants in rental units.[53] San Francisco also fought to eliminate the ban on construction so that the Friant Dam and Friant-Kern and Madera canals of the vital Central Valley Water Project could be finished in San Francisco's hinterland.[54] Although San Francisco and Los Angeles represented two very different urban forms, the one concentrated and the other sprawling, both insisted that federal driving restrictions be loosened so as to give them more gasoline. "This section is unique," Mayor Bowron wrote to the editor of *Life Magazine* in late 1942. It "has grown up, developed and expanded during the automobile age. The life of the people, the economy of the section, is dependent upon the continued use of the automobile." He admitted that "gasoline rationing is the proper method" to save auto and tire wear but argued that "Los Angeles and the surrounding area must have far different considerations than New York and Boston and other eastern cities." Otherwise, the City of the Angels could not keep up its splendid war work![55]

San Francisco tried a radically different tack to the same end of fuller gas tanks. Since "The City" would be a major target in case of enemy attack and since its inhabitants had been "instructed to be prepared for evacuation when required" and since its hills and steep grades plus "numerous traffic signals and arterial stops requires a higher average consumption of gasoline for each automobile," the city of St. Francis could not get along on the four gallons per week allotted to its car owners. It was simply not fair to allow them the same number of gallons as "residents of communities where the climate and topography aid in obtaining a greater mileage."[56] In effect, Los Angeles demanded more gasoline because it was a horizontal city and San Francisco, because it was a vertical one!

All of the cities had problems caused by wartime regulations, but each faced special challenges as well. San Francisco had long suffered inroads into its hinterland by Los Angeles, and this realization came to a head just as the war emergency built up. The Southland metropolis seemed to have representatives everywhere, grabbing every business opportunity they could lay their hands on, while San Francisco seemed strangely inert. At a time when most cities did not even maintain an office in the national or state capitals, the feisty Angelenos had a chamber of commerce branch in Salt Lake City, an area long noted for its close ties to San Francisco. As Senator Jesse Mayo of Angels Camp explained to a San Francisco supervisor, "San Francisco had, for too many years, been looking to the West [in general] and forgetting that the great backbone of its wealth could be the rural and mining counties."[57]

The City of St. Francis tried desperately to make up for its years of neglect, fighting back through the new Regional Service Organization. By 1941 the Southland's gains had finally sunk into the consciousness of the Board of Supervisors, and they anxiously sought to prevent the war from doing further damage to its relations with the interior. San Francisco had grown to prominence as a Gold Rush city, and when the priorities of war deprived the gold mining industry of steel needed to produce precious metals, it protested. The Board of Supervisors complained to Washington that "142,000 citizens in thirteen California counties within San Francisco's trade area are substantially dependent on mining activities for their livelihood." The "infinitesimal amount" of steel necessary to keep these people employed and the "depopulation of mining communities" and lowering of morale that might ensue from the government's noncooperation in these matters argued for a reallocation of enough steel to keep the industries going.[58]

The San Francisco Board of Supervisors petitioned the government to change the priorities, sent representatives to consult with the "back Country" about their needs, and dispatched envoys to Washington to devise ways to save the industry. They found the interior counties of Calaveras, Mariposa, Amador, Trinity, Tuolumne, and others facing a shutdown of their mines (which they swore could not be opened again once closed), a loss of their tax bases, and the closing of their schools, if the industry did not receive a little steel. Supervisor Robert M. Green of San Francisco also discovered the usual story of Angeleno penetration. To his surprise, he learned that almost all of the mining equipment used by these Bay City neighbors came from Los Angeles. The city of St. Francis was closer to the precious metals regions and it would have been easier to do business with that place, but as one mine owner put it, "You have to do business with your friends." As the supervisor learned to his chagrin, "The reason for this was that it seems that Los Angeles through the Chamber of Commerce or the Board of Supervisors continually [has] agents traveling through the gold mining fields," said Green. "They had received thousands, if not hundreds of thousands, of dollars that could be given to San Francisco," observed the legislator, "if we were to be more cooperative with the gold mining district."[59]

For the moment, San Francisco may have lost large amounts of machinery supply business, but it did not lack resourceful responses that would give the mining backcountry ample reason to regard "The City" as its friend. Long before the war ended, the Chamber of Commerce had adopted a very sophisticated plan, conceived by a Nevada senator, to help the miners, in this case those involved in the production of strategic metals as opposed to precious ones. This effort led to the idea of stockpiling ores, a practice that would grow into a big federal program in the Cold War period.

The plan called for the production of more strategic minerals than were needed for the war effort and the accumulation of reserves of such metals, starting during the war and continuing "after conclusion of the war until an adequate supply of each of these critical and strategic metals and minerals is on hand in a national stock pile." These materials were not to be "sold or dumped on the market in such a way as to disturb normal prices or sales of such metals or minerals by private industry." Nor were these ores to be bought from the lowest bidder if that person happened to be a foreign producer of the goods. To the extent possible, all such purchases were to "be made from domestic sources at current domestic prices and the continuance of domestic production, particularly after the war, should be thus encouraged."[60] Already, the urban politicians had found ways to transform international warfare into domestic welfare.

Since this program would have required the government to buy the minerals at domestic prices, which would be higher, and since it excluded the purchase of foreign minerals except insofar as they were available from domestic producers, it was obviously designed as a subsidy, or rather price support, whatever its national defense value might have been. The San Francisco Chamber of Commerce adopted this policy in early September 1943, and Senator J. G. Scrugham of Nevada introduced the idea into Congress as Senate Bill No. 1160, where it died in committee.[61] Of course the Chamber of Commerce denied that this proposal would have amounted to an outright grant, but it did admit that the government paid premium prices for minerals during the war, which is when the Chamber sought to initiate the program. Despite its disclaimers, the businessmen of the Chamber were proposing a form of price support for the mining industries of the West, rather similar to the famous silver purchases and agricultural supports of the New Deal period.

San Francisco representatives were moving on several fronts to help the gold regions when another interior problem arose. California launched the massive Central Valley Project in the 1930s to distribute water from the well-watered northern part of the valley to the parched southern one. This scheme was of great interest to the large agricultural corporations, which often maintained headquarters in San Francisco, as well as to valley residents, who were in general dependent on farm prosperity. However, the war also stopped construction of the Friant Dam and the Friant-Kern River and Madera canals in the San Joaquin Valley. Getting this project started again meant a lot to the hinterland that San Francisco sought to pacify. It is not too surprising that the Board of Supervisors tried to persuade the War Production Board to grant the necessary priorities. In this case the boosters argued that the parched interior valleys would make critical contributions of "food, fiber, and guayule rubber for the nation's war effort if water were available on the land." Only a very small amount of steel (330 tons) would be enough to place the dam and canals in operation. The way the boosters saw it, the steel could be considered a conservation device, since the canals and dam would raise the entire water table of the southern San Joaquin Valley, whereas it took up to 5000 tons of steel annually to deepen and repair water wells to keep pace with the dropping water table. The Madera Canal opened in 1944, but the Friant-Kern Canal commenced operation only in 1949.[62]

The same hinterland concerns motivated San Franciscans to lobby to include representatives of the California Cattleman's Association and the California Wool Growers Association on the board of directors of the Cow Palace. San Francisco's participation in the building of the Cow Palace had been designed "to promote closer relations between this city and the livestock industry and to encourage the industry to make San Francisco the livestock center of the Pacific Coast," so this further sop to the back country was understandable.[63] So was the attempt by the Board of Supervisors to get the Board of Education to extend public school vacation time on the pretext that it would aid in the national defense. In fact a longer summer break would benefit the interior recreation industry by allowing schoolchildren to spend more time at these places.[64] Finally, the city also found itself compelled to help with the harvests of its own hinterland.

One of the major ironies of the internment of the Japanese—Issei and Nissei—was that it hit hard the food production industry, one of the state's largest, at the very moment that the government drafted farm men and the defense industries lured other country males to town. California agriculture went from being labor-rich in the era of the Okies to labor-poor in the Second World War. The evacuation of the Japanese, who were heavily involved in agricultural production, led to make-shift efforts to fill the gaps.[65] One of these was the recruitment drives in urban areas carried on by organizations such as the San Francisco Wartime Harvest Council, which persuaded laborers—schoolchildren, housewives, young women, and others to replace the defense workers, soldiers, and Japanese who usually did the work.

The San Francisco Chamber of Commerce claimed initial success for this effort, but as late as May 1943, the Board of Supervisors admitted that the situation of "agricultural labor in the State of California is steadily becoming more acute." Despite the supposed efficacy of urban recruitment of agricultural labor, the San Francisco Board of Supervisors requested the federal government to send the troops, in this case "war prisoners," to alleviate the shortage. Whether the area leaders ever comprehended the delicious irony of importing German and Italian POWs to do the work of the Japanese whom the Roosevelt administration had recently interned is not known, but it would seem considerable indeed.[66] In any event, organized labor viewed the proposal as a threat to its interests and threw up a wall of opposition. Unions claimed that the "farmers" had already secured draft deferments and the "relaxation of existing laws permitting women and minors" to work, plus the importation of Mexican workers. Still, by mid-1944, the prisoner scheme had received a "qualified" certification from the Regional Office of the War Manpower Commission.[67]

Los Angeles was more concerned with a different "interior." That city was singularly blessed with war prosperity yet strangely suspicious of, perhaps even paranoid about, the world beyond the Great Wall of California. In Southern California, the "hurricane of war" left not debris and destruction but defense factories, pavements, bases and installations, Navy yards, star-struck G.I.s, modernized airports, modern dock facilities, new roads, and much else; but the area, especially Los Angeles, could never shake the colonial mentality of a dependent region at the mercy of some greater American power. Mayor Bowron sounded warning after warning that Washington was neglecting them, that Texas was out to get them, that the "interior" was in league against them, and that San Francisco was employing some mysterious means to deprive the City of Angels of military cargoes, camps, contracts, federal offices, and its destiny as an air center of the world. Given this mindset, the idea of "industrial decentralization" did not go over very well in Southern California.

The idea of industrial decentralization or dispersal was simple enough and fairly persuasive. Since the airframe portion of the aircraft industry had located so heavily in Southern California and other coasts, and since the war was expanding and enriching those coastal cities so marvelously, other sections of the country, both before and after the American entry into the conflict, looked at the enrichment with some degree of envy, perhaps even lust. Even before Pearl Harbor, critics of the overconcentration of the airframe industry inside the Great Wall of California had a valid point. It could readily be argued that, in an air age, a coastal location was inappropriate for such a huge part of the American aircraft industry. Not only did the Southland have such an enormous part of the industry, but no part of it was located more than a few miles from the ocean, from where it could be struck by carrier-borne planes. Since Los Angeles officials themselves continually reiterated the threat of air attack or even invasion, one cannot assume that the idea of urban vulnerability to attack was merely the invention of the fertile minds of scheming midwestern or Texas city politicians.

Neither was the idea of decentralizing the industry to other parts of the country to minimize that vulnerability, since the military and the government alike agreed on this necessity. Nonetheless, Los Angeles both feared and fought it. The Chamber of Commerce did not begrudge the interior its "war baby" industries, that is, those that had grown up with the conflict and would die with its ending. However, they did resent the attempt to strip L.A. of its "maximum productive capacity," which meant the aircraft industry, oil refining, or some other local enterprise that was necessary in either war or peace.[68] "Industrial evacuation," as the Chamber of Commerce incorrectly called decentralization, had no economic rationale, only a political one, it was claimed. The natural forces which had produced a great manufacturing center in Southern California must not be tampered with because the same forces dominated peacetime and wartime manufacturing, and any meddling with these immutable laws would undermine war production.[69]

Southland spokesmen hedged on the vulnerability of that region to attack. On the one hand, they insisted on the possibility of sneak attack in order to relocate the Japanese, and they wanted to trumpet the virtues of air power, even in early 1942, in order to remain on good terms with the military air forces. On the other hand, the same argument could be mobilized against them in the competition for government contracts, thus their ambivalence and sometimes inconsistency. For example, when Mayor Bowron argued for more helmets for his civil defense corps, he reiterated the refrain that Los Angeles was such an important defense center that it would surely be the subject of an attack from the air. Bowron was convinced in early 1942 that the Doolittle raid on Tokyo and the relocation of the Japanese in California "would naturally result in reprisals" in the form of a "token raid on the coast or even a more serious effort to destroy war industries and affect the civilian morale." Unfortunately, in this context, the climate, far from being the oft-claimed asset, was a hindrance. "Each year just a little later in the season," the mayor informed the federal director of civil defense, "there is usually a heavy fog bank off the Southern California coast which would protect the approach of aircraft carriers."[70]

Simultaneously, however, the Chamber of Commerce argued that Los Angeles was one of the safest places in the nation, being more air miles from Tokyo, Rome, and Berlin than nearly any other American city except San Diego, El Paso, and a few other western towns. Of course, this argument was almost completely without merit. Any attacking planes would take off from aircraft carriers rather than from enemy capital cities, and to this kind of sea-borne assault, Los Angeles was indeed very vulnerable, much more so than interior cities located some hundreds of miles inland.[71]

Nonetheless, Chamber president Carlton Tibbetts denigrated the potential of air attack, going so far as to argue that German air power had not substantially interrupted English defense production even though the German Luftwaffe repeatedly bombed British cities.[72] He also denied that military opinion supported the idea of industrial evacuation, though it obviously did. To Southland spokesmen, the political machinations of the urban Midwest and urban Texas explained why the government intended to fly in the face of the overwhelming economic logic that had put so much wealth inside the walls of Fortress California.[73] The Chamber called it "political pilfering," and to Mayor Bowron it was all part and parcel of the Washington prejudice against the Southland. "Texas wants our industries and so do other sections of the middle west [hardly anyone else ever considers Texas a part of the Midwest], but our oil is vital and if that is properly protected our industries, aircraft and shipbuilding, can be protected at the same time," he argued. "We must work together to prevent further sniping at Southern California's great industrial development. . . . The difficulty is that we do not have the voices in Washington [that is, Southlanders in important bureaucratic positions] that can be heard above the din," continued the chief executive. "Think of what could be accomplished in Southern California if we had one-half of the influence at Washington that Texas has." Bowron thundered, "We wouldn't need a Jesse Jones, either" (Jones was a Texas politician who had secured great resources from the New Deal).[74]

The Chamber of Commerce even went so far as to say that the enemy within that hampered production by politics, social planning, and jitters was more threatening than the enemy without, which wielded bayonets and bombers. This statement came at a time when the Chamber was trying to obtain the establishment of an aluminum sheet rolling mill at Los Angeles, to go with the "reduction or ingot plant" that the government had already promised them. This addition would centralize various phases of aircraft production by putting the aluminum mills next to the aircraft factories and eliminating unnecessary transportation costs.[75] Of course, it could be just as logically argued that aluminum production in the interior was more sensible, since it would be invulnerable to attack, and the cost of shipping finished products, such as ingots or sheet aluminum, to the Urban Southland would be less than that of shipping the unrefined raw materials to that place. And, obviously, centralizing more industry in the Southland would make that target more inviting. So it would appear that the immutable Urban California laws of economics dictated, at the same time, the *decentralization* of the aluminum industry from the Far Midwest (Pittsburgh) while mandating the *centralization* of the aircraft industry in Southern California.

In this event, the federal government devised a very subtle compromise of the industrial dispersal issue. Immediate orders for aircraft poured into the Southland, thus insuring its prosperity for the duration of the war. Then the military insisted on decentralizing the new wartime plants into the interior, giving them the protection that the military had demanded for them as early as 1938. Thereafter, the issue died down until the martial cities began to think about victory, demobilization, and the necessary postwar planning to bring it about.

One of the most astonishing examples of wartime competition occurred over ships. Both San Diego and San Francisco had already been "given" cruisers, in the sense that the Navy had named the ships after these cities. The *San Francisco* was involved in heroic action off Guadalcanal where "Fighting" Dan Callaghan, its San Francisco commander, gave his life to halt the Japanese advance into the South Pacific.[76] The battle-scarred navigating bridge of that indomitable ship stands on the shores of the Pacific today, looking out to sea. As we have seen, the launching of this vessel had an important political as well as military significance, as it was the occasion of San Francisco's bringing together the various warring parties of the Bay Area into an effective coalition dedicated to getting their share of military expenditures. The *San Diego* had a somewhat less illustrious career, being launched in the East, instead of in California, in July 1941.[77]

Whatever their ultimate fate, both San Francisco and San Diego could at least lay claim to having had a cruiser, and both gloried in their undoubted gallantry. However, this was one race to the swift in which Los Angeles was left behind. It had no cruiser until well into the war. Matters stood this way until June 30, 1943, when Secretary of the Navy Frank Knox appeared in the city to be honored at a luncheon at the Biltmore Hotel. After the usual remarks about the role of the City of the Angels in the war and a note on the geographically expansive nature of that city,

Mayor Fletcher Bowron shifted his remarks away from the land. "Just now, we are interested in extending the Los Angeles city limits to the Seven Seas, marked by a proud, modern fighting craft, a $40,000,000 cruiser of the United States Navy," intoned the feisty chief executive. "On your promise to name it, Mr. Secretary, we will pay for it during the month of July," Bowron pledged.[78] It is not known if the secretary got offers like this every day, but it is highly unlikely if for no other reason than the impressive sum of money involved. It is important to remind ourselves that $40 million represented a large amount of cash at that time. For example, the entire airport bond issue of 1941 came to only $3.5 million; the postwar airport expansion bond issue totaled a mere $12.5 million; and some of the military bases put into California cities at this time cost even less. Given the size of these figures, one can imagine the secretary's skepticism at the offer.

Yet the fearfully energetic city of Los Angeles did indeed raise the money. In fact, it raised over twice the necessary amount in a "special War Bond campaign" in Los Angeles City and County. The extra $40 million plus was "sufficient to build four of the latest type destroyers," named after Los Angeles naval heroes. To provide a sum for the cruiser's welfare fund, the mayor solicited every city employee plus every schoolchild in the city to contribute. In return, all would have their names entered on the permanent records of the cruiser *Los Angeles.* The Navy christened the ship in the Philadelphia Navy Yard on August 20, 1944, and it was set to sally forth against the Japanese on May 9, 1945, just as the Germans surrendered.[79] San Diego prided itself on its close relations with the Navy before and after the war, and so did San Francisco. But if either ever made a more generous and noble gesture to its service partner, the act is unknown to this author. In effect, Los Angeles financed a small navy of its own, consisting of five ships, capable of fighting at least a minor naval action, with little or no help from the rest of the country.

Aside from these major activities, the cities engaged in a host of miscellaneous struggles of self-aggrandizement. The Second World War was such an all-encompassing experience that it touched nearly everything. So did the influence of the urban rivalry. And as John Anson Ford anticipated, it was often difficult to tell where national defense left off and the Imperial City began. For example, in 1941, as the Los Angeles area geared up for the war, numerous borderline cases appeared. As usual, these illustrate both the nature of the Imperial City and the benefits that came to it as a result of war.

In March of that year the arid Southland suffered heavy flooding, which affected defense production. Lockheed found "portions of its production floor" under two feet of water. The County Board of Supervisors immediately asked the government to assist "speedily in extending a flood control channel up to and beyond the Lockheed plant in order that costly delays might not recur." Flood control would certainly guarantee against a recurrence of this disruption of defense production, but it would also work in very well with the long-term effort at water management of the Darwinian city, designed to rationalize that resource and therefore make the area more competitive. Whether the problem of chronic flooding was a real long-term threat to national defense production in an arid area, where rainfall had been known to drop below ten inches a year, is a question best left to the judgment of the reader.[80]

The same March rains also inconvenienced the Douglas plant being built at the

Long Beach Municipal Airport, since a recently completed drainage ditch could not carry off the water. This latter facility needed to be widened and lengthened to a "distance of six or eight miles." If the federal government undertook this job, it would certainly aid defense, but it would also be of great benefit to the contractors building a subdivision adjacent to the Douglas plant. Up in the Mojave Desert lay a similar example. The government had developed "a great bombing field at Muroc Lake" (near the present Edwards Air Force Base and current NASA shuttle landing site), but to get there "one must travel 40 or 50 miles over desert roads which now are narrow and inadequate." The County Board of Supervisors felt that the government should assist them in providing a good road to this site.[81] Of course, if another industry had been ensconced in the desert, the government would not necessarily have felt compelled to construct such an approach nor the county, to ask for it. Private industry did not necessarily build roads to its own factories nor provide other normal urban or county services like flood control or drainage ditches. Yet the national defense emergency justified the asking and, in many cases, the granting of such problematical requests.

Since both San Francisco and Los Angeles owned municipal water and power facilities, the war presented opportunities for both. In 1942, the federal government wanted a power plant in the Owens River Gorge to supply power to the defense industries of Southern California. This plant would add to the infrastructure of Los Angeles and help it provide the cheap power that lured industry. Even though the mayor wanted the nation-state to pick up the bill, his own Department of War and Power was willing and anxious to finance the plant.[82]

The city and county of San Francisco had a similar wartime opportunity and employed it to resolve temporarily one of its most intractable dilemmas. Since the 1920s public power had been an explosive issue at both the city and state levels of California politics. San Francisco had built a water system that also generated power, but each time it tried to get the voters to approve a bond issue for a system to distribute the power, the formidable Pacific Gas and Electric Company defeated the referendum.[83] This delay enabled that company to distribute the power produced by the city along with their own, since the city could not get a distribution system approved. Finally, the matter appeared before the courts, which ruled that the city could not sell its public power for private distribution by P. G. and E., as it had for over a decade. This decision left the City of St. Francis with power but without a market for it, and the war helped partially to resolve the problem.

In early 1942 San Francisco came forward with a proposal to sell the city's electricity to the government for the duration of the conflict, to be used to supply a Defense Plant Corporation "aluminum smelting plant" near Modesto. By April, arrangements were complete. San Francisco both found a market for its power and helped to realize a longtime California and western ambition of diversifying its manufacturing base by gaining heavy industry, especially aluminum needed for aircraft manufacture.[84] This solution seemed such a happy one that by October 1942, a committee of the Board of Supervisors proposed another like it. This one would involve the construction of an additional power plant at Red Mountain Bar, to be incorporated as a part of the city's Hetch Hetchy system. The plant wold also sell power to a Defense Plant Corporation aluminum mill, and that agency approved of the proposal; but by year's end the city had not yet received the "necessary priorities" from the War Production Board.[85]

More than its California rivals, Los Angeles recognized the truism that war is an eminently political process and tried to mobilize ever greater resources to promote its own development. Despite all that has been written about the rise and dominance of the modern nation-state and what was written and said at the time about the need for national unity, wartime Washington was awash in local politicians, boosters, labor leaders, and businessmen politicking their heads off for their own special interests or areas. If there was a national will expressed in that harried Potomac city, it was closer to an aggregation of these local wills and special interests than a national purpose, except for the will to win the war once the Japanese had forced the United States to fight it. Angelenos instinctively comprehended this reality well before it became one at Pearl Harbor.

They realized just as fully and intuitively that a genuinely centralized and powerful modern nation-state would be a threat to their own local and regional power bases. Well before the war broke out, local leaders were already talking about the hated regimentation that they expected from the war, warning of the influence of "social planners" in Washington, and fearing the tumult and upheaval that conflict might bring. Yet they also recognized the opportunity that might lie in global conflict; if war must come, they hoped to get the lion's share of the modern nation-state resources. Paradoxically, once war became inevitable, Los Angeles simultaneously fought the concentration of power in Washington and adroitly adapted itself to it. Despite loud misgivings about the god Mars, they welcomed his winged messenger, Mercury (god of commerce, cleverness, travel, and thievery), with open arms.

Much of the Los Angeles reaction to the global conflict took the form of political attacks on the federal government. Early on L.A. came to be very concerned about its "voice in Washington" and about its treatment at the hands of the government. Initially, Angeleno leaders concentrated on increasing the city's "representation" in the bureacracy of the hated nation-state. Nothing the wartime government did seemed right, and much appeared downright stupid. For example, in early 1942 the government was amassing an enormous amount of defense production and military installations in the Southland at a time when either air attack, invasion, or sabotage seemed possible if not imminent. This concentration was before the great victory at the Battle of Midway relieved these fears. Simultaneously with this heightened threat to security, the same federal authorities seemed bent on drafting the forces of order, the police—even older ones—into the military.[86] To the mayor of Los Angeles, such inconsistency seemed both precociously incompetent and wonderfully illustrative of the incomprehension with which the bureaucracy viewed his city. "We do feel, however, that the many serious problems in connection with the war industrial development in and around Los Angeles are not fully understood and appreciated to the extent that they are given adequate consideration at Washington," Mayor Bowron wrote to the editor of *Life* in late 1942. He repeated that refrain endlessly both before and after that date.[87]

To check his impression of underrepresentation, the chief executive commissioned a study of the *Official Register* of the Washington government and found only 27 out of 3800 names with even a slight connection to the Southland. Of these, "not a single person, from this metropolitan area, so far as I know, from all of Southern California, is in any position where he has any part in governmental policy making," he complained. "Show me one, just one, from Southern California, who helps make policy at Washington," he demanded before the service clubs in a speech at Santa Anna. The Los Angeles leader went on to explain to his suburban listeners that the area was divided up into too many governmental units, all looking out for themselves. "We want to boost the home town rather than Southern California, or California, or the Pacific Coast," Bowron insisted. The area needed a united approach, both to win the war and to face the future after they had done so. "We are sending out young men to fight. We should fight more effectively at home."[88]

To do so, the mayor leaned toward more regional approaches to the problem of influence in Washington. He never stopped looking out for his own "home town" in the distribution of the spoils of war, but as the conflict waxed, so did his enthusiasm for unity—of California, of the Pacific Coast, and even of the West—to face the problem of power in the nation-state. Not only did he warn suburban Santa Ana residents of the dangers of disunity within the metropolitan area, but as early as August 1942 he called a conference of California mayors at which he stressed the theme of unity again, even going so far as to declare the historical antagonism between San Francisco and Los Angeles at an end.[89]

By 1944 the mayor was sounding the same note for the Pacific coast at large, using almost the same phraseology he had previously employed to describe the problems of Los Angeles. In a letter to the Under Secretary of the Navy requesting the release of a serviceman to civilian life to organize the efforts of California cities to cope with the war, Bowron laid out his case. "The problems of the Pacific Coast cities are peculiar and unique and call for united action, and if possible, a uniform program," the mayor explained. "The cities of California are members of the League of California Cities and we are relying upon this organization to coordinate and secure cooperative action at the municipal level and as far as possible to develop the program."[90]

Even earlier, the mayor had seen the need for a regional program involving all of the West. "It has for some time been my feeling that the cities of the West have not been getting benefit from this organization proportionate to the larger cities of the East," wrote Bowron of the United States Conference of Mayors. It has "largely become a pressure organization, used to advantage by those mayors who go personally to Washington with requests for appropriations of local benefit or special consideration from various Federal agencies." Bowron proposed to Mayor W. C. Seccombe of San Bernardino that the West form a caucus within the mayors' conference as a whole. "We have serious and peculiar problems in the Pacific area that are not understood in other sections of the country," he lamented in the usual refrain.[91] Other western, urban sources sounded the same note of regionalism during the war.

This message was heard especially clearly in the case of the newly founded western steel industry. The war had brought large-scale modern steel plants to Fontana in San Bernardino County and the Geneva Plant near Provo, Utah. Both were subsidized by the federal government and both were looked to as a means of ending western colonialism by providing a critical manufacturing dimension that would help the West escape dependence on the East. Of course, the movement for industrial decentralization was a similar western initiative.

Thus, despite the struggles of the Darwinian cities, one could discern the faint outlines of a greater regional consciousness, perhaps prophetic of the emergence of what would later be called the Sunbelt. In the 1940s, it was still a very dim outline, however. The Imperial cities might talk of unity and cooperation, but throughout the war, they stuck to their own metropolitan imperial aims. To the extent that they seriously considered cooperating across urban boundaries, it was more to collaborate on a metropolitan-wide basis rather than on a Pacific coast or western one, not to mention a national one. As usual, Bowron was illustrative of the case. Just a few months before the mayor wrote to Washington of the need for cooperation among West Coast and California cities and requested the government to discharge a sailor to coordinate the "program" for California cities, he was complaining of governmental favoritism for San Francisco. The mayor denied being activated by boosterism, chamber of commerce propaganda, or sectional jealousy, but insisted that the war could be won quicker if more air traffic were routed through Los Angeles. "The war effort has suffered, time has been lost, much equipment has been needlessly used, with greater expense than necessary," said the chief executive, "merely because Army and Navy men arbitrarily determined that oceanic air transport shipments should all go out of San Francisco."[92]

The *Downtowner,* organ of the San Francisco Downtown Association, expressed perfectly the metropolitan view of the Darwinian cities in a 1943 issue. In an article entitled "Bay Area Coordination for Post-War Planning" the periodical carried a front-page map of the "West." It consisted of a circle around the city with a number of valleys radiating out from it and then the various states of the transmontane West radiating out behind each valley.

> The awakening of a regional consciousness is the first essential to the development of post-war San Francisco. The size, importance and power of this city is measured not alone by the number of its own citizenry but by the whole great population of the Pacific slope who use its facilities and look to its institutions for financial, industrial and agricultural leadership. Most particularly the people of adjacent communities and neighboring counties, which together with San Francisco comprise the San Francisco Bay Region, share a common destiny with the people of San Francisco. San Francisco should therefore seek to work in ever closer cooperation with the Bay Area communities and help to coordinate all of those matters in which we have an interest. This region must pull together for a common goal and prepare now for the great opportunities which the future offers.[93]

The West in this view was a tributary region whose watershed trickled into the valleys whose rivers surged into San Francisco Bay, whose waters flowed past "The City." The Second World War may have been a centralizing and nationalizing influence for some cities, but San Francisco still saw the West the way it had in the 1920s when Chamber of Commerce president Colbert Coldwell and James Bacigalupi had defined the "metropolitan conception." Los Angeles had the same idea; and if San Diego did not yet share it, it was perhaps because its two larger rivals had squeezed it out of the picture and because its boosterism was shifting to a qualitative basis. "The competitive tournament among world cities" still prevailed; the "survival of the fittest" still ruled the competition; and a "budding empire" remained the goal of each.[94]

Postwar planning reflected this outlook. The war had caused an unprecedented upheaval in Urban California. It had flooded the Golden State with new people, choked it with new industries, confronted it with novel sexual morals, disturbed it with crime, strained it by wearing out its infrastructure, embarrassed it with collective disorder, occupied it with soldiers, sailors, and flyers, frustrated it with federal directives, bewildered it with sustained and deep-seated change, and threatened it with technological revolutions. At war's end, the cities would be seething with resentment at the problems that the global struggle had left and vociferous in demanding government help to solve them. Yet all of Urban California realized that the global conflict had also bestowed advantages and assets, and each city was determined to hang onto them. Each would curse the federal government for the mess in which the war had left them, but each would plaintively beg for more of the economic resources that came with the mess. In short, each town fully understood that the prospects of war-related prosperity outweighed the predicaments. The California State Reconstruction and Reemployment Commission report on postwar planning in San Bernardino County, the nation's largest, captured the situation precisely when it called the county's gains "war winnings."[95] Holding onto them provided the central thrust for postwar planning in all of the cities.

The most surprising thing about postwar planning was how quickly it appeared. It did not await the scent of victory, nor even the faint aroma of it; postwar planning emerged almost as soon as the war began. San Diego had gained a lot from the world conflict even before formal American entry, and it led Urban California in planning to preserve the fruits of victory. So far as is known, San Diego established the first city postwar planning committee, on July 23, 1942, only about six weeks after the historic Battle of Midway had blunted the Japanese drive on Pearl Harbor. However, this surprising victory by American naval forces fighting with definitely inferior resources against a heavily favored and overwhelming Japanese armada was not then understood to be the decisive battle that it would later be recognized as. Of course, this data was long before the tide had been turned in the Solomons, or at El Alamein, or at Stalingrad and considerably before the coastal cities had quit worrying about invasion, raids, or sabotage from the enemy action.[96] In fact, in July 1942, the cities were still enforcing blackouts, collecting helmets, establishing block organizations, and sitting atop their tallest buildings anxiously watching for Japanese Zeros and submarine periscopes. Yet at this problematical moment, the San Diego Chamber of Commerce gamely decided that the struggle itself had been won and began to wonder what their city would win from it.

The consensus seemed to be that it would win a lot—one way or another. "San Diego has the alternative of becoming a ghost city after the war, or retaining its present industries and developing into a great metropolitan community," the Chamber of Commerce warned in its December report on postwar planning to the community.[97] The report is an interesting document, divided by the committee into four parts: (1) winning the war, (2) retaining existing payrolls after the war, (3) planning for postwar problems and for a "Greater San Diego," and (4) creating an organization to take appropriate action to retain existing payrolls after the war and to begin the work of organizing and making plans for other postwar developments. In other words, the report really had two parts—winning the war and keeping the winnings.[98]

To effect the latter, the Chamber appointed a twenty-man committee to make long-range plans for the future and collected a considerable war chest to implement its goals. The Chamber raised a $240,000 fund to create the city's blueprint for the future and proposed to secure another $120,000 later.[99] The twenty-man committee had an interesting, but not at all surprising, makeup. Four, or 20 percent, represented the defense interests of the Port of the Palms, including one retired vice admiral; Harry Woodhead, president of Consolidated Vultee Aircraft Corporation and a leader of the postwar drive for aerial rearmament; his assistant, David G. Fleet, son of the corporation's founder; and Fred Rohr, president of Rohr Aircraft Company. Four bankers shared the committee's responsibility along with the inevitable Phil Swing, the real father of Boulder Dam and because of its water, much of Southern California as well; two members of the San Diego Chamber of Commerce; two other politicians, including the mayor and chairman of the county Board of Supervisors; two building contractors; the curator of the San Diego Museum of Natural History; a representative of the Bach Company; the vice president and general manager of the San Diego Gas and Electric Company; a representative of the Spreckels empire; and a seemingly lonely and outnumbered "rancher." In reality, this latter "rustic" was also president of the Escondido Water Company and a director of the California Fruit Growers' Exchange.[100] If any one of these interests did not favor growth and the continued militarization of the city, it is not immediately apparent just who that might have been.

Obviously the committee represented business and, in the case of the officers of Consolidated Aircraft and Vice President Oscar T. Jensen of the Bank of America (not to mention the Navy), pretty big business. No labor leader shared the committee's work, and precious few non-business types did either. The curator was not flanked by representatives of women's clubs, neighborhood associations (so strong in San Francisco), black or Hispanic leaders, newspaper representatives, or even ministers. The Chamber of Commerce apparently did not consider these representatives important in determining the city's future, so businessmen overwhelmingly dominated. However, there can be little doubt that these businessmen fully represented the community's thinking on the matter of continued militarization. The many city referenda over the years which donated land to the services indicate as much, as do other unimpeachable sources.

Yet that pre-eminence does not equate with "big business" or national corporations. The literature of the military-industrial complex almost uniformly assumes that big business forms the linchpin of the interface between civilian and military sectors and, indeed, that big business is the primary beneficiary of this alliance. In sharp contrast, in San Diego small business was the key, at least in the sense that the local community understood the term. With the exception of the Bank of America vice president, the Consolidated executives, and the admiral, no other representatives on the San Diego Committee for Economic Development hailed from a major corporation.[101] In fact, the city was dominated by small businesses, and its principal spokesmen were quite aware of the pitfalls of either monopoly or big business in general. Some of the leadership rhetoric of the city sounded very much like that of the Progressive era in its suspicion of both big business and labor.[102]

San Diego newspapers were not represented on the committee, but they helped to articulate the urban view of postwar planning and to propagate the idea as well. The notion was an interesting paradox, or perhaps a series of paradoxes. Although the Harbor of the Sun overwhelmingly depended upon the Navy for its livelihood, it massively distrusted the nation-state that this service represented. Although cooperation between cities and the federal government has often been described as a natural alliance against the states that have hampered and cramped urban development, San Diego saw little that was natural about it. It is true that the local boosters wanted federal resources, like Navy patronage and public works, and they wanted the national government to create a favorable climate for investment and economic progress by lowering taxation, but that was about it. None of this enhancement implied an acceptance of a large federal role in determining the direction of urban development, qualitative or quantitative. Postwar planning meant local urban or possibly metropolitan direction, but did not include the suggestions or the orders of Washington bureaucrats.

Finally, although the war had brought great advances and great opportunities for further development, San Diegans neither anticipated nor appreciated the side effects that accompanied these gains. The conflict also brought about what they considered to be government by persons the city builders alternately called "socialistic planners" and "starry eyed little social planners" whose influence resulted in "government regimentation and class room planning," "new deal socialism," and "rigid government planning."[103] The boosters feared that the nation-state would entrust the "future of this nation to theorists and dreamers, who think only in terms of social welfare" and who seemed determined to handle the postwar employment and reconversion problems with a return to the dole of the 1930s.[104] The locals favored federal participation in the form of a postwar public works program, at least in 1943, but the primacy of the role of private capital in the process of reconversion was taken for granted. And, as the war ground to a close in the great tank battles of the Eastern Front, North Africa, and France and the analogous island hopping and carrier warfare of the Pacific, the idea of federal public works apparently declined.

Of course, some San Diegans believed in government participation and supported measures like the Wagner-Murray full employment bill of 1945. The supporters included the San Diego County Federated Trades and Labor Council and the *San Diego Journal*. However, they seemed to be in a definite minority.[105]

Not that war per se appealed to the urban developers. "No lasting prosperity ever was built upon a war economy," argued the *San Diego Union*, in what must be considered one of its worst predictions. "War at its best is destructive, even though it may be necessary."[106] San Diegans liked neither the regimentation nor the violence of the global conflagration, but when they looked around for an economic base for their visions of metropolis, they found themselves embracing just such a "war economy." Hance H. Cleland, president of the Chamber of Commerce and president of San Diego Gas and Electric Company, reported for the postwar committee in July 1944 that "San Diego County's postwar economy will rest securely on four bases." Two of the bases were military—"huge permanent naval installations . . . and a naval payroll much larger than before the war," together with industry, which in San Diego meant the defense aircraft industry. Tourism and agriculture represented the other two pillars, but even agriculture was dependent upon the military for a market and for help in obtaining water needed to develop fully San Diego County farming.[107]

The Chamber of Commerce also commissioned a $70,000 study by the planning firm of Day and Zimmerman from Philadelphia to spell out the economic opportunities of San Diego, and the firm came to very much the same conclusions as the Chamber had. The Philadelphians bravely talked of economic diversification, but the war had obviously narrowed rather than broadened the economic base of the region by intensifying both naval development in the harbor and hinterland and defense aeronautical industrialization. The consultants urged the locals to develop their retail facilities so as to prevent San Diegans from having to make their customary trips to Los Angeles to shop, encouraged the intensification of the tourist business, favored the development of closer links with Mexico and Latin America, recommended the further development of agriculture, cautioned against economic narrowness, and urged the widening of the industrial base.[108] Yet after the $70,000 had been spent, the words of a local planner were just as true as before the Chamber had parted with its cash. "San Diego always will be a navy-industrial community," stated city planning engineer Glenn Rick in March 1943, and "plans should be predicated on this assumption."[109]

Maritime martial dependence did not represent diversification, but it did mean that the city could realize one of its continuing development ambitions—on its own terms. Mere numbers of population growth was not enough. For years, San Diego had feared that its zeal for growth would undermine the amenities of the region that had brought so many thousands of settlers and tourists in the first place.[110] The Navy and aircraft industry allowed them to have it both ways. These economic activities represented industrialization, but without the distressing side effects that cluttered up the skyline of Pittsburgh or so befouled the atmosphere of St. Louis with sulphur-laden coal smoke as to necessitate the use of street lamps at midday. Other adverse spinoffs would appear at the end of the war, but these tended, ironically, to preserve rather than to destroy the amenities.

And these assets heightened another irony of San Diego's existence: its concurrent dependence on the government and discomfort with that state of affairs. Much has been written about the issue of home rule for American cities, implying both the dominance of cities by their home-state governments and the need to break that dominance. In this scenario, the federal government is always the kindly benefactor, trying to nurture urban independence from its state overlords.[111] However, in San Diego and Los Angeles, the cities chafed under federal control as well. If there could be such a thing as a "city-rights movement" to curb the growing power of the nation-state, it certainly found vent in Southern California in the war and postwar years. Particularly during the global conflict, the cities of Fortress California viewed war as a totalitarian pretext, which could be manipulated by the wrong bureaucratic forces to destroy the liberties of cities. But it should be emphasized that the cities did not regard the warriors as the problem, but rather the bureaucratic, "socialistic planners" whose hand the war seemed to strengthen.

That is why their solution to the problem was at the same time ironic, eminently practical, and pre-eminently naval. By remaining a "naval-industrial center," San Diego employed Navy patronage as the means to evade bureaucratic regimentation by "a small group of radicals" in the government. Or to put the matter another way, the city allied with one segment of the modern nation-state in order to avoid the clutches of another. And, of course, naval industrialism would also enable small business to avoid the embrace of large business. The Navy would provide the underpinning for small business, middle-of-the-road, democratic capitalism, urban liberties, and the Darwinian City all at the same time. The paradoxes and complexities of this situation obviously abound, but the idea was not at all an impractical one.

San Diego had been a planning-oriented city from early on, when department store owner George W. Marston had commissioned and privately financed the first study of the city by John Nolen in 1908. In 1926 the city government invited Nolen back to have another try at planning their town. The Border City thereafter implemented the plan piecemeal through prosperity and depression and was fully prepared with a list of needed public improvements when the war emergency began to transform the Harbor of the Sun. The federal government simply accepted these designs and geared its own construction to the San Diego plan, which had taken the Navy into account in the first place. Under this partnership, "civic improvements" fairly leaped ahead. "When the Federal Government announced it would build a waterfront highway to aid Navy traffic, the city produced, ready-made, its plans for a Harbor Drive, and Harbor Drive was tailored to the city's own specifications," explained a state reconversion study. "When the Federal Government needed streets, bridges, storm drains, sewers, harbor improvements, the city produced the plans—and the Federal Government did the building." And paid much of the impressive bill! Seventy percent of the $35.5 million, ten-year program was built "in half the time at less than half the cost to the city."[112]

Housing illustrated the pitfalls of not planning. In this realm the city did not have a blueprint already made up, and the federal government built the housing where there were "no sewers, no utilities, no shopping district, no schools, and no transportation." To avoid a repetition of this mistake when the next opportunity came for getting a ten-year program at half price, and to be prepared in case the federal government enacted a postwar public works program, San Diego made more lists.[113]

The city would need to cooperate with the Navy in investing the "huge sums" that were earmarked for airport improvements and for a long list of projects like street building, beautification, "a school system second to none" (to go with a Navy second to none), harbor construction, parks (like Mission Bay), sewer projects, and so forth. The overall program was a cross between a public works program and a city beautiful plan.[114] The Philadelphia consulting firm also recommended industry hunting, upgrading tourist and retail facilities, stimulating county agriculture, developing Mission Bay for recreation, and creating a harbor authority to gain full control over the bay (San Diego proper controlled only a part of the harbor). To implement these suggestions, the Chamber of Commerce collected a peacetime war chest of $240,000 to which $120,000 was to be added, hired a staff divided into sections with functional responsibilities for hunting industry and so forth, commissioned the Day and Zimmerman study, and established a branch office in Sacramento and another in Washington.[115] With such a program, San Diego would be no "ghost town" after the war, but rather "Greater San Diego, the Port of the Palms," a partnership between small business and a big Navy.

While San Diego began thinking about the future of this alliance well before the war ended, Los Angeles began considering postwar planning well before the conflict began. Although it did not establish a postwar planning committee before San Diego did, it saw the need for postwar planning as early as February 1941, ten months before American entry.[116] However, in most other respects its response to the postwar planning issue was remarkably similar to that of San Diego. Early on, Angelenos drew a distinction between "community planning" and "socialistic planning" such as the government would engage in.[117] Thus, as in the case of San Diego, the focus of postwar planning would be local, in this case metropolitan, in scope.[118] That meant that the City of Angels would also allot primacy in reconversion to free enterprise and would agree to a government role only insofar as it would protect and promote free entrprise through such acts as lowering tariffs and taxes, defense spending, and so forth.[119]

In the case of Los Angeles, there was considerable suspicion of planning per se. One spokesman argued that no one could know the shape of the future well enough to plan any significant portion of the economy to accommodate it; another urged planning for flexibility; and another promoted reconstructing the values of free enterprise.[120] The city was downright skeptical of the rumored federal works projects and accepted the idea only in limited form. Still another critic spoke disparagingly of the "postwar planning epidemic," and most seemed to sense the same totalitarian implications in government planning that disturbed San Diegans. Spokesmen saw both war and planning as totalitarian pretexts.[121]

However, Los Angeles did establish its own postwar planning list; and like that of its junior partner in Southern California, the list had to do with "war winnings." Like San Diego, the list included federal resources but not control or direction. In a January 1945 speech before "a capacity audience of 1000 Chamber members and officials, high ranking military officers, city, and county and state officials, war heroes and others," incoming president LeRoy M. Edwards led the charge into the postwar era. "We have during the war built this community into a great industrial center and we shall fight to maintain the hard won supremacy we have achieved during the war," promised the Chamber's fifty-second president. Keeping that position would require that the West "retains and develops a steel industry sufficient to meet the requirements of the Pacific Coast," an "airport second to none," and a lock on the aircraft industry. "We have achieved the leadership of the world in production of airplanes," said Edwards, "and we must make certain we do not lose that supremacy in the years to come." The Chamber leader went on to explain that "during the war our harbor has been turned into a great shipbuilding industry; . . . it is unthinkable that we allow our shipbuilding industry to decline as we did following World War I."[122]

Aside from these four major categories, the president listed a freeway system and the re-employment of veterans as prime necessities of peace. It is interesting to note that of the four critical necessities noted by the Chamber executive, every one had war and defense written all over it; and of the four, only the aircraft industry had come to Los Angeles before the military crisis began. Shipbuilding had been negligible in the City of Angels before the war; the Fontana steelworks in nearby San Bernardino County had been created for the war effort, and like the Geneva Steel works near Provo, Utah, it was heavily subsidized by the government; and the airport had little or no civilian traffic before the war proved the practicability of that mode of travel. War was the very making of these enterprises.

Los Angeles also had its own list of infrastructural improvements, which included a new civic center, an auditorium to strengthen the aesthetic side of the city's life, transportation improvements beyond the new freeway system, and improvements to the harbor to allow it to resume its role in overseas trade and to accommodate the "greatly expanded military operations likely to be maintained here after the war." Flood control, a new sewage treatment plant, and a miscellany of other projects rounded out the program.[123] Of course, Angeleno leaders fretted over the question of employment for returning veterans and produced a literature explaining how to deal with this problem.[124] However, the most important way to deal with veteran employment was to guarantee a booming economy. But that feat was largely an individual's job, undertaken with the help of "community" organizations like the Chamber of Commerce. "We are going to hear a great deal of 'planning' from now on," warned *Southern California Business* two weeks after the dropping of the first atomic bomb. "'Planning' will be the rallying cry of the advocates of statism. . . . 'Planning' also will attract those who are appalled by the size of the task which lies before us. . . . Both groups are wrong," argued the chamber journal. "The primary responsibility for planning reconversion rests with individual management. . . . That is your job—it begins today in your own place of business."[125]

San Francisco experienced about the same postwar planning activity as its rivals, but its experience differed at least somewhat in degree. "The City that knows how" got into the postwar planning business somewhat later than its two California competitors, getting down to work on the matter only in early 1943.[126] However, once into this process, it did a thorough job of assessing its own future. As with the other Darwinian contestants, the retention of the spoils of war took precedence over avoiding a postwar recession or employing its returning veterans. Those matters were not entirely neglected by postwar San Francisco planners, but they definitely had a lower priority than boosterism.

The Board of Supervisors' resolution calling for the establishment of a postwar planning committee set the tone. "The seaports of the western coastal apron of America will contend as rightful heirs for the estate of stupendous prosperity— inevitably inherent in the wake of total war," the supervisors informed the mayor. "It becomes the solemn duty of San Francisco to awaken to its destiny now; to summon her men of vision and action into counsel to the end that the mantle of preeminence shall fall upon the port of San Francisco when the guns are silent again."

The legislators went on to urge that "the impetus created under war conditions must be maintained when bombs cease to rain from the skies." Perhaps because it had been losing out vis-à-vis Los Angeles and San Diego, the San Francisco resolution noted also that there is "dire need for [the] resurrection of the inspirited enterprise that built this great city, and rebuilt it after the earthquake of 1906, in order to realize its "destiny."[127] Other leaders would reiterate this theme as the postwar era neared.[128]

Although many feared unemployment at one time or another, temporary or long-term, the belief in a postwar recession or depression was not strong in either the Southland or the Bay Area. Perhaps the key to the city builders' relative indifference to the unemployment issue was their attitude regarding the new migrants who had come to work in the war industries. Unlike immigration restrictionists worried about jobs or depression officials concerned about welfare costs, the Darwinian City boosters did not want to ship their new residents back home, since they provided larger markets, bigger labor pools, and greater representation in the Congress.

Most boosters, then, viewed the postwar period primarily as an opportunity that must be seized.[129] They also believed that urban design was the key to making the most of the opportunity. In the Bay Area as in the Southland, the war's conclusion stimulated the science of city planning. Like Los Angeles, "The City" compiled a master plan, and in fact the attempt to move from war to peace represented a turning point in the history of the city planning department. The Down Town Association had long campaigned for a strengthened city planning component in city government, and the postwar planning boom brought success to this fight. "This was accomplished by according that body the responsibility for the preparation of a postwar planning program based on recommendations of the various city department heads." As the *Downtowner* put it, "City Planning and Postwar Planning became practically synonymous during 1944."[130]

Urban design came to be seen in almost mystical terms. "A plan is a great deal more than at first it seems," rhapsodized the *Downtowner*. "A plan is a thing of power which, like the bursting seed in springtime, must grow into the beautiful flower of fulfillment. In its very creation forces are set in motion which will not be denied."[131] Since much of the postwar plan did ultimately grow to fulfillment, one must assume that someone along the way had more than a little gardening experience.

Regional cooperation in postwar planning was taken for granted, as various interested parties seized the opportunities of postwar conversion to strengthen the unity of a traditionally fragmented region. This included not only the cities of the Bay Area but the rural areas as well, for "the people of the nearby country in many respects depend for their well being on the prosperity of the city."[132] In San Francisco, however, there was an urgency that surpassed that in the Southland. "The City" had been torn by labor strife for at least a decade before the war and somewhat into that period; its port had lost ground to that of Los Angeles; its population had steadily declined compared with that of the City of the Angels, and worse still, it suffered actual, as opposed to relative industrial decline over the twenty-year interwar period. Fortunately the war had reversed that trend and revived industrialization in San Francisco, and it wanted to protect that renaissance. It also longed to eliminate the demoralization that had infected the area for too many years. As L. Deming Tilton, the director of city planning in San Francisco, put it, "Local belief in our destiny has been deplorably weak."[133] Rex Nicholson, head of the booster group called Builders of the West, noted a tendency to flounder: "We have been talking for two years, now let's act." Thomas P. Ludcke of the Junior Chamber of Commerce set the agenda when he asserted that "the *Bay Region* can be the industrial capital of the west!"[134]

The city builders stressed that private enterprise must carry the load in postwar conversion, but as in the Southland, the actual list of planning projects was eminently public. "The main emphasis in post-war construction must be to open opportunities for private enterprise on which a sound national economy can be based," urged the *Downtowner*. Thus, as in the Southland, public enterprise would plan, but in such a way as to help private enterprise create opportunities. The ideas contained in the plan suggested little that was new and would have been embraced by boosters in 1925 as easily as they were by those in 1945.

The Citizens Postwar Planning Committee recommended the building of a modern airport as the number-one postwar goal; they followed that with various transportation proposals, including rehabilitation of mass transit and construction of highways, streets, and motor terminals, and ended with further ideas on how to upgrade health, water, and sewer facilities.[135] The construction of the Bayshore Freeway was part of the longstanding attempt to link the city more closely with the Peninsula, especially to the new airport which was being built in San Mateo County, south of San Francisco. The airport and the Bayshore highway had been on the city builders' agenda since the mid-1920s, as had transit improvement, street modernization, and most of the remainder of the program.

The emergence of the redevelopment issue and of the second bay crossing idea were relatively recent, however. As in other center cities across the land, the 1940 census had come as something of a shock because it emphasized center-city decline in relation to suburban areas. The war prevented remedial action and actually added to the flight (decentralization) from the city, as San Francisco learned to its dismay in trying to solve its wartime housing crisis. However, even as the bombs fell on Dresden, Berlin, Tokyo, and London, San Francisco planners and boosters were visualizing a modest little blitz of their own against slums and blight that would ultimately clear large amounts of South of Market and other land for redevelopment. Similarly, the idea of a second bay crossing had emerged since the completion of the Bay Bridge to the East Bay in 1936.[136]

Neither naval nor aircraft industry considerations played as large a role in San Francisco's postwar thinking as they did in the South. Perhaps "The City" had given up on acquiring the aircraft industry and perhaps it took the Navy for granted, but it did not fight for aircraft factories nor advertise itself as a "Navy-industrial" town as San Diego did. San Francisco planners envisaged a federal role in postwar planning, especially in regard to the retention of the Geneva Steel Plant at Provo, Utah, and to highways and airports, which had first and second priority in the city's plans.[137] As in the case of the Southland metropolises, the implicit assumption of federal aid underlay a large part of the program, although this dependence was not trumpeted about. Moreover, San Francisco did not fear Leviathan in the way that San Diego and Los Angeles did.

Even the smaller jurisdictions of Urban California looked forward to a "greater" future. Vallejo, which had more than doubled its population under the impetus of war, looked to a postwar world in which it would retain its gains and finally achieve the economic diversification of which it dreamed. It will be recalled that at the time of its postwar study, Vallejo had, besides the Navy, only one flour mill and one small packing plant.

Like the other Darwinian cities, Vallejo dreamed of more. Not only was its postwar planning study a resounding booster document, but it was actually done by Rex Nicholson and the Builders of the West, one of the advocates of industrial decentralization of eastern industry to the West. "For the first time since it was founded, Vallejo has a local population of sufficient size to justify the expansion and diversification of all of its business and industrial potentialities," exulted the Nicholson postwar report on Vallejo. He went on to state an important premise upon which California cities based much of their success, when he noted that, "viewed constructively, this new population is the greatest adjunct to its natural assets that it is possible to have."[138] As most California cities realized, population brought political power, markets, labor pools, industrial skills, concentrations of capital, and, through letters home, free advertising.

A larger population would allow industrial diversification which would in turn lead to a greater number of service jobs and would help to provide the amenities necessary to keep the city a good place to live, especially for the Navy. "Vallejo must remember that the Navy has today a new and well equipped repair and maintenance base at Hunter's Point that can provide full service for both light and heavy war ships," the report cautioned. "Vallejo must also remember that the majority of the Navy officers and enlisted men would prefer to be headquartered at Hunter's Point, near San Francisco, because Vallejo lacks attractive residential and recreational facilities." That refrain was an old one in Bay Area interurban politics, and the report added urgency to it by asserting that "unless Vallejo improves the present unsightly, inadequate commercial, residential, and recreational sections, it has no right to expect the Navy to continue to maintain its main naval base at Mare Island." Looking to the city's wartime winnings, the report concluded that "Vallejo dare not content itself with a mere reverting to its former status."[139] The Navy-yard town, like its larger rivals for the affection of the Navy, moved to create a master plan to implement its program.

Although not well known, San Bernardino County by the 1980s had become an important standard metropolitan statistical area of one and a half million souls. As noted above, it too regarded its gains as "war winnings." "For untold ages the iron deposits of San Bernardino County remained untouched," noted the postwar planning study of that area. "The combination of war necessity and business courage made the dream [of steel production] into reality," continued the report. That meant 3000 jobs for the jurisdiction, and "even more important to the economy of the county and the State are the new processing and fabricating plants which the Fontana plant will make possible." Like Vallejo, San Bernardino County wanted to hold onto the windfalls of war and build a more diversified economy upon them.[140] Most of the California cities investigated here did too. Long Beach, Oakland, Alameda—to mention only some of the other urban areas largely affected by the conflict—had the same notions.

However, not every city did. Richmond, which was literally swamped by the conflict, was still awash by its aftermath. The north bay arsenal of democracy regarded itself as a "war stricken," "crippled" city, which had suffered the financial and "physical ravages of the bloodless war which has been waged within its city limits since 1941." Worse still, "Richmond's municipal financial ability was blitzed as severely by the war as the city's other facilities," making reconstruction impossible. "Everybody knows that World War II is everybody's war," noted the state reconstruction and re-employment commission, and Richmond demanded that everyone—that is, the United States government—should pay for the damage.

Unlike the other California cities studied, Richmond hoped only to get its head above water after the war and seemed to harbor no grandiose illusions about the future. It just wanted compensation.[141] Nonetheless, it was a distinct minority in a state full of "Imperial Cities" to whose intramural urban struggles postwar planning was to be a useful instrument.

Planning the Darwinian City, therefore, took precedence in each of the cities over more social and perhaps more rational approaches to the conclusion of the war. California boosters were not "dreaming the rational city," to employ Christine Boyer's phrase. Nor did matters like income redistribution, housing, and social services figure prominently, and usually they did not matter at all. However, in each of the major cities, a more social approach to planning existed side by side with that of the Imperial City. Despite its minority status, this more academic planning commanded the allegiance of many prominent Californians. It differed radically from the substance of Imperial City planning except in two respects, urban renewal and re-employment. Redevelopment, city and regional planning, re-employment, and public housing characterized more liberal planning efforts in Urban California. Redevelopment interested the booster planners, but not as much as other matters, and not as much as apparently was the case in other American cities.[142] Redevelopment appealed to California cities for the same reasons that it attracted other American urban areas, not because it would provide the means of improving the lives of center-city residents, who might live in poverty or close to it, but rather to improve the chances of cities in their struggles with each other.

In that respect, their approach differed fundamentally from that of the liberal planners, who wanted to make the cities rational and just, not economic Leviathans. The liberals had little interest in the contest among cities. Instead, they emphasized postwar employment, housing, redevelopment, and city and regional planning of both a more enlightened and more technical variety.[143] If the planners of the Darwinian City hoped to use planning to retain its wartime populations, the liberals wondered where they would be housed and employed. They worried too about downtown redevelopment; and, unlike their booster counterparts, they concerned themselves not only with the techniques of redevelopment, such as financing, federal aid, court precedents, existing redevelopment legislation, and so forth, but also with what would happen to the residents displaced from the clearance projects.[144] Also unlike their competitors for dominance of the postwar planning process, they cared more for planning in the abstract sense and believed more fully in its benefits.[145] And the scope of their planning horizons was broader too. Conservatives in California cities had already come to see the virtues of planning on a metropolitan basis, and they boosted the West in general. However, their concept of planning was much more local than that of the liberals, who foresaw, or thought that they foresaw, the need for planning on a Pacific Slope-wide basis.

The two parted company on the role of the federal government as well. The defenders of the Imperial City were coming to see the virtues of a federal role in downtown redevelopment because it appeared that it could not be done in any other manner. As Catherine Bauer somewhat sarcastically put it, if "there is no more profit in urban land and . . . downtown property owners must in desperation join their rural brethren as wards of the government, then we have indeed reached a major crisis."[146] Downtown property interests *did* come to see the virtues in a partnership with the federal government in order to avoid becoming "wards of the government."[147] This conversion troubled liberals somewhat. It seemed odd to them to see the former opponents of slum clearance, housing, and planning now embracing those ideas as their own, but not odd enough to cause the liberals to change their minds about the virtues of redevelopment. Nor to convince them that the modern nation-state might be a threat to their own values.[148] They were much more the champions of the notion of mixed enterprise between federal and local governments. And they were enthusiastic about a different kind of partnership, one in planning rather than metropolitan aggrandizement. The friends of the Darwinian City wanted federal resources to promote urban areas, but the liberals wanted federal guidance and aid for urban and regional planning to humanize, channel, and rationalize that development.[149]

A number of organizations carried the liberal banner into the postwar planning fight. The California Planning and Housing Association served as a statewide forum for liberal planning, and each city had its own version of this group, such as the San Francisco Housing and Planning Association. The city planning commission of the state also contributed membership to these liberal groups.[150] Quite a number of prominent or subsequently prominent Californians belonged to such organizations, such as L. Deming Tilton, director of the San Francisco city planning department and sometime member of the National Resources Planning Board; Melvyn Douglas, the actor; Mrs. Jesse Colman, wife of the veteran, conservative San Francisco supervisor; Paul C. Smith, editor of the *San Francisco Chronicle;* Catherine Bauer, the planner; her future husband, William Wurster, the architect; Mel Scott, who would become the dean of American city planning historians; Carey McWilliams, one of the greatest California historians; John F. Shelley, head of the San Francisco Labor Council and future congressman and mayor; Richard Neutra, the architect; scholar Max Radin; Helen Gahagan, the congresswoman; C. J. Haggerty, head of the California American Federation of Labor; Robert W. Kenny, the state attorney general; and John Anson Ford, the longtime Los Angeles County Supervisor.[151]

Despite all of this glitter, the liberal planners did not have much of an immediate impact upon postwar planning in the major California cities. They helped to publicize and promote the issue of redevelopment and they helped to spread the doctrines of academic planning, but even these achievements required conservative and booster help to put over. Otherwise, the liberals did not achieve much. Public housing made little headway, and rational planning itself was subordinated to the Darwinian City, as was the kind of federal-urban partnership they dreamed of. Compared with the impact of Imperial City planners in guiding postwar development, that of the liberals was puny indeed. One has only to glance at the cities of California today to see that it was the booster vision of postwar planning that prevailed. In San Francisco, for example, the airport was rapidly modernized from the end of the war; the Bayshore Freeway providing access to the Peninsula has long been a reality; a regional rapid transit subway and elevated system serving Bay Area center cities has been developed; the surface transit system has been rehabilitated; Market Street traffic problems have been alleviated, if not cured; a modern produce district was created and a spectacular new residential and business area was put in its place; the Broadway Tunnel was opened in 1952; a huge renewal area was created south of Market; the infrastructure has been modernized; and so forth. Postwar planning for economic growth succeeded. Social planning hardly got a start.[152]

The Darwinian cities of California had their own notions about the lessons of the war, and these had to do primarily with war winnings, not the rationalization or the humanization of the process of urbanization. This was what postwar planning was about in Fortress California—keeping new industries, retaining population gains, and cashing in on war-stimulated technologies and trends in the future. Even the California State Reemployment and Reconstruction Commission looked optimistically ahead in December 1944 to a future of full employment and the good life for all native Californians and the recent migrants as well. "Even within the next three or four years, the new processes which war has initiated may give Father the chance to retire earlier, to enjoy the fruits of his labor before he is too old," stated the commission report. "Mother, too, if she likes, may leave the factory and give more time to the children," the authors continued. "Social security programs can be broadened, and young people can stay in school longer. It is the kind of full employment for which Californians have been fighting."[153]

Obviously, this kind of planning differs considerably from the type that historians have written about. Unlike their liberal counterparts, the city builders accepted but did not depend overly on federal public works; they considered but did not greatly fear postwar unemployment; they accepted but did not concentrate upon downtown redevelopment (freeways were more important in L.A., the airport in San Francisco, and the harbor in San Diego); they did not like the idea of social planning; and so forth. Most important, they planned to win something from winning the war. Certainly they dominated the postwar planning process in city after city. Their agenda usually listed long-sought public works projects. Since this was the kind of planning that actually occurred, as opposed to only being written about, it has a better claim to the attention of urbanists than it has been given so far, especially compared with the social planning thought that has so far held center stage.

Perhaps, too, the postwar planning debate should not be considered a reflection of that between Robert Moses of New York and his critics. Like the tyro of New York City politics, the western urban planners suspected the leftist origins of social planning; but whereas Moses dreamed of the rational city, the booster planners had an agenda of their own, one that has so far been neglected by planning historians.[154] Like it or not, booster planning shaped the California metropolis and therefore should shape the agenda of planning historians as well. To do otherwise is to ignore the vast majority of urban planning in the Golden State.

The liberals had not expected this outcome. At least some viewed the war and the postwar planning problems as liberal opportunities. "War, we are often told, entrenches reaction," noted Dr. Harry Girvetz in an article written for the California Planning and Housing Association in late 1943. "But in Britain, Canada, and Australia there has been a steady movement away from reaction, all of which suggests that there is no necessary connection between war and the decline of liberalism." To Girvetz the war had been not so much the test case for the free enterprise system that the chambers of commerce deemed it, as the proving ground for the nation-state. "The great productive effort of which we are so justly proud is partially a result of the operations of the system of free enterprise," he noted. "But it is largely the result of an overall planning of our collective effort," in which the "hated, damned, reviled government—but government nevertheless set priorities, controlled prices and wages, guaranteed markets to producers, and froze workers in their jobs."[155] Despite the fears of some liberals that the war strengthened the other side, Girvetz saw the conflict in about the same light as the chambers of commerce, as creating a competing power center in the form of a more potent nation-state.

Yet if the war and postwar periods represented an opportunity for liberals, it did not emerge from the effort to reconvert California cities from a war to a peacetime basis. Harry Girvetz might urge liberals to "apply the spectacular lessons of wartime planning to the purposes of peace"; Robert W. Kenny might quote Daniel Burnham to urge Californians to "make no little plans"; and Catherine Bauer might claim "that a revolution is in process in the entire structure of housing and planning"; but in fact the lessons remained unapplied, the plans shriveled, and the revolution failed.[156] Certainly the war did not entrench reaction, but it did enthrone the Darwinian City.

PART II

THE CITY AND THE SWORD IN AN ERA OF DEFENSE: THE ATROPHY OF WAR AND THE HYPERTROPHY OF URBANIZATION

World War II created marked changes in California cities, especially those closely linked to the military services. Whether it liked it or not, Urban California was engulfed in the tide of military might flowing toward the Japanese-dominated lands of the Far East. The residue of this flow created vast new martial resources of almost every sort. At the close of the conflict, California lost many of these gains, but still retained an impressive amount. On this base, the Golden State built its current status as the richest and most powerful of American states. Indeed, if California were an independent nation, it would be one of the top ten economic powers in the world. Nonetheless, significant continuities accompanied the growth of the partnership between the city and the sword into the Second World War and beyond. Much of what happened from 1941 to 1961 was merely a continuation of trends already well under way in the interwar period.

The war itself did not come near to creating the close and enduring relationship between the civil and military sectors of American society. The federal-urban partnership had already begun to produce naval bases for San Diego and San Francisco, air force bases for Riverside and Marin County, aircraft industries for San Diego and the Los Angeles suburbs, shipbuilding contracts for the Bay Area and the Southland, and harbor improvements for all. Few important additions in the evolving partnership between the city and the sword did not hark back to these earlier developments, some of them fairly remote in the interwar epoch. Urban leadership created the close association between the city and the sword, and this in turn directed the riches of the nation-state to these California urban destinations. Nevertheless, for the duration of the conflict itself, the imperatives of war clearly overbore the necessities of urbanization. Change dominated continuity and, true to the formulae of Oscar Handlin, Donald Boulding, and others, forces beyond the control of California cities molded their present and their immediate future. From 1941 to 1945, war and the modern nation-state outweighed all other considerations.

These influences greatly accelerated the process of urbanization. California cities grew, although not at the rate that they had in the Progressive era, or in the absolute terms they would in the postwar years. That perhaps represented the most dramatic break with the past, but other important developments accompanied this transformation. Most important, the United States government regained much more freedom to plan its West Coast defense policies and to override local urban interests. However, this reassertion of national interest largely confirms the interpretation of urban power in the earlier period.

The great naval base at San Francisco grew spectacularly, and so did that at San Diego. Los Angeles also received massive military patronage, but at the same time it lost some of its previous assets. The government forced the decentralization of the aircraft industry with the advent of the war, and even earlier Los Angeles had permanently lost the fleet anchorage of the Pacific Navy. Now at the command of the soldiers, the cities did their bidding, but they did not entirely suspend their own intramural struggles. Each battled to capture as much of the war effort as they could accommodate and sometimes more, and each plotted a resumption of the "Darwinian" urban conflict upon the return of peace. At war's conclusion the competition did resume: for the old assets that the war had redistributed, for new assets like jet aircraft production and electronics, and for any other resources that became available, from government surplus to air force academies to regional government purchasing offices. Yet one thing changed dramatically. Great power war disappeared. Yet, paradoxically, cities grew rapidly because of the impetus of defense spending.

CHAPTER 6

••••••••••••••••••••••••••••••

From Warfare to Welfare:
The Revival of the Darwinian City

> The Down Town Association has been fortunate indeed in having among its leadership such men of vision who have dedicated it to the purpose of community development and created a force which carried the organization onward through the years working for the good of San Francisco. From the ashes of our greatest catastrophes these men have helped and are helping build a greater city.
>
> WM. G. MERCHANT
> President of the San Francisco Down Town Association,
> December 30, 1942

Although the Second Great War had temporarily upstaged the incessant struggles of the Darwinian cities, these entities reasserted themselves with the close of the conflict. It did so early on in shipbuilding, where the war had raised hopes highest and dashed them to the ground most forcefully. One of the first moves to reactivate the industry came in 1948 from the San Francisco City Board of Supervisors, which urged Congress to bring about a renaissance of Bay Area ship construction. Soon thereafter the port cities of the Coast banded together to pressure Congress, probably with support from another neglected region, the historic South.

Everything about the ensuing campaign was reminiscent of earlier struggles to win governmental favors for urban areas. In this case several urban groups from Seattle and Puget Sound, San Francisco, Oakland, Richmond and the Bay Area, Wilmington, San Pedro, and Long Beach in the Los Angeles area, San Diego, and Portland united to coerce Congress. Within each region, the usual bipartisan, non-ideological, non-vocational alliances prevailed. Chambers of commerce, newspapers, shipbuilding managers' associations, unions, veterans, civic groups, city governments, Democrats, Republicans, and liberal and conservative congressional representatives joined together in the fray. The revealingly named Pacific Coast Committee for Shipbuilding for National Defense was perhaps typical of these alliances.

In the 1949 phase of the fight, quite a number of city councils endorsed the West Coast's claims, but then and thereafter the San Francisco Bay Area clearly predominated in this struggle as it had in wartime shipbuilding. San Francisco, Oakland, and Alameda representatives waged this battle consistently; Long Beach representatives did so intermittently; and those of Los Angeles and San Diego did so even less. Among the interested pressure groups, labor stood out as vividly as the Bay Area did among metropolitan areas. As we have seen before, the linking of the city and the sword was not merely the work of greedy munitions makers and wealthy profiteers. Union men and labor representatives in the Congress viewed military spending as social spending. In the shipbuilding and merchant marine struggles, they took the lead in the process of transforming warfare into welfare.[1]

Many of the arguments advanced to revive the shipbuilding and merchant marine industries on the West Coast, and especially in Fortress California, smacked of déjà vu, beginning with the blanket justification of national defense. Spokesmen of the shipbuilding revival and the maritime renaissance that came to be associated with it disavowed any sectional interest and took their stand on patriotic grounds. A strong shipbuilding industry would serve the country well in time of war, argued the port city defenders. Both world wars had highlighted America's maritime unpreparedness, and the Korean War served only to strengthen that situation. These experiences must never be allowed to happen again, the argument went, but already there were bad signs. Even before the end of the Korean War, the maritime and shipbuilding industries had entered the familiar cycle of postwar decline. What the United States needed, according to these spokesmen, was to have a merchant marine perpetually ready and "second to none." It was the way these requirements were cast, plus the prospect of an active shipbuilding industry putting more people to work, that made the proposal all the more palatable. National security, however, took precedence over employment, at least in theory.

Shortsighted government attempts at economy and favoritism to shipbuilders in the Northeast had damaged the West Coast business. So had generous subsidies to European builders, given in an attempt to help revive their war-torn economies and to enable them to earn dollars for the purchase of American goods. Ignorance of the role of these two industries in time of war had hurt too. Moreover, expensive American construction and operation costs derived from a higher standard of living, while our allies and other foreign competitors tolerated lower living standards and gave greater subsidies to their carriers and builders, complained the city boosters. Under these conditions, Americans could not compete without government assistance. A neglected point, of course, was that national defense was designed to protect Americans from their enemies abroad, not to uphold their living standards.

However, although the employment rationale usually took a back seat to that of national defense, it always lurked just below the surface. For example, it is interesting to note that the maritime boosters saw no opposition between guns and butter and, in fact, ordinarily contended that their program provided an honorable way to combine the two. "Surely a sensible thing to do in the face of increasing unemployment," editorialized the *Oakland Post Enquirer,* "would be to revitalize our maritime establishments which would contribute so much to our prosperity and which are so utterly essential to our peace and security." This renaissance would "provide employment on a wide scale and at the same time avoid the wasteful evils of a political make-work program," the editor contended.[2]

Congressmen John F. Shelley of San Francisco, John J. Allen of Oakland, George P. Miller of Alameda, Clyde Doyle of Long Beach, and Bob Wilson of San Diego proposed various schemes to derive this aid. The United States government could extend greater subsidies to American flag ships and builders than those called for under the Maritime Act of 1936. For example, the government could allow shipbuilders a differential of 15 percent, whereas before the war the asking price of Pacific coast shipbuilders had been only 6 percent. Moreover, American foreign aid and mutual security guidelines should take into account the impact of these policies on American shipping and shipbuilding interests; military transportation of supplies and men should not be allowed to compete with private transport; and closed or threatened naval shipyards like those at Long Beach and, later, at Hunter's Point, should be reactivated or protected. And above all, the government should divide its private shipbuilding contracts between the Atlantic, Gulf, and Pacific coasts and the Great Lakes on the basis of national defense criteria, that is, on geographic bases rather than on low bidding or other economic grounds. The *Alameda Times Star* captured the spirit of this argument perfectly when it assured its readers that "an outlay of an added few million dollars is wholly incidental to the problem involved."[3]

Particularly for shipbuilding, this argument lay at the heart of what the coastal urban leaders wanted. It also represented a clever and perhaps disingenuous attempt to turn the urgent contemporary movement for a radical decentralization of defense industries to the benefit of the fortress cities of California. As early as 1939, Chicago and other interior places vociferously complained of the outrageous centralization of the airframe industry, a configuration that the war altered drastically. While peace brought a return to the older pattern, ironically the atomic bomb made a heavily centralized aircraft industry even more vulnerable than it had been in the era of conventional bombs. The government was forced once again to think seriously about deconcentration. As we shall see, Fortress California resisted that idea with genuine indignation. However, while denying the need for dispersal of the aircraft industry, Californians seized upon the principle as it applied to industries in which *they* were underrepresented, steel and shipbuilding among others.

Now the halls of Congress echoed with the cry for the decentralization of the boat construction business, which was highly concentrated along the northeastern coast of the country in "captive yards." These were dominated by Big Steel and other supposedly nefarious monopolists, to the detriment of all other coastal yards.[4] Just as before the war, this arrangement shortchanged the Pacific coast. Congressman Jack Shelley charged that not one private firm on the entire Pacific coast had even a single new ship construction job under way at the outbreak of the Korean War. California had fewer than 3000 persons employed in its shipyards. To put the matter another way, Shelley pointed out that in 1943 at the peak of shipbuilding activity during the war, Atlantic coast yards employed 513,000 people compared with 497,000 on the Pacific coast. One year after Korea, the former retained 70,000 workers, and the Pacific coast only 13,000.[5]

The onslaught to change this imbalance did not produce a triumph of the proportions of the seventy-group air force, but the spoils of this victory were not exactly marginal either. For example, press rumors that the Hunter's Point Naval Shipyard would be closed and its functions transferred to Vallejo and Mare Island quickly produced a San Francisco campaign to keep its own facility open.[6] The San Francisco yard remained active, but the Long Beach Naval Shipyard fell victim to the Navy's economy drive in the same year. However, by mid-1951 the latter was back in operation. The Korean War influenced this decision, even though it was not fought against a major or even minor naval power. Nor was the United States lacking Navy ships for the war or places to repair battleships, and Long Beach was the chief repair base for these obsolescent vessels. Perhaps a case could be made for the necessity of another Navy repair base, but for a war of this dimension, the facilities in San Diego, Puget Sound, and San Francisco Bay might easily have sufficed.[7]

In any case, the decision to reopen the Long Beach shipyard did not occur in immediate response to the outbreak of this latest Asian war, but rather in early 1951, after a six-month campaign by Representative Clyde Doyle of that city. The impact of the congressman's efforts can be surmised from the fact that the yard would shortly employ 3500 workers at a time when the California state unemployment offices listed 7000 to 8000 residents as out of a job.[8] In effect, the opening of one shipyard cut the state unemployment rate by half. Thereafter, government shipyards in California seemed to prosper, and the urban boosters turned their attention to the plight of the private shipbuilding industry.

Because that part of the business languished despite the Korean War and since certain metropolitan interests like the Los Angeles Chamber of Commerce objected on principle to government agencies doing work that private ones could perform, the shipbuilding fight shifted to different bases.[9] The Merchant Marine Act of 1936 had authorized further ship construction along with a 6 percent differential to enable West Coast builders to compete with the East, and the representatives of the California port cities defended every section of this act with tenacity and skill. When congressional economizers criticized the act as a "boondoggle" on behalf of shipbuilders, ship operators, and sailors, Shelley, Allen, and Miller pointed out that the act provided for the wherewithal to maintain the national defense and reminded the critics that sailors, shipbuilders, and shippers were hardly the only Americans receiving federal subsidies of one kind or another. Most attempts to amend the Merchant Marine Act were beaten off, at least through 1961.[10] This act also called for the maintenance in good condition of the American merchant marine, and that stricture in turn specified the retirement of vessels over twenty years of age. Shelley explained the need for ship replacement to the Congress in 1954 in justifying four new ships to be operated by the Moore-McCormack and Grace Lines and to be used for troop transports in case of emergency. "Ships, like most man-made machinery, are subject to wear and physical depreciation; and more important from the standpoint of national security, they rapidly become obsolete," he explained, as "technological improvements in design and construction are developed and, for wartime service, as the speed and efficiency of submarines increases and as other antishipping weapons became more potent." When the Eisenhower administration opposed him on the high ground of economy, the congressman from the Bay of St. Francis took even higher ground.

> Red ink on the Government's books is not as important to me as red blood needlessly shed through unpreparedness, and while some may think an unbalanced budget means political suicide, I prefer that to the national suicide we are now committing by failure to support our merchant marine.[11]

Whether or not the country stood in such dire peril without these four vessels is at least arguable, given the end of the Korean War and the increasing emphasis upon nuclear armaments, air power, and long-range weapons, but Shelley's rhetoric typified the port lobby's attempt to link their urban interests to the contemporary preoccupation with national defense. As early as 1949, the metropolitan-military complexes involved the Truman administration in the problems of national defense in metropolitan areas with high shipbuilding unemployment. This feat produced a thirty-five-ship program of construction, and the government assigned five of these contracts to the Bay Area. This agenda obviously did not end the supposed discrimination against the West Coast, but it did help Moore Drydock of Oakland, Todd Shipyard of Alameda, and Bethlehem Shipyard of San Francisco keep their doors open. As the period closed, the San Francisco coalition moved one step closer to the desired decentralization of the shipbuilding industry by gaining the assent of the House Armed Services Committee to the principle of dispersal.

> A healthy shipbuilding industry, that is, one ready for expansion and full-scale production, required that naval ship construction be distributed throughout the United States. . . . With the need enunciated above in mind, the Committee on Armed Services emphasized most strongly during the hearings and now repeats in this report its considered belief that the dispersal of ship-construction facilities in the various coastal areas in the United States is an essential element of our national security and that any construction contracts awarded persuant to this authorization should be distributed throughout these various coastal areas in such manner as to encourage the dispersal of vital shipbuilding facilities and to prevent undue and dangerous concentration in any particular area or areas of the United States.[12]

Congressmen Shelley, Allen, and Miller could not have stated their program any more precisely.

The campaign to salvage the merchant marine, "the fourth arm of our national defense," succeeded somewhat better. The Merchant Marine Act of 1936 provided, in addition to the shipbuilding subsidies, a minimum wage for sailors and operating subsidies for American ships to help them meet foreign competition and, if needed, to serve as auxiliaries in time of war. The martial ports' lobby vigilantly guarded these provisions and broadened them. Foreign-aid programs for Europe and Asia presented an ideal means of adding muscle to the fourth arm of defense. Since these programs represented national defense subventions to American allies, San Francisco and its maritime allies could easily argue that a part of this largesse should be dealt out to American enterprises of a similar character. That argument was the origin of the rule which stipulated that 50 percent of the tonnage of all American aid programs must be carried in American flag ships, manned by American crews. Congress adopted this rule in 1948, and year after year the metropolitan-military cities of California successfully joined with others to reaffirm this principle, which still prevailed as late as August 1954.[13]

It is impossible to state the exact monetary value of this provision, but it was considerable. Both friends and enemies of maritime subventions agreed that of the one-billion-dollar foreign aid ship transportation bill incurred between 1948 and 1952, $700 million had been paid to American flag ships.[14] Assuming that American ships really could not compete against foreign vessels without government aid, it would seem logical that hardly any of this money would have gone to American shippers in the absence of the 50 percent provision, the operating subsidies, and other government encouragements. Seven hundred million dollars represented an impressive sum in terms of contemporaneous economic and political buying power. Since these monies derived from the national government, it is obvious that the California urban coalitions that sought them cannot take sole credit for their enactment. However, neither did this form of federal influence represent an outside force over which cities exercised little or no control. Members of the metropolitan-military complexes spent considerable time and effort building urban alliances into metropolitan ones, and these, in turn, into statewide and then coastwide pressure groups to promote their local martial interests. The existence of massive federal resources in Washington is hardly open to question, but as in earlier instances, the targeting of these monies came out of a political process in which cities and metropolitan areas wield impressive power.

The Second World War paid handsome dividends to the California aeronautical industry and, in doing so, once again strengthened the ties between the city and the sword. Although the program of industrial decentralization conjured up the specter of new aircraft plants in the interior, those in the Southland received huge orders which vastly increased their capacity and output. The Southland urban masses trooped into the factories by the thousands—280,000 to be exact—at the peak of war production. At the same time, the other forces linking mars and metropolis continued to unfold. For example, Cal Tech became the manager of both the Southern California Cooperative Wind Tunnel and the Jet Propulsion Laboratory. Simultaneously, the von Karman connection continued to pay other important dividends. One of these derived from scientific research into the future of the American air force.

A meeting at La Guardia Airport in the summer of 1944 between two old Southern California hands revealed what was at stake. As usual, General Henry Arnold came right to the point. He had no more interest in the war then raging over the globe, considering it won, and therefore looked to the future to protect the country and, of course, the Air Force's part in its defense. The expertise he sought for this role "will come from the universities and the people at large," he explained to Theodore von Karman as they sat on the La Guardia runway in a parked Air Force limousine. "The next Air Force is going to be built around scientists—around mechanically minded fellows," the general continued. Arnold then informed the receptive Cal Tech scientist that he wished to establish a scientific advisory group for the Air Force which would help chart its future course by studying and planning air research. Von Karman thereupon set about organizing the Scientific Advisory Group (SAG) to the Air Force, which ultimately became the Scientific Advisory Board.

A slight ripple crested in the stream of mutual interest when Dr. Vannevar Bush, "head of the wartime Office of Scientific Research and Development," tried to limit military research to "the improvement of existing weapons," with new weapons development to be carried on by a civilian agency. Von Karman, who liked military men and institutions, predictably sided with the generals, and "Hap" Arnold apparently won the bureaucratic power struggle that ensued. Bush publicly retracted his statement, and the SAG became a reality.[15]

The California Institute of Technology shared disproportionately in its affairs. In the formative stages of this institution, von Karman worked most closely with four other men, two of them colleagues from Pasadena. Moreover, the interests of his university and its Southland metropolitan hinterland were well represented on an historic SAG mission to Germany in March 1945 to discover the extent of German progress in aeronautical research and development. Frank Wattendorf, H. S. Tsien (both of whom had worked closely with von Karman in establishing SAG), and von Karman represented Cal Tech and Metro Southern California; George Schairer represented Boeing and Seattle; and Hugh Dryden hailed from the National Bureau of Standards. In other words, Urban Southern California claimed three of the five-member mission who got to take the first look at the secrets of German aeronautical research. In urban history terms, the nation-state had one representative on the committee, Los Angeles had three, and Boeing, one. Small wonder if the other manufacturers of airframes and even the manufacturers of engines and their patron cities felt left out of this crucial voyage of exploration. At Braunschwieg and other German aerodynamic research centers, the SAG team learned a great deal. Of course, these discoveries had to benefit CIT as well because it put that institution in contact with a great deal of highly classified information about jet propulsion and rockets, two matters in which the Southland school had already become heavily interested. How much such inside information could profit one of the competitors was illustrated by the experience of Boeing, which benefitted perhaps even more fully. Schairer microfilmed German development of swept-wing airplanes which he rushed back to Seattle after telegraphing to his Puget Sound colleagues literally to halt work on their current models in order to take advantage of the new discoveries. That they did so is evidenced by the XB-47, the U.S.'s first sweepback-wing bomber, built by Boeing. Wing sweep proved to be a crucial aeronautical innovation, and representation on the visitation committee allowed Southern California and Boeing a privileged first look at German research in that field.[16]

The information together with the other SAG research that von Karman did also enabled him to affect markedly the future of the American Air Force and the very idea of air power. The resulting study argued that air power had been the decisive factor in the Allied victory on the Western Front and stressed the overall importance of technology in achieving that victory. These conclusions set the stage for the professor's plea for continued scientific research and development as the key to the military future. As von Karman often noted, such a judgment was not as self-evident as it seems today, and it had many influential opponents at the time. With the war ended, Congress did not want to fund expensive new projects; President Truman opposed expansion of the Air Force; and many Air Force officers still failed to see the long-range value of research. "A good many operational officers still lived in the old Air Force," noted a disappointed von Karman.[17] Even an airframe operative of the demonstrated abilities of president Dutch Kindelberger of North American initially "didn't like the idea of the government's spending money on research facilities instead of on planes."[18]

However, within a short time Washington was doing just that. Beginning with the efforts of Secretary Stuart Symington, the Air Force began to implement the von

Karman report, and it became the blueprint for the ensuing new Air Force. Obviously, Cal Tech and Southern California did not invariably benefit from the blueprint's implementation. For example, it lost the Arnold Engineering Development Center to Tennessee after a determined fight for a Colorado River location near the California border. The University of Tennessee promptly became space-minded, complete with its own wind tunnel, and in 1964 opened its own new "Space Institute." In an interesting confirmation of our thesis, von Karman felt that the Tennessee victory came from Senator McKellar's offer of the 40,000-acre Camp Forest site, an old World War II base.[19] Neither that tactic nor its success would have come as much of a surprise to Urban Californians.

Von Karman continued to build his interface between science, urban society, and the military as the years passed. He became head of the Technical Advisory Board of Aerojet, which had become Aerojet General after General Tire Corporation bought a controlling interest in January 1945. The Cal Tech professor also continued his services for the government. His Scientific Advisory Board apparently incubated the idea of the Rand Corporation, which grew out of curiosity on the board as to "what means could be employed by the Air Force to select and promote useful new ideas."[20] Frank Colbohm, "an ex-pilot with Douglas Aircraft Company, and a close friend of General Arnold" conceived the idea of a think tank that was eventually established in Santa Monica, where he served as its president from 1948 to 1967.[21]

Apparently von Karman merely presided over the discussions that led to the establishment of Rand, but he did take the leading role in the creation of AGARD, or the Advisory Group for Aeronautical Research and Development of NATO in early 1952, which was intended to be a kind of aeronautical scientific advisory board for NATO similar to the Air Force SAG.[22] Finally, the Cal Tech professor continued to expand his worldwide aeronautical acquaintances. For example, he helped to establish aeronautical research centers in Belgium and the Netherlands, and he also encouraged Spanish aerodynamicists. He collaborated with one on a book on the subject, which became a guide for that country, and claimed to befriend the Spanish scientists at a time when few others were willing to. All this was a part of von Karman's eternal campaign to facilitate international cooperation in the sciences. On one occasion, he even took the liberty of suggesting to the financially starved Turkish scientific community that the obvious way to break their monetary drought was to give the military a call. The aerodynamicist then acted upon his own suggestion and called together a conference of Turkish scientists and military men wherein the good professor alluded to the obvious identity of interest between the two groups. The Scientific Advisory Board of Turkey grew out of this meeting and, according to von Karman, greatly increased cooperation between the two groups.[23]

These activities obviously suggest that much of von Karman's work had little to do with the promotion of the interests of the Southland. The scientific patron saint of the American Air Force had his own not very subtly hidden agenda for the propagation of science, and that seemed to be his first priority. Von Karman claimed to believe that science held the keys both to American military superiority and to the eventual conclusion of peace. In the short run the scientists must produce more doomsday weapons, which would deter attack and allow the United States to speak from a position of strength. He harbored outright pity for his scientific colleagues such as Niels Bohr and Max Born:

> I have always felt that you cannot preach international cooperation and disarmament from a position of weakness. My Old Testament faith tells me that to get one's point across it is best to have a big stick. You don't have to use it, but you're freer to talk without interference. . . . Nothing in my view is so pathetic as an idealistic man talking of situations which he doesn't have the strength to control.[24]

One could question whether an arms race is something that any person or perhaps even any nation has "the strength to control," but von Karman thought that the growth of science would eventually show the way. If human beings could just get matters away from a nationalistic basis, where judgments were made on grounds of national interest, and onto an internationalist basis, where matters could be judged solely on scientific and technical grounds, then the dangers confronting his world could be overcome. How that internationalist millennium of the scientists was supposed to occur when technicians like von Karman kept putting ever more awesome means of destruction into the hands of nationalist American generals, not to mention those of Turkey and Spain, and while his Russian counterparts were doing the same, was never fully explained.

Von Karman would, perhaps, never have asked the question. Like Millikan, von Karman was either a man of extraordinary cynicism or one of touching faith in both God and science. He always believed that "God will do right by us and that we will survive the spirit of destruction."[25] In the meantime, while that ultimate disposition was being worked out, he was able to note, "I have never regarded my union with the military as anything but natural. For me as a scientist the military has been the most comfortable group to deal with. . . . at present I have found it to be one organization in this imperfect world that has the funds and spirit to advance science rapidly and successfully."[26] That part of the "imperfect world" that most benefitted from the rapid and successful advance of von Karman's projects was of course the metropolitan Southland, between which and the federal government von Karman formed a human pipeline.[27]

No sooner had agreement been reached on a seventy-group air force that would keep the factories of the Southland humming than another threat appeared to replace that of unemployment and industrial under-utilization. The new problem grew directly out of the doctrine of air power that the Southland and Bay Area boosters had so often advertised and championed. The dropping of the atomic bomb on Japanese cities had given the American Army Air Corps what they and the interwar air power theorists had long contended for—strategic capability. With the new doomsday weapons, air forces now possessed the capacity to end wars on their own account, without having to depend upon armies at the front or navies. These weapons also produced the ultimate union of the city and the sword. Heretofore, Urban California had labored to create the closest possible association with the military services. Ironically, in the process of building those ties, city boosters had made certain that under the new circumstances of air power war, urban areas would certainly be among the favored objectives of an enemy possessed of nuclear weapons and jet propelled delivery systems. Ultimately, most American cities would probably join them on the target, but the very nature of Fortress California ensured that it would get there first in the role of hostage for American good behavior.

The threat of destruction would eventually become bearable, but the accompanying danger was not. For years, the defenders of Fortress California had argued the reality of air power, and the many prewar air power demonstrations against their cities had imparted a realistic quality to those boasts. The atomic and hydrogen bombs greatly heightened the menace of air power. The work of the Southern California rocketeers such as Malina, von Karman, Foreman, et al., and their other American counterparts, together with the captured information on German rocket and jet-propulsion achievements, transformed the threat from great to unimaginable. This foreign military menace led directly to a domestic one. If air power constituted such a mortal danger to the airframe industry, which undergirded America's most important military service and sole source of deterrence, why should that business be concentrated to such a large extent in Southern California? The great military prosperity of Southern California, together with the wartime losses of population and money that the other sections of the country had sustained in order to allow the growth of Southern California, added a considerable urgency to the question. So did the seventy-group air force, which would provide a long-range and large-scale program of aircraft building in which other American cities and sections were determined to share. Between these influences and the Korean War, the Los Angeles aircraft companies alone stood awash in a backlog of five billion dollars in aircraft orders by mid-1952.[28] Small wonder that competing cities raised the cry of decentralization. After all, industrial dispersal would not only enrich them but make the United States less vulnerable to external attack as well.

This campaign did not threaten every Southland governmental entity in the same way, or to the same degree. In fact, some saw great potential advantages in the threat of government-enforced decentralization of the airframe industry. As the process of urban "scatteration" proceeded in Los Angeles without subsequent annexations, an increasing proportion of the county's residents lived outside of the city itself. Sometimes they resided in incorporated places and sometimes they did not, but in either case, the county of Los Angeles provided some of their city services. Urban growth, therefore, redistributed power away from the city to the county government, which ruled over an immense geographical domain larger than the states of Rhode Island or Delaware. The industrial decentralization crisis presented the county with yet another opportunity to expand its powers at the expense of the city and in the bargain to help save the aircraft industry for Southern California. Therefore, the doctrine of air power, together with jet propulsion and atomic technology, became enmeshed in a unique struggle to achieve metropolitan reorganization: within the Southland and between that region and other American metropolitan areas. The processes of urbanization and militarization collided head on and threatened the alliance between them.

As early as 1922, West Coast urban spokesmen had warned of the vulnerability of cities to air power destruction, often reiterated through a series of mock attacks on California cities.[29] Between this metropolitan-military make believe and the newspaper reports of very real aeronautical assaults on cities such as Nanking, Guernica, London, Rotterdam, and Berlin, the lessons of inter-war air power theorists Giulio Douhet of Italy and Billy Mitchell of the United States were taken to heart by American urban populations. If anything, the air power services were themselves even more convinced that "America's vital aviation industry would be destroyed almost instantly in the event of war." To forestall this eventuality, "the army and navy war plans divisions have perfected secret plans," based on current British planning, "for concentrating airplane factories in the Midwest where they would be safe from aerial bombardment," announced the booster *San Diego Union* in mid-1938.[30]

These military announcements came as a result of air maneuvers held the previous week, and of course, they put to rest the recurrent claims of Fortress California that the attempt to decentralize the aircraft industry had originated in the envy of "underdeveloped" American regions anxious to share in the manufacture of a glamorous new technology. Obviously, the military's decentralization policy also played havoc with the Urban Southland's contention that the aircraft industry had centered there because of the overweening natural advantages of the area, since it was precisely this geographic location next to the sea and on the nation's periphery that explained the area's susceptibility to military attack.

Nevertheless, if the military services originated the plan for aircraft deconcentration, jealous regions and cities in the interior supplied much of the enthusiasm for its implementation. The civilian movement for aircraft defense plant scatteration away from the coasts seems to have arisen in isolationist Chicago, an earlier aircraft center that had failed to keep pace with the cities of either coast. Representative Ralph E. Church of Chicago could deploy an unassailable phalanx of national defense logic to defend the heartland claim. By 1939, the interior had absorbed Douhet, Mitchell, and Hap Arnold and could quote the latter convincingly to the effect that "national defense has gone into the third dimension" beyond those of land and sea.[31]

It could hardly be disputed that most of the engine, propellor, and airframe divisions of the aircraft industry huddled together in a very few places on the two coasts, or close by, or that these selected locations would be splendid targets for weapons operating from the "third dimension" against factories, railyards, utilities, airfields, and other targets beyond the line of soldiers at the front. Church could bring the point home with even greater force by citing such works as J. M. Spaight's *Air Power and the Cities,* which spelled out the unmistakable urban implications of aerial warfare with ominous precision.[32]

Such attacks could be "made on a coastal factory even before the defense can be mustered," warned the Illinoisan.[33] Yet, as usual, the euphoria of economic development lay enmeshed in national defense rhetoric. "During the last several weeks much has been said about the need for research laboratories," Church reminded his colleagues in referring to the project that eventually became the Ames Laboratory.[34]

I am convinced that as a matter of progressive planning of our national defense the site for such a laboratory or laboratories should be selected in the interior of the country. The mere location of these facilities in the interior will itself give encouragement to the development of aviation industries inland and contribute much to encouraging the movement of those plants not located on our coasts. [Applause][35]

Doubtless, none of those cheers came from the California delegation to the House of Representatives who might have heard the speech. The supposed interest of the automobile industry in exploiting the defense boom by moving into aircraft production added to their gloom. It also increased the potential power that could be brought to bear on behalf of the "interior."

Other objections appeared as the war approached. "Los Angeles as a source of U.S. aerial armament remains an industrial phenomenon that overflows with contradictions," contended *Fortune Magazine* in early 1941. An industry that depended on metals should be in Gary or Detroit, they maintained. The magazine added its doubts that "the most vital of defense industries" should be concentrated in a nearly totally auto-dependent urban culture at a moment when defense considerations would shortly no doubt require "a curb on the use of passenger automobiles. There is no precedent in incongruity for what is happening in Los Angeles in 1941," mused *Fortune,* "except the eternal incongruities of Los Angeles itself."[36]

Angelenos, on the other hand, saw little contradiction in "making dive bombers in the land of Oz." Indeed there was "laughter in the arsenal" at the thought of the one-billion-dollar backlog in military orders, which was greater than the "assessed valuation of the city of Los Angeles" in March 1941.[37] The designs of interior cities and industries upon this bonanza led to a further development of the Urban Southland's rationale for their claim to 70 percent of the airframe industry. To requests for decentralization the Los Angeles Chamber of Commerce demanded "expansion of these plants where they are given recognition of the incomparable natural advantages of the area for that industry."[38] But beyond hardening the geographic thesis to protect their hold over the industry, the Chamber contended that the "manufacture of parts by the automotive industry and the location of assembly plants in the Middle West, for mass production of planes, is in disregard of the economic factors which normally dictate the location of industry."[39] The voice of the Southland booster held that "the expansion of the airplane industry on the Pacific Coast not only looks to the defense emergency but to the economies offered by this region for efficient peace-time operations."[40]

For the moment, wartime operations predominated and rekindled the enthusiasm of the interior for national defense, defined as the seduction of Southland factories.[41] The Chamber of Commerce not only rejected this outcry, which arose again in the wake of Pearl Harbor, but mobilized to concentrate as many other war industries in the Southland as possible. "The best areas for war-time production are the same ones for peace-time production," argued Dr. V. O. Watts, economic counsel to the Chamber. The economic advantages of areas rather than the "social planning theories" of Washington bureaucrats should determine the location of industries. The highly developed sections of the country should be allowed to profit from their superiorities, instead of giving "some industries to less fortunate regions," or in the doctor's phrase, "the more backward areas of the United States."[42] Whether Detroit, Fort Worth, St. Louis, Kansas City, Wichita, Memphis, and Tulsa would fit that description or not, they became new or expanded centers of wartime airframe production under the plan of decentralization enforced by the government.

Before this happened, however, Washington placed huge orders with the existing Southland factories so that this area really did not suffer from plant dispersal. Southern California experienced considerably more difficulty in accommodating the newcomers who poured in to work in the aircraft factories already there than it did from the loss of contracts to the supposedly "more backward areas of the United States."

Perhaps the forced industrial decentralization of the war or the prosperity of that conflict temporarily stilled the demand for further dispersal of industry. However, by 1943, the issue had rebounded into the political arena again, this time under the patronage of Nevada's powerful Senator Pat McCarran of Reno. The problems of both the war and after provided pretexts for the revival of the decentralization issue. In July of 1943 McCarran sent letters to fifty-five senators, suggesting that "a Senate bloc be formed to foster new and expanded facilities for the production of iron and steel in areas outside the acknowledged steel centers." The Senate Committee to Investigate the Effect of Centralization of Heavy Industry grew out of this effort. In October of 1943 "30 senators and from 50 to 75 Members of the House met in caucus to discuss a program of general industrial decentralization." Next, steering committees were created in each house; and on December 21, 1943, the Senate approved a resolution to set up the committee to "investigate industrial centralization." The group also established a "special subcommittee to establish and maintain cooperation with State planning boards and other such State and local agencies, both official and unofficial."

As McCarran explained it to the California legislature, the purpose of this group was to combat excessive centralization, both in government and economic life. It was a formal attempt to overcome what westerners had long regarded as their colonial status. As McCarran pointed out, the West contained a geographical domain larger than India, with huge resources of water power, space, and minerals. The West possessed a small population and wide-open spaces. By comparison, the East was overpopulated, congested, and hyperdeveloped. It tried to monopolize manufacturing processes and openly fought the West's efforts to achieve independence. The historic South labored under many of the same disadvantages, thought McCarran, and the two sections had enough in common to form an alliance to effect the changes that would overcome their common colonial status. At this point in time, both must combat the attempt by eastern economic powers and Washington governmental interests to use the widespread demand for reconversion to peace as an excuse to batten on even more bureaucratic and business concentration. A more decentralized government would be both more democratic and more efficient, held McCarran, because it would be closer to the people who best understood their own problems. Centralized government threatened efficiency, democracy, and states' rights. A better balanced economy would provide prosperity for both the East and West.

As might be expected, McCarran believed that the imperatives of national security also pointed to decentralization. "Our security in the Pacific demands a larger population in the Western States, demands more industry, more agriculture," contended the Reno senator. "The story of Soviet Russia's resistance might have been far different if Russia had made our mistake, and left Siberia undeveloped and made Siberia economically and militarily dependent upon Western and European

Russia." The need for reconversion was real enough, noted McCarran, but it must not serve as the pretext for extending the means of war—bureaucratic centralization—into a time of peace. "War, even among democratic peoples, is a totalitarian interlude," he concluded. "This necessary mood, this periodic but collectivist mood, is not the normal mood of this nation."[43]

Other representatives of the Urban West voiced similar objections, but on less theoretical grounds. Southland Congressman Cecil R. King noted the great geographic and corporate concentration of military contracts led by the War Production Board (WPB) in 1944. Although he admitted that the concentration of war contracts awarded by all governmental agencies had declined somewhat from 1940 to 1944, he still professed concern. According to King's figures, 100 large corporations won 85 percent of government contracts from June to December 1940, although these figures fell markedly to 75, 71, and 70 percent in 1942, 1943, and 1944, respectively. Even with this decline in corporate concentration, tremendous urban concentration remained. Government officials through mid-1943 awarded $101 billion out of $161 billion in contracts through the WPB offices in just six cities—Chicago, New York, Boston, Cleveland, Detroit, and Philadelphia. By contrast, the San Francisco WPB office dispensed only $20 billion; and the total of the offices at Denver, Kansas City, and Dallas amounted to only $15 billion. Minneapolis was awarded a paltry $1.66 billion, and Atlanta's figure amounted to only $7.5 billion. These figures confirmed in King's mind the discrimination against the South and West, which he said had been perpetuated by the war.

More to the point, King thought, was what would happen with the return of peace. He held that the War Production Board was staffed by representatives of the large corporations and by representatives of the overcrowded Northeast. The WPB was also maneuvering to gain control of the reconversion process, which would then be used to protect the same interests it had represented during the war itself. That would hurt the South, the West, and small businesses of which his Southern California district had a great number. More particularly, King worried that the West Coast cities would have to fight the Pacific War for several months after the northeastern cities had begun to assume a peacetime footing, thereby gaining control over formerly western markets, while those areas had to remain on a war footing.[44]

W. C. Mullendore, president of the Los Angeles Chamber of Commerce, disagreed with both King and McCarran. Centralization did not bother him because he regarded it as the natural outcome of economic forces, which, if left to run their course, would eventually help the West. They had already benefitted Los Angeles and Southern California. This area had captured a firm beachhead in the national economy even before the Second World War, and he felt confident that the region could maintain that position when peace returned. Regional specialization demanded interchange, and if the West and South tried to duplicate the economic functions of the East, this interchange could not occur. Mullendore particularly attacked the recommendation of the McCarran Committee that the federal government spend a little money to promote economic decentralization. Although he did not say so, the chamber president probably feared that decentralization would take the same form it had before the war when Chicago and other cities called for a dispersal of the aircraft industry away from what Mullendore considered its "natural" center. Whatever his reasons, his position in the Los Angeles Chamber of Commerce indicated that the western demand for decentralization was not unanimous.[45]

Apparently the issue died in the immediate postwar years. The 1947 National Security Act contained a provision for plant relocation which did not occasion much controversy. The 1950 Defense Production Act provided some authority to move plants around under the mobilization priorities for the Korean War. The Truman administration also raised the issue during the Korean conflict, but the debate did not become acrimonious until the 1951 extension of the same Defense Production Act.

Meanwhile, after the conclusion of the earlier conflict, the interior branch plants lost their prominence, and the industry again concentrated in the Southland. As in shipbuilding, the cancellation of war production orders caused a marked decline of airframe construction. However, aircraft production fell much less dramatically than shipbuilding. The latter business practically disappeared, while the airframe industry fell from 280,000 to some 75,000 at its postwar low point. At the same time, demand for autos and other wartime scarcities helped the economies of competitor cities like Detroit over the postwar reconversion with room to spare. Probably that good fortune, together with the overall decline of the airframe industry, conspired to blunt any resentment at the favored position of Southern California. However, with the adoption of the seventy-group air force, the profits of airplane manufacture began to rise again and with them the envy level of the cities that had been left out of the aeronautics industry's grand barbeque. By 1948, this development had set the stage for a return of the drama of metropolitan rivalry for domination of the airframe industry.

In the meantime several new elements arose to sharpen that competition. The first of these came clearly into focus in early 1946 in a letter palpably intended to re-create the kind of intense excitement that had prevailed in the wake of Pearl Harbor. The Association of Los Alamos Scientists donated to the City of Los Angeles a sample of New Mexico sand fused together by the first atomic explosion, together with a picture of Nagasaki. "This sample and picture should remind the people of Los Angeles that in another war their city would probably be destroyed in the first hours of conflict by atomic explosives dropping from the air in guided rockets or previously hidden in some cellar by enemy agents," warned president Willart Stout of the Los Alamos Scientists. "We know that no adequate defense against atomic explosives is now known or likely to be developed in the near future," he continued grimly, "and we believe, with most experts in this field, that only international control of these weapons can prevent the utter destruction of urban civilization within our lifetime."[46] That letter must have been small comfort to Mayor Fletcher Bowron, charged as he was with civil defense measures to protect city life from nuclear holocaust while simultaneously promoting the rocket and airplane industry to which Stout referred. His dilemma would grow with the passing years. As the rocket and jet propulsion experiments of Cal Tech, the Jet Propulsion Laboratory, the Southern California Cooperative Wind Tunnel, the aerospace companies, the electronics businesses, and other members of the metropolitan-military complex brought increasing sophistication to the destructive products of the Urban Southland, the outlook for civil defense worsened in direct proportion. The growing destructive capability of atomic and then thermonuclear weapons, developed in large part by scientists from the neighboring Bay Area, reduced those prospects to the point of nothingness.

By war's end, everyone knew of this new dimension of air power, but it was not enough of a threat to monopolize the public's attention. So until the explosion of the first Russian atomic bomb in 1949, the defenders of urban civilization did not dwell overmuch on its destruction. The events of 1949 forced them to do so, as very forbidding casualty predictions began to invade the sheltered world of Fortress California. Mayor Bowron described Target Los Angeles in 1950 in a speech calling for "more drastic and effective action in stamping out Communism." The area contained five million people; it was a center for the dispensation of information through the media; it contained huge aircraft and "allied industries" capable of delivering or deterring an atomic attack; and "here, too close for comfort are oil refineries producing high octane aviation gasoline."[47] If air power had put cities onto the front lines of national defense, the City of the Angels rested on the edge of the front trenches.

Its residents stood about as much chance of survival as the gray and tortured human beings who had occupied the actual trenches in the First World War. Perhaps less. The postwar cities of California witnessed a resurgence of the "science" of military disaster prediction, only this time without the mimic assaults. One expert assured his urban listeners that one atomic bomb possessed the explosiveness of all the bombs dropped on Great Britain in the Second World War; another noted that the enemy would strike again by surprise as at Pearl Harbor; another student of military science certified that the Russians had snorkel submarines that could surface and fire rockets onto the city; and several others promised that in the event of hostilities, at least seven of ten attacking planes would penetrate the American defenses around Los Angeles. These facts represented the good news. The bad news was that each atomic bomb (presumably modern airplanes could carry several) would create a literal crater of destruction three miles in diameter.

Given the pattern of aircraft and aerospace industrial location in the Southland, it would not have required many craters to obliterate 60 to 70 percent of the American airframe industry. Angelenos and Dieguenos often parried the thrusts of decentralizers by pointing to the decentralized urban morphologies created by their values, geography, and dependence upon the auto. The metropolis was too widely spread out to risk destruction of its aircraft factories. For example, Los Angeles claimed to be about 450 square miles in extent, and the metropolitan area was bigger still. Nevertheless, through 1953, most of the airframe industry clustered together on a relatively narrow strip of land in Los Angeles and its western suburbs, Long Beach, and San Diego, fronting the Pacific ocean. Convair, Solar, and Ryan in San Diego were most vulnerable and were actually situated at Lindbergh Field on San Diego Bay, only a few thousand yards from the open seas. Only Lockheed and Vega had inland locations, close together in the San Fernando Valley but only about fifteen aerial miles from Santa Monica Bay. Of the others, Douglas located plants in the oceanside communities of Santa Monica, El Segundo, and Long

Beach; North American established its factory at Los Angeles International Airport (the boundary of the airport was an ocean boulevard); Consolidated-Vultee (Convair), Solar, and Ryan placed their operations at Lindbergh Field; while Rohr sat farther south aside San Diego Bay.

Two other circumstances added immeasurably to the defenselessness of this critical industrial group. First, several of the great plants huddled close together. Only about a mile separated Lockheed and Vega in Burbank (the reader will doubtless recall the three-mile crater); Consolidated, Ryan, and Solar aircraft were virtually contiguous on Lindbergh Field; and an enemy pilot who missed these inviting targets would probably be over Rohr by the time he could turn around and head back. North American and Douglas-El Segundo were across the street from each other.

To compound the problem, by the 1950s the airframe industry had drawn a host of lesser firms to themselves as suppliers and subcontractors. Related industries have historically clustered together in American cities, thereby deriving external economies from proximity. The aircraft industry of Los Angeles was no exception to this rule. This practice rendered the corporate structure of the industry as a whole more decentralized, but did little to reduce the overall military vulnerability of the Southland. An enemy hit on any major plant would now take out several subcontractors as well, and an atomic bomb that missed Douglas still might cripple it by destroying the smaller plants on which it depended for parts. During the Second World War an enormous number of plants were concentrated within the Los Angeles area, roughly between Hollywood and Lynwood on the north and south and Maywood and Culver City on the east and west.[48]

By 1961, the industry had located several plants in more spread-out locations. Convair manufactured its Atlas missiles on Kearny Mesa in San Diego; Convair and Aerojet produced aerospace equipment or fuels in Pomona; and Lockheed tested some of its planes at Palmdale in the Antelope Valley. However, none of these sites was very remote from the seacoast, and all were vulnerable to the interdependencies of the metropolis. If the Russians destroyed the Lockheed plant in Burbank, its testing site in Palmdale would be rendered equally useless. The Southland metropolitan-military spokesmen might belittle the drive for industrial decentralization as merely the work of piggish "underdeveloped regions" trying to gather in government contracts, but by 1950 the problem of national defense had become just a bit more complex than that.

In large part, the products of the metropolitan-military Southland ensured its position in the industry. Yet as von Karman, Clark Millikan, Frank J. Malina, Hsue-shen Tsien, and their technocratic disciples continued to work their wonders in the fields of aerodynamics, jet propulsion, and rocketry, the tension between the city and the sword grew apace. The defenders of the concentration of the industry in Urban Southern California invariably stressed the asset of wide-open spaces for the testing of aircraft. However, in the thirty years since Donald Douglas had settled in Los Angeles, the process of urbanization had markedly reduced the veracity of that boast. For years the City of the Angels and its satellites had been the great exemplars of the decentralized American metropolis, with a scattered suburban pattern prevailing over most of the Southland. Los Angeles County planners had built

roads during the 1920s in advance of settlement and worked in other ways to facilitate the spread of the city according to the discipline of the automobile. In doing
so, they felt that they were fashioning a new and more modern kind of city that
would prove an example for the future.[49]

The jury is still out on that question, but by 1950 some unambiguous verdicts
had been rendered with regard to the compatibility of urban sprawl and the new
aviation and airframe technology. In 1948, the future seemed to belong to jet
planes, in whole or in part, and jets required different arrangements than the pro-
pellor-driven aircraft of the preceding era. They needed much more ground and air
space to take off and land, and they generated much more noise than their predecessors. Yet, as the Southland process of urbanization scattered urban agglomera-
tions in every direction, it devoured ever greater portions of land that the new technology required. So new land for jet airports became increasingly scarce at the same
time that urbanization multiplied the number of places in the metropolis where
noise from jet engines—or the accidental deposit of aircraft wreckage into the barbeque pits of suburban homes—would be resented by an affluent and self-assertive
city population.

Given the growing smog problems, which had been interfering with pilot visibility since World War II days, the threat of testing mishaps seemed real enough.
Moreover, as Los Angeles city with its municipal airport progressively realized its
ambition to become one of the great air transportation centers of the world, civilian
aeronautical traffic thickened over the urbanized area and created ever more competition between commercial and test aircraft for air space. Thus the peculiar
Southland process of urbanization would, and soon did, vastly intensify the competition for urban space both on and above the ground. The future could be seen
in a small way in the progressive loss of private airports in Los Angeles County.
Frequent complaints from the neighbors and continual temptations from the land
developers led to the closing of many formerly thriving private air fields in Los
Angeles County. Even the Los Angeles municipal airport was besieged by the endlessly multiplying Southland suburbs.[50]

To the unthinking devotee of progress, these new residential areas may have
seemed a blessing; yet to the airport promoters, the aircraft companies, and the
more reflective city builders these housing tracts were clearly a curse. To them, the
sprawling suburbs represented "urban strangulation" of the critical industry upon
which the metropolis depended and the newest transportation technology that
boosters and businessmen hoped to exploit. There is no question that they diag-
nosed the problem correctly. The aircraft companies themselves reached the same
conclusion, and even before the end of the Second World War began searching for
the wide-open spaces of which the Southlanders so often boasted.[51]

None of these problems would have been cause for alarm had these developments not occurred simultaneously with the development of the atomic bomb and
the perfection of jet propulsion to carry it. Southern California still contained lots
of open area for the construction of modern airports and for the testing of jet technology. Atomic technology made *any* Southern California airframe manufacturing
location arguable and the *concentration* of that industry downright dubious. The
newer doomsday machines and explosives should have rendered the question no

longer problematical. The metropolitan competitors of the City of the Angels took precisely that view. Both the cities of the "interior" and Los Angeles County now volunteered to help solve the problem.

The inland cities once again raised the cry of defense decentralization, while the county moved more circumspectly for dispersal within the Southland. Yet both would have relieved the already developed cities of Los Angeles, San Diego, Long Beach, Inglewood, Santa Monica, El Segundo, Pomona, and Burbank of a considerable portion of their assets. The county seems to have made the first move to do so. As early as 1943, T. C. Coleman, vice president of Northrop Aircraft, had written to county supervisor John Anson Ford chiding the Board for deleting a $500,000 expenditure for airports from its budget. The county was worried about economy at that moment in the war, and the supervisors had not reached a consensus that they should be in the airport business. To Coleman's charge, Ford replied that the Board had "its head in the sand."[52]

That imagery remained apt until mid-1948, when the county created a Department of Aviation, with William J. Fox as acting director. This turn of metropolitan events came at exactly the right moment to take advantage of an important national development. As a part of its recommendations to strengthen American air power, the Finletter Report deplored the postwar reversion to concentration in the airframe industry and recommended that future plant expansions be located away from the existing aircraft cities. The Finletter recommendations, with their promise of a redistribution of the airframe industry to areas that did not have any plants, led the County into developing the Palmdale Airport in the Mojave Desert.[53] Whether the aircraft companies foresaw the government's demand for dispersal when they originally invited the county to develop an airport system is not known, but they might well have.

In any case, events moved rapidly thereafter as Fox conceived and executed a brilliant maneuver in political economy. If successful, it would have gone far to redistribute the wealth of Southern California and to move toward metropolitan reorganization as well. The director's plan was simplicity itself. Like many other counties across the land, Los Angeles County had fallen heir to yet another military windfall: in this case a surplus but fairly well-developed airport donated by the War Assets Administration. "Rather than have them deteriorate for lack of unkeep, the Federal Government decided to declare them excess," noted Fox in a letter of explanation to the citizens of the Antelope Valley, "and to turn . . . such airports over to local governments in the hope that they could be made useful by civilian aviation and thus be available in the event they would be again needed for military purposes."[54]

Fox intended to achieve both of these aims as soon as humanly possible. Los Angeles International Airport badly needed modernization, especially if it were to accommodate the jet age, and as yet the necessary bond issue had not been passed to finance that indispensable upgrading. It was by no means beyond the realm of possibility that if another and rival airport, capable of handling jet traffic, opened sooner than the modernization of Los Angeles Airport could be carried out, it might attract some or even all of Mines Field's traffic to itself. That loss would undermine the case for a modernization of the city's airport, especially if the new facility was away from the urban agglomeration that threatened to engulf Mines Field. Of course, such a site could also take care of the need of the aircraft industry for a new jet testing site. This implication demonstrates once again the interplay of local and national influences.

In July 1948, Congress and the President were considering the new needs of air power documented by the Finletter Commission on Air Policy, including a proposal to create a new 143-group air force. Contemporaneously, the airframe industry was suffering considerably from the postwar collapse, and they and their metropolitan supporters naturally seized upon the 143-group air force proposal. Moreover, in 1948, just as the Finletter Commission report came under discussion, the County Board of Supervisors decided to get its hydra head out of the sand and create a division of airports. Simultaneously, each element of the trinity of air power was considering how far and fast to proceed with the development of jet propulsion. Brigadier General Fox was ahead of the game in this and knew almost exactly what would be involved. Jet planes would cost twice as much to build and therefore would be more valuable to local manufacturers than piston-driven planes. They required three times more labor hours to construct, which might have been of interest to Southland unions, and they needed two-and-a-half times as much plant space to construct. "The estimate of need for additional airport and plant facilities inspired the acquisition and development of Palmdale Airport," Fox noted.[55]

This Machiavellian maneuver to dispossess the central Los Angeles region of some of its aerospace manufacturers could also be portrayed as a means of defeating the cry of interior cities for decentralization. After all, an airport testing and perhaps manufacturing site that was really remote from the urbanized portion of Southern California would be less vulnerable to Russian attack or that from cities in the interior demanding decentralization. Locating aircraft industries at public airports was an old Southern California custom and therefore immune from the charge of socialism.

The county airport met these criteria very nicely. Located in Palmdale, which nestled in the Antelope Valley, it was conveniently close to the old Army Air Force testing grounds on the Muroc Dry Lake, which became Edwards Air Force Base in 1948 and which is currently used as a landing field for the space shuttle program. It is about seventy miles by highway from the built-up portion of metropolitan Los Angeles. A chain of low mountains, the Verdugo Hills, isolated the valley from the adjacent San Fernando Valley and a light year separated them in terms of urbanization: hardly any in the former and explosive growth in the latter.

Fox had devised a well-nigh perfect plan. The remote site could be used for testing without complaint by residents because there were not any, and manufacturing could be expected to follow testing, as it eventually did in part. From this beginning, the county would derive tax receipts that might have gone to the established cities of Los Angeles, Santa Monica, El Segundo, Long Beach, Burbank, San Diego, or possibly even some city out of the Southern California metropolitan area. With a new airport and testing site, the Antelope Valley would become a new growth center within the area, thereby building up county tax receipts from residences, businesses, service industries, and other facilities needed to serve the new growth area. The county bureaucracy would probably provide many of the services for this area, as it already did for the suburbs surrounding Los Angeles south of the Verdugo Hills. The idea would also accommodate the aircraft industry which badly needed new testing sites, free from the threat of urban strangulation. In order to achieve this end, the county would plan and zone specifically to keep the process of urbanization at bay by creating a "one-mile-wide buffer strip around the exterior boundaries of the airport" that would not allow "city type of development to encroach within a mile of the exterior boundaries of the Palmdale Airport site."[56]

Most important, the Palmdale project would provide "an *airport in being* (not just on paper), or of necessity the manufacturers would be compelled to seek locations already set up in business in Arizona or Texas." Thus the county promised to save this important industry for the Urban Southland, an industry that employed one-fourth of all "persons employed in manufacturing" and four times the number of people who worked in the motion-picture business. At that point, the Southern California airframe industry, two-thirds of which was located in the county, received 53 percent of all orders for "military aircraft." Obviously Fox's scheme involved important urban interests.[57]

One final point rounded out the grand design. It was recognized that the Los Angeles metropolitan area must have a modern airport, capable of handling jet aircraft, but the city of Los Angeles had so far not provided for one. "The need for additional air terminal facilities for the Los Angeles metropolitan area was becoming so critical that unless additional modern air terminal facilities were acquired, and soon," Fox explained, "the entire Los Angeles Metropolitan Area would suffer very seriously, economically and prosperity-wise, because of a lack of these needed facilities."

The Director of Airports did not put forth a demand for the entire jet business in the area, at least in the beginning. Instead, he proposed that the Palmdale Airport be used to land planes that had to be rerouted from the Los Angeles Basin and San Fernando Valley because of fog or other adverse conditions. Sometimes he denied this much interest in commercial aviation; however, his long-range intentions were clear even in the public statements he made. Los Angeles International Airport "and other existing airports were not and could not meet the ever-increasing demands of the aviation industry to furnish adequate facilities to serve the needs of this rapidly growing metropolitan area," Fox explained. Zoning would help accomplish all these things, Fox told his Antelope Valley audience. He then revealed his real purpose: "This prerequisite could be called 'Jacks are Openers' in this great game of vying for major industrial development in the Antelope Valley." If the United States Air Force could be interested in these developments, say to the extent of financing the construction of the aircraft companies' testing and modification facilities or establishing another air base in the Palmdale Field, so much the better. No one would have had to point this out to the Los Angeles Chamber of Commerce. They had invented this game and knew well what was intended. Perhaps no other scheme of the era so precociously sought to embody the dictum that the trinity of air power consisted of civil aviation, aircraft manufacture, and the air force. Of course, this trinity of air power would translate, in secular terms, into a unity of urban aggrandizement.[58]

Soon after the acquisition of the Palmdale Airport in 1948, the county began to implement its plans. Thereafter, Director Fox called a conference to discuss the project with representatives of Douglas, Northrop, North American, Hughes, and Lockheed. None of these companies signed on at this point, but each representative "manifested an intense interest in the County's leadership." By this time the director had raised his sights noticeably. Now he was thinking of "development, assembly, and testing of jet aircraft," whereas previously assembly had not been a part of the plan. This program was discussed at the conference of airframe representatives. Apparently the interest of the airframe manufacturers convinced the county to proceed with Palmdale, for the chief administrative officer of the county shortly launched a land acquisition program for the airport. Although none of the airframe companies signed a lease until 1950, the county proceeded to purchase territory specifically for the Lockheed Corporation in addition to the general purchase.[59]

As word of these discussions and purchases leaked to inhabitants of Antelope Valley, that part of the Mojave Desert witnessed a mini-boom, its residents hastening to exploit this new Southern California land rush. Like the Sooners of the Oklahoma land rushes, these Californians jumped the gun, for during the next three-and-a-half years, no aircraft company invaded their desert. Companies frequently expressed interest, however, and at the same time Director Fox initiated a correspondence with the Air Force Material Division at Dayton, Ohio, to sound out their readiness to build the testing and modification facilities for the companies. These negotiations waxed and waned, and the interest of the companies south of the Verdugo Hills "blew hot and cold" for more than three years. Fox continued to believe in his original plan, but corporate and federal vacillation convinced the director that when one of the companies or the government decided to invest in Palmdale, that decision would be made rather suddenly. Therefore, in order to have a chance to win the prize, Fox felt that the county must have an "airport in being," ready for occupancy, or risk losing the "great game" of industrial development to some other area in the Southwest.[60]

The county, therefore, marched steadily forward with its programs, adopting a complete plan for airport development in the area. Fox also asked the Board of Supervisors to fund a new jet airport instead of a field designed around a kind of propulsion that would soon become obsolete. In May 1951, John Anson Ford, General Fox, and other county officials dedicated the Palmdale Airport. Six months earlier, Fox had gained his first aircraft company when Lockheed signed a lease at the airport and promised to build a $400,000 hangar there. Shortly after the dedication of the airport, both Northrop and North American were negotiating for land at the Antelope Valley site. Moreover, both were simultaneously negotiating with the federal government to build the test facilities that would stand there. These overtures were done in collaboration with Fox, but it is not clear whether he or the companies initiated them.[61]

In any case, this correspondence and that of Fox himself, who had kept the Air Force authorities completely informed of his Palmdale plans, soon bore fruit, and in much the way that the General had expected. The Air Force suddenly became very interested, after itself blowing "hot and cold" for a couple of years, and in 1951 moved to consummate the deal. Up to this point, the Director of Airports had been entirely correct in his approach to the industrialization of the Antelope Valley. Just as he had expected, the decision to move to Palmdale came abruptly. At the same time, the county benefitted greatly from the existence of an airport already equipped for its job. Instead of waiting to build up a facility, during which time the Air Force and Lockheed might once again blow hot and cold or even warm up to some other part of the Sunbelt, the Palmdale Airport stood ready to receive its new tenants.

Unfortunately these newcomers had plans of their own for the landing field, which radically complicated those of General Fox. These "other generals," besides demanding a kind of zoning that would keep the process of urbanization at arm's length, also required that civilian aviation be banned. This meant that the Palmdale field would not be able to replace partly the civilian airport functions of Los Angeles International Airport. The Air Force sweetened this pill, but not enough to alter its fundamentally bitter taste. Due to the international emergency created by the Korean War, the government was willing to commit itself to the expenditure of $30 million over a period of three years to build the testing facility needed by the three aircraft companies who had signed up by January 1952. In return, the Air Force demanded a major concession from their booster allies. The county must turn over the entire airport to Air Force control, besides barring any civilian aviation. In part, this demand grew out of matters of internal airport administration, but it also stemmed from the Air Force's fear of "urban strangulation by commercial aviation."

The aircraft companies whom Fox had patiently wooed and accommodated for several years added the crowning indignity—they agreed to the Air Force's demands in toto. Military test aviation, civilian transport aviation, and residential development of a great urban crossroads like the Los Angeles metropolitan area would soon produce congestion in the thin air of the Mojave Desert and on the sandy soil around Palmdale Airport, jeopardizing defense activities. Therefore, the General had to compromise. The county's drive to crowd Los Angeles city out of a major portion of its air traffic would have to be halted or altered. As in so many other spheres of metropolitan life in the postwar era, the city and the sword were now in conflict. General Fox's plan to generate new urban growth through the standard booster strategy of an "airport starter" could not be made compatible with the need of the airframe industry and the Air Force for what the Southwest had always boasted of—wide-open spaces for testing, modification, and manufacture.

Of course, the county could have refused to accede to these conditions. The Air Force recognized this possibility and had already begun mobilizing massive pressure to prevent it. At a zoning hearing on November 5, 1951, Lieutenent Colonel Donald F. Marshall laid out the case for military zoning. After reminding the listeners of the critical importance of the aircraft industry to the Air Force and the crucial significance of the airframe industry to the Southland, the airman reviewed the usual facts about jet testing noise, extra ground space requirements, and aerial necessities. In conclusion, he dropped a not-too-subtle hint which, when added to the pressure for regional decentralization from other parts of the country, to civil defense questions, and to the government encouragement of plant dispersal, must have had a major impact on his listeners. "Faced with this problem, and not desiring to move the military aircraft industry to another section of the country, the air-frame industry and the USAF have worked out a solution," said Marshall. "This solution is to develop the Palmdale Airport for the adjusting and testing of U.S. Air Force aircraft fabricated in the Los Angeles Area." Southland civilians had often heard that refrain before, but never at a decibel level rivaling that of the jets them-selves.[62]

Put in this way, there was not much chance that the county would refuse either this request for military zoning or the subsequent and more momentous one for complete Air Force control of the Palmdale Airport. The $400,000 "flight station" opened in early 1951, and because of the fatal crash of a test pilot into a Van Nuys home, Lockheed rapidly shifted "all production flight work on jet fighters and train-ers" to the $30-million plant that the Air Force had built at Palmdale. As the Lock-heed official history noted, "Other aircraft firms later followed the Lockheed pat-tern by opening jet assembly and test plants away from the air traffic, smog, and encroaching residential tracts of the growing Los Angeles metropolitan area." The county's civilian aviation eventually grew up several miles away from Palmdale at a different airport, and the Air Force had its way in the short run on the issue of control of the field. Major urbanization did not occur adjacent to Palmdale, but rather several miles away at neighboring Lancaster near Edwards Air Force Base. The county even gave up control of the Palmdale Field to the city of Los Angeles, and by 1982 Palmdale formed a part of the Los Angeles system of four major air-ports that included facilities at Los Angeles International Airport, Ontario, and Van Nuys. In the 1970s the Palmdale Airport became the center of a controversy over Los Angeles's plan to turn the airport into precisely the kind of civilian airdrome for the future that Fox had fought to sponsor on behalf of the rival county and the Air Force had earlier vetoed.[63] Ironically and perhaps tellingly, the Palmdale Field by 1982 performed precisely the function of accommodating the overflow from Los Angeles International Airport that General Fox had envisioned for the county field. Whatever objections the Air Force had harbored had apparently been dissipated by the years.

Yet the first "Battle of Palmdale" yielded significant spoils for the metropolitan Southland. The County of Los Angeles did not benefit at the expense of the city of Los Angeles to the degree that it wanted, and therefore metropolitan reorganization within the area was not major. The county failed to seize a part of the city's civilian aviation, but it did acquire some manufacturing and testing, a major gain for itself. The work of Fox added measurably to the county tax base and thereby gained at the expense of the cities from which the airframe plants retreated. More important, the county provided a scheme that guarded the Southland's share of the aircraft industry at a time when that urban area was in danger of losing the business to com-peting cities.

The *Los Angeles Times* revealed what might have happened here in a 1954 headline announcing, "Douglas Gets Airport Space at Tucson." The article reported that the space would be used to build a plant that would eventually employ 3000 people.[64] "Douglas is moving its entire jet testing program out of the County to Arizona, because there is not space for it at any other location in or near Los Angeles County including Palmdale Airport," General Fox explained to a correspondent. "It is anticipated that the assembly of jet aircraft by Douglas will also follow and eventually go to Arizona." (It remained in the Los Angeles area.) He continued, "Had Los Angeles County not acquired and developed Palmdale Airport as a major jet testing and assembly activity, this same thing would have happened to Lockheed, North American and Northrop Aircraft Corporations."[65] One must, of course, discount the tendency of big-city politicians to claim credit for any beneficial developments that occur in their towns, but even after doing so, Fox's argument seems valid.[66]

There can be no question that the aircraft industry badly needed space in which to make the critical transition from piston engines to jet propulsion. Also, it certainly would have moved to some other location if the Southland had not proven receptive to its importunings. Many other cities possessed the capacity to meet the airframe industry's requirements and, as the Douglas example shows, were anxious to do so. Moreover, all of this took place just at the point the Korean War demonstrated that we were *perhaps* behind the Russians in the development of fighter planes and that jet propulsion might hold the key to the military balance of power.[67] As Fox had foreseen, the aircraft industry was in a great hurry to move once it had made up its mind.

The Palmdale drama unfolded just at the moment that the other cities around the country renewed their drive for defense decentralization. The urban competitors in this Darwinian struggle were clearly hungry and possessed of the muscle to satisfy their appetites, at least partially. Just as General Fox was signing his aircraft and Air Force allies to leases at Palmdale, the federal government was beginning to enforce a decentralization plan that eventually placed several components of the aircraft industry in other metropolitan areas. Lockheed, for example, moved a part of its operation to Marietta, Georgia, and opened a space branch at Sunnyvale in this same critical period of time. This move was a considerable victory for the Bay Area boosters who had secured the Ames Research Center, which specialized in space work. Contemporaneously, Boeing decentralized the production of the B-47 to its old wartime plant in Wichita in response to government prodding, and Chance Vought moved from Connecticut to Dallas.

The Marietta plant emphasized the seriousness of the government's demand for decentralization and therefore the degree of danger to the Southland's airframe industry. At the time of its completion, the Georgia factory was the "world's largest integrated airplane factory under one roof," covering seventy-six acres of floor space. Lockheed itself, as a part of the "Boeing-Douglas-Lockheed pool," produced B-47s in Marietta in response to the Korean War. By early 1951, this plant alone employed 10,000.[68] The outbreak of the Korean War prompted the government to request Lockheed to reopen and operate the World War II Bell Aircraft factory, evidence that the competitive cities in other parts of the country not only had the ambition to become airframe producers but possessed physical plants already in existence as well. The Second World War had produced both inland aircraft factories and surplus airports for testing. Lots of other places could have accommodated the industry if Los Angeles County had not, and the nature of the emergency meant that any delay on the part of the county could have easily thrown an even larger portion of the industry to another city. It seems clear, therefore, that the

Urban Southland would have lost much more had it not been for the efforts of the county and its Director of Airports. Fox brought his scheme to fruition precisely at the moment that the forces of decentralization were at a crest.

Just as the county menace to Los Angeles, Long Beach, Santa Monica, El Segundo, and San Diego began to fade, another and more dangerous threat appeared. Industrial decentralization in the name of national defense had provided a formidable rallying cry for competing cities and areas before the Second World War; now with the near-simultaneous emergence of thermonuclear weapons, jet propulsion, and the Korean War, this cause re-emerged with a vengeance. If primitive nuclear weapons jeopardized a concentrated aircraft industry, thermonuclear devices at least doubled the jeopardy. Not only did the aircraft industry concentrate in the Metropolitan Southland, but the rapidly developing electronics industry, especially the military segment of that business, which was crucial to the development of the new aerospace industry, largely grew up there as well. These new factories made "Target Los Angeles" doubly tempting. In other words, technological advancement in defense matters operated on both the urban target and the military weapon to maximize the danger.

In response, the military cities mounted a counter-campaign against decentralization. All this activity on behalf of the Southland metropolitan-military complex paid off richly in the short run. The Department of Defense officially recognized Southern California as "one of the most highly decentralized industrial areas in the nation," so much so that new defense installations were being planned for the area. The Pentagon was sufficiently pleased with the Chamber's "Defense in Space" that it used it as a model for other urban-industrial areas.[69] Almost a year after Truman's dispersal order, 32 of the leading 100 American defense contractors "maintained home offices or branch plants in the Los Angeles area including the fourth, sixth, and tenth largest." That figure did not count the "hundreds of other prime contractors and thousands of subcontractors and suppliers" in the area. These statistics added up to the even more impressive one of a five-billion-dollar backlog of orders at the aircraft companies alone. Yet, as will be explained later, Urban California, whatever its short-term triumphs, lost a considerable amount of its military resources as a result of this decentralization movement.

And the fight against this decentralization was considerably embarrassed by the civil defense position of the Southland. Mayor Bowron faced a very real civil defense problem, as did his counterpart in San Diego. As Bowron frequently pointed out, Los Angeles *was* indisputably a massive defense center; and despite its famous decentralized urban morphology, it suffered from numerous defects in an atomic age. These liabilities derived both from its architecture, its sprawling suburban living arrangements, and its much ballyhooed climate. Wood construction dominated Southern California architecture, providing an ideal tinder for atomic or thermonuclear firestorms. Federal flood control monies (somewhat ironic in a semi-arid climate) allowed developers to spread these flammable structures onto flood plains and into mountain canyons. This increasingly solid residential carpeting multiplied the combustible materials and reduced the natural firebreaks that would have been available if the natural character of the land had been more consistently respected. The Southland climate added the final bizarre touch to this civil defense nightmare. The entire area is naturally semi-arid and subject to dessicating Santa Ana winds that sweep out of the Mojave Desert and over the metropolitan area in summer and fall.[70] Between the aridity and wood construction, this megalopolis was extremely combustible. As it is, every fall the Southland area is subject to major forest fires that march right into the urbanized areas. One can only imagine the effect of a genuine thermonuclear attack. If a mild, dry climate provided natural advantages that allowed for the outside storage and assembly of aircraft and reduced the costs of heating and manufacturing, the same climate offered even more advantages to a Russian bomber pilot.

Therefore this economic interdependence vastly complicated the problems of civil defense. In large part, the interest in civil defense grew out of the concurrent problems of industrial dispersal. If local governments could present plausible civil defense plans to Washington, the martial metropolitan areas could not be penalized by the withholding of federal contracts, denied certificates of necessity, or deprived of government loans. Also, at least until the mid-1950s, sheer humanitarian concern over the effect of nuclear or thermonuclear attack created some predisposition to undertake civil defense measures to supplement the military defenses created to protect the metropolitan areas. Perhaps the case of the Los Angeles area was typical.

After World War II, the threat of war seemed to recede and civil defense had lagged accordingly. The Russians' bomb, the Korean War, and the campaign for industrial dispersal endorsed by the National Security Act of 1947 and by subsequent government pronouncements combined to make civil defense a serious matter in the Southland, yet not too serious. The problem was that civil defense was one military issue for which the Southland could expect little federal money, and this lack undoubtedly explains some of the reluctance to provide for it. Washington did not have a civil defense program that supplied large sums to urban areas. Initially civil defense was a state and urban problem. Given this situation, progress was understandably slow and the issue did not cause the kind of political excitement that dispersal did. The principal questions were whether civil defense could actually defend urban populations against an atomic or hydrogen bomb attack, whether the federal government should pay for this defense and how much, and whether military or civilian authorities should take control in case of a military emergency.

Both the lack of federal provisions and the fear of military control surfaced in 1950. Congressman Gordon McDonough introduced a resolution in Congress to provide for hearings that would lead to a "civilian defense program against an atomic-bomb attack."[71] In 1950 the Joint Committee on Atomic Energy decided to hold such hearings, and Mayor Fletcher Bowron testified at them, noting both the lack of a federal program and the danger of a military takeover of civilian functions in case of a nuclear attack. He also criticized the World War II program for spreading out civil defense monies to the whole country, instead of concentrating the funds in the defense centers that were vulnerable to attack. As Senator Bricker explained to the mayor, this scatteration policy was partly designed to mobilize a mass population in support of the war through the civil defense program by giving them a role to play in defense.[72]

In the meantime, both the City of Los Angeles and Los Angeles County governments initiated programs in 1950. In 1950, the Los Angeles County Department of Health published an *Atomic Warfare Primer* explaining how to protect the civil population. It was none too reassuring. While holding that civilian casualties could be reduced by 50 percent, the *Primer* went on to note many disquieting facts. Within half a mile of the blast of a primitive bomb, devastation would be complete, with major destruction lessening based on the distance from the center of the explosion. Even so, a three-mile-wide hole of literal obliteration would occur. A cloud 900-feet in diameter would be seen fifty miles away in the day and for two hundred miles at night. The explosion would produce winds of 800 m.p.h., falling to 100 m.p.h. one mile from the center of the blast. "Concrete, brick, or iron are better than wood" to withstand the effects of radioactivity, but wood held up better against the effects of a blast. Reinforced concrete or steel-frame buildings took the blast best, but the martial urban Southland was well known for its wood and stucco housing with a lot of brick thrown in. The *Primer* bravely explained that the canyons and valleys of the area and the spread-out character of the fragmented metropolis would help considerably. It then went on to admit that the danger from fire after an explosion was "extreme," that "general conflagration is to be expected from electrical circuits and leaking gas," and that radioactivity would remain present for a long time after the blast. Besides these problems, temporary blindness would afflict many, radioactive poisoning of water supplies was to be expected, and loss of hair would certainly occur in survivors near the center of the blast.[73]

Still, the county government assumed that it could minimize the numbers of these thirsty, blind, homeless, hairless creatures and, either through personal measures of protection of governmental ones, could reduce casualties by 50 percent. Thus the county, and city as well, began enrolling volunteers and assigning civil defense duties to government employees. However, the very magnitude of the programs cast considerable doubt on their chances of success. Much of the outcome would turn on whether the various civil defense workers would indeed go to their posts after an attack or, indeed, could even get there.

Whether these personnel would assume their civil defense duties instead of trying to protect themselves or their families is still an open question, which one fervently hopes will never be tested. Nevertheless, the City Council of Los Angeles created a Civil Defense and Disaster Corps on January 26, 1951, which designated the "existing departments of the City as Emergency Divisions of the Corps."[74] The Corps contacted 600,000 households about civil defense and passed out a booklet entitled "Survival Under Atomic Attack" to the householders therein. Over half a million block warden service cards were handed out together with other pamphlets; the Red Cross was mobilized to train 140,000 people in appropriate first aid techniques; fifteen courses were given in "atomic nursing"; medical supplies were inventoried; public education was carried on via "radio, television, in the press, with leaflets and speeches"; 200 fallout shelter signs were posted (for a city 454 square miles in extent, or one per 2.27 square miles!); and sixty-seven sirens were installed. The city appointed a rear admiral to head the corps and appropriated $61,000 to buy 230 additional sirens.[75] A plant-protection campaign further elaborated the preparations. In 1952, the Chamber of Commerce mobilized to arrange for the stockpiling of medical supplies at defense centers in Southern California, since at that time "all emergency supplies for the West Coast—including engineering and medical—are scheduled for concentration in one depot in San Jose."[76]

The County of Los Angeles established its own civil defense corps earlier by reorganizing its existing disaster corps set up to deal with earthquakes. It took measures similar to those of the city, and by the end of 1953 had enrolled over 40,000 people into its volunteer structure. These were the "hard core" of a volunteer group that they hoped would grow to one-quarter of a million people. Still, even under the best of circumstances, which seldom prevail in any war, let alone a nuclear one, the task was formidable. For example, the county estimated that it would require 100 first-aid stations to care for the wounded from one atomic blast; and at least 200 workers per station, "more than 20,000 first-aid workers would be needed for each atomic bomb, and this doesn't include hospital staffs." Since the Russians could be counted upon to hit the city with many bombs, it was quite possible that the required first-aid personnel would have equalled one-tenth of the pre-attack population.[77]

Literally blood-curdling pronouncements accompanied these preparations, perhaps to heighten public interest in civil defense. "The vehicles of warfare, augmented by the atomic bomb and guided missiles, have developed to a point where there is no such thing as being out of range of the enemy," warned a County of Los Angeles memorandum in 1953. "There are no 'Maginot Lines' anywhere in the world and no fixed barriers."

> Imagine even one atomic bomb being dropped on an American community—your city, for instance. Many thousands of persons would be killed instantly. Many thousands of others would be wounded and in need of immediate care. Many hundreds more would be trapped or buried in the wreckage. Every street within the major damage area would be completely blocked with rubble. Large fires would start within a matter of minutes in many places at once . . . a large part of the city's food supply might be destroyed or cut off. The water supply might be knocked out. Regular communications might stop entirely. Much of the transportation system certainly would stop. Thousands of survivors would suddenly find themselves homeless, without food, clothing, shelter, or money. . . . Try to picture the number of trained workers that would be needed to handle an attack situation. [Try indeed!][78]

By 1953, the city, the county, the lesser cities, and the unincorporated areas had organized civil defense measures "to meet catastrophes greater than any that ever have struck the United States."[79]

In spite of this terrifying rhetoric, the civil defense preparations did not involve anything as expensive and thorough as the Maginot Line, although they were perhaps as irrelevant. Between 1951 and 1959, the city of Los Angeles spent only $1,453,000 on civil defense, of which nearly $900,000 came from outside matching funds.[80] In 1953, the county budgeted a mere $105,000 to be matched by $114,000. In the minds of the county officials, the federal government provided too little money and direction to the program, although these same persons harbored considerable misgivings about the assumption of too much federal control in case of an emergency. It was admitted that the Army would assume control of civil defense in an actual attack, and this revelation caused great alarm, which the county tried to placate. Nonetheless, the county wanted more government funds pumped into the program, even though local officials and residents feared the specter of federal control to an extreme degree. Not much money flowed into civil defense during this period, however, and the three services specifically declined to share their appropriations with the cities in the Los Angeles area.

This left the possibility of new congressional appropriations, which Mayor Bowron and the county officials tried hard to obtain. Whether they seriously thought that civil defense would be effective, especially in view of the data that came out of the hydrogen bomb tests in 1954, is unknown, but at least civil defense might become another federally funded program for cities. Both city and county officials demanded greater federal appropriations on the usual grounds of the vulnerability of a major defense center to enemy attack. "Los Angeles, now a much more important industrial center and far more likely enemy target, is again facing the probability of being virtually on the front line," warned the mayor in late 1950. He then continued to make the usual claim on the federal purse.

> I know I speak for the vast majority of good Americans of the West Coast's largest metropolis in pledging fullest support of adequate military strength, regardless of cost, and preparedness, including immediate action in activating a national civil defense plan, including a program for civil training, and Federal financial assistance in providing adequate protection for the civilian population in those areas where enemy atomic attack might be expected as determined, not by political pressure, but by the judgment of our best qualified military experts. That is the thinking, the insistence, the demand of Los Angeles nine years after Pearl Harbor.[81]

Of course, "political pressure" had a lot to do with the fact that Los Angeles was a defense center in the first place. Moreover, the logic of pumping more money into a defense center directly contradicted the rhetoric which the Southland martial metropolis had mobilized against the threat of dispersal. In that argument, the Southland contended that it was not any more susceptible to attack than any other part of the country, and therefore it should be allowed to keep its inordinate share of military booty. But the logic shifted when boosters began trying to get more civil defense monies. In these situations, Los Angeles became a beleaguered defense center, whose vulnerability suddenly stood out vividly.

Both the civil defense measures of the area and their dispersal preparations contradicted another part of the Southland's martial program of those years. At the very time that the fragmented metropolis fought for more civil defense funds and for spacing out its industries to avoid total destruction in the event of atomic attack, it also strove for more defense contracts. On the one hand, the metropolitan leaders moved to make the city less vulnerable, while on the other they steadily labored to make it more vulnerable. From the First World War on, both Los Angeles, San Francisco, and San Diego had become increasingly aware of the importance of military spending. The preparations for World War II enhanced this perception greatly, and the war did too: the Los Angeles Chamber of Commerce, as we observed, even opened a Washington office devoted to helping local businessmen secure government war contracts. This department was continued and, during the Korean War, expanded. At the very time that the Southland martial metropolis was fighting for civil defense and against industrial dispersal, it was simultaneously working to carpet the floor of the area with ever more defense contractors. Through the Korean War, there seemed to be much less concern with this sort of activity in either San Diego or San Francisco.

Immediately after World War II, there was not much interest displayed in Los Angeles either. Each city acquired some surplus property from the government to aid veterans or other businessmen, but this issue never assumed primary importance.[82] War contracts were another matter. In all of this, there seemed to be a conscious effort to involve the small companies in the defense business. World War II had brought small businessmen into military contracting in large numbers, even though some had been there before that conflagration. The war presented the government with a painful dilemma. To win the fight against Hitler, Mussolini, and Tojo, Washington had to restrict many kinds of domestic businesses. These same war-effort limitations could easily have put many small firms out of operation, however, so the Roosevelt administration did the logical thing. It tried hard to recruit small businessmen into the defense-production system. Of course, local congressmen and senators also put enormous pressure on the government to do so. Therefore, both the nation-state and the cities had cooperated in the initial broadening of the base of the metropolitan-military complexes, both to spread around the war bonanza and to avoid the mass destruction of small business. The map of war subcontracting on page 135 illustrates how well the partners succeeded. However, small business had apparently drifted back into the domestic market.

As usual, Los Angeles took the lead to reinvolve them with the metropolitan-military complex. In May 1947, the Chamber of Commerce revived and reorganized the Military Affairs Committee, which "had reverted to paper status during the war as its normal functions were taken over by special groups."[83] The committee was to act "in a liaison capacity between the nation's military establishment and local businessmen and industry and to assist the army in the solution of appropriate problems." Predictably, the membership brought together military and civilian sectors of urban society. "Military personnel, including post commanders, specialist officers, and representatives of the regular army reserves and National Guard, and civilian personnel selected as a cross-section of the business community" were invited to join.

This liaison role expanded quickly. The Chamber noted that $12 billion had been earmarked for military spending in 1947–48 by the federal government. The Chamber thought that this spending might divert resources from some businesses and pledged that "the Chamber is prepared to help these firms fill the gap with military orders and assist others who are merely seeking greater sales for their regular items." It also noted that the military budget offered opportunities for many businessmen, from those selling machinery to consumer goods.[84] Thereafter, the Chamber published booklets, price lists, bid specifications, and government purchasing regulations and tried to bring together contractors and government purchasing agents.

Other organizations facilitated the same process. In early 1949, the Southern

California chapter of the Quartermaster Association of the United States invited metropolitan manufacturers to form themselves into industrial advisory groups to coordinate "supply questions" between the Army and businessmen. Representing the usual intimate interface in such groups, General Wayne Allen headed the Quartermaster Association at the same time that he served as chief administrative officer for the County of Los Angeles. The Chamber of Commerce heartily approved of this effort. "If Los Angeles is to maintain its healthy position as a small plant manufacturing area, and is to share in current as well as future government contracts," noted Ernest J. Armer of the chamber's Domestic Trade Committee, "it is important that our manufacturers join in this work."[85]

They seem to have done just that. Oscar Trippett of the Air Force Affairs Committee announced in February 1949 that area sales to the Air Force alone came to $54 million. The Chamber made a concerted effort to involve small businesses (500 employees and under) in this program, again with apparent success. Of the Air Force's expenditures, 66 percent of the contracts had gone to small businesses, and Trippet noted that 30 percent of the money paid to "large air frame manufacturers" went to small firms through subcontracting. The military fairs publicized the possible advantages for local businessmen; the Chamber of Commerce provided the kind of services for all businessmen that only large ones could afford through their internal economies; and the Navy procurement department in the Los Angeles area specifically set out to recruit small businessmen for military contracting.[86]

When the Korean War broke out, the Chamber expanded its services again. The high point of this procurement effort came in September 1951. In order to acquaint businessmen fully with the possibilities of military sales during the Korean War and to speed the buildup of contacts between supplier and service purchasing agents, the Chamber sponsored what amounted to a metropolitan-military fair. The "Military Opportunity Display" was held at the Hollywood Turf Club. Nearly 11,000 businessmen attended this four-day event, 4000 more than the number that went to similar affairs in Oakland, Chicago, New York, Seattle, and four other centers. The front page of *Southern California Business* pictured Major General William M. Morgan, Munitions Board Vice-Chairman Robert M. Hatfield, Major General William Morgan, and Chamber of Commerce president Trippet standing and smiling behind signs that read "PLANTS THAT MAKE THESE . . . [sieves, spatulas, dustpans] . . . CAN HELP MAKE THESE [Planes and army trucks]." Apparently many of the spatula manufacturers were converted because the Chamber described the fair as a great success and quoted businessmen to the same effect. "I'd been on the trail of that purchasing agent for three weeks," marveled one satisfied participant. "Then I walked into the Military Business Opportunity Display and in five mintues I was talking business with him."[87] Both exhibitors and businessmen overwhelmingly agreed that their business was greatly facilitated by the display. The Chamber put it on in cooperation with the Los Angeles Armed Forces Sub-Regional Council. Major General William M. Morgan of the Council summed up what they and the Chamber had in mind when he praised the fair for providing a fast way to get buyers and sellers together. The fair "contributed a great deal toward building a broad network of defense production in Southern California." It built "the kind of network that will let us increase production rapidly should a sudden demand arise."[88]

So, as the martial Urban Southland sought to gain civil defense monies and to reassure the federal government that it was not a vulnerable military target, it simultaneously strove to gain more defense contracts that would make an atomic attack both inevitable and bigger in the event of war. The "defense network" that General Morgan spoke of constituted a "martial carpet" over the Urban Southland which would permanently guarantee its military vulnerability. The boosters had created a metropolitan-military mass instead of dispersal. Now, instead of a few large contractors like Douglas and Lockheed, the area was literally covered with businessmen who had a stake in preserving the metropolitan share of government contracts, a vested interest in promoting defense spending, and a compelling reason to prevent a thoroughgoing dispersal of defense installations.

At first glance, that set of actions might seem contradictory, hypocritical, or even suicidally irrational. However, the kind of vulnerability that the Metropolitan Southland leaders worried about most was not the remote possibility of being hit by Russian missiles, but rather the more immediate threat of industrial dispersal. Since there had been several aircraft industry moves, prompted in part by federal dispersal initiatives and the support of rival cities, the loss of Southern California defense business seemed imminent. That being the case, civil defense concerns, opposition to dispersal, and the drumming up of ever greater military business were perfectly consistent with the city boosters' aim of building up and protecting the stake of Southern California in the defense business.

Historians, social scientists, and assorted Los Angeles baiters have long ridiculed the spread-out character of the Los Angeles region. But they have also traditionally overlooked the much more important economic unity of the place. The physical form of the metropolis may have been fragmented, but its military interests most certainly were not. Like a sample of New Mexico sand fused by the first atomic explosion, the blend that was the martial Urban Southland had become melded inextricably.

CHAPTER 7

The Trinity of Air Power, Plus One:
The Air Force, Air Commerce,
the Aircraft Industry, and the City

"Each loyal, optimistic American can turn himself into a one-man task force," wrote the editor and publisher of the *Los Angeles Mirror* to supervisor John Anson Ford in early 1954, "to sell the strength of our system of highly competitive free enterprise and the great glories of the future which are ours if only we will go to WORK and BELIEVE." Virgil Pinkley was describing a national economy to which the metropolitan economies of Urban California no longer corresponded. In 1954 the region depended heavily on military installations, the electronics industry, military shipbuilding, defense purchases, and aerospace. Perhaps these businesses were competitive to a degree, but they did not resemble the earlier free-enterprise economy that Thomas Nixon Carver and other local boosters described before the Second World War. In an economy heavily dependent on negotiated rather than competitive contracts, cost plus contracts, and cost overruns, Pinkley's words were closer to a parody than to the reality of the martial metropolitan economy in the year in which he spoke.

However, the Californian's words still applied to the competition among cities. That part of the metropolitan economies was still sharply competitive, immune in its way to the decline of the free market upon which so many historians and economists have remarked. Cities had not yet formed the monopolies and oligopolies characteristic of the business world in the mid-twentieth century. Nowhere did the truth of the Southern Californian's words come through more clearly than in the scramble of the various components of Urban California to get, keep, or enhance their military manufacturing. Given the industrial division of labor between the sections, it is not surprising that each specialized in different matters. San Francisco and San Diego were more concerned about shipbuilding, bases, atomic science, and installations, while Los Angeles concentrated on the aircraft and aerospace industries.

Shipbuilding and aircraft/aerospace, which had figured so prominently in the urban war effort of the three areas, continued to be important in the postwar and Korean War years. And, as they thrived, the political activity and economic boosterism of the urban areas spread to an ever wider realm. In 1920, it was possible to lure Donald Douglas to the Southland, and in the late twenties it was feasible to guarantee the continued presence of Lockheed by local action. After World War II the stakes rose. Now, to nurture a local defense industry it took local action *and* congressional pressure on issues that could range from airport legislation to defense bills to the Cold War. The preoccupations of boosterism had never been strictly local; when World War II approached, they had tended to widen, and after World War II, they exploded outward.

Some of the gains came effortlessly, however. This was in large part due to the extraordinarily wide foundations laid before the war. Several studies have attempted to explain the wonderful profusion of military-related institutions in California in the more recent period. These works have added greatly to our understanding of the complexity of this development, but they have suffered from a common lack of historical background. The gains of the postwar period *required* the developments of the earlier period. It would not have been reasonable to place the Ship Repair Facility in San Diego without the the Border City's previous acquisition of a large part of the Pacific Navy. By the same token, the procurement of the Ames Aeronautical Laboratory would have had little rationale without the prior seduction of the aircraft industry between 1920 and 1935 and the acquisition of the dirigible base by the Bay Area metropolis. Nor would securing Consolidated Aircraft in 1935 have had much logic without the antecedent construction of a flying boat harbor, the creation of open-shop labor conditions (which Consolidated's president desired), and the creation of a skilled labor market of ex-sailors through the annexation of the Navy. The militarization of California cities must be seen as a gradual, accretional process of foundation laying. Each new addition to the underpinnings below justified the construction of more rococo structure above.

By the fifties, much of what followed was ineluctable. The cases of the Jet Propulsion Laboratory, the Rand Corporation, and Ramo-Wooldridge illustrate this point. The former grew directly and, apparently inevitably, out of the decision of the Cal Tech trustees to recruit Robert Millikan and out of his decision to create an interface between the ivory tower and the world of industry, enlisting the aerodynamicist von Karman to do this job. Von Karman mentored the young rocket scientists at CIT; they in turn created usable rockets for the military, and out of this grew Aerojet. As Clayton Koppes has put it, the Guggenheim Laboratory at CIT became the "seedbed of American rocketry," just as Douglas had become the seedbed of the Southland aircraft industry. Even before the war ended, this fruitful environment would produce the Jet Propulsion Laboratory, which by 1980 had a budget of nearly $400 million.[1]

The sprouts grew quickly in a martial landscape. In mid-1943 the USAF urgently confronted von Karman with photos of some mysterious looking German sites in northern France. It was determined that these were missile pads, which would become the V-1 and V-2 launching areas. Although von Karman could not correctly identify the sites, the two military liaison officers at Cal Tech, W. H. Joiner and Robert Staver, thought something needed to be done and requested that the CIT rocket scientists submit a proposal to the Army for the development of jet propulsion. The two soldiers wanted Cal Tech to become the center of "missile research" and wished to establish this position before postwar funding cuts hampered the effort. Frank Malina, Hsue-shen Tsien and Theodore von Karman put together a proposal which the AAF Material Command rejected, but which the Army Ordnance Department accepted in early 1944. On July 1, 1944, the Jet Propulsion Laboratory began operation in the Arroyo Seco of Pasadena. The lab would eventually phase out most of its jet propulsion work in favor of electronics and other pursuits (it was to claim a leading role in the American aerospace program), but its initial role was in propulsion.

Its first efforts produced a flawed and virtually useless weapon called the Corporal. Nonetheless, the government promoted the lab to a higher rank. This time the Pasadena laboratory succeeded, producing the usable Sergeant missile, which the army desired to use with tactical nuclear missiles. The JPL, as it came to be called, went on to make important contributions to American space efforts, first with the Army and then under the aegis of the National Air and Space Aministration, created in 1958. However, it continued under the control of the California Institute of Technology.

Originally, Cal Tech agreed to take on this military task if much of the work of the laboratory would remain in the field of basic research rather than weapons development. The original Second World War military crisis was soon replaced with Cold War crises, and the laboratory became ever more linked to weapons development until it switched to space exploration in 1958. Gradually the lab outgrew the university, at least in budget size. In the momentous year of *Sputnik,* the JPL budget reached $24 million, while that of Cal Tech languished at the level of $11.6 million. Both that discrepancy and the military connection caused some consternation among the CIT professors and trustees, but the presidents, especially Lee DuBridge, favored the maintenance of the connection because of the easy money it provided the university through overhead. Clearly, the military connection allowed the institute to fund some of its own research activities through the overhead it received from the Army and later NASA.[2]

However, attaining the $400 million budget levels of later years did not come without some anxiety, especially during the late fifties. Just as the aircraft industry suffered a crisis of mission after World War II and again with the advent of missiles, and just as the University of California Lawrence Laboratory suffered a similar emergency with the maturation of atomic sciences, so the JPL faced a trying passage of its own. By the late fifties the lab had decided to get out of weaponry and into space. However, there was much competition for that mission and the JPL searched, sometimes desperately, for a sensational coup. In the words of Koppes, it required some "spectacular science" accomplishment, one that would assure its continuing role.

The historian of the lab has noted that at one point direct William H. Pickering "toyed with the idea of exploding an atomic bomb on the lunar surface, which would 'shower the earth with samples of surface dust in addition to producing beneficial psychological results.'"[3] Just whose psyche would have been constructively impacted by this explosion is not clear. In any case, the Russians saved the Pasadenans the trouble by producing a "spectacular science" exploit of their own in 1957. This feat not only saved the Californians the trouble of trashing the moon, but gave them a mission as well: they could now race the Soviets to the moon.

When the Vanguard attempt to catch the pesky Russians fizzled, the Army, Werner von Braun, and the JPL got the call. Thanks to the maneuvering of its director, the Army chose the lab to build the *Explorer* satellite, which the Army would fire into orbit. The effort proved successful, gave the JPL world-class status over-night, and assured its place in subsequent space explorations. From 1959 it oper-ated under the command of NASA, but the program had "quasi-military applica-tions."[4] Its budget rose accordingly, from $35 million in 1958 to $132 million in 1962. Of course this rise greatly helped to guarantee the well-being of the aircraft and aerospace industries that the boosters had recruited. As Clayton Koppes put it, "NASA was 'picking up the slack' in order to maintain a basic industrial sector—the aerospace industry—as aircraft production declined. Clifford Cummings's analysis of the relationship between the industry and the space program was borne out. The space program, particularly its manned component, was a godsend for the aircraft firms. As would become clear, Webb ran NASA with great solicitude for those politically powerful foundations of the military-industrial complex."[5]

Ultimately the RAND Corporation grew up in Santa Monica, in the midst of the Southern California metropolitan-military complex for about the same reasons that the Jet Propulsion Laboratory did—someone had already laid the foundations for the institution. RAND ultimately became the foremost think-tank for Cold War strategy, a position which paid large dividends for the metropolitan-military com-plex. If anything, the connection between this postwar development and prewar precursors was even closer than in the case of the JPL. From a national aspect RAND arose out of a desire of General Henry Arnold that the Army Air Force should keep up with the march of science into the future. Arnold believed that sci-ence would quickly expand the potential of weaponry and that the United States Army Air Force must keep up with that evolution. To help it stay abreast, Arnold turned to an old, and for this book familiar, acquaintance.[6]

In early 1944, while the war still raged, Arnold contacted Theodore von Kar-man to chair a committee to chart the future "research and development" require-ments of the about-to-be-created United States Air Force. Von Karman obliged and his committee generated a document that the historian of the corporation called the blueprint for "what would be called Air Force Project RAND."[7] As Fred Kaplan notes, the general idea of undergirding Air Force progress with science was "already afoot under the sturdy guidance of Arnold, [Edward] Bowles, and a few others, most notably Arthur Raymond, chief engineer at the Douglas Aircraft Com-pany in Santa Monica, and his assistant Frank Collbohm."[8] With Collbohm acting as intermediary, Donald Douglas eventually offered to "house an independent group of civilians to assist the Army Air Force in planning for future weapons devel-opment." Arnold accepted and the RAND Corporation began under the auspices of Douglas Aircraft. For various reasons a government or university setting was considered inappropriate and Douglas instead initiated the institution. As we have seen, Arnold and Douglas went back to the thirties and, as Kaplan notes, they were "hunting and fishing friends" whose children had recently married.[9] The liaison between Douglas and RAND "did not work out" and RAND became an indepen-dent corporation in 1948, but whether under Douglas or independent, the institu-tion was to become a crucial part of the metropolitan-military complex.

Not only did RAND keep the Air Force well supplied with technical plans for the future, it ventured one step further into the system of weapons procurement. Before World War II, weapons came from a process of military and corporation cooperation. The military created specifications to indicate their preferences and the aircraft manufacturers competed to meet the guidelines. Sometimes plane builders tried to modify their existing planes to meet the specifications or attempted to persuade the monopsonist buyers in the military that the machines already qualified. However, whichever one of the ways prevailed, the outcome was tactical. The military bought a weapon designed to fulfill a tactical mission. With the advent of the RAND Corporation the urban-industry-military interface moved one step beyond tactics to strategy. The new Santa Monica establishment became the fount of strategical thinking about the use of the weapons systems rather than simply the suppliers of machines that might or might not meet military requirements. That role helped guarantee pre-eminence for the Air Force and business for the martial metropolises.

One of the most important of these undertakings turned out to be thermonuclear. Even before the dropping of the atomic bombs, Edward Teller, a Los Alamos scientist, had moved beyond that feat to the creation of an even more destructive or "super" bomb. Teller and Stanislaw Ulam worked out the physics of the weapon, and Teller became its lifelong champion. By chance, the head of the small RAND physics section was in Washington the day the Russians exploded their atomic bomb in 1949 and so was the physicist. The RAND scientist Ernest Plesset, another Douglas alum, "brought Teller in touch, just after the Soviet explosion, with several high-ranking Air Force officers to talk about atomic energy and the Super."[10] When Plesset learned in 1951 that the fusion bomb was about to become a reality, he moved to insure that RAND would benefit from it. Plesset convinced the head of Los Alamos that when the bomb was proven practical, Los Alamos "should be in a position to interpret its implications." For that job the RAND group was ideally suited, said Plesset, and Norris Bradbury, the director of Los Alamos, agreed. Thus RAND got the job of explaining the destructive connotations of the new weapon. It never looked back. Subsequently its way of looking at nuclear and thermonuclear war became the national standard and its doctrine set the requirements for future weapons development.[11] A more congenial arrangement for the weapons producers of the martial metropolises could hardly be imagined.

Of course the development of scientific institutions and the hydrogen bomb certainly would have occurred whether or not the military cities of California had an interest in the matter. However, their *implications* would not have been so profoundly important for those cities had Donald Douglas not been recruited to the Los Angeles area in the first place. Thus as in so many other matters, it was the foundations of the metropolitan-military complex that proved decisive. Had Douglas gone somewhere else, the foundations for RAND and the super would have been laid elsewhere as well.

The location of the Thompson Ramo Wooldridge firm in Southern California after World War II grew out of similar processes. Both Simon Ramo and Dean Wooldridge were products of the aerospace engineering program set in motion years before by Robert Millikan and Theodore von Karman. In fact, like Malina, Forman, and Parsons, who founded rocketry, both were Cal Tech products, in this case Ph.D.s. They initially went to work for Hughes Aircraft, but left that company after World War II to create their own systems analysis outfit. They of course benefitted from the change from bomber power to missile power, since missile systems required so much more sophistication to manage. Both men had been advisors to the von Neumann Committee, which made the decision to upgrade the missile weapon vis-à-vis the bomber, so their larger opportunity came from the nation-state. However, the placement of their firm, and therefore the distribution of the military resources that derived from missilry, owed everything to Millikan, von Karman, Millikan's son Clark, and the other men who had turned Southern California into an aeronautical center.

The postwar booster methods reminded one of the prewar period, except now the partnerships were even more close and open. Air Force Day in 1945 smacked very much of the metropolitan-military festivals of the interwar years. In San Francisco a "daytime air display" was followed by an "Army Air Force Day dinner at the Palace Hotel at which Maj. Gen. Willis H. Hale, Commanding General, Fourth Air Force" was the featured orator. As the *Downtowner* explained it, "the purpose of the day will be to report to the American public the magnitude of air power's contribution to the victory in Europe and to the task that lies ahead of the Allied forces in advancing against Japan." Undoubtedly the speakers on this occasion did not minimize that effort, nor did the new Aircomet jet fighter, the C-47s, the B-29s, the P-61 Black Widow night fighters, and the Army Air Force gliders that entertained and thrilled the Bay Area public with air power displays in three scheduled shows on the afternoon of August 1, 1945.[12]

As usual, in matters touching on the Air Corps, Los Angeles did it better. "We salute, we honor those who conceived the future of air power," intoned Mayor Fletcher Bowron, "and are a part of the greatest force in the world for destruction and for the maintenance of stability and peace." Five days later American pilots would unleash over Hiroshima a new force in warfare that would, in turn, usher in a new era in armed conflict among nations. The chief executive did not mention this forthcoming event in his remarks at the Air Force Day celebration, but he described the alliance of the city and the sword in unmistakable terms. Bowron began by recounting the "tremendous contribution" of Los Angeles to the victory in Europe, listing the types of planes produced in the area, the famous aircraft built there (including the "flying White House" and the planes of the Doolittle Raid on Tokyo), and the 272,000 people (some 40% female) employed in these tasks. These instruments of war had brought victory, but this was not the end of it by any stretch of the imagination, for the Southland martial metropolis intended to stay in the front of developments thereafter as well. "It might sound like boosting, but verity and confidence compel the averment [the mayor favored arcane language] that Los Angeles will continue to maintain a secure and leading place in the air world of tomorrow. . . . Despite our modesty, our frankness makes impossible the suppression of these facts. They are known by the United States Army, for this city has been selected as one of the four in America for major sponsored demonstrations of this, the 38th anniversary of the Army Air Force."[13]

The Army Air Force lost no time in proposing a joint program for the future of aviation. Hoyt Vandenburg, deputy chief of Air Staff and nephew of the famous isolationist senator, spoke bluntly about the needs of the Air Force. This time the setting was pure Southern California. The scene had shifted from the airport to the world famous Coconut Grove nightclub at the Ambassador Hotel. Freddy Martin and his orchestra provided the musical backdrop for this martial occasion, and Clark Gable supplied a Hollywood aura. Gable called aviation a "power for peace" and Mayor Bowron repeated his praise before Vandenburg stood up to speak.

Vandenberg's remarks partook of none of the fantasy of the Hollywood surroundings, but rather represented a well-thought out, carefully conceived list of political and economic goals for the metropolitan-military complex. The lieutenant general warned that the mistakes that followed World War I must not be repeated. After that conflict the United States "practically threw its infant air force away. . . .

Past experience shows that our aircraft industry was brought to a virtual standstill by our surplus equipment." He elaborated: "We had enough, we built nothing new. And I do not mean for just a year or two after 1918—the problem confronted us until 1932—14 years later. For instance, in 1932 there were still 3,000 liberty engines at hand, which meant that the vital experimentation which must go on in such fields had been choked off." The "great Los Angeles Aviation Industry is a matter of first concern to you, as it is to us," the general assured his audience. "The continued well-being of that industry is vital not only to the prosperity of Los Angeles but to the welfare of the country. We must be perfectly clear on this point. America must be number one in the air."[14]

The general then went on to point out some of the elements in the program to keep America number one. The surplus must be eliminated so as not to compete with new manufacturing of planes; electronics was "an important consideration in any phase of air power"; and a strong air force with good equipment and training would be needed. But "this must be backed by a sound and progressive aircraft industry and a full research program. Civil aviation and transport must also be encouraged."

> We are checking our combat needs constantly so that when Japan is defeated, we trust that we shall not have too great a surplus in planes and equipment, so that industry can go right on with the production of newer and better aircraft.
> However, we realize that to accomplish this we will have to scrap much equipment. An aggressive policy must be followed in disposing of our surplus aircraft.[15]

The general clearly foresaw the future of "rockets and jet propulsion that will move at supersonic speeds, carry more deadly loads, and they may be controlled by the crew or by someone thousands of miles away." He also accurately predicted the future of rapidly changing military technology that would demand an endless new supply of weaponry. To point up the lesson Vandenburg quoted Herman Goering, who had told his postwar interrogators, "If they had only given me six months more!" and concluded by making the usual doomsday prediction. "The potentialities are so great that any lag in our research and experiment may mean nothing less than National disaster."[16] No one had to point out to this audience of Angelenos that it would mean nothing less than local industrial catastrophe as well.

President Eugene E. Wilson of the Aircraft Industries Association of America carried a similar, if somewhat more optimistic and comprehensive message to the San Francisco Bay Area. He did so a week after the second atomic bomb had demonstrated over a second Japanese city the ultimate connection between war and urbanization. In a speech to a joint meeting of the San Francisco Chamber of Commerce, the San Francisco Commercial Club, and the Bay Area Aviation Committee broadcast over KQW radio, Wilson spoke of a trinity of air power. "Today Air Power, that trinity of air force, air commerce, and aircraft industry, has proven itself the decisive factor in future world security," Wilson assured his audience. (The "plus one" of our chapter title, which adds the city itself to the proposed trinity, was axiomatic for those who listened to and understood Wilson's message.)

> Air force can make it unprofitable for nations to seek through conquest what they might better gain by enterprise. Air commerce, by speeding world trade, can tear down these artificial restraints which have hampered exchange of goods and fostered war. Aircraft industry can provide new investments and jobs and, with out enterprises, founded on industrial research, show the way to endless economic frontiers.[17]

Like Vandenburg before him, Wilson emphasized the threat of "enormous surpluses of plants and products, drastic cutbacks, [and] an uncertain future." Government over-regulation seemed to be the principal problem in this uncertain future, but loss of initiative by private enterprise could complicate matters as well. Wilson's prescription for the continued health of the trinity was like that of Vandenburg, but broader.

> We need expanded domestic and foreign air commerce. We need a sound private industry to maintain technical leadership and the ability to expand in emergency. We need to express our policies in law and then define responsibilities and authority to maintain them. Government should provide an orderly procurement of its own needs. It should fix responsibility on industry to keep in the forefront and it should provide the cooperative atmosphere in which this responsibility can be discharged.

If these prerequisites could be met and the problems of reconversion overcome, Wilson thought that a brilliant future beckoned to San Franciscans, one worthy of their western pioneer ancestors.

> Today we in the aircraft industry hand you a new instrument and with it we hand you a challenge. Look out thorough Golden Gate beyond the setting sun and you will see prospects more glittering than any the world has yet seen. With these new Argosies of Air Power you can create new trade, new industries, new jobs, new security, and peace.

Or, as Wilson described it, "the Pax Aeronautica."[18]

The Los Angeles Chamber of Commerce echoed both men. John C. Lee, President of Menasco Manufacturing Company (an aircraft industry manufacturer) and chairman of the Aviation Committee of the Los Angeles Chamber of Commerce, noted in September 1945 the three essential paths to continued prosperity for the Southern California aircraft industry:

> First, the resourcefulness of the aircraft designers and builders; Second, sound government policy decisions on the disposal of surplus airplanes, engines, and accesso-

ries, and on continued experimental and developmental manufacturing carried out by private companies—not government agencies; *Third, support of the community in the natural geographical competition for aircraft business.*

Of course, Lee made more explicit the booster dimension—the "trinity plus one" aspect—that the others had only implied, but otherwise he put forth much the same program, one which clearly linked the fortunes of urban areas to the vicissitudes of the Cold War.[19]

Although they seldom employed the term Pax Aeronautica to characterize their activities, Angelenos, San Franciscans, and San Diegans certainly worked consistently to propagate the trinity of air power. Because of the dissimilar economics of the three metropolitan areas, each placed a different emphasis upon these three elements. Los Angeles was more consistently trinitarian, San Diego was somewhat less so, and San Francisco, lacking an aircraft industry for most of the period, concentrated more on commercial aviation and only to a lesser extent on air power. Nonetheless each city accepted the trinity for the most part. There were certainly no unbelievers amongst them or even any unitarians.

The post-World War II performance of the aircraft industry seemed to justify the worst fears of the high priests of the air power trinity. At first the industry moved briskly on the basis of its few uncancelled military contracts and the backlog of orders for private and commercial civilian planes. For a time, industry spokesmen made much of the potential of this latter market. Tom Humphrey, of the Aircraft Industries Association, noted in March 1946 that "several California manufacturers . . . are convinced that within five or 10 years the greatest potential market for aircraft will be in the personal plane field, and are planning accordingly." Humphrey also spoke of an "Aeronautical Revolution" in the industry. The business "has performed another miracle," he went on. "It has weathered, since V-J Day, the most drastic contraction ever experienced by an American industry," due to the cancellation of $9,000,000 worth of military contracts. This brought aircraft manufacturing down from its wartime peak of 1,500,000 workers (all over the nation) to 150,000, although it hoped to rebound soon to 200,000. At that point, it was doing three-quarters of a billion dollars worth of business, of which military orders amounted to $500,000.[20]

Optimism could not carry the industry much farther than the month of March, however, and soon both the industry and local politicians complained of the collapse of one part of the trinity. "Los Angeles has a big stake in the aircraft industry," Mayor Bowron reminded an audience at an Air Force Association rally in early 1947. "Naturally we are interested in protecting that industry because of its effect upon the economy of Southern California," but, more important, he believed that an unhealthy aircraft industry would not be able to meet its national defense role. "While many of us thought business was good during the past year, the majority of the companies reported losses . . . only three reported profits for the year 1946." Cancellation of government orders and government sale of surplus planes, which competed with the new plane market, hurt the industry badly while the elusive civilian market had not yet materialized. "The industry cannot be supported by the limited number of orders for commercial planes," he admitted. As usual in these circumstances, he reminded his audience of the threat of nuclear annihilation and praised the Air Force Association for "taking up the fight for the purpose of promoting and maintaining America's air power." The mayor expected the 100,000 Army Corps veterans living in Southern California to back his fight as well.[21]

Nor would they struggle alone. The Chamber of Commerce, the city and county governments, labor unions, local congressmen, the American Legion, the media, and others would eventually take up the cause. The Chamber of Commerce would play a key role. Following prewar practice, the chamber was subdivided into working committees, of which two directly represented the interests of air power. An Air Force Committee and an Aviation Committee worked to promote the specific interests of the Air Force and the broader well-being of the general field of aviation.

The aviation subcommittee had, in fact, been hard at work on this latter problem since the late 1920s. By the postwar era, the committee contained a very impressive membership indeed, including almost every conceivable representative of aviation in metropolitan Southern California. For example, three of the big six manufacturers of the Los Angeles area—Douglas, Northrop, and Convair (Convair had a plant in Pomona)—sat on the aviation committee. They were joined by representatives of commercial airlines such as Trans World Airways; smaller manufacturers such as Menasco Manufacturing Company; representatives of the California Flying Farmers; unions such as the United Auto Workers and the International Association of Machinists; veterans groups such as the American Legion; aviation representatives of the major oil companies such as Shell and Union; freight haulers such as the Flying Tiger Lines; one University of Southern California professor; Clarence Belinn, the pioneer helicopter operator in Southern California; a few banks; the Santa Fe and Matson transportation interests, the editor of *West Coast Aviation* Associates; and officers of the Goodyear Tire and Rubber Company. The chairman of the Long Beach Chamber of Commerce Aviation Committee, the manager of the Los Angeles Airport, the chief engineer, Wm. J. Fox, of the county Regional Planning Commission, the Deputy City Attorney of Los Angeles, and one federal bureaucrat served as "advisers." Perhaps no better example of the metropolitan-military complex could be cited. Here the interests of civilians and defense came together.[22]

Nor could a better indication of their concern be shown than the record of the aircraft industry in 1946 and 1947. In both years the aircraft manufacturers sustained serious losses, although 1948 brought a return of black ink with the retooling for the new seventy-group Air Force. In 1946 the industry built a paltry 1,330 planes; the next year, they constructed 2,102, which they hoped would rise to 2,400 in 1948. The Aircraft Industries Association reported "heavy financial losses" for the years 1946–47, for which the modest profits expected in 1948 would not make up. In order to understand the decline of the business in the three years after World War II, it should be recalled that peak wartime production came to an annual figure of 96,318 craft built in 1944. A large number of civilian planes were manufactured in 1946 and 1947, but thereafter this market rapidly dwindled. At its height in 1944, the industry was the largest in the United States in "dollar value of output." Aircraft manufacturing collapse after the war represented a sharp decline, similar to that in shipbuilding. These problems led to a drive at both the local and national levels for government bailout programs.[23]

Although there were no military personnel on the Aviation Committee, the Air Force clearly understood the significance of its business to the martial metropolis and it did not hesitate to state that importance in a semi-public forum. In early 1949, in an attempt to mobilize urban support for the new and expanded Air Force procurement program, Colonel Thomas H. Chapman, chief of the Western District Air Force Procurement Office, stated that matter rather bluntly. "The objectives of the Air Force can only be met by a smoothly operating procurement team, including industry and its assisting agencies and organizations, such as the Chamber of Commerce," he explained. "The aircraft industry is the backbone of the procurement program in this area. We are striving to assist in stabilizing this industry by proper planning of the five-year program, by trying to eliminate feasts and famine," the colonel continued. "Over 75% of the airframe weight and dollar value of the 1949 procurement program—centered in the completed aircraft—is on the West Coast. Approximately 50% of this workload is in the Southern California area."

After explaining some of the details of the seventy-group program that had been laid over from the last Congress, the procurement officer let the other shoe drop. "The job of the Los Angeles Procurement Office is to administer contracts so as to assure prompt delivery of a quality product. The Air Force desires to be a good neighbor, an asset to business and a friend of the community as well as guardian of the air." The five-year program would eventually "level off" at 5200 planes per year, enough to keep the industry healthy and stable. However, the United States Air Force needed help in return. "Action on the following suggestions will further the Air Force Procurement Program," the colonel concluded.

Assist in providing approved legislation that will assure a continuity of adequate defense measures; develop an aggressive program to alleviate skilled manpower shortages and, in conjunction with the Aircraft Industry and the U.S. Department of Labor, anticipate requirements for the AF's five-year aircraft program and support local training programs to develop the technicians from among the local citizens; assist the local aircraft industry to locate critical materials in this country, or the State Department in securing them from foreign sources; prosecute an energetic program involving better housing conditions, better transportation, better consumer services, and better employee services, in order to create the highest state of morale and esprite [sic] de corps among employees which in turn means a higher production rate per employee; expose subversive activities that are jeopardizing our freedom.[24]

Along with William Kettner, Ed Izak, and Bob Wilson of San Diego, Richard Joseph Welch of San Francisco, Charles Curry of Sacramento, and Chet Holifield of Montebello, Carl Hinshaw was at least a "million-dollar congressman." In fact, he was probably closer to a "billion-dollar congressman," although we have no way of making an accurate dollar measurement of his value. Despite the fact that his career is almost totally unremarked upon by historians of all kinds, including those of California, Hinshaw was one of the most influential aviation representatives at a time when aviation legislation was among the crucial subjects before the United States Congress. He was, in short, the pre-eminent Capitol Hill guardian of the trinity of air power. If Theodore von Karman was the scientific father of the American Air Force, John Carl Williams Hinshaw was one of its legislative parents. As a founding father, Hinshaw had lots of help, but then so did George Washington.

It would perhaps be convenient and comforting to attribute Hinshaw's career to some streak of supposed malevolence—right-wing extremism, militarism, or anti-communism—and it is true that Carl Hinshaw was both conservative and anti-communist. However, his dedication to these causes was not as overt as that of some other politicians. His anti-communism did not rival that of Joseph McCarthy, Martin Dies, or Jack Tenney; his conservatism did not burn as brightly as that of Robert Taft; and if he admired the military, he was much less outspoken in that admiration than Theodore von Karman. Moreover, his motivation in adhering to the trinity of air power would seem to be much more prosaic. In truth, Hinshaw's career conforms much more closely to that of the classic booster, a devotee of the Darwinian City.[25]

The legislative father of the American Air Force was himself born in another noted booster city, Chicago. By the time of his election to Congress in 1938, he had lived in another, Tucson, and had finally made his way to a third. Like some other important promoters of the Los Angeles urban region, Hinshaw resided in Pasadena. Having worked in Chicago in various branches of the automobile business, he had switched to real estate and insurance by the time he arrived at his California rustic retreat. Of course, real estate is one of the businesses most dramatically benefitted by urban growth, while being least tied to any single city within a metropolitan region. Realtors operate across city lines and therefore are in a position to gain the rewards of explosive growth wherever it occurs. In some ways, the history of Los Angeles can be seen as the history of real estate promotion by just such people.

Hinshaw entered the armed forces in World War I and later belonged to several soldiers' organizations, including the American Legion, Veterans of Foreign Wars, Regular Veterans Association, and World War Engineers Association. He also belonged to the usual city clubs—Elks, Eagles, Masons, Sons of the American Revolution—and some unusual ones, such as the Princeton Terrance Club, the Overland Club, the Society of Automotive Engineers, the Congressional Flying Club, and the Astronomical Society of the Pacific. Although his father was a prominent Quaker, Hinshaw belonged to the Methodist Church. His civic activities indicate his booster base even more fully. He worked for certain "local improvements," served as a "member of the Tournament of Roses Association" and "chairman of the California Chamber of Commerce highway legislation committee," was director of the "Pasadena Realty Board," the Pasadena Chamber of Commerce, and the "California Real Estate Association," and "executive chairman of [the] Arroyo-Parkway Association."

Any one of these jobs could have won him the designation of booster, including that on the Rose Bowl Association, since the Rose Bowl was also a booster activity. However the Arroyo-Parkway Association is especially illustrative of Hinshaw's broad range of activities. The Arroyo Seco Parkway, which is now the Pasadena Freeway, connects the center city of Pasadena to downtown Los Angeles and is considered by some experts to be the first American freeway. Historically, American boosters, especially those in the real estate business, have been largely involved in building transportation facilities. After 1920, the builders of Los Angeles consciously attempted to fashion that city around the automobile, and the freeways constituted the ultimate instrument in this attempt to hold together the fragmented metropolis. In this respect, Hinshaw was as well placed to promote the interests of his metropolitan region as he later would be as a member of the subcommittee on aviation of the House Committee on Interstate and Foreign Commerce.[26]

It is interesting to note in this connection that Carl Hinshaw was not a former employee of the aircraft industries of Southern California, nor a former flying soldier, nor a veteran of the civilian aviation business. He may have had investments in airframe manufacturing or civil transportation or passenger airlines, but it takes no such connection to explain his efforts. His own business was tied to urban growth, and his career, from the Rose Bowl to the freeway to his anti-union activities, was calculated to promote it.[27]

Hinshaw's efforts were also designed to prevent urban decay or decline, and that was the pressing problem in the wake of the postwar slide of the aircraft and civilian aviation industries, at least in the minds of the boosters who followed those fields. Carl Hinshaw began immediately after the war ended to remove these difficulties. While General Vandenberg, Mayor Bowron, and the Chamber of Commerce occupied the public spotlight, Hinshaw moved behind the scenes in Congress to strengthen the sagging trinity of air power. His most notable contribution came in the movement to foster a comprehensive review of American aviation policy, civilian and military. The ultimate origins of the postwar air force program are difficult to find. Apparently, the idea had already been agreed upon by the Army Air Force even before the war ended. The industry itself also clearly foresaw its postwar dilemmas. Although aviation spokesmen frequently alluded to an expanding civilian airplane market after the war, they knew that they would continue to depend upon military orders.

More than a year before the war ended, a Senate investigation of demobilization problems found that the aircraft industry expected to have more than its fair share of them. The war had blown up the business from forty-fourth amongst manufacturers to first, and yet peacetime promised no business to return to, such as the automobile industry possessed. Moreover, aircraft manufacturers could not convert themselves to something else; they had to build planes, or at least they thought they had to. Conversion of military planes to civilian uses promised only small return. The civilian plane market needed more air-mindedness, more airports, and more aids to aviation, in short, many assets that had not been there when the war commenced. Harry Woodhead, president of Consolidated-Vultee of San Diego and member of the board of directors of the Aeronautical Chamber of Commerce of America, explained the solution very clearly. "We wish to point to the major handicap under which the industry is laboring in all its planning activities," observed the San Diegan. "Namely, the lack of any information on the size of the postwar air force of the United States, and the nation's technological program for aviation development." He added that "without such information, all planning—both for military and for civil aviation—lacks a sound basis."[28]

In case the senators had not been thinking much about the solution to this problem lately (July 10, 1944), the aircraft industry representatives had one ready made for the occasion. As Eugene E. Wilson, chairman of the Board of Governors of the Aeronautical Chamber of Commerce of America and vice-chairman of the United Aircraft Corporation, explained the plan, it amounted to about the same one that he would advocate after the war and that the Congress would accept from the Congressional Aviation Policy Board and Finletter Commission in 1948. Even though there was in July of 1944 no Red Menace, Cold War, or other Leftist threat to American security and power, the industry indicated that the United States must remain first in air power once the war ended. Outlining what he would later call the trinity of air power, Wilson urged the maintenance of a strong Air Force, development of civil aviation, and protection and promotion of the aircraft industry. Even the specifics were similar— research and development, airports, navigational aids, foreign and domestic air commerce, air mail, and personal flying aids.

Testifying before this committee, Wilson openly stressed a greater respect for sea power, both naval and aerial, than he would later. For the most part, however, Wilson concentrated on the many benefits that air power would supply to the American people. It would make them safe against enemy attack (as yet he would not specify who the enemy would be); it would save them money in the bargain; it would protect their jobs; and it would allow them to reap the rewards implied in the "broad advance of our civilization." This latter windfall would accrue through the "elimination of frontiers and the promotion of international friendship and understanding" brought about by the airplane. "Future peacetime aviation will make the world smaller and people separated by thousands of miles, and differences in languages and customs, close neighbors." In short, the aviation industry would create a kind of international melting pot of amity and understanding.[29]

One is entitled to to question whether new airborne weapons systems, planned in an endlessly evolving sequence, are calculated to promote good will and understanding or new arms races. But it is clear in any case that the aircraft industry knew it was in trouble even before the Germans and Japanese threw in the towel and was therefore searching for a rationale to the prolong the wartime aviation bonanza.

Before they did so, in the spring of 1945, a group of bureaucratic agencies concerned with aviation formed, "through interdepartmental agreement," an air coordinating committee to delve into the questions raised by Woodhead, Wilson, and others and to probe the future of American aeronautics. Truman gave this effort administrative sanction on September 19, 1946, by executive order number 9781. The President also broadened the group's charge to achieve "the fullest development and integration of United States aviation policies and activities." This Air Coordinating Committee reported periodically until replaced by the Congressional Aviation Policy Board and the Finletter Commission.[30]

That process began as early as 1946 when the Senate held hearings on the propriety of establishing a National Air Policy Board. John Northrop, president of yet another Los Angeles area aircraft firm, favored a permanent aviation board under presidential auspices. Above all, he stressed the problem of the industry after World War II. Inflation was a special menace. The aircraft industry was hit by the general price increase of the postwar years, but had its own unique inflationary difficulties as well. Modern planes required ever more technology, which increased the cost of both material and labor. Ever greater scientific input raised the costs enormously.

Northrop made the usual suggestions, although he did not frame them in language identical to that of these other experts. The industry needed "incentives": the ability to foresee the future demand for aircraft, "continuity" to engage in long-term projects, "production" sufficient to keep alive a "basic industry," and facilities, especially for research. Of these matters, research was overwhelmingly the first priority for Northrop. According to Northrop, the United States had lagged in the research field during World War II, and although our own mix of mass production and research was enough to pull us through, the outcome had been a close thing. New German weapons like rockets and jet planes at the end of the war could have been disastrously successful, given just a bit more time for development and perfection. Besides wanting more money to carry on research and a definition of government policy on what kinds of planes would be needed, Northrop also wanted the research activities of the government decentralized. At present, NACA had too much control over these matters. Although they had done a good job, decentralization was needed to mobilize more of the best brains in the aviation field, especially those in the universities.

> SENATOR CLYDE M. REED: May I inquire what some of these schools that are well equipped for this research work are?
>
> MR. NORTHROP: Yes. California Tech is one. MIT is another. Stanford is a third. The University of Minnesota is another.

Northrop framed these recommendations in the context of world affairs. To him, the alternative to his proposals was "national suicide." Nonetheless, it is relevant to note that the Northrop firm was much more concerned with research than the average aircraft firm was.[31] Moreover, at this point the California Institute of Technology was completing wind tunnel facilities to be used by all of the Southern California aircraft companies and supervised by that university. More money and decentralization of research would not have hurt either of these aeronautical specialists.

The next year the Committee on Interstate and Foreign Commerce held hearings to create a review board to give statutory life to the President's Air Coordinating Committee. As might have been expected, this operation was closely supervised by Pasadena's John Carl Williams Hinshaw. The committee chairman, Charles A. Wolverton of New Jersey, may have had an interest in the hearings too because of the Curtiss-Wright factories in Paterson, but he allowed Hinshaw to orchestrate them. The Los Angeles booster did so with considerable skill. The witnesses were uniformly favorable to the creation of a national aviation policy review board. Still, Hinshaw dogged every step of their testimony, making certain that the witnesses did not get off the track, seeking clarifications for the record, and leading the experts when they seemed to lose their way. Hinshaw's handling of Army Air Corps General Oliver Echols, retired, who testified as the president of the Aircraft Industries Association of America, Inc., was especially skilled. Obviously, the former Army Air Corps officer left out some important parts of the testimony, so the Pasadena conservative patiently led the general from one critical point to the next until the record contained the requisite testimony. Just as obviously, the booster knew as much as and probably more about aeronautical matters than did the general.[32]

In any event, Congress was persuaded to establish the National Aviation Policy Board, which recommended a big program of aviation improvement and defense. Although Carl Hinshaw had envisioned the congressional board as the successor to the President's Air Coordinating Committee, Truman apparently decided that he wanted a committee of his own and set up the Finletter Commission, essentially to duplicate the investigation conducted by the congressional National Aviation Policy Board. Whether the two boards did better work than one would have is not certain, but they arrived at similar conclusions.

At the same time that the aircraft industry of the metropolitan Southland moved to bring its case in front of the federal government, urban leaders set out to back them up. On December 12, 1944, the Aviation Conference for the State of California convened in the Hollywood Roosevelt Hotel. Mayor Fletcher Bowron set the tone for the meeting and for the continuing battle to protect local air power and aviation interests. The urban chief executive noted that in the past California had been hurt at the national level and by divisions within the state. However, at present the separation between northern and southern California was narrowing, and simultaneously the various states of the Pacific slope were moving toward ever greater cooperation.

The mayor did not take long to get to the point. California aviation interests must unite to ensure that they receive a fair hearing from both the state legislature and Congress. "So far as I can see," explained Bowron, there is no State in the Union that has a greater stake in aviation." Still, "the relative importance of this state has not been fully and properly appreciated," especially in Washington, which tended to think that the state did not present a united front. "A well developed California view point" was an absolute necessity, he assured the delegates. "At the municipal level much is being done in this regard. We who have to do with the problems and policies of the cities realize that we all must stand together," the mayor argued. "Otherwise, the cities of the East, as they have been doing years past, will get what they want and we will get what is left or will get recognition on the same basis or formula, whereas our situations, our problems, are peculiar and unique." He explained that "down Texas way, they fight among themselves, but when the interest of Texas is involved, they appear at Washington or in any national conference as a single unit," concluded Bowron. "That is what we should do here in California."[33]

That is apparently what they were already doing, since the California Aviation Conference had been jointly sponsored by the National Aeronautic Association and eight California urban chambers of commerce, at the instigation of the Aviation Department of the Los Angeles Chamber of Commerce.[34] And what was expected of these cities was made plain at the outset. "Air power is peace power," said James L. Straight, western manager of the Aeronautical Chamber of Commerce of America. "The mighty air power which is tipping the balance for the Allies in this global war is the ideal tool for maintianing the peace after victory" for the first time in history, the "first real hope of a means of preserving peace."

This realization, spreading throughout the world, is placing upon every citizen an obligation to support the progress of aeronautics so that America may not only enjoy the commercial fruits of the air age, but provide the world with the one mechanism which has made permanent peace seem attainable. Air power is a thing of the people—not a scientist's dream or a militarist's monopoly. The message of air power must be carried to the people, and to the small communities who can and should be on the air map, and playing their parts in the air power that represents the power to maintain peace.[35]

One might wonder how much an "airport" in Weed Patch, California, or Grapevine, Texas, would have contributed to either air power, in the strictly military sense, or to the cause of peace, but it is obvious that such institutions would give citizens of these places a stake in aeronautical progress. In a way, this kind of aviation popularization had already taken place in the Urban Southland, where Los Angeles County alone had fifty airports, not to mention those in adjacent counties like San Bernardino and San Diego. Commentators on the so-called military-industrial complex have usually assumed that it *was* a "scientist's dream" and even more a "militarist's monopoly," but in Urban California it was quite accurately "a thing of the people."

The airport directors, aircraft executives, city boosters, airline executives, and so forth were impressed enough to direct that such conferences should be annual in the future and to give the Los Angeles Chamber of Commerce Aviation Department responsibility for organizing them.[36] Thereafter, Los Angeles boosters kept up a drumfire on behalf of air power. Although he was careful to praise the role of sea power on occasion, Bowron subscribed wholeheartedly to the trinity of air power. "I express the civilian point of view and speak as a respresentative of local government," the mayor said. "Los Angeles, as the center of what has become one of the leading industrial areas in the entire country has a big stake in the aircraft industry," the chief executive told an Air Force Association Rally at the Shrine Auditorium in early 1947.

Naturally we are interested in protecting the industry because of its effect upon the economy of Southern California, but of far greater importance is the fact that unless the aircraft plants are kept going, unless the aircraft industry continues research and is continually concerning itself with improvement and development, we will not be prepared to supply military planes when needed. The industry cannot be supported by the limited number of orders for commercial planes . . . . the only way to properly support the industry in order to have planes when needed, is to place orders for new military planes in sufficient number each year to supply the Air Force with the latest and the best models and keep ahead of other nations in research and development.

Bowron then went on to outline the problems of the aircraft industry, in language virtually identical to that used by industry officials such as Eugene Wilson. The sale of government surplus planes curtailed the need for new craft; most of the aircraft companies had lost money during the year (unbeknownst to Bowron till lately); federal policy had to be clarified; and air power must be upheld. The mayor ended with his own version of the theory of deterrence couched in urban terms.

Probably too much has been said about the atomic bomb, because in the minds of many people nothing else matters. It must be remembered, however, that the atomic bomb is useless for defense, and—speaking on behalf of one of America's largest cities, . . . an urban section greater in population that any one but nine states of the Union—we are interested in defense. And the only adequate defense will be a greater, more efficient Air Force with the most advanced planes in the world.[37]

Nor did the mayor fight for these goals alone. The Chamber of Commerce continued steadfastly to support air power proposals and, as can be seen from the participants in Air Force Day, 1947, had several important allies. "Los Angeles is one of the principal centers in the country where an organized program is planned" for Air Force Day, the Chamber's organ informed its readers. That institution would take an energetic role and the other "active participants" would include "the County of Los Angeles, City of Los Angeles, Aircraft Industries Assn., Air Force Association, Air National Guard, Air Reserve Training Detachment, and the Civil Air Patrol."[38] Although the Chamber of Commerce frequently denounced government expenditures and the growth of government, even that related to wars, it also endorsed the air power program of Hinshaw, the aircraft industry, and other Southern California aircraft boosters which could be implemented only through massive federal spending. Proving that nothing is too incongruous for politics, particularly that of California cities, so did one of the strongest Los Angeles unions, the International Association of Machinists (IAM), Industrial Lodge 727, of the aircraft industry.[39] Whether the union-busting Chamber of Commerce felt comfortable with the militant Chamber-hating IAM, and vice versa, is not known, but one must remain skeptical. Interestingly enough, the union embraced the seventy-group air force before the *Los Angeles Times* did. Perhaps reflecting a broader perspective that recognized the importance of both the Navy, Army, and Air Force to the metropolitan Southland it had done so much to create, the *Times,* in both 1948 and 1953, supported compromises that called for a more balanced force between the three services in the former year and between the latter two in 1953.[40]

In any case, when Colonel Thomas H. Chapman, chief of Western District Air Force Procurement, made his famous appeal to the Chamber of Commerce Air Force Affairs Committee for support of the Air Force program, the groundwork of such support had already been laid. The colonel did not need to remind the members of the Chamber committee that "the aircraft industry is the backbone of the procurement program in this area" or that the "Air Force desires to be a good neighbor, an asset to business and a friend of the community, as well as guardian of the air." The chamber and its Air Force Affairs Committee already knew both of these facts and had long earnestly endeavored to be just as good a "neighbor" and "guardian of the air." In fact, a better neighbor and guardian would be hard to imagine.[41]

It was in this already pro-Air Force and Air Power context that Hinshaw, together with Senator Owen Brewster of Maine, initiated legislation that would bring about a comprehensive review of American aviation policy by the Congressional Aviation Policy Board, which it brought into being. On this body, Brewster served as chairman and Hinshaw as vice-chairman and "head of the key combat Aircraft Subcommittee." The congressional body produced a report that was much like that of the Finletter Commission, established by the President to cover the same ground. To say that the 1948 report of this congressional group was favorable to the interests of aviation is to put it mildly. This document contained literally something for everyone in the aircraft and aviation industries and for the Air Force as well. Of course, the policy recommendations were not immediately implemented (neither those of the congressional committee nor of the Finletter Commission), but they served as a sacred text for air power advocates through both the Truman and Eisenhower administrations. Whenever economy-minded public servants questioned growing military expenditures, they encountered a solid wall of expert opinion drawn from these reports, defending the higher outlays.

That the document protected the interests of Southern California is not suprising. For example, the subcommittee on combat aviation included fifteen persons of whom five were current or old California hands. Hinshaw chaired the group and sat with J. H. (Jake) Kindelberger, president of North American and longtime resident of the Los Angeles area; Professor Clark B. Millikan, the son of the builder of Cal Tech, who had helped von Karman build the first wind tunnel in this area; General of the Army Henry H. Arnold, who had commanded at March Field near Riverside before moving to Washington and who had recently retired to California; and Admiral John H. Towers, retired, who had likewise spent many years in the Southland, some of them formative for the aviation business, air power, and the aircraft industries. Arnold and Towers represented competing forms of aeronautics, but both were air-power men.

The subcommittee on manufacturing included Hinshaw, Arnold, Kindelberger, Towers, and Robert Ellsworth Gross, the man who created the modern Lockheed Corporation out of its bankrupt predecessor.[42] They were five of seventeen. But if metropolitan Southern California was over-represented on this important body, the aviation industry was even more so. That the committee would come up with recommendations for diminishing the role of the Army and Navy, granting subsidies for the aircraft and air commerce industries, giving airports to cities, bankrolling research, and so forth, is not surprising considering only three out of the twenty-four-person council of advisors even vaguely represented interests outside the aeronautical realm.

Ten representatives and senators made up the formal Congressional Aviation Policy Board; nine representatives and senators sat ex officio on the board, and 24 outside experts made up the council, which advised the board members. The ex officio members from the House and Senate came in about equal proportions from the appropriations and armed services committees, so they might have been expected to keep an eye on the air-power buffs. However, the ex officio members did not sit on the subcommittees that *did the actual work of constructing the report.* More curious still, the outside experts who sat on the council, although not on the Congressional Aviation Policy Board, even ex officio, *did* sit on the working subcommittees that drafted the final report. In other words, the board represented the aircraft industry more than it did the Congress. The final report would affect the future of transportation in the United States, provide thousands of jobs for union men, deepen the government's involvement with research, favor certain geographic sections of the country over others, and, not least, influence the arms race. In short, it would affect a broad spectrum of national interests. Yet the men who wrote the recommendations of the Congressional Aviation Policy board represented a very narrow range of interests.

Intriguingly enough, however, the impetus for this congressional review of aviation policy came from both civilian and military sources. As the report tersely put it, civil aviation and aircraft manufacture stood on the brink of disaster in 1947 at the same time that the world situation had changed for the worse.

> Within 2 years after cessation of hostilities in World War II, general concern over national security and the threatened bankruptcy of the aircraft industry and carriers of the United States, indicated [the] necessity for review of national aviation policy by the Congress. . . . Before Board study had proceeded far beyond preliminary stages, it became apparent that the primary problem of national aviation policy was one of providing well-balanced military and naval air forces rather than one of finding means to maintain an aircraft industry. If the former were accomplished, the health of the latter would be assured.[43]

Although the board specified that it did not mean to diminish the role of the other services, it resoundingly declared that only air power could prevent an attack on American cities, industries, communications lines, and so on. The congressmen would have preferred peaceful means to forceful settlement of international quarrels and hoped that the United Nations would eventually evolve the capacity to civilize the practices of what Hans Morgenthau called "politics among nations." In the meantime, air power would have to do the job. All of this was, of course, intensely interesting to the city builders of California. Their cities still harbored many aircraft factories employing thousands of people who nurtured perhaps as many dreams about the future of the air. Any diminution in the prospects of this third dimension threatened all three. As in the case of the post-World War I period, then, the threatened relative decline of a great metropolitan area, the actual decline of the Second World War's largest manufacturing industry, the plight of the newly created Air Force, and the anxiety of a muscular (but probably also muscle-bound) and threatened nation-state combined to align all these elements together on behalf of air power. And it was not long before the primacy of air power came to be admitted by both federal policy makers and a large segment of the public as well.

Perhaps this conclusion was inevitable, given the world situation in 1945–47. Although the Army Air Force did not play a *decisive* role in the European theater of World War II, it had played an important one there and something close to a decisive one in the Pacific. The latter experience seemed to be more indicative of the future. Rapidly evolving science would surely make future weapons more deadly and their means of delivery more speedy, sophisticated, and certain. Moreover, population concentration, the irreducible measure of urbanization, seemed certain to continue, thereby making cities ever more inviting targets for attack. Armies and navies could partly defend against such an eventuality, but they were not thought capable of deterring an airborne assault. That proposition was more debatable for the Navy than for the Army, but at any rate it was generally believed to be true by the congressional and presidential policy makers of the postwar era.[44] Ironically, therefore, although the original theorists of air power had not conceived of it as a weapon to be used against urban populations, the experience of World War II, the process of urbanization, and the march of science had definitely made it into one.

It is perhaps impossible to sort out definitively the cause and effect relationships in these matters, yet certain things seem clear enough. Science, technology, and war had certainly made air power formidable and cities vulnerable to it. By the same token, the fact of urbanization had made the threat of air power into a reality. Without the modern age of the city, the flyers would have had a much less prestigious raison d'être, because without the overgrown targets in urban-industrial areas, especially in World War II, the strategic rationale of air power would have been much less compelling. In a less urban epoch, airplanes could easily have ended up like the glorified cannon that Great War commanders favored, a tradition that both German and Soviet military establishments stuck to until the end of World War II. Although few historians dwell overmuch on this role of the city in history, there is a certain cause and effect mutuality to the relationship and, despite the complexities, even a neat circularity. The Atomic Age is also the Urban Age.

The report of the Congressional Aviation Policy Board revealed both this urban-atomic interface and the mutual dilemma of decline, relative and absolute. It also revealed real fissures in the competing military perspectives that prevented any agreement on the overall aircraft and dollar needs of the armed services. Consequently the board presented alternate plans written by the Air Force and Navy respectively. Both provided for a marked increase in aircraft procurement. The Navy plan would have approximately tripled new aircraft procurement and was essentially defensive. As the report described it, "This plan is designed to provide a force sufficient to (a) withstand an initial blow intended to cripple the United States, (b) form the basis for a strong Territorial defense, and (c) provide effective retaliation, but not a sustained offensive action."[45] The Air Force urged something more ambitious. It would have more than quintupled (528%) the new airframe budget and would not have been defensive, but was rather designed to "mount promptly an effective, continuing, and successful air offensive against a major enemy." The Congress ultimately accepted the Air Force program, which came to be called the "seventy-group program," a figure which referred to the number of combat aviation groups that the Air Force would receive.[46]

On other matters the board reached consensus, most importantly on the unity of air power and, by the same token, the indivisibility of civil and military society. Dozens of books and hundreds of articles have been written about civil-military relations, but in this conception, which city boosters had originated long ago, the two were essentially one. As the committee members noted:

> National air power is an entity not fundamentally divisable as a weapon, or as a carrier. Materials, organization, and craftsmanship which go to make a great aviation industry are as readily turned to the combat plane as to the transport. Airway facilities which gave scheduled dependability to civil air lines also give tactical dependability to military forces. Airports which serve the burden of natural and international traffic can also base tactical or strategic combat squadrons. Transport fleets which serve commerce in peace can tie together tactical and administrative requirements in war.[47]

From these premises the committee went on to deduce the need for a wide range of other recommendations. "Scientific leadership" in the field of aviation had to be maintained, and the aircraft manufacturing industry had to be able to meet Air Force and Navy needs in time of peace and to possess a "degree of expandibility as to supply adequately, and without delay in emergency, the requirements of the military air forces." The "airways, weather stations, airports, and essential facilities of air navigation and control" were to be maintained and aviation programs should be fostered in the educational system. Moreover, "domestic and foreign air commerce should receive a helping hand from the government and small businessmen should be singled out for benefits from the program." The specifics under these general recommendations included benefits for everything from the development of atomic powered aircraft (one of Hinshaw's favorite projects) to helicopter research (soon to be initiated as mass transit in Los Angeles) to weather research to aviation safety to air parcel post service. In short, the committee tried to foster every aspect of aeronautics that they could think of, and in the course of ninety-two specific recommendations they do not seem to have omitted very much.[48]

Many of these suggestions had a solid foundation in the interests of security and national defense. There is no question that the United States in 1947 faced very real foreign policy dilemmas, particularly how to balance the massive land armies of the Russians with a kind of military might that was both affordable and acceptable to Congress and to a nation of taxpaying voters hardly captivated by the idea of universal military training. The American people disliked peacetime military service, and, especially after the fall of China, it was hard to see how the United States could match the land armies available to their enemies of the moment. Like it or not, the Cold War developed after the end of World War II and the United States had to create some kind of military capability within the context. Perhaps air power was the only possible response to competitors with larger and more docile populations willing to serve long terms in large land armies.

Still, men like Carl Hinshaw could not but chuckle at the degree to which the program benefitted both the national interest and that of the Darwinian City. The various other constituencies of metropolitan Southern California must have chortled as well. The City of Los Angeles badly needed a new and modern airport just at this moment; the members of the International Association of Machinists dearly wished to staunch the flow of jobs from the aircraft industry; the aircraft manufacturing industry desperately hoped to avoid going over the brink of bankruptcy; the California Institute of Technology needed monies for its outstanding aeronautical research programs; 100,000 World War II Army Air Force veterans wanted work in the field the war had taught them to love; Los Angeles, San Diego, and Long Beach all aspired to develop the Urban Southland into a major hub of air transportation; the cities of Burbank, Pomona, Santa Monica, Long Beach, San Diego, Inglewood, Chula Vista, and El Segundo wanted to protect and promote their aircraft industry–supported tax bases; and the entire Southern California area wanted their many war workers and veterans to be gainfully employed now that the Japanese had surrendered. The seventy-group program looked like a marvelous way to achieve these goals and to do so at the expense of the remainder of the country, whose taxes would largely pay for these windfalls.[49]

And windfalls they were, too, because much of the program did not make an overwhelming amount of military sense. For example, even as early as 1947 the Air

Force and its supporters assumed that war with the Soviet Union would be short, nasty, and aerial. The Air Force expected that a Soviet-initiated attack would be a sneak attack à la Pearl Harbor to which the United States would respond with massive retaliation. One side or the other would get the upper hand in this exchange, and it would all be over before the entire resources of either country could be pressed into service as in the Second World War. That is, of course, what atomic air power was all about. It would achieve a quick *decisive* result solely through aeronautical means. If this were the case, then civilian airports would be of little value and an upwardly flexible aircraft manufacturing industry would be of less value still.

In a nuclear exchange, the aerospace industry would be expendable rather than expandable because it would be the obvious target for a first strike. Obviously, there would be little value in attacking military targets and omitting the factories that produced military material. Civilian airports might be used to disperse military planes, that is, if the victims of an attack had prior warning, but otherwise would not see workhorse service in such a conflict. Certainly airports and civilian aviation would not be used to shift massive numbers of troops around as during World War II. The war would be over before they could pack their duffel bags. And if the conflict was short, then air transport by civilian planes adaptable to military uses would also not likely occur either. So the provisions for aiding domestic and foreign air commerce had only the foggiest sort of military rationale. Putting the pilots of such businesses in the air reserve would not have had much of an effect either. Much of the thrust of these recommendations was based on conventional war assumptions, even though atomic air power precluded conventional war.

There were interesting questions from the military side as well. Although in 1948 the Russians were nearing their goal of possessing the atomic bomb, they had few long-range planes to deliver them onto a foreign target. Moreover, they did not have these in any numbers until the second Eisenhower administration and did not have enough for an attack on the United States mainland until well into the 1960s.[50] That was not a fact discovered only in the recent past; it was known at the time of the postwar aerial buildup. As the admissions of the air-power supporters in congressional debates demonstrate, even extreme Air Force partisans recognized that in 1948 the Soviet air force was overwhelmingly dedicated to tactical support of ground forces rather than to intercontinental strategic missions. Even the fighter defenses of the country lagged behnd this tactical priority. It could have been argued that a seventy-group air force would be used to balance Soviet conventional power in Europe, but this is not generally the argument that prevailed.[51] The report is further suspect from a military standpoint because it did not come out under the auspices of the House and Senate armed services committees, but rather orginated in an appointed board that circumvented these committees. The Congressional Aviation Policy Board prepared a document that would have decisive long-term implications for all military policy, even though it represented aviation interests almost exclusively. No Army representative sat on the committee, and the report easily relegated the Army to third-class citizenship behind the Air Force and Navy.

Luckily for Carl Hinshaw, Jake Kindelberger, Robert E. Gross, Clark Millikan, and the rest of the metropolitan Southland, the Russians helped to put the recommendations of the Congressional Aviation Policy Board through the Congress in 1948. Although there were very fundamental interests at stake and although there was considerable speech making about the board's recommendations, surprisingly little actual debate occurred. Yet considerable opposition existed. Apparently the opponents chose not to fight the measure on the floors of the Congress, but rather to obstruct the later passage of legislation which would have funded the recommendations.

Nonetheless Hinshaw exerted himself fully to secure passage, explaining details, clarifying congressional thinking, supplying facts, reiterating the underlying principles of air power, and endlessly hovering about the fringes of the discussion, ready to lend a hand where needed. Interestingly enough, help was not needed in gaining congressional acceptance of the principles of the seventy-group air force. The Russian presence and the imminent Russian development of the atomic bomb loomed over the debate, although the Berlin Blockade did not influence the outcome since it began in June 1948, over a month after the debate on the seventy-group air force had concluded. Congressmen presented various rationales for the seventy-group air force: that we must not repeat the unpreparedness of the pre-World War II period; that the Air Force had become the first line of defense; that Congress must not go against the weighty advice of so many eminent experts; that Russia was fast building up its air force and nearing completion of an atomic bomb; and that the Army and Navy were irrelevant to nuclear warfare.[52]

Under the impetus of these arguments, the seventy-group program easily flew to victory. Obviously, with a lopsided vote, there was neither a partisan nor ideological division over the acceptance of the air-power program. Even hard-core California Labor-liberals such as Helen Gahagan Douglas of Los Angeles and Franck Havenner of San Francisco spoke for the program and joined equally hard-core conservatives such as Hinshaw of Pasadena and John J. Allen of Oakland in voting for it. Only afterward did the opposition begin to appear or, in the case of the Navy, to surface. This opposition remained for the next several years.

To Hinshaw's alarm, he found that there were several sources of this antagonism. For one thing, the Truman and Eisenhower administrations were sometimes in favor of considerably fewer Air Force groups than the aircraft industry, the air power advocates in the Congress, and the Air Force. Indeed, the seventy-group program passed the Congress in 1948 over the objections of the Secretary of Defense, who believed that fifty-five groups were adequate. This split recurred several times more, and an even more difficult one opened between the Air Force and the Navy. When it saw the seventy-group program, the Navy felt left out, and its congressional spokesmen and officers therefore fought hard to keep the Air Force in check. As Hinshaw ruefully put it, "Those admirals have got awful sharp sabers and they know how to use them."[53] So did the economizers, some of them in Hinshaw's own party. For example, Senator Leverett Saltonstall of Massachusetts continually reiterated that he believed in air power too, but not to the point of bankrupting the Treasury. Others emphasized the need for a balanced American military force. They pointed out that the Air Force must not grab the lion's share of service monies, since the Army and Navy had important roles to play also. Of course, this was exactly what the Air Force wanted to do, since it believed that nuclear war made the other branches of the military irrelevant. By no stretch of the imagination, therefore, could one argue that the post-World War II triumph of the Air Force and consequent emphasis upon air power was simply the result of the Cold War, nuclear weapons, jet technology, or the necessities of the modern nation-state. The final victory of the Air Force in 1956, which diminished the power of the Army, required all sorts of political allies—bureaucratic, industrial, military, congressional, and metropolitan.[54]

John Carl Williams Hinshaw needed no reminder of this elementary fact of American political life. Although the vote on the seventy-group Air Force had been overwhelming—343 to 3 in the House (with 84 abstentions) and 76 to 2 in the Senate—the Los Angeles booster soon found his seventy-group air force grounded. The Navy's premier defense role may have been eroded by air power but the admirals recognized that their own first line of defense lay in the Congress, where they battled the Air Force for several years. In June 1948 Hinshaw attacked the idea of a super carrier, a pet Navy project, on grounds of cost and vulnerability only to find himself opposed by Admiral Willis W. Bradley, retired, Hinshaw's fellow congressman from sea power–sensitive Long Beach.[55] Then, although the Congress formally accepted the seventy-group air force, it did not vote the money to fund it. Now Hinshaw was desperately trying to defend a far smaller fifty-five group air force and was in danger of losing even that compromise figure. "At this time, right today," exhorted the city builder, "the aviation industry in the United States is in the very dangerous position of having to lay off thousands of employees because orders have run out."

Even though the President's own Finletter Commission agreed with the Congressional Aviation Policy Board on the necessity of the seventy-group, the President himself deserted this concept in the 1949 budget. He asked for only forty-eight groups, although a disproportionate number of those were in the strategic category. Senators such as Leverett Saltonstall urged a balanced force and economy in military spending, and Hinshaw found himself having to invoke diverse foreign policy menaces to get a hearing. "Even if we ignore the ominous atomic deadline [for the Russian acquisition of the atomic bomb], what other world conditions justify cutting out air power?" agonized the Pasadenan. "Does the ever-growing Red might in the Far East encourage such reductions? Are we completely confident that the cold war is over in Europe?"

Hinshaw's concern is not hard to understand, nor was that of other Southern Californians. In discussing the announcement of the Russian explosion of the atomic bomb in 1949, Manchester Boddy summed up the predicament of the Southland Martial Metropolis. "'I see that it's now official,'" wrote one of Boddy's readers. "'Russia has the atomic bomb. That should mean that we workers in the about-to-be-shut-down Terminal Island Navy works do not have to worry any more. This is no time for economy. It's an emergency. We will have to stay on the job.'" Boddy explained that "nearly 6,000 workers will be thrown out of employment if the Navy closes down at Terminal Island." He went on to explain his concern:

> I refer to it only because it is a perfect example of the part defense plays in our national economy. I am sure that everyone of the 6,000 threatened workers on Terminal Island wishes the atom bomb had never been created. I am sure that all concerned wish that Russia were a peace-seeking democracy with whom the great family of civilized nations could walk, hand in hand, down or up the road that leads toward universal peace. I am equally sure that since the atom bomb does exist, and since Russia does threaten the peace of the world, military preparedness will become an indispensable factor upon which a large segment of the economy of the Nation will depend.[56]

Figures released in 1952 by the Los Angeles Chamber of Commerce indicated vividly just how great that reliance could be. In June of that year, the aircraft and parts industry of the County of Los Angeles represented nearly 59 percent of all new manufacturing in the county, and 160,000 employees worked in the industry in the same year, far and away the largest manufacturing employer in the county. At that point, the world-famous motion-picture industry employed 31,000 people, and petroleum 19,000.[57] Ere long, the figures would grow even more astonishing. Fully 275,000 earned a living in this branch of "military preparedness" by 1955, and more still were added during the 1960s. These figures do not count San Diego or San Francisco workers, nor do they take in all defense employment, which would include military personnel, shipyard workers, employees of the electronics industry, and others; but it is enough to convey the importance of federal defense in ths supposedly laissez-faire metropolitan economy.[58]

Nor had the metropolitan anxiety declined in proportion to the flood of military monies that saturated the Southland. Citing myriad figures to prove the importance of his Eighteenth Congressional District which centered on Long Beach, Representative Clyde Doyle demanded in 1951 that the West Coast, Southern California, and especially Los Angeles County "be given due heed and consideration in all matters relating to national expenditures, branches of national offices of administrative government, transportation and freight rates, flood control, and so forth."[59] Although a county studded with military installations, naval and private shipyards, airplane factories, and a budding electronics industry might be assumed *already to have been given* "due consideration," this was apparently not how the defenders of the martial metropolis viewed the case. Despite their military bounty, they felt aggrieved by the federal bureaucracy. Los Angeles's long struggle for prestige and status vis-à-vis San Francisco contributed to this sense of malaise amidst military prosperity.

> Since the Mother Lode and Barbary Coast days the east has thought of San Francisco as the big city on the Pacific coast. To this day people for miles in every direction say they are going "to the city" when they go to San Francisco," complained a *Los Angeles Daily News* editorial in the midst of the Korean War. "Something has happened since Jack London made the place famous and Nob Hill was the center of the social

universe. . . . Population and the stream of economic life in the West have moved south and southwest, and people have moved with it."

The editor went on to remind the East of the relative strength of the Los Angeles vote for President Truman in 1948 compared with that of San Francisco and to add that the county contained 44 percent of all factory workers on the West Coast. Chamber of Commerce president Oscar Trippett complained that the federal government considered Los Angeles a "hick town or a suburb" of San Francisco. The congressional delegation from the martial Southland even organized "a march on the White House as a body to impress upon the officials there the facts" of economic life and political power in the Southwest. Representative Gordon McDonough echoed these joint claims individually. A more latent threat of political muscle in the interest of metropolitan expansion and dominance could hardly be imagined, or a more open admission of the continuing importance of urban rivalry despite the growing power of corporate and bureaucratic America.[60]

Nor was Southern California the only area worrying about the loss of airplane contracts due to a lack of federal "recognition." The metropolitan anxiety affected the competitors as well. In supporting larger outlays for the Air Force, Henry "Scoop" Jackson informed the House of Representatives "that the announcement was made by the Air Force a month ago [September 1949] that the B-47, which is a jet bomber, will not be built in Seattle because the air defenses in that area are not adequate. . . . Our area is vulnerable to air attack," he continued, "because of a current lack of airplanes, radar fence, and airfields." His colleague, Representative Hal Holmes of Washington, also supported larger Air Force appropriations.[61]

Even with such allies, Hinshaw's progress remained slow. Nonetheless, he continued to hammer home the air power thesis. In January 1949, he introduced a resolution to establish another congressional air policy board and presented legislation to provide government aid to companies developing a civil air transport plane that could be converted to military uses upon the outbreak of a crisis. By March, he was back at work, quoting American Federation of Labor support for a seventy-group air force and promoting the B-36 bomber, despite its critics, because it was the only American bomber that could range from the United States to the Soviet Union and back. To get the aircraft industry tooled up, he reminded his colleagues that the British orders and captial invested to expand American aircraft production in 1938 had saved us precious years in meeting our own production needs in World War II. He also quoted others to good effect, especially I. I. Rabi's attack on P. M. S. Blackett's arguments, which Rabi interpreted as minimizing the effectiveness of the atomic bomb. Hinshaw continually reminded his House colleagues that A-Day—that is, the day when the United States needed to have a force "capable of dealing with possible atomic attack on this country," was nearing. The *Los Angeles Times* joined this effort to secure the seventy-group Air Force with a rousing declaration that "it seems to us that adequate air power is as essential in the crusade to save the world from communism as the plan to ease the suffering of poverty-ridden millions." Despite this aid and his best efforts, Hinshaw had to settle for a House authorization of fifty-eight Air Force groups in 1949.[62]

Hinshaw and his allies finally elevated the figure to seventy in 1950, but not because a stubborn President and his Secretary of Defense had conceded the argument. For no sooner had the Senate accepted the fifty-eight group program, and the President had signed the legislation, than Truman decided against the idea, opted for forty-eight groups and impounded the nearly $745 million authorized by the Congress for the larger number. In fact, according to the Semiannual Report of the Secretary of Defense for the last half of 1949, the government was not even spending enough to maintain forty-eight groups, much less seventy. Hinshaw was just as dogged as the President. He noted that without quick replacements the Air Force would be reduced to just 2000 modern combat planes by the process of obsolescence. He pointed out that the Navy's air arm was equally close to obsolescence. The booster also criticized the government for publishing figures that misled the public into believing that new orders had been placed when they actually had not been. This was a "cruel hoax" upon the unemployed aircraft workers and the businessmen who depended upon them, the Pasadenan claimed. Above all, the booster stressed the need for lead time in preparing the Air Force. Normally, it required about two years, from the placement of the order to delivery, for the government to acquire an aircraft of a model already developed and in use. To conceive, design, test, and manufacture a new model took up to five years.[63]

Hinshaw hammered these points home over and over again and warned the Congress and public that the program of achieving seventy first-line groups for the Air Force must be initiated now. Despite this need for lead time, in spite of Hinshaw's reputation in the Congress as an aviation expert, and notwithstanding the deprivation of the unemployed aircraft workers and contractors, it required the Korean emergency of the summer of 1950 to force the President to accept the congressional program. On June 30, 1950, the House approved "a conference report on House Resolution 1437 which established in law the 70-group program," and on July 11, 1950, the President signed the bill into law. At that point in the beginning of the Korean war the strength of the Air Force stood at forty-eight groups.[64]

But even seventy groups represented a compromise, since that figure represented the number of planes needed for a peacetime Air Force and peace no longer existed. Therefore, the figure continued to edge upward during the next few years until the magic number for the air power advocates had risen to 143 groups of first-line planes. By 1951, the country was escalating toward a ninety-five group Air Force, and already the groundwork was being laid for an even larger increase. With eighty-seven groups and building toward ninety-five, Senator Henry Cabot Lodge and Commander Earle Cooke, Jr., of the American Legion both described the United States as a "second rate air power." That charge touched off a flurry of articles, speeches, and learned arguments demanding a further increase to between 138 and 150 groups. According to Hanson Baldwin, the *New York Times* military expert, these higher numbers would require the abandonment of the balanced force idea, which had guided administration policy up to this point in 1951. It was a concept certain to be resisted by the Army and Navy, whose responsibilities were being increased by the new commitments to defend Europe. The target figure of 140 was agreed to late in 1951, but not without considerable conflict among the services. The Joint Chiefs of Staff reached consensus on the higher target only after Secretary of Defense Robert Lovett informed them that if they could not agree on a figure, they must request the civilian authorities to set it for them. The unhappy prospect of politicians establishing military doctrine was enough to bring accord. Although the 140 target greatly increased Air Force appropriations at the expense of the other two branches, it was probably a compromise. It vastly increased the neglected tactical air forces, which would have helped the Army then being called on to carry out new responsibilities in Europe while simultaneously fighting in Korea. This new emphasis was not necessarily detrimental to the interests of Urban Southern California aircraft builders because they built both tactical and strategic airplanes.[65]

What all of this arcane discussion about air force groups meant for the aircraft industry was literally quite astounding. Robert E. Gross, the grizzled Lockheed industry veteran, explained it all to a Chicago audience of the American Bankers Association in October 1952. Given his modest beginnings in the industry, fighting for contracts day to day to keep the ailing Lockheed Corporation alive, Gross must have savored the sound of his own words. According to his information of the moment, Gross assured the bankers that the government would spend $56 billion on defense next year, and 48 percent of this total would go to the aircraft industry. Of course, the urban impact of these funds would be even more astonishing because such a huge part of the industry lay nestled within the Great Wall of California. Comparative figures on such things are seldom available, but one wonders if there was ever a time in the history of Western Civilization when the military expenditures of a free-spending great power were so absurdly maldistributed, in either their urban or industrial impact. Since Chicago had once aspired to be an aircraft manufacturing center, one can only imagine the envious local reaction to Gross's words.

Yet the current bonanza was only the beginning. The Lockheed president both looked forward to an ever-expanding future and compared it with a cramped past. Until the present, Gross argued the aircraft industry had been on a feast-or-famine basis. Before the Second World War the business had fasted until just before American entry and then gorged. It fasted again almost to the point of starvation in 1945, 1946, and 1947, when American air power fell while that of the Soviet Union grew. "We let our stream run so dry, however, that back in 1946 and 1947 it looked as though America wouldn't even have a small Air Force." But a group of far-sighted men took note of the worsening conditions in 1947 and began to urge immediate rebuilding of our Air Force, Gross explained. "The President's Temporary Air Policy Commission headed by Thomas Finletter and the Hinshaw-Brewster congressional board came up with virtually the same recommendation: namely, rebuild aircraft production on a gradually intensified scale." He then recounted the struggle to get the President to accept the congressional legislation. All this stop-and-go motion had cost the taxpayer dearly, since the industry had to catch up when the Second World War and the Korean conflict forced an acceleration of production. Aerospace manufacturing needed instead a sufficient volume of production, steady orders, and, "finally, a long-range air program that would support the constant research and development necessary to produce airplanes of the future."

"Enact and support this long-range air program, and I can bring you great promise of wondrous things that can and will be done." Among these, Gross mentioned the possibility of space flight, the early advent of luxurious jet airliners, guided missiles to reduce the cost of air defense and eliminate the possibility of losing a crew of ten to twenty men, and personal, individualized aircraft—"everyman's airplane," as he put it. "Science, her tempting finger beckoning us forward, will show us new fields in which to work. . . . In my heart I know there is a whole new world waiting for us in the mysteries of the air," promised the Lockheed chief. "New airplanes and power systems are but on the threshold of this long corridor of searching, which at the other end may well hold the very secret to eternal life." The written record does not reveal whether Gross or his audience grasped the irony of searching for eternity on the wings of Lockheed war planes, but they must have been convinced by his ringing declaration that "this is the age of air."[66]

That conclusion seemed to be shared by Congress through 1952 as well. The higher air-power appropriations appeared to be accepted with little controversy. The feast continued until the assumption of office by Dwight D. Eisenhower in 1953. With the conclusion of the Korean War, it might be assumed that there would be a reversion to lower spending levels for all of the services. Indeed, the new President had promised to lower taxes and balance the budget, and now he and Secretary of Defense Charles Wilson set out to do so. Reducing the military budget would have been painful, no matter how even-handed the process, but the cuts fell mostly on the Air Force. That service had enjoyed large funding during the Korean War, and now the administration proposed to cut their budget by fully one-third, from approximately $16,778,000,000 to $11,688,000,000. Although the program had not been clearly thought out at that point, the New Look military policy of the Eisenhower government eventually came to stress nuclear over conventional weapons. "Getting more bang for the buck" was the way the program was characterized. Whatever the ultimate size of strictly military bang, the fewer "bucks" certainly produced an impressive political explosion in the Congress.

Since the days of the presidential and congressional postwar study committees, an Air Force bloc had been building in the Congress. For the most part, but not invariably, its members came from districts with either Air Force installations or aircraft industries to defend. These included House members such as Hinshaw and later Clyde Doyle and Samuel Yorty of metropolitan Los Angeles; Melvin Price of East St. Louis; George Mahon of Colorado City, Texas; Overton Brooks of Shreveport, Louisiana; Harold Patten of Tucson, Arizona; Frank W. Boykin of Mobile, Alabama; and Senate members Lyndon Johnson of Johnson City, Texas; Burnet Maybank of Charleston, South Carolina; A. S. "Mike" Monroney of Oklahoma City; and Stuart Symington of suburban St. Louis. These men, together with allies in the Congress, bureaucracy, and Air Force, created a rather marked blowup.[67]

No single member of Congress did more to detonate this explosion than Samuel Yorty of Los Angeles. Although a relative newcomer to the House of Representatives and therefore not in a position to present a prestigious committee report on behalf of air power, Yorty nonetheless drove home his point as well as any senior member. The Angeleno congressman lined up an impressive array of military witnesses, including generals Carl Spaatz, Matthew Ridgeway, Hoyt Vandenberg, and lesser commanders, to provide "expert" testimony against the Eisenhower-Wilson cuts. When not marshaling witnesses, the feisty Southlander was accusing the Republicans of unrealism—wanting to cut the budget and taxes and still maintain an adequate defense force. At other times he hammered Secretary Wilson for his supposed favortism to the big taxpayers, accused the administration of trying to gain economy at any price, and pointed to the crucial role air power played in the recent history of Great Britain. He also highlighted the excellent performance of the Air Force in the Korean conflict and publicized reports of new and ever more threatening Russian progress in nuclear weapons and delivery systems.

Other occasions found Yorty warning that the Wilson cuts would dangerously weaken NATO and citing economic statistics to prove that the country could easily bear the burdens necessary to maintain air superiority. Like Hinshaw before him, Yorty reminded the House of the long lead time necessary to produce planes and longer time needed to create new ones, questioned the view that the Russians were becoming less threatening, and generally did everything he could to produce an impression of impending doom if the Air Force lost any funding.[68]

There was certainly lots of ghastly material on hand to work with. Yorty could point to the newly developed route over the polar ice cap that shortened American reaction time in case of Soviet attack and complain that the Eisenhower cuts would hurt American research and development along these lines. He also could round up articles by such unlikely allies as Irving R. Levine to document the inadequacy of the new military budget and produce statements by prestigious national columnists like Joseph Alsop to demonstrate the ever-lengthening range of Soviet bombers. Nor would the future mayor shrink from scaring the public more directly. "Last time it was Pearl Harbor," the Angeleno reminded his constituents. "We had better realize that next time it will be American industrial centers."[69]

Other Los Angeles leaders helped the representative to make the point. "There must be no letdown in our preparations for defense, or offense," urged the editor of the *Long Beach Independent* as the Korean War neared a close. "We have brought on three wars by being weak. Now let us try keeping out of war by being strong." While paying lip service to the Eisenhower attempts to curb spending, the same newspaper editorialized against the very popular tax cuts being advocated at the time. "The danger of war, that makes these expenditures necessary, also brings us full employment, overtime and spending money, far greater in volume than ever before," explained the editor in a blunt admission of the transformation of warfare into welfare. "It is common sense that we pay for this year's budget from those earnings"; to delay payment "is passing the debt on to your kids." Not every community would share in the prosperity of this bonanza, but if taxes remained high, Long Beach certainly would.

The *Los Angeles Daily News* was not even this subtle. "Can it be, as Senator Stuart Symington bitterly charged in assailing the reductions in funds for the Air Force," questioned the editor, "that the Republican administration intends to meet Russian bombers 'with a firmly balanced budget?'" The Hearst-owned *Los Angeles Examiner* suggested the answer to this query. We "still do not have the essential assurance, the vital confidence, that the administration accords air power, and especially that of atomic bomb carrying aircraft, the enormous importance it deserves," the editor cautioned. "And we wish to repeat as energetically as we can that the Hearst newspapers want this Nation to have not only the best Air Force but the biggest and the best." In giving grudging assent to the idea of a Korean War truce, the *Los Angeles Times* left no doubt how it felt about the role of this air power in the next war. "If we must swallow such a pact [the Korean settlement] to stop the bloodshed it should be made perfectly clear that the first violation of it will bring a rain of bombs on Peiping and, perhaps, Moscow," the editor warned.[70]

The pressure of Yorty, Hinshaw, Doyle, and others in Congress and in the newspapers did not produce an immediate decisive change in administration policy, but it did help to initiate a long-term realignment of American defense posture. Up to this point, American military expenditures had been balanced rather evenly between the three services, as frequent complaints from air-power advocates indicated. When the Korean War ended, the Eisenhower administration tried to cut back on all the services, but the budget reductions fell most heavily on the Air Force. The cuts triggered a revolt by the Air Force, led by General Hoyt Vandenberg, the Air Force Chief of Staff, and air-power advocates in the legislative branch. After all, Congress had all along supported higher Air Force spending levels than either the Democratic or Republican administrations were willing to countenance. As a result, Eisenhower was caught between both international and national pressures. The Russian presence obviously justified a large martial establishment, but domestic pressures demanded both less and more defense spending at the same time. The demand for economy is well known, but historians have neglected the simultaneous pressure from defense constituents for *higher* spending, especially for the Air Force. Yet is was there, and it certainly helped to force a complete reappraisal of all defense policy. This process led to the abandonment of the idea that each of the services should have an equal share of the defense pie and, instead of drastically slashing Air Force funding, radically diminished that of the Army. The policy sacrificed Army interests to those of the air power services—the Air Force and the Navy—and then devised a new military doctrine to explain this development.

This outcome did not appear until the fiscal year 1956 and came to be called the "New Look." The system reduced the importance of conventional ground forces and increased that of nuclear and thermonuclear weapons, both for conventional and strategic forces, maintained the importance of strategic air power, and enhanced that of fighter defense (continental defense). In the future, no more ground wars like Korea were to be courted and none like the Second World War either. The arming of "conventional" forces with atomic weapons would see to that. In financial terms, that meant cutting the budget from about $50 billion to $40 billion, a goal which the Eisenhower administration held to until 1961. More important, the vast majority of the cuts came at the expense of the American Army. Its share of the budget fell from $16,242,000,000 in 1953 to $8,702,000,000 in FY 1956.[71]

Whether this outcome represented a deal between the Air Force and the Navy at the expense of the Army is unknown, but the Army was the principal financial loser. It is interesting to note that both the *Los Angeles Times* and the *San Diego Union* endorsed the supercarrier and the nuclear-powered submarine, which were the Navy's way of adapting to the jet age and thermonuclear weapons and thereby maintaining a foothold in the crucial realm of air power.[72] Without them, naval air power would soon have become obsolete because the older submarines and carriers could not accommodate the new jet airplanes or missiles coming into use. In buying into the supercarrier, both newspapers were protecting the interest of a service vital to their urban futures and at the same time helping to stabilize the aircraft industry upon which both were also dependent.

Of course, the entire New Look was wonderfully well adapted to the interests of metropolitan Southern California and to a lesser extent to those of the Bay Area as well. The Navy and Air Force were overwhelmingly dominant among the services in the former, and the Navy was dominant in the latter. No sensible person would claim that California urban pressure groups achieved this reorientation of American defense policy strictly on their own. On the other hand, it would have been unlikely that the Air Force, national security bureaucrats, cabinet secretaries, or even popular Presidents could have accomplished the realignment individually. They needed congressional assistance, especially from heavily urbanized and militarized states such as California. And it bears repeating that the New Look very closely approximated the interests of several California metropolitan areas, as that interest was defined by their key actors: John Carl Williams Hinshaw, Samuel Yorty, Chet Holifield, Fletcher Bowron, Robert E. Gross, the *Los Angeles Times*, the *San Diego Union,* and the chambers of commerce.

Clearly, the idea made more sense as a doctrine of urban defense than as a national security proposition. The United States has so far fought five wars in the twentieth century and all have been conventional conflicts. In addition, it has felt called upon to project its conventional power in Grenada, the Dominican Republic (under presidents Wilson and Lyndon Johnson), Haiti, Cuba (in the Progressive era and at the time of the Missile Crisis), Mexico, Libya, and Lebanon (under Eisenhower and Reagan). The lesson of both Korea and Vietnam was that nuclear weapons have a very limited utility as a way of ensuring dominance. They are relevant for great power relations, but the massive area of the Third World is off-limits to them. Therefore, if conventional martial power is the only kind of military influence that nations can ordinarily use, a New Look doctrine of force is not sufficient to maintain the national interest. Moreover, the unusable New Look has always been overfunded. Eisenhower himself recognized this problem, and his scientific advisors such as Herbert York, George Kistiakowsky, and James Killian have been unanimous in their memoirs in condemning the inflated budgets of the Pentagon and, we might add, the pressure groups allied to it.

Ike and his advisors are witnesses whose testimony we need hardly question. Eisenhower's military credentials speak for themselves, but it might be pointed out that Kistiakowsky fled the Bolshevik Revolution in Russia after fighting on the side of the Whites against the Reds and York actually ran the weapons laboratory that manufactured American thermonuclear weapons. All four were men whose expertise and patriotism are beyond reproach.[73]

It also bears repeating that the New Look outcome was not inevitable. As Samuel Huntington points out, some kind of "new look" was bound to appear, but not necessarily *the* New Look. Several alternative choices were available at the time that would not have jeopardized American security. One was to maintain large conventional land forces, an option that the Russians chose never to discard. Another was to go slower with the Air Force and air-power buildup. Another still was to buy less complicated equipment, since more complex weapons do not increase national safety anyway. High-tech equipment is often in the shop instead of ready for combat.

There was a tremendous hue and cry in the late fifties and early sixties about bomber gaps and missile gaps, foreshadowing the 1980 election-year "window of vulnerability."[74] Neither the Democratic "missile gap" and "bomber gap" of the late fifties and the 1960 election nor the Republican "window of vulnerability" of the 1980 election turned out to have any substance. Both these earlier "problems" were political blarney perpetrated upon the American public by politicians out of office. Even so staunch a defender of the United States as Barry Goldwater admitted that in the fifties the Air Force had more money than it knew what to do with; Russell Long of Louisiana and Paul Douglas of Illinois agreed. Senate Majority Leader William Knowland, himself no cowering dove, defended the Eisenhower cuts in the 1954 budget. After all, Ike was a rather respected judge of national security matters.[75]

In short, nothing on either the international or domestic front made inevitable a distribution of military resources in such a manner as greatly to enrich the major California metropolitan areas, as well as several others. The outcome was the result of a political drama in which the representatives of these urban areas played a very important role. They could not have known where the process would end up when Hinshaw, Air Force representatives, chambers of commerce, mayors, and congressmen initiated it; but the process did turn out to put a disproportionate share of military wealth in California cities. To argue that this joining of the city and the sword was simply the outcome of an interaction between national security bureaucrats, Presidents, and cabinet secretaries on the one hand and Russian and international developments on the other is not very plausible. And to contend that the martial metropolis was merely the outcome of deterministic economic forces, locational factors, social change, or any one of the other large, impersonal forces that imply a lack of human agency and are usually cited to explain American urbanization is equally unpersuasive. Just as Fortress California had representatives and leaders to attract and develop infant aircraft manufacturing, it also had leaders willing and able to protect and promote the interests of a mature aircraft industry. The trinity of air power had many effective defenders within the Great Wall of California. And they all exercised their free will in doing so.

The creation of general "national" policies that would guarantee urban prosperity, as well as national security and even oversecurity, was probably the most important way in which the martial metropolis sought to manipulate federal policy in the interest of the Imperial City. Yet there were lesser but still important ways as well. Air Force groups of 70 or 143 could set overall spending levels of great importance, but profitable adjustments could also be made in the lower levels of defense policy. To achieve this adjustment, Carl Hinshaw and his fellow Californian, Chet Holifield of suburban Montebello, strove to brighten the prospects of those parts of the aircraft industry which specialized in overhaul and repair.

The Navy long had experience with the competition between government Navy yards and private shipyards for contracts. Now the same problem appeared in the aircraft industry. When Truman rejected the larger Air Force appropriations before the Korean War broke out, the aircraft industry still considered itself on short rations. That perception made aircraft repair, modification, and overhaul worth fighting over, and here again the Pasadena aviation expert led the way into battle. Hinshaw discovered in the 1950 budget estimates that government shops received eight times as much of the overhaul business as private contractors. He advocated awarding more work to the latter, since he believed that they were more efficient and would thus reduce costs; a greater proportion would produce more efficiency and therefore cost reductions. But he obviously wanted the business for his own area. World War II had built up the Los Angeles area system of subcontracting and aircraft parts manufacturing, and Hinshaw hoped to preserve more of the overhaul and repair business for these less-known, but still very important members of the Southland aircraft industry.[76]

More important, private contracting would guarantee against another problem—nationalization of the aircraft industry. Although no one seemed about to propose such a step, Hinshaw argued that the practice of giving overhaul work to government bases or to private contractors using government-owned plants would be the first step toward a nationalization of the entire industry. During the war the government constructed and owned hundreds of plants and afterward turned over many to private enterprise. However, many were kept, and these were rented to the private contractors at a minimal sum. Chet Holifield charged that by this practice the government "subsidizes one type of private industry against another type by furnishing them jigs, dies, tools, and plant facilities at a dollar a year cost, and putting them in competition with private industries who have their whole capital investment to charge off when making bids on Government contracts." Hinshaw claimed that both capital and labor opposed this type of thing. Capital opposed it because it lost business and was threatened with nationalization and labor and because it preferred the benefits it got under free enterprise to those it could get under semi-public enterprise.

This dilemma was very reminiscent of the experience of San Francisco during the interwar period. "The City" had lost out completely in the private aircraft industry, in no small part because of the refusal of San Francisco bankers to finance Lockheed's transition to the metal airframe. Yet, as a consolation San Francisco received a kind of aircraft manufacturing establishment in the Alameda Naval Air Station, which did much overhaul, modification, and repair work on planes, and in the Ames Aeronautical Laboratory, which pursued research. Just as Southern California had its Jet Propulsion Laboratory, the Bay Area, despite its general weakness as an airframe center, possessed the very important Ames Center. Having no Donald Douglas or Cal Tech, the Bay Area fell back on government for its share in the aeronautical industry.

From the remarks of the congressional debate, other cities had apparently pursued the same strategy. The old aircraft factories were in the interior where the industry had decentralized during the war to avoid Japanese attack. When the war ended, these plants shut down, but were subsequently opened again, presumably in response to the new aircraft programs voted in 1948 and thereafter. Now the overhaul phenomenon offered them a way back into the Treasury, and several took advantage of the opportunity. In addition, again like San Francisco, the competitive cities had acquired public facilities to compensate for the private ones they missed out on. For example, Tinker Air Force Base in Oklahoma City employed 13,000 workers in 1950 and was heavily involved in overhauling and repairing Air Force vehicles, especially those recently used in the Berlin airlift. This was precisely the kind of thing that Hinshaw complained about, and his complaint drew a sharp response from defenders of other Darwinian cities. When the Pasadenan criticized the practice of allotting most overhaul work to public enterprise, Representative A. S. Mike Monroney of Oklahoma City responded that the private contractors were not big enough to do the kind of sophisticated industrial tasks that the 13,000-person Tinker Air Force Base crew could perform. Hinshaw retorted that private contractors could certainly do this work, specifically noting Pacific Airmotive as one example. Pacific Airmotive was one of the largest parts makers for the aircraft industry in Southern California. Hinshaw also pointed to Long Island contractors who could do the same jobs, but Monroney remained unmoved. Obviously, other cities outside of California also appreciated the advantages of a partnership between the city and the sword.[77]

Yet it is doubtful whether many appreciated this connection as fully as did the representatives of the Darwinian Southland, especially Representative Hinshaw. One of his colleagues paid tribute to him in 1948. "Almost single-handedly he convinced the Members of the House that we must be properly prepared in the aviation field, in the event of an emergency and to do so, we must have a production line in being, one that can be expanded rapidly if the emergency comes," explained Representative Leroy Johnson of Stockton in outlining Hinshaw's contribution to House acceptance of the seventy-group air force plan. While the controversy over that idea still raged, Hinshaw undertook another job of persuasion. The Congressional Aviation Policy Board had recommended government aid for the development of a commercial transport plane for passengers and cargo that could be converted to military uses in case of an emergency. Hinshaw initiated the process of acquiring such a vehicle by introducing House Resolution no. 6501 along with Senator Owen Brewster, who introduced a companion bill in the Senate requesting hearings on the project by the "Subcommittee No. 5—Air Matériel" of the House Committee on Armed Services. The ensuing testimony revealed the usual pattern of piggybacking.[78]

Robert E. Gross led off at the 1948 hearings with a statement that the commercial airlines were nearing bankruptcy and that they needed new planes to succeed. Apparently, all portions of the trinity of air power considered themselves on their last legs in the postwar years. The private sector could not finance the development of these planes, neither the airlines themselves nor the aircraft companies. New machines cost in the neighborhood of $30 million to $40 million to develop, and the manufacturers could not withstand that price, especially since it took two prototypes upon which to work out designs. Economically, this government subsidy would produce a healthy air passenger industry and would possibly create a whole new freight business to boot. This would enable American commercial airlines to "meet competition from abroad" and enhance our prestige as well.

Happily for the trinity of air power, this commercial project supposedly possessed immense military value as well. A new plane would help the airlines develop fresh overseas routes. "Their worldwide operation and experience is an invaluable springboard for military operations," noted Gross. In addition, in the event of an emergency, the planes could be taken over by the military for transportation of troops. Finally, Gross foresaw an interaction between civilian and military plane technology. "Many of the engineering advances which give high performance in new military fighters and bombers are adaptable to new passenger and cargo transports," he explained to the congressmen. So convinced was Gross of the interchangeability of this technology that he was willing to go along with the Hinshaw bill's provision, "which gives the Air Force, . . . the responsibility for its [the passenger-cargo plane] development, but it takes into account the advice and interests of other segments of aviation." Gross maintained that "by providing the best prototype, it will insure that our air lines have equipment equal to or superior to advanced passenger and cargo transports now being developed in other countries and at the same time provide a national asset, both now and in the event of trouble."

However, as Hinshaw brought out under questioning, these feats could not be accomplished without the government bearing the cost of development. In return, Washington would not need to purchase a fleet of transport planes, but could borrow them for the length of any military emergency. Vice president Arthur E. Raymond of Douglas took the same line, but with some deference to free-enterprise scruples. After largely accepting the provisions of the bill, Raymond went on to complain of the "abnormal" circumstances that forced the companies to ask for federal assistance. "We in the aircraft industry are not voluntarily in the position of desiring any handout on the part of the Government," Raymond protested. "We are anxious to stand on our own feet. We are very anxious to take normal business risks. We are very anxious to keep a normal competitive situation in the aircraft industry." If this venture helped commercial aviation to get on its feet, such a subsidy might not be necessary in the future. "I certainly hope so," he pleaded.

Of course, as we have seen, government assistance was entirely routine rather than abnormal. Albert E. Lombard, the military sales manager of Consolidated-Vultee, agreed with the need for a subsidy, but did not mention the free-enterprise scruples. Nor did Admiral Lawrence B. Richardson, president of Fairchild Engine and Airplane Corporation, or Burdette S. Wright, vice president of Curtiss-Wright Corporation.[79]

For that matter, neither did the various military and civilian representatives of the government who followed. All assumed that the nation-state would have to pick up the costs of the operation. So did Mendel Rivers, who spoke forcefully in favor of the legislation. The legendary congressman from Citadel Charleston knew a little something about the city and the sword himself. "If we are going to continue to have the finest airplanes in the world . . . , the Congress of the United States has to make the money available because neither the industry nor the operators can furnish the capital," urged the South Carolinian. "The greater and more laudable objective is to keep the industry in a healthy condition, because if we do not we are going by the board," he predicted.

None of the bureaucrats or service people disagreed with this perspective, but they did have considerable trouble stating exactly what kind of a plane would be needed and whether it could be used by both the military and civilians. Under questioning, the officers stated that the Air Force could use the plane designed for the civilians, but it seemed uncertain how much. Major General K.B. Wolfe, Director of Procurement and Industrial Planning, United Sates Air Force, testified that flying cargo to Europe or Japan required a "different kind of a ship than would be needed for transporting cargo between cities within the continental United States." Nor would the aircraft in question be useful for taking soldiers or cargo into combat. That task required a special plane, designed specifically for the job. Moreover, sometimes the government witnesses called for two different planes, one for military purposes and one for civilian ones. These contradictions confused even the sympathetic members of the House Subcommittee and forced repeated interventions by Carl Hinshaw to straighten out the record. As usual, he was equal to the task, questioning, leading, interposing, correcting, and lecturing the officers and supplying very accurate and specific information from his own encyclopedic store.[80]

From the testimony given to this committee, it is difficult to judge the military value of the subsidies proposed for the development of a transportation aircraft. It seems relatively clear that the main concern of all was the transportation of cargo, not people. And the supporters of the legislation—from the Civil Aeronautics Board to the Air Transport Association of America to the Air Force to the aircraft manufacturers—had high hopes indeed. They believed that an efficient cargo plane would promote the national defense, would keep America number one in air cargo, would vastly accelerate the development of the business in this country, and would bring down the price of the service thereby. It might also provide another, commercial market for the aircraft manufacturers, allowing them to escape their abject dependence on the military market. The civilians argued as well that this greater aviation activity would create a trained reserve of pilots to man the craft in wartime. Nonetheless, the case did not seem an open-and-shut one.

The military value of the plane would be confined to transportation within the United States during a World War II-style conflict and possibly to those areas abroad that were not combat areas. Combat aircraft and transatlantic transport had to be done by specially built planes. The Air Force wanted a backup fleet of transports in case of emergency. Still, the basic rationale seems to have been economic; the aircraft industry needed another market to supplement the newly recovered one that the seventy-group Air Force program and its predecessors had brought them. Some of the civilian witnesses bemoaned the state of the cargo business, claiming operating losses and near bankruptcy. However, the testimony of the Civil Aeronautics Board documented a rather different story. They portrayed a rather rapidly growing industry. "There have been numerous estimates made by assorted experts as to the eventual size of the air-cargo industry—domestic and international," noted the CAB statement to the subcommittee. "Irrespective of which estimate is picked, it is apparent that the industry offers one of the best opportunities for substantial growth over the next few years." The brief went on to point out that air-cargo tonnage had doubled between World War II and 1947, but noted that rising costs of airplane manufacture threatened to put "a brake" on the development of the industry.

Thus, to keep pace, the industry wanted a subsidy in the form of a super trans-port to carry cargo so efficiently that it would prevent European firms from getting into the market, take over a part of the American transportation business that already existed, and provide the manufacturers with a craft superior to any pro-duced abroad. It is quite obvious that there were already plenty of planes to carry the cargo. In fact, witnesses complained of a glut left over from World War II. What the industry wanted was a new aircraft that would make all of the others, including those abuilding in Europe, obsolete.

Although the manufacturers complained of the abnormal conditions pushing up prices, many of the problems were normal business difficulties, including airline specifications, underestimates, unanticipated design problems, strikes and other labor troubles. None of this was abnormal, and neither these problems nor the gen-eral inflation of the time constituted a different set of difficulties than those under which other businesses operated. The aircraft industry frequently complained of its special injuries; but it would seem that many of them were not so special, and some were self-inflicted. They were an overgrown business that wanted government assis-tance in finding a mission and in fighting off their expected decline during times of peace. Nor did they shrink from trying to horn in on the markets of other carriers. As Congressman Leroy Johnson of Stockton put it, "In my state this is the cherry season, and they could move those cherries across to here almost as cheaply by air as they could by train." Vice president Raymond of Douglas Aircraft answered that it is "undoubtedly true that there is an enormous potential market for air cargo commercially and the problem of cracking that market is one of getting the proper aircraft." Thus, in this interpretation, the cherry season in Stockton took on a national defense relevance that might have escaped even the most intelligent observers.[81]

Apparently they continued to miss this vital connection, for by 1950 the plane had not been built. Nor was this failure due to a lack of national defense crises. By the time of the August hearings of the next committee that investigated the prob-lem, the Berlin Airlift had proven the utility of air-cargo transport, and the Korean War was demonstrating it again. As Delos W. Rentzel explained it in 1950, the Eightieth Congress did not pass the legislation because "the industry—I speak of that considering the Government agencies involved as well—has been unable to get together on a program on which they could agree." He pointed out that "the point of view has changed several times in the past 3 years." Lack of agreement, in turn, defeated the bills introduced into Congress in 1948 and 1949.

One of the agencies failing to agree was the Air Force, for whom the new plane was supposedly being designed. Just as the 1948 testimony hinted, the Air Force did not believe in an aircraft that could at the same time be both "sword and ploughshare." By 1950 that ambivalence had turned into Defense Department opposition. The department did not oppose subsidies to the aircraft industry to develop a commercial transport, but it did not favor a plane that was a hybrid of commercial and military vehicles. At best they favored the development of two dif-ferent machines.[82]

Even such an air power devotee as Secretary of the Air Force Stuart Symington thought that the proposition was of limited value. "The anticipated benefits from such a program can be expected to accrue, initially and with certainty, to the civil airlines, and to the national security only in event of emergency," the Secretary testified in January 1950. At that point, Symington did not perceive an Air Force deficit in "lift capacity." The secretary made this statement before the outbreak of the Korean War, but it was made after the Berlin Airlift, so the air-power champion was well informed about the needs of the Air Force. Eventually a more modest interim solution emerged.[83]

In 1950 legislation was introduced into both houses of Congress which would subsidize the aircraft industry to the tune of $12 million to develop commercial transport (feeder-line passenger) and cargo aircraft. The national defense rationale was repeated less ardently in this case, though the inability of private aircraft companies to develop the planes without government assistance was ritualistically reiterated. However, both the sums involved and the subsequent history of commercial aircraft indicate that the subsidy was hardly crucial. In the first place, $12 million spent over a period of five years was not a very large amount of money to firms of the magnitude of the aircraft companies. Such modest infusions of capital can hardly have been a life-or-death proposition to corporations such as Boeing, Douglas, Lockheed, or Convair, especially since no one of them could lay claim to the entire sum. Second, despite the repeated protestations that the aircraft industry needed government aid to get into the business of building a new postwar transport plane, specifically a jet-powered one, they were able to do just that. Boeing built the 707 series, the first American commercial jet transport, which came onto the market in 1959 without the kind of subsidy deemed indispensable by the industry from 1948 to 1950. As John B. Rae has noted, Boeing, Lockheed, and Douglas has extensive experience with jet engines by virtue of their strictly military contracts and were able to move successfully into the field of jet transport. There definitely was a swords-into-ploughshares transfer of technological training between military and civil fields. Boeing gained this training in part with its experience in large plane manufacture of the B-47 and B-52 bombers. Lockheed did likewise through its work on the Air Force transport, the C-130. Moreover, it is clear that the companies, especially Douglas, delayed their move into this business in large part because of their own business strategies. National defense seems to have had little to do with the matter, except insofar as the companies used their military experience to move into civilian fields. They certainly did not need another special subsidy to achieve their goals in civil aviation; nonetheless, they would not turn down a windfall from the government.[84]

Despite the lack of a rationale for this kind of handout, the industry eventually got just that. The cargo-plane issue sputtered on throughout the fifties without the subsidizers gaining the victory. However, it is important to remember than even without a new plane, the air-cargo and passenger transportation industries gained valuable data from military operations of airplanes comparable with the civilian ones in question. For example, the Pentagon ran something called the Military Air Transportation Service, which ferried soldiers, sailors, marines, and Air Force personnel to distant posts and carried some of their cargo as well. Since the experience of these many years of transportation service was readily available to the civilian flyers, this in itself was a subsidy to the domestic carriers. Of course, it illustrates once again the close interface between civil and military sectors in this realm. The soldiers were not exactly transforming their swords, but they certainly were providing data from which to develop better ploughshares.

And by 1961, when President Eisenhower complained of the burgeoning influence of the military-industrial complex, the cargo-plane issue had finally come home with yet another subsidy. The House Armed Services Committee hearings of that year authorizing spending for aircraft included testimony from the redoubtable Carl Vinson that Lockheed had been awarded a contract to develop a new transport plane. The chairman's description of the craft could easily have been taken from the 1948 hearings. After citing the various deficiencies of the seven- to eleven-year-old planes currently in use, Vinson described the new one:

> A new cargo transport is needed to provide the payload/range and speed required to support the Army and the Air Force in both general and limited war.
>
> To satisfy the intent of presidentially approved courses of action regarding the national airlift posture, the design philosophy of this new transport is directed toward satisfaction of military requirements and the needs of commercial carriers. Procurement of this optimum cargo aircraft for the civil reserve fleet will greatly strengthen the national airlift capability.

Although the committee members strongly denied it, someone had already leaked information to the media that the contract would eventuate in the purchase of 100 machines at a total value of one billion dollars. Lockheed received only the developmental contract, but there obviously was more where that came from. At the same time, the government was considering adding to its special "air mission fleet," which flew long range. This would have been a small order, for which the Douglas DC-8, Boeing 707, and Convair 990 were all under consideration.[85]

And by that time, the practice of developing civil and military transports together was well established. *Jane's All The World's Aircraft* is full of examples of the codevelopment of civilian and military aircraft. For example, Convair developed the 240/340/440 series right after World War II, flew the initial prototype in 1947, and delivered the first "licensed" plane to American Airlines in 1948. The firm sold some 176 planes of the 240 variety and 209 planes of the 340 version to various private airlines. It then marketed many military versions of the 240/340/440 as well—48 T-29As, 105 T-29Bs, 119 T-29Cs, 93 T-29Ds, 26 C-131s, 36 C-131Bs, for a total of 427 planes. Whether subsidized upfront or simply paid for at the time of delivery, these military craft supplied a means of spreading the development cost of civilian aeronautics to the military, since those charges would be passed along to the consumer, both military and civilian.[86]

Civil aviation constituted the third leg upon which the trinity of air power stood. In 1945 it rested uneasily, as indeed it had for most of the history of civil aviation in the United States, on a primitive system of urban airports. During the war, the government had taken over the airports as well as airline equipment and personnel and moved large numbers of passengers. This action validated the concept of air travel and opened seemingly endless vistas to the hungry postwar aviation business. When the war ended the industry grew, but it did not immediately hit the takeoff point on its own.

Like the market for personal flying, the market for passenger and cargo transportation proved disappointing. It seemed destined to remain that way, at least for a considerable time to come. As late as the early 1960s air cargo had not developed very far, and as early as 1948 "experts" in the field of aviation held that the field of passenger transportation had already reached the saturation point. In 1948, the airlines employed only about 300 airplanes to carry all of the passengers in the United States, fewer than at the outbreak of the war. In addition, from 1945 until the early fifties, the manufacturers had to face the added question of the future of jet propulsion in civilian aviation. Jet transports would vastly increase the cost of building aircraft, and this cost would have to be spread over a thin market. At the end of 1945 the *California Magazine of the Pacific* noted that the San Francisco International Airport handled only 2000 passengers a day; in the same year a congressman estimated the traffic at St. Louis at less half of that figure. With a market like this, one can understand the reluctance of the aircraft companies to design and test new jets for the business, or even to improve on existing models of passenger or cargo transports. In fact, several companies, including Convair, had tried to do so immediately after the war and lost considerable money for their trouble.[87]

The lack of a suitable airport system posed one of the most intractable problems that city builders and the aviation industry faced. In fact, this problem constituted an obvious bottleneck, blocking the development of both the aircraft industry and civil aviation. Without adequate airports, the prospects of those businesses would certainly be limited by the aircraft and airport technology of the era of the Douglas DC-3 and DC-4. Jet planes would not take to the air with tiny passenger and cargo loads, nor could they ascend or land at primitive airports.

Urbanists of all kinds have frequently, and perhaps usually, attributed urban growth to vast impersonal forces shaping the course of modern American history. Industrialization, the march of technology, developments in transportation, the rise of the modern nation-state, demographic trends, market "forces," capitalism, population migration, and several other large trends have been used to explain the phenomenon of urbanization. By the same token, the idea of urban self-generation has often been denigrated. The city as dependent variable created by a set of independent ones is perhaps close to the prevailing view of the process of urbanization.

Yet, as we have seen, the process is not this simple. Sometimes the process of urbanization is a dependent variable, sometimes it is an independent one, and sometimes a coordinate or tantamount variable.* In regard to other aspects of the trinity of air power, the process of urbanization was often a dependent variable, or at best a tantamount one. The Cold War dominated the postwar aircraft buildup and commitment to air power, and urban influence could only add to the overall total, although the additions are often estimated at 100 percent. Yet with civil aviation, the positions were reversed. Cities preceded aviation and had well developed and adequate transportation networks long before aviation was ever discovered. Moreover, population concentrations and cargo terminals had to exist in order for the aviation business to function. The same might be said of the interstate highway

---

*As used here, the term "tantamount" means equivalent in value, meaning, or effect. It is necessary to illustrate influences which are neither dependent nor independent, but rather more nearly equal.

network, but it was even more true of air transportation. Highways need terminals, but are accessible along their lengths to farmers, villagers, and townsmen bypassed by the road itself. This plural access is not true of civil aviation, for which there is no equivalent of the rural or town cloverleaf. Passenger and cargo airports are located in cities and, almost always, *only* in metropolises; and the bigger the city, the more fully elaborated the air transport. In this case, "transportation" grew up as the subordinate variable, dependent upon a pre-existing urban network and the presence of a modern nation-state interested in promoting economic growth. So if there is a vast impersonal force in this interpretive puzzle, it is the process of urbanization itself.[88]

Both these prerequisites for aviation development existed in 1945. Although the development of passenger aviation would revolutionize American travel habits, few historians, aside from Paul Barrett, have seen fit even to mention the process whereby this latest "transportation revolution" unfolded. An important part of the process can be seen in the congressional debates over aid to airports, starting with that of 1945, which did not eventuate in legislation until the next year. Homer Lea of Santa Rosa, who had helped build up the military presence in the San Francisco Bay Area between the wars, introduced the legislation in the House, and Pat McCarran, one of the builders of the West and creator of the industrial decentralization controversy of 1944, did the same in the Senate. As he frequently did in important aviation matters, Carl Hinshaw also played a key role, both in the congressional hearings preliminary to consideration of the bill and in the congressional debates themselves. Obviously, the bill had impeccable booster origins.[89]

Two broad considerations of national interest permeated the discussion. One was defense, and here the usual arguments were reiterated. The nation must stimulate the aircraft industry by providing landing space for their products because of the possibility of future wars. A war would require an expandable aircraft industry, and air transport would enhance our capacity for supply during military crises. Expanded aviation would also train both pilots and mechanics for the next military emergency, and last, but far from least, airports would create jobs for returning servicemen. Yet most of the congressmen used a more economic rationale to justify this latest federal-urban program. Some of these looked at the airport subsidy, which would have run up to 50 percent in some cases, as a way of improving the conditions of doing business. It would speed up business transactions, create jobs, stimulate new industries, hasten the flow of information, and so forth.

Many others saw these same factors in even more nationalistic terms. An airport program would keep America number one in the air, keep the country moving forward, encourage a new transportation revolution, and generally speed the passage of travelers around the country. The speakers acknowledged that this program would undoubtedly center upon cities, but they usually stressed the national benefits, either to the economy or to defense. Critics stressed the cost of the program and the fact that it would circumvent the state part of the federal system by establishing direct ties between city and national government.[90]

One lonely Missourian, however, got at the more substantial explanation for the bill. It had to do with the Darwinian City rather than with defense, federalism, national prestige, national economics, or any of the more frequent justifications for the bill. After complaining of the expense of the measure, Clarence Cannon argued, "We not only have enough airports but we have as large and as adaptable airports as civil aviation will require for many years to come." He called the measure "pork." "[F]unds made available under the pending bill," said Cannon, "would be used merely to enlarge and enhance and aggrandize existing ports to promote the commercial and civil interests and ambitions of enterprising municipalities and chambers of commerce." Some of the most "enterprising" and "ambitious" of these civil and commercial interests hailed from California.[91]

Each of these vigorous metropolises had a postwar airport project, and what is more, each was aware of the others' progress. "The future of Los Angeles is dependent in no small degree upon the early construction of a modern airport," Mayor Bowron reminded the city council in early 1945. "The citizens of San Francisco, Seattle, Chicago, Detroit, New York, Dallas, Oklahoma City, Kansas City, and numerous other cities" already had airport projects under way. Not content with this warning, he went on to a more dire prediction: "If we stop to argue the point, we will be left at the post in the competitive race for a secure position in the business, industrial, and commercial world." Bowron's booster counterparts in San Francisco and San Diego could have written the same speech. "Many key cities have already provided funds for airport expansion to accommodate the forthcoming larger airplanes," observed the Special Subcommittee of the Bay Area Aviation Committee. "In order to receive the new super aircraft, San Francisco Airport must provide landing strips comparable to those from which such aircraft take off, or these aircraft will have to land elsewhere." "Competition among American cities for the aviation industry already is becoming very keen," the San Francisco Postwar Planning Committee wrote to Mayor Roger D. Lapham, and then went on to catalogue the cities that recently passed or were considering new airport bonds. It is not too surprising that Los Angeles was at the head of the list, and both L.A. and San Francisco were high on San Diego's list.[92]

City-booster expectations for these "sky harbors" ran the gamut from civilian to military. In the Bay Area, civilian concerns dominated, but in the cities to the south, the two aims came into much closer balance. San Francisco, which had not only the burgeoning southern cities to worry about but also booming San Jose and cross-bay Oakland, saw the new airport as essentially an economic multiplier. Certainly the field would supplement the activities of the marine port of San Francisco, and together they would cement the commercial primacy of the Bay City and Bay Area. San Francisco also had the added motive of overcoming the geographic disadvantages that accrued to it from its location on an isolated peninsula. "The City" had been denied the terminal of the transcontinental railway in 1869 because Oakland was more conveniently located. Although the older city finally claimed a terminal of its own, which delivered passengers and freight into the city by way of San Jose, many people and much freight came across the waters.

Aviation offered the possibility of eliminating that annoying stop at Oakland by allowing air cargo and passengers to debark directly into San Francisco, or at least into San Francisco Airport in contiguous San Mateo County. Therefore, the plane offered a new technological weapon in the long battle with Oakland. However, the project promised a general economic boost for the transbay area. Even though the airport was not within the city limits, it could help the entire peninsula area, of which San Francisco was such an important part. In the short term, 5000 construction jobs were expected to come out of the project, and another 20,000 private positions were hoped for when the bulldozers and trucks disappeared. United Airlines alone already employed 1800 persons at the field. Three other carriers also operated from the airfield in 1945, and several more waited for the completion of the new field. Of course, the positions created by the improvement of the airfield would bring both commercial and industrial jobs. Airplane repair and overhaul would grow simultaneously with the retail shops in the airport and the commercial facilities around it. In addition, the airport would increase trade, and as a result, "the activity of banking and finance will keep pace. Credits will be required by the vast expansion." Finally, the airport was expected to be a major profit-making enterprise for the city.[93]

Mayor Roger Lapham, city planners, chamber of commerce types, and labor leaders emphasized civilian over military concerns, but the latter did enter in. In fact, the city had parlayed its control over Treasure Island into a military improvement of the field even before the war ended. The Navy asked for Treasure Island in perpetuity, and in return for it, put $10 million worth of improvements into San Francisco Airport. That, in turn, made the field into a center for the wartime activities of the Military Air Transportation Service, and the Army and Navy had "spent considerable sums at San Francisco airport developing patrol bases." An improved airport would ensure that these institutions stayed put. It would also provide work for returning veterans. "All public bodies are being urged to plan public works projects as a means of taking up the slack in employment during the period following V-J Day," explained the Special Sub-Committee of the Bay Area Aviation Committee in mid-1945. A modern terminal promised "jobs for skilled workers, many of whom will be our own sons back from the airforces of the war."

Of course, the airport was already a stage for military aviation spectaculars, such as that put on for Air Force Day, 1945, when 25,000 people showed up to inspect the sinews of air power. And the port could serve for military transportation operations in case of another conventional war. The Bay City accepted the trinity of air power even if it did not have the factories that undergirded that doctrine in the Southland.[94]

As the airport struggle moved southward, the military rationale grew space. Los Angeles had the same civilian economic aspirations from aviation as did San Francisco, but its military rationale was considerably more compelling. As the earlier discussion of the trinity of power reveals, Angelenos were acutely aware that any development that facilitated the use of aircraft would help them. Airports were especially important to them because of the expected postwar boom in civilian plane construction. If the factories inside the Great Wall of California were going to get the job of putting these new "super" planes into the air, someone had to find a place to bring them down. And the factories *must* get the jobs because the nation needed an expandable aircraft industry in case of war and in order to keep American military technology ahead of its Soviet competitors. Of course, every aviation advance would also benefit the California Institute of Technology, the Jet Propulsion Laboratory, and the other suppliers of brain power to air power. The air fields of the Southland fortress were even more closely tied to the future of aviation in the area because they were military manufacturing and testing sites as well as passenger and cargo termini. The local city builders *had* to build up their airports to retain their manufacturing clients, who turned out predominantly martial implements.

This had long been the case. Clover Field in Santa Monica had been built to serve the Douglas firm, and of the former Douglas employees who formed the "competition" in the Southland aircraft manufacturing field, nearly all had similar arrangements with other municipal airports. At the end of World War II, Los Angeles Airport did not even handle passengers. It was largely a military manufacturing site. Until 1946, most of the passengers in the area traveled through the Lockheed Air Terminal in Burbank. Los Angeles Airport had begun as a leased property on private land in 1928, had gained from various New Deal programs, and had acquired title to its own site in 1937. The city moved to make it a first-class airport, but World War II intervened. In 1943 Mayor Bowron organized an aviation committee to plan for an international airport. Negotiations with the airlines to transfer from Lockheed Air Terminal to Mines Field promised to give that place some new tenants. Until then, it has mostly military ones. North American arrived in 1935, and the opening of the Douglas branch at El Segundo brought another tenant in before World War II. Both used the field for military and other testing and their plants were adjacent to the air strip. Long Beach Municipal Airport provided a similar service to the Douglas branch in that city.

There can be little doubt about the military reasons why boosters in these cities favored the creation of modern terminals or even federal aid to airports. Their modern military aircraft manufacturing districts depended upon both. "The local aircraft industry—employing 305,000 persons with a total payroll of more than $15,000,000 per week—depends extensively on airport facilities for its operation," explained W. W. Shepherd, chairman of the Chamber of Commerce's Aviation Committee in the midst of the 1949 airport bond campaign. Of course, he need not have bothered. The connection between the city and the sword in the Urban Southland was hardly a military secret.[95]

San Diego represented the principle better still. The chief aircraft manufacturers there included Convair, Solar Aircraft Company, Ryan Aeronautical Company, Rohr Aircraft, and the Navy, in the sense that repair and overhaul constituted manufacturing. Lindbergh Field, San Diego, represented a long-term commitment by that city to the acquisition of the aircraft industry and the Navy as well. The harbor commission controlled the airport, and, as we have seen, was extremely growth-minded. By the postwar era that body had developed the field into one immense manufacturing district which housed every aircraft manufacturer in the country with the exception of Rohr in suburban Chula Vista. Convair, the county's leading industrial employer and producer of the B-24 and the Catalina and Coronado flying boats, was entrenched on a fifty-four-acre site north of the field. Ryan Aeronautical, the builder of the *Spirit of St. Louis* and, more recently, designer of the Navy's "first plane to use jet propulsion," hunkered down to the south. Solar Aircraft Company, which in 1947 held "a dominant position in the production of aircraft accessories," mounted guard on the east. The Nelson-Kelley plant, which specialized in "repairs and major overhauls, hangar storage, and parachute packing" as well as retailing

Convair Stinson personal planes, occupied another part of the airport. The Navy completed the encirclement of that facility with its seaplane facilities on the bay side. Of course, these facilities had been provided by the city and were under the control of Lindbergh Field for use by either the Navy or Convair's flying boats, most of which were sold to that service.

All of these groups used Lindbergh Field for flight testing, and both of the services used it for flying. The whole complex faced across the bay to North Island Naval Air Station and the carrier anchorages where many of its products would ultimately end up. The spatial relationships could not have been more symbolic. The aircraft companies surrounded Lindbergh Field and in turn were encircled by the city of San Diego. It was hard to determine where the city left off and the sword began in this highly integrated military-metropolitan industrial district in the heart of the Port of the Palms, the premier manufacturing center of the county.[96]

It is little wonder, then, that the martial metropolises of the Golden State were enthusiastic about airport improvement. Nor is it surprising to find the high priority accorded such development. The Citizens Postwar Planning Committee reported to Mayor Lapham in 1945 that the airport should have the number one priority among postwar public works essential to the city. And, the committee recommended this number-one priority over such perennial and crucial urban goals as traffic rationalization, downtown redevelopment, regeneration of mass transit, and improvement of major streets and highways. Twenty years earlier, these problems were overwhelmingly dominant and airport construction was hardly thought of at all. If anything, Los Angeles, without a real airport of its own in 1945 and studded with aircraft factories, put an even higher priority on airport improvement. Perhaps San Diego was a bit more complacent because the federal government had completely rebuilt Lindbergh Field in 1944, but it too wanted airport development.[97]

San Francisco, Oakland, and Los Angeles moved rapidly to supply this needed facility, but San Diego lagged behind somewhat. The Federal Airport Act of 1946, which Carl Hinshaw and Clarence F. Lea fought to enact, provided generous aid to urban airport projects. For larger airports, the national government could contribute up to 50 percent of the cost of most aspects of construction. This was no more than fitting because smaller entities like towns and counties also received generous treatment under the act, and the big-city airports served urban, and rural areas, none of which could afford a major airdome of its own. The legislation is of special interest to the study of urban competition because of the intense battle for airport facilities after World War II. Each city desperately wanted to develop a means of harnessing this new transportation technology on behalf of its own imperial designs. Yet, as Mayor Fiorello La Guardia pointed out, New York's airport was useless unless someone else had a place to land planes that departed from there. Therefore, each contestant needed its competitors to develop enough to handle shipments and passengers from the rest. San Francisco wished to capture more freight and passenger traffic than Los Angeles, but it needed L.A. to be able to handle the greater tonnage dispatched from the Bay City. Nearby cities were a different matter, however.[98]

Neighbors troubled San Francisco in particular. Between 1939 and 1947 it had lost 182 manufacturing establishments while its suburban counties had gained over

400. "The City's" manufacturing decline was both relative and absolute. Even though the airport rested in San Mateo County, San Francisco needed it badly to counteract the industrial losses it had sustained. In keeping with these facts and with its number-one postwar planning priority, the airport project sped toward completion. The public accepted the 1945 bond referendum by a five-to-one majority, and by the early fifties the facility had become an imposing one. By late 1947 the airport had the eleventh largest San Francisco payroll, just below that of the maritime port and greater than that of "the banking and hotel business." At that point, the city had invested $25 million in the sky harbor in addition of $7 million of federal monies. In that year the airport manager, Bernard Doolin, estimated that the facility brought over $34 million of new monies into San Francisco and the peninsula. By the mid-sixties, the skyharbor was valued at $100 million; it handled 146,000,000 pounds of freight a year, had an annual payroll of $120 million, employed 16,000 people, and handled sufficient passengers to make it the "fourth largest air hub in the United States."[99]

San Francisco's downtown area tried to further develop this commitment to aviation by acquiring a field for personal flying at Treasure Island, recently given up to the Navy in return for improvements to San Francisco International Airport. Since the new airport would concentrate mass air travel several miles away in San Mateo County, the Downtown Association wanted at least to capture the personal flying traffic for the center city. In this case, the Navy stuck to its guns, and Treasure Island did not become a civilian flying center. The predicted movement away from the center city did occur, however. Ninety percent of the employees of the airport lived in San Mateo County and many of the businesses served were located there. Moreover, as its founders had predicted, the airport also drew new businesses and industries to its immediate area. Oakland, whose airport had initially outstripped that of "The City," now lagged behind. Nonetheless, it developed its facility into a modern one also.[100]

Los Angeles, with its heavy stake in manufacturing the products that flew out of airports, did not lag behind. Its 1945 bond issue of $12.5 million passed by a six-to-one majority before San Francisco's bond issue went through, and by the late 1950s Los Angeles, too, had a $100 million investment in its international airport. Only a third of this money came from the federal government. Sectionalism within the city of Los Angeles stalled the project for a time in the early fifties. In 1950, a $13 million bond issue failed because it would have placed yet another Los Angeles project in the basin "across the hill" from the San Fernando Valley. The next bond issue took that objection into consideration. The city acquired an airport in Van Nuys from the War Assets Administration in 1949 and used that field to placate the residents of the San Fernando Valley. The city government promised the Valley that this former martial asset would be developed into a commercial and general aviation airport, which it subsequently was. Eventually the city's collection of airports would expand to four, including those at Ontario, Van Nuys, and Palmdale. So the martial influence helped to bring about public acceptance of a $50 million bond issue and helped further to spread out the already fragmented metropolis. Like its freeways, suburbs, and life-style generally, the Los Angeles airport system is also decentralized.[101]

To exemplify the point further, Santa Monica improved its own airfield to help its service partner. Where the original Douglas plant sat, Santa Monica undertook an $857,000 expansion of its Clover Field airport, an action which nicely illustrates the principles of the martial metropolis. The Army had taken over the municipal golf course for the duration of the war, and afterward it had ceded that land to the city to be used to expand Clover Field for Douglas Aircraft. The city accepted $150,000 of federal money as compensation for the "loss" to the aircraft industry of this recreation facility (badly needed at the time in the Los Angeles metropolitan area) and Douglas in turn chipped in another $175,000. As the *Los Angeles Aviation Progress,* the chamber's aeronautical booster periodical, smugly noted, this "swap" allowed "the city to acquire the necessary property without resort to a bond issue." And, of course, the trade did not hurt Santa Monica's relations with Douglas either.[102]

The experience of Long Beach and San Diego points up the urgency of airport projects for all parties concerned. Both were enthusiastic supporters of the trinity of air power, but both had crowded facilities as well. In each case it proved impossible to maintain both military and civil air activities at a desirable level, and the Darwinian City had to give up one or the other. Long Beach Airport, which had a branch plant that manufactured Douglas aircraft products, was also the site of military flying and installations. At the same time the process of urban strangulation was well advanced there, investing the airport with a wooden ring of residences.

Douglas's testing did not seem to have threatened these sturdy householders. But Air Force jet-plane pilot-training maneuvers certainly did. In fact, in this instance, the fears of General William Fox, the Los Angeles County airport impresario, proved to be unfortunately, but quite literally, well grounded. On January 12, 1954, an F-87 jet trainer crashed into a residential neighborhood at Nineteenth and Raymond Avenue in historic Signal Hill, a city surrounded by Long Beach and the site of the famed oil boom of the twenties. The accident demolished six houses and killed nine people along with some of Long Beach's ardor for national defense. In fact, fifteen such incidents, most of them involving the military, had occurred since 1944, taking a toll of twenty lives. The city wanted to hang onto its military assets, but in the face of this carnage, something had to be sacrificed. In this case, the military jet-training exercises proved to be expendable. City officials and the press now called for their removal, while hoping to maintain the other military activities at the airport.[103]

Urbanization, then, did indeed jeopardize the continued existence of even large airports, and therefore the trinity of air power itself. In fact, local authorities and boosters had long known this fact, which made the development of new, large public airports critical. In 1940, Los Angeles County had fifty-seven airports, but in 1952 only twenty remained. Officials predicted that, except for the large public airports, they, too, would disappear within five years. The high cost of flying, the decline in public interest, and the inability of the airplane to adapt to the needs of masses of urbanites who made short-haul journeys all helped to explain this disappearance.

So did the process of urban strangulation. In Los Angeles County, subdivisions, industrial parks, highways, and other large land users inexorably besieged the twenty survivors. For a time, William Fox proposed and actually gained some success in implementing a program of dedicating airport runways as "public ways" which local authorities would maintain and protect from changes such as that which put the Bellflower Airport out of business in 1952. However, many private fields did not come into this scheme, and the local governments eventually cooled toward it. Hence private airports found themselves forced to close down and sell out, by either political or economic pressures upon their lands. Jet technology increased the urgency of the airport issue. Jets needed more, not less, room in which to take off and land. They were also bigger, faster, and therefore more dangerous in a crash, and they generated loud and unpleasant noises in operation.[104]

These various problems made the operation of airports more risky and the future of aviation more problematical. If the local authorities wanted to continue to subsidize private flying, mass flying on the airlines, military reserve activities, and martial manufacturing on public sites, some means must be found of defending the aviation interests from the hordes of urban householders and businessmen surging round the airport perimeters. Public fields represented the best answer to these problems. They alone could mobilize sufficient capital to provide large landing fields; they alone could prevent urban strangulation through zoning or land use changes, and they alone possessed the power of eminent domain necessary to enlarge upon the airports in time of need. As Long Beach learned, even a public airport could be forced to surrender something to an enraged citizenry.

For much the same reasons, San Diego sacrificed part of its civilian aviation interests for the military. With North Island Naval Air Station and Lindbergh Field facing each other across the bay, San Diego flying conditions had become extremely crowded as early as 1945. To solve this problem, officials hoped to build a new civilian airport remote from Lindbergh Field's downtown location. By the early fifties, however, the partnership between the city and the sword had become so close and comprehensive that hardly any suitable land remained available. In 1945 the federal government owned a staggering 40 percent of the total area of the county, and urbanization and mountains took up most of the remainder. San Diego, which had given away so much valuable land to the Navy, now found itself forced to go back, hat in hand, to that service with a request for retrocession of some Navy property to the city or for the right to share use of the military airfields.[105]

The Navy, which possessed major fields at North Island and Miramar Naval air stations, responded with outrage to the latter suggestion, made in a 1956 planning report, but offered to retrocede another site suitable for a new international civil airport. In the meantime, the city encountered more and more difficulty in keeping Lindbergh Field abreast of the changing demands made upon it for the accommodation of increasingly modern planes. In 1957 the Civil Aeronautics Administration rejected plans for the development of Lindbergh Field into a jet-age airport and agreed to the project only when San Diego promised that it did not intend to keep the airport as its "master airport" permanently, a pledge so far unkept. In 1960 the Navy offered to decommission Brown Field, near Tijuana, Mexico, and the city moved toward making this its major jetport. However, by 1987 Lindbergh Field still served as the only airport.

The Brown Field proposition faced many difficulties. Its air traffic would have to be integrated with that of Tijuana Airport, making it a truly international airport, and "strong local resistance" would have to be overcome. In the meantime, Lindbergh Field had been transformed into a jetport but could not handle the largest fully loaded commercial planes. The Harbor of the Sun had captured the Navy and the aircraft industry, but at the expense of civil aviation. One part of the trinity of air power, air commerce, had fallen victim to the other two, aircraft manufacturing and air power. As the booster history of the city sadly confessed, "The civil dream of a jet airport which would open the door to the entire Pacific basin was fading, even though the annual number of passengers using the airport had climbed to almost 700,000." As in the case of the railroads, "San Diego, again, in an air age, was at the end of the line."[106]

Not in any military sense, however. San Diego's airport had protected its investment in the service connection very nicely and so had the airports of Long Beach, San Francisco, Oakland, and Los Angeles. National defense did not constitute the only motive for airport construction nor the only lever that city builders could use to pry loose appropriations from urban taxpayers or congressmen. Nonetheless, the service connection did provide one important rationale for the development of an airport system. The strength of the rationale varied with the urban areas in question, from very important to less so, but nowhere was it unimportant. The martial metropolis recognized the obligations inherent in their faith in the trinity of air power and fulfilled them very well.

Nor did the other cities interested in landing-field air fail to stress the national defense factor. Urban California was by no means unique in this respect. Mayor Fiorello La Guardia of New York gave defense as one of his principal reasons for favoring the airport act of 1945, and do did the representative of Chicago. The justification appeared throughout hearings for airdrome assistance in 1945. It came both from the representatives of urban-vested aviation interests and from aircraft manufacturers, road builders interested in constructing airplane runways, airline companies, bureaucrats, congressmen, and most other spokesmen for federal aid.

It would appear that the close alliance between municipal airports and military services existed in other aircraft building centers as well. Wichita, a longtime participant in plane manufacture, is a case in point. In the spring of 1945, the city and the Army jointly ran the flying field and each occupied half of the administration building. The city of Wichita expected that ratio to decline after the conflict but expected the soldiers to remain in lessened numbers. At least two aircraft manufacturers used the municipal airport as a site for building and testing planes. These included the Boeing factory, which employed 28,000 people turning out the famed B-29 bombers. The airdrome also contained an Air National Guard building which would revert to that organization after the Army evacuated it.

As in other cases around the country, the Army had greatly improved this airport during the war, thickening the runway to enable it to handle B-29s and therefore the largest civilian aircraft as well. The interface did not stop there either. The city of Wichita sold gasoline to both military and civilian flyers, thereby earning much of the money that put the airport in the black financially, and the airport also serviced both civilian and military planes. As in the case of San Diego, the city had built the airport originally to cash in on as much of the development of the aircraft industry as possible, and this is exactly what it did during and after World War II.

It is impossible to enumerate all of the ways in which the defense effort influenced cities and vice versa, but suffice it to identify an few of considerable importance. The services operated about 540 airports in early 1945, in addition to the 434 municipal and commercial airports used by them. Civilians looked forward eagerly to the acquisition of the 540 service airports as defense surplus, and the War Surplus Property Act actually provided means to turn over defense airports to adjacent municipalities. Another key link came through the use of private airports and municipal airports to train pilots in World War II. In all, the war produced some 3,000,000 Army Air Corps veterans, and of these, 300,000 had received pilot training at the aforementioned airports in private flying schools. Many would go on to careers in civil aviation serving the urban areas whose flying schools had originally trained them.

Obviously, cities depended upon the military, but just as obviously, the dependence was mutual. Training those 300,000 pilots through some other system might not have been impossible, but it would have been both costly and time-consuming to create airports, flying schools, and experienced pilots to do this job. In any case, such a conversion never proved necessary and cities went merrily on tranforming yet another aspect of warfare into welfare.[107]

One of the oddest connections between military and urban development came in the field of helicopter transportation. The Los Angeles Airways began the "world's first scheduled helicopter service airline" in 1947, but this initial service carried only mail. In 1953 and 1954, the firm added freight and passenger service. Clarence Belinn, president of Los Angeles Airways, Inc., saw the helicopter as the answer to the transportation problems of a fragmented metropolis. Belinn predicted that the streets, highways, and freeways of the area would soon be choked with automobile traffic and that the higher altitudes of air space would be clogged by the rapidly multiplying long-range passenger airplanes. This compound, vertical congestion left only the intermediate area between choked ground highways and cluttered high altitude air lanes, and this was precisely the realm where the helicopter held sway.

Belinn also thought that the geographic immensity of the Los Angeles area would reinforce this tendency to travel beneath the rotors. In a metropolitan region of four counties (Orange, Los Angeles, Riverside, and San Bernadino) which alone was larger than four of the New England *states* combined (R.I., Mass., Conn., N.H.), a region already suffering from snarled traffic, only the helicopter could speed passengers on their way. Conventional propeller-driven small planes could help too, but the airports necessary for these craft were being gobbled up or strangled by the process of urbanization. Thus, just as the trolleys had been forced to give way to the auto in the endlessly sprawling Southland metropolis, now the auto would give way to the helicopter, at least in part.[108]

Los Angeles Airways operated between Los Angeles International Airport and other points in the Southland "megalopolis," as Belinn termed it. However, by the mid-1960s the line had multiplied its outlets and it planned other expansions that would carry passengers to San Diego, the Antelope Valley, San Bernadino, Barstow, and Santa Barbara. By 1964 the company had carried a total of 673,000 passengers in its ten years of service to that clientele. This number swelled greatly toward the end of this period, but the three-year total of passengers from 1962 to 1965 came to only 487,000. By way of comparison, five of the supposedly obsolescent freeways of that era handled an average of 583,000 passengers in a single day.[109]

Possibly it would be some time before the auto gave way to the helicopter, but even with these unimpressive results government officials accorded Los Angeles Airways a federal subsidy, based in part on the national defense utility of helicopters. The aid began in 1954, and as the Civil Aeronautics Board noted in 1958, the line had "greatly aided civil and national defense" as well as helping to speed the mails and contributing to the advancement of helicopter technology. Supposedly the Los Angeles Airways provided valuable maintenance and operating information that saved millions of dollars during the Korean War and it even served as a kind of mechanics seminar for the Army during that conflict. As the president noted in testimony to the aviation subcommittee of the Senate Commerce Committee, "Special pilot training was performed for the military during the Korean War. The U. S. Army stationed officer observers in an OJT [on-the-job training] program in all aspects of helicopter maintenance and flight techniques."[110]

It is possible that the company's own estimate of the usefulness of the "commuter" line in serving the military was not entirely fanciful. Outside commentators such as *Air Transport World* argued that "the accelerated de-bugging of newer turbine helicopters (by Los Angeles Airways) has saved the U.S. and other free world military establishments hundreds of millions of dollars." *American Aviation* argued in 1965 that "any real objective looks at the helicopter experiment over the years have proved beyond doubt that the value to the military alone has been in excess of the subsidy money paid out to the carriers." John B. Rae notes in his history of American aviation that the helicopter needed extensive testing after World War II, a conflict in which it had played a very limited role. Since the commuter helicopters flew many more miles than their military counterparts and since Los Angeles Airways made their experience available to their service opposite numbers, it is quite possible that the urban commuter line did significantly help to prepare the helicopter for the expanded role that it would play in the Korean War.

In any case, Los Angeles Airways certainly got paid for being helpful. In return for all of its services to both the military and civilian development of this technology, the line received some $12 million in federal subsidies from 1954 to 1964. By 1965 two other lines, operating in New York and Chicago, also received aid from the federal government and a fourth, in the San Francisco–Oakland area, functioned without it.

It is interesting to note that despite the limited utility of this kind of urban transportation, Los Angeles Airways received a government subsidy. Its stipend was begun at a time when both trolley and bus-borne urban mass transit were declining and before mass transit claimed subsidies from the Washington bureaucrats. Not until the early 1960s did Washington become interested in mass transit of any kind, although mass transit moved many more passengers than did helicopters. Moreover, in Los Angeles these latter vehicles seem to have been of use primarily in moving people, especially businessmen, from airport to airport or from an airport to some other urban destination, a kind of flying airport limousine. Nonetheless, helicopters provided a modest economic stimulus to the martial metropolis, while further cementing the partnership between the city and the sword in yet another area.[111]

Perhaps enough has been said to document convincingly the claim that Californians did not share the traditional American suspicion and fear of the military and actively sought to align themselves with the services. Yet as we have seen, that alignment could cause major problems for cities even while it provided a marked stimulus to the process of urbanization. At the conclusion of World War II and in some cases before that point, urban Californians awoke to some of the consequences of the Imperial City. Their dreams had not exactly turned into nightmares, but they had definitely lost some of their simplicity. The war had vastly accelerated the concentration of installations, factories, airstrips, and other military facilities as well as the development of camps, bases, and cantonments, with much of their own infrastructure including streets, sewers, and lights, and their own schools and police. These assets meant more retail sales, more bank deposits, more commercial traffic over the docks, more construction opportunities, more defense contracts, and more people, but they also left problems in their wake.

California city builders wasted no time in pointing out these problems to the federal government. Although all of the martial metropolises suffered from the complications of war, San Diego felt its impact more than the two larger urban areas. In early 1946, Mayor Harley E. Knox reminisced that "like a tropical hurricane the war effort swept over San Diego, tearing at its normal way of life, uprooting carefully laid plans, disrupting municipal services. . . . NOW the gale has subsided. Around us is the wreckage and debris that must be swept up."[112] Nor did he and other San Diego officials leave any doubt as to who should wield the broom. The San Diego associate superintendent of schools spoke for all but a few urban California officials when he complained that "the situation is unfair to the taxpayers of San Diego. The personnel is assigned there in the national interest. The naval locations are there because of the strategic importance to national defense." He went on to argue, "The citizens of San Diego are paying their Federal taxes on the same basis that the other taxpayers of the Nation are paying them. This way they are being asked to add to the support of the national institutions, national defense institutions, by direct payments for the support of their dependent personnel."[113] The message remained simple. War and defense were national rather than local problems, and the nation-state should assume responsibility for the local consequences to the process of urbanization and the condition of urbanism that this national phenomenon produced. And it often did so.

CHAPTER 8

....

"Born in Sin": Nuclear Power
for Imperial Cities

Civilian atomic energy has always been pre-eminently an urban matter. Hardly anyone seems to have noticed that fact until modern nuclear plants began to loom over countless metropolitan horizons. At that point, the connection between the new source of power and the aging urban centers of the country was finally recognized. Even then, the recognition was largely negative. Atomic power presented a threat to population centers, and both critics and defenders took to the hustings to explain the threat or the benignity of the reactors in their backyards. As in the case of nuclear war, critics thought that urban dwellers had become hostages to chance, lunacy, operator error, corporate mismanagement, or terrorist malice.[1] Defenders thought the risks were bearable. Yet long before the age of atomic-power consciousness and the attendant fear of a meltdown disaster—of which an urban population would multiply the magnitude—American cities exercised a decisive effect upon the development of this novel source of electric energy.

Proponents of atomic energy (there were hardly any opponents originally) saw many advantages for it, mostly of a national or international nature. Developing atomic energy for civilian purposes would demonstrate to the world that American and, therefore, democratic technology was superior to Russian. Demonstrating peaceful uses of the atom would mitigate the rising panic about the arms race. It would salve the consciences of the scientists who brought this means of destruction into being by turning an awesome threat into a magnificent resource. And it would help end poverty and war in the world by bringing about prosperity, especially in the Third World, and by removing the causes of conflict through material uplift. Of course, it would ultimately create further well-being in the United States by providing cheap power for industrialization and perhaps transportation.

Initially, atoms would not be so helpful because of the large sources of conventional fuels in America and the consequent low costs of electricity. In the long run, the United States would share in this cornucopia, but in the short run it could benefit by exporting reactors, technology, and technique to underdeveloped countries, where power costs were much higher. Primitive nuclear technology would be competitive here from the beginning and American business would make money supplying reactors to economically primitive countries. In this wonderful scenario, everyone would win, except the pesky Russians, who would be checkmated in the Cold War, outmaneuvered in the Third World, and shown up everywhere for the backward ideologues that they were.[2] Many historians of nuclear power development have picked up on these original political arguments and turned them into the reigning interpretive explanations of domestic nuclear power.[3]

Although most of the early interpreters of nuclear power and later historians of that technology live in an urban civilization, they seldom mention the role of cities in its development. Yet that role was considerable. If one looks at a map of the 94 American nuclear power plants licensed as of March 1986, one will see that they were built to serve masses of people crowded into metropolitan centers.[4] Nor is this urban-nuclear axis a recent phenomenon. The first American nuclear power facility, as opposed to research or military reactors, was the Shippingport, Pennsylvania, plant, built by the Duquesne Light Company to serve Pittsburgh.[5] When atomic power began to "go civilian" in 1954, of the first large "prototype power reactor plants" (Shippingport was the first) six of seven were located in urban areas.

These plants were industrial to the extent that industries consumed some of their power and large firms such as Westinghouse shared responsibility for constructing them, but each plant was to be operated by an urban utility company such as Commonwealth Edison (Chicago), Detroit Edison, or Consolidated Edison (New York). Obviously, these corporations did not build these plants to service farms, small towns, or factories per se, but rather to exploit the aggregate demand of great masses of people in urban areas.[6] In doing so, these modern firms simply followed the lead of the original inventors of electrical power who also began with an urban market and the very most crowded part of it at that.[7] Moreover, the number of plants continued to grow, especially in the 1970s, even in the face of so-called deindustrialization. Since industry was in decline in places like Detroit, Pittsburgh, and New York at the very moment of the advent of nuclear power, mere industrialization cannot have been the critical cause of which atomic energy was the effect.

Technical considerations reinforced market ones. As a new largely untested technology, nuclear power would be unreliable. The original plants would often be shut down for testing, repairs, improvements, and fine tuning attendant to a pioneering stage of technology. Therefore, initially nuclear power would be intermittent power and consequently could be attempted commercially only in a large city system. In a metropolitan utility, nuclear power would constitute only a part of the overall electrical supply and in case of a shutdown, could be easily replaced by conventional sources. As the originators of civilian atomic energy often pointed out, large systems were required for the realization of their dreams of cheap power. With a few exceptions these were to be found in urban areas. In addition, as Dr. Walter H. Zinn, head of the Argonne National Laboratory explained, bigger nuclear generating plants had a better chance of achieving economical nuclear electricity than smaller ones. Ordinarily, only big towns could afford larger plants.

Congressman Holifield put the matter bluntly to a group of small cooperatives and one small municipality, who had applied to the Atomic Energy Commission (AEC) to build demonstration reactors under the 1954 program. "The co-ops have no business in this program. . . . The reason they have no business in this program is because this is an expensive program," explained Holifield. "You are playing with thousand-dollar chips and the co-ops have two-bit chips." More pointedly in 1957, Holifield, in opposing the cooperatives' operation of experimental reactors, reminded them that "rural cooperatives do not have reserves of money for investment" and entry into "this highly problematical field."

In addition, the ratio of fuel to population was different with nuclear power.

Since reactors needed only a small amount of fuel, plant operators did not have to face the prospect of transporting tons of coal to generating sites and therefore they could be more flexible in locating the plant in "proximity to load." As Eugene M. Zuckert, member of the AEC explained it, the cost of land, local ordinances for health and safety, and the presence of adequate cooling water were also factors but these would not alter the fact that "competitive nuclear powerplants, installed to meet the large power demands characteristic of metropolitan and industrial centers, would be located, as is true of most new conventional generating capacity, near but not in such centers."[8]

Yet not all American urban areas benefitted equally from "Atoms for Peace" and not all expressed an equal interest in them. In general, peaceful atoms appealed to several classes of cities and regions. Areas with few conventional sources of power—water, oil, natural gas, or coal—had expensive fuel costs and therefore high expectations about nuclear energy. New England cities, for example, suffered from the highest electricity costs in the nation, twice the national average, and therefore entertained commensurate hopes for atomic power. Other areas possessed one or more conventional fuels, but were running out or being forced to turn to something else. For example, the Pittsburgh Renaissance movement was trying to clean up that city's atmosphere, and eliminating sulphurous coal smoke was a critical part of this effort. Chicago lacked natural gas, oil, and water power and was under the same necessity as Pittsburgh to purify its environment. New Mexico had little oil or coal and only a small amount of water power. And California, to give a final example, had no nearby coal, was running through its oil and natural gas supply, and faced increasing competition from other southwestern states for the water power of the Dry West.

In addition, all of these areas wanted to outstrip their competitors, especially the cities.[9] Urban California had always recognized the necessity of cheap power and its imperial cities jumped at the chance to exploit a new one. The AEC awarded one of the first large-scale reactor demonstration projects to Pacific Gas and Electric of San Francisco, a city disadvantaged by high electrical costs in its struggle with Los Angeles, which derived cheap power from its Owens Valley water system and the Colorado River dams. However, the contract with PG&E and the giant construction firm of Bechtel and Company represented only the tip of the iceberg. From the very beginning, Urban Californians had shown a keen interest in the new technology, and they would continue to do so through the 1960s at least.

California representatives in the Congress led the way, none more forcefully than Representative Craig Hosmer of Long Beach, who perhaps had a more dramatic demonstration of the power of the atom than anyone else in the Congress. "My interest in this subject first was excited when, as a naval officer, I was among the first Americans to visit Hiroshima after V-J Day," he noted nine years later. Hosmer went on to work for the Atomic Energy Commission in Los Alamos, New Mexico, and then became a naval reserve officer, whose "naval reserve training duty . . . included on-the-spot study of the Navy's atomic powered submarine." Hosmer's experience was typical of the civil-military interface in Urban California, but he was by no means the most important link between the two.[10]

The veteran members of the Joint Committee on Atomic Energy (JCAE) of the

United States Congress were that link. They carried on the critical work of encouraging both peaceful and military uses of the atom, channeled information and probably contracts to their constituencies, marshaled witnesses to present "expert" testimony to reinforce their authority, pushed the AEC to greater efforts, spoke out for the development of a new technology, and in general served as a linchpin between the military and the cities.

From the very beginning, California represented a disproportionely large presence on this critical committee, which oversaw *all* American nuclear matters, public and private, civilian and service. From the committee's first appearance in the *Congressional Directory* in 1947, all the way through1956, Californians made up one-sixth of its membership. Two representatives, Carl Hinshaw and Chet Holifield, hailed from the Southland, from Pasadena and Montebello, respectively. The third, Senator William Knowland, came from an Oakland suburb. Both the San Francisco Bay and Los Angeles areas had important atomic interests and key congressmen to represent them. Moreover, their longevity on the committee enhanced their influence. As Chet Holifield pointed out in 1957, several of the members of the Joint Committee on Atomic Energy had more continuity on the committee than anyone in the AEC had in their jobs. In a new and rapidly changing field of technology, this advantage could hardly be overestimated.[11]

Still, the legislators' other qualifications ranked high in any congressional rating. Senator William Knowland of prestigious Piedmont, California, brought important assets to his position. His residence in the heart of the San Francisco Bay region accorded him considerable power in itself. Knowland grew up in the Bay Area, graduated from the University of California, and by the time of his elevation to the United States Senate, served as assistant publisher of the *Oakland Tribune,* a powerful conservative voice in California politics. Knowland had previously been a member of the California State Assembly and a member and chairman of the executive committee of the Republican National Committee. He served three years as an enlisted man in World War II, and in 1945 Governor Earl Warren appointed him to fill the senatorial term of Hiram Johnson, who had died in office.

The Bay Area native reached the apogee of his power in the Senate, serving as both Republican minority and majority leader. To argue that such a person was well positioned to represent the growing atomic interests of the University of California, its far-flung laboratories (Los Alamos, Livermore, and Lawrence, to name the best known), or the new installations that developed after World War II would be to belabor the obvious.[12]

Democrat Chet Holifield of the Los Angeles suburb of Montebello could claim at least as pivotal a position. Like Knowland, a suburbanite, but unlike him a liberal, Holifield was a vigorous supporter of civilian atomic power and extremely knowledgeable in the field of atomic technology per se. He too served as a charter member of the JCAE, of which he eventually became chairman, and Holifield was consistently one of its most active and well-informed members. In addition, he served as a member of the President's Special Evaluation Commission on Atomic Bomb Tests at Bikini Atoll and as congressional adviser on the United States delegation to the 1955 International Conference on the Peaceful Uses of Atomic Energy, at Geneva, Switzerland. The Montebellan's overlapping congressional committee assignments provided further influence, since Holifield chaired the congressional committees investigating the subject of civil defense against nuclear attack as well as the House Military Operations Subcommittee of the House Government Operations Committee. By 1955 the liberal Democrat was also chairman of the JCAE Subcommittee on Authorizing Legislation, which scrutinized and passed on every piece of legislation on atomic matters.

His booster connections were equally impeccable. Of his four daughters, one was married to William Mulholland, whose parent was, for all intents and purposes, the father of Urban Southern California; the senior Mulholland's water system had underwritten, and indeed guaranteed, the continued growth of the Southland. A second daughter was the wife of Donald Lee Douglas, son of the airplane manufacturer who had been brought to Los Angeles by the *Times* boosters in 1920. Like Knowland and Hinshaw, Holifield was not only a link between civilian and military society but an equally sturdy and open conduit between the resources of an exploding nation-state and the appetite of the growing Darwinian metropolis.[13]

John Carl Williams Hinshaw was a more enigmatic and less public figure than his colleagues on the Urban California bloc of the JCAE, but he was probably even more influential. Hinshaw's impressive booster credentials have already been described; he also possessed the educational background necessary to understand technical matters, having received a B.A. in civil engineering and having served in the U.S. Corps of Engineers in the First World War. Hinshaw was a recognized authority in the fields of aeronautics, radio, and navigation as well.[14]

His congressional colleagues knew Hinshaw as an expert on engineering, aeronautics, and atomic matters, and no less an authority on atomic technology than Hyman Rickover praised Hinshaw's ability to deliver to the services. As the admiral informed a congressional subcommittee shortly after Hinshaw's death, "Although I used to accuse him of being for the Air Force, he was really for everybody, and helped us in the Navy a great deal." In fact, Hinshaw aided the Navy enough for Rickover to propose that a laboratory or possibly the first nuclear-powered aircraft carrier be named for the Pasadena congressman. Since Hinshaw not only sat on the JCAE but sometimes chaired its reactor and research and development subcommittees, he was critically situated to exploit the evolving technology of nuclear power, even before the other commitee members did so.[15]

Another committee assignment illustrates the link between national leadership and local urban benefits even more fully. When the United States investigated the possibility of developing weaponry beyond the atomic bomb, the JCAE appointed a subcommittee to study "the feasibility of the hydrogen bomb." Given the preceding narrative, one should not be surprised to find that Hinshaw became "ranking minority member" of this subcommittee, but it is at least mildly astonishing that the other presiding member was also a Californian. Chet Holifield "was the chairman of that particular subcommittee," the Montebello resident later recalled. Together they traveled "to practically all of the Atomic Energy installations" and "interviewed our Nation's foremost scientists on this particular subject." One need not emphasize the advantage that these contacts would have given the California urban bloc, nor how much this trip resembled the journey Theodore von Karman and others took to Germany to interview the captured German scientists and to inspect their work.

Hinshaw's congressional colleagues regarded him as one of the most respected and influential of their numbers and his obituary testimonials read like H. H. Bancroft's *Chronicles of the Builders*—or *Plutarch's Lives*, for that matter. His eulogizers commended him for his hard work, courageousness, honesty, grasp of subject matter, lack of rancor, and technical expertise in the fields of engineering, aviation, aeronautics, atomic energy, and conservation. However, it is fitting that Hinshaw himself considered atomic energy and aeronautics to be his first priorities. As no less an authority than Sterling Cole, sometimes Republican chairman of the JCAE put it, Hinshaw was passionately devoted to "the development and application of the two great technical developments of our time, the miracles of two great technologies—aviation and atomic energy." Cole went on to elaborate his insider's view even more categorically, especially with regard to the latter. "Carl Hinshaw saw and recognized perhaps more clearly than anyone else, the impact that the application of nuclear power to industrial development would have on the economic well-being of the world," Cole concluded. "His contributions to the development of nuclear reactors for peaceful purposes are beyond cataloging."[16]

Nonetheless, the California bloc rapidly put together just such a catalogue, one that went beyond the achievements even of Hinshaw. Chet Holifield summed up perfectly the importance of nuclear science and political representation in a rare admission of the relationship between military and urban development. "California's large stake in atomic energy is reflected in the fact that three of the State's congressional representatives are members of the Joint Committee on Atomic Energy," he explained in a candid report on the rapid proliferation of atomic science and technology in the Golden State. Moreover, "the 16th semiannual report of the Atomic Energy Commission lists about a dozen important advisory groups to the Commission," he continued, "covering all phases of the national atomic-energy program, with one or more Californians on each board or committee." Between the persons giving the advice and the congressmen voting on it, Metropolitan California was well represented, to put it mildly.[17]

Although Hinshaw "was for everybody" when it came to the Navy and Air Force, both of which had vital strongholds within the Great Wall of California, he and his colleagues were not out to help every region. The Pasadenan's battle against industrial decentralization had demonstrated Hinshaw's regional biases and his colleagues were equally dedicated to the dominance of their region and its cities. However, they did not wear such sentiments on their congressional sleeves. Rather they almost invariably took a more statesmanlike view of civilian atomic energy. They talked of cheap power for national economic development, of ending poverty in the world, of creating reactor markets abroad for American business, of winning the prestige derby with the Russians, and of maintaining America's scientific pre-eminence.[18]

One does not have to doubt the patriotism or sincerity of such men to point out that even if all of these *national* goals were attained through the development of atomic energy, certain *metropolitan* goals would be achieved as well. Not every region would benefit from nuclear energy, nor would those who did profit do so at the same time or to the same degree. Some regions would prosper more from this energy than others, and among the beneficiaries some would reap their harvest earlier than others. The California bloc on the JCAE was fully aware of the civilian and miltary atomic interests in their districts and they needed no prompting to remind them that these regional interests would profit quickly and in disproportionate measure from the national goals they emphasized in the Congress.

By 1945 and certainly by 1954, there was a considerable atomic interest in Urban California. Cal Tech had acquired several nuclear physicists, such as Robert Bacher and President Lee DuBridge, a member of the Advisory Committee to the AEC, and the University of California had amassed a literally amazing nuclear empire. The university possessed the Lawrence Radiation Laboratory on campus and managed, under the directorship of Berkeley professor Robert Oppenheimer, the Los Alamos Weapons Laboratory in New Mexico which had manufactured the World War II atomic bombs. At war's end, when the United States decided to develop the hydrogen bomb, a second weapons laboratory would be created in the Bay Area at Livermore, operated by the University of California and run by a Cal Tech professor, the controversial Edward Teller.

Of course, the university had gained many of these nuclear resources in the Second World War as a result of the Manhattan Project to develop the atomic bomb. However, the targeting of those nation-state resources was determined by local decisions, primarily that of the Berkeley physics department to upgrade its scientific reputation by hiring publishing scholars. The departure of Ernest O. Lawrence from Yale in 1928 for the University of California was the critical development in the creation of this nuclear expertise at the university. It is not known if his appointment came in the same manner as the Cal Tech recruitment of Robert Millikan, Theodore von Karman, and other scientists. As we have seen, the CIT trustees had initiated this scientific recruitment process specifically to build up the Los Angeles metropolitan region. Whether the wooing of Lawrence, who was refused early promotion at Yale and departed rather than wait for one in due time, had anything to do with the pressure to develop the metropolitan Bay Area rapidly is not known. It is entirely possible however, since the metropolitan elites of universities and cities tend to think alike, but the proposition cannot be documented at this moment.

In any case, whether Lawrence came to build cities, in the fashion of Millikan through applied science, or simply to pursue pure science in the older university mode, his coming brought much in train. The Second World War mobilized University of California physicists on behalf of the victory and at the same time brought undreamed-of opportunities within its servants' range. By 1945 these nuclear interests were already impressive and the politicians of Urban California wasted no time in representing them in Congress. It's interesting that both Carl Hinshaw and Chet Holifield knew E. O. Lawrence, who testified before their various committees and with whom they corresponded. Hinshaw knew the Berkeley physicist well enough to dine with the Lawrences in Berkeley on one occasion.[19]

With rare exceptions, however, neither these congressional figures nor any other Californians dwelt overmuch on the local implications of the supposed national interest importance of atomic energy. Senator John F. Kennedy of Massachusetts was one of the few congressional figures to speak in a frank, businesslike manner about such interests and his candor drew from the California nuclear bloc an equally frank admission. As we shall see in the discussion of the employment of defense contracts to combat regional urban unemployment, Senator Kennedy willingly mobilized the military resources of the nation-state to prop up the sagging economic fortunes of his New England urban power base. Those same misfortunes also drew his attention to the issue of nuclear power.

In 1954, the AEC began to think seriously enough about civilian nuclear power to set up several pilot projects involving the firms mentioned above and others as well. Since the Commission included no New England firms on its early list of demonstration sites, Senator Kennedy appeared before the JCAE to plead for the inclusion of his section. It is not known if Kennedy knew of Robert Millikan or had read his autobiography, which had appeared four years earlier, but the Massachusetts politician certainly understood the principle that the physicist had elaborated. If a geographic section lacked material resources it must compensate for this defect by a more precocious development of its human and intellectual ones, so that the advantages of technology could offset the disadvantages of geography. Nor did Kennedy believe that economic considerations alone should determine who got what in the division of civilian atomic spoils. "I believe it is the duty of Congress to insure that selection of the participating companies . . . is based upon the total national interest," the future President argued to a JCAE hearing in 1954, "not merely upon an examination of which companies are most able to make an attractive bid for participation."

Kennedy went on to explain that the "selection of companies and sites for reactor experimentation should be based, at least in part, upon prevention of concentration of these programs in any one geographical area, upon the particular power needs of any geographical section of this country, and on other considerations of national policy." In that latter category the Bostonian included "the need to provide assistance to areas of the country suffering from serious unemployment."[20]

Predictably, every one of these principles expressed on behalf of the "total national interest" was also designed to benefit that of New England. Its cities already endured high unemployment and high electricity rates, compared with those of the South, the West, and the Midwest. As the senator noted, Boston, Brookline, Newton, and Somerville had the highest residential electricity rates in the nation. "Of the more than 150 Federal hydroelectric projects in this country, there is not a single project in New England," Kennedy continued. "Our distance from the coalfields and high transportation rates for bringing coal necessary for steam generating plants and the absence of really choice hydroelectric sites, of course, contribute to the increasingly high cost of electric energy in New England."[21]

To overcome these disadvantages and the lack of petroleum reserves in Boston's suburbs, Kennedy had several propositions. He wanted a New England representative to be let in on the pilot atomic electricity program, even if it could not make an economic bid for that right. Kennedy recognized the bill before the JCAE as "one of the most important pieces of legislation pending before this Congress," and he did not want his political base ignored. To make doubly certain that Congress did not make this mistake, Kennedy urged that the legislation include safeguards that would prevent companies identified with certain regions from muscling a stranglehold upon the atomic technology that would ensue from the demonstration projects. On the positive side Kennedy held out the enticement of early nuclear development in his section. Since power costs in the remainder of the nation were much lower than in New England, nuclear power would not initially be economically competitive with conventional fuels in those areas, but Kennedy felt that it would be more attractive to a high cost power area like his own.[22]

"I might say that I think your remarks are very direct and pertinent to the issue. . . . this is a new source of energy that can be used without regard to the peculiar natural resources of a region," Chet Holifield replied to the senator. "And it can be transported anywhere, and it can have longtime generation from a very small amount of material." The liberal congressman pointed out, as he would many times, that competitive nuclear power would not be available for five to ten years but that when such electricity became economical, "it should be available first to those who need it the most in the Nation and then secondly to all of the people of the Nation."

Although the California representative professed to believe that Southern California had adequate electrical power from Hoover Dam, his "section" shared at least some of the characteristics of New England. The Urban Southland had very little coal; its oil supplies were being used very rapidly; it already felt the pinch in natural gas, and its water power sites were limited. Even its Hoover Dam ace-in-the-hole had to be shared with the increasingly aggressive Arizonans, and was not itself an endless source of energy to drive the unlimited ambitions of this urban section. Holifield also knew that nuclear power would not be economically competitive for a long time, perhaps into the seventies and eighties, and by that time Southland cities might well be feeling an energy pinch.

There is no question that the Golden State anticipated tremendous new development and wanted nuclear science to help mold that future. As the California Assembly resolved in 1955, "the State of California, with its tremendous past growth and certain future growth, has the duty to provide its people and industries with all possible benefits from the new and important field of nuclear research." Such an efficient energy source must have been very attractive to the almost completely urbanized Southern California.[23] Nuclear power could not have been a more dramatic application of the principle of using science to overcome a region's geography.

Perhaps just as important, California cities could benefit immediately and directly from nuclear science. In mid-1955 its utility corporations could gain experience from the technology that would pay economic benefits down the road; its university departments could find many applications to their own research; its aerospace industry could profit by experimenting with nuclear propulsion; its medical schools could profit from nuclear medicine; its construction firms could build pilot plants in California and elsewhere in the United States; and its large corporations could build and operate some of the pilot plants for both power generation and research.

Such completely nonurban fields as water transportation, irrigation, and mining might also benefit. "Even the weapons work—on fission and fusion—may have direct peacetime application," reported Robert Gordon Sproul, president of the University of California system, to the state senate in 1958. "There is strong hope that in the near future nuclear bombs will be so cleared of unwanted radiation that they may be used for major peacetime earth-moving projects in such areas as canal building and mining." These optimists no doubt overlooked the possible effects of atomic explosions on the infamous fault lines of the state. In any case, the availability of economic atomic electricity constituted only a part of the appeal of nuclear science. Scientists and politicians alike assumed that each part of the industry would reinforce the rest and that all would progress together.

The mutuality between civilian and military atoms seems particularly evident. One could perhaps argue that civilian nuclear power and military power were two different things and therefore the former did not represent another adaptation of a military necessity to a metropolitan one. However, the two were closely and perhaps intimately related. Although plows are not exactly an urban technology, the peaceful use of the atom is one of the purest possible examples of the principle of turning swords into plowshares.

City boosters recognized fully the mutualities of military and civilian nuclear power, but Chet Holifield understood it better still. When President Eisenhower slashed funds from the 1953-54 defense budget which would have financed research on nuclear-powered planes and aircraft carriers, the Montebello congressman responded bluntly that this cut "means a stretchout in atomic power-progress, a postponement of the day when the atom will do useful work for industry and the public." The liberal Democrat insisted that "the technical lessons that we learn in building atomic power plants for military vehicles have direct application to atomic power in other fields."[24]

Perhaps nothing illustrated this principle better than America's first "commercial" reactor at Shippingport, Pennsylvania, built by Westinghouse for the use of the Duquesne Light Company to supplement its supply of electrical power for the Pittsburgh area. Although the polemical literature of civilian nuclear power charges that the government and industry exaggerated the ease with which economical electrical power could be produced and predicted that this feat would not be achieved at an early date, the documents refute this claim.[25] Neither the AEC nor the JCAE believed in the advent of economic nuclear power within ten years of 1954, and the AEC went so far as to predict that by 1975 nuclear power would constitute only 2 to 10 percent of America's electrical energy. Chet Holifield thought that the date would be even more remote. It is possible that federal and business spokesman on occasion mentioned more optimistic figures, but the overwhelming bulk of the evidence points to the conclusion that the AEC and JCAE had a much more realistic view of the matter.[26]

The Shippingport reactor illustrates this "realism" and documents the interdependence of civil and military technology. Since the only models in 1954 were military, civil atomic power in America began with a martial reactor, specifically a design taken from the first atomic submarine. However, the *Nautilus* reactor possessed different properties than would be desirable for a civilian nuclear plant. The former had to be light and compact in order to fit into a submarine; the Pittsburgh metropolitan area had considerably more space and did not impose comparable weight constraints either.[27]

As nuclear expert Kenneth W. Davis, Director of Reactor Development, AEC, explained, "The pressurized water reactor has a real advantage for a compact reactor, but not necessarily for a cheap reactor." Dr. Walter H. Zinn, director of the

Argonne National Laboratory, echoed this sentiment: "economics was not really considered in selecting the *Nautilus* plant."[28]

The naval contribution did not go unappreciated by the JCAE. Senator Henry Jackson and Representative Melvin Price, chairmen respectively of the Military Applications and Research and Development JCAE subcommittees, claimed in 1957 that the Navy had already been "primarily responsible for developing the technology of pressurized-water reactors, which had given the United States world leadership in both military and civilian "atomic power." The two went so far as to urge that the AEC "should consider the immediate assignment to the Naval Reactors Branch of the development and construction of a new civilian reactor concept."[29]

Whether or not city boosters wanted this degree of military dominance in this new field, there is no question that the Urban California bloc and the JCAE wanted to maintain American atomic leadership. Although the AEC and especially its chairman, Lewis Strauss, are sometimes caricatured as the devils in the plot to put over civilian nuclear power, the congressional members of the JCAE usually took the lead in this matter. Indeed, often they had to force, bully, threaten, prod, or pressure the AEC or the administration into action that one or the other did not want to take. Some of the historical literature on civilian nuclear power has noted this JCAE zealotry, but has seldom noted the parochial geographic interests that these congressmen represented. Therefore, much of the literature talks of civilian nuclear power in terms of competition with the Soviets, capturing world leadership in atoms, providing economic help for Third World nations, creating reactor markets for big business, and aiding big business in general. Such a perspective focuses almost exclusively on the "bigger" picture, of capitalism, the Cold War, international relations, and national history. Even when talking about the use of political influence, the language often vaguely specifies not individuals or cities but classes of people, such as "politicians," "bureacrats," "businessmen," and "military men."[30]

However, in the mid-1950s, none of these groups was interested in nuclear power. Indeed many politicians were either opposed or skeptical; many naval officers fought the application of nuclear propulsion; and most businessmen in the early years were indifferent. Like any congressional program, nuclear power required a constituency and much of this came from urban areas that stood to benefit disproportionately from the development of this new science. Historians have long understood that public rhetoric is not a sufficient gauge of political reality, but the historians of nuclear power have often taken it in that manner. Undoubtedly public postures and private convictions partially converged, but the story is just a bit more complex than the public rhetoric about the Cold War, capitalism, or diplomacy would indicate. When Chet Holifield retired in 1973 after thirty years' service in the Congress, his eulogist, Representative Carl Albert, himself a seasoned and experienced veteran of congressional politics, stated a cardinal rule of congressional politics and even survival. After citing the extraordinary number of national and international achievements of this remarkable man, Albert noted that the "19th Congressional District, which he is privileged to represent, has always been Mr. Holifield's foremost concern."[31]

Holifield's district, which de facto covered Los Angeles proper, was replete with high-technology laboratories and companies, think tanks, aeronautical and aerospace laboratories, high-powered universities, defense contractors, military installations, retired service officers, and construction firms, all of which were vitally concerned with developments in nuclear science. So was the constituency of Carl Hinshaw in neighboring Pasadena and that of William Knowland in the Bay Area, whose University of California alone managed three renowned radiation and nuclear laboratories. To argue that members of the California Urban bloc considered only national and international implications of nuclear energy and not those of their own congressional districts would be well-nigh idiotic. Indeed, successful politicians must find national, international, philosophical, and often cosmic reasons for actions that benefit their own districts, whether they believe in the rationales, as Holifield and Hinshaw probably did, or not.[32]

It is often a complex task to trace the manner in which these men went about realizing their dreams of civilian nuclear power. Sometimes they voted against a nuclear-related matter like ship propulsion on technical grounds; occasionally they opposed a bill that would give public or private power interests too much of a role, and sometimes they hesitated to spread limited resources too far. But in general they enthusiastically supported the advance of nuclear science, both military and domestic.

Between 1945 and 1952, the two Californians dealt mostly with military applications, and even beyond that date they continued to foster the growth of nuclear military science. Although historians have almost universally failed to note the strategic contributions of one or both of California's two most able advocates of nuclear power and science, they have insisted upon the central role of the JCAE.[33] The documents fully support this latter contention. If anything, the JCAE made an even more critical contribution, in part because by 1957 most of the members had had more experience in dealing with atomic science than most members of the AEC and almost all those of any given political administration. As usual, Holifield articulated the matter best. "As the chairman of the Atomic Energy Commission recently suggested, the joint committee has acted as a board of directors," the Montebello clothier explained in 1957.

> Therefore, acting as a board of directors, your Congressional members have, time after time, decided that the Atomic Energy Commission, under both Democratic and Republican executives, was failing to initiate programs vital to the national welfare. We necessarily took the initiative in recommending and supporting expansion of weapons stockpile [sic]; building of the atomic submarine, *Nautilus,* and additional nuclear vessels; starting on the hydrogen bomb; starting a second weapons laboratory at Livermore, Calif.; building the Shippingport power reactor; building the great production plants at Portsmouth, Paducah, and Savannah River; the first 5-year reactor program; the building of an aircraft propelled by nuclear power; and many other programs of lesser magnitude.[34]

On another occasion, Holifield reiterated the claim and added to it. "Let me call the attention of the gentleman to three different instances in which the Atomic Energy Committee pushed the Atomic Energy Commission into worthwile endeavors," Holifield noted in a congressional debate.

The construction of the H-bomb. We went against the wishes of the Atomic Energy Commission and the 15-man scientific board and achieved our purpose just 9 months before the Soviets. We went into the program of developing additional material. In the case of the submarine and the airplane we have pushed the Commission into these fields and we have pushed the Defense Department into the development of tactical weapons.

Carl Durham, another JCAE veteran, expert on nuclear matters, and longtime member of the House Military Affairs Committee, put the H-bomb matter even more strongly. "On February 1, 1950, the Congress overruled the Commission and backed the committee, and we developed the hydrogen weapon." AEC chairman Lewis Strauss himself admitted as much in a 1957 speech in the Bay Area when he noted, "In December of 1952, the Joint Committee on Atomic Energy of the Congress had acknowledged in a published report that there existed in the United States 'no major project whose purpose is to achieve a reactor directly advancing industrial power.'" Only after that statement did Chet Holifield introduce the idea into Congress in 1953, which then became law in 1954.[35]

Lest the reader lose sight of the all-important political question of who gets what, when, and where, it would perhaps be instructive to observe that, of the various "products" mentioned in these two extended Holifield quotes, California produced most, sometimes exclusively, and benefitted from all. These included the civilian reactors built by San Francisco's Bechtel Corporation, the atomic bombs constructed at Los Alamos, the hydrogen bombs fabricated at Livermore, tactical nuclear weapons constructed at Livermore, nuclear-propelled aircraft built at Los Angeles, and nuclear aircraft carriers put together at Mare Island Naval Shipyard. The state did not directly produce the *Nautilus* class submarines, but General Dynamics, a defense conglomerate that had grown up in San Diego, did. California weapons laboratories also benefitted from the weapons-grade materials produced at Portsmouth, Savannah, and Paducah. Of course, the five-year civilian reactor program did for that industry what the five-year program did for the aircraft industry in the mid-twenties: it put it on a firm foundation. Once again, we can see that the resources of the nation-state were easily domesticated to urban uses. We can also understand why Holifield and Hinshaw were anxious to speed up these "scientific" and "national defense" developments.

Some of the "lesser" achievements were not all that trivial. In 1953, the Navy passed over Hyman Rickover, the father of the Nuclear Navy, for promotion to admiral. Thereupon, his political allies sailed to his defense. A recent study pictures the legendary admiral as a foul-mouthed, imperious, greedy, corrupt, and vainglorious man, but no hint of these traits seeped into the congressional defense of Rickover. Representative Sidney Yates went to his defense in the House, and others soon followed. Representative John McCormack of Massachusetts complained that the Rickover case was just like one in which an Army general working for the Cambridge Research Laboratory in the Boston area was passed over because of a rivalry for research contracts between that place and New York. He thought that this disagreement smacked of military domination of government.

Melvin Price of Illinois, another active member of the JCAE, added his weight to the Rickover side of the argument, and, as usual, Chet Holifield weighed in with a decisive summary of the pro-Rickover case. The nuclear submarine "will be a revolutionary form of undersea craft that will make obsolete the submarines not only of our own country but of all other nations in the world," argued the transplanted Kentuckian. "It will put the United States . . . in a position far ahead of any nation in the world in this type of craft, and it may revolutionize completely the concept of naval warfare." To refuse promotion to the initiator of these developments would be "incomprehensible."[36] Needless to say, this high-minded rhetoric paid off, for the Navy shortly changed its mind and promoted Rickover.

Holifield and other Californians such as Sam Yorty found it equally unthinkable that anyone should cut the 1953-54 defense budget. Although President Eisenhower was a military man who understood the need for a strong national defense, he nonetheless felt that appropriations for the atomic airplane and aircraft carrier could be reduced. As his scientific advisors document, the general consistently opposed these weapons. The aircraft had been plagued with problems since its inception in 1946, and eventually President Kennedy scrubbed it in 1961. Its defects had been well known since 1948, but Holifield leaped to its defense in 1953 and to that of atomic-powered aircraft carriers. "Certain phases of reactor development, looking toward atomic-powered aircraft carriers and airplanes, have been eliminated," complained Holifield. For him, that spelled nothing less than a "dangerous retreat from national-security goals and a threat to continued progress in atomic development."[37] When the demand for civilian atomic power appeared in 1953 (Holifield thought it was too early at that point) and threatened to divert technicians, fissionable materials, and funds from military purposes, Holifield warned that "our supply of atomic weapons, while considerable in some forms, is dangerously inadequate both as to quantity and variety."[38] In light of the 1980s that argument would seem to be dubious at the very least, but it certainly demonstrated the Californian's zealotry in protecting the interests of military nuclear science.

Nor did Holifield or the JCAE demonstrate less enthusiasm for the development of civilian nuclear science. As we have seen, the JCAE usually led the AEC on such matters and even prodded them into action. Major prodding began in about 1952. Up to that point, military imperatives dominated the development of nuclear affairs. In 1952 the United States exploded the first hydrogen bomb, and by 1954 it had tested the weapon several times and stockpiled enough of them. This cache of bombs was enough to protect the country and to allow it the luxury of pondering some of the civilian applications of the military technology it had developed. In a very real sense, the hydrogen bomb allowed the emergence of civilian atoms.[39]

The shift toward this goal appeared in a furor outside the halls of Congress to realize the peaceful promise of the atom. A number of business firms, some of them, including General Electric, involved in nuclear matters since the Second World War, led the way. Dow Chemical, Monsanto Chemical, and a few other large corporations reinforced the G.E. thrust. However, not many other companies joined this movement, at least not in a serious way. Although a number of small firms eventually appeared in the industry, large ones dominated the scene from the beginning. Only such corporations or the government had the resources to do anything big in a field of experimental technology, which necessitated extraordinary security and safety precautions and which required an investment of substantial sums of money without guaranteeing large returns. "We had to beg them to take over in 1946," observed Carl Durham of the difficulty of getting private enterprise involved in the nuclear program. A firm as small as a utility company could operate a civilian reactor, but the architects, contractors, and equipment suppliers tended to be impressively large organizations.[40]

Both the size of the companies and the general reluctance of others to join them in a risky venture created problems from the beginning. Although the AEC supposedly had authority to push peaceful atoms forward on its agenda, it had a difficult time recruiting a reluctant business community. American capitalists as a group had no particular affinity for the atom, so not many volunteered to develop this new science. But if only a few firms entered a field destined to be dominated by large corporations, that created a threat of monopoly over this essentially government-sponsored technology. For several years this fear generated conflict in the Congress and even within the JCAE.

In 1953 Chet Holifield raised the issue of civilian nuclear power in Congress. At that point he felt that peaceful uses of the atom for electrical power were a long way off and he did not yet want to open the field to private enterprise. The liberal Democrat believed that letting private enterprise into the atomic field would result in several negative developments. First, it would give an advantage to the large corporations who pioneered the atomic wilderness and who would benefit from exposure to government techniques, patents, procedures, and power to create a monopoly or near-monopoly situation in the industry before free enterprise got a foothold. In the second place, Holifield felt that, in the early fifties, private enterprise lacked the resources, and discipline to produce rapid progress in the field of nuclear enterprise. So his initial opposition to business participation in the peaceful atoms program stemmed from his conviction that the government, with its larger resources, greater experience in this field, and more acute sense of urgency about the exploitation of this new technology would make atomic electrical power a reality faster than private enterprise.[41]

Both national and local experience underlay this conviction. The Montebello congressman was very impressed by the Manhattan Project of the Second World War and thought that public enterprise could harness the potential of the peaceful atom much more rapidly than private enterprise could. Having lived in the Urban Southland since 1920, Holifield knew well what public enterprise could do to develop a section of the country by providing water, electrical power, a harbor, and incentives to industry. Of course the federal government had infinitely greater resources than city, county, or state governments or private enterprise, and Holifield wanted to mobilize these larger federal revenues to support Southland urban development schemes.

Predictably, an urban Californian, Chet Holifield, placed the issue of peaceful atoms on the congressional agenda in 1953. In the spirit of developing civilian nuclear energy, but doing so more rapidly under government auspices, the liberal Democrat observed that civilian uses "has been the subject of numerous newspaper articles now for several weeks." Holifield argued that "it is about time that someone on the Atomic Energy Committee asked for time on the floor of the House to bring before the Congress . . . and the American people some very important information on this particular subject." In 1954, the Congress enacted legislation to accelerate the development of civilian nuclear electrical power, but even before that moment, the AEC began to speed up its own timetable.[42]

This first, hesitant, yet major step by the AEC into the realm of the peaceful atom came at the instigation of the JCAE, which was perennially dissatisfied with the AEC's progress. In that year the AEC contracted with utilities and industrial or construction firms to create pilot reactors. If one Southern Californian put the issue on the congressional agenda, John Carl Williams Hinshaw, the other Southlander on the committee, shared the credit for getting it onto the AEC agenda. No less an authority than representative Carl Durham of Chapel Hill, North Carolina, another astute JCAE veteran, recalled "that the Commission's five-year experimental reactor program was initiated by my friend and colleague, Sterling Cole [of New York] and our late friend and colleague, Carl Hinshaw."[43]

Some of the initial contractors pulled out of the program by 1956, and the AEC added two other groups to the list. Possibly due to the prompting of Senator Kennedy, Yankee Atomic received a contract to develop a large prototype reactor. Others went to the state power cooperative in Nebraska, and to Westinghouse and Pennsylvania Power and Light to supply Philadelphia. The Shippingport, Pennsylvania, plant of Westinghouse and Duquesne Light Company, the Indian Point plant of Consolidated Edison (25 miles north of New York City), the Dresden, Illinois, plant of Commonwealth Edison and others (close to Chicago), and the Monroe, Michigan, plant of Detroit Edison and Monsanto Chemical remained from the original list.

With the exception of the Nebraska state government cooperative, an urban utility constructed each of the large prototype power reactor plants and built them to serve major metropolitan areas. The Hellum, Nebraska, cooperative plant was the smallest and least expensive. Although some of the original contractors dropped out of the program by 1956, some such as Bechtel and PG&E would re-enter it as builders of plants or suppliers of equipment. Even without counting the Westinghouse and Pennsylvania Power and Light facility, for which figures were not available in 1956, the Hinshaw-cosponsored large prototype power reactor plant program represented a quarter-billion-dollar investment, most of it government money.[44]

This represented a good start, but the JCAE wanted even more pioneers in the atomic wilderness and soon set about encouraging them to take to the woods. That urging brought a second round of civilian atomic power agitation in 1954. It also led to a serious conflict within the JCAE over sponsorship of these new pathmaking ventures. One part of the committee, led by Chet Holifield, hoped for public construction of the new plants, while another faction led by chairman Sterling Cole of New York wanted private development. It required two years of struggle between these two basically pro-nuclear factions to resolve the issue in favor of private enterprise sponsorship.[45]

The two sides joined the issue in 1954, when the New York congressman introduced a bill into the House of Representatives to develop civilian nuclear energy by encouraging private enterprise into the field and by allowing American allies to share in many of its nuclear power secrets. Up to that point, the government had dominated the development of this new source of energy and had guarded closely its atomic discoveries. Washington had denied this information even to the British right after World War II and had subsequently gone into a large atomic program of their own. Since at least some Americans believed that nuclear power ultimately would become a very big business, it seemed important to get American industry into the game early.

Experts expected that the United States—which had some of the cheapest energy in the world—would develop nuclear power slowly, because of the competition of abundant coal, oil, and water-generated electricity. In the rest of the world, however, electricity was dear, so boosters hoped these areas would be interested in higher-cost nuclear energy. In effect, foreign atomic markets would nurture an American nuclear manufacturing sector into being while it waited for an American market for nuclear energy to develop. But in order to create a foreign market in the first place, the U.S. would have to share its nuclear technology, fuels, and even development funds with foreign nations. All of this led logically to the 1954 bill to prod private investors into a field that they sensibly hesitated to enter and to push American atomic technology abroad.[46]

Holifield and Hinshaw accepted the necessity of developing foreign markets for American and, it might be said, Californian nuclear products, but they parted company on the issue of allowing private enterprise into the field of atomic science. Hitherto, private enterprise and universities had done most of the work for the AEC, but that body maintained control of these projects. Now in 1954, the friends of free enterprise proposed that business be allowed to initiate and control its own nuclear projects—especially power-generating plants instead of military or research reactors, military propulsion systems, and so forth.

For several reasons, Chet Hollifield took the lead in opposing this departure. In 1954, he thought it was too early for private enterprise to enter the field. Although Holifield is correctly considered by scholars to have been one of the most important political supporters of nuclear power, he nonetheless consistently predicted that economically competitive nuclear power could not be produced before the 1970s or 1980s. Therefore, he felt that turning the civilian nuclear power industry over to private enterprise would result in a slowdown of its development. In a cheap fuel country, business would not have enough incentive to develop the industry rapidly and would not have or would not be willing to devote major resources to such a long-term proposition. Holifield wanted nuclear power accelerated, but he believed that only the government could achieve this speedup. The federal arm possessed the money; they had imperative diplomatic reasons for moving rapidly; and they had the political authority to set timetables and force contractors to live up to them. Holifield felt that business had dragged its feet in the first round of the large power reactor prototype program.[47]

Just as important, he feared that, once allowed into the field, private enterprise would exclude public power enterprise. In many respects, his fight against the JCAE bill introduced by Sterling Cole in 1954 sought to put public power into the nuclear industry. Among other things, he brought the representatives of the Los Angeles municipal bureau of power and light to Washington to testify on behalf of his own position. The Montebello clothier also opposed the 1954 bill on ideological grounds. He feared that only large buinesses could afford to enter the field at this early experimental stage and that they would get an unfair advantage over the potential competition. By being exposed to the government hardware and technique developed so far, they would be in a position to patent and monopolize some of this technology and secure a stranglehold over the industry. Holifield wanted it to remain open to small business and to public power as well. Hinshaw largely sided with the sponsors of the bill who believed that private enterprise could move the industry ahead more rapidly than federal enterprise. Yet the whole purpose of the bill, as he saw it, was to let private enterprise into the industry and to accelerate its development.[48]

Something of a compromise issued from this debate. The House and Senate easily accepted the provisions to share American technology abroad, although not without some opposition. Congress went on to invite private industry to play a leading part in the drama of the atom, but included a role for public power. Many congressmen suspected Holifield of using nuclear science as a means to create a huge new public power industry, but, the representatives nonetheless accorded public enterprise a role in nuclear power development.[49]

Despite the rumpus, neither private nor public groups moved very rapidly to explore the field. This indifference led the JCAE to the AEC to recruit more groups into the program. Still, the going remained slow. By 1956, a few large firms had been lost and a few gained, bringing the total number developing large prototype power reactors to seven and a string of lesser entities that had begun negotiations with the AEC to join their larger brethren. These included the small cities of Mount Holyoke, Massachusetts; Piqua, Ohio; Anchorage, Alaska; and Orlando, Florida; the University of Florida; and rural cooperatives at Hersey, Michigan, and Elk River, Minnesota. Taken together, these small prototype power reactor plants represented a total investment just slightly less than the one Consolidated Edison plant at Indian Point, New York.[50]

These disappointing results forced the JCAE to find ways to tempt reluctant concerns into this new "miracle" industry. For a time the committee thought that the dual-purpose reactor would supply the proper inducement to these wary businesses. An atomic reactor could produce electricity, or plutonium, or both, although some commentators held that all reactors produced plutonium. The government used this rare material to manufacture nuclear and thermonuclear weapons, and herein lay what some atomic boosters felt was a profitable way out of their uneconomic dilemma. The reactors built to supply the public with electricity could at the same time manufacture plutonium for the government. At various times, the nuclear lobby charged that the services did not have enough weapons-grade material, so the dual-purpose reactor would solve both problems at once. The civilian reactors could produce plutonium, which in turn could be sold to the government for a "fair price," and the money gained from this transaction would go to compensate for the noncompetitive costs of civilian atomic electricity. Thus the new industry would receive another windfall in the form of subsidized plutonium prices and, at the same time, it would ensure a large supply of plutonium for the military.

This was undoubtedly one of the most ingenious schemes ever conceived for subsidizing an industry in the United States, and perhaps one of the most insidious. Plutonium, which appears only rarely in nature, is almost entirely a man-made substance, and it is an extremely dangerous one. The prospect of this material getting into a city water supply or into the hands of an urban terrorist who might manufacture it into a nuclear weapon seems not to have concerned the JCAE in these early years. And, as Carl Hinshaw argued in the debate over the new atomic energy act of 1954, "If you are going to enable them [private enterprise] to go ahead and build the reactors and produce cheap power, then you have to subsidize them in the form of a contract for the repurchase of the special material [plutonium] produced, at a fixed price." Holifield was less joyous about this departure than he had been about some of his other nuclear enthusiasms, but he allowed that such a compensation might be necessary. Such a subsidy should be watched carefully, he noted, and the public should be made fully aware of the opportunity to share in it. The AEC itself was torn on the question of the dual-purpose reactors. However, the commission eventually decided upon single-purpose reactors, for reasons that are not entirely clear. As Holifield observed, the plutonium subsidy "indicates some of the legislative labor pains which this committee is having in trying to give birth to an unsubsidized private industry in the atomic energy field."[51]

Two years later the baby had still not arrived, and Congressman Holifield adopted fresh techniques to induce its appearance. In 1956, the Californian, in cooperation with Senator Albert Gore of Tennessee, sponsored a bill to create five new federal government nuclear reactor demonstration projects to supplement the faltering efforts of the private sector. The Gore-Holifield bill would have poured another $400 million into an industry that was already floating in subsidies and it sought specifically to "accelerate" the development of atomic electricity. Unfortunately for the nuclear boosters, this legislation divided the House of Representatives right down the middle and split the JCAE from the AEC. Holifield carried a majority of the JCAE with him, even in the face of stern opposition from other members of the committee and the AEC.[52] He fared less well with the whole Congress.

The proposed program would have expended the $400 million to develop three new types of reactors not then being worked up by the AEC. These would have sold power not to the public but rather to government installations, and the advocates of the legislation considered the program to be one of research and development. The usual arguments about beating the Soviets and British enlivened the debate, and as usual with this technology, earlier precedents for government subsidization were called forth. As Chet Holifield pointed out, the government had recently coaxed the uranium industry into being, and as Carl Durham, a staunch advocate of free enterprise, echoed, "We have faced the problems we are trying to meet in this bill before you in the development of our railroads, of electric power, and in the great industrial growth of our vast airplane industry." At another point he noted that "most of these things like atomic energy, radar, and so forth, are born sometimes I think in sin, because most of them have had their birth during war," but now it was time to use this doubtful progeny "for the benefit of humanity."[53]

However, in one of his rare congressional speeches, Carl Hinshaw more specifically captured the essence of the arguments of these "ardent atomic-energy advocates." The Pasadena native put the matter in 1970s terms of declining resources and increasing demand. He cited figures on the tremendously increasing demand for energy in the United States. Coal, he admitted, would not soon run out, but hydroelectric power had been developed to its limits, and petroleum resources were being rapidly depleted. In his estimation, the U.S. had only about twelve years of petroleum resources left and was becoming dangerously dependent on unstable areas such as the Mideast. Coming from Southern California, which had a fully developed source of hydropower, no coal, and declining petroleum resources, Hinshaw was in a perfect position to understand the squeeze between growing urban demand and stable or shrinking supply.[54]

In agreeing with Hinshaw, Melvin Price of East St. Louis, another JCAE graybeard, acknowledged that they were really arguing about cities. "Mr. Hinshaw . . . went pretty much to the nub of the problem we are facing," Price explained, "and he answered very convincingly a statement . . . to the effect that this Nation has no power shortage." When challenged to show where the scarcity existed, Price retorted, "I might say any city in the country. Does the gentleman from Iowa realize many of the large cities within the last year at times have almost gone to the point of rationing power?" When pressed on the issue he reiterated that, "in some of the largest metropolitan areas of this country, you hardly have enough power at certain times of the day to operate an electric shaver" and added that "every city in the country faces that situation at times." He went on to note that industries searching for plant locations often have to have additional electrical stations built to supply their need.[55]

The urban condition also entered into the calculations of the opponents of the Gore-Holifield bill. Referring to the Monroe, Michigan, plant, a future powerful congressman exploded: "We of Detroit," fumed John Dingell, "are concerned about the calloused disregard which seems to be prevalent in some areas of high policy in this town regarding the safety of the 7 million residents of metropolitan Detroit." Others shared this concern, but it was not urban safety that motivated the majority of opposing speakers.

The most vocal opposition to the bill in fact came from the coal-producing districts, especially those of Pennsylvania. Generally speaking, these representatives favored government-sponsored research and development of atomic energy, but they vociferously opposed federal construction of plants and sale of electricity, even to government subsidiaries. The mining spokesmen reiterated their anger at former Washington programs to create hydroelectric power, which cut into their markets already contested by gas and oil. Government subsidization of yet another competitor of coal and government attempts to sell reactors abroad, which would further encroach upon American coal markets, were simply intolerable. Other opponents argued that the bill would put Washington into the public power business (it would not have); that the U.S. already led the Russians and British in the race for the atom; and that the bill would undermine the role of private enterprise in the economy. Still others thought Gore-Holifield would divert scarce scientific talent from defense. However, it would seem that the objections of the coal industry and the fear of public power were the most important concerns of the opposition. As one of the coal district spokesmen put it, using their taxpayers' money to subsidize a new fuel industry into being was "a little like paying for your own funeral."[56]

In the end, it was Congress, rather than the besieged Pennsylvanians, that buried the Gore-Holifield bill, but only by a small margin. The California delegation divided by 17 votes against the legislation to 12 in favor. A change of only seven California votes would have carried the day for Holifield and Hinshaw, both of whom voted for the act.[57]

Yet the defeat of the Gore-Holifield bill did not discourage the JCAE in any way. The next year they came back with another bill, this time the historic Price-Anderson Act to provide government indemnity to those injured by nuclear accidents. As the earlier debate had revealed, representatives showed growing concern for the problem of urban safety from nuclear accidents. Chet Holifield found this issue to be a very difficult one. The nuclear industry could not progress without firm insurance provisions, and everyone concerned considered the lack of these to be an insurmountable roadblock to the creation of a nuclear industry. The sponsors of the Price-Anderson Act always treated the possibility of a major accident as "remote," "highly unlikely," or a mere "mathematical possibility," but they knew that atomic electricity could not proceed without assurance against the "impossible."

Doubtless the insurance community did not consider the chances of disaster quite so "unlikely" because they categorically refused to provide full coverage against this "remote" eventuality. In fact, a consortium of 139 companies, including the mammoth and prestigious Lloyd's of London, would provide only $60 million worth of coverage for any plant. Perhaps the private reactor operators did not consider the possibility of catastrophe quite so "highly unlikely" either, because they refused to step out in the march to nuclear progress unless the government, or someone, supplied coverage against an eventuality they thought to be remote. However, they did admit that if an accident occurred it could be calamitous. As Willis Gale, chairman of Commonwealth Edison of Chicago, explained, "the likelihood of a major nuclear incident is extremely remote. However, if one should occur, the potential damage might be extreme."[58]

So the only way out was another government subsidy, this time in the form of a $500 million indemnity for parties harmed by a nuclear accident. Nor is the full generosity of the government to the industry indicated by this figure. The JCAE realized that an accident might cause more damage, and in that case, Congress would certainly provide a further indemnity beyond the $500 million. Even more astonishing, the operators of the plants paid no premiums to the government to provide this insurance. Carl Durham argued that the newness of the business made an actuarially sound schedule of payments impossible. Since "it would not be likely that the fund would ever be used," the government would simply be collecting a huge fund of money that "would be idle." Perhaps more to the point, Durham argued that "private enterprise" could not afford the payments. "If the Government tried to collect sums from the reactor operators which would quickly provide a fund from which tremendous losses could be paid," argued Durham, "the reactor operators would not be able to make that kind of payment." In addition, in response to a question about how the Joint Committee had arrived at their figure, instead of one "much higher than $500 million," Melvin Price explained "that [a higher figure] throws too great a scare out to the public." That might be considered damage control before the damage occurred. The sponsors of the bill realized from the beginning that a nuclear disaster might create much more than $500 million in damage, but they refused to legislate for a higher figure nonetheless.

To justify this handout, the pro-insurance group of the JCAE (17 out of 18) cited the usual arguments about the necessity of government aid for a new and untried technology à la the railroads, airplanes, and electricity. More important, they argued that the pursuit of the peaceful atom would stop unless the government guaranteed the indemnity. It is curious that Holifield, the "ardent atomic-energy advocate," who had just introduced a bill to accelerate the development of that medium, who had helped push ahead on the creation of the hydrogen bomb, and who would later forge ahead again on other things of the sort, parted company with his equally eager JCAE colleagues on this issue. He did so on specifically urban grounds.[59]

The Montebello representative was a complicated man and his positions on civilian nuclear power faithfully reflected this complexity. It is inadequate to characterize him, as some historians have done, as an undiscriminating nuclear booster. He consistently sought to promote atomic power within the context of the public interest by fighting against big-business monopoly, trying to preserve a place for public power within the new business, and attempting to limit the number and size of government subsidies to large private concerns. In the Price-Anderson case, the congressman sought to protect an even more important public interest, that is, the right to protection against the mass damage, destruction, and death which a major nuclear accident, however "remote," might involve. On the other hand, he had also always tried to use nuclear power to boost the national interest and the interest of Southern California. Price-Anderson put Holifield squarely up against the limits of his philosophy with regard to his urban environment.[60]

The act did so because, by 1957, it seemed clear to Holifield that the imposing nuclear power plants which he had fostered were going to be located in large metropolitan areas like the one he represented. The Southern Californian wanted atomic power *for* cities, but not *in* cities. Aside from his JCAE position, Holifield also chaired the House committees investigating civil defense against atomic attack, and in this capacity he learned much about the effect of radiation on the populace. That the impact would be devastating needs no reiteration here, and Holifield therefore moved to eliminate this threat from the nuclear power program. The AEC triggered the incident that brought Holifield to a parting of the ways from his joint committee colleagues. The AEC Scientific Safeguard Committee had declared the Lagoona Beach reactor, forty-odd miles from Detroit, to be unsafe. However, the commission itself overruled that decision and gave the Detroit Edison firm "a construction permit on it anyway." Holifield feared that the AEC might let the firm go ahead and operate the plant under unsafe conditions, just as they had allowed the building of it to go ahead. In a supremely ironical development nine years later, Lagoona Beach did indeed partially melt down. It was damaged so badly that it never opened, despite the $132 million that had been invested in it.[61]

"I do not want to stop this reactor business," Holifield informed his House colleagues. "I want to keep on making them. I want the Government to build them and I want private industry to build them, but I know what happened in the case of the Lagoona Beach reactor." As he had since at least early 1956, Holifield argued that the reactors should be in remote areas, away from population centers. He explained that either a bomb or a civilian reactor created "deadly radioactivity that can go through several feet of concrete and steel" and went on to elaborate that the "inside of a reactor becomes contaminated to a degree equivalent to the contamination of a bomb." So long as the material was contained within the reactor all would be well, but a reactor "could run away, become so hot that it would melt down. It could explode and release radioactive clouds of gas and contaminated material." The results could be awesome, 100,000 killed and widespread contamination of the earth and its structures, for "an undetermined length of time."

Holifield argued that the Edison plant could "decimate the city of Detroit," and he cited a study by the National Academy of Science to back up his contention that plants should head for the hinterlands. The National Research Council of that body made the usual claim: that a catastrophic accident "is highly unlikely in a properly designed reactor." But it went on to say that "nevertheless, the barest chance of it happening in a highly populated area is intolerable." Holifiled even cited the figures of Commissioner Harold S. Vance of the AEC to the effect that "the damages from one nuclear accident could reach $7 billion." The latter figure derived from a study by the Brookhaven Laboratory of the AEC and had been commissioned by the commission itself to determine the risk involved in nuclear power.[62] Another AEC estimate of the time placed the damage at anywhere from $10 million to $10 billion.

When congressmen argued that the Dresden reactor was forty-five miles "remote" from Chicago and the Lagoona Beach reactor was forty miles from Detroit, and therefore safe, Holifield was not pacified. He retorted that one million people lived within a thirty-mile radius of each of the five plants in the AEC program. Suburbanization had done its silent work, and a facility in the midst of such an area put a huge populated region at risk. The problem of urban placement was exacerbated by the primitiveness of the technology and the inexperience of its operators. "We just do not know whether they will be safe or not because we have not built any of their contemplated size," explained the congressman. "We are shooting in the dark."

> We are going into the unknown with these types of reactors. In no instance have all of the vital components such as the fuel rods, the valves, circulatory system, moderating elements, the level of continuous heat operation, and so forth been tested. We have not tested them. We do not know. That is why the insurance companies will not cover these reactors to the extent that the people who are building them want them covered.[63]

Coming from an ardent pro-nuclear man, that was damning evidence indeed. Although Holifield expressly stated that he would not accept the Price-Anderson Act in any form, he did try to amend it into a more palatable bill. For one thing, he attempted to force private insurance companies to accept more of the insurance burden so that the government would not get stuck with so much of the tab in case of a serious accident. Second, he sought to increase the authority of the Reactor Safeguards Committee which advised the AEC. However, it should be stressed that even with the amendments, the Montebello Democrat opposed the bill.[64]

It is difficult to follow Holifield's strategy during this part of his relationship with nuclear power. He clearly favored its development, yet he was fighting legislation that all and sundry agreed would eliminate the most serious "roadblock" to progress in the field. So how does one explain his behavior at this point? The most plausible explanation is that Holifield knew that he had not the slightest chance of defeating Price-Anderson; rather, he hoped to make a point by his opposition. He feared that, if passed, Price-Anderson would allow utilities to locate plants wherever they wanted. As we have seen, cities were the logical sites, and Holifield knew that, with insurance to hedge against a future accident, the operators would place their power-generating stations in metropolitan areas. In a sense the phenomenon of nuclear power was clearly a response to the urban market; yet the city masses were also the most important liability to nuclear power. So it was logical, if not politically feasible, for Holifield to argue that without this enormous government indemnity program, a utility company would be forced to site its facility in "an isolated position where it will not explode in the neighborhood of the people who are liable to get killed." Holifield's argument was economically reasonable as well. Coal plants such as the Pawnee, Illinois, power plant are sometimes located far from metropolitan areas and must ship their power over one hundred miles to the metropolitan market, in this case Chicago.[65]

Because not many House members shared Holifield's forebodings of catastrophe, the House debate sputtered on to fill only fifteen pages with a final resolution inimical to the California Democrat. Price-Anderson supporters noted the absolute necessity of the indemnity in order to get the program going; they reiterated the remoteness of the danger of a tragedy; and they claimed that a plant could not blow up in the manner of a bomb. As Carl Durham pointed out, no scientist had yet argued that a nuclear explosion could occur. "They say it simply cannot result because of the difference in the structure and the fissioning material." However, even as staunch a supporter of nuclear power as Melvin Price admitted that a chemical explosion, as opposed to a nuclear one, could happen. As he starkly acknowledged, "I think any of them could blow up." Still, that admission caused no explosion of sympathy for Holifield's position, and the bill passed the House with a minimum of discussion and without a record vote. The Senate took even less time, did not debate the bill at all, and also accepted it without a record vote. Thus, one of the most important pieces of legislation in the twentieth century, one which would subsidize into being a multi-billion-dollar industry by the 1980s, became law with hardly a word, much less a whimper.[66]

It is ironic, but nonetheless quite consistent, for the United States Congress to treat the issue of reactor safety in urban areas with what amounted almost to contempt; ironic, because while both houses of Congress enacted many, in fact too many, measures to protect the same urban areas from Russian nuclear weapons, they refused to take seriously the threat of atomic power plants to cities. Yet Americans had always had a considerable dislike for their cities, so subjecting them to the danger of nuclear catastrophe, however "remote" that danger might have been, was very much in keeping with past attitudes about the place of the metropolis in American culture. Exposing cities to this kind of ultimate tragedy perfectly expressed the widespread American scorn for "the urban condition."[67]

One of the most important JCAE contributions to the nuclear industry was dramatic and favorable publicity. Holifield certainly knew how to obtain and control these assets. In April 1960 the Montebello representative was temporary chairman of the JCAE, in which capacity he held a rather unusual congressional hearing of one day's duration. The session occurred aboard the USS George Washington, fifty-five nautical miles from New London, Connecticut, and 400 feet beneath the surface of the ocean. This dramatic (and undeniably fishy) location was selected to highlight to the congressmen and senators the fact that the *George Washington* was slated to be the first Polaris missile-firing nuclear submarine, giving the United States a marked strategic edge. "It was evident to us that the nuclear-powered submarine provides a superb platform for the ballistic missile," Holifield noted, "and that the marriage of submarine nuclear propulsion developed by the Atomic Energy Commission and the Polaris missile under development by the navy provides the United States with a potent deterrent."

That same occasion provided the feisty Admiral Rickover with an opportunity to speak. Rickover was a Navy establishment outsider, and Holifield, the JCAE, and the AEC had long been his staunch allies. The carefully staged hearing allowed the Admiral to give vent to his grievances with the navy establishment and to strengthen his links to the AEC and JCAE, who fed him one question after another designed to strengthen the Admiral's standing with Congress and the country.[68]

As we have seen, the Montebello congressman opposed the means to, but not the ends of, nuclear development, and he soon showed how loyal to nuclear power he remained. After all, Holifield was one of the few politicians, scientists, or technicians to articulate the urban dimension of nuclear power. In his speech placing that topic on the congressional agenda in 1953 he had noted that "locked up in a small amount of fissionable uranium was an enormous energy potential that could be harnessed to generate electric power for whole cities." He went on to point out that it would also "propel great ships and submarines and aircraft." neither his loyalty to the city nor his loyalty to the sword wavered in the aftermath of Price-Anderson. Indeed he would soon be advocating some of the most questionable, or at least potentially dangerous, departures in his long campaign for atomic electricity.[69]

In 1957 the House Appropriations Committee cut the budget submitted by the JCAE. The latter had split 11 to 7 over its own financial recommendations, and a floor fight ensued with the JCAE majority, this time including Holifield, struggling to get the monies restored. As an instance of JCAE zealotry, this case is not unusual, but it further exemplifies the enthusiasm of the Montebello liberal for atomic science, despite his temporary and probably only pro forma apostasy from the Price-Anderson Act. The controversial issues in this case were increased plutonium production and the development of a plutonium-burning reactor, a fast breeder reactor, and a natural-uranium as opposed to enriched-uranium reactor. Each of these issues involved a critical safety problem, perhaps as crucial as the issue of urban placement. Nonetheless, Holifield supported them all.[70]

As Melvin Price noted in requesting the restoration of the plutonium cuts, Edward Teller, Ernest O. Lawrence, and Mark Mills had testified to the JCAE that the weapons program needed "a substantial increase in plutonium production," both for the Eisenhower "clean bomb" which required more plutonium and for the general weapons program of the government. Of course, Teller and Lawrence ran important atomic science programs in the San Francisco Bay Area, and Holifield sided with them in this case. He explained that "additional plutonium facilities will be necessary if we are to expand the small nuclear weapons program which will give us the flexibility of choice in brush-fire war situations, relieving us of major dependence on large strategic nuclear weapons." At the same time that Holifield offered this justification of increased plutonium production, he put forward the JCAE's scheme for creating a plutonium-burning reactor. Although building a civilian reactor *to burn* this material would seem to be inconsistent with the concept of a military shortage of plutonium, Holifield pushed ahead anyway. If "an armistice should happily occur in the cold war," he said, or if the country reached "the ceiling of desired weapon inventory," military plutonium "now being produced could be converted into peacetime reactor fuel in electric generating plants."[71]

Yet, as Holifield knew, the country was likely to have more civilian plutonium than it knew what to do with, and the plutonium-burning reactor would be the answer to this oversupply. As he explained it, the burning of uranium 235 in a reactor created a byproduct of plutonium, for which the only current use "is in bombs." Obviously the country would face a situation of overproduction rather than the reverse because "under the law every one of these reactors that are built by private companies, practically every one of them, produce plutonium. The government has to buy that plutonium under the law." If a plutonium-burning reactor could be developed the material could be used for "peacetime application." In a sense, the plutonium reactor would be an answer to the waste-product problem of the conventional ones.[72] Of course, this condition of overproduction did not yet exist, because very few nuclear power plants were on line in 1957. Therefore, Holifield's attack on the long-range abundance of plutonium was quite consistent with his concern over the current shortage. One was a contemporary problem and the other was a future one.

At the same time that Holifield pushed for a device that would burn this extraordinarily deadly substance, the Southern Californian sought to create more of it. A fast breeder reactor could achieve this goal and do it in a very tempting manner. A breeder produced even more plutonium while burning uranium, and the government had already been hard at work developing one. Unfortunately the first experimental breeder was also one of the first American reactors to come to grief. "On the fast breeder reactor there was one laboratory model and it ran wild and melted down," Holifield advised his congressional colleagues. "There are $29 million in the bill to complete a second laboratory model to try to see if they can make this fast breeder reactor work safely."[73]

Unlike the breeder and plutonium-burning reactors, the final item on the 1957 JCAE agenda was designed for the export market. As previously noted, nuclear boosters understood that the United States might not produce economical nuclear electricity until the 1970s or 1980s because of the cheapness of generating electricity from abundant conventional fuel sources. However, high-cost areas of the world might need, and therefore produce, atomic energy much quicker on account of the differential. Therefore, it appeared that an export market for nuclear reactor manufacturers, construction firms, machinery suppliers, and architects might develop before one appeared at home. If the evolution of this technology turned out to be this perverse, with the mechanically less progressive nations interested in developing a more sophisticated technology ahead of the most advanced nation in the world, there just might be a market in it for the United States.

Not all of that prediction would ultimately come true. Nevertheless, that is how matters appeared in 1957, and Holifield and the JCAE majority hoped to use this foreign demand to create American nuclear manufacturing, construction, and engineering businesses based upon the export market. In time, a domestic demand would appear, and when it did, the United States would have already nurtured into being the expertise to supply it.[74]

The typical American reactor, however, did not suit this export market. "All of our reactors are on the basis of unriched fuel, but it costs a tremendous amount of money to make it [ordinary uranium] into enriched unranium." Some countries could not afford this expensive fuel and would instead turn to plants which used "natural uranium." To avoid losing this segment of the reactor trade, the "ardent advocates of atomic power" sought to get yet another subsidy from the government. This would be goverment development of a reactor that would burn natural instead of enriched uranium and thus allow American manufacturers to compete for these other foreign markets. Holifield explained, "A reactor that uses natural uranium can get the natural uranium anywhere in the world where they have uranium. This puts our manufacturers on a competitive level not only in the enriched field but also the natural uranium field."

Employing slightly more altruistic terms, Holifield framed the matter as an "atoms for peace program," in which "American manufacturers can make these reactors and export them to have-not nations, to neutral nations, to nations that do not have any coal or oil supply and cannot get it because of the cost of transportation." Great Britain, he observed, already possessed the technology to monopolize this field, so the United States needed to develop a natural uranium reactor.[75]

From a strictly business point of view, these arguments seem valid. The nascent nuclear energy industry needed government support, subsidies, research programs, and much else to make it economical, and the American government certainly had previously subsidized countless other businesses. However, Holifield's advocacy of the plutonium, fast breeder, and natural uranium reactors does not square with the metropolitan safety perspective that he had adopted in the Price-Anderson debate. A fast breeder reactor could produce plutonium that could be diverted into urban water supplies or terrorist bombs in some ship in a city harbor; and a natural uranium reactor, or indeed any kind, would produce fissionable products that might be converted into bombs that the so-called "have-not nations" could aim at each other's cities, or perhaps our own. The dream of atoms for peace could just as easily end up as a nightmare of terrorism and proliferation. Of course it did not take an Abu Nidal, or any other Middle Eastern terrorist, to recognize the nationalist, as opposed to economic meaning of this new technology.

And these were only the major services of the urban atomic congressmen to nuclear science and therefore to California cities. The *San Diego Union* and Representative Bob Wilson argued for a larger atomic role for the Navy, including the use of atomic warheads for anti-submarine warfare, and boasted of the contribution of the Navy's San Diego facilities in preparation for this eventuality. Craig Hosmer echoed this praise of the navy's nuclear role, especially that of the soon-to-be-built guided missile cruiser *Long Beach,* named after Hosmer's hometown. If the AEC suffered in recruitment and retention of scientific talent even a little bit, they could count on a Californian like Charles Gubser to introduce legislation to make the AEC more competitive with its private enterprise rivals. Sometimes other Californians got ahead of even the zealous JCAE.

Neither did it take a city planner to understand the urban implications of these actions. Much, if not most, of the nuclear discussion that Holifield, Hinshaw, Hosmer, and other Californians couched in national interest or humanitarian rhetoric in the halls of Congress related directly to their own home districts as well. It has been argued throughout this book that local urban interests have consistently diverted "national" resources to their home districts by various means, thereby transforming warfare into welfare. To put it another way, these urban promoters, the guardians of the Imperial City, have been able to mobilize national resources on behalf of their own urban development schemes. "Atoms for peace," nuclear power, or what one hyperbolic congressman termed a device "more wonderful, more inexplicable, than any Biblical miracle" led straight back to the metropolitan congressional districts of Los Angeles, San Diego, and San Francisco Bay.[76]

It would be well-nigh foolish to argue that such grizzled Washington veterans as William Knowland, Carl Hinshaw, Chet Holifield, and Craig Hosmer were unaware of the miraculous implications for their home districts of the positions they took and the efforts they put forth in the national capital. The ramifications of the atom in metropolitan California were already both lucrative and complex by 1954, and by 1957 they were even more so. As usual, Chet Holifield best articulated these myriad developments. As he put it in explaining his anti-monopoly fight on the 1954 atomic energy legislation, "Many people in my district, in personal talks and letters, have shown that they understand the fundamental issues at stake." They certainly should have, for as Holifield observed, "California is one of the leading States in the Union in atomic-energy activities." That was something of an understatement.[77]

Already by 1954, "California contracts represented nearly 10 percent of the Atomic Energy Commission's unclassified research work," a bonanza that represented thirty-nine contracts "with California educational institutions and research establishments." The University of California at Berkeley was "one of the most important organizations in the national atomic-energy program," the Montebello congressman noted with even more pronounced understatement. The University of California at Berkeley, under a contract with the AEC, operated the Los Alamos Scientific Laboratory in New Mexico, the Livermore Laboratory, and ran the radiation laboratory in Berkeley. The University of California Medical School at San Francisco was already a leader in the field of atomic medicine, especially that devoted to treating cancer, and the University of California's "atomic energy project" at Los Angeles Medical School covered "the complete range of the applications of atomic energy in the field of biology and medicine." The radiological laboratory at San Francisco was one of the "best-equipped facilities of its kind in the world."

Both Stanford and Cal Tech held their own in the atomic competition. "Two of the most important centers for both classified and unclassified research work in California are the California Institute of Technology and Stanford University," Holifield noted. Elsewhere in the state, the Navy conducted ordnance research at the Inyo-Kern area and the government tested ballistic weapons for atomic warheads at the Salton Sea area. By 1954, over 100 firms were using radioactive isotopes supplied by the AEC.

By that same date the Livermore Weapons Laboratory and the North American Aviation Corporation of Downey operated lower-power reactors, both built by North American. North American would soon build another, this time one of the five experimental reactors planned by the AEC under the 1954 program to bring private enterprise into the field. The facility would be located near the company's "field test laboratory in the Santa Susana Mountains, north of Los Angeles." It would be operated by Southern California Edison. The Bechtel Corporation, Pacific Gas and Electric, the Kaiser Engineers, Inc., and the Fluor Corporation already worked in this field, some of them producing equipment, "particularly in the field of atomic instruments." Nuclear physics had also expanded into the general field of industry. "The value of the atom in making industrial production jobs easier, faster, and cheaper is recognized by leading California industries," Holifield boasted. "Thus the petroleum industry, important in our State, uses radioactive instruments and materials in prospecting, well drilling, pipeline operations, and refining processes."[78]

The fascinating and extensive ramifications of atomic science can be seen further by looking at their impact upon one Urban Southland firm, North American Aviation. As President J. L. Atwood testified in 1953, even at that early date, his supposedly aeronautical company was already head over heels into atomic science. As noted elsewhere, they were building an atomic airplane; they worked on atomic guided missiles; they operated an atomic reactor in their Downey plant for research; and they were later scheduled to build several reactors. The firm had also contributed "various designs for reactors to perform many services for both military and peacetime applications. Designs of small reactors, suitable for medical, industrial, and academic research with atomic radiation have been made, some of which are now being proposed for actual construction." By 1953 the firm employed a force of 300 personnel in a 50,000-square-foot area of their main plant in Los Angeles. Among other things, the company had done research in electromechanics, aerophysics, and electronics and had produced several important breakthroughs, perhaps worth quoting verbatim.

> Our accomplishments in atomic-energy work include design and development of a pilot plant suitable for construction; design, construction, and operation of a water-boiler-type reactor producing neutrons for research and development work for all types of reactors; design and construction of research reactors for research, medical, and industrial uses; designs and component development for plutonium and power producing reactors; evaluation of economics of atomic-power plants utilizing uranium and thorium; nuclear-physics experiments with reactor components; development of reactor safety devices and low-cost chemical processes; and experimentation with reactor materials.[79]

Hollifield looked ahead to even more spectacular atomic feats. The Army Corps of Engineers and the AEC had asked for bids on a "package atomic reactor that can be transported by the Army to remote places, such as Greenland, and used to provide heat and power." Simultaneously the AEC had commissioned development of a 60,000-watt reactor, "enough to supply a fair-sized city." Last, but not least, the new power already provided contracts to those in the field of propulsion. The *Nautilus* had charted these unknown waters, and its admirers claimed that "the time may not be too far off when ships, airplanes, and locomotives will be driven by atomic power." North American, together with the Cincinnati nuclear propulsion laboratory of General Electric, had already made a start on the nuclear airplane. Commissioned in 1946, this project eventually claimed one billion dollars and provided contracts to Convair, General Dynamics, North American, and probably many subcontractors in the Southland. General Electric, Pratt and Whitney, and Fairchild likewise exacted a toll from this experiment in atomic air travel. Incidentally, the plane of which Carl Hinshaw was the acknowledged "father" never left the ground, but one billion dollars—over four and a half billion in current dollars—left the federal Treasury for the Southland and other contractors who kept the program alive long after it was proven unfeasible.[80]

Several other atomic projects flew much better and, like those that appeared by 1954, landed in one of the California metropolises. Between 1954 and 1957, when it could be accurately said that civilian nuclear science had been firmly established, the field proliferated extraordinarily. Hyman Rickover himself, in describing just the rise of factories to supply his program, testified to the JCAE that "you would be amazed if you really knew how extensive this private manufacture has grown." All of this development directly benefitted the California martial metropolises. By 1957, the venerable Mare Island Naval Shipyard was hard at work constructing "a guided-missile submarine" post-*Nautilus* class. In the interest of providing some balance in this picture, it might be mentioned that the Livermore Laboratory built the warhead for the *Polaris*-class missile.

In 1957, General Electric began constructing an important plant in San Jose. In that year, G.E. moved its atomic manufacturing factory and headquarters to the South Bay city. In the same year, G.E. began building "laboratory facilities, the tools of the atomic trade," on a 1600-acre site in East Bay Alameda County. The two developments were intimately related and the importance of this private research institution and factory can hardly be exaggerated. The laboratory illustrated the diversification of Bay Area industry away from its public base in Berkeley and Livermore, and the fabrication plant represented the creation of a high-technology component in local manufacturing. The San Jose plant by 1957 employed 1000 persons making reactor cores, test reactors, reactor equipment, "nuclear fuel elements," control-rod drive systems, liquid metals equipment, and other materials, many of them, including the reactor itself, destined to be used at the Vallecitos Laboratory.

General Electric and Pacific Gas and Electric owned the latter, and it featured a complex pattern of quadrupartite cooperation between those firms, Bechtel, and the AEC.[81] Originally PG&E and Bechtel began nuclear consultations with the AEC in 1951, and from these talks emerged a nuclear industry group called the Nuclear Power Group, Inc. The Vallecitos Laboratory grew out of these endeavors, and other important things, out of that. The laboratory was a proving ground for the boiling-water reactor, data from which was to be supplied to the Dresden, Illinois, operators of Commonwealth Edison.

In effect, then, the reactor at Vallecitos was a "pilot plant" for Dresden. That not only put PG&E and Bechtel on the ground floor of atomic energy, it put them on the elevator to the upper levels as well. PG&E became a partner in the Dresden venture and Bechtel built it. Bechtel went on to become extraordinarily important in the fabrication of future plants all over the world. Vallecitos also gave the Bay Area a pre-eminent position in the nuclear power market. The reactor furnished 5000 kilowatts of power that Pacific Gas and Electric distributed to 47 Northern California counties.

All in all, this endeavor provided atomic energy watchers with several famous firsts.[82] Vallecitos supplied the first privately produced atomic electricity in the United States; it ran the first boiling-water reactor; and it was the first privately financed reactor in America. Its creators saw it as a significant milestone on the road to what Governor Goodwin J. Knight called an "atomic peacetime." One can only echo that judgment, especially for the metropolitan Bay Area. Its precocity in nuclear physics had brought these windfalls, just as it had secured those of the war period. And its politicians and boosters would hang onto these resources now that they had been secured.[83]

The Vallecitos Atomic Laboratory would be devoted to research and development. It would include, among other things, a model boiler reactor, similar to the Dresden reactor, designed to provide research insights into that reactor and others like it. The Vallecitos power plant alone brought business to 60 subcontractors, 52 of them from California, and 47 of those from the Bay Area.[84]

Even the Livermore Laboratory diversified away from its military base and into civilian applications of nuclear technology. By 1962, Livermore, in addition to its weapons work, had at least one nuclear propulsion program going to develop the "nuclear ramjet propulsion field"; investigations to develop civilian nuclear energy; Project Sherwood, "for generating energy from controlled thermonuclear reactions"; and Project Plowshare, to use nuclear technology in mining, water, irrigation, excavation, and the mass production of radioisotopes. A Livermore press release of 1962 described its fusion research as "probably the most diversified controlled thermonuclear research program in the world."[85]

The transformation of the Livermore Laboratory and Los Alamos was illustrative both of the rapid evolution of the field and of the continuing need for political support from local congressmen. Much of the diversification of the nuclear science industry grew out of opportunity, but that at Los Alamos and Livermore came in response to threatened decline. The Eisenhower administration cut the atomic science budget for 1958, a development that presented problems enough. Beyond that, the AEC had successfully stimulated into being private laboratories, such as that of General Electric at Vallecitos and General Atomic at San Diego, which now competed with commission labs for government work. Between budget cuts, competing private institutions, and disarmament proposals, by mid-decade the weapons institutions were worried. In late 1955, the Atomic Energy Commission surveyed its various laboratories to learn of their long-range plans. Director N. E. Bradbury of Los Alamos answered bluntly. "Although the developmental demands upon the Laboratory are very heavy today and five or ten years of very hard work can be foreseen, the future beyond that point looks somewhat unrewarding."

> Fissionable material will go on and on being made until the efficiency of atomic weapons will become of academic interest. Everyone will ultimately have all the weapons in all the variety wanted, and the number will probably be more than the world can safely tolerate being used. Inspection, control, atomic disarmament, are words continually in the public eye and, in one form or another, an announced objective of our government. The steady advance of our potential enemy—along with our own advance—in the atomic field points to the eventual decline of this technique as a unique source of international dominance. Moreover, there does not appear to be any unscaled peak on the horizon in 1955 comparable to the challenge of a thermonuclear weapon a decade ago. In all frankness, the things the weapon laboratories are now doing and foresee doing are modifications, variants, and extensions of basic ideas going, back, in some cases, many years.
>
> Because of this prospect, and because the Laboratory must have an intelligible, realistic, and exciting future for its staff if they are to remain and work hard on weapons *now* [emphasis in the original], we have increased our interest and effort in the reactor field, the nuclear propulsion fields, the Sherwood field, and in basic research. However, in most of these fields, we are unclear as to the eventual relationship the Commission desires between its laboratories and industry.
>
> In short, if atomic weapons are abandoned, what should Los Alamos then be in a position to do? How should we plan today?

Perhaps no better statement of the dilemma of modern Urban California could have been formulated. Disarmament could cause real problems and so could technological advances away from the specialties of the Golden Land. Predictably, both Livermore and Los Alamos diversified from concentration on weapons to atomic energy, fusion power, basic research, Project Plowshare, and nuclear propulsion. Even in 1962, after the nuclear aircraft had supposedly been canceled, the Livermore Laboratory was still at work on nuclear ramjet propulsion. In this context, the actions of Chet Holifield to stimulate progress in the uranium, breeder, and plutonium reactor fields and to secure more plutonium for small weapons development are much more understandable. Both E. O. Lawrence, the head of the University of California nuclear empire, and Edward Teller, supposed father of the thermonuclear bomb, needed more plutonium for their work on small nuclear weapons. However, in the long run the laboratories had to diversify from instruments of destruction. Holifield's interest in nuclear propulsion and reactors and that of the University of California in employing atomic science in medicine, excavation, mining, and water management came in response to a very real crisis of decline in the Berkeley nuclear empire.[86]

These facilities added greatly to the atomic science complex of California cities. Reactor research would put the Bay Area in the forefront of civilian nuclear power development, and so would the equipment manufacturing plant. Holifield and others had warned that the AEC atomic energy program might develop a number of monopolies or semi-monopolies on the outside in the private sector. That is exactly what happened, to the great benefit of both G.E. and the California cities. By 1986, General Electric and Westinghouse, two of the earliest entrants into the field of atomic manufacturing, had literally monopolized parts of the reactor equipment supply business. The March 1986 edition of *Licensed Operating Reactors,* published by the Nuclear Regulatory Commission, listed four principal categories of contractors to nuclear power plants. Turbine and nuclear steam system suppliers both were equipment contractors categories, and the two electrical powerhouses had practically cornered this market. Of 94 licensed reactors, Westinghouse and G.E. had supplied 40 and 31 nuclear steam systems, respectively, and they had even more completely monopolized the turbine supply. Westinghouse produced 43 of these, and G.E., 46.

The Bechtel Corporation had a more dominant position in the other two contractor categories. The AEC had commissioned Bechtel, along with PG&E, to serve as contractors in the original civilian atomic energy reactor program of 1954. Also, both helped to build the Dresden reactor that supplied Chicago. From that point on, the San Francisco construction firm never looked back. By 1986 Bechtel had served as architect-engineer for 32 of the 94 licensed plants and constructor for 30. No other firm came close to this total in either category. North American also participated in the early program as a constructor for the Santa Susana reactor and was scheduled to build the reactor for Piqua, Ohio, and the Nebraska cooperative, but did not appear prominently thereafter.[87]

In this holiday season of nuclear enthusiasm there seemed to be no limit to the number of applications of this mysterious but promising technology. If atoms could run a portable Arctic generator, move mountains of construction debris, and propel a submarine, what other blessings were in the offing? Just as the successful perfection of the *Nautilus* power plant touched off a mild interest in civilian nuclear power, it also ignited a maritime propulsion boom. If a reactor could power a submarine, it could also propel surface ships such as carriers, cruisers, and destroyers, and by 1956 the Navy had at least sixteen other nuclear ships and subs on the drawing boards. Naturally this development interested the representatives of shipbuilding and maritime towns such as Vallejo, San Francisco, and expecially New London, Connecticut, where the *Nautilus* and its successors were built. If atoms could drive a war ship, why not a peace ship like the one that President Eisenhower hoped would sail around the world demonstrating American technical superiority and good will?

In more commercial waters, Golden State defenders of maritime interests had fought since the 1920s to resurrect the American merchant marine, and Californians like Jack Shelley took a prominent role in this crusade. Now they too hoped to go nuclear, as the military would say. The nuclear-powered merchant ship, both passenger and cargo carriers, became a part of this revival effort. Representative Horace Seely-Brown, whose district included New London as well as a laboratory developing the atomic aircraft, noted with pride that his ancestors had developed the Yankee Clipper and their descendants were now building nuclear ships for the

Navy. He hoped that Congress would allow them to construct others for the merchant marine, for both commercial and military auxiliary purposes. As usual, he and the other proponents of this idea cited the military utility of the merchant marine and pointed to the disastrous decline in American civilian shipping after both world wars. As usual, the defenders of the nuclear-powered merchant ship, contended that the merchant marine was the fourth arm of American defense and that the fourth arm must be as strong as the other three. Predictably, John J. Allen, Jr., conservative representative from Oakland, California, joined them in this advocacy.

On this occasion, however Holifield and Hinshaw did not. The two nuclear drummers had to draw back because of the feared impact of such a program upon the military nuclear propulsion program already under way. Citing Hyman Rickover, they argued that a new program for nuclear-powered merchant ships would be premature by at least five years because it would take valuable scientific personnel away from the navy program. Besides, the navy's program already comprehended what the merchant marine advocates wanted because the Navy was working on propulsion systems that could be applied to peacetime purposes. Thus in backing the navy in this dispute, the California JCAE bloc was also supporting what its members thought was the more orderly and rapid development of the nuclear ship. Obviously, when forced to choose between military and civilian applications, they defended the interests of the services, but either way they would have been promoting the rapid evolution of nuclear science. In any case, it is obvious that California urban congressmen helped to provide a firm foundation for the development of nuclear science, which by 1957 had proliferated into an amazing number of fields, most of them beneficial to Golden State cities.

This list of activities does not, of course, exhaust the "amazing" proliferation of atomic science in urban California, if for no other reason than that it does not cover classified atomic science. However, it provides some of the flavor of those years when the "Biblical miracle" of atomic energy was unfolding in the nation's most urban state. One cannot make a direct connection between each of these government-sponsored scientific developments and the California bloc in Congress and on the JCAE in all cases, but it is clear in some. Hinshaw, Holifield, Hosmer, and Knowland, as members of the JCAE, helped to guide the country toward a nuclear future. Specifically, they helped to secure the second weapons laboratory at Livermore; they pushed ahead on the H-bomb (Hinshaw and Holifield were in effect the subcommittee that recommended this departure); they encouraged nuclear propulsion; they tried to accelerate the civilian uses of nuclear power; they fought for new technologies like the fast breeder, plutonium burning, and natural uranium reactors; and in general they forced the AEC to move faster than it wanted to.

And in doing so, they were not simply making national legislation or creating public policy in an abstract sense. They represented urban geographic districts possessing very specific atomic interests, which would be benefitted by the "public policy" initiatives that they supposedly took on behalf of the modern nation-state. If the Urban Californians urged the creation of more demonstration reactors, they knew there was a good chance that Bechtel would build them and the G.E. plant in

San Jose would supply their equipment. If they argued for greater plutonium man-ufacture, they knew that it would probably go to increase the production materials of either the Los Alamos or Livermore weapons laboratories. If they supported the *Polaris* missile-toting submarines, they could be certain that the Livermore Weap-ons Laboratory would manufacture the warhead. If they pumped for atomic sub-marines or airplanes, there was a good chance that the Mare Island Naval Shipyard or the North American Aviation Corporation would construct them. If they fought for greater funding for atomic research and development, they knew that it was highly probable that the R&D would be done by the Cal Radiation Laboratory, the California Institute of Technology, the Stanford Research Associates, or the Gen-eral Electric Laboratory at Vallecitos. And if they urged that more money be put into nuclear medicine and biology, it would quite likely be spent at the University of California Medical School in San Francisco or in Los Angeles.

When they struggled to enlarge the nuclear role of the Navy, they knew that they were benefitting friends in San Diego, Long Beach, Vallejo, Livermore, and Oak-land. And when they argued that "we cannot apply factual estimates nor rigid forms of normal justification to the justification of funds to explore the unknown," they were laying the groundwork for an increased funding of scientific endeavor that would have benefitted countless laboratories in all three of these essentially high-tech urban areas. And when they worked to produce an export market for Ameri-can nuclear technology, they knew that G.E. in San Jose might construct the reactor and Bechtel might design and build the plant in which it functioned. When they fought against atomic budget cuts, they knew that they were helping keep the lab-oratories and factories running at full tilt. When they argued government indem-nities for nuclear plants they knew that this protection would stimulate the range of atomic activities in their home districts. And when they strove to open the Amer-ican West to uranium mining, they were aware that the Los Angeles Chamber of Commerce was already rallying its readers to the existence of this new opportunity. Thus representative Sterling Cole said that Carl Hinshaw's "contributions to the development of nuclear reactors for peaceful purposes are beyond cataloging." Above all, they were important to Urban California.

How far beyond, we shall probably never know. Still, the historical record con-tains certain hints of the amounts of money spent in these combined nuclear endeavors. By March 1958, the San Francisco Operations Office of the U.S. Atomic Energy Commission in Oakland could report that it had poured nearly half a billion dollars into California for "all purposes—plant, equipment, and operations." Cur-rently these expenditures ran to $100 million a year. Most of the funds had gone to Northern California, largely because of the University of California laboratories at Berkeley and Livermore. The University of California system president reported a similar figure that month. Three years earlier, in 1955, the California state legisla-ture had directed the University of California system to investigate the fields of atomic science that might be worthy of state support, and now President Robert Gordon Sproul reported back on the educators' progress. Atoms for war were doing much better than atoms for peace, but the university was doing even better from both. Sproul reported that university nuclear work financed by the Atomic Energy Commission alone totaled $91 million. The figure did not include the myriad activ-ities of private enterprise in the field.[88]

Other constituencies were just as acutely aware of these benefits, especially those that did not get them. Nevada, whose inhabitants received radioactive fallout regularly in order to feed enough data into the Livermore and Los Alamos weapons laboratories, received hardly any atomic payoff in return. Nevada had served as a gaming playground for Urban Californians for at least forty years, a place where they could indulge their passion for games of chance without having to endure permanently the glittering side effects. It had now become a weapons playground. There, winds blow from west to east, whisking fallout away from California and onto the Nevadans. It is impossible to believe that the Californians in science did not appreciate the beauty of this arrangement, and it is certain that the Nevadans resented it.

That state, where almost everyone lived in cities and towns, had even more extreme resource shortages than California: no oil, no natural gas, no coal, little water power potential, and a remote location from western sources of each. On the other hand, it had the same growth ambitions that metropolitan California did. As Nevada Senator Dana Bible explained to Congress, "We want enterprising residents, who want to see their State grow and prosper and attract industry. We cannot do this without ample power." Not only was the state a high-cost power area, it lacked the technical base that large urban areas would have guaranteed it. "Small power firms in Nevada do not have at their disposal men who are qualified to outline and draw plans for negotiating contracts with the Atomic Energy Commission," complained Bible.[89]

Nevada's disadvantage vis-à-vis Urban California can be seen in the bargains it made with the government. "Nevada residents do not want to become the dumping grounds for the Atomic Energy Commission's experimental weapons program," Bible warned. Yet they were at least willing to cooperate in these tests, which numbered 60 by 1956. However, the state wanted something nuclear in return. "If the State of Nevada can bear the brunt of atomic blasts and a necessary testing program for nuclear weapons," stated the senator, then "the Atomic Energy Commission should also awaken to the needs of [the] State and direct some effort toward establishing a portion of its experimental work along peaceful lines, such as a reactor in a section of Nevada to be chosen at the Commission's direction." In other words, Nevada was reduced to swapping its continued cooperation in remaining a test site for some slight nuclear concession in return. Meanwhile, California, which was rolling in atomic benefits, could go on enjoying them and the stimulus to growth that they provided, while at the same time retaining the use of Nevada as both a gambling resort and a "dumping grounds."[90]

The contrast between have and have-not atomic states emphasizes once again the geography of American atomic development. In the vast majority of cases, nuclear power did not develop in states that lacked large urban populations or that contained large water, coal, oil, or natural gas resources. And of the two, the correlation of urbanization and atomic electricity is the strongest. Most American nuclear plants today are located east of the famous 98-100 meridian demarcation of the Dry West. Only ten of 94 reactors are situated in the vast area which constitutes about half of the territory of the Untied States. Even there, they are close (around 35 miles) to principal metropolitan areas such as Portland, and Phoenix; and even closer to Sacramento (25 miles) and San Luis Obispo (12 miles).

Eastern plants stand in the same relationship to their urban markets, with reactors ranging from 10 to 25 miles from New Orleans, Charlotte, New York City, Rockford, Toledo, Wilmington, N.C., Chattanooga, Newport News, and Omaha. Obviously, the prediction of AEC Director of Reactor Development W. Kenneth Davis that atomic plants would be located near, but not in metropolitan areas came true with what an increasing number of people in late twentieth-century America have come to regard as a literal vengeance. The Chernobyl "incident" in the Soviet Ukraine during the 1980s makes it obvious that the ten-mile disaster planning limit of the Nuclear Regulatory Commission is ludicrous and that all America's nuclear plants are a major risk for some metropolitan community.

Thus it is clear that the U.S. atomic energy program has had a very pronounced urban dimension. Without city markets, the evolution of this technology would have been markedly different. By the same token, without the promotional activities of the Imperial City, the movement would have been noticeably slower. Urban California boosters grasped this technology as a means of realizing their dreams of growth and clearly move it forward. It is pretty well understood that military spending during this period of time greatly exceeded military necessity. Even insiders like Eisenhower science advisors Herbert York, George Kistiakowsky, and James R. Killian indicate that many defense programs were simply unnecessary.[91] Whether it was producing extra plutonium for weapons that were not used, building nuclear aircraft that did not fly, or providing insurance without premiums, the city boosters sought to increase spending for nuclear science. It was a vastly subsidized business, and urban congressmen aided in creating these subsidies. Perhaps more than any other members of Congress, California legislators helped to lay a broad and rich foundation for the new field of nuclear science.

Therefore, to treat the evolution of American civilian atomic energy without regard to its urban geography is simply inaccurate. One need not argue that diplomatic reasons for nuclear power are invalid, that the United States did not want to best the Soviet Union, that industry would not ultimately require a new energy source, that individual scientists like Lawrence, Teller, and Rickover had no influence, or that bureaucratic maneuvering had nothing to do with the advent of this "Biblical miracle." All of these causes entered into the matter. However, the urban dimension is also a major part of the complex growth of atomic energy. It may have been the most important of the many causes; despite the influence of individuals like Lawrence and Teller, of the Cold War, of diplomacy, and of bureaucracy, major nuclear plants simply do not exist where there are no cities. Cities in general supplied the markets for this novel energy source, and the Darwinian City provided much of the imperative to develop it.

CHAPTER 9

....

San Diego and the Continued Quest
for Military Riches

California cities have pioneered in the domestication of the art of war, and San Diego has led the way in California, using essentially military resources to make itself into a great American urban center. More than any other Golden State city, the Port of the Palms has linked its fate to that of military development. It has been and is the quintessential martial metropolis. As a result, a city located in the most remote corner of the nation has become one of its largest despite its lack of resources, centrality of location, or head start in the race for world-class status. Just as conflict formerly militarized cities, now cities have civilianized war, and, ironically, nowhere more so than in the militarized city of San Diego. This process has been vivid in other California metropolitan areas and throughout the American South and West and has helped to encourage the shift of population and wealth to those so-called Sunbelt areas. However, no other place has outstripped the Harbor of the Sun in its recruitment and transformation of military resources.

San Diego commenced this transformation in the Progressive era. Although the Border City likes to attribute its success to its natural resources, namely climate and scenery, it has precious few assets of the kind that had helped to create great cities prior to the twentieth century. It has no nearby deposits of coal or iron, little level land, not much water, no adjacent river highways, no strategic location on the routes of trade or international migration, no proximity to the great markets of the United States or the world, and meager railroad network. It did not even possess a world class harbor. San Diego Bay required successive dredging operations to make it useful in an era of steel ships, so even the most strategic resource of the Harbor of the Sun was small compared with San Francisco Bay or the harbor of New York City. However, as has been detailed in an earlier chapter, San Diego did have dedicated leadership who were determined to make it into a world-class city. They sometimes quarreled over whether it should cater to industry or retirees because smokestacks might destroy the natural beauty of the place, but growth of some kind seemed eminently desirable.

Although social commentators and historians have accorded the Second World War a great influence in shaping the contemporary world, it did not change some things even a little bit, Or, perhaps the more they changed, the more they stayed the same. One such matter was the San Diego approach to the competitive process of urban development and the close connection to the military services that this association involved. San Diegans had long labored to create a tight interface between the services, especially the Navy, and the city after the war, and the Harbor of the

Sun continued to look upon its relationship with the military as symbiotic. E. Robert Anderson, San Diego officer of the Navy League, captured the local sentiment vividly in a letter to Congressman Bob Wilson. "If, during my term of office, I can give muscle to the 'civilian arm' of our Navy, then I will have served San Diego," wrote the newly elected national vice president. "And to serve San Diego is to serve our national defense because our city and the nation's security are like twins." The Navy Leaguer could not have summed up better the effort to use the presence of the Navy, and defense in general, as the cement of urban community, an effort that elaborated further the already impressive community of interest between the city and the sword.[1]

In his farewell address to the nation in 1961, President Dwight Eisenhower called attention to the partnership between civilian, government, and military elements, which he termed the "military-industrial complex." This was not the first time the President had warned of this new economic force, but it was the one that stuck in the minds of press and public and the one that has come to characterize this civil-military relationship ever since. However happy the phrase might have been as a way to educate the public, it oversimplified the matter in several important ways. Ike described a monolith, whereas the nature of the military-industrial complex was much more pluralistic. He stressed the military partnership with industry, thus neglecting everything else. He conveyed a sense of "we" and "they," which has characterized discourse about the relationship from that point onward. And he gave the impression that the military-industrial complex was made up only of the rich and powerful, as opposed to the common people. The President was correct that a relatively powerful alliance had grown up between the civil and military sectors in the United States, but the term military-industrial complex implied a number of very fundamental misapprehensions about the new powerhouse in American political and economic life.

None was more unfortunate than the idea that the military-industrial complex served primarily wealthy munitions makers, politicians, and government bureaucrats at the expense of everyone else. Neither the "we" and "they" aspect of his description nor the rich-poor dichotomy holds up under investigation. Historians have recently come to study nearly every imaginable social institution from the "bottom" up, and that approach is a useful corrective to Eisenhower's original conceptualization of the military-industrial complex. This perspective reveals the broad urban, social bases of the civil-military interface and the welfare dimension of twentieth-century warfare as well.

The "metropolitan-military" complex comprehended elites of all kinds—educators, businessmen, servicemen, politicians, chamber of commerce activists, scientists, labor unionists. It also encompassed masses of non-elites. They often voted subsidies to the metropolitan-military complex, and they always clamored for ever more defense monies for their city. Nowhere did this support of the "little people" reveal itself more dramatically than in San Diego.

Any threat of a reduction in force at one of the local bases, any threat to its missile or airplane programs, any demand to move a part of the fleet to Long Beach, or any whisper of a redistribution of shipbuilding contracts away from the harbor of the Sun prompted a flurry of protests to the government. The language of these missives is both poignant and revealing. For example, the proprietor of a music company wrote to Wilson in early 1961 that his business had dropped off by 35 percent, that his work force was being laid off, and that two firms on his block would shutter their windows if conditions did not improve. "We have an idle aircraft industry that the Government should recognize in some positive manner," lamented Robert Mitchell. "I am writing to stress the urgent need for defense contracts," wrote James W. Bleford, bemoaning the "extent of unemployment" in San Diego. "Our industry consists, so very much more than most, predominantly of Military and Defense contracts." A union labor man added, "If Convair is working strong then I will be working."[2]

Many, perhaps half, of the correspondents were women. One wrote stressing the advantages of living in San Diego and explained that her family had put down roots in the city. "We love San Diego . . . we have had a baby . . . my mother has joined us . . . we have built a new home here . . . we are college graduates. . . . However, our almost blissful existence here has been marred by the fear that my husband, along with thousands of others will lose his job" at Convair. "This is such a marvelous place to live, and we certainly hope we can continue here," concluded Mrs. Paul W. Bergstedt. The wife of a twenty-year veteran at Convair asked, "Will it come to giving up our home, our children's education which we happily sacrificed for, so they could be part of the future of our country?" It was not fair for a man to invest twenty years in a job, "just to find yourself washed up and out in the cold," she observed. "Here's to a bigger and better Convair and more contracts from the Defense Dept."[3]

An Army veteran of twenty-three years already considered San Diego a "Lost County." Democracy itself seemed to hang in the balance. "If it be in your representative's [Congressmen Bob Wilson] power to give new birth to the unemployed in this county," concluded Master Sergent W. W. Law, paraphrasing Abraham Lincoln, "it would long be remembered that, government of the people, by the people, for the people, shall not perish from this earth." Moving from the Gettysburg battlefield to a closer one, the soldier added that "no county in the United States can offer the relaxation to our defense workers like San Diego County, with its many Parks, National Forest Camp Grounds, State Forestry Parks and Camp Grounds, and Seashores." Between amenity and democracy, the Harbor of the Sun seemed to have it all. Many of the pleaders believed that Convair had been unfairly cheated out of its fair share of contracts by sinister political influences, especially after the new Kennedy administration took power in 1961. "I feel that the talents of a large engineering force, such as the one at Convair, should be utilized for the good of our country," wrote the wife of an engineer. Obviously, the national well-being and that of her husband were closely linked.[4]

These letters document the widespread popular belief in the Harbor of the Sun that what was good for Convair was good for the USA. They also emphasize the belief that political manipulation was used to deny the company its fair share of contracts. In reality, this discrimination is unlikely. At the very moment of this urban "crisis of contracts," only 8 percent of the San Diego work force was unemployed, and the company had a backlog in early 1961 of over one billion dollars in military contracts. While the mass backers of the martial metropolis complained that San Diego was becoming a ghost town and that "Convair had not received a contract in years," the *San Diego Tribune* reported that this firm "spent a record $936,000,000 with suppliers in 1960," mostly in San Diego. For those with short memories, the *Tribune* pointed out that the previous record had been set at $862.2 million—the year before.[5]

The letters also document the fact that San Diegans as a whole understood quite clearly the close connection between the city and the sword and their heavy dependence upon military contracts. They were not manipulated by some greedy elite, but rather were willing participants in the creation of a fortress city. Finally, this view of the metropolitan-military complex from the bottom up reveals a completely special-interest approach to national defense matters. Hardly anyone judged the matter of local contracts within the context of overall defense spending policies. Although San Diego leaders often had a clear idea of defense strategy and tactics, their constituents had not the foggiest notion of what these were. They instinctively assumed that if Convair or San Diego did not get the contract, "politics" had cheated them out of their "fair share," and that being the case, politics should restore it to them again. The mass of citizens at that place partook of the defense feast as willingly as any of the other diners—military, industrial, bureaucratic, political, or scientific—and with the same insatiable appetite.

The mass adherence to the metropolitan-military complex can be seen in an even more stark light in the ceremonial interface between the city and the sword. Just as pre-World War II residents had involved themselves heavily in staging bomber shows over the World's Fair, sham battles, and practice marine landings, so did their postwar successors. None rallied the entire metropolitan area more successfully than Air Power Day, 1953. Other cities traditionally have staged their own peculiar celebrations—a Taste of Chicago, A Taste of Peoria, the Pekin, Illinois, Marigold Festival, the Newport and Covington, Kentucky, Oktoberfest, the Pennsylvania National Pike Festival—in which the downtown streets are blocked off and the citizens assemble to enjoy the town cuisine, beer, flowers, and crafts, listen to the municipal band, and enjoy the afternoon sunshine. In San Diego, it was Air Power Day. This civil festival grew out of the fiftieth-anniversary celebration of "Controlled Powered Flight" and the seventieth-anniversary celebration of "Controlled Winged Flight." Cities across the nation joined in this celebration, but California cities joined in more than most. Of the forty-six events scheduled nationwide, California cities provided sixteen and co-sponsored a seventeenth. Golden State cities staged dances, air shows, factory open houses, lectures, and public school observances. And of the California total, San Diego put on over half.[6]

The crowning event, Air Power Day itself, took place at Miramar Naval Air Station later that fall. To say that the event succeeded or that it involved the urban masses would be something of an understatement. The Jaycees expected a crowd of some 125,000 people but instead found themselves mobbed by an estimated 300,000. More sea and air power observances followed over the years, several of them attracting similar crowds. On a more prosaic level, the maritime museum, the offices of local clubs, the Historical Society, the Chamber of Commerce, and other urban institutions displayed naval and military relics in order to keep the Navy story before the community. Year after year, the boosters continued to join the emotional, recreational, and vocational life of the urban masses to the military in an ongoing series of pageants designed to bolster the city's fortunes in the Darwinian struggle for urban hegemony.[7]

Anyone who has spent any time in San Diego knows that no special pains are needed to keep the Navy story before the community because the Navy is an inescapable presence. A harbor cruise reveals a submarine base, a carrier anchorage, North Island Naval Air Station, hummock ammunition bunkers, docks and ships galore, barracks ships, shipbuilding firms, and dry docks. A drive down the boulevard bordering the harbor reveals an almost wall-to-wall naval presence from just below Seaport Village to the San Diego-Coronado Bridge. In the bay, ships ply the waters and retired admirals cruise their sailing vessels; overhead, naval helicopters buzz and jets scream; and downtown, sailors throng the streets and crowd the beer joints.

So, as San Diego grew, not only would the Navy prove inextricably bound up with the city's everyday work life, but the recreational and historic consciousness of the city would become equally tied to that service as well. The people of San Diego would participate just as fully in the metropolitan-military complex as the elites, whether through their pleas for work, their attendance at the martial festivals, their participation in harbor cruises, or their visits to the Museum of Fine Arts in Balboa Park. They would be kept in touch with the Navy in their public schools, in visiting their congressmen, or in walking past the display cases of the Fleet Reserve Association, the Military Order of the World Wars, or the Navy League.[8]

Both the mass participation in the metropolitan-military complex and the transformation of military assets into civilian ones can be seen anew in the politics of military surplus. The requests for surplus government assets ranged across the spectrum: religious and secular, charitable and business, public and private. The military resources started out as weapons all right, but eventually were turned to economic, fraternal, and even genuinely benign purposes. Urban leaders traditionally complain of the adverse impact of the military on their communities, but that influence could quite often be rather helpful.

For example, Midway Motors needed several hundred trailers for a large engineering project; the Ramona Municipal Water District required some good government steel pipe; and the Gyrotor Helicopter Company (makers of military and civilian craft) wanted an HSL-1 helicopter. The tuna industry needed both air and naval power to pursue its catch: planes to spy out the fish and tugboats to catch them. The American Legion wanted surplus uniforms to replace their own stock and horns for their youth drum and bugle corps; the San Diego Heart Association wanted a safe to store their donations securely; and the Fletcher Hills Elementary School urgently required a "surplus Navy aircraft" for playground equipment. So did the Community Methodist Chapel of the Hills in Descanso, preferably a P-40 or P-51. The South Bay Young Men's Christian Association begged for a surplus bus in order to serve its suburban district. Meanwhile, the San Diego Home for the Blind hoped for a former housing site lot on which to build a home, and the Boy Scouts angled for a ship.[9]

The American Association of University Women wished to know how to get in on the general phenomenon of surplus; the Clairmont High School hoped for some woodworking equipment; and the City of San Diego hankered after a spare Navy tugboat. And James W. Turpin, M.D., desired to secure "as much surplus material as possible from the hospital ship, *Repose,* being decommissioned in San Diego, the materials to be used in treating Chinese refugees in Hong Kong." Perhaps the most unique request came from an enthusiast who wanted the military to stop destroying its surplus parachutes and make them available to sky divers like himself. He was firmly convinced that the parachutes would produce a distinct leveling influence on society, Milton Nodacker explained, since "surplus parachutes give the low-budget sky diver a chance to compete with his richer neighbor." "They would also make parachutes available at lower cost to private pilots for a greater margin of safety in cross-country flying, and local flying too." Of course the daredevil grounded his ultimate justification in the realm of military security. "Another case for the release of surplus parachutes for civilian use is the potential of trained parachutists for national defense, who would make a valuable . . . reserve. For this reason alone, the armed services should do all they can to promote, rather than hinder, sport parachuting." One does not have in these efforts a literal example of beating a genuine sword into an authentic ploughshare, but the parachutes, buses, medical supplies, playground equipment, woodworking machines, tugboats, irrigation pipe, hospital supplies, land for the blind, and planes for the tuna dawn patrol at least come close.[10]

Nonetheless, popular participation and acquiescence in the metropolitan-military complex does not negate the fact of elite domination of it. In the immediate aftermath of the Second World War, San Diego struggled to recover from the hurricane of urban development that this event had triggered. After some low-grade complaining that the Navy had left their city in the lurch to deal with the problems that the *military* had caused, the Port of the Palms settled down to its normal routine of ingratiating itself with the Navy and monopolizing its property.

Although the Navy had poured millions into the infrastructure of the Harbor of the Sun by 1945, it would subsequently add many more crucial elements to its holdings. By 1954, government investment in Marine and Navy installations in the Eleventh Naval District had risen to "about one billion" dollars; it paid out annually another two hundred million plus to "uniformed and civilian personnel" in the district. And much more was on the way.

On April 1, 1954, the government commissioned the United States Naval Repair Facility to "perform emergency and voyage repairs to any active fleet vessels" and "general repairs for all ships" of the Pacific Reserve Fleet based at San Diego. This "facility" was a quintessential example of how San Diego parlayed one unassuming naval asset into a larger one and then a larger one still. San Diego had begun in World War I with the usual land grant, this time of ninety-eight acres, for use by the Emergency Fleet Corporation. The site became an anchorage for servicing destroyers and other small vessels and then in 1921 changed to a submarine and repair base. Finally, in 1954 it became a full-fledged repair base which could mend ships up to cruiser size. This installation represented an important consolation for the private industrial base that the city had not been able or willing to attract, and it was a clean industry at that, one that would not disturb the geraniums. The auxiliary air station at Miramar Field began as Camp Kearny in World War I and reverted to the Navy prior to World War II. It then became a bona fide naval air station in 1952, to be used to provide an on-shore home base for carrier planes when they were in port. Without this base, the carriers would not have come to San Diego, a fact that the boosters well appreciated.

The Naval Electronics Laboratory, opened in 1949, provided another important element to the growing naval oligopoly in the Harbor of the Sun and at the same time gave it a piece of the electronics industry, then concentrated in rival Los Angeles County. Like Miramar and the fleet repair base, this institution grew out of previous Navy ones, in this case the Point Loma Radio Station, which was "the first radio station on the Pacific Coast to handle transcontinental traffic." In 1940 it became the Navy Radio and Sound Laboratory and was absorbed by the Electronics Laboratory in 1949.[11]

An important further addition to the growing integrated naval presence arrived through the attempt to modernize the naval base. The advent of nuclear-propelled submarines and aircraft carriers triggered two of the most significant modernizations of the port. The rise of nuclear propulsion forced a number of adjustments upon the military services and, in turn, opened up a series of opportunities for the martial metropolises. Nuclear power might propel submarines, aircraft carriers, and, until 1961 it was hoped, airplanes. Each of these technical innovations required new port facilities, and each generated scientific spinoffs that would benefit a city ever watchful of its opportunities. Of course, San Diego had always been vigilant and was again when Admiral Hyman Rickover's new nuclear-powered Navy got big enough to raise the question of where and how to berth the ships in ports. That juncture provided the opportunity that San Diego needed, and it moved expeditiously to exploit it.[12]

First, the city had to secure the status of home port for the atomic submarine fleet. When Admiral Arleigh Burke, Chief of Naval Operations, set in motion the plan to build the piers necessary to handle atomic submarines at Ballast Point, San Diego stood ready to lend a hand. As the president of the San Diego Navy League explained to Wilson, "The continuation of San Diego as the home port for the Atomic Submarine Fleet should be assured by the building of these piers." As the fleet moved to an ever more nuclear basis, the home port issue loomed larger. The *San Diego Union* explained exactly what was at stake: "San Diego is the home port for a fourth of all U.S. submarines, a third of the Navy's submarine tenders and more than two-thirds of the subs in the Pacific Fleet." The city could and did argue that its current possession of the fleet sonar school and the Navy Electronics Laboratory strengthened its claim to the piers and the subs. It also championed the Navy's argument that the current sub tenders with their twenty to thirty submarines cluttered and clogged the harbor and that the piers would alleviate this congestion. As usual, the Navy expressed its interest forcefully. Captain Norvell G. Ward, commander of the Navy's first *Polaris* sub squadron, pointed out at a Military Order of the World Wars dinner, "If you want the nuclear submarines to call here, you'll need the pier at Ballast Point." In seven to ten years, he continued, "nuclear subs will have replaced the conventional diesel undersea craft."[13]

By the time the captain spoke these words, San Diegans were already mobilizing behind the scenes to bring the piers to Ballast Point. In fact, Congressman Wilson had been at work for two years before Admiral Burke's request, and the Chamber of Commerce Military Affairs Steering Committee had been working for at least one. Others soon joined them. As the Chamber, the mayor, the Navy, and Wilson went public, James S. Copley swung his powerful *San Diego Union* and *San Diego Evening Tribune* behind the piers. Also, the *San Diego Independent* argued that "surely the piers are important enough to San Diego's economy and the West Coast defense to have the piers put in the 1960 budget." Dr. Roger Revelle, Scripps Institution director, informed a congressional investigating committee that nuclear subs would "command the seas within 10 years." In what he must later have rued as an unfortunate prophecy, the good doctor went on to predict that "atomic submarines will achieve speeds approaching those of aircraft." The *Independent* explained the Scripps connection to the metropolitan-military complex. As "Scripps becomes more and more essential to our underseas warfare picture, the stronger our argument for the sub piers here will become."[14]

As so often in the past, Congressman Wilson could find a strategic theory to match the political and economic ambitions of the metropolitan area. "The present uneasy international situation, in my opinion, demands a speeding up of ASW [anti-submarine warfare] training," warned the modern William Kettner. Since the Pacific Fleet "ASW Forces which train in the San Diego area are to be trained with nuclear submarines," the city must have the piers. Otherwise the nuclear subs would be based in Hawaii, and they and the ASW forces would lose training time and "nuclear power core life" sailing to their rendezvous.[15]

With the Navy, the congressmen, the Copley press, the *Independent,* the San Diego Chamber of Commerce and its journal, *San Diego Business,* the American Legion, the Military Order of the Two World Wars, the mayor, the San Diego Council of the Navy League, certain businesses, and so forth lined up in battle order behind the sub piers; the metropolitan-military complex had collected a formidable political coalition. Moreover, as so often seemed the case, it had attracted little local criticism. Some San Diegans worried that the piers would "conflict with residential areas," "interfere with harbor traffic," or provide atomic pollution, but the Navy and boosters deftly parried each of these half-hearted thrusts. Lest national security was not enough to carry the point, the *Union* added, "It's later than we think. Seattle and other West Coast cities are anxious to replace San Diego as the hub of Pacific naval activity." In fact, the ever pesky San Franciscans already had an atomic submarine pier.[16]

Congress literally torpedoed the sub base out of the 1960 budget but the San Diegans were not discouraged. "This is where the fine arts of public relations and political maneuvers will come into play," predicted the *Independent,* "with each national region putting forth its case in the strongest possible terms." That of San Diego must have been strong, for by July 1960, the city had won. Acknowledging the political nature of the process, the assistant chief of naval operations thanked Wilson: "Without your fine help, I am sure we would have been in trouble." By 1963, Wilson and San Diego were well on the way to yet another sub pier. Hopefully, San Diego could parlay these assets into a nuclear sub building capacity, and the city might "become the West Coast equivalent to New London, Conn." So the "fine arts of public relations and political maneuver" continued as the period came to an end.[17]

As early as 1957, the Chamber of Commerce made the acquisition of nuclear carrier wharves a high priority. The city and the Navy were soon hard at work trying to find ways to squeeze even bigger ships into an already crowded military harbor. As in the case of nuclear submarines, the carriers would add to the guaranteed annual income that the Navy provided, and the carrier dock would assure the guarantee. Climate alone would not ensure the acquisition of the carriers, so the city must revamp its harbor, explained Ralph J. Phillips of the San Diego Chamber's Military Affairs Department (ironically abbreviated by the Chamber to MAD). Nor did the martial metropolis fail to meet these needs. It did, and in late October 1958, Congress approved a $7,000,000 appropriation to begin the carrier docks; a dredging appropriation followed in 1960. As usual, the Darwinian competition spurred the city on, in this case the fear of Long Beach's acquiring the carriers. With the dredging and docks, that obscenity would not occur.[18]

Equally unthinkable scenarios threatened the city's shipbuilding industry. San Diego was not a great shipbuilding center after World War II, but it did aspire to a bit more of this industry. Congressman Wilson helped spearhead these efforts, often in regional coalitions with other California cities. In 1953 the Martinolich Shipbuilding Company of San Diego thanked Wilson for the "contract for two A M Minesweeping Vessels," and in 1959 he received credit for the largest contract that the National Steel and Shipbuilding Company (NASSCO) firm had ever received. The shipbuilding interest soon turned their attention to bigger game in the form of a nuclear powered supercarrier of the *Forrestal* class. Coast cities and builders stood together in this battle, and by 1955 Wilson had made good headway with the current Secretary of the Navy. By 1959 San Diego shipbuilders had had enough success to lure the Convair firm into creating a hydrodynamics department to bid on ship contracts.[19]

Besides the struggle for individual contracts, San Diego and its coast allies had to beat off the advances of other regional alliances. In order to develop a West Coast shipbuilding industry that would be available for defense, Congress in 1936 granted the area a 6 percent advantage in bidding upon government contracts. Arguing that the geographic and cost factors that had justified the 6 percent differential had disappeared, a southern and eastern congressional coalition tried to repeal the law in 1960. Their attempt created a West Coast counter-alliance that included chambers of commerce, unions, and companies in each of the three leading California metropolitan areas.[20] Congressman Wilson prevented this law from coming to a vote, but as the period ended in 1961, the easterners and southerners were up to the same tricks.[21]

West Coast cities also competed for home porting the Navy's ships; and since San Diego had so many, it was the goal of its neighbors to acquire a few. Long Beach did so when San Diego was distracted and fat from the Korean War. "The Great Long Beach Ship Raid" did not permanently harm the Border City, but it did prompt it to take stock of its position and to improve its relations with the Navy. Illustrative of the close ties between civilian and military society, the city chose retired Admiral Ray Tarbuck to report on its relationship with the Navy. In doing so, Tarbuck gave one of the frankest admissions on record of the political nature of much of the Navy's business. The admiral explained that ships had home ports, operating bases, and home yards, or three basic ports per ship. In addition, no harbor except New York's could hold the entire fleet at once, so it had to be divided up between many cities. "Political and economic pressures have influenced the designation of home ports and yards in the past," explained the officer. "They have even affected the strategic location of warships awaiting battle. In lean years, Navy yards have been closed or reopened on a political basis, usually with the change of administration or congressman."

On the other hand, noted Tarbuck, "from a local point of view there are times when an increase in naval activity at a port may look highly political, while it is the result of an impartial command decision," In that case, "before press release, it is not unusual to notify the local congressman in advance, so he might collect from his constituents any reflected glory." Regardless of party, "his amity is always welcome when the next naval appropriation bill comes up for approval." Tarbuck soothed San Diego's fears by assuring them that Long Beach could never capture the major portion of the Navy and urged cooperation. "By playing ball with them, and presenting a united front for Southern California, the San Diego–Long Beach position is strengthened with a view to keeping what we have in the south and acquiring more."[22]

Nonetheless, the Long Beach threat recurred later in the decade when it became known that the commandant of the Eleventh Naval District lived in inadequate quarters on North Island, where his ears were continually jarred by the takeoff and landing of jets. Fearing that his discontent might lead to pressure to remove the headquarters to Long Beach, where the commander's ears would not take such a beating, the city builders were soon moving to provide him with a better home. Surely this must be one of the most unique exercises in "public housing" on record in American cities.[23]

Dredging, master planning, and port government reorganization were not unique, however, and these flowed just as inevitably from competition among cities as did the drive for shipbuilding contracts, the procurement of bases, or the home porting of ships. The vaunted Harbor of the Sun required much dredging to enable it to accommodate the increasingly larger ships of the modern Navy. The necessity of digging deeply enough to berth supercarriers led the city into another fight for dredging appropriations from Congress. The city recognized this need in the early fifties, but since congressional approval required action against other cities competing for the same funds, the appropriation was delayed until 1960, when the national legislature provided $5,000,000 to do the work. The chairman of the chamber's military affairs committee highlighted the welfare-warfare connection. "One supercarrier will materially benefit the San Diego economy by providing a multimillion dollar payroll," and it would benefit the West Coast and American defense posture as well. Dredging would also help the city's tourist industry by depositing soil which could be used to create new harborfront land for tourist attractions and to diversify the city's economy, both perennial local ambitions. Master planning grew apace. The Chamber of Commerce revived its Metropolitan Planning Committee, apparently at the insistence of its Harbor Committee; not surprisingly it was headed by another retired admiral. In 1963, "a plan of development was created."[24]

The establishment of a unified port authority came harder, but that too claimed major San Diego efforts from the Tarbuck Report onward. County representatives introduced legislation to create a unified harbor authority in 1955, but it was not passed and ratified in a referendum by voters until 1962. Although the often magisterial Richard Pourade's *History of San Diego* makes no mention of the Navy as a critical stimulus to the creation of the port district, it is clear, as Bob Wilson's correspondence proves, that the Navy was indeed the principal reason for the creation of this new governmental entity. Both the city and the Navy needed a plan, but the Navy needed it worse.

By 1961, then, San Diego had literally provided a very comfortable berth for the Navy in its magnificent bay. Overall investment totals are not available, but the Navy supplied a startling summary of its growth and development in San Diego from 1953 to 1958. The Navy had sunk $144 million into permanent investments at the various installations; it spent a cool $1.3 billion annually in Southern California; and it pumped in almost $259 million per annum in payrolls, "exclusive of pay to forces afloat, retirement benefits, and family allotments." It also attracted per month some 7000 visitors to see servicemen stationed or inducted there. Yet even these mind-boggling figures greatly underestimate the Navy's full impact on the urban community. In 1957, the district commandant estimated that the Navy added 215,000 people to San Diego County, which equaled more than 20 percent of the county's population and 37 percent of the city's population. Nor did these figures count the large and growing military retirees' colony. Put another way, the 215,000 amounted to more people than lived in the contemporary Las Vegas metropolitan area; it was more than the combined total of all the California counties of 20,000 persons and under; and it was very close to the median size of all American standard metropolitan areas.

The Navy also helped to provide ordinary city services such as health care, police in the form of the shore patrol, and water; it subsidized urban purchasing power through the service exchanges and surplus disposal policies and entertained the city on many occasions. In what is perhaps one of the most redundant recorded suggestions in American History, the manager of the chamber's Military Affairs Department summed up the Navy's influence in his city in 1958: "When we take stock of assets providing impetus to our upward spiral which has made San Diego the fastest growing major city in the nation, we should not overlook the importance of the armed services."[25]

Nor did the services overlook the influence of the city on their own "upward spiral," which made defense the fastest growing industry in the United States. Although historians have tended to emphasize the overweening importance of the nation-state on twentieth-century American life and especially on urban history, the reverse has also been true. The national government owes much to the backing it has received from cities. The notion that cities are simply the victims or the beneficiaries of the actions of larger entities such as class, demography, migration, international economics, the state, or central governments is not tenable. Certainly the powerful military establishments recognized the critical importance of their own urban constituencies. After thanking Congressman Wilson for the *Congressional Record* speech "stressing the importance of seapower and emphasizing the essentiality of the carrier forces and Marine Corps," Chief of Naval Operations Arleigh

Burke went on to state that "your outstanding ability to present the case for sea-power to Congress is invaluable to our National Security, and most gratifying to the whole of the Naval Establishment." It was also obviously the quid pro quo for all of the favors that service had bestowed on the ambitious Border City.[26]

Wilson aided the air arm of the country just as consistently and efficiently, and that too did not go without notice. If anything, the procurement practices of the Air Force and its contractors were even more political than those of the Navy. Both the little people who manned the Convair, Ryan, Rohr, and Solar factories and clung desperately to their houses, jobs, and hopes through the usual feast or famine of defense contracting and the corporate executives and scientists for whom the feasts were greater and the famines shorter recognized the political nature of the business in which they labored. Complaining to Wilson of the "substitutions" made in Convair's Wizard anti-missile program, J. W. Bond, Jr., Chief of Physics for the Convair Division of General Dynamics, protested that "I believe the important point to be made is the need to remove political considerations from defense contracts."

Nor was politics confined to the minor details of modifying anti-missile systems. Less than two months before Bond's letter, one of his bosses, W. H. Patterson, assistant to the division manager of Convair-Astronautics, had also written to "Dear Bob." Far from disavowing politics in the defense industry, this one enclosed a two-page draft of a speech on defense matters written by Convair, to be delivered by President Eisenhower. Bill Patterson sent another copy to Vice President Richard Nixon. Although the proposed draft spoke of the need for a military force balanced among the Army, Air Force, and Navy and genuflected to the importance of truth, foreign aid, and a strong economy in the struggle against Communism, most of the speech dealt with rockets, *Polaris* missiles, intermediate-range ballistic missiles, and intercontinental ballistic missiles. The talk called for greater defense spending for such hardware in 1959 and, if necessary, higher taxes in order to pay for them. "This as you well know is expensive and will require an even greater sacrifice by all of us in the future," intoned the Convair executive, hopefully speaking through the President. "I feel that it is you, the American public, who must know and be kept advised of this state of affairs." Of course, in outlining "this state of affairs," Bill did not refer to the fact that Convair manufactured most of those products which would "require an even greater sacrifice by all of us in the future." [27]

Wilson acknowledged the same overriding importance of influence in thanking Herb Kunzel, president of Solar Aircraft, and his "executive team" for "your very generous assistance" during his campaign for re-election in 1958. "It is support such as this which certainly will make me work even harder to bring more jobs and contracts to San Diego." And when those jobs did not roll in, his constituents did not hesitate to remind the congressman of the political process. Johnnie M. May of the final assembly section of one of the San Diego Convair plants and twenty-eight colleagues wrote Wilson in late 1961 to inform him that they supported the American government, paid taxes, had fought for the country, and would again. "We are prowd [sic] of our company," said May, but he wondered why "every firm except the one we work for is getting contracts from the government." He went on to say that "we are like a bunch of rats on a sinking ship, we don't know wheather [sic] to jump off and swim for shore, or stay with it and sink to the bottom." The intent of their letter was to gain "us equality."[28]

Wilson responded that Convair had received a tremendous amount of government patronage over the years, which was very true; but unfortunately, that truth did not exempt the representative from both popular and union criticism. The congressman had succeeded very well in mobilizing the resources of the nation-state on behalf of urban development, and as the International Association of Machinists let him know, he must do at least that well in the future.[29]

He and San Diego both did well in the era of jets and missiles. The government built the F-102 fighter there. This plane eventually evolved into the F-106, which the company continued to manufacture until the Kennedy administration. By that point, it had become one of the largest projects Convair had ever undertaken. Nonetheless, with changing technology, even big contracts were vulnerable, and eventually the Department of Defense decided to stop building the F-106 fighter in 1961, and replace it with anti-ballistic missiles. With the Democrats in full cry about missile and bomber gaps in the late fifties, however, it was no easy time to cancel a major contract held by one of the nation's premier defense cities. Congressman Wilson knew that his town would get new contracts to replace the F-106, but he feared a three-year gap before the old contracts played out and the new began. So Wilson, too, joined the chorus of protest over the vulnerability of the United States in order to prolong and perhaps modify the F-106 while waiting for the new business to come on line.[30]

Modification came first. Wilson argued to the government that the F-106 could be modified to be used as a trainer for the B-70 bomber or to serve as a tactical fighter. The first ploy failed because the Kennedy administration subsequently scrubbed that plane. In effect, Wilson had tried to piggyback one obsolescent technology onto another one. He had more luck with the tactical fighter, eventually persuading the government to buy thirty-five more F-106s for conversion. Beyond that, the Congressman continually warned of the unemployment that cancellation would create, of the threat of the Russian manned bomber, which made the F-106 still relevant, and of the even greater menace of Castro's Cuba within easy flying distance of the nation's southern shore. The congressman went so far as to try to help the fighter by attacking the newer technology, the Bomarc missile, manufactured by Boeing.

The government eventually scrubbed the Bomarc, but that action did not save the F-106. However, Wilson did argue forcefully enough to get over $100 million put into the Eisenhower budget of 1961 to build more fighters; but the incoming Kennedy administration, after a long and agonizing review, declined to spend the money. Although his constituents, especially the International Association of Machinists (IAM), fumed over the decision, Wilson felt that San Diego had done very well under Eisenhower and could look forward to similar success under the Democrats. He seemed to know whereof he spoke. In early 1962, just as the F-106 ran out, the government invited Boeing and Convair to make studies of a new fighter, the even more star-crossed TFX. When Eisenhower came to office, 35,000 San Diegans labored in defense industries; by 1961, 110,000 did. And even if the F-106 disappeared, defense spending in the Port of the Palms had a certain continuity—as the contractors phased out one system, they phased in another.

The Atlas missile overlapped the obsolete technologies very effectively. The immediate origins of that dreadnought weapon go back to early post-World War II days and ultimately to the success of San Diego in luring the then Consolidated Aircraft Corporation to its shores. In effect, Convair won the contract for American's first intercontinental missile, and San Diego won the firm that captured the contract.[32] Interestingly enough, although San Diegans claimed the absolute necessity of building and keeping the Atlas, some well-informed scientists did not even think it should have been built. According to Herbert York, Eisenhower's science advisor and onetime director of the Livermore weapons laboratory, the United States built about twice as many missile systems as it needed to defend itself. Ultimately the country developed six different systems, whereas York thought it required only three. Among others, it did not need the Atlas, a liquid-fueled missile designed to fill a developmental gap until the more manageable solid-fueled weapons came on line. The rocket had other enemies. According to special assistant for science and technology George Kistiakowsky, the Ballistic Missile Division of the Air Force was one of them. However, both aide Bryce Harlow and Vice President Richard Nixon favored them.[33]

Just after World War II, the government gave Convair a contract to develop an American version of the German V-2 rocket, and the firm labored on this project until funding ran out in 1948. However, Convair kept together its team of scientists and was rewarded for its loyalty when the Korean War revived the contract. So did the invention of the hydrogen bomb, which provided a much lighter but more powerful weapon. In 1953, Convair recommended that the government initiate a crash program to build missiles, and they won the contract to do so. Several other defense giants shared the contract with Convair, but that firm held 22 percent of the prime contracts and let out 30 percent to subcontractors.

Although local boosters talked of this weapon as a counter to the Soviets, city boosting played a large role too. San Diego created the Kearny Mesa Industrial Park to house just this kind of project. Convair opened their Atlas plant there in mid-1958 on land sold to them by the City of San Diego. Beginning with a startup force of 300, the Atlas project soon employed over 14,000, including 6,000 on Kearny Mesa. From the outset, chamber officials believed that the Atlas would move beyond its purely military application to a more civilian one of boosting vehicles into space. Nor did city builders neglect the wider urban payload of the missile. It would be a large construction job, attract skilled labor, lure smaller industries to the city, and "guarantee us leadership in growth for the next few years," argued the chamber president.[34]

Atlas did just that, as San Diego enjoyed record industrial growth in both 1956 and 1957. Even before the Kearny plant opened in July 1958, San Diegans looked ahead to further windfalls from the weapon. A number of San Diegans suggested the necessity of a new West Coast site to test the dreadnought, a suggestion that the Navy snapped up. By mid-1958 the new Navy testing site, near Lompoc, was nearing completion, thus both eliminating the necessity of testing the weapons on the East Coast and giving California another asset. None of the competing cities acquired the facility, but they all benefitted by its proximity. Moreover, Convair alone received a $48 million contract to help ready the station. Eventually the Atlas became one of the country's ICBMs and also propelled the manned *Mercury* capsule into space, thus fulfilling the booster promise of beating swords into ploughshares and gaining considerable publicity for their city in the bargain.[35]

Perhaps it was too much publicity. By the end of the decade several converging pressures greatly increased the competition for military contracts. Two of these pressures were the defense contracting success of California and the losses of competing regions, especially New York State (that is, suburban Long Island). In addition, changing technology made relatively new weapons obsolete, and budget pressures by the President jeopardized them further. This loss triggered a free-for-all between the boosters of the Atlas and those of the Titan, built by Martin of Baltimore but manufactured in Denver with engines constructed in the Los Angeles area. Since the government did not need both missiles and both would soon be replaced by the solid-fueled Minuteman, neither felt secure and each attacked the other. Wilson went on the assault against the Titan as early as 1959 and Convair moved to increase the range of their weapon from 5000 to 9000 miles, while increasing its warhead capacity.

This effort did not beat out the Titan, and the 1959 ratio of thirteen Atlases to fourteen Titans smacked of a political compromise. So each side nullified the other, but both gained, since original projections for the missiles ranged from only six to eight squadrons. The Atlas also beat out the competing Vega rocket for the chore of boosting space vehicles when the government cancelled the Vega. In fact, military rockets boosted most of the original vehicles into space. Eventually, Secretary of Defense Robert McNamara would rule against the Atlas in the mid-1960s; but even before then, the principle of compensation seemed to be operating, as Convair was one of four defense conglomerates asked to bid on the *Saturn II* project and already in 1961 had a foothold in the *Saturn I* program.[36]

Simultaneously with the Atlas-Titan battle, a disgruntled New York State delegation, led by senators Jacob Javits and Kenneth Keating, miffed at the loss of that state's pre-eminence in the war business, mobilized to reclaim its lost contracts from the Golden State. The New Yorkers charged that the close cooperation between California government and industrial leaders had resulted in that state's lead. California countered that its excellence in the martial arts had given it the advantage. Both these explanations were correct, but a third is important too. Douglas, Consolidated, and Lockheed, the core of the California weapons industry, were either lured to the Golden State in the twenties and thirties or persuaded to stay there by city boosters. Technical skill may explain how they prospered in the munitions business, but city boosting explains why Urban California profited so inordinately from them. The California share of the industry had risen from 13.6 percent during the Korean War to 21.4 percent, while that of the Empire State had fallen from 15.3 percent to 11.6 percent. This new battle was heating up just as the period ended in 1961, and its issue would await a later time.[37]

The period did witness the conclusion of the nuclear aircraft (ANP) episode. This time San Diego lost, but not before it had profited from the affair. The ANP was an attempt to mate two new technologies, nuclear and jet, which for a time seemed a promising venture. In fact, for a while, San Diegans were interested in powering the Atlas with nuclear propulsion, and Convair actually secured a contract to work on a space platform powered by controlled (we should hope) nuclear explosions. However, most of the city's political and economic clout went into the ANP. From the beginning, insoluble technical problems plagued what Herbert York called the "elusive nuclear airplane," not the least of which was how to shield the pilot and what to do if the plane crashed, especially in a residential neighborhood. Since San Diegans were already up in arms about the passage of North Island jets over Point Loma, one can only imagine their reaction to the crash of a nuclear-laden plane amongst their palm trees and bungalows. Fortunately for them, the contractors never solved the technical problems. Yet, despite the obviously poor chances of the ANP, political and economic influences kept it alive. On one occasion, Robert Wilson himself beat back the government's attempt to freeze funds for the Airplane, Nuclear Power; and among politicians like Wilson, the AEC, the Department of Defense, and the JCAE, they kept alive this ill-fated technology from 1948 to 1961, when the Kennedy administration accepted the Eisenhower recommendation to scale down the project to minimal research funding.[38]

However, the contractors and their competing cities, Convair and San Diego among them, must have taken some consolation from the one-billion-dollar-plus expenditure that the government literally sank into the ANP. Even in defeat, Convair's success illustrates its overall impact upon the Port of the Palms. In 1959, at the end of the period, Convair paid out $270,918,016 in wages to 47,150 area employees. As usual, one of the foot soldiers in the metropolitan-military host summed up this impact much more eloquently than any statistics could have. "I have watched San Diego grow from a sleepy semi-military, semi-retired peoples' town to a modern industrial city," wrote W. W. Whittier. During those years, "no single business or activity has contributed so dramatically except the navy to our city's growth or its world-wide recognition as a center of industrial might," a role which demanded a "recognition of the value of the company to the city, the United States and the free world."[39]

The elaboration of a more personal kind of welfare proceeded apace. As might be expected, Bob Wilson prided himself on being a conservative in politics, a man who owed nothing to unions. Nonetheless, they owed something to him, and so did other working people in San Diego's defense industries. Not only did he and other city boosters consistently fight to increase the number of jobs in the city, they struggled to prevent layoffs, to secure better services for employees, to raise military pay, to enhance service fringe benefits, and generally to secure decent working conditions for employees of the metropolitan-military complex.

Reductions in force (RIFs), especially at the 2000-plus Repair Facility, a key building block in the naval oligopoly of San Diego, drew the instant attention of the city boosters. These episodes illustrate well the conflict between welfare and warfare. When the Navy had to cut back, it cited efficiency, budgetary, and military reasons for its reductions. The urban civilians countered this rationale in welfare language: they had kids in school, pregnant wives, house payments, elderly parents, and so forth, and could not afford to be laid off. However, the Navy, perhaps quixotically, insisted on operating on an efficient military basis, and that insistence generated conflict. With what must be considered egregious timing, that service announced a big cut at the repair facility during the 1956 election campaign, a decision that local politics promptly forced them to rescind. They tried again in 1957 and once more were forced to scale back their cuts, but doggedly persisted into 1962 with another layoff, this time in the form of a reorganization.

As usual, ideology did not complicate the city's attempt to transform further warfare into welfare. Despite his own distaste for unions, Wilson worked with the North Island Association, the International Association of Machinists, and the American Federation of Government Employees, just as he did with the conservative city booster press, to avert RIFs. The sometimes tearful thanks he received from these people illustrate both his success and his predicament. Whatever he called himself, the conservative, anti-union booster often functioned as a labor congressman.[40]

That necessity flew in the face of what the city considered the better strategy for gaining contracts.

> Today a considerable effort is being made in Washington by many states hard hit by unemployment to have defense contracts awarded on a formula of geographic distribution with emphasis on distressed areas. San Diego is not in a position to outcompete these other areas for these so-called hard luck contracts. As a result, the whole California delegation in the Congress has continually stressed the need that contracts be let on the well established competitive basis practiced heretofore.

Thus, in spite of his many welfare activities, Wilson and his booster allies had to uphold publicly the larger good of competitive bidding and military qualitative excellence.

Fortunately for the Harbor of the Sun, one could achieve other welfare gains in some realms while seeming to serve the national interest. Military pay, retirement benefits, job classifications, and fringe benefits opened an area for welfare efforts which could be justified on grounds of military efficiency, service morale, and fair play to the nation's defenders. As usual, the boosters could count on the cooperation of various San Diego pressure groups. The 8000-member North Island Association, the Admiral Kidd Club, the American Legion, the *San Diego Bulletin,* the Navy Civilian Administrators Association, the Fleet Reserve Association, the IAM, and the Employees Association of the Naval Repair Facility could be counted upon for both support and pressure on bread-and-butter military matters. So could even civilian-seeming groups like the San Diego Chapter of the American Institute of Industrial Engineers. Of the sixteen officers, directors, committee chairmen, and members of the board of governors of that organization, fifteen worked for Rohr, Ryan, Convair, Narmco, Solar, and the Naval Air Station. Nor did this list of pressure groups come close to exhausting the reserve of political muscle in the city. Their activities would have gladdened the heart of any New York City liberal; pay raises, retirement benefits, job classifications, equalization of benefits for active and retired personnel, travel allowances for military families, post commissary activities, and even the decrepit state of the North Island cafeteria claimed the attention of the martial metropolis. So did housing, since a shortage could lead to a turnover of the work force that might jeopardize contracts. Traditional welfare was perhaps not the booster's favorite issue, but they took it very seriously where it impacted on their metropolitan-military constituency.[41]

City builders were much more enthusiastic about the realm of education. In the late fifties, they put together one of the classic metropolitan-military campaigns on behalf of higher education. Southern California urban boosters had long believed that the California Institute of Technology in Pasadena was one of the key elements in the success of Los Angeles's defense industries. Cal Tech had lured new firms to the area, provided scientific advice, created new defense businesses, and generally made itself useful to the martial metropolis. It now became the model for a comparable institution in the Border City. The national shortage of trained scientists provided the ostensible reason for the creation of a new branch of the University of California, but the real reason lay much closer at hand. Convair and the other military businesses suffered from a shortage of trained scientists, one aggravated by their Atlas boom. They felt that their own businesses would be better served by the products of a new, world-class university, and their current scientists would have a place to upgrade their skills and develop their interests.

Of course, the city builders also knew that such a center of learning would benefit the entire martial metropolis. As Robert Biron, sometime vice president of Convair and later vice president of the new University of California at San Diego, predicted, that place would ultimately have the same "dollar impact" on San Diego as Convair itself. And it was just the right kind of dollar impact. Local leaders believed that research and development and education were largely recession-proof businesses that would provide the city an entrée into the age of automation; would spin off innumerable new firms; and would be a clean industry (like the Navy) that would not throttle the city's flora.[42]

Exactly when the plans for the University of California at San Diego originated is not certain, but this idea surfaced in early 1955. It would seem to have had quadrupartite origins with the city of San Diego, the San Diego Chamber of Commerce, Board Chairman John Jay Hopkins of General Dynamics, and assemblyman Sheridan Hegland. They campaigned, along with much of the city's elite, to get the California Board of Regents to accept the idea, which they did in mid-1956. However, the university at that point had neither the cash to initiate another branch nor the land to put it on. Yet they got both, and, incidentally, got the university started, in a typical San Diego fashion.

First, Hopkins offered to create a new research laboratory, a new branch of General Dynamics, called General Atomic, right in the San Diego area. However, he stressed the absolute necessity of a major university close by to provide an appropriate resource for his nuclear scientists. He also needed land, and here the ever shrewd and generous city government of San Diego chipped in about 300 acres. That gift satisfied a part of Hopkins's requirements; and when the regents agreed to create the university, the city donated another 450 to 500 acres next to the La Jolla campus for the new school. This donation got the university over one hurdle, and Hopkins helped with the next. His business empire gave the university $1,000,000 to begin operations; and by 1965, 2,258 students were in residence. One does not have to be a land economist to understand the value of these gifts, especially those of the city. Approximately 800 acres of prime real estate in the city's most prestigious suburb of La Jolla represented a large sum at the time and an even greater value for the future. This public contribution was decisive, as was its gift of land to General Atomic.[43]

Nor should we entertain any illusions that this campus was designed to serve the general educational needs of the community. San Diego State University already carried out that mission well, and UCSD did not intend to be burdened down with a lot of undergraduates trying to find themselves. Rather it was to be an "atomic age graduate school," as the *Evening Tribune* termed it, one designed for "ultrasonic, intercontinental, fissionable, fusionable 1956," in the words of the other Copley paper. Both President Robert Gordon Sproul of the California system and John Jay Hopkins recognized that the new university would create a tight interface between itself and industry and both stressed its national defense relevance. Roger Revelle, director of Scripps Institute, which served as the nucleus of the new school, argued that Americans must either "learn mathematics or learn Russian," thus giving the school a more general national defense twist. However, the students could learn mathematics at any number of California places. The reason they would learn it at San Diego instead of Chico or Oroville or Blythe or Lone Pine had more to do with corporate and urban ambition. "San Diego can give thanks to the satisfaction of moving forward with the assurance of a stability unequaled by most American cities," argued Mayor Charles Dail. "This is a model of progress, exceeded only by our continued efforts to keep San Diego at the top." Even an outsider like President Sproul understood that the "expansion of the Scripps campus would be a powerful stimulant to the already vigorous growth of this dynamic community." President Love of San Diego State put the matter in Turnerian terms when he noted that, since the nation had reached its territorial limits, the new frontiers of the future were "upward, not outward." Perhaps that was so, but in a way the frontier in question was not so new after all. It may have been stretching more upward than outward, but it was still an urban frontier being described: the same as the one Richard Wade identified many years ago in writing about the Ohio and Mississippi river valley cities.[44]

Similarly urban was the sister institution to UCSD, the new John Jay Hopkins Laboratory of General Atomics. The idea for this lab originated with John Jay Hopkins rather than with the city, but the latter quickly grasped it when it became available. Hopkins was both a businessman and an idealist. Although his corporation manufactured many of the most deadly weapons of the Cold War, he did not believe in their ultimate effectiveness. Hopkins thought that Communism fed upon the uneven development in the world between have and have-not nations and that only the solution of the problems of the underdeveloped world could secure peace. As he put it, only an ethical balance of power, not a balance based on weaponry, would hold. Energy seemed the key to Third World development, and, though fusion and solar power might ultimately help, only atomic power would be available in the near future. So Hopkins became an evangelist for this form of energy, and his atomic laboratory represented a way to unlock the secrets of nuclear science for a developing world.

Hopkins hoped for a world development agency to finance the purchase of nuclear reactors for the have-not nations which would make them prosperous and therefore neither aggressive nor susceptible to Communism. Of course, such an institution would also subsidize the purchase of the goods that his company produced; nonetheless, he had a rather enlightened view of the Cold War. San Diego, however, viewed the laboratory as another means to further uneven development between itself and American places such as Montana and Utah. As George W. Sears of the Chamber put it, the "establishment of the laboratory can well mean that San Diego's future industry will be developed along the most up to date and most scientific lines, assuring the community a position of world leadership in the field of scientific and technological development."

Needless to say, the city went after General Atomic with the usual magnificent gift of precious urban land, about 300 acres of it, nearly half a square mile. In explaining the choice of San Diego, Hopkins stressed that a "combination of physical features needed for the laboratory, attractive surroundings, climate and the farsightedness of the San Diego community were the principal factors leading to the acceptance by the corporation of the San Diego area." Of course, with the exception of the farsightedness, all of these assets could have been obtained in many spots along the California coast. The laboratory came to San Diego because both the leadership and the masses of the city devoutly wished to have it and because it was a part of a package deal to acquire the university branch. The voters showed their own "farsightedness" when they ratified the magnificent land donation by a margin of six to one, as they had ratified the gift to the university.[45]

There seemed to be a cycle of defense investment in all of the many metropolitan-military endeavors. Perhaps the evolution was not predictable or consistent enough to be termed a model; nevertheless, a clear pattern seemed to exist. Initially, San Diego fought for some martial addition to its stock of contracts, bases, ships, berthing spots, laboratories, universities, amphibious bases, ship repair facilities, missile plants, and landing fields. Having gained them, the city builders sought to enlarge them, edging the naval repair facility ever upward toward the status of a full-fledged Navy yard, expanding the capacity of the Atlas, and so on. If products were at stake, they would seek to sell more of them, often in contravention of government policy, as in the case of the F-106, while at the same time resisting any diminution of their prize. San Diego lost some contracts during the period, but, to my knowledge, they did not lose a single base or installation.

Upon losing a contract, however, they could usually expect compensation or a consolation prize. Bob Wilson explained the process to Republican County Chairman Robert Finch when the latter wrote to Wilson to seek his help in keeping alive the Snark missile upon which 20,000 Los Angeles County jobs supposedly depended. Wilson promised to do everything he could to help, but pointed out the probability of the Snark's demise. "We have a similar crisis approaching in regard to Convair contracts, but so far we in Southern California have been extremely fortunate in obtaining new contracts to replace jobs that become obsolete," consoled the San Diegan.[46]

Wilson spoke correctly on both counts. The Snark did disappear, and Southern California gained many new contracts both to replace it and to solve Convair's "crisis." From 1957 to 1961 the aircraft industry of California lost exactly 95,000 jobs and gained back 94,000 more defense jobs in aerospace, electronics, and missile industries, a loss of a paltry 1,000 positions. At that moment the Los Angeles Chamber of Commerce was trumpeting the decline of California defense industries as if a *real* crisis had overtaken the state.[47]

Obviously, the crisis was imaginary because the principle of compensation had obtained. Further evidence of this can be gleaned from the virtual torrent of

Defense Department contract verifications that flooded Congressman Wilson's desk in the early Kennedy years. Hardly a letter spoke of a dollar amount less than one million, and some reached upwards of $500 million. On October 17, 1962, the DOD explained that it had "obligated" $29 million to Convair to develop test manuals for the Atlas; in July it announced an obligation of $467 million for the manufacture, delivery, and checkout of the Atlas; on May 29, 1962, it noted the obligation of $48 million for the development of the new Navy test site at Vandenberg Air Force Base; and on December 11, 1961, it revealed the obligation of $78 million to General Dynamics under the Centaur program. These impressive totals represent compensation with a vengeance.[48]

Seen over a span of years from 1945 to 1961, San Diego's martial empire strikes the observer as a very coherent one, and it was acquiring a lucid rationale to go with it. In short, San Diego had its own strategic theory to back its economic interests. Although he had plenty of support in the city, Congressman Wilson expressed this theory best. In fact, he had been one of the leading theoreticians for the Republican defense strategy put forth in the 1956 election. The representative was one of the most forceful spokesmen for the Eisenhower defense policies of getting more bang for the buck. However serviceable that idea may have been to a Republican administration, it was more useful still to an urban area whose industrial and commercial base was integrated around certain categories of military spending. Wilson spoke often of defense against the Russians, but the weapons that he advocated were almost always only those which his district manufactured or wielded. Overwhelmingly, he emphasized the importance of sea power and air power and championed a concept of weapons balance: between defense and offense, between fighters and bombers, between manned airplanes and unmanned missiles, between new and older weapons, and so forth.

Here again, however, the coincidence between the interests of his district and its corporations and the weapons advocated was far stronger than the strategic logic that supposedly underlay his advocacy. For example, the Wilson logic of balance argued against phasing out the manned bomber (Convair manufactured the B-58 in Fort Worth) and in favor of a partnership of missiles (Convair built the Atlas in San Diego) and manned bombers. At the same time he favored a balance between Air Force and Navy nuclear weapons, which up to 1961 meant an equilibrium between Polaris and Atlas missiles. He also argued for a solid fighter defense to defend against "total annihilation." Yet the congressman did not favor a new and upscale fighter to protect against the supposedly ever more sophisticated Russian menace; rather, he touted the tried-and-true F-106 made in San Diego. In 1961, the Russians could not field a massive bomber and missiles threat, but they were notoriously fond of and ludicrously oversupplied with tanks and infantry. Yet Representative Wilson found no need to balance these weapons, the principal ones upon which the Soviets relied. By the same token, it made little strategic sense to have a strong Navy, even leaving aside the perennial behemoth carrier issue, to project American power if the United States had inadequate land forces to project.[49]

The most enticing aspect of "balance" was that between new and obsolescent weapons. "Because of lead times, and other technical considerations it is constantly essential that we maintain a family of offensive weapons in various states of their life cycle," explained Wilson. "By the same token, it is equally essential that we have a similar family of defense weapons in the same stages." That kind of technological balance within the U.S. arsenal was at least as well calculated to promote an arms race as to increase security. However, this "balance" was well designed to produce an endless supply of technological windfalls for the metropolitan areas that manufactured these "families" of weapons. As Wilson had explained to Robert Finch, Southern California had always had good success in replacing obsolescent contracts with new ones, a process for which the representative's strategic theory was perfectly fitted.

CHAPTER 10

Getting on Target: Nuclear Weapons, Jet Technology, and the Metropolis

Exactly where did the California struggle come out and how illustrative is the California case of the rest of the country? California is often considered unique among American states. Was its love affair with the metropolitan-military complex another example of this exceptionalism? Or was the Golden State simply ahead of its time, as it so often is, in adopting customs that the rest of the country would embrace a few years later, a pacesetter, as Gerald Nash put it? These questions can best be answered by looking at the continuing importance of urban rivalry and, in so doing, examining the origins of the Sunbelt-Frostbelt controversy. The idea of the Sunbelt emerged rather suddenly onto the American scene. Even an educated American could have grown up, served in the Army, gone to college, and weathered the storms of McCarthyism, Sputnik, the Vietnam War, Watergate, Japanese economic competition, and inflation and still not have heard of the term Sunbelt, much less of the economic and political shifts underlying its popularity. Then suddenly in the 1970s the idea of the Sunbelt was everywhere.

Analysts and pundits never reached a majority explanatory consensus. Politicians blamed the phenomenon on discriminatory federal spending policies which redistributed the wealth of the midwestern, New England, and Middle Atlantic states to the South and West. Economists had a different set of answers, centering on such matters as energy prices, cheap labor, open spaces, truck and highway transportation, changing manufacturing processes, the branch plant movement, interstate migration patterns, cheap land, climatic advantages, and rising farm prices. Commentators on the left stressed the significance of good climates for investment and business, by which they meant weak labor unions and right-to-work laws; others cited western and southern amenities. But most everyone emphasized defense spending.

Besides this agreement on the partial military causation of the Sunbelt phenomenon, commentators on the whole agreed on its timing. The Sunbelt problem had emerged in the early 1970s. These pundits also concurred that political influence had much to do with the shift and that representatives from the South and West had somehow gathered enough of it to help effect an historic regional shift in American cultural patterns. The movement had produced an economic realignment from a developed to an underdeveloped region, or two regions, both of which had long considered themselves to be colonial appendages of the North.[1] Not much seems to be known about the specific circumstances in which this political influence was wielded and over whom. However, it seems to be agreed that it was there in overwhelming amounts, enough to help two American dependencies overcome their northern masters. Until the rise of the Sunbelt, no American region had ever been displaced in the hierarchy of American economic power. The East had been forced eventually to share some of its power with the Midwest, but overall it still held sway until the Second World War. This fact, too, makes the shift to the South and West an historical matter of first importance and so does its military underpinning. If government expenditures have been important in creating the Sunbelt and if military spending has been the key to federal discrimination in favor of that region, then the event is all the more singular. No American region heretofore has been that dependent upon military patronage.

Therefore, the Sunbelt phenomenon, that is, the shift of power and wealth to the South and West, certainly deserves all of the attention it has received since about 1973. Yet the explanations of this power shift leave something to be desired. The historian will instinctively suspect that such a fundamental alteration of the balance of power could not have taken place in such a short time without more warning, indications of decline, or public controversy. Was there no warning of the outbreak of the "second war between the states" before the early seventies? And, more intriguing, how did the underlying process of military redistribution work? What were the times, places, and circumstances of this political coup? Did western areas openly court the military and did eastern areas avoid this connection? Did only the Sunbelt metropolitan areas recognize the immense developmental potential of defense spending? Did eastern centers such as Detroit, Chicago, and Boston fail to note the huge defense contracts generated by the Second World War and again by the Korean conflict? Did the more liberal regions of the country simply shun the development and employment potential of defense spending? Or did the South and West just outmuscle the more populous and wealthy regions of the United States, stretching along the industrial belt from New England to the Mississippi River? Or alternatively, did these latter get outwitted, perhaps because they were caught napping or were distracted into other areas of political gain? If defense spending is a crucial factor in the power shift to the South and West, these are important questions which are not answered satisfactorily in the literature on the Sunbelt. Perhaps an historical perspective can begin to answer some of these queries.[2]

The investigation has already been initiated for the Sunbelt as a whole in a number of books, especially *Sunbelt Cities* and Carl Abbott's *The New Urban America.*[3] In particular, Bradley Rice and Richard Bernard and their collaborators have documented the longstanding interest of western and southern cities in defense spending, as has my own research. As we have seen, from the voyage of Theodore Roosevelt's Great White Fleet in 1907-9 until 1961, these metropolitan regions competed vigorously for a share of the federal defense budget.[4]

So did non-Sunbelt cities, although these efforts are not pilloried in the Sunbelt literature about the maldistribution of military wealth. Representatives of eastern and midwestern cities and states were neither morally above the contest for war riches nor unaware of their importance. They too fought energetically for martial contracts, defended their military bases with commendable enthusiasm, and remained wary of any congressional legislation that might put them at a disadvantage in this struggle. In fact, the East and Midwest were never *unaware* of the need for vigilance in this area or of the potential to be gained from defense spending. As early as 1939, Chicago spokesmen had questioned the equity and strategic necessity of aircraft contract distribution. However, during the war, the East and Midwest fought against industrial decentralization when, in the name of defense, the South and West tried to deconcentrate the industries of the country, supposedly to make them less vulnerable to Nazi attack. In truth, they were more interested in making themselves less susceptible to control from the power centers of the United States. The Frostbelt fought back just as forcefully; indeed, throughout the war the controversy over the urban geographic distribution of military spending continued to rend the fabric of national unity.[5]

Thus, not only did the South and West gain military installations and contracts from at the least the 1930s on, they also engaged in a *sectional* struggle for these assets with the older power centers of the country. It is not certain exactly how far back this competition goes, but it dates at least from 1939.[6] And it continued in some form or other through the 1950s. The conflict was overt, explicit, and bitter; and the contestants even employed many of the same charges and terms that surfaced in the Sunbelt debate of the 1970s and 1980s. The remainder of this chapter will concentrate on some examples of this competition. These case studies will center on industrial dispersion to protect against nuclear or thermonuclear attack and on federal government manpower policies. These are by no means definitive or even relatively complete studies of the controversy, but they do at least uncover some of the circumstances, timing, and origins of the later struggle and perhaps reveal some unexpected participants as well. Just as important, they document the culmination of the Darwinian competition in the Golden State and relate the California struggles amongst cities to those in the remainder of the United States.

As we have seen, industrial decentralization or dispersal became a reality before World War II. The American military concluded that the defense industries were highly centralized in a few vulnerable places, especially those along the coasts. For example, airframe production centered in Seattle, San Diego, and Los Angeles on the West Coast and suburban Long Island and Baltimore on the East Coast. Theoretically, a few enemy strikes could cripple much of this vital defense industry. Pearl Harbor did not lessen this anxiety, but even before that event, Washington began to spread the industry throughout the interior of the United States. Decentralization might reduce the military vulnerability of production centers, lessen manpower shortages, and spread the contracts to heretofore unblessed cities. The coastal builders received large orders in the short run; but once they reached capacity, the government built its new plants at Wichita, Dallas, Fort Worth, St. Louis, Kansas City, and Tulsa, for example. This change did not damage the coastal firms, since they usually built the branch plants in the interior. However, it did detract from the aircraft metropolises and threatened to establish new centers of production that would remain competitive in the postwar years. In the short run, this fear proved groundless. When World War II ended, the government did not have enough money to keep even the parent plants operating, much less the branch plants in places like Tulsa.[7] However, the advent of the Cold War, with its nuclear and thermonuclear weaponry, greatly enhanced the vulnerability of the industry. Once again, the government moved to reduce that threat. This move touched off a seven-year controversy that pitted the urban parts of the South and the West, minus California and Washington, against those of the Midwest and Northeast.

The nuclear age endangered the martial metropolises in two related ways. Such urban areas were, of course, principal military targets in case of the outbreak of war, but they were also prime economic targets if peace continued indefinitely. Of the two dangers, the latter was the most realistic and persistent; yet the two together caused endless concern. For years, non-military cities had enviously watched the defense-related prosperity of the martial metropolises mount and, on occasion, had tried to capture some of it. In 1950 the defense industry was concentrated in California, Washington State, and a corridor of urban industrial areas in the northeastern, Middle Atlantic, and midwestern states. Much of the industry huddled together on or near the coasts of the country, and nearly all of it was concentrated in urban areas. In other words, the industries upon which the United States depended for its defense were much more vulnerable to attack than was the country as a whole.

This defenselessness was not a serious problem in World War II, because Germany possessed no weapons like long-range planes or aircraft carriers that could reach American shores. While the Japanese did have these weapons, their use against transoceanic targets would have been rather difficult. However, the newer, postwar weapons were vastly more menacing. Nuclear weapons and jet technology, whether in planes or missiles, enormously enhanced the exposed military position of these urban defense centers and, in the process, made them simultaneously vulnerable to their urban rivals.

Both nuclear weapons and jet technology were prestigious products of California cities, and the latter certainly knew their destructive potential. In 1946 a group of Los Alamos scientists presented Mayor Fletcher Bowron with a sample of sand fused together by the initial atomic test in New Mexico. Charged as he was with maintaining urban employment and simultaneously protecting the citizens of his city, Mayor Bowron must have found this artifact of the modern world somewhat confusing. So did the federal authorities. If they seriously attempted to secure the country against nuclear and jet technology, it would mean dismantling some of the concentrated Northeast and Pacific Coast military industries and moving them to more protected interior locations. On the other hand, emphasizing the economic side of defense—that is, production—meant even more centralization and therefore heightened military vulnerability.

It did not take the envious cities and regions long to decide on their own choice. They could now argue even more forcefully than they had in the World War II era that decentralization of defense industries was in the national interest. And, as before, they could hope that this dispersal would benefit their own relatively unindustrialized or depressed cities. Urban development and national defense now stood together on behalf of decentralization.[8]

Before civilian Washington could construct guidelines on this dilemma, the Air Force grasped one horn and thereby touched off the battle. In 1948, it began its own decentralization policy. It pressured Boeing into producing the B-36 bomber in the interior at a World War II Wichita plant rather than in the highly exposed Seattle area. Similar demands led to the migration of Chance-Vought from Connecticut to

Dallas, the relocation of Consolidated Aircraft's B-36 production from San Diego to Fort Worth, the construction of General Electric's turbojet engine plant at Kansas City, and the "contemplated move of Lockheed Aircraft from Burbank, California, to Tulsa."[9] These real or threatened blows to the established defense centers forced them to protect themselves.

Seattle led the martial cities in fortifying themselves against the defense policies of their own government. In 1949, Puget Sound interests, including the Chamber of Commerce and city hall, hit on the idea of dispersing military contracts *within metropolitan areas* in order to avoid decentralizing them *between geographic areas.*[10] By spreading out the contracts and installations within metropolitan areas, the martial cities could avoid losing them to other geographic regions, because it would allow the defense centers to claim that they were now less defenseless militarily. In the meantime, the federal government had continued to worry about "defense in depth," or dispersal. Just as its anxiety crested, Washington, D.C., discovered the Seattle plan. The government was so impressed by the Seattle idea that it became the basis for the "national industrial dispersion policy." The administration naturally turned to Puget Sound because of its expertise on the matter and brought to Washington several Seattle boosters to work for the National Security Resources Board, the government agency currently responsible for the dispersal program. Ethan Allen Peyser, Presley Lancaster, Jr., and Jack Gorrie set about writing the federal guidelines for dispersal. Needless to say, these rules guarded Seattle's economic interests more than they protected the congested areas from nuclear attack.[11]

California did not lag far behind the Pacific Northwest in producing its own plans for urban defense in depth. The Los Angeles Metropolitan Area Industrial Dispersion Committee helped industry to find "safe industrial sites within that area."[12] Like Los Angeles, San Francisco contributed another model dispersion plan. Appropriately, it was worked out jointly by the Bay Area Council, "an organization dedicated to the economic interests of the nine counties that open on San Francisco Bay," and the Stanford Research Institute.[13]

Announced on August 10, 1951, the federal guidelines specified that new defense plants or expansions of old ones could not be located within ten miles of "densely populated" or "highly industrialized areas."[14] However, the rules contained many escape clauses, and the federal government did not directly administer them. It influenced them through the power to withhold contracts, allocate materials, and grant tax breaks. Nonetheless, each plant had to be certified by a local dispersion committee, formed for each metropolitan area. Of course, this was a little like letting the fox guard the henhouse.

In the case of Philadelphia, the Chamber of Commerce served as the local dispersion committee; in the case of Chicago, the Industrial Development Committee of the chamber performed the same function. Philadelphia refused even to send a target map to the national government. Not too surprisingly, the urban bastions found this plan congenial, and fifty-two metropolitan areas had formed dispersion committees by the beginning of 1952. The proponents of the plan always insisted that it meant dispersal *within* metropolitan areas rather than a geographic redistribution (or decentralization) of defense monies of *other* sections. Events proved them correct. Of the nearly eight billion dollars' worth of new plant or plant expansion contracts given out in the next six months, most went to the existing defense centers, with only a fraction going elsewhere. Yet even this modest dispersal proved too much for center cities, which resisted the loss of any more industry to their already growing suburbs.[15]

The Korean War tended to reinforce, rather than reduce, the concentration of military production. Dispersal policies were always torn between immediate production goals and long-range defense objectives. Due to the Asian emergency, government officials felt that they must place the immediate mobilization needs of the conflict ahead of the long-range goal of protecting the United States from nuclear attack. In addition, the agencies responsible for dispersal overlapped, lacked authority, and, more important, were short of funding and staff. They were often headed by able men like Arthur Fleming, but lacked most other resources. Therefore, most of the Korean defense work took place in the established industrial martial metropolises. For example, defense plants were allowed to expand into Houston, "the largest petrochemical center in the United States; Nassau County, Long Island, an aircraft target center; and Rochester, one of the three largest producing centers of industrial instruments."

Between the urban insiders who wrote the guidelines, the local dispersion committees which enforced them, and the war emergency, the historic defense centers did not suffer. However, when the defense administrators stated that the metropolitan-military complexes fared well in the struggle for contracts, they were only half correct. They were right quantitatively and wrong qualitatively. The campaign for decentralization, launched by Chicago before the Second World War and revived by the Air Force after it, was steadily bearing fruit. Some of this agitation now began to appear in the thickets of the Pentagon and congressional politics.[16]

As in the Second World War, areas that did not share fully in the military bonanza resented the fact. These places had suffered a loss of population in the war and did not want to repeat the experience during the Korean struggle. Their bitterness and determination not to lose out on this latest defense boom injected an acrid sectional note into the war, one which soon spilled over into Congress. On July 11, 1951, Congressman Albert Rains of Gadsden, Alabama, offered an amendment to the Defense Production Act of 1950, under which the government carried on the struggle. The amendment would have strengthened the authority of the President to locate *new* defense plants so as to aid in minimizing unemployment and to take account of the new security threat from the skies by dispersing defense production geographically. Rains took his cue from the Truman guidelines and from numerous critics who favored extreme dispersal.

The southern and western legislators in Rains' coalition reasoned that if a little dispersal was good, a lot of dispersal was better. After all, the Air Force had already initiated its own dispersal program. And it had further assured the country that, in case of attack, seven of ten enemy planes would reach their American targets and that each atomic bomb would produce a crater three miles across. Not unreasonably, spokesmen from the South and West argued that nothing short of geographic decentralization would shield American defense industries and cities from such a first-strike disaster. However, it would not protect the defense cities from their envious urban competitors, since it would also give southern and western municipalities a larger portion of the defense pie.[17]

Both the rhetoric and the geography of this struggle are reminiscent of the contemporary Sunbelt controversy. Cities in the South and West had developed later than those in other parts of the country and, with the exception of the urban areas of the Pacific Coast, were not heavily industrialized. The have-not cities therefore viewed the new defense industry as a surrogate for the factories that had so far passed them by. The cities of the Northeast, Midwest, and Pacific Coast also viewed the matter largely in economic rather than military terms. "The Federal Government talks through the Office of Defense Mobilization and to other agencies of getting the critical industries out of cities. These industries are high tax producers," noted Socialist Mayor Frank P. Zeidler of Milwaukee in 1956. "If they go, then the tax base of the city is lost, and consequently every urban official fights the dispersal of industry even though it may be important for the defense of the country." In case there were any doubts about the urban nature of this matter, the government published a list of "congested areas" in 1955 that read like a *Who's Who* of big American cities. Thus, despite the protestations about national defense, the congressional debate became one of urban development, that is, urbanization versus de-urbanization. Put familiarly, the argument turned a question of warfare into one of welfare.[18]

The congressional debate broke down on several lines. Generally speaking, less industrialized and urbanized areas opposed heavily industrialized and urbanized ones; the South and West minus California and Washington struggled with the Northeast, Midwest, and Middle Atlantic states; and depressed areas sought the economic means of thriving ones. The have-nots lost the opening round. Southern and western congressmen led but did not stand united against the rival sections, and the amendment lost. Apparently many Southerners and Westerners preferred to see the contracts go to the established centers rather than to interrupt defense production.[19]

In the meantime, upon conclusion of the Rains debate, the President acted. Perhaps to forestall further congressional legislation and to placate what his successor would call the "military-industrial complex," Truman issued his own dispersal policy on August 18, 1951. This directive effectively safeguarded the interests of the defense cities. It also carefully dissociated the administration's own formula from the more radical idea of industrial geographic decentralization found in the Rains Amendment. Truman's plan aimed to find "dispersed sites around such existing industrial centers as Detroit, New York, Pittsburgh, and San Francisco." Nonetheless, this compromise did not really provide for defense in space, and therefore administration concern continued.[20]

The increasing destructiveness and technological sophistication of new weapons heightened this anxiety. Jet planes were proven in the Korean War; the hydrogen bomb was tested by the United States and the Soviet Union in 1952-53 and was perfected thereafter; and intercontinental rocketry was literally just over the horizon by the end of the Asian fighting. These developments forced the administration to confront the dispersal problem anew. While an atomic bomb would create a three-mile-wide urban crater, a hydrogen bomb would produce one ten miles across. These facts made the Truman ten-mile urban limit obsolescent, with every prospect of becoming more obsolete with each advance of the arms race. The experts now considered a thirty-mile interval between plants to be necessary.

Even this figure was undoubtedly a compromise because a hydrogen bomb, in even the most spread-out American metropolis such as Los Angeles, would have created such destructive havoc in the infrastructure—bridges, roads, streets, communications, sewers, waters systems—and amongst the work force that a plant that was missed under the thirty-mile limit rule could well stand idle for want of those other indispensable necessities. Nor did this estimate take into account the casualties among defense subcontractors which could drastically affect production by denying critical parts needed to build weapons. The Eisenhower administration shared these concerns, as did a number of people outside the government, such as those of the *Bulletin of Atomic Scientists* and Fordham University expert Neal P. Hurley. When the Korean truce eliminated the need for heavy production in established defense centers, it set the stage for a reconsideration of dispersal policy.[21]

Administration sources had employed the lure of accelerated tax write-offs for new and expanded defense facilities in dispersed areas since 1950, and they continued this practice thereafter. In addition, Secretary of the Air Force Harold Talbott, civil defense head Val Peterson, and President Dwight Eisenhower publicly advocated the need for greater defense in space. So did Marshall K. Wood, the Chief of Mobilization Planning, and the Otto Nelson Committee, created to assess the state of civil defense, which reported in early 1956. The Nelson Committee went further, advocating some dispersion of civilian industries as well, since these would be vital to the restoration of normal conditions after a thermonuclear attack.

Predictably this campaign caught the attention of vested defense interests, like the Los Angeles Chamber of Commerce, which began a counter-campaign of their own. So did West Coast labor, such as the International Association of Machinists and the Council of Aircraft Unions of the Pacific Coast. As Neal Hurley has written, everyone seemed to agree with the theory of dispersal, but not when it applied to "their own region, city, or industry." Undeterred by this clamor, on January 11, 1956, the Office of Defense Mobilization issued guidelines under Mobilization Order I-19 that accepted the principle of *geographical* as opposed to *metropolitan* dispersal. It went beyond even the thirty-mile limit. Moreover, since government defense contracts were awarded through this office, these policies carried weight. However, even in the opinion of the administrator in charge of the program, as well as civil defense officials, something more was required. This urging was all the encouragement that the South and West needed to mount yet another assault on the "congestion" of the established defense cities.[22]

J. William Fulbright, who later led the fight against the Vietnam War, also captained this attack on the martial metropolises. Unlike his later battle, he was not trying to gain peace, but rather to capture some of the spoils of war. The Arkansas senator and his allies sought to amend the 1950 Defense Production Act by putting Congress on record in favor of geographical dispersal. Supposedly, congressional support would strengthen the hand of the Office of Defense Mobilization in its attempt to implement the January guidelines. The debate that followed resonated the same arguments as the 1951 Rains Amendment struggle.

Fulbright's coalition warned of the destructiveness of the H-bomb, pointed to the greater vulnerability of American urban targets since the opening of the Circle Route over the North Pole, and argued that the United States should not put all its eggs in one basket. "If the taxpayers' money is used why should not the Government insist upon construction of a facility somewhere other than in the target area?" queried the famous budget guardian H. R. Gross of Waterloo, Iowa. "Why not?" Representative Albert Rains agreed. The amendment said to the taxpayers of America "that where we spend your dollars for defense, we must spend it in those places where it will not be subject to atomic attack." "Our enemies are taking every precaution to protect their war plants by dispersal," pointed out William Dawson of Salt Lake City. "'Why should we permit our defense industries to be concentrated in the coastal areas where they are sitting ducks for an atomic attack?"

The senators also minimized the impact of their amendment by specifying that it apply only to new plants and expansions and reminded their opponents that every relevant government department supported the principle of geographical dispersion. However, Senator Carl Mundt of South Dakota got closer to the real point when he reminded the Senate that the process of urbanization had long worked against certain parts of the country.[23]

> California, the East, and other areas of the Nation are heavily populated with the sons and daughters of rural America, who were forced to leave their home states to secure employment in defense industries—a fact which up to now the Department of Defense has pretty well ignored. I repeat, the word is "ignored." The Middle West has been pretty well ignored in the locating of defense fabricating plants. The defense plants are supported by all the taxpayers, not merely the taxpayers of the coastal States which now have a plethora of defense industries.

In the minds of Mundt and the decentralizers, "national defense and progressive development" were what the argument was all about. However, now national defense could be harnessed to the progressive development of their own previously neglected urban areas, instead of California, the Pacific Coast, and the East.[24]

Mundt's opponents knew this fact full well, and they marshalled the same arguments that carried the Congress in 1951. California led the charge, providing fully a fourth of the speakers in the House debate and much of the élan as well. Some twenty of twenty-six opposition debaters represented major metropolitan districts. To a greater degree than in the Senate, the House members put their urban-industrial cards on the table. The proponents of decentralization could afford to take the high ground of national defense, but the opposition came out frankly for the urban-industrial interests they represented.

Geographic dispersal would amount to socialist planning, disrupt the flow of production, and raise defense costs by spreading out producers. Moreover, decentralization would politicize the economic life of the nation and necessitate massive expenditures for infrastructure like streets and utilities in the new defense centers that would have to be built. Despite this general interest rhetoric, these speakers had concerns closer to heart. "The idea of sectionalism is repugnant to me," said future House Speaker John McCormack as he set out to defend the interests of New England. Threatened a Detroiter, "I am not going to vote for anything that will put the great automobile business of Detroit in a goldfish bowl and circumvent their expansion. With decentralization, "your labor will and your management will be forced to move," agreed Carl Hinshaw of Pasadena. The amendment would "result in the denial of defense-production contracts not only to our great industrial firms in Connecticut but throughout New England," agreed Horace Seely-Brown of Connecticut. Edward Boland echoed the same alarm for Greater Springfield, Massachusetts. Albert Cretella of New Haven chimed in that there "is no question that this is a back door attempt to further pirate industries."

Noting that the Defense Department would spend five billion dollars on guided missiles in 1957, Gerald Ford asserted that decentralization would "mean that industrial States, including the State of Michigan, will be precluded from participating in this kind of production for the Armed Forces." Elmer Holland professed to see the decline of Pittsburgh and especially the ruination of its Golden Triangle renewal project in the amendment. Donald Jackson, of the Los Angeles suburb of Pacific Palisades, echoed these sentiments for the aircraft industry of his area. Carl Hinshaw of Pasadena thundered, "[The policy is] an outrage upon the industrial areas of the United States. It would make farm communities out of the industrial areas and industrial areas out of the farm areas." "Dispersal would disrupt the economy of all the large industrial areas in the Nation," agreed Gordon McDonough of Los Angeles. "Moving a plant out of St. Louis to a weed patch somewhere is no solution," echoed Lenoir Sullivan of that city. Senators Thomas Kuchel and William Knowland protested just as hard in the Senate.[25]

Representatives of metropolitan Providence, Los Angeles, and Cleveland brought the opposition arguments into ever clearer sectional and urban focus. "We in Rhode Island have long been suffering from the problems which necessarily attach to a 1 or 2 industry State. We know intimately the burden inflicted by the flight of the textile industry to mills in the South and the movement of the center of the machinery-manufacturing industry to the Middle-West," explained John Fogarty. Decentralization could "deal a death blow to the hopes and aspirations of many of our Rhode Island communities which are so desperately striving to pull themselves up virtually by their own bootstraps to secure a place of economic stability." Chet Holifield of the Los Angeles suburb of Montebello pointed out that "the laborers in these industries live in urban centers. That is where they have lived for some time in connection with our war production."

Finally, Cleveland's Charles Vanik noted that American national defense was designed to protect its urban centers and that dispersal would greatly alter the patterns and process of urbanization in the United States. "We must remember that the national defense of America was designed to protect our industrial cities. We have a tremendous investment in the establishment of jet air bases and in the establishment of NIKE defenses to protect the cities of America," he reminded the House. "If we disperse defense production industries, it means that we are going to have to disperse and weaken national defense installations" and to "*develop new urban areas*" which will require new military and civilian installations." That, of course, was exactly what the sectional coalition of small city, town, and agrarian military-industrial have-nots had in mind. They were, it seems, struggling to get on target.[26]

The geography of the vote vividly revealed its sectional bases. In both houses, the electronics and aircraft states of Washington and California stood with most of New England and the urban industrial belt stretching to the Mississippi River. Sixty-four senators favored the amendment, and nineteen opposed. In the House it won by the narrow margin of 210 to 207. Surprisingly, in the very House where the numerical advantage of the Northeast, Midwest, and Pacific Coast states was strongest, they failed to present a united front. Illinois, Indiana, Ohio, Michigan, Pennsylvania, and New York provided Fulbright's House allies with 29 of 210 votes, nine from Pennsylvania alone. The switch of even two of the yea votes in any of these states would have reversed the outcome. On the other hand, the Frostbelt-Pacific Coast alliance gained hardly a single vote in either house south of Virginia, west of the Mississippi River, and east of the Pacific Coast tier of states. Although this geographic section does not exactly fit all definitions of the Sunbelt, it does approximate much of the shift of national resources to the South and West noticed in the 1970s.[27] Ironically, despite what the Sunbelt is supposed to have done to resuscitate the Republican party, it was the Democrats who made up the bulk of the southern and western voters in these struggles. If we include in the South and West those areas south and west of a line running from Maryland to the Ohio River around Illinois, south of Iowa and then along the western boundaries of that state and Minnesota, the Sunbelt had a senatorial bloc of 60 votes. Fully *90 percent* of these voted for dispersal. This compares with 81 percent of Democrats who voted yes on dispersal, along with 53 percent of the Republicans. In the House of Representatives, the South and West had a total of 183 votes. Of this number *75 percent* voted for dispersal and only 21 percent voted against, most of them from California and Washington. The rest abstained. From an overall partisan standpoint, 60 percent of the Democrats voted for the amendment as did 33 percent of the Republicans, while 33 percent of the Democrats and 60 percent of the Republicans chose opposition. Roughly 7 to 8 percent of both parties abstained. So the vote exemplified more sectional consistency than partisan, but nonetheless the Democrats were much more strongly identified with dispersal and therefore with the fortunes of the Sunbelt, a fact that they perhaps have come to regret.

In its geographic bases, its rhetoric, its sectional overtones, its concentration upon the defense budget, and even its sectional inconsistencies, the struggle was a preview of the better known one of the seventies and eighties. However, in the latter controversy, the urban dimension was usually not stressed. Nonetheless, in both cases it was the welfare of cities that primarily interested the proponents. If a shift of resources to the South and West occurred, it would indeed benefit their cities, which, as Representative Vanik patiently explained, would be built up thereby. And the other cities of the nation would stagnate or even become deurbanized. For all of Ms. Sullivan's anxiety, defense industries do not grow up in weed patches, unless they are on the outskirts of cities. By 1951 and certainly by 1956 Americans had come to see the defense budget as at least as much a matter of urban welfare as of warfare.[28]

But this habit is supposedly an already well-known western and southern behavior pattern. What about the cities of the Northeast and Midwest? Was their struggle against decentralization merely defensive? Or did they too have their own schemes to pirate industry from the South and West? They certainly did, and their free-booting took the form of Defense Manpower Policy No. 4. In fact, this attempt to steal industry had even less of a defense rationale than did the idea of geographic decentralization. The Frostbelt scheme would have concentrated even more defense production in the prime urban target areas in order to relieve unemployment and nourish sick industries.

The principle which underlay Defense Manpower Policy No. 4 dated back at least to the Second World War. During that conflict the government attempted to allocate both its prime and subcontracts so as neither to exacerbate labor shortages in the arsenals of democracy nor to worsen unemployment in cities that had fewer contracts. With the onset of the recession of 1949, the Truman administration reverted to this approach. It tried to channel all government spending into the areas hardest hit by economic troubles.[29] The longstanding problems of the New England textile cities and the problems of the automobile industry created by the Korean War added intensity to this thrust. Due to management problems, higher labor costs, and foreign and southern competition, New England textile mills had lost ground to their rivals. The Korean War added material shortages, especially of steel, which forced a curtailment of automobile production and employment. These influences brought about pressures to mobilize defense monies to alleviate unemployment, revive industries, and aid the growth or maintenance schemes of city builders.

Defenders of these urban vested interests proposed various therapies. For example, Thomas Lane of Massachusetts sought to route federal purchasing to jobless areas and attempted to extend unemployment benefits beyond the normal span of payments. He also tried to get the Secretary of Labor to enforce the Walsh-Healy Public Contracts Act to ward off southern textile competition, to channel defense monies into high unemployment areas, to get the Department of Defense to spend more on textile products and even to stockpile them as it did strategic minerals.[30] As we have seen, Urban California had benefitted from the stockpiling of minerals since the Second World War. Representative John Dingell and Senator Blair Moody, both of Detroit, similarly attempted to increase the amount of federal monies available to pay unemployment benefits in areas negatively impacted by the Korean War.[31] Others put forth different remedies, but for the moment Defense Manpower Policy No. 4 became the favorite military spending panacea.

In the case of Detroit, the Korean War did indeed disrupt automobile production for a time. However, the argument did not have much merit for the textile industry because southern textiles profited from the Asian struggle while New England textile spokesmen claimed to be hurt by it. In any case, most commentators admitted that New England textile problems stemmed primarily from causes other than the war. Moreover, New England already enjoyed large defense spending, though not necessarily in textile towns. Strictly in terms of military spending, New England has long been a part of the Sunbelt.[32]

Nonetheless, New England spokesmen led the fight for DMP No. 4. Their action brought both federal relief and sectional conflict. Fortunately for the urban centers of the Midwest and Northeast, the defense mobilizer in 1952 happened to be Charles Wilson, formerly of General Motors.

In February 1952 he issued in final form DMP No. 4, to the satisfaction of the New England representatives. Under this arrangement, surplus labor areas were informed of the low bid for a certain contract and then its firms were allowed to match that price and secure the award. This procedure brought a chorus of protests that such a procedure was socialistic and violated the sanctity of secret bids. Worst of all, it showed sectional economic favoritism. The outburst apparently had its effect, for the Truman administration subsequently declared certain industries to be unaffected by its February ruling, among them textiles and shoes. New Englanders were furious. Nonetheless, the strategy of channeling defense contracts into areas of high unemployment remained a successful strategy through the Eisenhower administration. As a matter of fact, when the Sunbelt controversy began in the 1970s, DMP No. 4 was still the favored counter-strategy for the Rustbelt cities.

Once again, both the rhetoric and voting of Congress revealed the sectional bases of the struggle. With the exception of California, they were the same ones that agitated the question of geographic decentralization. The debate pitted the cities of the South and West against those of the Northeast and Midwest. This time the positions were reversed, with the Northeast and Midwest trying to shanghai the defense contracts of the South and West. Otherwise, the process and the rhetoric are reminiscent of the recent Sunbelt controversy. "The Civil War is being fought all over again in the field of economics, and the South is gaining victories," Representative Thomas J. Lane of Lawrence, Massachusetts, assured his colleagues in 1952.[33] Seymour E. Harris, chairman of the Committee on the New England Textile Industry, told a congressional hearing, "In view of the much more rapid economic gains in the South, in view of the disproportionate gains in military outlays, new construction, and defense contracts generally in the South, some easing of the pressure on labor and other scarce factors would facilitate the carrying through of war contracts in the South. "Any labor released in textiles [in the South by the working of DMP No. 4] could much more easily find opportunities for work in defense industries in the South than in New England."[34]

Like the recent debate, the former one echoed the charge against the South of unfair competition, especially in regard to wages and unions. Representatives of New England cities and industries reiterated over and over again the charge that the South was in violation of the wage standards of the Walsh-Healy Public Contracts Act. Others said that the peculiar "business climate" of the section—that is, the absence of unions—created unfair competition for the other sections. Like their successors who imply unfairness when defense dollars for each state do not equal their tax proportions, these earlier representatives hammered away that defense expenditures discriminated against New England. William F. Sullivan of the National Association of Cotton Manufacturers even demanded a quota system to ensure fair treatment.[35] And Solomon Barkin of the Textile Workers Union of America went further, proposing that "the procurement policy must be designed to aid civilian industries maintain their full health and status."[36] That union policy was very close to a military Keynesianism. The mayor and an alderman of Lawrence, Massachusetts, followed capital and labor to the stand to reiterate the demand for "equal" treatment.

Boston representative John F. Kennedy made the same point. Kennedy testified in 1952 to a Surplus Manpower Committee hearing that "a substantial number of defense contracts could be channeled to these distressed areas through preferential negotiation as planned under Defense Manpower Policy No. 4." He hinted that sectional pressures had caused the policy to be "suspended."[37] The future President reiterated this belief in an April 1954 *Atlantic Monthly* article entitled "New England and the South: The Struggle for Industry." He went on to sketch a more comprehensive attack on the problem of regional decline and competition. Kennedy tried to avoid the kind of sectional rhetoric that had characterized the DMP No. 4 debate, but he did single out the South for criticism. He argued that low wages, anti-union activities, failure to provide welfare for workers, land grants to factories, and other supposed southern practices undermined rather than strengthened the long-term prosperity of the South. However, he admitted that these policies might produce jobs in the short run.

The representative did not use the word "pirating," but he certainly implied it. The federal government was partly responsible for this situation, Kennedy argued, by its policy of lavishing monies on the South. The Boston Democrat, perhaps in a utopian mood, urged an end to the unfair *artificial advantages* of the South, so that the sections could indulge in a sporting competition for industry, based on their *natural advantages* and their developed skills and resources.[38]

Although Kennedy and other New Englanders eschewed any sectional animosity in their campaign, they certainly stirred up some by their rhetoric. Much of the controversy seemed to be between Massachusetts, especially the city of Lawrence, and North Carolina, with South Carolina and Georgia taking a lively interest as well. When northern representatives stressed the inequity of defense spending, Herbert C. Bonner of Washington, North Carolina, countered with statistics that indicated that the New England states, mostly Massachusetts and Connecticut, had received three times as much money in defense contracts in 1950-51. Massachusetts alone got as much as the five southern states running from North Carolina to Mississippi, and Connecticut gained one and a half times as much.[39] Thurmond Chatham, of Winston-Salem, documented that the National Association of Wool Manufacturers, based in New York City, opposed the distribution of contracts on a negotiated basis to distressed areas. They believed that this suspension of competitive bidding would lead to unemployment in efficient areas, which would lose defense awards to the original unemployment zones. This change would merely shift the distress from one locale to another, costing the taxpayers more and undermining the defense effort.[40]

Nor did Southerners exactly agree to the charges of unfair labor competition. The *Raleigh News and Observer* reminded the New Englanders that southern mill workers were not "a pitiful company of the outrageously exploited," and that despite the continuing wage differential between the sections, southern wages had risen markedly. Moreover, "the New England textile industry which now complains of the competition of the South maintained its profits and kept down its wages for years by importing successive waves of immigrants ready to work for almost any wage at all." The *Observer* and other Southerners maintained that it had developed its own industry rather than pirating it from New England.[41]

Southern representatives rejected the charge of government favoritism for the South and countercharged that DMP No. 4 itself represented sectional discrimination. Throughout the debate, sectional bitterness was both implicit and explicit, sometimes painfully so. Representative Paul Brown of Elbertson, Georgia, argued that the textile problem was industry-wide and not confined just to New England. "Why should one state in New England," he asked, "have a preference in law as against a State in the West or a State in the South?" Brown went on to remind Massachusetts that "We have in the South, it is true, a great many mills, but many of these are running less than 3 days a week".[42] This "defense manpower policy represents an outrageous maneuver of throwing people out of work in one section of the country in order to give jobs to another," thundered Representative Burr P. Harrison of Winchester, Virginia.[43] Of course, he was absolutely correct in this assessment, as had been the case with industrial decentralization advocated earlier by the South and West.

Henderson Lanham of Rome, Georgia, charged that John F. Kennedy and the "CIO bosses of Pittsfield, Mass.," had halted the transfer of a plant from the latter place to Rome, Georgia, by blocking the issuance of federal tax amortization certificates to the General Electric plant in question.[44] Mendel Rivers of Charleston, South Carolina, joined the fray to remind the New Englanders that "economic law moved their industries in some other direction" and to demand that these economic laws not be set aside. He would support a relief program for the communities adversely affected by the Korean emergency, but not any tampering with the principle of competitive bidding. "If you do this thing to us, you are creating wounds that will be aggravated in the future and we will not forget it," warned Rivers.[45]

Some very important western representatives joined this southern defense. Chet Holifield, William Knowland, Barry Goldwater, Dennis Chavez, Jack Shelley, and several others saw DMP No. 4 in the same light as did the historic South. Although this group did not make a very tidy ideological mix, they stood together against the principle of undermining competitive bidding. Jack Shelley and William Knowland, who faced each other across San Francisco Bay and an even greater ideological and partisan gulf, are perhaps representative. Shelley, the former head of the San Francisco Labor Council and future mayor of that city, thought that DMP No. 4 had been issued long after the disruptions of mobilization had passed. Moreover, San Francisco shipbuilders could not be assured of getting a contract on which they were the low bidders until some builder from a surplus labor area had a chance to meet the bid. Even though the local shipbuilders, like the New England textile industry, had long suffered from hard times, not being designated a surplus labor area ruined the Bay Area's chances. San Francisco Area electronics firms had suffered the same fate.[46]

Although his state had not fought with the Confederacy in the Civil War and labor leader Shelley did not share the Southerners' view of unions, he did partake of their sectional perspective on DMP No. 4. "Only one area west of the Mississippi has been so approved [as a surplus labor area]. Only one area in all of the Southern States is included," complained the liberal Democrat. "These eastern and midwestern cities designated comprise relatively limited sections of their own States." Shelley felt that he had been tricked into supporting the retention of the policy when it was considered for congressional action.[47]

Shelley's cross-bay conservative Republican neighbor, William Knowland, the majority leader of the Senate, objected to DMP No. 4 just as vigorously. He opposed giving the President that much power to shift contracts around, and he felt that such a policy struck a blow at the free-enterprise system by eliminating fair competition. These were obviously arguments to protect his constituency, since California representatives usually championed competitive bidding, but he also openly admitted the sectional implications of the policy. When Burnett Maybank of Charleston, South Carolina, noted that under the policy "distressed areas will be able to take business from other areas," such as California, Knowland answered that "the Senator from South Carolina is correct."[48] Other Westerners joined in, as Barry Goldwater and Dennis Chavez fretted about the loss of parachute contracts from Arizona and New Mexico cities.

They need not have worried. Senator Leverett Saltonstall put the matter to a vote on July 22, 1953, and it lost by 25 yeas to 62 nays. The vote, like the rhetoric of the argument, had a sectional cast. Most of Saltonstall's support came from Pennsylvania, New York, and New England, plus Michigan, where he received 15 of his 25 votes. Four more came from Illinois, Indiana, Kentucky, and Minnesota and another five from Nebraska, South Dakota, Montana, and Washington. As in the concurrent struggle over dispersal, some sections were not monolithic; but the Frostbelt tended to support Saltonstall, and everyone else, to oppose him. DMP No. 4 did not get a single vote in the states of the Southern Confederacy and got only four out of a possible 34 in the West.

Thus the attempt to get congressional sanction for DMP No. 4 failed, although the government had already accepted the principle administratively and did steer contracts to labor surplus areas. Initially, however, the outcry against DMP No. 4 apparently worked to contain the program to the implementation stage. As noted previously, the government deleted textiles and shoes from the distressed areas list, and the total amount spent in distressed areas remained small. As one frustrated member reminded the House, the government had channeled only $52 million to such areas by mid-1953.[49] Nonetheless, despite the minimal nature of this victory and the congressional setback, the idea of using defense monies countercyclically to combat unemployment persisted in government policy. Having lost in Congress, the depressed cities lobby once more went to the administration and again succeeded.

In November 1953, the government modified its tax write-off program. This policy had stimulated the swift expansion of defense plants in all twentieth-century wars by allowing private enterprise to amortize rapidly the cost of the plants that they built for the government. This policy allowed breakneck conversion of industry to war and avoided federal construction of the plants. During the Korean War, defense in space was made a secondary aim of the tax amortization guidelines. Illustrating perfectly the transformation of warfare into welfare, in late 1953 the Eisenhower administration added a function to the "multipurpose tax writeoff program." In the words of historian Neal Hurley, "In addition to stimulating defense production, encouraging dispersal, and defraying the extra costs of protective construction, accelerated amortization was to be employed . . . in aiding chronically distressed labor areas." Now a defense plant built in a depressed labor region would be eligible for fast tax write-offs.

Unfortunately for dispersal, the depressed labor regions often turned out to be the best targets for the Russians as well, including such cities as Detroit, Philadelphia, and Terre Haute. "As the program has worked out in actuality, the labor objective of amortization has received priority whenever a clash arose between this objective and that of industrial dispersal." Obviously, the government was spending defense funds countercyclically in a kind of metropolitan-military Keynesianism. Despite the colossal threat of thermonuclear weapons, welfare won out over warfare.[50] The Defense Manpower Policy No. 4, like the fight over decentralization to avoid nuclear attack, prefigured much of the later Sunbelt-Frostbelt controversy. Both parties to the struggle had come to recognize the potential role of military spending in influencing the growth of the Sunbelt or the Northeast-Midwest corridor. Both were already converting warfare into welfare, a transformation that is so obvious in the Sunbelt debate of recent years. Although the rhetoric of both sides spoke of national defense, each was more anxious to protect certain cities and their parent regions from the other than to defend the United States against the Soviets. Moreover, other issues, such as unemployment compensation, fair labor standards, federal spending on dams, price supports, shipbuilding and merchant marine subsidies, tax policies, transportation rates, general industrial decentralization, and the distribution of scientific research monies were viewed from the same sectional and urban perspective. Obviously, the argument over military spending was part of a much larger sectional debate over the realignment of American culture.

From the above, it is clear that the Northeast and Midwest did not become interested in defense spending only after the economic troubles of the 1970s. The move of industry to the Sunbelt was already well under way by the fifties, and the Northeast and Midwest were acutely aware of the threatening potential of this shift. The resulting Sunbelt debate over deindustrialization broke out in the 1950s, not in the 1970s. As we have seen, the problems created some interesting political alignments. The ethnic bloc of the Northeast and Eastern Midwest, usually considered politically liberal, stood solidly in the dispersal fight with the Pentagon, big business, the military contractors, Southern California, and Washington.

The issue also shows how complicated the so-called military-industrial complex often was. Southern representatives, usually considered hawks and conservatives, sided with Trans-Mississippi westerners against the Pentagon and military contractors. More important, they won. General Motors and the heavily concentrated military contractors of the maritime West and the martial corridor, stretching from Connecticut to St. Louis, did not have the political muscle to prevent what they obviously considered very damaging to their interests. If such a thing as a military-industrial complex ever did exist, its power in 1956 was not enough to beat back this threat from an alliance of town, country, and small-city politicians from the unindustrialized South and West.

To the extent that either policy was implemented, it represented a redistribution of wealth, since both the South and West were underdeveloped. Therefore, both represented a kind of welfare or social democracy. However, in this case, the social democracy came out of the barrel of a silent gun and benefitted several noisy sections at the expense of the established cities of the Northeast, Midwest, and Pacific coast. This transformation of warfare into welfare explains the unseemly haste of the cities of the South and West to get on the target of thermonuclear weapons and to cling to their dangerous position there so tenaciously. Also, like the recent controversy, this earlier one demonstrated how difficult it is to gain Sunbelt or Rustbelt sectional unity. Just as the Northeast-Midwest in the 1970s, and even today, struggles against internal disunity as often as against the South and West, in the fifties it did too. By the same token, California, the paragon Sunbelt state, sided with the Rustbelt in the first conflict and with the Sunbelt in the second. The Frostbelt lost the fights over both dispersal and DMP No. 4 due to its own lack of solidarity.

It is perhaps impossible to gauge the long-range impact of these matters on our story because of the complexity of tracing the exact trail of either defense spending in depressed areas or dispersal on specific or general contract acquisition thereafter. It is doubly difficult because of the political blarney surrounding each of the issues. The decentralizers tended to minimize the importance of their measure so as not to arouse too much anger in the defeated urban areas, and the metropolitan-military Keynesians tended to exaggerate as well. However, there is good circumstantial evidence that both of these issues of the California metropolitan-military complexes continued to be important.

Dispersal is perhaps the most enigmatic of the two problems. It is mysterious because the struggle created such a furor and such bitterness in 1956 and then dropped from sight thereafter. If the issue was so important to proponents and opponents in 1956, why did they not go on fighting over it thereafter? Some of the harshest rhetoric of the 1956 congressional session was expended upon dispersal, and then suddenly the issue dropped out of sight. It is also puzzling because of the contradictory evidence that subsequently appeared on the matter. For example, in 1958 John Dingell, ultimately the influential congressman from Detroit, introduced material into the *Congressional Record* which claimed to show that the dispersal policy lacked sufficient authority and therefore was not working. However, he then went on to complain that the provision was hurting Detroit's effort to recover from its 1958 depression woes. From this conflicting testimony, it would appear that the dispersal amendment was working both not well enough and entirely too well.

Since decentralization was only one among a series of criteria for contract allocation, which included the responsibilities of aiding distressed labor areas and maintaining a sound economy, it would be impossible in the confines of the book to trace its influence beyond 1961. That must remain for future studies. However, it is possible to trace a significant portion of the decentralization impact between 1948 and 1962, and beyond that to hypothesize about its influence based upon the known nature of the spending process and on two recent inquiries.[51]

Earlier in this chapter it was pointed out that the Korean War did not create a large-scale reallocation of the military wealth of an increasingly urban nation. In a quantitative sense that is correct, but in a qualitative sense it is profoundly misleading. The campaign for reallocation was initiated by Chicago just prior to World War II and revived by the Air Force just after it had borne considerable results all along. These results began in the war years and culminated in the 1950s. The first of these had been the policy of decentralizing aircraft production away from the supposedly vulnerable coasts. This rationale made only a little sense for the East Coast and not much more for Southern California.

On the East Coast only German sea or air power could conceivably have posed a conventional threat to coastal factories like those on Long Island, and the Germans did not have a long-range bomber force (the ability to fly from Europe to North America and back nonstop developed well after World War II). Moreover, they possessed no aircraft carriers that could have brought their planes any closer. Although they did possess several formidable surface ships, like the new but tactically obsolescent battleships that so troubled the British (and still do even from a watery grave), it would have been suicidal for these to attack Long Island, even presuming they could have slipped across the Atlantic unseen to shell the factories and presuming again that they could have come within range.

The Japanese did possess a carrier-borne air force that might have eluded the American defense screen to get to Seattle and perhaps even to Los Angeles, though with more difficulty. Sabotage was not a threat on the Pacific coast because the Japanese all were in camps, although it was somewhat more of a danger on the East Coast. These remote risks led the defense authorities, with the backing of the air power–envious cities, to decentralize aircraft production away from the coasts. Although it was accorded little significance beyond the period of war, this decision laid a foundation for the decentralization of the aircraft and aerospace industries, upon which the hungry postwar cities quickly built.

It is highly significant to note that several of these critical post-1950 decentralizations shared two characteristics: their new productions began in World War II plants that the receiving cities had fought for earlier, and the production to be carried on there was most advanced. This was not a distribution throughout the country of ordinary branch plants. In short, their success in attracting wartime plants allowed these cities to lay the foundation for their leap into the postwar technological tomorrow.

The campaign to revive industrial decentralization had multiple origins. The booster cities had always favored it, that is, if they had not yet received their share of the aeronautical pie. Both civil defense and the Air Force helped to initiate the campaign. The Air Force obviously did not want its sources of supply too heavily concentrated in a few places in case of attack, and civil defense officials shared the same concern. Throughout the period, the civil defense debate revolved around three methods of protecting non-combatant populations. One approach stressed the evacuation of city populations; a second sought to create a bomb and fallout shelter program; and a third pressed for the dispersion of industry, government offices, populations, and other targets. Politicians like Chet Holifield could stress one dimension of this triad, like shelters, but usually civil defense officials called for a combination of the three.[52] Despite the view of civil defense historians that not much dispersal occurred, considerable movement took place.

The Boeing Corporation followed the Seattle-designed strategy of dispersing within its own immediate area by putting major branches in Renton and Everett, Washington, home of the military-minded Democratic Senator Scoop Jackson. The Air Force pressured a further removal of a part of the Boeing empire to Wichita for the construction of the B-36 in vacant World War II plants, and Wichita became one of the manufacturing divisions of Boeing. Ultimately the B-52 would be built there as well. By 1952 that Great Plains city had carefully grafted this military dimension on top of its already well-developed light plane industry.

Other cities plunged forward in Wichita's wake. Soon Chance-Vought relocated not only a branch but the entire company operation, from Stratford, Connecticut, to Dallas. Consolidated later put its bomber operations at next-door Fort Worth, and much later Bell Helicopter joined these ranks to form another of the famous metropolitan-military complexes, a special concern of the recent Democratic speaker of the House of Representatives, Jim Wright of Fort Worth. General Electric located its turbojet engine plant at Kansas City, another of the World War II aircraft production centers. Martin Aircraft made an even more obvious Sunbelt move. As late as 1956–57, Baltimore remained the firm's only base of operations. That was before the Titan intercontinental ballistic missile. Late the next year, the firm occupied a factory in Denver to build the Titan, and a site was acquired in Orlando, Florida, adjacent to Cape Canaveral, "to meet Martin's commitments in the field of electronics, nuclear engineering, and missiles, as well as piloted aircraft." In 1962–63, the firm executed another brilliant, urban, Sunbelt decentralization maneuver by moving a part of its works to Marietta, Georgia, and changing its company name to Martin-Marietta. At that time, both Richard Russell, chairman of the Senate Armed Services Committee, and Carl Vinson, chairman of the House Armed Services Committee, hailed from that state.[53]

The Southern California companies followed a rather more complex strategy of decentralization, more akin to that of Seattle. It was well calculated to mend their political fences with the air power–envious cities and simultaneously to protect the martial cities of their own state. It will be recalled that the California metropolises had eagerly complied with the Seattle strategy of dispersal within metropolitan areas in order to avoid geographic decentralization. Now, however, with two major congressional battles demanding geographic decentralization and with Air Force, civil defense, and administration pressure, it was no longer possible to avoid geographic decentralization. So the California firms, like those in Seattle, *merely added geographic decentralization to the policy of dispersal within metropolitan areas.* Some of their firms' assets decentralized "abroad" to exotic places like Tulsa, Tucson, Sunnyvale, Palo Alto, and Marietta. However, many branches were also dispersed *within* the California metropolises which that state's congressmen had sought to protect in the Rains debate of 1951 and the Fulbright decentralization battle of 1956.

Lockheed followed perhaps the most complex strategy. In line with General Fox's efforts, in 1951 it dispersed its final assembly and testing operations from Van Nuys in the San Fernando Valley to Palmdale in the Antelope Valley of the Mojave Desert, north of the Los Angeles megalopolis. Another division sprang up in suburban Maywood, this one dedicated to avionics and electronics, and by 1954–55, it had even acquired a Beverly Hills factory! By 1957–58, it had decentralized a part of its missile division from Van Nuys to Palo Alto and Sunnyvale, California, adjacent to the Ames Aeronautical Laboratory that the northern metropolis had won in 1941. It further decentralized within the Golden State by creating another missile division operation at Santa Cruz and still another at Bakersfield in 1952–53. That latter move put a plant close to, although not directly within, the congressional districts of Leroy Johnson, spokesman for the San Joaquin Valley and another member of the House Military Affairs Committee.

Having "saved" considerable resources for Southern California cities, in 1951–52 Lockheed also decentralized both geographically and politically by moving its B-47 bomber production plant to Marietta, Georgia, close to Atlanta, where another martial metropolis, one which could count on the backing of both Senator Russell and Congressman Vinson, was abuilding. And by 1957–58, it was already dispersing its activities within the Atlanta area by undertaking nuclear-powered air development in Dawsonville, Georgia, some 40 miles northeast of Atlanta.

Altogether, then, the firm had decentralized *out of* the L.A. megalopolis to Palo Alto, Sunnyvale, Bakersfield, Santa Cruz, Dawsonville, and Marietta, while dispersing *within* the Southland metropolis to Maywood, Beverly Hills, and Palmdale, and within the Atlanta region as well. This was a subtle strategy, both politically and economically. It kept most of the firm's production in proximity to other sophisticated aerospace corporations, subcontractors, and aeronautically minded universities such as Stanford, from which it drew external economies. It also kept the corporation close to powerful congressmen and representatives from San Francisco Bay, Bakersfield, and Atlanta. Besides Russell and Vinson, fellow Armed Services Committee member George P. Miller, a Democrat from Alameda, resided right across the bay from Sunnyvale, and San Joaquin Valley spokesman Leroy Johnson, Republican from Stockton, lived one district away from Bakersfield. They could be counted upon to keep an eye on those neighboring urban interests.[54]

Douglas and Consolidated (which ultimately became General Dynamics) followed much the same strategy of dispersal within the California metropolises and decentralization outside of them. In 1954, Douglas announced its intention to create a branch in Tucson and sent one to Tulsa in 1951 to produce the Boeing-designed B-47. By 1962, it had opened a missiles division in Charlotte, North Carolina; and it already had considerable dispersal within the Los Angeles region, with plants at El Segundo, Long Beach, and Santa Monica. In 1951, Consolidated moved to put its small missile division in Pomona, east of Los Angeles, and established its B-36 and B-58 bombers division in distant Fort Worth, where it already had a plant from World War II. It will be recalled that one of the principal advocates of the "bomber gap" theory was none other than Lyndon B. Johnson, Senate majority leader and future President. Paul Kilday of San Angelo, Texas, also sat on the House Armed Services Committee. Daingerfield, Texas, hosted another Texas-Convair partnership, this one an Ordnance Aerophysics Laboratory and wind tunnel for the Navy.[55]

Of the other firms within Fortress California, North American, Hughes, and Northrop followed the standard Southland pattern. In 1951, North American created a Columbus, Ohio, division to share aircraft production responsibilities with its main office in Los Angeles and dispersed within the region by putting its autonetics division in Downey and its Rocketdyne division at Canoga Park. Northrop moved its headquarters from Hawthorne to Beverly Hills, while keeping its Norair manufacturing division in Hawthorne, California. It also dispersed a division to develop target drones to Ventura, and a field laboratory to the Santa Susana Mountains of Ventura County, north of the main Los Angeles settlement. Finally, it created another Rocketdyne division in Neosho in the far southwest corner of Missouri, as close to the South and West as it could be without actually being in it, and another division at McGregor, Texas. Northrop started late, only in 1958–59, but moved rapidly once it began. After that date it opened branches at El Segundo, Pasadena, Los Angeles International Airport, and Edwards Air Force Base within the Southland megalopolis and at Holloman Air Force Base, New Mexico, El Paso, Texas, and Cape Canaveral. By 1962 it had added facilities at Palmdale in the metropolis and at Amarillo, Texas, while closing out Holloman and El Paso.

Other firms also adhered to the familiar pattern. Hughes Aircraft kept a headquarters at Culver City just south of Los Angeles and decentralized its missile manufacturing division to Tucson in 1961–62. Aerojet fell into the same line. It began with a headquarters and works in Asuza, just east of Los Angeles, and by 1962 had added local plants in San Ramon and Downey, another California works at Sacramento, and an Atlantic Division in Frederick, Maryland. Even one of the more modest firms, Marquardt, which made engines, added a branch at Pomona and another at Ogden, Utah, not far from Senator Bennett's home in Salt Lake City.[56]

Thus, however forcibly Representative John Dingell (in the late 1950s) or current analysts of the military-industrial complex might argue that decentralization was not being implemented, in reality it was substantial. The weed patches, as the frustrated Ms. Lenoir Sullivan called them, were sprouting concrete, asphalt, subdivisions, shopping centers, and sleek new factories, just as Representative Vanik had feared. Moreover, this development had come about in response to the decentralization pressures in Congress from hungry urban congressmen, the Air Force, civil defense officials, and the administration.[57] The great debates of 1951 and 1956 had most certainly borne fruit, winged in some instances, but fruit nonetheless.

Throughout this book we have seen the way in which cities mobilized military resources for the purpose of growth and urban welfare. The political nature of this process of contract allocation was dramatically confirmed for me at a recent banquet in Texas. A woman in the audience who had heard my speech, which was essentially the San Diego chapter of this book, approached me to offer her own experience in support of what I had said. She said that her husband had worked for General Dynamics for over twenty years and that his experience corresponded to everything that I had said about San Diego and the process of defense contracting.

The moment was unusual, a breach; California defense contractors usually denied the charge of political influence at the same time that they frantically urged their own congressmen to make greater use of it. One has only to recall the General Dynamics speech written for President Eisenhower. California congressmen also denied the charge, all the while exercising as much political muscle as they could flex.

As we shall see in the discussion of Urban New York's reaction to its loss of defense pre-eminence, their congressional delegation was much more forthcoming about the relentlessly political nature of the military contracting process. Given that self-evident truth, we can assume that after 1961 southern and western representatives made full use of any provisions that would give their sections an edge, including the statutory requirement to take defense in space into account, just as congressmen from areas of urban unemployment could and did use the distressed labor areas provision to secure leverage of their own.

Although not concerned with the battle over industrial decentralization, two recent investigations that cover a period of nearly fifty years, from 1940 to 1988, lend further credence to this point. These studies did not recognize the importance of the decentralization struggles—indeed, one denied it—but their findings willy-nilly confirm its importance. The big winners in contract allocations from 1950 to 1980 were about the same as those who voted for decentralization with Rains in 1951 and Fulbright and Bennett in 1956. There is not an exact correlation here, but it is close; and the major exception helps to prove the rule. California held its own in the competition, and the remainder of the Sunbelt gained markedly, especially the West. So did Massachusetts, the heartland of the metropolitan-military Keynesian strategy of countercyclical spending in distressed areas. On the other hand, the Midwest and the Middle Atlantic states, especially New York, lost big. If Senator William Fulbright himself had structured American defense spending after 1956, he could not have arranged it much more favorably for the congressional constituencies that he led into battle in 1956 to do just that.[58]

The Massachusetts and new England "miracles" undoubtedly had something to do with the policy of spending defense monies in depressed areas. In a sense, New England had the best of both worlds. It had a powerful position in shipbuilding, which was a foothold in the older metropolitan-military economy, and a strong place in electronics, that is, a foothold in the new. The region also had high unemployment in the textile cities, which enabled it to qualify for distressed urban areas spending. Ironically enough for the future, both the strong areas and the weak spots in the New England economy allowed it to lay claim to more government monies.

And they were hardly the only ones who claimed such funds. Once the idea got out, the notion of countercyclical defense spending to combat urban distress quickly spread. In 1961, Congressman Bob Wilson, no slouch himself at "creative spending," noted that everyone in the capital was employing the same countercyclical ploy to enhance their share of contracts. Incongrously, liberal New York State led the way. In 1959, the *New York Times* informed the public that 100 large firms secured three-fourths of the defense contracts, and that, of the twelve leading firms, five were West Coast corporations: Boeing, Lockheed, North American, Douglas, and Hughes. General Dynamics had the largest part of its aerospace operations in California, with a major component in the Dallas-Fort Worth area and its shipbuilding in New England. Although several of the top dozen contractors had New York City or State connections, Baltimore possessed number twelve, Martin, and New England and Virginia held a large portion of the shipbuilding, New York legislators singled out California for hogging the defense barbeque.[59]

Certainly they could cite conclusive evidence of New York's declining and California's rising share of the defense market. Between 1951 and 1958 New York's proportion of defense contracts declined from 18.2 percent to 11.6 percent, while the California portion rose from 13.2 percent to 21.4 percent. The *New York Times* speculated that this flap over contracts was motivated by Nelson Rockefeller's competition with Richard Nixon for the 1960 Republican presidential nomination.

Nonetheless, both states mobilized to protect or promote their own contracting business. Led by Senator Kenneth Keating, New York congressmen united to form a bipartisan congressional caucus.

The irrelevance of party and ideology in this action was revealed in the nature of the appointments to the committee's leadership. Arch-conservative Republican John Taber of Auburn and arch-liberal Democrat Emmanuel Celler of Brooklyn were named to the five-person steering committee, each with the right to designate one more person. "We can now negotiate with Federal agencies from a position of strength," argued one representative. "When we now take up problems, we will not be speaking as individuals, but will have the solid backing of the New York delegation." The *Times* noted the unprecedented nature of the occasion. "The New York Republican said it was probably the first time that the New York members of congress from both parties had sat down together to act for a common purpose." That the precedent was shattered over a metropolitan-military issue was itself significant.

The importance of this movement was not lost on the Southland cities that still dominated aerospace production within the Great Wall of California. Indeed, the uproar began in February when the *Los Angeles Times* published the news of the New York mobilization. The West Coast reaction came swiftly. As the *New York Times* tersely put it, the "Los Angeles Chamber of Commerce announced this week the formation of an 'industrial task force to defend California's missile and aircraft defense business from further attacks by New York and other eastern legislators.'" Nor were they in any doubt as to who the culprits were. As industry officials put it, the New York action came not from the state per se, but from the suburban "Long Island bunch"—Republic, Grumman, and Fairchild.

Soon the San Francisco, Oakland, and California chambers of commerce were involved in strategy talks, and the Los Angeles task force was busily engaged in putting together its own "documentary presentation to Federal officials of California's 'qualifications' for continued defense business." This was followed by standard statements of California's case by both industry and political spokesmen. The Golden State received such a high proportion of the contracts because they were more efficient producers, said its leaders. Moreover, with subcontracting, perhaps 70 percent of the defense dollars were spread around the country. In any case, these monies could not be traced. "A breakdown of how much of California's prime-contract dollars end up elsewhere is virtually impossible," the industry conveniently claimed. (In reality, most of the subcontracting monies seemed to stay close to home.)

Before long, Los Angeles had produced California's own sorrowful tale of economic woes, purporting to demonstrate its worsening defense industry position. As previously noted, this argument certainly did not prove that the Golden State suffered in the metropolitan-military competition. It proved the exact reverse, since the state's defense bastions had held their own. The recent studies of prime contracting further document the point, if that were needed, for the next thirty-five years.[60]

Like John F. Kennedy and other Masschusetts predecessors, the New Yorkers viewed defense spending as a political panacea for economic troubles. Senator

Keating explained that "the best efforts of elected officials at both the state and national levels . . . must be applied if New York is 'to avert an unemployment crisis and stop its economic slide.'" And both the problem and the solution seemed to be political, rather than economic. John Taber explained to the *New York Times* that "neither the state Administration nor New York business people had shown the aggressiveness required to get an adequate share of Federal business for the state." He said he regarded the channeling of more contracts to New York as "the most immediate and pressing problem we have to face." "We don't want any ghost towns in New York," he said. The threatened towns included Buffalo, Utica-Rome, Amsterdam, Auburn (Representative Taber's home town), Elmira, Gloversville, and the Ogdenburg-Massena-Malone area.[61]

These quasi-apparitions and their live allies employed two very real integrated strategies. One was to keep up the drumfire of pressure for countercyclical defense spending in urban areas, a strategy that continued to be effectively used in Washington. The other was to demand that Congress force the Defense Department to let more contracts through a process of competitive bidding rather than on a negotiated basis. According to the Empire State critics, the DOD let some 85 to 91 percent of defense contracts on a negotiated basis, which they felt put their Long Island planemakers at a disadvantage. The New Yorkers were probably mistaken in this tactic, since California had a very strong competitive position to begin with.

By the end of the Eisenhower administration, New York was beginning to get results. Senator Jacob Javits introduced legislation in the Senate to compel more "competitive bidding wherever possible." A week after the Javits resolution passed the Senate, the House, under the prodding of Carl Vinson, ended the Korean War emergency legislation that had allowed the DOD to bypass the requirement of competitive bidding. Apparently all of this activity paid off, as Javits reported that the New York share of defense spending had risen by 15 percent in the 1959–60 fiscal year, "compared with an 11 percent drop for California." Nonetheless, the New York City resident was still not satisfied that the DOD had channeled enough money into distressed areas.[62]

In the meantime, other American sections found even more inventive ways to forward the claims of their own defense cities or aspiring ones. Some were quite ingenious. For example, one congressman proposed an "amendment to the military construction bill that would require Congress to authorize individual missile and aircraft expenditures, even after the appropriations for these weapons were passed." Another was an amendment to the Renegotiation Act, which would have benefitted Boeing, Lockheed, Douglas, North American, Temco, Martin, and Grumman. Then Senator John Sparkman began a probe of defense procurement in mid-1959, ostensibly to help the small businessman, whom he said the government had slighted.

This argument was problematical, since one-third of the defense spending since 1957 had gone to small business, an impressive figure in view of the fact that they were ordinarily not large enough to handle the huge prime contracts. Sparkman's ploy was well calculated to aid the cities of the South and West, since they were not yet such a big-business preserve as other sectors of the nation. Moreover, Urban California would not be hurt by this legislation either because it was so heavily dependent upon defense spending that it had many more small subcontractors who might benefit from the small-business provision. At the same time, Representative Edward F. Hebert of Louisiana opened a probe into the practice of hiring ex-military men into defense firms, and the General Accounting Office began investigating waste in procurement practices.[63]

Perhaps the most ingenious, and certainly the most cynical, way of getting more defense contracts was through the illusion of civil defense. It will be recalled that Representative Holifield was one of the workhorses of the extremely pro-nuclear JCAE and also a nuclear booster in his own right. In 1959, a subcommittee of the Joint Committee on Atomic Energy, chaired by Chet Holifield, began reporting on the consequences of an attack that employed some of the "devices" that Holifield was boosting. These were predictably gruesome, but contained some some rays of hope as well.

In line with recent Air Force declarations, the civil defense report claimed that a nuclear war was survivable. The Air Force had actually claimed that, after an appropriate period of cleansing, the nuclear radiation from a war would not be much worse than normal doses received from industry, the sun, or rocks. Holifield's panel asserted that proper civil defense actions could reduce the casualties from 25 to 3 percent of the total population in a thermonuclear exchange. The proper precautions included a new $20 billion congressional program to provide fallout shelters!

This may have been a brave humanitarian idea, but it would also have deluged Southern California, and to a lesser extent, Northern California, cities with shelter monies because they were more vulnerable and inviting targets. If California indeed possessed 21 percent of defense contracts, it would certainly be entitled to 21 percent of the monies to shield that defense investment, not to mention its share of defense funds to protect its numerous military installations. Moreover, the report itself further helped the metropolitan-military complexes because it cast nuclear war as more survivable and less "unthinkable," thereby making the California weapons of destruction more in demand.[64]

All of this activity got the attention of the Department of Defense and defense contractors as well. Suddenly, concessions appeared everywhere. For example, Aerojet announced in August of 1959 that it would survey the country to find small businesses and distressed areas into which it could subcontract its military work. The United States Navy began a similar campaign on behalf of small business about one month later. The Defense Department as a whole made a comparable announcement in late 1959. Finally, in mid-1960, which was also in the presidential campaigning season, the Eisenhower administration announced through the Office of Civil and Defense Mobilization that areas "that had persistent high unemployment would receive preference in the placement of Government contracts and Federally financed plants."

It should be remembered that John F. Kennedy, the Democratic candidate in the current contest, had been one of the architects of the policy of countercyclical defense spending in urban areas. It would thus appear that the Republicans were stealing his thunder. The distressed-areas tactic certainly came back to haunt the Massachusetts Democrat in other phases of the election. In the waning days of the campaign, Republicans "distributed leaflets in California defense plants saying 'Jack Wants Your Job.'" The "pamphlets alleged that Mr. Kennedy favored transferring defense work to the East." JFK retorted with characteristic wit that "the only job I'm after is President Eisenhower's," but the charge hit home. The Democrat called the tactic "despicable," although we can hardly doubt that it was quite true. Simply put, this incident of the campaign was triggered by the Darwinian competition between California's booming military cities and Massachusetts's distressed textile ones.[65]

It was also the immediate background for the famous Eisenhower farewell address, which provided the country with the timeless phrase "military-industrial complex." The President was quite clearly dismayed about defense lobbying from almost the beginning of his first term. By his second, he was downright angry. Between DMP No. 4, the dispersal fight of 1956, the 1959 New York campaign, the Sparkman and Hebert investigations, and the bomber and missile gap ploys, the President had plenty to steam about. As early as 1959 he began searching for the appropriate language with which to strike back. His first attempt seemed to be the phrase "munitions lobby," initially employed sometime in 1959. Subsequently he employed the term military-industrial complex.

As this book has held throughout, when Ike hit upon this memorable phrase for the defense spending derby, he also seriously mislabeled it. The phrase "military-industrial complex" implies a monolith, an alliance of certain nefarious groups like scientists, bureaucrats, congressmen, and businessmen, united to militarize the country. In fact, what one finds operating is no such thing. Competition among defense contractors and their sponsoring cities was always acute, and there is little evidence that they were united over anything. When Lyndon Johnson complained of a bomber gap, we cannot doubt that the bombers that he worried most about were those produced by the metropolitan-military complex in Dallas-Fort Worth, including Bell Helicopter, Chance-Vought, and Convair. And when Sam Yorty denounced Ike's budget cuts, we need not doubt that the ones that concerned him most were those that affected the defense-studded district of Los Angeles, from which he hailed. In short, Eisenhower was correct about the use of undue political influence on behalf of military contracting, but wrong in his description of it. It was not a unitary institution, as he implied, but a nation full of Darwinian urban areas, heavily dependent upon defense spending. In California cities, that fight went back at least to the coming of the Great White Fleet. The fight over defense spending was every bit as much a contest of urban rivalry as it was a product of national politics or the Cold War.[66]

Although the shift of American power and wealth to the South and West has been of momentous importance, American historians writing of the 1950s have often, if not usually, slighted or ignored it.[67] This chapter is intended to encourage them to end this neglect and, at the same time, to remind contemporary commentators who have taken up the Sunbelt and deindustralization themes that the Sunbelt struggle did not suddenly emerge full-blown in the 1970s, but rather has origins that go back at least to the urban rivalry of the early 1950s.

Conclusion

It is the argument of this book that the city leaders of California have consistently employed federal military resources to help create the urban empires to which they aspired. It is also the contention of this book that a further focus on the city and the sword will help to move the discipline of urban history beyond traditional emphases that have been fruitful but limiting.

It seems clear that Urban California leaders, sometimes knowingly and sometimes unknowingly, followed something close to the San Diego formula for successful city building. They systematically constructed their cities, carefully placing each military asset into the whole and thereby laying the foundations for modern California urbanism. They structured the city environment so that military activities would thrive there, just as towns of the South once organized themselves to accommodate the cotton or tobacco factories or Northern ones sought to adjust to the railroads. The following maps of the military installations, factories, think tanks, and collaborating universities are illustrative. Social scientists frequently ask why certain cities have corralled such a disproportionate share of the market for military supplies and services. Their answers range all over the spectrum, but they do not fully comprehend the structures of the metropolitan-military cities.

By the end of the period investigated in this book, the California cities had extraordinary external economies for the production of military goods and services. The literature of both history and economies is full of examples of corporate integration, both vertical and horizontal. However, these ideas have seldom been applied to an urban region, either to explain the extraordinary economic power of an urban area or to account for the preternatural success of certain cities in the race for military wealth. Yet the idea, especially that of vertical integration, is quite applicable to the development of the California martial metropolises. In the same way that Andrew Carnegie created a steel empire that eventually included components at all levels of his operation—iron ore reserves, mining operations, Great Lakes ore boats, railroads and railroad cars, smelting and manufacturing plants, and a distribution network—the cities of California became vertically integrated as well. And if one looks at the cities in terms of their regional hinterlands and their overlapping urban hinterlands, the idea of urban or metropolitan-military vertical integration becomes even more plausible.

Both the Bay Area and Southern California qualify as vertically integrated martial metropolises, but the latter stands out because it comprises two contiguous and intertwined metropolitan economies geared to a significant extent to the needs, real or imagined, of the military services. The notion of imagined or "mock" needs does not imply that there will never be a need to project American military power into

346

The Metropolitan-Military Complex: San Francisco Bay c. 1961

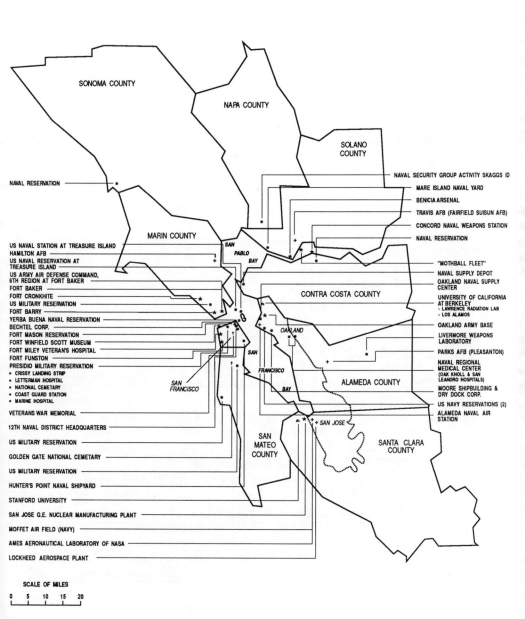

SONOMA COUNTY

NAPA COUNTY

SOLANO COUNTY

NAVAL SECURITY GROUP ACTIVITY SKAGGS ID

MARE ISLAND NAVAL YARD

BENICIA ARSENAL

TRAVIS AFB (FAIRFIELD SUISUN AFB)

CONCORD NAVAL WEAPONS STATION

NAVAL RESERVATION

NAVAL RESERVATION

MARIN COUNTY

SAN PABLO BAY

US NAVAL STATION AT TREASURE ISLAND
HAMILTON AFB
US NAVAL RESERVATION AT TREASURE ISLAND
US ARMY AIR DEFENSE COMMAND, 6TH REGION AT FORT BAKER
FORT BAKER
FORT CRONKHITE
US MILITARY RESERVATION
FORT BARRY
YERBA BUENA NAVAL RESERVATION
BECHTEL CORP.
FORT MASON RESERVATION
FORT WINFIELD SCOTT MUSEUM
FORT MILEY VETERAN'S HOSPITAL
FORT FUNSTON
PRESIDIO MILITARY RESERVATION
 ▪ CRISSY LANDING STRIP
 ▪ LETTERMAN HOSPITAL
 ▪ NATIONAL CEMETARY
 ▪ COAST GUARD STATION
 ▪ MARINE HOSPITAL

VETERANS WAR MEMORIAL

12TH NAVAL DISTRICT HEADQUARTERS

US MILITARY RESERVATION

GOLDEN GATE NATIONAL CEMETARY

US MILITARY RESERVATION

HUNTER'S POINT NAVAL SHIPYARD

STANFORD UNIVERSITY

SAN JOSE G.E. NUCLEAR MANUFACTURING PLANT

MOFFET AIR FIELD (NAVY)

AMES AERONAUTICAL LABORATORY OF NASA

LOCKHEED AEROSPACE PLANT

CONTRA COSTA COUNTY

"MOTHBALL FLEET"
NAVAL SUPPLY DEPOT
OAKLAND NAVAL SUPPLY CENTER
UNIVERSITY OF CALIFORNIA AT BERKELEY
 - LAWRENCE RADIATION LAB
 - LOS ALAMOS
OAKLAND ARMY BASE
LIVERMORE WEAPONS LABORATORY
PARKS AFB (PLEASANTON)
NAVAL REGIONAL MEDICAL CENTER (OAK KNOLL & SAN LEANDRO HOSPITALS)
MOORE SHIPBUILDING & DRY DOCK CORP.
US NAVY RESERVATIONS (2)
ALAMEDA NAVAL AIR STATION

OAKLAND

SAN FRANCISCO

SAN FRANCISCO

SAN FRANCISCO BAY

ALAMEDA COUNTY

SAN JOSE

SAN MATEO COUNTY

SANTA CLARA COUNTY

SCALE OF MILES

0   5   10   15   20

The Metropolitan-Military Complex: Los Angeles c. 1961

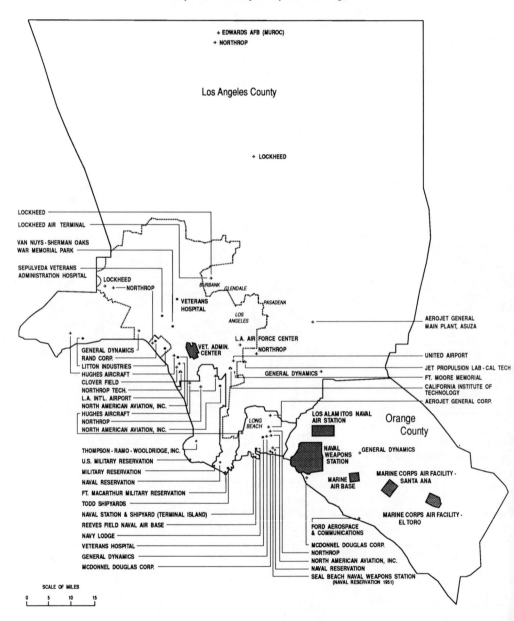

→ EDWARDS AFB (MUROC)
→ NORTHROP

Los Angeles County

→ LOCKHEED

LOCKHEED
LOCKHEED AIR TERMINAL
VAN NUYS - SHERMAN OAKS
WAR MEMORIAL PARK
SEPULVEDA VETERANS
ADMINISTRATION HOSPITAL
LOCKHEED
→ NORTHROP
BURBANK
GLENDALE
VETERANS
HOSPITAL
PASADENA
LOS
ANGELES
AEROJET GENERAL
MAIN PLANT, ASUZA
VET. ADMIN.
CENTER
L.A. AIR FORCE CENTER
→ NORTHROP
UNITED AIRPORT
GENERAL DYNAMICS
RAND CORP.
LITTON INDUSTRIES
HUGHES AIRCRAFT
CLOVER FIELD
NORTHROP TECH.
L.A. INT'L. AIRPORT
NORTH AMERICAN AVIATION, INC.
HUGHES AIRCRAFT
NORTHROP
NORTH AMERICAN AVIATION, INC.
GENERAL DYNAMICS →
JET PROPULSION LAB - CAL TECH
FT. MOORE MEMORIAL
CALIFORNIA INSTITUTE OF
TECHNOLOGY
AEROJET GENERAL CORP.
LOS ALAMITOS NAVAL
AIR STATION
Orange
County
THOMPSON - RAMO - WOOLDRIDGE, INC.
U.S. MILITARY RESERVATION
MILITARY RESERVATION
NAVAL RESERVATION
FT. MACARTHUR MILITARY RESERVATION
TODD SHIPYARDS
NAVAL STATION & SHIPYARD (TERMINAL ISLAND)
REEVES FIELD NAVAL AIR BASE
NAVY LODGE
VETERANS HOSPITAL
GENERAL DYNAMICS
MCDONNEL DOUGLAS CORP.
LONG
BEACH
NAVAL
WEAPONS
STATION
→ GENERAL DYNAMICS
MARINE
AIR BASE
MARINE CORPS AIR FACILITY -
SANTA ANA
MARINE CORPS AIR FACILITY -
EL TORO
FORD AEROSPACE
& COMMUNICATIONS
MCDONNELL DOUGLAS CORP.
NORTHROP
NORTH AMERICAN AVIATION, INC.
NAVAL RESERVATION
SEAL BEACH NAVAL WEAPONS STATION
(NAVAL RESERVATION 1951)

SCALE OF MILES
0   5   10   15

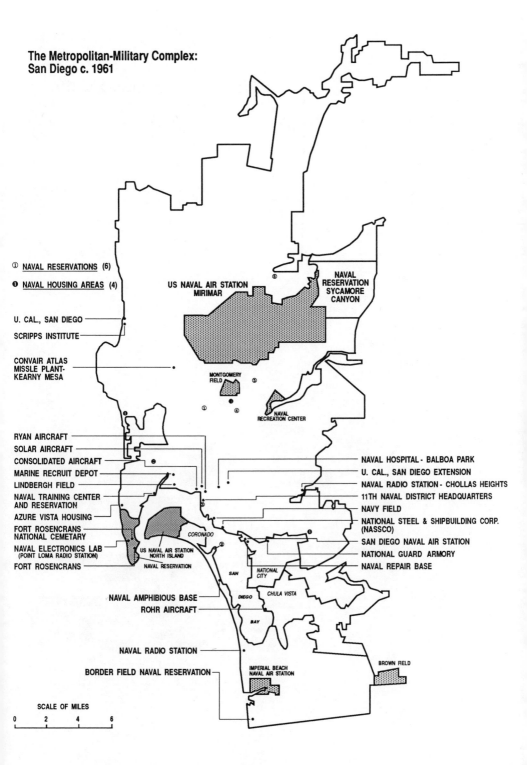

The Metropolitan-Military Complex:
San Diego c. 1961

① NAVAL RESERVATIONS (6)
❶ NAVAL HOUSING AREAS (4)

U. CAL., SAN DIEGO

SCRIPPS INSTITUTE

CONVAIR ATLAS
MISSLE PLANT-
KEARNY MESA

US NAVAL AIR STATION
MIRIMAR

NAVAL
RESERVATION
SYCAMORE
CANYON

MONTGOMERY
FIELD

⑤

④ ①

NAVAL
RECREATION CENTER

RYAN AIRCRAFT

SOLAR AIRCRAFT

CONSOLIDATED AIRCRAFT

MARINE RECRUIT DEPOT

LINDBERGH FIELD

NAVAL TRAINING CENTER
AND RESERVATION

AZURE VISTA HOUSING

FORT ROSENCRANS
NATIONAL CEMETARY

NAVAL ELECTRONICS LAB
(POINT LOMA RADIO STATION)

FORT ROSENCRANS

NAVAL HOSPITAL - BALBOA PARK

U. CAL., SAN DIEGO EXTENSION

NAVAL RADIO STATION - CHOLLAS HEIGHTS

11TH NAVAL DISTRICT HEADQUARTERS

NAVY FIELD

NATIONAL STEEL & SHIPBUILDING CORP.
(NASSCO)

SAN DIEGO NAVAL AIR STATION

NATIONAL GUARD ARMORY

NAVAL REPAIR BASE

CORONADO

US NAVAL AIR STATION
NORTH ISLAND

NAVAL RESERVATION

SAN

DIEGO

BAY

NATIONAL
CITY

CHULA VISTA

NAVAL AMPHIBIOUS BASE

ROHR AIRCRAFT

NAVAL RADIO STATION

BORDER FIELD NAVAL RESERVATION

IMPERIAL BEACH
NAVAL AIR STATION

BROWN FIELD

SCALE OF MILES

0   2   4   6

The Military Hinterlands, c. 1961

BEALE AFB

McCELLAN AFB

MATHER AFB

TRAVIS AFB

SAN FRANCISCO BAY
URBANIZED AREA

CASTLE AFB

FORT ORD

U.S. NAVAL AIR STATION
(LEN MOORE)

HUNTER LIGGET
MILITARY
RESERVE

CAMP ROBERTS

NAVY ORDINANCE TEST RANGE

NAVY ORDINANCE TEST STATION
MOJAVE RANGE B

FORT IRWIN MILITARY
RESERVATION

EDWARDS AFB (MUROC)

VANDENBURG AFB

MARINE CORPS
TRAINING CENTER

COOK AFB

LOS ANGELES
URBANIZED AREA

GEORGE AFB

NORTON AFB

OXNARD AFB

NAVY
WEAPONS
STATION

CHOCOLATE MOUNTAIN
AERIAL GUNNERY RANGE

MARCH AFB

PACIFIC COAST
MISSILE TEST RANGE-
PT. MUGU

SALTON SEA

USMC - CAMP
PENDLETON

SALTON SEA
TEST BASE

SAN DIEGO
URBANIZED AREA

SCALE OF MILES

0   20   40   60   80   100

the rest of the world. Such a conviction would be unrealistic. It merely acknowl-
edges the fact that the most sophisticated and expensive weapons we possess have
never been fired in battle conditions and perhaps will never be fired more than once
and then counterproductively for each antagonist. The weapons sit unemployed in
silos, in firing tubes, or on airstrips. Producing better weapons usually does not gain
any adversary a meaningful advantage because the other side develops the same or
counter weapons. For most of the Cold War, new weapons did not change the balance of power.

For example, between Los Angeles and San Diego, the martial metropolis could
build transport planes (Convair), trainers, fighter planes, bombers, drones, and missiles. In this latter field it could build everything from intercontinental ballistic missiles to ship-to-ship missiles to ship-to-plane missiles to hand-held missiles. At Cal
Tech it could find aerodynamicists to shape these weapons; at Ramo Woldridge it
could find systems analysts to integrate the various weapons systems; at the myriad
electronics firms in the area or the Navy Electronics Laboratory in San Diego, it
could construct electronic spines and guidance systems; from the Rand Corporation it could mobilize the integral minds who could devise tactical missions appropriate to the individual weapons, to various combinations of armaments, and to
strategic rationales for the ensemble. The Air Force could test its planes and missiles
at Edwards Air Force Base at Muroc Dry Lake, just as it had tested strategic bombing theories there before World War II. Or it could determine the air speed of these
products at the Salton Sea measured test course. The Navy could try out its weaponry at China Lake, and the Pacific Missile Test Range at Lompoc could accommodate tests of intercontintental missiles fired by each of the services. Other testing
could occur at the Chocolate Mountain Aerial Gunnery Range. If the weapons
required underwater sophistication, the Scripps Institute of Oceanography at La
Jolla had been collecting this lore since the Progressive era.

The Jet Propulsion Laboratory in Pasadena provided first jet propulsion and
then electronics technology of all kinds. The Aerojet General Corporation, the
Rocketdyne Division of North American, Lockheed, and the Marquardt Corporation of Van Nuys manufactured engines, and Aerojet also produced the fuel. If
the propulsion were nuclear, as it was for the new submarines and aircraft carriers
and hopefully for the nuclear aircraft, the General Atomics Laboratory in San
Diego and the Lawrence Radiation Laboratory at Livermore, as well as nuclear
divisions at North American and several other corporations, provided another kind
of lore.

The Southland martial metropolis did not have the shipbuilding capacity of
Mare Island, Hunter's Point, and the private yards of the Bay Area, but between
Todd Shipyards at Los Angeles, NASSCO in San Diego, and the Long Beach Naval
Shipyard, the Southland could also build naval vessels. When these broke down or
required overhaul, this job could be done at the San Diego Naval Ship Repair Facil-
ity. Within the services the same kind of integration and self-sufficiency prevailed.
San Diego could handle battleships, cruisers, destroyers, guided missile ships,
nuclear and coventional submarines, and aircraft carriers. It could also accommodate the planes that accompanied one or all of these weapons at Miramar Naval
Air Station or at North Island Naval Air Station. In addition, it possessed a full

industrial operation that supported both the seagoing and the airborne weapons. For its employees, it offered PXs where they might enjoy bargain prices, Balboa Hospital when they were sick, employee associations when they were disgruntled, and housing when they required shelter. And for a mystified public who might not otherwise have understood all of these legions of military resources, the cities offered very good entertainment. The Reuben Fleet Space Theater and the Aerospace Museum in Balboa Park supplied eye-popping space exploits to keep the public "informed" about the progress of the scientists. Of course, they labeled space the "new frontier," an always appealing phrase well calculated to provide the man in the street a vicarious linkage with the single most revered experience of the American West.

Of course, it could be argued that this vertically integrated urban-military system occurred simply due to the vagaries of the international economy, the even more whimsical behavior of the modern nation-state, the tides of elite emigration or demography, the grinding struggle between classes, or the mystifying evolution of uneven development.

None of these forces, however, can really explain the growth of the California metropolitan-military complexes. That development can be understood only historically, in terms of foundations, bases laid to be built upon in the future. For example, it made sense to put the Jet Propulsion Laboratory in Southern California and the Ames Laboratory in the Bay Area only because the aircraft industry was already there, largely inside the Great Wall of California. And the aircraft industry was there because the *Times* had lured Douglas to the Southland, because the Burbank boosters had persuaded Lockheed to remain in the San Fernando Valley, because the Los Angeles financial markets had refinanced Lockheed, and because the city of San Diego and its private boosters had seduced Consolidated Aircraft to a rendezvous at the border.

By the same logic, unless the Navy had occupied San Diego to the level that it did in World War I, it would not have made sense to make the later decisions creating a Naval Electronics Laboratory (out of the radio station), a Naval Ship Repair Facility, a submarine base, an atomics laboratory, or a carrier facility. Without the extensive dredging campaign of the city it could not even have berthed the World War II-class carriers, nor could it have acquired the planes that accompanied the carriers. Miramar Naval Air Station required the preceding development of the harbor to accommodate the aircraft carriers whose planes Miramar was intended to base. In every sphere both urban boosters and military planners structured a vertically integrated urban economic system that would accommodate ever more external economies to military needs.

Again, one hopes that this book will suggest some new ways of practicing the urban historian's trade. The influence of the military in twentieth-century America has been enormous, and that field of inquiry should not be left to other subdisciplines to monopolize. Whether one takes the approach that I have or one that emphasizes economics, class conflict, uneven development, industrialism, or modernization, urban historians should make the military's influence on cities and the cities' influence on the military an important part of their inquiry. After all, it is not as if the urban-martial connection is an isolated phenomena. Whether as forts in the nineteenth century or metropolitan-military complexes in the twentieth, American cities have been firmly touched by the phenomenon of war and defense. Not only have San Francisco, Los Angeles, and San Diego been largely structured around war and defense, but so have Seattle, Denver, Albuquerque, Orlando and Jacksonville (Florida's largest city), Jacksonville, Goldsboro, and Fayetteville (North Carolina), Charleston (South Carolina), St. Louis, Cincinnati, Brooklyn, Boston, Norfolk, Washington, D.C., Colorado Springs, Minneapolis-St. Paul, New Haven and Hartford (Connecticut), Springfield (Massachusetts), the Nassau County metropolitan suburb of New York City, Atlanta and its suburb of Marietta, Bath (Maine), and Rock Island (Illinois) and its Quad City neighbors. All have been significantly and sometimes decisively influenced by military developments.

And this catalogue does not even include less well-known cities and towns, such as Belleville, Illinois (Scott Air Force Base); Rantoul, Illinois (Chanute Air Force Base); Junction City, Kansas (Fort Riley); Clarkville, Tennessee (Fort Campbell); Brownsville, Texas (one of the new battleship groups); or lowly Waynesville, Missouri (Fort Leonard Wood), whose very existence is tied to their military partners.

Even a city like Chicago, generally regarded as having lost out in the race for military wealth, has or had Fort Sheridan, Great Lakes Naval Training Station, and Glenview Naval Air Station within its limits or close by in the suburbs.

Historians have long recognized, although not systematically developed, the importance of the topic of the military to postwar *national* history. If anything, it proves much more important to *urban* history, because that is where the military money impacted. Urban historians with certain admirable exceptions like Philip Funigiello, Carl Abbott, Bradley Rice, and Richard Bernard have ignored this very rich field, a field where they could make a unique contribution.

When they do make this effort, both urban and national historians will find, not a military-industrial complex, as President Eisenhower courageously and presciently termed the phenomenon, not a monolith, but rather a polycentric configuration that changes consistently over time. This pluralistic entity is better termed a "metropolitan-military complex" because cities and metropolises were the fundamental bases of these alliances. There may have been a transient monolith at budget negotiations when it came time to pass the annual appropriations for the military establishment. And there certainly were fleeting alliances between cities and between sections. However, the essential nature of the process was competitive. Cities and their hinterlands fought each other for the spoils of war.

Even Eisenhower's farewell address for which the term "military-industrial complex" was coined, was fundamentally conditioned by this rivalry. The President may have defined the problem monolithically, but the biggest flap over armaments in his later years was a struggle between the armaments-producing suburbs of New York City and the weapons-making regions of Los Angeles and San Diego, who, as we have seen, were by this point well along in their successful attempt to transform warfare into welfare.

It remains to answer the question of how much influence the city, the nation-state, and the boosters had on this process. How did the division of labor work out? And how did the three influences interpenetrate? One cannot summarize the entire process, but one can perhaps review enough of the major events of the era to convey a better understanding of the subject.

In certain matters, the exigencies and the vagaries of the modern nation-state clearly exercised a decisive influence. World War I created an up-to-date navy too large for one coast to monopolize. That produced the fundamental resource for which California urban navalists contended. World War II greatly enhanced the Navy, Army, and Air Force, and the Cold War vastly altered them qualitatively to a high-tech basis. By the same token, both world wars, Korea, and the Cold War created a demand for aircraft, aerospace vehicles, and electronics to guide them. The various emergencies of the nation-state likewise created other windfalls for California cities. These included street improvements, surplus property, defense highways, airport improvements, headquarters, and so forth.

However, the nation-state created these national assets without a specific target for them. They were merely military resources that could have been located in many other places than the ones where they came to predominate. That is especially true of the aircraft and aerospace industry. The cities themselves helped to determine where these resources would be placed.

Some urbanists have argued that cities do not act, that they are benefitted or hurt by individuals or are buffeted by vast impersonal or structural forces like industrialism. Anything else is anthropomorphizing the city. That is a valid point in many analyses, but not in this one. Cities did act as an independent influence in the story of the metropolitan-military complex. For example, when the Navy steamed westward in 1919, its porting was already determined by a vast impersonal force, but not an outside one. That force was the city, whether considered as a way of life, a site, a process, or a reality combining the three. There was no likelihood that the Navy would choose Mendocino or Eureka or Big Sur for a base site. That service needed modern harbors, warehouses, supply firms, labor forces, dredged channels, lighthouses, berthing spaces, housing, buildings for headquarters, sophisticated railroad and highway networks, recreation outlets, and much else that only a major city could supply on the massive scale required.

Those requirements meant that the militarization of the California coast would reinforce rather than alter the existing pattern of urbanization. The nineteenth-century railroads in the United States did not substantially re-create the existing urban network. Whether American towns like New York, French ones like New Orleans, or Spanish ones like San Francisco, the cities usually drew the rails inevitably to themselves. That was true of the militarization of California as well. The Navy accommodated itself to the existing city system. So did the aircraft industry. All of the fledgling aircraft firms of the twenties located in cities in Southern California and, once there, stayed. When Consolidated came to San Diego, it created a list of cities over 100,000 to look at and finally chose the Border City. Incidentally, when they were forced to decentralize, first by the Second World War and then by the Cold War, the aircraft and aerospace firms conformed to the same pattern. The existence of the city was an indispensable asset to aircraft manufacture as it was to the Navy, and for about the same reasons.

Aircraft historians and locational analysts have often pointed out that the aircraft and aerospace industries are essentially footloose. That may be true in a regional sense, but not many of them are so footloose that they can avoid locating in a big city. Their flexibility does not give them the freedom to locate in a weed patch, to employ Ms. Lenoir Sullivan's rhetoric. For a whole host of reasons, they depend upon a pre-existing urban network.

Yet the urban-military story was not dominated by these two vast impersonal forces, the nation-state and the process of urbanization, as important as they may have been. Human agency in the form of boosters played the most important role. Without the booster effort, San Diego would not have attracted the Navy and therefore become a great city, one of the ten largest in the United States. By the same means, Vallejo was able to block the aspirations of the mid-bay cities to become the great naval base of the Pacific. The others were forced to settle for a substantial, but less impressive chunk of the Navy. In the Los Angeles area the boosters brought the aircraft industry to Santa Monica, kept it in Burbank, and refinanced it as well. Boosters likewise secured Consolidated for San Diego. They recruited Robert Millikan, and he enlisted Theodore von Karman to build Cal Tech into an aerospace power. Von Karman, in turn, helped to create Aerojet and served as a pipeline for scientific information to the Southland.

Human agency played a similar part in the decision to split the Navy in 1919. By harping on the Japanese threat, the advocates of the Yellow Peril thesis helped to rationalize the decision to send the fleet into the Pacific where it could be fought over by the rival cities. The credits go on and on, but the point is clear. Human agency—the efforts of individual boosters, individual politicians—vastly affected the business of the modern nation-state and the process of urbanization.

A final point: Often the three forces were tied together. For example, the exigencies of the nation-state clearly created the Cold War. However, there was no rigid division between the necessities of the nation-state and those of the Darwinian City. If the presidential scientific advisors and many other commentators are correct, the nation-state spent perhaps twice as much on armaments as was required for defense. The rest represented a windfall to contractors, universities, and martial metropolises. And of course city representatives helped to create the conditions that would impel these national assets in their own direction. Sam Yorty whipped up the lather of the Cold War to prevent defense spending cuts, and Bob Wilson whipped it up again to secure contracts for San Diego. Carl Hinshaw served as vice chairman of the committee investigating American rearmament, and he, Chet Holifield, and William Knowland served on the Joint Committee on Atomic Energy which helped to legitimize the uses of nuclear power. In similar fashion, the human agency of the boosters was closely connected to the reality of the city. They were its representatives, and its fortunes were their marching orders.

Thus, the nation-state and the boosters created resources and opportunities; the existence of the city determined specifically where these could be put and exploited; and the nation-state and the boosters split the decisions of who got what, when, where, and how.

Notes

Introduction

1. Jonathan Green, comp., *A Dictionary of Contemporary Quotations* (London: David and Charles, 1982).

2. As used in this book, the term *urbanization* refers to the physical, demographic, and economic process of growth—to the process of city building. The term *urbanism* refers to the conditions of urban life.

3. Robin Higham, *Air Power: A Concise History* (NY: St. Martin's Press, 1972); Samuel P. Huntington, *The Common Defense: Strategic Programs in National Politics* (NY: Columbia Univ. Press, 1961); Walter Millis, *Arms and Men: America's Military History and Military Policy from the Revolution to the Present* (NY: Capricorn Books, 1956); Col. James A. Donovan, *Militarism, U.S.A.* (NY: Scribner, 1970); Richard J. Barnet, *Roots of War: The Men and Institutions Behind U.S. Foreign Policy* (NY: Penguin Books, 1980); B. H. Liddell-Hart, *History of the Second World War* (NY: Putnam, 1970); Philip Barker, *Alexander the Great's Campaigns: A Guide to Ancient Political and Military Wargaming* (Cambridge, Eng.: P. Stephens, 1979); Raymond Aron, *Clausewitz: Philosopher of War* (Englewood Cliffs: Prentice Hall, 1985); Reuben Brenner, *Betting on Ideas: Wars, Inventions, and Inflation* (Chicago: Univ. of Chicago Press, 1985); Geoffrey Blainey, *The Causes of War* (NY: Free Press, 1973); Reginald Bretnor, *Decisive Warfare: A Study in Military Theory* (Harrisburg, Pa.: Stackpole, 1969); David G. Chandler, *The Art of Warfare on Land* (NY: Hamlyn, 1974); J. R. Hale, *Renaissance War Studies* (London: Hambledon Press, 1983); Wm. V. Harris, *War and Imperialism in Republican Rome, 327–70, B.C.* (Oxford: Clarendon Press, 1979); Watson O'Dell Pierce, *Air War: Its Psychological and Social Implications* (NY: Modern Age Books, 1939); Edmund Silberner, *La Guerre dans la pensée economique du XVI siècle* (NY: Garland, 1972); Richard W. Simkin, *Race to the Swift: Thoughts on Twenty-first Century Warfare* (London: Brassey's Defence, 1985); Werner Sombart, *Krieg und Kapitalismus* (NY: Arno Press, 1975).

4. See Richard Wade, *The Urban Frontier* (Cambridge: Harvard Univ. Press, 1959); John W. Reps, *Cities of the American West: A History of Frontier Urban Planning* (Princeton: Princeton Univ. Press, 1979); Bradford Luckingham, *The Urban Southwest: A Profile History of Albuquerque, El Paso, Phoenix, and Tucson* (El Paso: Texas Western Press, 1982); James R. Barrett, *Work and Community in the Jungle: Chicago's Packinghouse Workers, 1894–1922* (Champaign: Univ. of Illinois Press, 1987); Barbara Berg, *The Remembered Gate: Origins of American Feminism: The Woman and the City, 1800–1860* (NY: Oxford Univ. Press, 1978); Carl Abbott, *The New Urban America: Growth and Politics in Sunbelt Cities* (Chapel Hill: Univ. of North Carolina Press, 1987); Scott Bottles, *Los Angeles and the Automobile: The Making of the Modern City* (Berkeley: Univ. of California Press, 1987); Mark I. Gelfand, *A Nation of Cities: The Federal Government and Urban America, 1933–1965* (NY: Oxford Univ. Press, 1975); David R. Johnson, *American Law Enforcement: A History* (St. Louis: Forum Press, 1981); Thomas S. Hines, *Burnham of Chicago: Architect and Planner* (Chicago: Univ. of Chicago Press, 1979); Roger Lane, *Violent Death in the City: Suicide, Accident, and Murder in Nineteenth-Century Philadelphia* (Cambridge: Harvard

Univ. Press, 1979); Christine Rosen, *The Limits of Power: Great Fires and the Process of City Growth in Urban America* (Cambridge: Cambridge Univ. Press, 1986); Michael Feldberg, *The Turbulent Era: Riot and Disorder in Jacksonian America* (NY: Oxford Univ. Press, 1980); Kenneth T. Jackson, *The Crabgrass Frontier: The Suburbanization of the United States* (NY: Oxford Univ. Press, 1985); Sam Bass Warner, *Streetcar Suburbs: The Process of Growth in Boston, 1870–1900* (Cambridge: Harvard Univ. Press, 1962); Henry C. Binford, *The First Suburbs: Residential Communities on the Boston Periphery, 1815–1860* (Chicago: Univ. of Chicago Press, 1985); Robert Fishman, *Bourgeois Utopia: The Rise and Fall of Suburbia* (NY: Basic Books, 1987). For a more extended list see notes 5, 6, 9, 11, & 12.

5. Adrian Cook, *Armies of the Streets* (Lexington: Univ. Press of Kentucky, 1974); Elliott Rudwick, *Race Riot at E. St. Louis, July 2, 1917* (Carbondale: Southern Illinois Univ. Press, 1964).

6. For example, see Jesse D. Clarkson and Thomas C. Cochran, *War As a Social Institution: The Historian's Perspective* (NY: A.M.S. Press, 1941); R. Aron, *Clausewitz;* William Brown, *War and Peace: Essays in Psychological Analysis* (London: A. C. Black, 1939); Nasli Choucri, *Population Dynamics and International Violence* (Lexington, Mass.: Lexington Books, 1974); Robert Ginsburg, ed., *The Critique of War: Contemporary Philosophical Explorations* (Chicago: Regnery, 1969); James F. Dunnigan, *How To Make War: A Comprehensive Guide to Modern Warfare* (NY: Morrow, 1982); James F. Dunnigan, *A Quick and Dirty Guide to War: Briefings on Present and Future Wars* (NY: Morrow, 1985); Sigmund Freud, *Civilization, War, and Death* (London: Hogarth Press, 1953); John K. Macksey, *The Guiness History of Land Warfare* (Enfield, Eng.: Guiness Superlatives, 1973); Michael E. Howard, *War and the Liberal Conscience* (London: Temple Smith, 1978); Michael Glover, *The Velvet Glove: The Decline of Moderation in War* (London: Hodder and Stoughton, 1982); Carol R. Berkin and Clara M. Lovett, eds., *Women, War, and Revolution* (NY: Holmes and Meier, 1980); Edward Glover, *War, Sadism, and Pacifism: Further Essays on Group Psychology and War* (London: Allen and Unwin, 1946); Louis Golding, *Sorrow of War: Poems by Louis Golding* (London: Methuen, 1919); Geo. Wm. Gray, *Science at War* (NY: Harper, 1943); Charles H. Hamlin, *The War Myth in United States History* (NY: Vanguard Press, 1936); Ernest Hemingway, *Men at War: The Best War Stories of All Time* (NY: Crown, 1942); Albert Einstein, *Why War* (Paris: International Institute of Cooperation, League of Nations, 1933); Niccolò Machiavelli, *Arte Della Guerra e Scritti Politici Minori* (1521; Milano: Feltrinelli, 1961); Maj. Ralph Hermon, M.D., *Fatal Partners: War and Disease* (Garden City: Doubleday, 1941); *Marxism-Leninism on War and the Army* (Moscow: Progress Publishers, 1972); Edwin D. Mead, *Washington, Jefferson, and Franklin on War* (Boston: World Peace Foundation, 1913); Henry Meyer, *Voltaire on War and Peace* (Bambury, Oxfordshire: Voltaire Foundation, 1976); Emmanuel Miller, *The Neuroses in War* (NY: Macmillan, 1940); Emilio Mira y Lopez, *Psychiatry in War* (NY: Norton, 1943); Gilbert Murray, *The Ordeal of This Generation* (NY and London, 1929); Geo. W. Nasmyth, *Social Progress and the Darwinian Theory: A Study of Force As a Factor in Human Relations* (NY: Putnam, 1914); Keith L. Nelson, *Why War: Ideology, Theory, and History* (Berkeley: Univ. of California Press, 1979); Alan Newcombe, *An Inter-Nation Tensionometer for the Prediction of War* (Oakville, Ont.: Canadian Peace Foundation Research Institute, 1972); Wm. V. O'Brien, *The Conduct of the Just and Limited War* (NY: Praeger, 1981); Keith F. Otterbein, *The Evolution of War: A Cross Cultural Study* (n.p.: H.R.A.F. Press, 1970); Leo Perla, *What Is National Honor: The Challenge of the Reconstruction* (NY: Macmillan, 1918); Paul R. Pillar, *Negotiating Peace: War Termination As a Bargaining Process* (Princeton: Princeton Univ. Press, 1983); Koca Popovic, *Revision of Marxism-Leninism on the Question of the Liberation War in Yugoslavia* (Belgrade: Jugoslavenska Knjiga, 1949); Ralph C. Preston, *Children's Reactions to a Contemporary War Situation* (NY: Columbia Univ. Press,

1942); Rodolfo Quintero, *El Hombre y la Guerra: Estudio Antropologico* (Caracas: Universidad Central de Venezuela, 1965); Sidney Rogerson, *Propaganda in the Next War* (London: G. Bles, 1938); George Seldes, *Iron, Blood, and Profits: An Exposure of the World Wide Munitions Racket* (NY: Harper, 1934); Alex Strachey, *The Unconscious Motives of War: A Psychological Contribution* (London: Allen and Unwin, 1957); Lewis F. Richardson, *Arms and Insecurity: A Mathematical Study of the Causes and Origins of War* (Pittsburgh: Boxwood Press, 1962); Martin Middlebrook, *The Battle of Hamburg: Allied Bomber Forces Against a German City in 1943* (NY: Scribner, 1980).

7. B. H. Liddell-Hart, *History of the Second World War* (NY: Putnam, 1970), vol. 2: 589–612, 682–98.

8. Wm. McNeill, *The Pursuit of Power: Technology, Armed Force, and Society since A.D. 1000* (Chicago: Univ. of Chicago Press, 1982); Sir George Clark, *War and Society in the 17th Century* (Cambridge: Cambridge Univ. Press, 1958); J. R. Hale, *War and Society;* Michael Howard, *War in European History* (NY: Oxford Univ. Press, 1976); J. W. Winter, ed., *War and Economic Development: Essays in Memory of David Joslin* (Cambridge: Cambridge Univ. Press, 1976).

9. Paul Hohenberg and Lynn Lees, *The Making of Urban Europe, 1000–1950* (Cambridge: Harvard Univ. Press, 1985); see also the work of Susan G. Davis, *Parades and Power: Street Theatre in Nineteenth-Century Philadelphia* (Philadelphia: Temple Univ. Press, 1986); James R. Barrett, *Work and Community in the Jungle: Chicago's Packinghouse Workers, 1894–1922* (Champaign: Univ. of Illinois Press, 1987); Olivier Zunz, *The Changing Face of Inequality: Urbanization, Industrial Development, and Immigrants in Detroit, 1880–1920* (Chicago: Univ. of Chicago Press, 1982); Fishman, *Bourgeois Utopias;* Deil S. Wright, *Understanding Intergovernmental Relations* (Monterey, Calif.: Brooks/Cole, 1982); Bernard Bailyn, *The Origins of American Politics* (NY: Knopf, 1968).

10. Patricia Nelson Limerick, *The Legacy of Conquest: The Unbroken Legacy of the American West* (NY: Norton, 1987).

11. Jackson, *Crabgrass Frontier;* Zane L. Miller, *Suburb: Neighborhood and Community in Forest Park, Ohio, 1935–1976* (Knoxville: Univ. of Tennessee Press, 1981); Fishman, *Bourgeois Utopias;* Binford, *The First Suburbs;* Michael H. Ebner, *Creating Chicago's North Shore* (Chicago: Univ. of Chicago Press, 1988); Matthew Edel, Elliott D. Sclar, and Daniel Luria, *Shaky Palaces: Homeownership and Social Mobility in Boston's Suburbanization* (NY: Columbia Univ. Press, 1984); Carol O'Connor, *A Sort of Utopia: Scarsdale, 1881–1981* (Albany: State Univ. of New York Press, 1983); Daniel Schaffer, *Garden Cities for America: The Radburn Experience* (Philadelphia: Temple Univ. Press, 1982); Jon Teaford, *City and Suburb: The Political Fragmentation of Metropolitan America, 1870–1900* (Chicago: Public Works Historical Society, 1978); Stanley Buder, *Pullman: An Experiment in Industrial Order and Community Planning, 1880–1930* (NY: Oxford Univ. Press, 1967); Joseph L. Arnold, *The New Deal in the Suburbs: A History of the Greenbelt Town Program, 1935–1954* (Columbus: Ohio State Univ. Press, 1971).

12. To mention only one book from each genre, see Michael Feldberg, *The Turbulent Era;* David R. Goldfield, *Cotton Fields and Skyscrapers: Southern City and Region, 1607–1980* (Baton Rouge: Louisiana State Univ. Press, 1982); Arnold R. Hirsch, *Making the Second Ghetto: Race and Housing in Chicago, 1940–1960* (Cambridge: Cambridge Univ. Press, 1982); Ronald H. Bayor, *Neighbors in Conflict: The Irish, Germans, Jews, and Italians of New York City, 1929–1941* (Champaign: Univ. of Illinois Press, 1988); Ricardo Romo, *East Los Angeles: The History of a Barrio* (Austin: Univ. of Texas Press, 1983); Thomas Bender, *Toward an Urban Vision: Ideas and Institutions in Nineteenth-Century America* (Lexington: Univ. Press of Kentucky, 1975); Sylvia Doughty Fries, *The Urban Idea in Colonial America* (Philadelphia: Temple Univ. Press, 1977); Gunther Barth, *City People: The Rise of Modern*

City Culture in Nineteenth-Century America (NY: Oxford Univ. Press, 1980); Harold Platt, *The Electric City* (Chicago: Univ. of Chicago Press, 1991); Wm. Issel and Robert Cherny, *San Francisco, 1865–1932: Politics, Power, and Urban Development* (Berkeley: Univ. of California Press, 1986); Norbert MacDonald, *Distant Neighbors: A Comparative History of Seattle and Vancouver* (Lincoln: Univ. of Nebraska Press, 1987); Gerald D. Nash, *The American West in the Twentieth Century: A Short History of an Urban Oasis* (NY: Prentice Hall, 1973); Douglas Henry Daniels, *Pioneer Urbanites: A Social and Cultural History of Black San Francisco* (Philadelphia: Temple Univ. Press, 1980); Patricia Mooney Melvin, *The Organic City: Urban Definition and Neighborhood Organization, 1880–1920* (Lexington: Univ. Press of Kentucky, 1987); Richard M. Bernard and Bradley R. Rice, eds., *Sunbelt Cities: Politics and Growth Since World War II* (Austin: Univ. of Texas Press, 1983); Luckingham, *The Urban Southwest;* Carl Abbott, *The New Urban America;* Barbara Berg, *The Remembered Gate;* Scott L. Bottles, *Los Angeles and the Automobile;* Mark I. Gelfand, *A Nation of Cities;* David R. Johnson, *American Law Enforcement;* Thomas Hines, *Burnham of Chicago;* Roger Lane, *Violent Death in the City;* Christine M. Rosen, *The Limits of Power;* Marc A. Weiss, *The Rise of the Community Builders: The American Real Estate Industry and Urban Land Planning* (NY: Columbia Univ. Press, 1987); Stanley K. Schultz, *Constructing Urban Culture: American Cities and City Planning, 1800–1920* (Philadelphia: Temple Univ. Press, 1989); Robert B. Fairbanks, *Making Better Citizens: Housing Reform and the Community Development Strategy in Cincinnati, 1890–1960* (Champaign: Univ. of Illinois Press, 1988).

13. Gavin Wright, *The Political Economy,* 182; for urban historical examples of bipolar analyses striving for hegemony see Marjorie Murphy, "Gender Relations on an Urban Terrain: Locating Women in the City," *Journal of Urban History,* 13:2 (Feb. 1987): 197–206; John F. McClymer, "Social Space and the Development of Working-Class and/or Urban Culture," *Journal of Urban History,* 14:3 (May 1988): 406–12.

14. Eric Monkkonen, *America Becomes Urban: The Development of U.S. Cities and Towns, 1780–1980* (LA: Univ. of California Press, 1988), 89–158.

15. Clayton R. Koppes, *JPL and the American Space Program: A History of the Jet Propulsion Laboratory* (New Haven: Yale Univ. Press, 1982), 96–97.

Chapter 1. The Metropolitan-Military Complex: A Mutual Dilemma of Relative Decline

1. Kenneth E. Boulding, "The City as an Element in the International System," in Martin Meyerson, ed., *The Conscience of the City* (NY: Braziller, 1970); Oscar Handlin, "The Modern City as a Field of Historical Study," in Oscar Handlin and John Burchard, eds., *The Historian and the City* (Cambridge: Harvard Univ. Press, 1963), 3; Olivier Zunz, *The Changing Face of Inequality: Urbanization, Industrial Development, and Immigrants in Detroit, 1880–1920* (Chicago: Univ. of Chicago Press, 1982), 1–11, 399–403; Sam Bass Warner, Jr., *The Urban Wilderness: A History of the American City* (NY: Harper and Row, 1972), 267–76; William Issel and Robert W. Cherny, *San Francisco, 1865–1932: Politics, Power, and Urban Development* (Berkeley: Univ. of California Press, 1986), 101–218.

2. Mark I. Gelfand, *A Nation of Cities,* 30–66.

3. City of Los Angeles, Bureau of Community Analysis, *The Economic Development of Southern California, 1920–76,* vol. I: *The Aerospace Industry* (LA: City of Los Angeles, 1976), 9–12.

4. *San Diego Union,* June 4, 1935.

5. Handlin, "The Modern City As a Field of Historical Study," 3.

6. Richard C. Wade, *The Urban Frontier: Pioneer Life in Early Pittsburgh, Cincinnati, Lexington, Louisville, and St. Louis* (Chicago: Univ. of Chicago Press, 1959), 315–19.

7. Roger W. Lotchin, "The City and Sword in Metropolitan California, 1919–1941," *Urbanism Past and Present* 7:2 (Summer/Fall 1982): 1–16.

8. Nash, *The American West in the Twentieth Century: A Short History of an Urban Oasis,* 65–77.

9. Ibid.

10. Association of Bay Area Governments, *Regional Plan 1970–1990: San Francisco Bay Region* (Berkeley, 1970), 7.

11. Nash, *The American West,* 65–77.

12. *San Francisco Business,* 10:14 (April 13, 1925): 8–9 (hereafter *SF Business*); State of California, *California Statistical Abstract, 1970* (Sacramento, 1970).

13. U.S. Dept. of Commerce, Bureau of the Census, *Census of Population: 1950,* vol. 2, *Characteristics of the Population* (Washington: U.S. Govt. Printing Office, 1952), 9–11.

14. Ibid.

15. Ibid.

16. U.S. Dept. of Commerce, Bureau of the Census. *Sixteenth Census of the United States,* vol. 1, *Population* (Washington: U.S. Govt. Printing Office, 1942), 215–26.

17. *San Francisco Journal of Commerce,* Jan. 27, 1920, p. 2 (hereafter *SF Journal of Comm*).

18. Robert A. Hart, *The Great White Fleet: Its Voyage Around the World, 1907–09* (Boston: Little, Brown, 1965), 54–55.

19. Jack McNairn and Jerry McMullen, *Ships of the Redwood Coast* (Stanford: Stanford Univ. Press, 1945), 79–81, 100–109.

20. According to some estimates, up to 85 percent went to labor. For the expected multiplier, see Ralph R. Eltse, March 5, 1934, 73rd Cong., 2nd sess., 1934, *Congressional Record* 78:4:3751–52.

21. *SF Jour. Comm.,* April 7, 1920, p. 1.

22. Roger W. Lotchin, "The City and the Sword: San Francisco and the Rise of the Metropolitan-Military Complex, 1919–1941," *Journal of American History* 65:4 (March 1979): 1007.

23. Ibid., 118.

24. Ibid., 4.

25. Ibid.

26. Robert Wiebe, *The Search for Order 1877–1920* (Westport, Conn.: Greenwood Press, 1967).

27. Roger W. Lotchin, "The Darwinian City: The Politics of Urbanization in San Francisco Between the World Wars," *Pacific Historical Review,* 48:3 (Aug. 1979): 381.

28. For the development of county government in Los Angeles County, see John Anson Ford, *Thirty Explosive Years in Los Angeles County* (San Marino: Huntington Library, 1961). The immense domain of Los Angeles County may yet provide the ultimate test of whether metropolitan government actually will solve urban problems.

29. State of California, *Statistical Abstract: 1970* (Sacramento, 1970), 13–17.

30. Ibid.

31. Ibid.

32. Quoted in *SF Business* 6:20 (May 18, 1923): 7, 10, 20.

33. Ibid., Nov. 11, 1925.

34. Maynard McFie [former president of the Los Angeles Chamber of Commerce], "Pinning Faith to a Growing Harbor," *Southern California Business* 3:1 (Feb. 1924): 70–78 (hereafter *SC Business*).

35. Lotchin, "The Darwinian City . . . ," 361.

36. Ibid.

37. "Days of Delight on the Magic Isles," *SC Business* 4:6 (July 1925): 26.

38. Visiting Among Northern Friends," ibid. 2:4 (May 1923): 22–23; ibid. 1:12 (Dec. 1922): 11–12.

39. Lawrence Kinnard, *History of the Greater San Francisco Bay Region,* vol. 2 (NY: Lewis Historical Publishing Co., 1966), 102–286; John B. McGloin, S.J., *San Francisco: The Story of a City* (San Rafael: Presidio Press, 1978), 107–234.

40. Benjamin F. Cooling, ed., *War, Business, and American Society: Historical Perspectives on the Military-Industrial Complex* (Port Washington, N.Y.: Kennikat Press, 1977), 1–180; Paul A. C. Koistinen, *The Military-Industrial Complex: A Historical Perspective* (NY: Praeger, 1980), 1–124.

41. For American pacifism, see Charles Chatfield, *For Peace and Justice: Pacifism in America, 1914–1941* (Knoxville; Univ. of Tennessee Press, 1971); and John Kendall Nelson, *The Peace Prophets: American Pacifist Thought, 1919–1941* (Chapel Hill: Univ. of North Carolina Press, 1967).

42. William Kettner, *Why It Was Done and How* (San Diego: Frye and Smith, 1923), 19–20ff.

43. The Japanese often expressed regret at the transfer of the fleet or some part of it to the Pacific Coast.

44. The class-based interpretation of urban history goes back at least to the work of George Mowry, *The California Progressives* (Berkeley: Univ. of California Press, 1951), and it has flourished recently in the writing of Olivier Zunz, *The Changing Face of Inequality: Urbanization, Industrial Development, and Immigrants in Detroit, 1880–1920* (Chicago: Univ. of Chicago Press, 1982); Ira Katznelson, *City Trenches: Urban Politics and the Patterning of Class in the United States* (NY: Pantheon, 1981); William Issel and Robert Cherny, *San Francisco, 1865–1932: Politics, Power, and Urban Development* (Berkeley: Univ. of California Press, 1986); M. Christine Boyer, *Dreaming the Rational City: The Myth of American City Planning* (Cambridge: MIT Press, 1983).

45. *SF Jour. of Comm.,* Feb. 2, 1920, p. 1.

46. Frank R. Devlin to Hiram Johnson, June 20, 1920, Hiram Johnson Correspondence and Papers, Bancroft Library, University of California (hereafter Johnson Papers).

47. *San Francisco Daily Commercial News,* June 10, 1920, p. 1 (hereafter *Daily Commercial News*).

48. *SF Journal of Commerce,* Oct. 10, 1921, pp. 3, 7; Oct. 20, 1921, p. 12; Oct. 21, 1929, p. 3.

49. *San Francisco Examiner,* Dec. 21, 1922, Sec. 1, p. 10.

50. *San Francisco Labor Clarion,* Nov. 11, 1921, p. 13.

51. For San Francisco radicals, see District Council No. 2, Maritime Federation of the Pacific, "The Yanks Are NOT Coming!" (San Francisco: Maritime Federation of the Pacific, 1940), 2–15.

52. For Los Angeles area left-wing comment which is fervent on the international situation, but oblivious to the buildup of the metropolitan-military complex, see various 1939 issues of *Hollywood Now:* Aug. 11, p. 4; Aug. 18, pp. 1, 4; Sept. 1, pp. 1, 4; Sept. 8, pp. 1–2; Sept. 22, p. 2; Oct. 6, p. 2; Oct. 13, pp. 1, 2, 4; Oct. 20, p. 2; Nov. 3, pp. 1–2; Nov. 10, p. 2; Dec. 8, p. 2; Dec. 15, pp. 1–2; and 1940 issues: Jan. 12, pp. 1, 4; Jan. 26, p. 2. The last issue, for example, denounced the U.S. Steel Corporation, "which profits from hostilities," but made no mention of the local urban employers like Lockheed, Douglas, North American, and Consolidated, which also benefitted from war, and which, unlike U.S. Steel, had considerably less civilian business.

53. *San Francisco Chronicle,* Oct. 24, 1921, editorial, p. 18.

54. Leslie B. Newman, Secretary of the Navy League of the United States, Western Section, to James D. Phelan, April 9, 1925, James Phelan Papers, Bancroft Library (hereafter Phelan Papers).

55. Nathan Glazer and Daniel P. Moynihan, *Beyond the Melting Pot: The Negroes, Puerto Ricans, Jews, Italians, and Irish of New York City* (Cambridge: MIT Press, 1963), 3–23.

56. *San Francisco Journal of Commerce,* Jan. 19, 1920, p. 1; ibid., Jan. 27, 1920, p. 2; ibid., Feb. 2, 1920, p. 1; ibid., March 22, 1920, p. 1; ibid., May 20, 1920, p. 1; ibid., Nov. 17, 1920, p. 2; *San Francisco Daily Commercial News,* Feb. 2, 1920, p. 1; June 10, 1920, p. 1; ibid., Nov. 18, 1920, p. 1.

57. *Chronicle,* Oct. 19, 1921, p. 13; *Journal of Commerce,* Oct. 8, 1921, p. 4; ibid., Oct. 10, 1921, p. 3; ibid., Oct. 29, 1921, p. 1; ibid., Feb. 14, 1922, p. 3; ibid., Oct. 10, 1922, Sec. I, p. 17; *San Francisco Examiner,* Dec. 31, 1922, p. k-4; Oct. 28, 1922, Sec. I, p. 28; ibid., Nov. 24, 1922, Sec. I, p. 4; ibid., Dec. 19, 1922, Sec. I, pp. 7, 15; *One Army Spirit,* vol. 1: no. 3, p. 1; *Daily Commercial News,* Sept. 1, 1922, p. 4.

58. Ibid.

59. For an excellent discussion of this intra-ethnic tension, see Ronald Bayor, *Neighbors in Conflict,* and Charles H. Trout, *Boston, The Great Depression, and the New Deal* (NY: Oxford Univ. Press, 1977).

60. For the city and country conflict of the twenties see Don Kirschner, *City and Country: Rural Responses to Urbanization in the 1920s* (Westport, Conn.: Greenwood, 1970), 1–21 and passim.

61. *San Francisco Examiner,* Dec. 21, 1922, Sec. I, p. 10.

Chapter 2. Capturing the Navy: San Diego

1. Clarence Grange, Secretary of the Finance Committee of the Official Committee for the Reception of the Fleet, to James D. Phelan, March 23, 1908, Phelan Papers.

2. William R. Braisted, *The United States Navy in the Pacific, 1909–1922* (Austin: Univ. of Texas Press, 1971), 5–6.

3. Speech of the Honorable James D. Phelan in the 64th Congress (Washington: U.S. Govt. Printing Office, 1916), 1–8; U.S. Senate, diverse senators speaking on "Naval Appropriations," July 17, 1916, *Congressional Record,* vol. XIII: pt. 11, pp. 11195–11207.

4. Ibid.; Braisted, *The United States Navy,* 458–60.

5. Braisted, *The United States Navy,* 535–48.

6. Dept. of Commerce, Bureau of the Census, *Fourteenth Census of the United States . . . , 1920,* vol. I, *Population* (Washington, 1921), 81, 95.

7. Kettner, *Why and How It Was Done,* 11.

8. Greg Hennessey, "San Diego, the U.S. Navy, and Urban Development: West Coast City Building, 1912–1929," forthcoming in the *California History.*

9. Walter Millis, *Arms and Men: A Study in American Military History* (NY: Capricorn Books, 1956), 1–70; Samuel Huntington, *The Soldier and the State: The Theory and Politics of Civil-Military Relations* (Cambridge: Belknap Press of Harvard Univ. Press, 1957), 223–30, 290–94; Col. James A. Donovan, *Militarism, U.S.A.* (NY: Scribner, 1970), 3ff.

10. Richard F. Pourade, *The Rising Tide,* vol. 6 of *The History of San Diego* (San Diego, Union-Tribune Pub. Co., 1967), 1–26.

11. Ibid.

12. Ibid.

13. Kettner, *Why and How It Was Done,* 9–10.

14. Naval Affairs Committee, *Hearings Before the Sixty-sixth Congress on Estimates Submitted by the Secretary of the Navy, 1920* (Washington: U.S. Govt. Printing Office, 1950), 2070.

15. Kettner, *Why and How It Was Done,* 1–181.

16. Ibid., 15.

17. Robert Caro, *The Power Broker* (NY: Random House, 1974), 91–180.

18. House Naval Affairs Committee, *Hearings Before the Sixty-sixth Congress on Estimates . . . , 1920,* 925.

19. Kettner, *Why and How It Was Done,* 33, 89, 116.

20. Josephus Daniels, *The Wilson Era: Years of Peace—1910–1917* (Chapel Hill: Univ. of North Carolina Press, 1944), 299–320.

21. Ibid.; Josephus Daniels, manuscript diary, Jan. 14, 1921, Folder 100, Daniels Papers, Southern Historical UNC; Hennessey, "San Diego."

22. For a definitive account of the impact of the Navy on San Diego, see Hennessey, "San Diego."

23. Edward J. P. Davis, *The United States Navy and U.S. Marine Corps at San Diego* (San Diego: Pioneer, 1955), 29; Braisted, *The United States Navy,* 229–30, 473–74, 480–82; J. S. McKean et al., Special Board of Inspection of Naval Bases, etc., on the Pacific Coast, to the Secretary of the Navy, Oct. 18, 1919, Office of the Secretary of the Navy, Secret and Confidential Correspondence, 1919–1926, General Records of the Department of the Navy, RG 80, Box 73, National Archives.

24. Charles Glaab and A. Theodore Brown, *A History of Urban America* (NY: Macmillan, 1983), 26–51.

25. William Kharl, *Water and Power: The Conflict Over Los Angeles Water Supply in the Owens Valley* (Berkeley: Univ. of California Press, 1982), 1–180ff; Robert Fogelson, *Fragmented Metropolis: Los Angeles, 1850–1930* (Cambridge: Harvard Univ. Press, 1967), 97–98, 233–34; Vincent Ostrom, *Water and Politics: A Study of Water Policies and Administration in the Development of Los Angeles* (LA: Haynes Foundation, 1953), 1–26.

26. House Naval Affairs Committee, *Hearings Before the Sixty-sixth Congress on Estimates . . . , 1920,* 1–28.

27. *San Diego Union,* May 27, 1938, sect. I, p. 3; editorial, "Splitting the Fleet," *LA Times,* Dec. 26, 1938, sect. 2, p. 4.

28. Pourade, *The Rising Tide,* 3–50; For San Francisco's manifest assets for a naval base see *Hearings Before the Sixty-sixth Congress on Estimates . . . , 1920,* 1097–1107.

29. Kettner, *Why and How It Was Done,* 21–40.

30. Ibid., 46–49.

31. Davis, *The United States Navy and U.S. Marine Corps at San Diego,* 17–18.

32. Martin K. Gordon, "The Marines Have Landed and San Diego Is Well in Hand: Local Politics and Naval Base Development," paper delivered to the Thirteenth Annual Military History Conference, Boston, Mass., April 28, 1979, pp. 1–14.

33. Kettner, *Why and How It Was Done,* 101–5.

34. Davis, *The United States Navy and U.S. Marine Corps at San Diego,* 29–30.

35. Joseph W. Brennan, "What a Dime Can Do . . . ," *San Diego Magazine,* June 1931, pp. 5–7.

36. *San Diego Union,* July 13, 1935.

37. San Diego Harbor Dept., *The Port of San Diego: Harbor and Industrial Data, 1940–41* (San Diego, 1941), 29.

38. *San Diego Union,* Oct. 18, 1935.

39. Ibid., Oct. 27, 1934.

40. *SC Business* 2:3 (April 8, 1940): 1.

41. Ibid; *LA Times,* Feb. 2, 1938; Nov. 25, 1937; May 9, 1937; *San Diego Union,* May 27, 1938, Sec. I, p. 3.

42. Kettner, *Why and How It Was Done,* 101; Gordon, "The Marines Have Landed," 111.

43. Roger W. Lotchin, "The Metropolitan-Military Complex in Comparative Perspec-

tive: San Francisco, Los Angeles, and San Diego, 1919–1941," *Journal of the West* 18:3 (July 1979): 26.

44. Peter Hall, Anne Markusen, Scott Campbell, and Sabina Dietrich, *The Rise of the Gunbelt* (NY: Oxford Univ. Press, 1991); Daniel Todd, *Defence Industries: A Global Perspective* (London: Routledge, 1988), 131–99.

45. Kenneth E. Boulding, "The City as an Element in the International System," in Martin Meyerson, ed., *The Conscience of the City* (NY: Geo. Brazilier, 1970), 27.

46. Oscar Handlin, "The Modern City as a Field of Historical Study," in Handlin and John Burchard, eds., *The Historian and the City,* 26.

47. Even such an important matter as the establishment of Camp Kearny during the First World War was delayed until San Diego and Los Angeles put aside their differences over the site. Till that moment, their competition for the base in effect vetoed it.

48. National Guard planners also feared attack from the south, and National Guard units held maneuvers in that area to prepare for invasion from that direction. See David P. Barrows to Brigadier Gen. Sherman Miles, Acting Asst. Chief of Staff, G-2, Feb. 28, 1941, Barrows Papers (Bancroft Library).

49. Todd, *Defence Industries,* 133–99.

Chapter 3. Creating the American Singapore:
The San Francisco Bay Area and the Quest for Naval Riches

1. "Historical Outline of the Proposed Naval Base Development Project in San Francisco Bay," Dec. 12, 1923, Office of the Secretary of the Navy, Secret and Confidential Correspondence, 1919–1926, General Records of the Department of the Navy, RG 80 (National Archives).

2. 66th Cong., 2nd sess., House, Naval Affairs Committee, *Hearing on Estimates Submitted by the Secretary of the Navy, 1920* (Washington, 1920), 2346–47.

3. City of San Diego, Harbor Department, *The Port of San Diego: The Southwest Terminal for Navigation, Transportation and Aviation. Naval Operating Base* (San Diego, 1928), 48.

4. Ibid.

5. 64th Cong., 2nd sess., Senate, *Congressional Record,* pp. 10–15.

6. U.S. Senate, Senator James D. Phelan speaking on "Naval Appropriations," 64th Cong., 2nd sess., March 2, 1917, *Congressional Record,* vol. LIV: pt. 5, pp. 4721–23.

7. Ibid.

8. 64th Cong., 2nd sess., Joint Committee on Pacific Naval Base Sites, *Report of the Joint Committee: Naval Base, San Francisco Bay* (Washington, 1921).

9. *San Francisco Chronicle,* Nov. 7, 1923, p. 1.

10. The decisiveness of the influence of Vallejo and its congressman, Charles F. Curry, was universally admitted. That point is documented by evidence from sources of all kinds. The Navy insiders were particularly impressed with the influence of Curry and the reality of the veto of Vallejo and Mare Island. A Navy memorandum of 1930 made the point perfectly.

Despite the repeated recommendations of the Secretary of the Navy, all proposals to acquire the Alameda site have been disregarded or have failed of passage in Congress. This has been mainly due to the determined and consistent opposition of political and local interests representing VALLEJO AND MARE ISLAND . . . the city of Vallejo is still opposed to the construction of a Naval Base at Alameda.

Memorandum from Director, War Plans Division, to the Chief of Naval Operations, Oct. 18, 1930, General Correspondence, 1926–40, General Records of the Navy Dept.

11. 72nd Cong., 3rd sess., Committee on Naval Affairs, *Hearings on Sundry Legislation*

Affecting the Naval Establishment, 1929–30 (Washington, 1930), 2723; memorandum of the General Board, No. 18, 1930, General Correspondence, 1926–40, General Records of the Navy Dept.

12. Memorandum of the Chief of Bureau of Yards and Docks to the Secy. of the Navy, Sept. 24, 1929, Secret Correspondence, 1927–1935, General Records of the Navy Dept.

13. Ibid.; and memorandum, War Plans Division to the Chief of Naval Operations, Oct. 18, 1930, General Correspondence, 1926–1940, General Records of the Navy Dept.

14. Memorandum from the Senior Member of the Board for the Development of Navy Yard Plans to the Local Board for Development of Navy Yard Plans, Twelfth Naval District, April 4–17, 1929, Secret Correspondence, 1927–39, General Records of the Navy Dept.

15. Commandant, Twelfth Naval District and Naval Operating Base, San Francisco, to Chief of Naval Operations . . . , March 7, 1933, Secret Correspondence, 1927–39, General Records of the Navy Dept.

16. The entire decision-making process which brought about the re-evaluation of the base situation in San Francisco Bay began at least as early as 1928 with a Navy General Board review of the situation. After consideration by various bodies local and national, the process came to a head in a memorandum from the Chief of Naval Operations to the Secy. of the Navy, June 26, 1931, General Correspondence, 1926–1940, General Records of the Navy Dept.

17. Besides the popular support for the Oakland Supply Depot, the Chamber of Commerce, the newspapers, the congressional delegation, the Oakland City Council, and the Alameda County Board of Supervisors supported the acquisition of the supply depot. See letter of the Oakland Board of Port Commissioners to the Oakland electorate, Oct. 22, 1936, Institute of Governmental Studies, University of California at Berkeley (hereafter IGS).

18. For an able treatment of the important but much misunderstood Reber Plan see David R. Long, "Dam It!: The Story of John Reber and the San Francisco Bay Project," M.A. Thesis, Univ. of North Carolina, Chapel Hill, 1988, pp. 84–138.

Chapter 4. Dive Bombers in the Land of Oz: Los Angeles and the Aircraft Industry

1. Eric Monkkonen, *America Becomes Urban: The Development of U.S. Cities and Towns, 1780–1980* (Berkeley: Univ. of California Press, 1988), 85–86.

2. John B. Rae, *Climb to Greatness: The American Aircraft Industry, 1920–1980* (Cambridge: MIT Press, 1968), 1–19.

3. John S. Pettengill, "The Impact of Military Technology on European Income Distribution," *Journal of Interdisciplinary History* 10:2 (Autumn, 1979): 201–25.

4. City of Los Angeles, Community Analysis Bureau, "The Economic Development of Southern California, 1920–1976," vol. I, *The Aerospace Industry* (LA, 1976), vii–xii, provides a good outline of the peculiar economic disabilities of southern California. The War Production Board coined the phrase, "The great wall of California," in 1945, ibid.

5. Rae, *Climb to Greatness,* 58–118; Arlene Elliott, "The Rise of Aeronautics in California, 1849–1940," *Southern California Historical Quarterly,* 52 (March 1970): 1–32.

6. Rae, *Climb to Greatness,* generally ignores the booster influences on aircraft localization. See also, Nash, *The American West,* 230, for the geographic argument.

7. Rae, *Climb to Greatness,* 1–19.

8. Standard & Poors Corporation, *Industry Surveys,* vol. 158, no. 24, sec. 1 (June 21, 1990): A-17, A-22, A-25; Ibid., vol. 158, no. 20, sec. 1 (May 21, 1990): E-33.

9. Rae, *Climb to Greatness,* 77–97.

10. Ibid.

11. City of Los Angeles, Community Analysis Bureau, "The Economic Development of Southern California, 1920–1976," vol. I, *The Aerospace Industry* (LA, 1976), vii–xii.

12. For the Angeleno leadership see Robert Fogelson, *The Fragmented Metropolis: Los Angeles, 1850–1930* (Cambridge: Harvard Univ. Press, 1967); Frederic Cople Jaher, *The Urban Establishment: Upper Strata in Boston, New York, Charleston, Chicago, and Los Angeles* (Champaign: Univ. of Illinois Press, 1982), 577–710.

13. Fogelson, *Fragmented Metropolis,* 85–186.

14. Ibid., 1–84; Carey McWilliams, *Southern California Country: An Island on the Land* (NY: Duell, Sloan and Pearce, 1946), 70–165.

15. Nash, *The American West,* 1–5.

16. City of Los Angeles, Community Analysis Bureau, "The Economic Development of Southern California, 1920–1976," vol. I, *The Aerospace Industry* (LA, 1976), vii–xii.

17. For the decline of the aircraft industry following World War I, see Rae, *Climb to Greatness,* 1–8.

18. George H. Prudden, "Aviation As a Business," *San Diego Magazine* (Aug. 1927), 36; Harris M. Hanshue, "Development of Passenger Transportation in California," *SC Business* (Aug. 1928), 9.

19. Unsigned editorial, *SC Business,* 7:7 (Aug. 1928): 7.

20. James Flink, *Americans Adopt the Automobile, 1895–1910* (Cambridge: MIT Press, 1970), 87–103.

21. Unsigned editorial, *SC Business* 8:4 (May 1929): 7.

22. Ibid.

23. E. V. Rickenbacker, "When Traffic Takes to the Air," *SC Business* 4:8 (Sept. 1925): 7.

24. *SF Examiner,* June 1, 1927, editorial page; *SC Business* 7:7 (Aug. 1928): 26; *San Diego Union,* Oct. 25, 1935, Sec. 1, p. 3.

25. Rickenbacker, "When Traffic Takes to the Air," 7–8, 46.

26. *SC Business* 7:7 (Aug., 1928): 12–13, 50; Henry H. Arnold to Wm. M. Henry, April 13, 1932, Henry H. Arnold Papers, Library of Congress (hereafter Arnold Papers).

27. H. H. Arnold to Major Gen. Malin Craig, Commanding General, 9th Corps Area, Nov. 3, 1932; Arnold to A. C. McIntosh, Air Officer, 9th Corps Area, March 16, 1933; Dudley M. Steele to Arnold, July 18, 1932, Arnold Papers.

28. *SF Examiner,* March 24, 1923, p. 1; ibid., May 16, 1923, sect. 2, p. 7; *SF Call and Post,* March 12, 1925, p. 12; *SF Chronicle,* Oct. 26, 1925, sect. 2, p. 2.

29. *SF Examiner,* May 20, 1932, sect. 1, p. 7; *San Diego Union,* Jan. 23, 1933, sect. 1, p. 1; *SF Examiner,* Feb. 19, 1933, sect. 1, pp. 1, 11.

30. *LA Times,* April 27, 1937, sect. 1, p. 1; Jan. 1, 1937, sect. 1, p. 4; ibid, April 23, 1937, sect. 2, p. 1; ibid. May 22, 1937, sect. 1, pp. 1 & 7; May 11, 1937, sect. 1, p. 3; May 13, 1937, sect. 1, p. 7.

31. Ibid., May 6, 1938, sec. 2, p. 1; Sept. 9, 1938, sec. 1, p. 1; *San Diego Union,* Jan. 23, 1938, sect. 1, p. 10. Throughout the period, metropolitan newspapers voiced support of more adequate defense preparations. This backing became more pronounced, more insistent, and more consistent as World War II loomed.

32. As was previously noted, George Hearst was an honorary naval officer of the State of California. He was also a member of the Golden Gate Chapter of the National Aeronautic Association, the U.S. branch of the Federation Aeronautique Internationale. Earle Wright to Directors, Golden Gate Chapter of the National Aeronautic Assn., Dec. 5, 1932, Arnold Papers, Box 3.

33. Editorial, *San Diego Union,* July 28, 1935, sec. 1, p. 4; United States 75th Cong., 1st sess., 1938, *Congressional Record* 83:9:678–682; editorial, *San Diego Union,* Aug. 27, 1941, sect. 2, p. 2; Nov. 25, 1938, sect. B, p. 3.

34. *SF Examiner,* May 13, 1923, sect. N, p. 14; Warren Jefferson Davis, *Japan, the Air Menace of the Pacific* (Boston: Christopher Publ. House, 1928), 122–23, 141ff; ibid., 101–14.

35. "Remarks of Fletcher Bowron at National Defense Week Program, "Los Angeles Municipal Airport, Feb. 24, 1940; Bowron, Speech at the Armory, Exposition Park, Los Angeles, April 7, 1941 (all Bowron material is to be found in Bowron Collection); *L.A. Daily News,* Sept. 22, 1941, Los Angeles County; Office of the Superintendent of Schools," Defense Digest," no. 1, Sept. 1941, Foreword and pp. 5–7.

36. Van Hogan to H. H. Arnold, March 12, 1932, Arnold Papers, Box 4.

37. Henry H. Arnold, *Global Mission* (NY: Harper, 1949), 136 ff; Henry H. Arnold and Ira C. Eaker, *This Flying Game* (NY: Funk and Wagnalls, 1936), 156–57; Louis Vanderhood to Arnold, Aug. 4, 1932; Arnold to Carl McStay, Auto Club of Southern California, July 22, 1932; Louis Vanderhood to H. H. Arnold, Aug. 4, 1932; Arnold to Carl McStay, Auto Club of Southern California, July 22, 1932, Arnold Papers, Box 4. *SC Business* 8:10 (Nov. 1929): 9–11.

38. Arnold, *Global Mission,* 148–53. "As regards strategic bombardment, the doctrines were still Douhet's ideas modified by our own thinking in regard to pure defense. We felt, out in the 1st Wing, that we were doing much to furnish the practical tests for, and proofs of, the Maxwell Field theories. A different attitude from Douhet's toward bomber escort and a very different view of precision bombing resulted . . . we became convinced—at least I certainly did—that long-range, heavy bombers must have not only increased fire power and mutual support, but also a fast maneuverable fighter escort which could go with the bombers to their targets. . . . Those who thought it was a miracle that long-range fighter escort for our bombers appeared over Germany at just the critical moment in the fall of 1943 apparently do not realize that, like the B-29, this was something we started developing before the war. I should have prefered never to send any unescorted bombers over Germany" (ibid.).

39. U.S. Army, Ninth Corps Area, Annual Report, 1925–1926, R. G. 94, Office of the Adj. General, Central Files, 1926–1929, Box 1529. It is, of course, questionable whether the promotion of "commercial aviation" was a military function and it is at least as dubious whether the military had any business comparing speed factors that would have put auto, steamship, and railroad transportation in a bad or disadvantageous light. These considerations did not bother the military, though, however much they might have angered auto, railroad, and steamship competitors for passenger and freight transportation.

40. William Beard, unpublished mss, "Los Angeles Municipal Airport," 1–2; for the demand for federal aid, see San Francisco Board of Supervisors (hereafter SF Bd. of S.), *Journal* 33 . . . (Jan. 3, 1938): 16–17; and Bowron, "A National Airport Program . . ." 1–23.

41. For the later period, see Bowron, ibid., 12.

42. *SC Business* 8:10 (Nov. 1929): 9.

43. Editorial, *SF Chronicle,* May 4, 1927, sect. 2, p. 22; ibid., June 2, 1927, sect. 2, pp. 2–3; editorial, ibid., May 4, 1927, sect. 2, pp. 22. *San Diego Magazine* 3:9 (Aug. 1927): 20, 39; for the impact of dynamic airplane technology on fixed airport facilities see Fletcher Bowron, "A National Airport Program . . . ," 21.

44. For the pattern of air power dispersement in Northern California, five months before Pearl Harbor, see the maps in the *SF Chronicle,* June 29, 1941.

45. Dudley Steele to Arnold, July 20, 1932, and same to same April 8, 1932, Arnold Papers; Dudley Steele, "As I Remember It" (manuscript autobiography), 7; Dudley Steele, interview (typescript), 19, Bowron Collection.

46. Charles A. Lindbergh, *Autobiography of Values* (NY: Harcourt, Brace, Jovanovich, 1976), 105.

47. Arnold to Westover, Aug. 6, 1932; Arnold to Carr, May 27, 1932; Arnold to Lt. Col. C. P. George, Aug. 1, 1932, Arnold Papers. It should be noted that these three letters cover

the period from May to August, a considerable period of time during which ideal flying conditions did not prevail, at least in the humble opinion of the commander of all the Air Corps units in Southern California. It is perhaps adding insult to injury to note that despite the glorious climate the Army Air Corps commander also suffered from hay fever. See also J. E. Schaefer to Arnold, May 25, 1932, Arnold Papers; Dudley Steele, "Interview," p. 23, Bowron Collection; *The American City* 63 (Oct. 1948): 117; and 38 (April 1928): 144.

48. Dept. of the Navy, Bureau of Aeronautics, "History of the Use of North Island, San Diego, California, for Flying Activities of the Army and Navy, Aug. 20, 1932," Office of the Secretary of the Navy, Confidential Correspondence, 1927–1939, RG 80 (National Archives): 4; Kettner, *Why and How It Was Done,* 77; "Flying Activities," 4.

49. Kettner, *Why and How It Was Done,* 74–76, 77–98; the story in Kettner's autobiography is based on verbatim quotes from a letter written to Kettner by J. B. Lippincott.

50. Kettner, *Why and How It Was Done,* 77–98.

51. Ibid., 73–76.

52. Ibid. These pages contain a series of verbatim quotes from the records, letters, and documents of the participants. The whole is contained in a letter from Lippincott to Kettner, Nov. 15, 1918.

53. "Flying Activities," 21–22.

54. Ibid., 25.

55. Gordon Swanborough and Peter M. Bowers, *United States Military Aircraft Since 1908* (NY: Putnam, 1963), 376–77. The Platt-MacArthur agreement of January 1931 conveyed this responsibility to the Army Air Corps.

56. "Flying Activities," 12, 16, 20.

57. Ibid., 10, 25; MacArthur objected that "it is hard enough to get money for legitimate Army purposes, without our having to contribute to other branches of government" (pp. 25–26).

58. Ibid., 28; *San Diego Union,* June 9, 1934, sect. 1, p. 1. The news story quoted and paraphrased San Diego Congressman George Burnham; ibid., Dec. 28, 1934, sect. 1, p. 1.

59. Rae, *Climb to Greatness,* 77–119; Wm. G. Cunningham, *The Aircraft Industry: A Study in Industrial Location* (LA: Lovin L. Morrison, 1951), 19–21.

60. Arnold Papers, Boxes 1–6; for an interpretation stressing the importance of information in economic location decisions, see Alan R. Pred and Gunnar E. Tornquist, *Systems of Cities and Information Flows: Two Essays* (Royal University of Lund, Sweden, Dept. of Geography, C.W.K. Gleerup, Lund, 1973), 1–64. I do not have a telephone log for March Field for the years Arnold was commander. However, it seems reasonable to assume that he would not have had an entirely different set of contacts with whom he communicated by telephone as opposed to written or verbal means.

61. T. Claude Ryan to Arnold, Nov. 9, 1932; Arnold to Ryan, Nov. 10, 1932, Arnold Papers.

62. Arnold to Donald Douglas, June 6, 1932, Arnold Papers; Arnold to Dougas, Nov. 29, 1932, Arnold Papers; Arnold to M. J. Ritterath, Jan. 16, 1933, Arnold Papers; Arnold to Spaatz, Nov. 13, 1933, Arnold Papers; the letter went on to outline the advantages of the Douglas plane.

63. Ibid.; Spaatz to Arnold, Dec. 7, 1933, Arnold Papers.

64. Arnold to Spaatz, Dec. 12, 1933, Arnold Papers.

65. Rae, *Climb to Greatness,* 79–84.

66. *Fortune Magazine* 23:3 (March 1941): 180.

67. Paul Rhode, "The Aircraft Industry in California," paper presented to the Triangle Area Economic History Workshop, Nov. 5, 1990, pp. 16–21.

68. William Wagner, *Reuben Fleet and the Story of Consolidated Aircraft* (Fallbrook, Calif., 1976), 222.

69. Robert A. Millikan, *The Autobiography of Robert A. Millikan* (NY: Prentice Hall, 1950), 215–16.

70. *Who's Who in California: A Biographical Directory, 1928–1929*; for the *LA Times* activities in promoting Southern California see Robert Gottlieb and Irene Wolt, *Thinking Big: The Story of the Los Angeles Times, Its Publishers and Their Influence on Southern California* (NY: Putnam, 1977). The role of the *Times* in developing Southern California is well known, but this book presents a very complete account.

71. Millikan, *Autobiography*, p 241.

72. Ibid., 230.

73. Ibid., 238–51.

74. Theodor von Karman, with Lee Edson, *The Wind and Beyond: Theodore Von Karman: Pioneer in Aviation and Pathfinder in Space* (Boston: Little, Brown, 1967), 147.

75. Ibid.; Daniel Guggenheim Fund for the Promotion of Aeronautics, *Final Report, 1929* (1930), 1–2.

76. Ibid.

77. Von Karman, *The Wind and Beyond*, 140–46; Millikan, *Autobiography*, 243–44.

78. Von Karman, *The Wind and Beyond*, 141–47; *LA Examiner*, June 18, 1926, sect. VI; pp. 1, 5. The article is by Edwin J. Clapp. See also Doyce B. Nunis, Jr., ed., *Los Angeles and Its Environs in the Twentieth Century* (LA: Ward Ritchie Press, 1973), 6–12, 27–30. This enormous bibliography lists only about seven items on aviation, aircraft, or airports published about Southern California before the Clapp article of 1926.

79. Von Karman, *The Wind and Beyond*. 124–29.

80. Ibid., 156–57.

81. Ibid., 160–65.

82. California Institute of Technology, *The Guggenheim Aeronautical Laboratory of the California Institute of Technology: The First Twenty-five Years* (Pasadena, 1954), 9.

83. Ibid., 28–30.

84. Arthur Raymond, "Engineer for the DC Series," interview, Oral History program, Claremont Graduate School, 1964, pp. 4, 10, 37; CIT, *The Guggenheim Aeronautical Laboratory*, 5, 36.

85. Von Karman, *The Wind and Beyond*, 169.

86. Millikan, *Autobiography*, 243–44; von Karman, *The Wind and Beyond*, 169–72. It is interesting that some histories of the DC-3 and its predecessors do not credit Cal Tech with a part in the plane's success. See Lt. Col. Carroll V. Glines, Jr., and Lt. Col. Wendell F. Mosely, *Grand Old Lady: The Story of the DC-3* (Cleveland: Pennington Press, 1959), 17–30. This work does not even acknowledge the existence of Cal Tech, much less of its individual scientists. Rae's definitive *Climb to Greatness* does not mention von Karman or the wind tunnel or other tests in the Guggenheim Laboratory. He did note that Klein and C. Millikan worked on Douglas's legendary craft. I have accepted the opinion of the scientists who were involved in the project.

87. Von Karman, *The Wind and Beyond*, 230–41.

88. Ibid., 245–254.

89. Ibid., 256–59.

90. Ibid., 260.

91. Rae, *Climb to Greatness*, 58–76. John B. Rae (p. 71) argued that within a few years of its appearance, the DC-3 carried "95 per cent of the nation's civil air traffic."

92. Arthur E. Raymond, interview, 16–17.

93. Crosby Maynard, comp. and ed., *Flight Plan for Tomorrow: The Douglas Story, a Condensed History* (Santa Monica, 1962), chap. 2; Donald Douglas, "Planes Twelve Months

in the Year," *California Magazine of Business,* 28:3 (March 1938): 5–6, 38–39; for a similar argument for Arizona, see Bradford Luckingham, *The Urban Southwest: A Profile History of El Paso, Albuquerque, Tucson, and Phoenix* (El Paso: Texas Western Press, 1982), 75–95. A Douglas official declared that "we came here for the flying conditions and the airport facilities but we've been pleasantly surprised by other advantages. The labor supply, for instance. We can recruit engineers, electronics people, machinists anything we need. Workers like it here and don't want to move away." That argument replicates the well-known amenities theory of Edward Ullman. The Hughes people were even more appreciative of the climatic advantages of Tucson. As Luckingham notes, "a Hughes plant manager noted that precision electronics manufacturing requires a 'controlled temperature and a low humidity' and the 'climate in this part of the country is most ideal.'" As Luckingham summarized the situation, "suitable conditions for both work and play seemed to meet in Tucson, as elsewhere in the urban Southwest, and the site and situation appealed to many technical and professional people and their families." See also, Rene Francillon, *McDonnell Douglas Aircraft Since 1920* (London: Putnam, 1979), 7; Frank Cunningham, *Skymaster: The Story of Donnell Douglas* (Philadelphia: Dorrance & Co., Pub., 1943), 98–99; Rhode, "The Aircraft Industry in California," 14.

94. Francillon, *McDonnell Douglas Aircraft Since 1920,* 3; Cunningham, *Sky Master,* 57–101.

95. Maynard, *Flight Plan,* chap. 2; Gottlieb and Wolt, *Thinking Big,* 155.

96. *Fortune Magazine,* vol. 23, no. 3 (March 1941): 180; Maynard, *Flight Plan,* chap. 2; Gottlieb and Wolt, *Thinking Big,* 156; Rhode, "The Aircraft Industry in California," 13–14; Francillon, *McDonnell Douglas Aircraft,* 7–14.

97. John Oliver La Gorce, Assoc. Ed. *National Geographic Magazine,* Washington, D.C., to Bill Henry, July 13, 1944; Waldo D. Waterman, Washington, D.C., to Bill Henry, May 31, 1966, Bill Henry Papers, Special Collections Department, Occidental College Library.

98. Rae, *Climb to Greatness,* 3; Gottlieb and Wolt, *Thinking Big,* 156; John B. Rae, "Financial Problems of the American Aircraft Industry, 1906–1940," *Business History Review* 39 (Spring 1965): 106–11.

99. Rae, *Climb to Greatness,* 67; The Security Pacific 9 (successor of Security First National) Richard Miller, "A Career in Aviation," interview, Oral History program, Claremont Graduate School, 1963, pp. 2–3.

100. Rae, "Financial Problems," 110; Rae, *Climb to Greatness,* 67–68.

101. The story of the critical TWA order is based on Gottlieb and Wolt, *Thinking Big,* 156; Carroll V. Glines and Wendell F. Mosely, *The Legendary DC-3* (NY: Van Nostrand Reinhold, 1979), 13–41; Howard Serling, *Howard Hughes Airline: An Informal History of TWA* (NY: St. Martin's, 1983), 13–31; Trans World Airlines Flight Operations Department, *Legacy of Leadership: A Pictorial History of Trans World Airlines* (n.p.: Wadsworth, 1971), 61–75; Ralph S. Damon, *"TWA": Nearly Three Decades in the Air* (NY: Newcomen Society in North America, 1952), 10–21; Works Project Administration, comps., *Who's Who in Aviation* (Chicago: Ziff-Davis, 1942), 148–49.

102. Von Karman, *The Wind and Beyond,* 168–76.

103. Rae, *Climb to Greatness,* 57–76.

104. Millikan, *Autobiography,* 244; von Karman, *The Wind and Beyond,* 168–76; *Who's Who in Aviation,* 1942–43, p. 321.

105. Frank P. Goss to Theodore von Karman, Aug. 8, 1941, Theodore von Karman Papers, California Institute of Technology Archives, Box 80, Folder 21.

106. Edwin J. Clapp, "LA Should Be Home of Aircraft Industry," *LA Times,* June 13, 1926, sect. VI, pp. 1, 5.

107. Gottlieb and Wolt, *Thinking Big,* 32–52 and 82–105; Robert M. Fogelson, *The*

Fragmented Metropolis: Los Angeles, 1850–1930 (Cambridge, Mass.: MIT Press, 1967), 129–32; Robert E. Lee Knights, *Industrial Relations in the San Francisco Bay Region* (Berkeley: Univ. of California Press, 1960), 226–35; Grace H. Stimson, *The Rise of the Labor Movement in Los Angeles* (Berkeley: Univ. of California Press, 1955), 289–406.

108. For the Douglas struggle against organized labor and the eventual unionization of the aircraft industry in metropolitan Los Angeles see the excellent, but as yet unpublished dissertation, James Richard Wilburn, "Social and Economic Aspects of the Aircraft Industry in Metropolitan Los Angeles During World War II," Ph.D. dissertation, University of California at Los Angeles, 1971, pp. 114–55.

109. Clapp, "Los Angeles Should Be Home of Aircraft Industry," 1, 5; Wyndham Mortimer, "Reflections of a Labor Organizer," interview completed under the auspices of the Oral History program, UCLA, 1967, pp. 139–76; Cunningham, *The Aircraft Industry,* 16–18.

110. Ibid., 193.

111. Lockheed Aircraft Corporation, *Of Men and Stars: A History of Lockheed Aircraft Corporation* (1957), chap. 2, pp. 2–11.

112. Ibid., chap. 2, pp. 11–15.

113. Ibid., chap. 3, pp. 1–7.

114. Carl Squier, "Lockheed Aircraft Company," interview, Oral History program, Claremont Graduate School, 1962, p. 6; *Of Men and Stars,* chap. 3, pp. 7–10.

115. Ibid., chap. 4, pp. 1–16.

116. Robert E. Gross to Courtlandt S. Gross, June 26, 1933, Courtlandt Gross to Robert E. Gross, Nov. 8, 1934. Robert E. Gross Papers, Box 4, Library of Congress.

117. R. E. Gross to Randolph C. Walker, Feb. 1, 1934, Gross Papers, Box 4; *Of Men and Stars,* chap. 1, p. 6.

118. The Reconstruction Finance Corporation loan probably needed local endorsement as well. "I am not making any prophesies and I am not sure how much the recommendation of the local agency is worth," wrote Gross of his application. "But I am prepared to state that no loans can be granted in Washington without this recommendation." Gross to Thomas F. Ryan III, Nov. 26, 1934, Gross Papers, Box 5. In the case of a similar loan to Consolidated at about the same time, it took the intervention of the local congressman to secure the RFC monies.

119. Gross to Randolph Walker, Aug. 6, 1937, Gross Papers, Box 5.

120. Gross to Courtlandt Gross, May 29, 1934, Gross to Robert Proctor, May 2, 1934, Gross Papers, Box 5.

121. Gross to Randolph C. Walker, March 3, 1935, Gross Papers, Box 5.

122. Gross to Courtlandt Gross, April 3, 1935, Gross Papers, Box 5.

123. Gross to Lawrence C. Ames, April 18, 1935, Gross Papers, Box 5.

124. Courtlandt Gross to Robert Gross, Aug. 15, 1935; Gross to C. Gross, Dec. 9, 1935, Gross Papers, Box 5.

125. C. Gross to R. Gross, April 14, 1937; R. Gross to Randolph C. Walker, June 2, 1937, Gross Papers, Box 5.

126. *San Diego Union,* sect. 1, pp. 1, 5; Wm. Wagner, *Reuben Fleet and the Story of Consolidated Aircraft* (Fallbrook, Calif.: Aero Publishers, 1976), 175–77.

127. *San Diego Union,* sec. 1, pp. 1, 5.

128. Wagner, *Reuben Fleet,* 175–77.

129. Ibid., 175–77, 181; *San Diego Union,* Oct. 20, 1935, sect. 5, p. 1.

130. Wagner, *Reuben Fleet,* 93–95.

131. Ibid., 107–72.

132. Editorial, *San Diego Union,* Oct. 27, 1934, sect. 1, p. 4.

133. *San Diego Magazine* 3:9: 6–7, 38–39.

134. Ibid., 12–14, 40–43; *San Diego Union,* Oct. 21, 1935, sect. 1, p. 5; Wagner, *Reuben Fleet,* 175–77.

135. Editorial, *San Diego Magazine* 4:3: 22; Wagner, *Reuben Fleet,* 175–77.

136. James J. Horgan, *City of Flight: The History of Aviation in St. Louis* (Gerald, Mo.: Patrice Press, 1984), 2–35.

137. *San Diego Union,* Oct. 21, 1935, sect. 1, p. 5; Wagner, *Reuben Fleet,* 201–6.

138. The official version of the Ames Research Center story is contained in Edwin P. Hartmann, *Adventures in Research: A History of Ames Research Center, 1940–1965* (Washington: NACA, 1970), 1–30. Needless to say, this is an authorized history of Ames, published by the successor to NACA, the National Aeronautics and Space Administration, in the NASA Center History Series. In the University of North Carolina Library the book is classified as a government document.

139. Ibid.

140. Ibid.

141. Ibid.

142. *LA Times,* May 11, 1937, pt. I, p. 3. For the campaign to demonstrate the vulnerability of West Coast cities, see ibid., April 27, 1937, pt. I, p. 1; April 28, 1937, pt. I, p. 12; May 10, 1937, pt. I, p. 4; May 13, 1937 (that raid hit aircraft factories and the San Pedro docks); May 21, 1937, pt. I, p. 1; May 22, 1937, pt. I, pp. 1, 7; *San Diego Union,* May 21, 1938, sect. I, p. 4.

143. 76th Cong., 1st sess., 1939, *Congressional Record,* 84:8:8522–24; *SC Business* 2:41 (1940): 1; Wagner, *Reuben Fleet,* 243.

144. *SC Business* 2:17: 1.

145. Rae, *Climb to Greatness,* 123–24.

146. Hartman, *Adventures in Research,* 37.

147. Cunningham, *The Aircraft Industry,* 24.

148. Ibid., 198.

149. Benjamin F. Cooling, *War, Business, and American Society: Historical Perspectives on the Military-Industrial Complex* (Port Washington, N.Y.: Kennikat Press, 1977), 59–72; Clapp, "Los Angeles Should Be Home of Aircraft Industry," 1–5.

Chapter 5. "Mars Has a Hand in Your Pocket": Urban California in the Second Great War

1. Los Angeles, Office of the Mayor, Conference of Mayors of the Larger Cities, Aug. 21–22, 1942, 26.

2. Ibid., 27.

3. Ibid.

4. John Anson Ford, address over Radio Station KFVD, April 24, 1941, pp. 1–4, Ford Papers.

5. Fletcher Bowron, "Remarks at Memorial Day Services at the Colliseum," May 5, 1944. (All Bowron material is to be found in Bowron Collection unless specified otherwise.)

6. Fred Powledge, *Model City* (NY: Simon and Schuster, 1970) pp. 45–64.

7. *San Diego Union,* April 25, 1943, sect. B., p. 1.

8. *Southern California Business* 3:14 (June 23, 1941): 1–2 (hereafter *SC Business*). The same issue carried the opinions of six Los Angeles bankers praising the new service as one essential to local contractors.

9. Ibid. 3:12 (May 26, 1941): 1–2; 13 (June 2, 1941): 1; and 14 (June 9, 1941): 1–2.

10. *SC Business* 3:47 (Jan. 26, 1942): 2.

11. *California Defense Digest* 2:2 (Jan. 15, 1942): 4; Haynes Collection, Univ. of California at Los Angeles.

12. *San Diego Union,* April 8, 1944, p. B-2.

13. *SC Business* 5:36 (Oct. 4, 1943): 1, 3; 5:40 (Nov. 1, 1943): 1, 4; 5:41 (Nov. 8, 1943): 1, 2; 5:43 (Nov. 22, 1943): 3.

14. W. C. Mullendore to Bernard M. Baruch, Office of War Mobilization, April 17, 1944, an open letter reprinted in *SC Business* 6:14 (April 17, 1944): 1.

15. *San Diego Union,* April 8, 1944, p. B-2.

16. Mullendore to Baruch.

17. Remarks of Reps. Carl Hinshaw, Ed Izak, Gordon McDonough, March 1, 1945, 79th Cong., 1st sess., *Congressional Record* 91:2:1626–29.

18. SF Bd. of S., *Proceedings,* 36:1 (Jan. 6, 1941): 32–33.

19. Ibid., 36:17 (May 5, 1951): 724.

20. *The Downtowner,* Sept. 1, 1943, 1.

21. *SF Chronicle,* June 29, 1941, p. D-12.

22. SF Bd. of S., *Proceedings,* vol. 36 (Oct. 20, 1941): 2094–95; *The Downtowner,* Nov. 12, 1941, p. 1.

23. SF Bd. of S., *Proceedings,* vol. 36 (Nov. 3, 1941): 2161–63.

24. *Western Construction News,* March 1942, pp. 104–6. Lotchin, "The City and the Sword," 1012.

25. Ibid., SF Bd. of S., *Proceedings,* vol. 36 (Nov. 3, 1941): 2162.

26. *Western Construction News,* March 1942, pp. 104–6.

27. For the career of Robert Moses, see Robert Caro, *The Power Broker;* the Burnham Plan for San Francisco is analyzed in Judd Kahn, *Imperial San Francisco.*

28. SF Bd. of S., *Proceedings,* vol. 37 (April 24, 1942): 694.

29. Ibid., June 15, 1942, p. 1460.

30. Ibid., April 24, 1942, p. 694; and Aug. 24, 1942, p. 1881.

31. *San Diego Union,* Jan. 6, 1943, p. A-1.

32. Ibid., Sept. 19, 1943, p. B-1.

33. Ibid., Jan. 9, 1944, p. B-1.

34. SF Bd. of S., *Proceedings,* vol. 38 (June 14, 1943): 1590–1603; Kinnard, *Greater San Francisco Bay Region,* vol. 2, pp. 400–403.

35. Ibid.

36. Bowron to E. N. Kemp, President, American Airlines, Feb. 6, 1943.

37. Ibid.

38. Bowron to Donald M. Nelson, Chairman, War Production Board, April 3, 1942.

39. Bowron to Morgan Adams, L.A. city representative in Washington, D.C., Sept. 9, 25, 1952.

40. Bowron to Chesebro, City Attorney, L.A., Aug. 10, 1942.

41. *SC Business* 4:25 (Aug. 3, 1942): 1.

42. Ibid. 5:14 (May 3, 1943): 2.

43. Bowron to the Board of Harbor Commissioners, City of Los Angeles, May 3, 1943.

44. Fletcher Bowron, untitled remarks on the occasion of the 150th anniversary of the Bureau of Supplies and Docks of the U.S. Navy, Feb. 23, 1945.

45. Bowron to T. D. Gatchel, Bureau of Supplies and Accounts of the U.S. Navy Dept., March 12, 1945.

46. Bowron to Leroy M. Edwards, April 26, 1945.

47. Fletcher Bowron, remarks at a dedication ceremony for a public housing site in the harbor area of L.A.

48. SF Bd. of S., *Proceedings,* vol. 38 (June 1, 1943): 1349.

49. Ibid., vol. 38 (Sept. 13, 1943): 2095–96.

50. Ibid., vol. 38 (Oct. 25, 1943): 2348–49.

51. Ibid., vol. 38 (Dec. 27, 1943): 2634–35.

52. Remarks of Reps. Carl Hinshaw, Ed Izak, and Gordon McDonough, on war housing, March 1, 1945, 79th Cong., 1st sess., *Congressional Record* 91:2:1626–29.

53. SF Bd. of S., *Proceedings,* vol. 37 (Dec. 21, 1942): 2750.

54. Ibid., vol. 38 (Jan. 18, 1943): 93.

55. Bowron to "Editor," *Life,* Oct. 14, 1942.

56. SF Bd. of S., *Proceedings,* vol. 37 (Dec. 21, 1942): 2753–54.

57. Robert M. Green, Report Supervisor, in a Meeting of the Miners Association of California, March 26, 1942, in SF Bd. of S., *Proceedings,* vol. 37 (March 30, 1942): 496–99.

58. Ibid., vol. 37 (March 23, 1942): 454.

59. Ibid., vol. 37 (March 30, 1942): 496–99.

60. *Post War Economic Policy and Planning. Hearings Before a Subcommittee of the Special Senate Committee on Post-War Economic Policy and Planning* on S. Res. 102. 78th Cong., 1st sess., 1943, pp. 130–32.

61. Ibid.

62. SF Bd. of S, *Proceedings,* vol. 38 (Jan. 1, 1943): 93; Bean and Rawls, *California* . . . , 330.

63. SF Bd. of S., vol. 38 (Jan. 18, 1943): 100.

64. Ibid., vol. 37 (June 8, 1942): 1370–72.

65. Ibid., vol. 37 (June 22, 1942): 1529.

66. Ibid., vol. 38 (May 24, 1943): 1131–32.

67. C. J. Haggerty, Secretary, California State Federation of Labor, "Undercover Campaign to Import War Prisoners in California Exposed," *West Coast Sailor,* May 12, 1944, p. 7.

68. *SC Business* 4:1 (Feb. 23, 1942): 1–4.

69. Ibid.; Bowron to James M. Landis, Director, Office of Civil Defense, April 18, 1942.

70. *SC Business* 4:1 (Feb. 23, 1942): 1–4.

71. Ibid., 3:48, pp. 2–3.

72. Ibid., 4:1, pp. 1–4.

73. Ibid.; 3:48, pp. 2–3.

74. Fletcher Bowron, remarks to the service clubs of Santa Ana, Feb. 19, 1942.

75. Bowron to Prof. A. G. Christie, Dept. of Mechanical Engineering, Johns Hopkins University, April 27, 1942.

76. Franklin D. Roosevelt to Daniel J. Gallagher, SF Bd. of S., Dec. 26, 1942, in SF Bd. of S., *Proceedings,* vol. 37 (Jan. 18, 1942): 100. The telegram from the President is worth repeating verbatim.

My dear Mr. Gallagher:

Your telegram of December seventeenth, regarding the erection of a monument to perpetuate the magnificent achievements of the U.S.S. *San Francisco,* its officers and men, has been received. I am delighted to advise you that the Secretary of the Navy has informed me that in compliance with your request certain outer sections of the navigating bridge of the USS *San Francisco* will be made available to become a part of the proposed monument. This is a most fitting tribute to the epic performance of the *San Francisco* and the heroic deeds of its officers and men. Our fight for freedom and democratic government is made all the more glorious by such heroes as Admiral Callaghan, Captain Young and the officers and men who served under them.

77. *San Diego Union,* July 27, 1941, sec. 1, p. 1.

78. Bowron, "Remarks of Mayor Fletcher Bowron on the Occasion of the Luncheon Honoring Secretary Knox, . . ." June 30, 1943.

79. Bowron to Vierling Kersey, Supt. of Schools, LA, May 9, 1945.

80. John Anson Ford, address over Station KFVD, Los Angeles, May 9, 1941, pp. 1–4. Ford Coll.

81. Ibid.

82. Bowron to A. G. Christie, April 27, 1942.

83. Bean and Rawls, *California,* 329–32; and Lotchin, "John Francis Neylan"; SF Bd. of S., *Proceedings,* vol. 37 (Feb. 2, 1942): 292–93.

84. Ibid., vol. 37 (April 6, 1942): 517–18.

85. Ibid., vol. 37 (Oct. 19, 1942): 2348–49.

86. Bowron to James C. Sheppard, Director, Ninth Civilian Defense Region, S.F., April 22, 1942.

87. Bowron to "Editor," *Life,* Oct. 14, 1942.

88. Bowron, remarks to the service clubs at Santa Ana, Feb. 19, 1942.

89. Los Angeles, Office of the Mayor, "Conference of Mayors . . . ," 1942, pp. 26–71.

90. Bowron to Undersecretary of the Navy Ralph A. Bar, Nov. 7, 1944.

91. Bowron to W. C. Seccombe, Mayor, San Bernardino, Dec. 6, 1943.

92. Bowron to Sen. Harry S Truman, Chairman, Special Committee to Investigate the National Defense Program, April 29, 1944.

93. *The Downtowner,* Jan. 24, 1943, pp. 1–2; see also "The Horizon—1943: 'Westward the Course of Empire Takes Its Way,'" ibid. (Dec. 30, 1942), 1; "S.F. Must Take the Lead in Consolidating Pacific Coast War Time Gains," ibid. (Sept. 1, 1943), 1.

94. Lotchin, "The Darwinian City," 360.

95. California State Reconstruction and Reemployment Commission [CSRRC], "The First Step and the Unfinished Task," Pamphlet No. 5 (Nov. 1944): 6–8.

96. SD Chamber of Commerce, "Post War San Diego: Report of the Temporary Post War Plans Committee," Dec. 3, 1942, p. 1 (hereafter "Post War San Diego").

97. *San Diego Union,* Dec. 4, 1942, p. A-1.

98. "Post War San Diego," 2.

99. SD Chamber of Commerce, Committee for Economic Development (Postwar Planning Committee), "Blueprinting San Diego's Future," July 7, 1944, p. 1.

100. Ibid.

101. Ibid.

102. "Jobs and the Little Man," *San Diego Journal,* Dec. 6, 1945; *San Diego Union,* Oct. 18, 1943, p. B-2.

103. *San Diego Union,* Jan. 2, pp. B-2; Aug. 22, p. B-4; Aug. 31, p. B-2; and Oct. 25, 1943, p. B-2.

104. Ibid., Aug. 31, 1943, p. B-2.

105. "Full Employment—a World Issue," *Labor Leader,* Sept. 9, 1945; "Jobs and the Little Man," *San Diego Journal,* Dec. 6, 1945.

106. Ibid., Oct. 18, 1943, p. B-2.

107. "Blueprinting San Diego's Future," 3.

108. CSRRE, "Planning Pays a Profit: The Story of San Diego," Pamphlet No. 8, pp. 8–25.

109. "S. D. Warned of Need for Post-War Plan," *San Diego Union,* March 11, 1943, p. B-2.

110. Ibid., Nov. 16, 1942, p. B-2.

111. Roscoe C. Martin, *The Cities and the Federal System* (NY: Atherton Press, 1965), 86–135.

112. "Planning Pays a Profit," 1–5.

113. Ibid.

114. "Post War San Diego," 9–17.

115. "S.D. Metropolis Seen After War: Move To Retain, Expand City's Present Development Launched by Chamber," *San Diego Union,* Dec. 4, 1942, p. A-1; "Planning Pays a Profit," 8–23.

116. "Chamber Planning Now for Time When Peace To Bring New Problems for Solution," *SC Business* 2:48 (Feb. 17, 1941): 1.

117. Ibid.

118. *SC Business* 4:47-A (Jan. 11, 1943): 2–3: Dr. D. F. Pegrum, "The Basis of the Los Angeles Metropolitan Economy" (Industrial Department, LA Chamber of Commerce), 14–16.

119. *SC Business* 5:29 (Aug. 16, 1943): 1–3; Wm. C. Mullendore, Los Angeles Chamber of Commerce, "The American Way Is Not the Easy Way," speech delivered to the Chamber of Commerce, March 14, 1944, pp. 10–14. LA County Merchants and Manufacturers Assoc., "Post-War Factors," *M&M Survey Analysis,* no. 18 (July 11, 1945): 14–16.

120. "Postwar Planning versus Mobility," *SC Business,* 5:29 (Aug. 16, 1943): 1–3.

121. "Doherty Assails Planners' Using War to Destroy Free Enterprise," *SC Business,* 5:5 (March 1, 1943): 1, 4.

122. "Edwards Inaugurated As President: New Chamber Head Says Private Industry Proves Worth in War Production Tasks," *SC Business* 7:4 (Jan. 22, 1945): 1, 3.

123. Ibid.

124. LA County, Merchants and Manufacturers Assoc., "Veteran Employment Policy," *M&M Survey Analysis,* no. 15 (Dec. 14, 1944): 1–11; LA County Committee for Interracial Progress, "Statement of Philip M. Connelly, Secretary-Treasurer, LA CID Council (Los Angeles, 1945), 1–3.

125. "Freeways, Transportation, Harbor in Plans: Program to Include Auditorium, Health, and Flood Control," *SC Business,* 7:34 (Aug. 20, 1945): 1, 3.

126. "Analysis of Post-War Problems," *Downtowner,* March 10, 1943, p. 1; SF Bd. of S., *Proceedings,* vol. 38 (April 5, 1943): 758–59.

127. Ibid. (June 21, 1943), 1661–62.

128. CSRRC, "The Bay Region Takes Stock," Pamphlet No. 3, Aug. 1944, p. 20.

129. Ibid., 5–11; S.F. Postwar Planning Committee, "Report to Mayor Roger Latham," Aug. 20, 1945, p. 22; "Reconversion in the San Francisco Bay Area," *Downtowner,* Sept. 12, 1945, p. 1, 4; Truman R. Letts, Executive Secretary to Mayor Roger D. Lapham, "San Francisco Looks Ahead," *California Magazine of the Pacific,* vol. 35, no. 9, pp. 27–29.

130. "DTA's 1944 Progress Report," *Downtowner,* Jan. 17, 1945, p. 2.

131. "San Francisco's New Year's Resolution," ibid., Dec. 26, 1945, p. 1.

132. L. Deming Tilton, Director of Planning, City and County of SF, "San Francisco Plans Its Future," *California Magazine of the Pacific,* 33:12 (Dec. 1943): 15.

133. "The Bay Region Takes Stock," 4–5, 20.

134. Ibid.

135. "Report to Mayor Roger D. Lapham," Aug. 20, 1945, pp. 1–27.

136. Chester McPhee, Supervisor, City and County of SF, "We Need Urban Redevelopment Legislation in California," Memorandum to Accompany Preliminary Outline of Urban Redevelopment Bill (to be introduced into the California legislature, prepared by the San Francisco City Planning Administration), June 5, 1944, pp. 1–3, University of California at Berkeley, Institute for Governmental Research Collection (hereafter IGRS Coll.); "San Francisco Must Prepare for Postwar Transportation," *Downtowner,* June 20, 1945, p. 2.

137. "Bayshore Freeway," *Downtowner,* Nov. 7, 1945, pp. 1, 4; "Post-War Road Build-

ing To Supply Work for Two Million," ibid., Dec. 5, 1945, p. 2; L. Deming Tilton, "Freeways," ibid., p. 3.

138. City of Vallejo, Board of Planning Commissioners, Builders of the West, *Master Plan* (San Francisco, 1945), Sept. 14, 1945, p. 2.

139. Ibid., 2–6.

140. CSRRC, *The First Step and . . . the Unfinished Task. A Report . . .* (Sacramento, 1944), 6–12.

141. CSRRC, *Richmond, California—A City Earns the Purple Heart. A Report . . .* (Sacramento, 1944), 18–20.

142. Philip Funigiello, *The Challenge to Urban Liberalism: Federal-City Relations During World War II* (Knoxville: Univ. of Tennessee Press, 1978), 218–36.

143. The California Housing and Planning Association in its literature, for example, almost completely ignored the struggle between cities and did not boost the same kinds of public works projects that interested the city builders. Edward Howden, Secretary and Director, California Housing and Planning Association (hereafter CHPA), "Urban Redevelopment," Memorandum no. 1, April 23, 1942, pp. 1–6. John Haynes Coll. Institute for Govt. Research, UC California Housing and Planning Association, "Minutes of Fresno Meeting of LA Board of Governors and Advisory Council of the CHPA," April 11, 12, 1942, pp. 1–9.

144. CHPA, Catherine Bauer, "Urban Redevelopment: Crisis in Land Economics Produces Hansen-Greer Plan and Others," 2.

145. CHPA, "Minutes of the Fresno Meeting . . . ," 1.

146. Ibid., 5–6.

147. Ibid., 1.

148. CHPA, Bauer, "Urban Redevelopment . . . ," 1.

149. CHPA, Robert W. Kenny, "Swords into Ploughshares That Will Turn Up Jobs," reprint of editorial in *Business Week,* Oct. 29, 1943, pp. 1–4.

150. CHPA, "Urban Redevelopment," Memorandum no. 1, p. 1, Haynes Coll.

151. Edward Howden to Anne Mumford, March 17, 1942, Haynes Coll.; Howden to Dear Friend, June 30, 1942: CHPA, "California Must Plan Now," 1942, pp. 1–2; Harold I. McGrath, Executive Director, CHPA, to Gov. Earl Warren, June 2, 1943; CHPA, "California Must Look Ahead," 1–2.

152. CHPA, Girvetz, "Political Aspects . . . ," 4; CHPA, Kenny, "Swords into Ploughshares . . . ," 4; CHPA, Bauer, "Urban Redevelopment," 5.

153. CSRRC, "How Many Jobs for Californians," Pamphlet No. 5, Dec. 1944, p. 23.

154. For the differences between liberal and booster planners see Funigiello, *The Challenge to Urban Liberalism,* 187–216.

155. Ibid.

156. The entire issue of postwar planning deserves more study than it has so far received. The idea of postwar planning was being discussed at every level of government from at least 1943 on and sometimes before that point. City governments and chambers of commerce led the way in the urban realm; state committees planned for the states; the federal government held hearings and tried to plan on a national level; and businesses tried to plan their own private responses to the cessation of the fighting. The multiplicity of these efforts makes any coherent discussion of postwar planning very difficult. For example, business interests made little reference to the possibility of mass unemployment after the war, but were very interested in matters like federal permission to build up the necessary cash reserves with which to convert to peacetime pursuits; in lower taxation; with less governmental interference in the economy; in the idea of returning the national role in the economy to the status of impartial arbiter and fact gatherer; in international cartels; in the timing of the reconversion process, which might prejudice West Coast industries because they would have to stay at the task till the war

in Asia was won; in tariffs; in discriminatory freight rates; in the disposal of surplus federal property after the conflict; in the monetary policy; and so forth. Labor representatives usually voiced the most fear of unemployment and had the fewest specific suggestions for coping with it, except to favor a large federal role in the postwar drama. They almost always took a narrow view of the problem, although on occasion they might voice booster proposals, as did John F. Shelley at the 1943 hearings. The state of California was far along with postwar planning by 1943, including highway and public works construction planning, the creation of postwar committees, the earmarking of specific revenues to create public works, and the establishment of veterans' preference systems. The chambers of commerce, city government, and liberal responses have been discussed above. Ironically, although the chambers of commerce distrusted the long-haired planners, the chambers themselves indulged in the most comprehensive planning of any of the groups interested in the reconversion process. As the testimony of the San Francisco Chamber of Commerce representatives before the 1943 Senate postwar planning and economic policy hearings demonstrates, the Chamber took a very comprehensive view of the process of postwar planning. If the liberal planners stressed redevelopment; if the state emphasized highways; if the businessmen wanted adjustments in government policy that would favor their enterprises; if labor wished for employment schemes—the booster planners took all into account. See *Postwar Economic Policy and Planning,* 1–240. It would appear that only the Imperial City organizations such as the San Francisco Chamber of Commerce and Downtown Association and the Los Angeles and San Diego chambers of commerce understood the full complexity of postwar planning or even chose to think seriously about it. Others were content to think about their own small piece of the puzzle.

Chapter 6. From Warfare to Welfare:
The Revival of the Darwinian City

1. Rep. John F. Shelley, "Maintenance of an American Merchant Marine," April 6, 1950, extension of remarks, 81st Cong., 2nd sess., *Congressional Record* 96:14:A2621–22.

2. *Oakland Post Enquirer,* Aug. 18, 1949.

3. *Alameda Times Star,* June 28, 1949.

4. "Resolutions submitted to the Pacific Coast District Metal Trades Council," Jan. 16, 1950, in Hon. John J. Allen, Jr., "Shipbuilding and Ship Repair on the Pacific Coast," March 22, 1950, extension of Remarks, 81st Cong., 2nd sess., *Congressional Record* 96:14:A2116.

5. Rep. John Shelley on "Ghost Ships and Ghost Men," July 10, 1950, 81st Cong., 2nd sess., 1950, *Congressional Record,* 96:7:9865–67; and Shelley, "Navy Shipbuilding and Repair Policy," April 6, 1954, 83rd Cong., 2nd sess., ibid. 100:4:4742–44.

6. SF Bd. of S., *Journal* 44:53 (Dec. 5, 1949): 986, 989, 1007–9.

7. Rep. Clyde Doyle on the "Long Beach Shipyard Reactivated," Jan. 17, 1951, 82nd Cong., 1st sess., 1951, *Congressional Record,* 93:1:401–2.

8. *Long Beach Press-Telegram,* Jan. 5, 1951.

9. *SC Business* 15:13: 4; 15:9:1–2, records the "ideological" opposition to government shipbuilding at the expense of private construction firms. Concern with the continued problems of the private shipbuilders can be found throughout the *Congressional Record* from 1949 to 1954, especially in the speeches of Reps. John F. Shelley, George Miller, and John J. Allen.

10. Remarks of Reps. Shelley and Allen on H. R. 9987, "Private Financing of New Ship Construction," July 30, 1954, 83rd Cong., 2nd sess., *Congressional Record* 100:10:12843–46.

11. Extension of remarks of Rep. John F. Shelley on "Vessel Replacement Under the

Merchant Marine Act, 1936," July 26, 1954, 83rd Cong., 2nd sess., *Congressional Record* 100:9:12128–3.

12. Remarks of Rep. John F. Shelley on "Navy Shipbuilding and Repair Policy," April 6, 1954, 83rd Cong., 2nd sess., *Congressional Record* 100:4:4742–44.

13. Extension of remarks of John J. Allen, Jr., on "The Cost of Using American Flag Ships," Aug. 12, 1954, 83rd Cong., 2nd sess., *Congressional Record* 100:11:14313–15.

14. Ibid.

15. Von Karman, *The Wind and Beyond,* 272–83.

16. Ibid., E. P. Hartman, *Adventures in Research,* 102.

17. Von Karman, *The Wind and Beyond,* 298–307.

18. Ibid., 302.

19. Ibid., 298–300.

20. Ibid., 299–300.

21. *Who's Who,* 192.

22. Ibid., 302.

23. Ibid., 322–39.

24. Ibid., 338.

25. Ibid., 35.

26. Ibid.

27. Ibid.

28. *SC Business* 15:30 (July 30, 1952): 1.

29. *SF Examiner,* Nov. 19, 1922, sect. 1, p. 14.

30. *San Diego Union,* May 21, 1938, sect. 1, p. 4.

31. Rep. Ralph E. Church on "National Defense and the Aviation Industry," June 27, 1939, 76th Cong., 1st sess., *Congressional Record* 84:7:7991–93.

32. James M. Spaight, *Air Power and the Cities* (London, 1930), 224–35. Spaight argued that air power would not be used against cities because cities were not the prime targets. Factories, airdromes, etc. were the main military targets and would therefore be attacked instead of cities. One cannot read his book, however, without being reminded of the potential destruction that airplanes could rain upon urban areas, and, of course, in the Second World War, both sides adopted the tactic of terror bombing and practiced it early and often.

33. Church, "National Defense," 7991–93.

34. Ibid.

35. Ibid.; Rep. Ralph E. Church on "National Defense and the Aviation Industry," July 1, 1939, 76th Cong., 1st sess., *Congressional Record* 84:7:8522–24.

36. *Fortune* 23:3 (March 1941): 90.

37. Ibid., 92, 174.

38. *SC Business* 2:41 (Dec. 30, 1940): 1. Emphasis in original.

39. Ibid.

40. Ibid.

41. *SC Business* 4:2 (March 2, 1941): 2.

42. Ibid. 4:27 (Aug. 17, 1942), 2, for the campaign to further concentrate war production in the Los Angeles area see LA Chamber of Commerce, "Concentration of Civilian Industry," 1–10.

43. 78th Cong., 2nd sess., *Congressional Record* 90:10:A2313–16.

44. Ibid., part 9, pp. A1830–31. Similar apprehensions about reconversion came from the representatives of the South. See the extended remarks of Rep. Sam Hobbs of Alabama, Sept. 18, 1944, ibid., pt. 2, pp. A4263–65. Hobbs even quoted Lincoln to the effect that the nation could not endure half slave and half free. According to Hobbs, Connecticut's share of war contracts alone amounted to more than that of "the 10 Southern States put together."

45. Ibid.; speech of W. C. Mellendore to the Senate Committee to Investigate Industrial Centralization, San Francisco, Nov. 16, 1944, ibid., pt. 11, pp. A45-3-35.

46. Willard Stout to Fletcher Bowron, Santa Fe, Jan. 12, 1946.

47. Fletcher Bowron, speech to the annual national convention of the American Legion, LA, Oct. 9, 1950.

48. Aircraft War Production Council Inc., "Location of Prime, Feeder and Parts Aircraft Plants in the Los Angeles County Area," map. Bowron Coll., Box 59.

49. Scott Bottles, *Los Angeles and the Automobile: The Making of the Modern City* (LA: University of Calif. Press, 1987), 211–54; David Brodsly, *L.A. Freeway: An Appreciative Essay* (LA: Univ. of Calif. Press, 1981), 63–149.

50. Rep. Craig Hosmer on "Air Force Disasters at Long Beach Municipal Airport," Feb. 22, 1954, 83rd Cong., 2nd sess., *Congressional Record* 100:2:2092.

51. Rep. Craig Hosmer on "Reducing Airport Hazards," Jan. 29, 1954, 83rd Cong., 2nd sess., *Congressional Record* 100:15:A720.

52. John Anson Ford to T. C. Coleman, Ford Collection, The Huntington Library.

53. LA County Dept. of Aviation/William J. Fox Acting Director/, "To the People of Antelope Valley," Aug. 24, 1951, p. 1; Fox to John Anson Ford, Sept. 12, 1949, Ford Collection.

54. Ibid., 9.

55. Ibid., 7.

56. Ibid., 9.

57. Ibid.

58. Ibid.

59. William J. Fox to Ray Darby, May 4, 1948. Ford Coll., Huntington Library.

60. Fox, "To the People of Antelope Valley," 7. Lockheed, the first signee at Palmdale, may have been negotiating with the County as early as December 1948. LA County Chamber of Commerce, *Los Angeles County Aviation Progress* 18:5 (Dec. 1947): 1, 7.

61. William Fox to Ford, May 29, 1951; John W. Myers, Vice President, Northrop Aircraft, Inc., to Brig. Gen. Fox, July 11, 1952; D. P. Sternbert, Executive Advisor, North American Aviation, to Fox, Aug. 14, 1951.

62. Lt. Col. Donald F. Marshall, "Statement at 5th November 1951 Zoning Hearing: Palmdale Airport" of the County of LA, p. 1.

63. Robert C. Fellmeth, ed., *Politics of Land: Ralph Nader's Study Group Report on Land Use in California* (NY, 1973), 436–55.

64. *LA Times,* May 21, 1954.

65. Fox to Jessup, May 25, 1954, Ford Collection. Emphasis in original.

66. This point cannot be made definitively without consulting company records, but the available evidence points clearly in this direction.

67. Lockheed Aircraft Corp., *Of Men and Stars: A History of Lockheed Aircraft Corporation,* chap. 9, p. 2.

68. *LA Times,* Sept. 4, 1949; *Of Men and Stars,* chap. 9, pp. 2–3.

69. *SC Business* 13:48 (Nov. 28, 1951): 1.

70. David W. Lantis, Rodney Steiner, and Arthur Karinen, *California: Land of Contrasts* (Belmont, 1963), 226, 228.

71. 81st Cong., 2nd sess., *Congressional Record* 96:1:497–99.

72. Testimony of Fletcher Bowron to the Joint Committee on Atomic Energy, March 17, 1960, p. 10 of a transcript.

73. LA County Health Department, *Atomic Warfare Primer,* 1950.

74. City of LA, Office of Civil Defense, *Annual Report, 1951,* pp. 1–19.

75. Ibid.

76. *SC Business,* 14:38 (Sept. 24, 1952): 2.

77. County of LA, "The Effect of Atomic Bomb Tests Upon Los Angeles County Disaster Civil Defense Authority," typescript in John Anson Ford Papers, Huntington Library.

78. Ibid.

79. Ibid.

80. R. J. Carreon, Jr., Chairman, Civil Defense and Disaster Board to Mayor Norris Poulson, Jan. 31, 1959. Letter appears in LA Office of Civil Defense, "Survival in an Atomic Age," 1959.

81. "Statement by Mayor Fletcher Bowron," Dec. 7, 1950.

82. *Downtowner,* July 25, 1945. *SC Business,* Nov. 5, 1945, p. 1; SF Bd. of S., *Journal* 41: 50 (Nov. 25, 1946): 3314–16; ibid., 42:11 (March 17, 1947): 604.

83. *SC Business* 9:22 (May 28, 1947): 2.

84. Ibid. 9:35 (Aug. 25, 1948): 1, 3.

85. *SC Business* 9:8 (Feb. 23, 1949): 3.

86. Ibid. 9:6 (Feb. 9, 1949): 2.

87. Ibid. 13:39 (Sept. 26, 1951): 1,3.

88. Ibid. 13:40 (Oct. 3, 1951): 4.

Chapter 7. The Trinity of Air Power, Plus One:
The Air Force, Air Commerce, the Aircraft Industry, and the City

1. Clayton R. Koppes, *JPL and the American Space Program: A History of the Jet Propulsion Laboratory* (New Haven: Yale Univ. Press, 1982), 1. My discussion of the JPL is based on Koppes.

2. Koppes, *JPL,* 67.

3. Ibid., 82–85.

4. Ibid., 85–91, 101.

5. Ibid., 115–16.

6. Fred Kaplan, "Scientists at War: The Birth of the Rand Corporation," *American Heritage* 34:4 (June/July 1983): 49–64.

7. Kaplan, "Scientists at War," 53.

8. Ibid.

9. Ibid., 54.

10. Ibid., 59.

11. Ibid., 59–64.

12. *Downtowner,* July 25, 1945, p. 4; "Annual Message [of Mayor] to the Board of Supervisors," Jan. 14, 1946, in SF Bd. of S., *Proceedings,* 41:2: 90.

13. Remarks of Mayor Fletcher Bowron at Air Force Day Program, LA Airport . . . Aug. 1, 1945.

14. Harry Walstrom, Freddy Martin, et al., "Freddy Margin—Ambassador," Aug. 1, 1945, pp. 1–14, typescript of radio program, Bowron Papers.

15. Ibid.

16. Ibid.

17. Eugene E. Wilson, "Peace . . . Through Air Power," SF, Aug. 16, 1945, broadcast over Station KQW, pp. 1–14; *Downtowner,* Sept. 5, 1945, p. 1.

18. Ibid.

19. Aviation Dept. of LA County Chamber of Commerce, *Los Angeles County Aviation Progress* 16:41 (Sept. 5, 1945): 1 (hereafter *Aviation Progress*); *SC Business* 7:38 (Sept. 17, 1945): 21; "Chamber Leader Pledges Support for Aviation," ibid., 12:28 (July 12, 1950): 1, 4; resolutions of Long Beach Chamber of Commerce, Dec. 29, 1947, in extension of the

remarks of Rep. Willis K. Bradley, Dec. 29, 1948, 80th Cong., 2nd sess., *Congressional Record* 97:1:37.

20. Tom Humphrey, "Aeronautical Revolution," *California Magazine of the Pacific* 36:3 (March 1946): 63–65.

21. "Remarks by Mayor Fletcher Bowron at Air Force Association Rally," Shrine Auditorium, Feb. 25, 1947, pp. 1–2.

22. "Aviation Committee," *Aviation Progress* 17:2 (June 1947): 1–2.

23. "1948 Review," ibid. 20:2 (Jan. 1949): 2; Rae, *Climb to Greatness,* 172.

24. "Air Force Procurement," *Aviation Progress* 20:2 (Jan. 1949): 1.

25. To the best of my knowledge, I originated the term "Darwinian City." See Lotchin, "The Darwinian City: The Politics of Urbanization in San Francisco Between the World Wars," *Pacific Historical Review* 48:3 (Aug. 1979): 357–81. Judd Kahn's term "Imperial City" is equally appropriate. See Kahn, *Imperial San Francisco: Politics and Planning in an American City, 1897–1906* (Lincoln: Univ. of Nebraska Press, 1979). The idea is generally accepted among urbanists, but, as yet, it has not brought about rethinking of the doctrine of urban impotence, despite the genuine relevance of the one idea to the other, and of their generally antithetical nature. If a city like Los Angeles could create an artificial harbor where there was no natural one, attract millions of settlers through advertisement of its climate, and develop a water supply that could turn a semi-arid area into an urban garden, it can hardly be described as impotent.

26. Anna Rothe, *Current Biography: Who's News and Why, 1951* (NY, 1952), 276–78.

27. Ibid.

28. Military Affairs Committee, *Hearings on Demobilization and Mobilization before the Senate Military Affairs Committee,* 4–14.

29. Ibid.

30. Committee on Interstate and Foreign Commerce, National Aviation Council, *Hearings Before the Committee on Interstate and Foreign Commerce on H.R. 2220,* 80th Cong., 1st sess., 1947, pp. 6–7, 30.

31. *Hearings To Establish a National Air Policy Board.*

32. *Committee on Interstate and Foreign Commerce, National Aviation Council,* Hearings, pp. 1–43.

33. Bowron speech to the First California Aviation Conference, Dec. 12, 1944.

34. "Aviation Conference Now Annual Affair," *SC Business* 6:50 (Dec. 25, 1944): 2.

35. Speech of James L. Straight, quoted in address of John Anson Ford over Station KPAS, Dec. 13, 1944, pp. 1–5, Ford Papers.

36. "Aviation Conference Now an Annual Affair," 2.

37. "Remarks by Mayor Fletcher Bowron at Air Force Association Rally," Shrine Auditorium.

38. "Air Force Day Luncheon to Honor Fliers," *SC Business* 9:29: 1.

39. For Chamber of Commerce complaints about big spending and big government, see "Washington Representative Warns Against Long-Range Spending Plans," *SC Business* 11:9 (March 2, 1949): 2, and "editorial," ibid. 11:19 (May 11, 1949): 1. For the Chamber's support of legislation to assist "aircraft manufacturers and air carriers in developing a transport plane which could be diverted to military use," see "Legislative Aid to Develop New Aircraft Sought," ibid. 10:31 (July 28, 1948): 3; for their endorsement of a "long-range" spending program (five years) to stabilize the aircraft industry see "5-Year Aircraft Schedules Urged," ibid. 11:1 (Jan. 5, 1949). For the endorsement of the 70 group Air Force program by the machinists, see "Air Policy Forgotten," *American Aeronaut* Aug. 2, 1949, p. 2.

40. Editorials, *LA Times,* April 17, 1948; Dec. 17, 18, 1953.

41. "Air Force Procurement," *Aviation Progress* 20:2 (Jan. 1949): 1.

42. Congressional Aviation Policy Board, *National Aviation Policy: Report of the Congressional Aviation Policy Board of the Congress of the United States Pursuant to Public Law 287,* Report 949, 80th Cong., 2d sess., 1948, p. iv.

43. Ibid.

44. The Russian strategy in the Cold War before the USSR acquired atomic weapons and for long thereafter was to balance American nuclear superiority with Soviet conventional superiority in Europe. If the U.S. attacked the Soviet Union with nuclear weapons, the Red Army would occupy Western Europe in retaliation. For purposes of the argument being made here, it is important to remember that there were viable *military* alternatives to a massive buildup of American air power with its consequent diminution of the role of conventional forces, especially that of the army. A balance of superior conventional forces and a modest air power superiority might have been just as effective as the attainment of air power superiority and concession of conventional superiority.

45. Aviation Policy Board, *National Aviation Policy,* 7.

46. Ibid., 4.

47. Ibid.

48. Ibid., 1–53.

49. Southern Californians and westerners in general had always claimed to be more "air minded" than easterners. Perhaps this was due to the greater distances encountered in the West. It was practical for a businessman to board a train in Philadelphia, Boston, Chicago, New York, or Washington, to go to these cities. The California cities, however, were separated from the rest of the country by miles of uninhabited territory, which made train travel much less efficient.

50. Edgar M. Bottome, *The Balance of Terror: A Guide to the Arms Race* (Boston: Beacon Press, 1971), 35–38.

51. For the congressional debate over the 70 group Air Force, see debate on H.R. 6226, April 15, 1948, 80th Cong., 1st sess., *Congressional Record* 94:4: 4531–48.

52. Ibid.

53. Rothe, *Current Biography,* 277.

54. It is interesting to note that some writers with a national security orientation attack the problem of postwar rearmament as if it had no metropolitan dimension or even a congressional one. Samuel Huntington, for example, writes about this process of rearmament as if it were simply an interaction among the events of the Cold War, the military services, the presidency, and certain interested bureaucrats, such as the national security staff, State Department staffers, and Treasury officials. Public opinion, industrial pressure groups like the Associated Aircraft Industries, and congressional, state, or metropolitan influences are almost entirely nonexistent in his accounts. Although President Eisenhower recognized the existence of a munitions lobby, or what he later called a military-industrial complex, Huntington allows such groups no influence in the formation of military policy between World War II and the end of the fifties. One need only mention that the largest congressional delegation and the delegation destined to replace it in that role, New York and California respectively, had a vital interest in protecting and promoting the aircraft industry. Southern California was by far the largest airframe manufacturing center in the country. Even in the midst of the postwar aircraft industry doldrums, it employed 65,000 people, the largest number among Los Angeles Area industries and more than twice the number employed by the motion picture business. It had an annual payroll of $300,000,000; it ranked "first as a source of new money brought into Southern California"; and it was "also the center of American aeronautical research and development" in 1947. San Diego also had a large stake in the aircraft industry. As noted elsewhere, Mayor Bowron claimed that there were fully 100,000 Army Air Force veterans in Southern California and an Air Force Association to represent

their interests. One can assume, therefore, that together with San Diego, the Los Angeles metropolitan area possessed some political influence in matters aeronautical. LA Chamber of Commerce Industrial Department, *Los Angeles Industries of National Importance* (LA: Chamber of Commerce, 1947), 1–2; "Remarks by Mayor Fletcher Bowron at Air Force Association Rally," Shrine Auditorium; Samuel P. Huntington, *The Common Defense: Strategic Programs in National Politics* (NY: Columbia Univ. Press, 1961).

55. Rep. Carl Hinshaw on supercarriers, June 3, 1948, 80th Cong., 2nd sess., *Congressional Record* 94:6:7081–83.

56. Editorial, *LA Daily News,* Oct. 10, 1949.

57. *SC Business* 14:31 (Aug. 6, 1952): 1–2.

58. David L. Clark, "Improbable Los Angeles," in Richard M. Bernard and Bradley R. Rice, eds., *Sunbelt Cities: Politics and Growth Since World War II* (Austin: Univ. of Texas Press, 1983), 268–308.

59. Extension of the remarks of Rep. Clyde Doyle, Feb. 2, 1951, 82nd Cong., 1st sess., *Congressional Record* 97:11A:623–24.

60. Editorial by L.E.C., *LA Daily News,* Feb. 14, 1951.

61. Remarks of Reps. Henry Jackson and Hal Holmes, Oct. 10, 1949, 81st Cong., 1st sess., *Congressional Record* 95:11:14142.

62. Rep. Hinshaw introducing House Joint Resolution 22 & 73, Jan. 1, 1949, 81st Cong., 1st sess., *Congressional Record* 95:1:25; extension of the remarks of Rep. Carl Hinshaw, March 16, 1949, 81st Cong., 1st sess., *Congressional Record* 95:13A:A1523, extension of the remarks of Rep. Hinshaw, Jan. 17, 1949, 81st Cong., 1st sess., ibid. 95:12A:A241–42; Rep. Hinshaw on H. R. 1437, March 16, 1949, 81st Cong., 1st sess., *Congressional Record* 95:2:2639; extension of the remarks of Rep. Carl Hinshaw, April 7, 1949, 81st Cong., 1st sess., *Congressional Record* 95:13A:2079–81; Marvin Miles, "Skyways," *LA Times,* Jan. 23, 1949.

63. Oct. 10, 1949, 81st Cong., 1st sess., *Congressional Record* 95:11:14146, 14151–52; Remarks of Rep. James Van Zandt, July 25, 1950, 81st Cong., 1st sess., *Congressional Record* 96:8:1103–5; Remarks of Rep. Carl Hinshaw, May 9, 1950, 81st Cong., 1st sess., *Congressional Record* 96:5:6731–33.

64. Van Zandt, *Congressional Record* 96:8:1103–5. This speech by Van Zandt is the best overall discussion of the 70 group Air Force up to mid-1950 that I have found. This speech was, of course, a criticism of President Truman, but I have found no rebuttal of it. Van Zandt was a member of the House Armed Services Committee, so he was in a position to know the facts. It is important to emphasize that the numbers referred to the level of forces that would be achieved at the end of a five-year program. For example, President Truman in refusing the higher figure in 1950 was agreeing to the creation of a forty-eight group Air Force in 1956. See U.S. Congress. House. Excerpts from House Report 1797 of the Committee on Appropriations, quoted in extension of the remarks of Rep. Hinshaw, Dec. 15, 1950, 81st Cong., 1st sess., *Congressional Record* 96:12:16674–75; John G. Norris, "Lead-Time Reduction—How Pentagon Fashions a Miracle," *Washington Post,* June 1, 1953.

65. Hanson Baldwin, "How Big an Air Force?—Argument Is Reopened—Case for and against the 150 Group Program Weighed by the Pentagon," *New York Times,* July 29, 1951; Joseph Alsop, "Matter of Fact: One-Hundred-and-Forty Group Air Force," *Washington Post,* Oct. 1, 1951.

66. Robert E. Gross, "What Price Air Power—Are We Getting Our Money's Worth?," quoted in extension of remarks of Rep. Carl Hinshaw, Oct. 9, 1951, 81st Cong., 1st sess., *Congressional Record* 97:15A:A6253–56.

67. Dept. of the Air Force report quoted in extension of the remarks of Rep. Samuel Yorty, May 20, 1953, 83rd Cong., 1st sess., *Congressional Record* 99:11A:2838–39; This estimate is based primarily upon the pro air-power activity of these members of Congress as doc-

umented in the *Congressional Record.* Considerations of space preclude a full listing of the activities of these men, but a sampling of their efforts can be seen in: Extension of the remarks of Rep. Frank W. Boykin, Feb. 26, 1953, 83rd Cong., 1st sess., *Congressional Record* 99:9A:A946–48; Senate, Remarks of Sen. Lyndon B. Johnson, March 16, 1953, 83rd Cong., 1st sess., *Congressional Record* 99:2:1979–80; Extension of the remarks of Rep. Harold A. Patten, April 27, 1953, 83rd Cong., 1st sess., *Congressional Record,* 99:10A:A2193; Extension of the remarks of Rep. Melvin Price, May 13, 1953, 83rd Cong., 1st sess, *Congressional Record* 99:10A:A2592–93; Remarks of Sen. Stuart Symington on Air Force appropriations, June 25, 1953, 83rd Cong., 1st sess., *Congressional Record* 99:6:7241–46.

68. Considerations of space preclude a full listing of the activities of Congressman Yorty, but an extension of the remarks of Rep. Yorty can be seen on the following days: May 20, 1953, 83rd Cong., 1st sess., *Congressional Record* 99:11A: May 25, 1953, June 15, 1953, pp. A2845–46, A2838–39, 3046–47, and A3437–38.

69. Extension of the remarks of Rep. Yorty, June 8, 1953, 83rd Cong., 1st sess., *Congressional Record* 99:11A:A3248–49.

70. Editorial by Lawrence A. Collins, Sr., "Peace Without Victory," *Long Beach Independent,* June 11, 1953; unsigned editorial, "Pay Your Own Debts," ibid., July 13, 1953; editorial by Robert L. Smith," GOP Defense Slash Is Cause for Alarm," *LA Daily News,* June 29, 1953; unsigned editorial, "Biggest and Best," *LA Examiner,* June 15, 1953; unsigned editorial "What Are We Signing in Korea?," *LA Times,* July 8, 1953.

71. Samuel P. Huntington, *The Common Defense,* 33–92; the budget figures appear on p. 79. Paul A. Carter, *Another Part of the Fifties* (NY, 1983), 31–36.

72. Unsigned editorial "The Case for the Carriers, I," *LA Times,* Dec. 17, 1952; unsigned editorial, "The Case for the Carriers, II," ibid., Dec. 18, 1952; editorial by Rembert James, "Giant Flattops Seen Essential to Naval Superiority in War," *San Diego Union,* May 7, 1953; and editorial by Frank Macomber, "Navy's First, the *Forrestal* To Be Ready Late in 1954," ibid.

73. Herbert York, *Race to Oblivion: A Participant's View of the Arms Race* (NY: Simon and Schuster, 1970); James R. Killian, Jr., *Sputnik, Scientists, and Eisenhower: A Memoir of the First Special Assistant to the President for Science and Technology* (Cambridge: MIT Press, 1977); George B. Kistiakowsky, *A Scientist at the White House: The Private Diary of President Eisenhower's Special Assistant for Science and Technology* (Cambridge: Harvard Univ. Press, 1976).

74. Huntington, *Common Defense,* 87; James Fallows, *National Defense* (NY: Vintage Books, 1981), 35–106. Fallows, often using DOD sources argues very persuasively that loading down American weapons with ever more technology of ever more sophistication reduces rather than enhances weapons performance. It also greatly increases their cost. According to the studies cited by Fallows, the F86 Sabrejet of the Korean War is still the best fighter jet America has produced despite the expenditure of enormous sums to improve upon it. He also notes that some weapons are so expensive that they cannot be fired in practice and thus conceivably could be used in actual combat by a person with no experience of ever having fired one. Nonetheless, the ever more complicated weapons are very helpful to the economies of cities that manufacture electronics, aerospace equipment, ships, and tanks.

75. Edgar M. Bottome, *The Balance of Terror: A Guide to the Arms Race* (Boston: Beacon, 1971), 35–38, 84–86; Carter, *Another Part of the Fifties,* 35; as a member of the Air National Guard and former member of the Air Force, Goldwater criticized the Air Force. "I have great admiration for the Air Force, and I have taken great pride in having served in the Air Force. However, I do not believe the fact that I am a former member of the Air Force, and am now an active member of the Air National Guard, dictates that I should stand in awe or say 'salam' to everything that comes from across the river in the Pentagon. I have seen the

waste that goes on in the Air Force." Mr. Symington: "So have I." Remarks of Sen. Goldwater, July 22, 1953, 83rd Cong., 1st sess., *Congressional Record*, 99:7:9457; Remarks of Sen. Paul Douglas and Sen. Russell Long on Air Force appropriations for fiscal year 1954, July 23, 1953, 83rd Cong., 1st sess., *Congressional Record* 99:7:9591–95; Remarks of Sen. William Knowland on Air Force appropriations for fiscal year 1954, July 22, 1953, 83rd Cong., 1st sess., *Congressional Record* 99:7:9462.

76. John S. Day, *Subcontracting Policy in the Airframe Industry* (Boston: Harvard Univ. School of Business Administration, 1956), 15–42.

77. Remarks of Reps. Hinshaw, Holifield, and Monroney on Air Force appropriations, May 9, 1950, 81st Cong., 2nd sess., 96:5:6753–55.

78. Committee on Armed Services, Subcommittee No. 5—Air Materiel, *To Provide for the Development of Civil Aircraft Adaptable for Auxiliary Military Service, Hearings on H. R. 6501*, May 22, 1948, 81st Cong., 1st sess., pp. 7105, 7114.

79. Ibid., 7109–17, 7117–24, 7134–39, 7124–34.

80. Ibid., 7143–48, 7152–77.

81. Ibid., 7121–25.

82. Committee on Interstate and Foreign Commerce, Subcommittee on Transportation, *Development of Improved-Type Aircraft, Hearings on H. R. 8536*, 81st Cong., 2nd sess., July 25, Aug. 7, 17, 1950, pp. 15, 21–22.

83. Ibid., 100–103.

84. Ibid., 6; Rae, *Climb to Greatness*, 205–20. Rae portrays the industry as largely responsible for its own success, despite its heavy dependence upon government orders. He does not mention the hunt for transport or helicopter subsidies.

85. 1961 Appropriations *Hearings*, 1545–53.

86. Leonard Bridgman, comp. and ed., *Jane's All the World's Aircraft, 1959–1960* (London: Sampson Low, Marston, 1960), 278–81.

87. James H. Turner, "San Francisco—International Air Center," *California Magazine of the Pacific* 35:12: 16–17. Turner was Manager of Utilities for the City and County of San Francisco and a member of the Regional Service Commission. Remarks of Rep. Jennings Randolph on airport aid, Oct. 16, 1945, 79th Cong., 1st sess., *Congressional Record* 97:7: 9710; Committee on Armed Services, Subcommittee No. 5—Air Materiel, *To Provide for the Development of Civil Transport Aircraft Adaptable for Auxiliary Military Service*, 7124.

88. Roscoe C. Martin, *The Cities and the Federal System* (NY: Atherton Press, 1965), 81.

89. The term "transportation revolution" is George R. Taylor's, taken from his book of that name. Although both the automobile and the airplane stimulated transportation revolutions of their own, the term has not caught on to describe latter-day events. 79th Cong., 1st sess., History of Bills and Resolutions," *Congressional Record* 91:14: Index, pp. 751, 896; for Hinshaw's role, see "Debate on Federal Airport Aid," Oct. 16 and 17, 1945, 79th Cong., 1st sess., *Congressional Record* 97:7:9700–9718, 9728–54; and Committee on Interstate and Foreign Commerce, *Federal Aid for Public Airports, Hearings on H. R. 3170*, 79th Cong., 1st sess., May 15–16, 22–25, 29–31, and June 1 and 5, 1945, pp. 9–17 passim, 185, 405.

90. The debates, Oct. 16–18, 1945, can be read in *Congressional Record* 97:7:9700–9718, 9728–54, 9792–9808, and ibid., 91:3:4111–20.

91. Ibid., 9708.

92. Fletcher Bowron to L.A. City Council, April 11, 1945; Special Subcommittee, Bay Area Aviation Committee, "Report of the Special Subcommittee," June 7, 1945, p. 2, IGS Library, Univ. of California at Berkeley; Citizens Postwar Planning Committee, "Report to Mayor Roger D. Lapham," Aug. 20, 1945, p. 23.

93. For San Francisco's rivalry with Oakland see Robert W. Cherny and William Issel, *San Francisco: Presidio, Port and Pacific Metropolis* (San Francisco: Boyd and Fraser, 1981), 1–107; Turner, "San Francisco . . . ," 16–17.

94. Ibid.; Special Subcommittee, Bay Area Aviation Committee, "Report . . . ," 3; Mayor, "Annual Message to the Board of Supervisors," Jan. 14, 1946, in SF Bd. of S., *Proceedings,* vol. 41, no. 2, p. 90.

95. R. E. Swanson, "Los Angeles International Airport," 1–11; "Need for Airport Bonds Stressed," *SC Business* 15:16: 1–2.

96. *Lindbergh Field: City of San Diego Municipal Airport* (San Diego, 1947), 5–21; San Diego City Manager, *Annual Report, 1948–49,* p. 41; San Diego Harbor Department, *Port of San Diego: Harbor and Industrial Data* (1948), 5–56.

97. Citizens Postwar Planning Committee, "Report . . . ," 22–27; Bowron to the L.A. City Council, April 11, 1945.

98. Martin, *Cities and the Federal System,* 104–5; Committee on Commerce, Subcommittee on Aviation, Federal Aid for Public Airports, *Hearings before a Subcommittee of the Committee on Commerce,* Senate Bill #34, 79th Cong., 1st sess., March 13–14, 16, 20–21, and 23, 1945, pp. 128–29, 159.

99. Lawrence Kinnard, *History of the Greater San Francisco Bay Region,* (NY: Lewis Historical Publishing, 1966), vol. 2, pp. 452–57; Mayor, Annual Report to the Board of Supervisors," Jan. 14, 1946, in SF Bd. of S., *Journal of the Proceedings,* 41:1: 43; "S. F. Airport in Big Business Bracket," *Downtowner,* Nov. 12, 1947, p. 2.

100. Kinnard, *San Francisco Bay,* vol. 2, p. 456; remarks of Rep. George P. Miller on Transocean Air Lines economic difficulties, July 2, 1954, *Congressional Record* 100:7:9681–82.

101. Swanson, "Los Angeles International Airport," 10–11.

102. "Clover Field," *Aviation Progress* 15:12 (June 1945): 3.

103. Unsigned editorial, "Reducing Airport Hazards," *Long Beach Press-Telegram,* Jan. 29, 1954; "Secretary Talbott's Long-Distance Advice," ibid., Feb. 1, 1953; extension of the remarks of Rep. Craig Hosmer (Long Beach) on Air Force disasters at Long Beach Municipal Airport, Feb. 22, 1954, 83rd Cong., 2nd sess., *Congressional Record* 100:2:2092. Residents must have felt that they lived in a battle zone. Hosmer documented crashes at Wardlow and Olive, 67th and Lime, 223rd and Santa Fe, Brayton Avenue, Lakewood Boulevard, and 19th and Raymond, not to mention others closer to the air field.

104. William J. Fox to John Anson Ford, Oct. 14, 1952, Ford Collection, Huntington Library.

105. Richard F. Pourade, *City of the Dream,* vol. 7 of *The History of San Diego* (La Jolla: Copley Press, 1977), 159–63.

106. Philip R. Pryde, ed., *San Diego: An Introduction to the Region* (Dubuque, Iowa, 1976), 162–66; Pourade, *City of the Dream,* 163.

107. U.S. Congress, Senate, Committee on Commerce, Subcommittee on Aviation, Federal Aid for Public Airports . . . , 180–90, 129, 311.

108. Statement of Clarence M. Belinn, President of Los Angeles Airways, Inc., before the Aviation Subcommittee of the Senate Commerce Committee, March 8–9, 1965, pp. 1–15 and Los Angeles Airways, Inc., "Helicopters and the National Transportation Picture," pp. 1–9, both in Bowron Papers.

109. Belinn, "Statement," 3; John B. Rae, *The Road and Car in American Life* (Cambridge, Mass.: MIT Press, 1971), 319.

110. Belinn, "Statement," 2, 8–9.

111. *Air Transport World,* March 1965, p. 56; *American Aviation,* March 1965, p. 48; Rae, *Climb to Greatness,* 163, 200–203; Belinn, "Statement," 3, 11.

112. City of San Diego, Office of the Mayor, City Planning Department, "The Responsibility of the Federal Government in the Transition from War to Peace," 1.

113. Committee on Education and Labor, Special Investigating Committee, *Federal Assistance for Educating Children in Localities Affected by Federal Activities, Hearings on H. R. 4115,* 81st Cong., 1st sess., Oct. 10–17, 1949, p. 1079.

Chapter 8. "Born in Sin": Nuclear Power for Imperial Cities

1. Peter Pringle and James Spiegelman, *The Nuclear Barons* (NY: Holt, Rinehart and Winston, 1981), 422–44.

2. Various members of Congress speaking on amending the Atomic Energy Act of 1946 as amended, H. R. 630, 83rd Cong., 2nd sess., July 22, 23, 27, and 28, 1954, and Aug. 13, 16, and 17, 1954, *Congressional Record* vol. 100, part 9, 11483–87, 11655–11753, 12241–44, 14338–64, 14583–14606.

3. Pringle and Spiegelman, *The Nuclear Barons;* Bertrand Goldschmidt, *The Atomic Complex: A Worldwide Political History of Nuclear Energy* (La Grange Park, Ill.: American Nuclear Society, 1982); Herbert York, *Race to Oblivion: A Participant's View of the Arms Race* (NY: Simon and Schuster, 1970); Frank G. Dawson, *Nuclear Power: Development and Management of a Technology* (Seattle: Univ. of Washington Press); Gerard H. Clarfield and William M. Wiecek, *Nuclear America: Military and Civilian Nuclear Power in the United States, 1940–1980* (NY: Harper and Row); Richard G. Hewlett and Oscar E. Anderson, Jr., *The New World, 1939/1946: A History of the United States Atomic Energy Commission,* vol. I (University Park: Pennsylvania State Univ. Press 1962); Richard G. Hewlett and Francis Duncan, *Atomic Shield, 1947/1952: A History of the United States Atomic Energy Commission,* vol. II (University Park: Pennsylvania State Univ. Press, 1969).

4. Map in the author's possession.

5. Clarfield and Wiecek, *Nuclear America,* 191–93.

6. U.S. Nuclear Regulatory Commission, *Licensed Operating Reactors* (Washington, D.C.: U.S. Govt. Printing Office, 1990), sec. 1, pp. 2–9; sec. 2, pp. 1–497; sec. 3, pp. 1–9.

7. Harold Platt, *The Electric City* (Chicago: Univ. of Chicago Press, 1991).

8. Joint Committee on Atomic Energy, *Accelerating Civilian Reactor Program, Hearings Before the Joint Committee on Atomic Energy on S. 2725 and H. R. 10805,* 84th Cong., 2nd sess., 1956, pp. 71, 81. Rep. Chet Holifield on "Authorizing Appropriations for the Atomic Energy Commission," 9 Aug. 1957, H. R. 8996, 85th Cong., 1st sess., *Congressional Record* 103:11:14256; *Accelerating the Civilian Reactor Program,* 81; Rep. Holifield on civilian nuclear power, 27 July 1956, 84th Cong., 2d sess., *Congressional Record* 102:11:15175–76; Joint Committee on Atomic Energy, *An Act To Amend the Energy Act of 1946: Hearings Before the Joint Committee on Atomic Energy,* on S. 3323 and H. R. 8862, 83d Cong., 2nd sess., 1956, p. 582.

9. Roy Lubove, *Twentieth-Century Pittsburgh;* map of American fuel resources.

10. Rep. Craig Hosmer on the "Use of Atomic Energy for Electric Power," 11 March 1954, 83d Cong., 2nd sess., *Congressional Record* 100:3:3153–58.

11. Joint Committee on Printing, comp., *Congressional Directory,* 84th Cong., 2nd sess. (Washington: U.S. Govt. Printing Office, Jan. 1956), 10.

12. Gerald Nash, *The Twentieth-Century West: The History of an Urban Oasis.*

13. *Congressional Directory,* 1956, p. 15.

14. For an assessment of Hinshaw's career by his congressional colleagues, see Rep. Gordon McDonugh et al. on "The Late Honorable Carl Hinshaw, of California," 9 Jan. 1957, 85th Cong., 1st sess., *Congressional Record* 101:1:415–23.

15. Joint Committee on Atomic Energy, *Naval Reactor Program and Shippingport Pro-*

ject: Hearings Before Subcommittees of the Joint Committee on Atomic Energy on Progress Report on [the] Naval Reactor Program and the Shippingport Project, 85th Cong., 1st sess., 1957, pp. 1–2.

16. Sterling Cole, "The Late Honorable Carl Hinshaw, of California," 421. It is fascinating to contrast the heartfelt, generous, and informative testimony on Hinshaw's career with the meager record of his own remarks in the *Congressional Record* or the many JCAE committee hearings. His colleagues, almost to a man, attested to Hinshaw's influence in the House but Hinshaw seldom spoke, and then usually confined himself to brief remarks, technical questions, clarifications, pithy examples, and requests for yet more information. Perhaps this reticence explains why historians have hardly ever mentioned the man. Holifield's role, by contrast, has drawn more attention. See, for example, Frank Dawson, *Nuclear Power,* and Clarfield and Wiecek, *Nuclear America.*

17. Rep. Chet Holifield on "Will Atomic Energy Serve or Destroy Humanity?," 20 Aug. 1954, 83d Cong., 2nd sess., *Congressional Record* 100:12:15785–87.

18. Rep. Holifield on "Atomic Energy and Private Enterprise," 1 June 1953, 83d Cong., 1st sess., *Congressional Record* 99:5:5858–63. Coal industrial spokesmen were the most important exception to the rule of avoiding vested interests in congressional debates about nuclear power. Rep. James E. Van Zandt of Pennsylvania and the JCAE paid particularly close attention to the impact of nuclear energy on the coal industry. So did other Pennsylvania and coal-state congressmen. Even they, however, did not oppose the research and development phase of the industry, only subsidies to nuclear power that would cut into coal markets at home and abroad.

19. The story of Lawrence's coming to Berkeley and his work there is told in Nuel Pharr Davis, *Lawrence and Oppenheimer* (NY: Simon and Schuster, 1968); Herbert Childs, *An American Genius: The Life of Ernest Orlando Lawrence* (NY: E. P. Dutton, 1968); Daniel J. Kevles, *The Physicists: The History of a Scientific Community in Modern America* (NY: Alfred A. Knopf, 1978); Raymond T. Birge, *History of the Physics Dept.* (Berkeley: Univ. of Cal. Physics Dept., n.d.), vols. 1–4.

20. Joint Committee on Atomic Energy, S. 3323 and H. R. 8862, To Amend the Atomic Energy Act of 1946, *Hearings Before the Joint Committee on Atomic Energy. . . . on S. 3323 and H. R. 8862 to Amend the Atomic Energy Act of 1946,* 83d Cong., 2nd sess., 1954, pp. 772–81.

21. Ibid.

22. Ibid.

23. Ibid.; *Journal of the Assembly of the Legislature of the State of California, 1955* (Sacramento: State of California, 1955), 5801.

24. Rep. Holifield on the question "Are We Ready To Give the Atom to Private Enterprise?" 6 June 1953, 83d Cong., 1st sess., *Congressional Record* 99:5:6367–70.

25. Clarfield and Wiecek, *Nuclear America,* 177–79.

26. Joint Committee on Atomic Energy, S. 3323 and H. R. 8862, To Amend the Atomic Energy Act of 1946, especially the testimony of AEC member Eugene Zuckert, pp. 583–85; Rep. Holifield on "The Atomic Age," 28 May 1953, 83d Cong., 1st sess., *Congressional Record* 99:5:5782; Rep. Holifield on "Atomic Energy Commission Proposals on Atomic Power," 22 June 1953, 83rd Cong., 1st sess., *Congressional Record* 99:5:7029–31. For a more optimistic prediction from a Los Angeles-area congressman, see Rep. Craig Hosmer on "The Use of Atomic Energy for Electric Power," 11 March 1954, 83d Cong., 2nd sess., *Congressional Record* 100:3:3153. "The day is close when commercial electric power will be generated at power plants using nuclear fuels," Hosmer claimed.

27. JCAE, *Accelerating the Civilian Reactor Program,* 100–101.

28. Ibid.

29. Sen. Henry Jackson and Rep. Melvin Price to Carl Durham, JCAE, *The Naval Reactor Program and the Shippingport Project;* Sen. Henry Jackson, Chairman, Military Applications Subcommittee, and Melvin Price, Chairman, Subcommittee on Research and Development, JCAE, to Representative Carl Durham, Chairman, JCAE, in JCAE, *The Naval Reactor Program and the Shippingport Project* (U.S. Govt. Printing Office, 1957), iii–v.

30. Peter Pringle and James Spigelman, *The Nuclear Barons* (NY: Holt, Rinehart, and Winston, 1981), 107–264; Bertrand Goldschmidt, *The Atomic Complex: A Worldwide Political History of Nuclear Energy* (LaGrange, Ill.: American Nuclear Society, 1982), 67–156, 253–312; Gerard H. Clarfield and William M. Wiecek, *Nuclear America: Military and Civilian Nuclear Power in the United States, 1940–1980* (NY: Harper and Row, 1984), 177–229. The latter book notes some of the political pressures, but not their urban origins.

31. Rep. Carl Albert speaking on "The Honorable Chet Holifield's Distinguished Public Service Record," March 7, 1972, 92nd Cong., 2nd sess., *Congressional Record,* 118:6:7428–29.

32. An excellent technical review of nuclear power is Bertrand Goldschmidt's *The Atomic Complex: A Worldwide Political History of Nuclear Energy.* Despite its subtitle, the book is written from the perspective of policy and contains very little actual politics. Goldschmidt writes as an insider to the French program and therefore provides extraordinary insight from that perspective, but is blissfully unaware of the very real constituency pressures that beset the American program.

33. Chet Holifield appears in some of the secondary literature, but Carl Hinshaw does only rarely. Clarfield and Wiecek, *Nuclear America,* give Holifield his due; as does Dawson, *Nuclear Power,* but most of the literature does not. See Daniel Ford, *The Cult of the Atom: The Secret Papers of the Atomic Energy Commission* (NY: Simon and Schuster, 1982); Stephen Hilgartner, Richard C. Bell, and Rory O'Connor, *Nukespeak: Nuclear Language, Visions, and Mindset* (San Francisco: Sierra Club Books, 1982); York, *Race to Oblivion;* Irvin C. Bupp and Jean-Claude Berian, *Light Water: How the Nuclear Dream Dissolved* (NY: Basic Books, 1978).

34. Rep. Holifield on a "Review of the Atomic Energy Program and the Latest Authorization Bill" (H. R. 8996), 5 August 1957, 85th Cong., 1st sess., *Congressional Record* 103:10:13685–88.

35. Rep. Holifield on "The Civilian Power Acceleration Program," 24 July 1956, 84th Cong., 2nd sess., *Congressional Record* 102:10:14276; and ibid.

36. Rep. Holifield on "Captain Hyman G. Rickover," 12 Feb. 1953, 83d Cong., 1st sess., *Congressional Record* 99:1:1029; for a critical assessment of Rickover see Patrick Tyler, *Running Critical: The Silent War, Rickover, and General Dynamics* (NY: Harper and Row, 1986), 75–163ff.

37. Holifield, "Are We Ready To Give the Atom to Private Enterprise?," 6337–70; and "Atomic Energy and Private Enterprise," 5858–63. Much of the debate that arose from the introduction of the nuclear power issue into the Congress can be followed in Joint Committee on Atomic Energy, *Atomic Power Development and Private Enterprise, Hearings Before the Joint Committee on Atomic Energy, . . . on Atomic Power Development and Private Enterprise,* 83d Cong., 1st sess. Most of the arguments that appeared in the 1954 congressional debates over this subject came up first in this hearing or the preceding hearings and debates in 1953.

38. Holifield, "Are We Ready To Give the Atom to Private Enterprise?," 6367–70.

39. For the story of the nuclear "aircraft," see York, *Race to Oblivion,* 60–74; Clarfield and Wiecek, *Nuclear America,* 172–74; Pringle and Spigelman, *Nuclear Barons,* 218–19.

40. *Atomic Power Development and Private Enterprise.* See especially the testimony of John Foster Dulles, 683–87, and that of Rep. Carl Durham, 502.

41. Ibid., 80–81.

42. Rep. Holifield on "Atomic Energy," 5 May 1953, 83d Cong., 1st sess., *Congressional Record* 99:4:5741.

43. Rep. Carl Durham on authorizing appropriations for the Atomic Energy Commission, H. R. 8996, 8 Aug. 1957, 85th Cong., 1st sess., *Congressional Record* 103:10:14162.

44. *Accelerating the Civilian Reactor Program,* 56–57; Joint Committee on Atomic Energy, *Development, Growth, and State of the Atomic Energy Industry, Hearings Before the Joint Committee on Atomic Energy . . . ,* 84th Cong., 1st sess., 1955, p. 341.

45. Various House and Senate members on amending the Atomic Energy Act of 1946, as amended, H. R. 9757, 22 July 1954, 83d Cong., 1st sess., *Congressional Record* 100: 9:11483–87, 11655–11753, 12241–44, 14338–64, 14583–14606, passim.

46. Ibid.

47. Ibid., 11483–86, 11662–67, 11673–74 11686–90, 11694–11717.

48. Ibid.

49. Ibid.

50. *Accelerating the Civilian Reactor Program,* 56–57.

51. S. 3323 and H. R. 8862, to Amend the Atomic Energy Act of 1946, pp. 911–12.

52. Rep. Howard Smith on civilian atomic power acceleration program, H. R. 12061, 24 July 1956, 84th Cong., 2nd sess., *Congressional Record* 102:10:14246.

53. Ibid., 14246–88 passim.

54. Ibid., 14255–57.

55. Ibid., 14257.

56. Ibid., 14246–88 passim, 15285.

57. Ibid., 14288.

58. The various aspects of the insurance question are covered in Joint Committee on Atomic Energy, *Governmental Indemnity, Hearings Before the Joint Committee on Atomic Energy. . . . On Governmental Indemnity for Private Licensees and AEC Contractors Against Reactor Hazards,* 84th Cong., 2nd sess., 1956. See, for example, the testimony of Willis Gale, Chairman, Commonwealth Edison Co., of Chicago, pp. 185–92.

59. Ibid., 333; Rep. Holifield on "An Act To Amend the Atomic Energy Act of 1954," H. R. 7383, July 1957, 85th Cong., 1st sess., *Congressional Record* 103:8:10714–20, 10722–25.

60. Clarfield and Wiecek, *Nuclear America,* 196; "An Act To Amend the Atomic Energy Act of 1954," 10714–20, 10722–25.

61. Ibid.; for the Laguna Beach story see John G. Fuller, *We Almost Lost Detroit* (NY: Reader's Digest Press, 1975), especially 196–245, which describe the actual meltdown. This reactor was almost diabolically sited to maximize the tragedy of a meltdown in an urban area.

62. "An Act To Amend the Atomic Energy Act of 1954." Commissioner Vance's testimony on the Price-Anderson Act appears in *Governmental Indemnity,* 317–24; one AEC "estimate" on property loss which was floating around the upper echelons of the Berkeley atomic empire ranged from ten million to ten billion. See Berkeley, Donner Laboratory memo from Hardin B. Jones to E. O. Lawrence, Jan. 12, 1957, and attached letters and summary of AEC findings.

63. "An Act To Amend the Atomic Energy Act of 1954," 10714–20, 10722–25.

64. Ibid.

65. Ibid.

66. Ibid., 10715, 10718, 10725; Senate, 8 Aug. 1957, 85th Cong., 1st sess., *Congressional Record* 103:11:15057–59.

67. I am indebted to Leonard J. Duhl for the phrase "the Urban condition." See his *The Urban Condition: People and Policy in the Metropolis* (NY: Simon and Schuster, 1963). For

the classic argument that Americans traditionally disliked their cities see Morton and Lucia White, *The Intellectual Versus the City* (NY: New American Library of World Literature, 1964); Peter J. Schmitt, *Back to Nature: The Arcadian Myth in Urban America* (NY: Oxford Univ. Press, 1969); Paul Boyer, *Urban Masses and Moral Order in America, 1820–1920* (Cambridge: Harvard Univ. Press, 1978). For a contrasting view see Thomas Bender, *Toward an Urban Vision: Ideas and Institutions in Nineteenth-Century America* (Baltimore: Johns Hopkins Univ. Press, 1975).

68. Joint Committee on Atomic Energy, *Naval Reactor Program and Polaris Missile System: Hearing Before the Joint Committee on Atomic Energy,* 86th Cong., 2nd sess., April 9, 1960, pp. v–vi, 1–34.

69. "Atomic Energy and Private Enterprise," 5858.

70. For the dangers of various kinds of reactors, see Fuller, *We Almost Lost Detroit,* 14–18, 88–95, 196–245; on other dangers, see Pringle and Spiegelman, *The Nuclear Barons,* 179–97, 231–37.

71. Various representatives on "Authorizing Appropriations for the Atomic Energy Commission," H. R. 8996, 9 Aug. 1957, 85th Cong., 1st sess., *Congressional Record* 103:11:14247–62 passim, 14250, 14252–53, 14256–57.

72. Ibid., 14252.

73. Ibid., 14256.

74. Ibid., 14247–62.

75. Ibid., 14252.

76. Rep. Holifield on "Will Atomic Energy Serve or Destroy Humanity?," 20 Aug. 1954, 83d Cong., 2nd sess., *Congressional Record* 100:12:15785–87.

77. Holifield, "Will Atomic Energy Serve or Destroy Humanity?," 15785–87.

78. Ibid.

79. *San Diego Union,* May 18, 1955; Rep. Craig Hosmer on "The Modern United States Navy," 29 July 1957, 85th Cong., 1st sess., *Congressional Record* 103:10:12945–47; Rep. Craig Hosmer on "Nuclear Navy Paces United States Atomic Industry," 22 July 1957, 85th Cong., 1st sess., *Congressional Record* 103:9:12384–88; Rep. Charles Gubser on "Scientific and Technical Personnel," 31 Jan. 1956, 84th Cong., 2nd sess., *Congressional Record* 102: A1345–46.

80. York, *Race to Oblivion,* 60–74; *The Naval Reactor Program and the Shippingport Project,* 7, 13; *Accelerating the Civilian Reactor Program,* 178–82.

81. *Atomic Power Development and Private Enterprise,* 324–36.

82. Ibid.; *Accelerating the Civilian Reactor Program,* 53–57, 178–82.

83. George White, General Manager, Atomic Power Equipment Department, General Electric Company, "Remarks at the Dedication of the Vallecitos Atomic Power Plant," 1–2; Lewis L. Strauss, Chairman, AEC, ibid., 1–8; Norman R. Sutherland, President and General Manager, PG&E, ibid., pp. 1–2; J. P. Yates, Executive Vice President, Bechtel Corporation, ibid., pp. 1–3; Goodwin J. Knight, ibid., 1–3; Cramer W. LaPierre, ibid. 1–3, all dated Nov. 25, 1957; General Electric Company and Pacific Gas and Electric, "The General Electric Development Boiling Water Power Reactor," Nov. 25, 1957; and General Electric Company, "Atomic Power Equipment Department," 1–5, E. O. Lawrence Papers, Bancroft Library.

84. Pacific Gas and Electric and General Electric Atomic Power Equipment Department, "List of Major Subcontractors of the Vallectios Atomic Power Plant," 1–2, Lawrence Papers.

85. University of California Lawrence Radiation Laboratory, Livermore, "Press Release," Aug. 24, 1962, pp. 1–5, E. O. Lawrence Papers.

86. N. E. Bradbury to T. H. Johnson, Director, Division of Research, U.S. Atomic Energy Commission, Nov. 21, 1955; H. F. York and N. E. Bradbury to W. Kenneth Davis,

Director, Division of Reactor Development, AEC, Aug. 14, 1956; Alvin M. Windberg, "Some Problems in the Development of the National Laboratories," 1–3; Lewis Strauss to E. O. Lawrence, Aug. 7, 1957, Lawrence Papers.

87. Sen. Dana Bible on "Atomic Testing and Atomic Power for the State of Nevada," 16 Aug. 1957, 85th Cong., 1st sess., *Congressional Record* 103:11:15056–57.

88. California Senate, *Journal of the Senate, 1958,* pp. 144–46.

89. Ibid.; *Mineral County Independent,* Aug. 7, 1957. The Nevada struggle for a piece of the atomic pie started as early as 1953, when Sen. George W. Malone, Gov. Charles H. Russell, and the Atomic Power Utilization Committee of Reno launched a campaign both with the AEC and the JCAE to secure the first large civilian pilot reactor. They made the argument, later repeated in 1957, that Nevada deserved a share of the peaceful uses of the atom if it were to serve as the testing ground for the more warlike ones. Sen. Malone even resurrected the by now hoary western cry of industrial decentralization. Since "most of your atomic-energy brains right at the moment, . . . are within submarine shooting distance of either coast," argued the senator, "like your Cal-Tech, your University of California, your Massachusetts Tech [*sic*]; and it will become an item in case we really have any trouble with anyone, and we are talking about it all the time." *Atomic Power Development and Private Enterprise,* 441–57.

90. Ibid.

91. York, *Race to Oblivion.* The point of overkill runs throughout this fascinating personal account, but see especially pp. 27–46 and 228–39; James R. Killian, Jr., vigorously echoes York and Kistiakowsky on this point of excessive defense spending. See James R. Killian, Jr., *Sputnik, Scientists, and Eisenhower: A Memoir of the First Special Assistant to the President for Science and Technology,* 237–39.

Chapter 9. San Diego and the Continued Quest for Military Riches

1. E. Robert Anderson to Bob C. Wilson, May 18, 1959, Robert Wilson Collection, Box 3, Archives Department, San Diego State University. (All Wilson material in Wilson Collection unless specified otherwise.)

2. Robert Mitchell to Wilson, March 16, 1961; Harve R. Dunlap to Wilson, March 18, 1961, Box 33.

3. Mrs. Duane W. Anderson to Wilson, March 21, 1961; Mrs. Paul W. Bergstedt to Wilson, March 18, 1961, Box 33.

4. Mrs. Rose Bauer to Wilson, March 17, 1961; Carl D. Bauer to Wilson, March 17, 1961; William Nugent to Wilson, March 17, 1961; Mrs. Joanne Thompson to Wilson, March 22, 1961; Mrs. Helen Krumweide to Wilson, March 22, 1961, Box 33.

5. Wilson to Ray Pekrul, Recording Secretary, International Association of Machinists, San Diego, Jan. 23, 1961, Box 56. "Convair Pays $936 Million to Suppliers," *San Diego Evening Tribune,* March 15, 1961, sect. b, p. 5.

6. J. H. Doolittle to Wilson, Aug. 13, 1953; "To [the] 50th Anniversary Chairmen: Some of the 50th Anniversary Events and Activities Planned During the Remaining Quarter of the Year . . . ," Oct. 1, 1953, Box 12.

7. George May, San Diego Junior Chamber of Commerce, to Wilson, Aug. 13, 1953; Ray Booth, SD Jr. Chamber of Commerce, to Wilson, Dec. 4, 1953; Wilson to Ray Booth, Dec. 11, 1953; Wilson to Paul W. White, Executive Editor Station KFMB, San Diego, Dec. 17, 1953, Box 12.

8. Commander R. H. Mereness, Assistant for Information, Twelfth Naval District to Rear Adm. W. M. Eller, Director of Naval History, Navy Dept., Washington, D. C., Sept. 14, 1959, Box 43.

9. Marty Kingsbury to Bob Wilson, Nov. 30, 1957; James W. Smith to Wilson, Dec. 19, 1958; John H. Raifsnider to Wilson, Sept. 24, 1960, Box 33; Forrest Lockard, "Air Officer Views Gyrotor System," *San Diego Tribune,* Dec. 22, 1960; American Tunaboat Association to Wilson, May 11, 1961; Wilson to Capt. Diego Xavier, May 22, 1962; American Legion "Memorandum to All Member of the United States Senate and House of Representatives," March 12, 1959; William Bollen to Wilson, June 20, 1961; H. Jack Hardy to the Bureau of Supplies and Accounts, Material Redistribution Division, Washington, D.C., Feb. 3, 1955; Wilson to Adm. C. S. Cooper, Bureau of Aeronautics, Washington, D.C., May 17, 1957; Rev. W. L. Truman to Bob Wilson, Nov. 5, 1957; Wilson to Jim Snapp, Jr., March 12, 1959; Wilson to Charles Finucane, Assistant Secretary of Defense, March 2, 1959; Mrs. Martha Kirchmann to Wilson, Aug. 12, 1957; Dr. Ralph Schrock to Wilson, Feb. 2, 1960, Box 33.

10. Mrs. A. H. Keith to Wilson, June 17, 1959; Allan C. McAllister to Wilson, Sept. 14, 1960; William B. Macomber, Asst. Secy. of Defense to Wilson, Nov. 10, 1960; Dr. James W. Turpin to Wilson, July 31, 1961, Milton W. Nodacker to Wilson, June 25, 1962, Box 33.

11. Davis, *The United States Navy . . . at San Diego,* 32, 37–38, 47, 57, 60–61.

12. Wilson to Robert J. McPherson, Past President, San Diego Industrial Development Council, Inc., April 16, 1958, Box 33.

13. G. C. Erickson, President, San Diego Council of the Navy League of the United States to Wilson, March 13, 1959, Box 33; Lester Bell, "Nuclear Sub Base Proposed for S. D.," *San Diego Union,* March 8, 1959, sect. a, p. 28; "A-Sub Pier Called 'Must' for City," *San Diego Tribune,* May 20, 1959, sect. a, p. 3.

14. Editorial, "Submarine Pier Vital: Keep Pace with Atomic Navy," *San Diego Union,* July 15, 1959, sect. b, p. 2; editorial, "We Need the Pier," *San Diego Independent,* Sept. 1, 1959, p. 4.

15. Bob Wilson, "Statement of Congressman Bob Wilson: The Need for Nuclear Submarine Pier at San Diego, California," before House Armed Services Committee, May 31, 1960, Box 33.

16. "Submarine Pier Vital"; Oliver King, "NI 'A-Sub' Berth Out," *San Diego Independent,* April 10, 1960, sect. a, p. 1; "Flotilla Commodore Rejects 'Choice' Idea," ibid., March 3, 1960, sec. a, p. 1; "Kuchel's Support Asked on Sub Pier," *San Diego Union,* May 20, 1960, sect. a, p. 24; "Navy Bares Plan for Sub Piers Here," *San Diego Tribune,* Feb. 11, 1959.

17. Wilson to Rear Adm. E. W. Grenfell, Assistant Chief of Naval Operations, July 5, 1960, Box 33; "We Need the Piers!," *San Diego Independent,* Sept. 1, 1959, p. 4.

18. Robert J. McPherson to Wilson, March 17, 1960, Box 33; "Submarine Pier Vital"; Edward G. Martin, "S. D. A-Sub Pier Project Postponed," *SD Union,* April 4, 1963.

19. Anthony Martinolich to Wilson, June 23, 1953; C. Arnholt Smith, President, National Steel and Shipbuilding, to Wilson, July 9, 1953; Charles S. Thomas, Secretary of the Navy, to Wilson, July 8, 1955, Box 24. "Shipbuilding Firm Has Record Backlog, Plan To Hire 1,500," *SD Business* 26:4 (April 1958): 3; Roger D. Fuller, Hydrodynamics Group Engineer, Convair, to Wilson, May 19, 1959, Box 56.

20. Edwin M. Hood, President, Shipbuilders Council of America, "The Case for the Private Shipyards," remarks before the Western Shipbuilding Association, Sept. 1961, pp. 2–4, Box 26.

21. Port of San Diego, Resolution No. 8183, New Series, attached to letter of John Bate, Director of the Port of San Diego, to Wilson, June 7, 1960; Wm. F. Hood, Executive Secretary, Local No. 9, Industrial Union of Marine and Shipbuilding Workers of America, to Wilson, April 8, 1960, Box 59.

22. Rear Adm. Ray Tarbuck, USN, ret., "Analysis of the Transfer of Naval Vessels from San Diego," July 1952, pp. 1–9, Box 57.

23. Wilson to John Bate, Director of the Port of San Diego, May 9, 1953; C. T. Leigh, President of the San Diego Chamber of Commerce, to Wilson, Nov. 2, 1953, Box 57.

24. "Many Benefits to San Diego Seen in Navy Harbor Dredging Project," *SD Business* 28:18 (Sept. 1960): 8; "Chamber Metropolitan Planning Committee Reactivated," ibid. 21:3 (March 1953): 4; Richard F. Pourade, *The History of San Diego,* vol. 7, *City of the Dream* (La Jolla; Copley Press, 1977), 200–201; Walter P. Davis to Bob Wilson, May 24, 1955; Wilson to Davis, June 10, 1955; Vice Adm. R. F. Good to Rear Adm. Chester C. Hartman, Commandant, Eleventh Naval District, Feb. 6, 1956, Box 57.

25. "Tremendous Investment in San Diego by Navy Emphasized in Tarbuck Report," *SD Business* 26:7 (July 1958): 1–2. The San Diego Chamber of Commerce commissioned this latest Tarbuck Report, in which the admiral explained the city's good fortune with the Navy on the basis of its climate and operating conditions and "an overall receptiveness to the Navy and Marine Corps." He also reiterated the need for continued development of civil-military planning to ensure the Navy's future in the city. "Navy Increasing Investment in San Diego," *SD Business* 26:10 (Oct. 1958): 1–2; Rear Adm. M. E. Arnold, Commandant of the Eleventh Naval District, to Wilson, March 21, 1962; U. S. Dept. of Commerce, Bureau of the Census, *Statistical Abstract of the United States: 1964* (Washington: U.S. Govt. Printing Office, 1964), 14–15; U.S. Dept. of Commerce, Bureau of the Census, *Eighteenth Decennial Census of the United States, Census of Population,* vol. I, *Characteristics of the Population* (Washington: U.S. Govt. Printing Office, 1961), 195–99.

26. Adm. Arleigh Burke to Wilson, Aug. 20, 1959, and attached draft of a Wilson speech to the House of Representatives entitled "Marine Combat Strength," no date, Box 17.

27. J. W. Bond, Jr., to Wilson, Feb. 2, 1958; W. H. Patterson to Wilson, Dec. 27, 1957, and attached untitled, undated speech, Box 56.

28. Wilson to Herb Hunzel, Nov. 13, 1958, Box 59; Johnie M. May to Wilson, Nov. 27, 1961, Box 56.

29. Col. Robert H. McCutcheon, USAF, Acting Director for Procurement Policy, Office of the Asst. Secy. of Defense, to Wilson, Dec. 12, 1961, Box 56; "Collins Charges 'Wilson Fiddles While Constituents Burn,'" *Silvergate Union News: International Association of Machinists* 8:4 (Feb. 16, 1962): 1.

30. "Industrial Buildup Seen for San Diego Area," *SD Business* 26:4 (April 1958): 1; "Big Anti-Missile Job Restored to Convair," *San Diego Evening Tribune,* March 28, 1958, sect. 1, p. 1; "In Dynamic San Diego," *SD Business* 4 (1959): 5; Secy. of the Air Force, Memorandum to the California Congressional Delegation, untitled, undated, but probably 1959; Convair Memorandum, "Production Capacity Study: Wizard II," Oct. 1, 1957, Box 56.

31. Wilson to John V. Naish, President, Convair, April 4, 1960, Box 56; Convair, Memorandum, "USAF F-106 All-Weather Interceptor: Status," May 20, 1960, Box 56; W. H. Patterson to Wilson, May 25, 1960; T. G. Pownall to Wilson, May 31, 1960; Wilson to Gerald R. Ford., Jr., June 21, 1960, Box 56; O. [Oliver] M. Gale to Wilson, Memorandum for Congressman Bob Wilson, June 16, 1960; Col. Paul S. Deems, USAF, Memorandum for Mr. Gale, June 16, 1960, Wilson Coll., Box 56. York, *Race to Oblivion:* 49–59; Wilson to Richard Nixon, Memorandum, "Action on Convair F-106 Appropriation," June 29, 1960; Jim Wright to Wilson, Feb 23, 1961; Wilson to Wright, March 1, 1961; Sen. Dennis Chavez to Robert S. McNamara, March 21, 1961, Wilson Coll., Box 56; Wilson to Thomas S. Gates, Jr., Secretary of Defense, Aug. 22, 1960; "AF Studies New Role for F-106," *Aviation Duty,* Feb. 14, 1961, p. 285; Assistant Secy. of Defense to Chavez, March 9, 1961; Wilson to Mrs. C. E. Pennick, San Diego, Sept. 15, 1961; Major Gen. Thomas C. Musgrave, Jr., to Wilson, Jan. 31, 1962; Wilson to Ray Pekrul, Jan 23, 1961, Box 56.

32. Roger W. Lotchin, "The City and the Sword in Metropolitan California, 1919–1941," *Urbanism Past and Present* 7:2 (Summer/Fall 1982): 1–16.

33. "In Dynamic San Diego," *SD Business* 27:2 (Feb. 1959): 5; Convair, "News Release," Jan 4, 1960, pp. 1–2; "House Unit Backs B-52, B-58, Plans Cutback in B-70," *Wall*

Street Journal, May 4, 1961, p. 26; York, *Race to Oblivion,* 75–105; George B. Kistiakowsky, *A Scientist in the White House,* 243–44, 271.

34. J. V. Naish, President, Convair Division of General Dynamics Corporation, "Statement Before the Subcommittee for Special Investigations, Committee on Armed Services, House of Representatives, May 9, 1959," manuscript copy, pp. 1–21, Wilson Coll., Box 56; Kistiakowsky, *A Scientist in the White House;* "In Dynamic San Diego," *SD Business* 26:7 (July 1958): 7.

35. Wilson to Rear Adm. J. S. Russell, Chief of the Bureau of Aeronautics, Dept. of the Navy, May 3, 1956; Rear Adm. C. S. Cooper, Acting Chief of the Bureau of Aeronautics, to Wilson, May 9, 1956; *SD Tribune,* May 22, 1958; Rear Adm. J. P. Monroe, Commander, Pacific Missile Range, Point Mugu, Calif., to Wilson, March 31, 1959, Box 44.

36. Historians have documented the Eisenhower proclivity for a balanced budget and Kistiakowsky's diary makes the point specifically for the B-70 and B-58 bombers, the nuclear carrier, and many other weapons. See, for example, Kistiakowsky, *A Scientist in the White House,* 160–62; Naish, "Statement"; "Martin Girds for Titan Crisis," *Business Week,* Jan. 9, 1960, pp. 69–71.

37. Robert Harman, "New Yorkers in Drive for California Missiles Business," *LA Times,* Feb. 4, 1959; "Work on Titan Will Proceed, Wilson Advised," *SD Union,* Feb. 10, 1959; "N. Y. Moves To Halt 'Trend' of Arms Work to California," *SD Union,* May 8, 1959, sect. a, p. 5; Lester Bell, "Missile Budget Is Sufficient, Pacific Range Chief Says," *SD Union,* Feb. 10, 1959.

38. "Wilson Encouraged on Atom Seaplane," *SD Union,* Dec. 11, 1957; Frank Macomber, "Rep. Wilson Plans Parley on A-Plane," *SD Evening Tribune,* Dec. 9, 1957, sect. a, p. 5; Wilson to Eisenhower, Dec. 1, 1957; Eisenhower to Rep. Melvin Price, March 5, 1958; Eisenhower to Wilson, March 10, 1958, Wilson Coll., Box 33; untitled Convair press releases, July 2, 1958, April 10, 1958, Aug, 31, 1959, Wilson Coll., Box 43; Kistiakowsky, *A Scientist at the White House,* 123, 146, 182, 204; York, *Race to Oblivion,* 160–74. Both York and Kistiakowsky document the enormous political pressure surrounding this project, and, for that matter, most others.

39. W. W. Whittier to Wilson, Feb. 23, 1962; Convair news release, Jan. 4, 1960, Wilson Coll., Box 56.

40. E. O. Arnold, Employees Association, U.S. Navy Ship Repair Facility, to Wilson, Sept. 7, 1956; Rear Adm. A. G. Mumma, Chief of the Bureau of Ships, to Wilson, Sept. 7, 1956; E. O. Arnold to Wilson, Sept. 9, 1956; Joseph A. Breault to Wilson, Sept. 12, 1956; Arthur M. Johns to Wilson, Sept. 15, 1956; A Future Rifee to Wilson, Sept. 18, 1956; Memo from E. O. Arnold to Wilson, Aug. 24, 1956; Frank Macomber, "Navy To Reduce Civilian Staff at Repair Facility," *SF Evening Tribune,* Sept. 15, 1956; Robin Goodenough, Mayor of Coronado, to Wilson, Sept. 10, 1956; Wilson to Goodenough, Oct. 3, 1956; F. H. Watts, President, Southwest Iron and Steel Corporation, to Wilson, Sept. 6, 1956; Wilson to C. A. Brooks, Sept. 28, 1956; Sen. Thomas Kuchel to E. O. Arnold, Feb. 14, 1957, Box 33.

41. Wilson to Robert B. Freeman, March 15, 1962, Box 56; extension of the remarks of Rep. Bob Wilson on service academy pay, July 27, 1953, Cong., 1st sess., *Congressional Record* 99:12:A4924; extension of the remarks of Rep. Bob Wilson on fringe benefits in the armed forces, May 24, 1954, 83rd Cong., 2nds. sess., *Congressional Record* 100:A3789; *San Diego Bulletin,* June 11, 1954; Michael F. Catania, National President Fleet Reserve Association, to Wilson, March 7, 1955, Box 57; R. L. Becht, President, San Diego chapter of the American Institute of Industrial Engineers, to Wilson, May 6, 1958, Box 33; Wilson to W. Kirby Vaughan, President, North Island Association, May 27, 1975; W. Kirby Vaughan to Wilson, May 18, 1957; Wilson to Rear Adm. George A. Holderness, Chief of Industrial Relations, U.S. Navy, May 12, 1955, Box 33; Wilson to Ernest C. Pherson, the Two-Time Vet-

erans Association, Feb. 13, 1958, Box 3; draft copy of "Statement of Congressman Bob Wilson Before the House of Representatives," May 12, 1960, pp. 1–2; Harry L. Wingate, Jr., Chief Clerk, Senate Committee on Armed Services, to Wilson, June 29, 1960, Box 33; extension of the remarks of Rep. Bob Wilson on pay increases for personnel of the Armed Services, March 15, 1954, 83rd Cong., 2nd sess., *Congressional Record* 100:A1954; "Sub Pay Denied Bathyscaph Diver," *SD Union,* May 28, 1960; "Initial Chamber Housing Survey Completed," *SD Business* 20:3 (Sept. 5, 1952): 1, 3; "Critical Shortage Over According to New Report," ibid., 21:7 (Sept. 1953): 1; "Housing Report Indicates Upturn in Single Family Dwellings Here," ibid. 22: 6 (June 1954): 5; "Rental Housing Shortage Seen As Labor Force Here Increases," ibid. 24: 6 (June 1956): 12; "Wilson Gets Conferee Assignment," *SD Union,* Aug. 1, 1958.

42. Richard Pourade, *City of the Dream,* 223; editorial, "San Diego Enters the Era of Science," *SD Union,* Aug. 25, 1956, sect. b, p. 2.

43. Henry Love, "Expanded Scripps Graduate School of Science Approved by Regents"; "Initial Need Is 12 Million, Revelle Says," "New Industrial Horizon Foreseen," "State College Unaffected by Scripps Plan," "San Diego Enters Era of Science," *SD Union,* Aug. 25, 1956, sect. a, pp. 1–2, sect. b, p. 2.

44. "Community Unites To Put Over Idea; 12 Million Expansion Okayed; Civic Leaders Join in Lauding Action," "Revelle Voices Thanks for Aid," "Regent Vote Wins Praise of Hegland; Expansion of Campus Bright News for Area"; editorial, "Community, State and Nation Can Rejoice in U.C. Decision," *SD Eve. Tribune,* Aug. 25, 1956, sect. a., pp. 1–2, 8; "Chamber Applauds U. of C. Action: Science, Technology School at La Jolla Wins Approval," *SD Business* 24:9 (Sept. 1956): 1–2. The city of Coronado also made a bid for the new university, which apparently never received serious consideration. Walter A. Vestal, Mayor of Coronado, to the Board of Regents, University of California, Jan. 25, 1956; T. H. Hugford, Assistant Director, Budget and Fiscal, University of California, to Sheridan Hegland, March 1, 1956; Patrick J. Sullivan, Director of Public Relations, General Dynamics Corporation to R. K. Kelly, University of California, July 18, 1956; untitled General Dynamics press release, July 18, 1956, pp. 1–3; memo from Robert G. Sproul to the Regents Committee on Education Policy [recommending the expansion to San Diego], Sept. 10, 1956, President's Files, University of California Archives, Bancroft Library; "City Moves for A-Lab on Torrey Pines Mesa," *SD Eve. Tribune,* Feb. 10, 1956, p. 1; James W. Archer to Robert Gordon Sproul, President, University of California, Feb. 23, 1956, President's Files, Bancroft Library; "University Campus Plans Get Backing," *SD Business* 26:9 (Sept. 1958): 1–2; editorial, "Community, State and Nation Can Rejoice in U. C. Decision," 8; Pourade, *City of the Dream,* 222–23; Charles C. Dail to Sproul, Sept. 28, 1956, President's Files, CUB; Dr. Malcolm Love, "A Nation's Progress: Science Conquers U.S. Frontiers," *SD Union,* Feb. 19, 1956, sect. c, pp. 1, 3.

45. John Jay Hopkins, "Toward a New Heaven and a New Earth," a proposal for the creation of a World Energy Community Presented at the World Symposium on Applied Solar Energy, Phoenix, Ariz., Nov. 3, 1955, pp. 1–16; "The Truth Shall Make You Free," an address by John Jay Hopkins on Founders' Day at Occidental College, April 21, 1955, pp. 1–14; James W. Archer to Robert G. Sproul, Feb. 23, 1956, President's Files, CUB; "City Moves for A-Lab on Torrey Pines Mesa," 1; "In Dynamic San Diego: General Atomic Dedication, Guided Missile Plant Plans Are July Highlights," *SD Business* 24:8 (Aug. 1956): 8; "In Dynamic San Diego: Record Atomic Reactor Flash Marks Lab Dedication," ibid. 27:7 (July 1959): 3; "Nuclear Lab for San Diego Is Approved," ibid. 24:3 (March 1956): 1.

46. Robert H. Finch to Wilson, March 31, 1958; Wilson to Finch, April 5, 1958, Box 44.

47. LA Chamber of Commerce, "Report to: The California Congressional Delegation," March 14, 1961, pp. 1–7, Wilson Coll., Box 12; Wilson to Ray Pekrul, Jan. 23, 1961, Box 56.

48. Robert H. McCutcheon, Acting Director for Procurement Policy, DOD, to Wilson, Dec. 12, 1961; Thomas G. Corbin to Wilson, Oct. 17, 1962; Perry M. Hoisington II to Wilson, July 13, 1962; Hoisington to Wilson, May 29, 1962; Hoisington to Wilson, Dec. 11, 1961, Box 56.

49. Robert Wilson, "Marine Combat Strength," manuscript version of a speech Wilson delivered to Congress, attached to Arleigh Burke, Chief of Naval Operations, to Wilson, Aug. 20, 1959; Robert Wilson, untitled manuscript version of a speech to the House of Representatives, Aug. 15, 1961, pp. 1–6, Box 17; extension of the remarks of Bob Wilson on defensive problems, Aug. 17, 1961, Cong., 2d sess., *Congressional Record* 107:A6476–77.

Chapter 10. Getting on Target:
Nuclear Weapons, Jet Technology, and the Metropolis

1. John Hekman and Alan Smith, "Behind the Sunbelt's Growth, Industrial Decentralization," *Economic Review* (Federal Reserve Bank of Atlanta) March 1982, pp. 4–13; Carl Abbott, *The New Urban America: Growth and Politics in Sunbelt Cities* (Chapel Hill, 1981), 1–13; Richard M. Bernard and Bradley R. Rice, *Sunbelt Cities: Politics and Growth Since World War II* (Austin, Tex., 1981), 1–30; Clyde E. Browning and Will Gesler, "Sunbelt-Snow Belt: A Case of Sloppy Regionalizing," *Professional Geographer* 31 (Feb. 1979): 66–74; For purposes of this paper, the use of the term Sunbelt indicates the general shift of resources within the United States from the Northeast and Midwest to the South and West. South refers to the states of the Confederacy, and West to that portion of the United States west of the first tier of Trans-Mississippi states.

2. Hekman and Smith, "Behind the Sunbelt's Growth," 4–13; Alfred J. Watkins, "'Good Business Climates': The Second War Between the States," *Dissent,* Fall 1980, pp. 476–85; Edward Ullman, "Amenities As a Factor in Regional Growth," *Geographical Review* 44 (Jan. 1954): 119–32; Horace Sutton, "Sunbelt vs. Frostbelt: A Second Civil War?," *Saturday Review,* April 15, 1978, pp. 28–37; Joel Havemann, Neal R. Pierce, and Rochelle L. Stanfield, "Federal Spending: The North's Loss Is The Sunbelt's Gain," *National Journal,* June 26, 1976, pp. 878–91; Joel Havemann and Rochelle L. Stanfield, "'Neutral' Federal Policies Are Reducing Frostbelt-Sunbelt Spending Imbalances," *National Journal,* Feb. 7, 1981; "A New Milestone in the Shift to the Sunbelt," *Nation's Business* 65:5 (May 1977): 69; Gurney Breckenfeld, "Business Loves the Sunbelt (and Vice Versa)," *Fortune,* June 1977, pp. 132–46; Bob Gottlieb, "The Phoenix Growth Machine," *The Nation,* Dec. 29, 1979, pp. 675–88; "The Second War Between the States," *Business Week,* May 17, 1976, pp. 92–123; "The Sun Belt Today—Still a Land of Opportunity, but . . . ," *Changing Times* 35:9 (Sept. 1981): 25–30.

3. Bernard and Rice, *Sunbelt Cities;* Abbott, *The New Urban America.*

4. Robert A. Hart, *The Great White Fleet: Its Voyage Around the World, 1907–09* (Boston, 1965), 162–78; Roger W. Lotchin, "The City and the Sword: San Francisco and the Rise of the Metropolitan-Military Complex, 1919–1941," *Journal of American History* 65:4 (March 1979): 996–1020; Lotchin, "The Metropolitan-Military Complex in Comparative Perspective: San Francisco, Los Angeles, and San Diego, 1919–1941," *Journal of the West* 18:3 (July 1979): 19–30; and Lotchin, "The City and the Sword in Metropolitan California," *Urbanism Past and Present* 7: 2 (Summer/Fall 1982): 1–16; Fletcher Bowron to Vierling Kersey, May 9, 1945, Bowron Collection, Huntington Library.

5. "Statement of W. C. Mullendore," quoted in extension of the remarks of Rep. John M. Costello, Nov. 22, 1944, 78th Cong., 2nd sess., *Congressional Record,* 90:11:A4503–5; "Address of Sen. Pat McCarran to the California Legislature, June 9, 1944," quoted in extension of the remarks of Sen. Joseph C. O'Mahoney, June 21, 1944, ibid. 90:10:A3213–16.

6. Remarks of Rep. Ralph E. Church on "National Defense and the Aviation Industry," June 27, 1939, 76th Cong., 1st sess., *Congressional Record* 84:7:79991-93.

7. Rae, *Climb to Greatness,* 119-72.

8. Neil P. Hurley, S.J., "The Role of Accelerated Tax Amortization in the National Industrial Dispersion Program," Ph.D. dissertation, Fordham University, 1956, pp. 50-51, is a first-rate study of the dispersal controversy, although it concentrates on tax amortization as a device to effect dispersal rather than on urban competition.

9. Jack Gorrie, "America's Security Resources," quoted in extension of the remarks of Sen. Warren Magnuson, June 16, 1952, 83d Cong., 1st sess., *Congressional Record* 98:10:3733-35.

10. Remarks of Sen. Harry P. Cain on "The Industrial Dispersal Program," Aug. 14, 1951, 82nd Cong., 1st sess., *Congressional Record* 97:4:11043.

11. Ibid.

12. Edward T. Dickinson, Vice Chairman of the National Security Resources Board, to Sen. Thomas H. Kuchel, Feb. 20, 1953, in Modern Military Records Division, Central Files, 1949-1953, Record Group 304, Records of the Office of Civil Defense Mobilization, NA.

13. William J. Platt, "Industrial Defense: A Community Approach," *Bulletin of Atomic Scientists* 9:7 (Sept. 1953): 261-64.

14. National Security Resources Board, Press Release for Friday, June 6, 1952, pp. 1-2, Central Files, 1949-1953, RG 304, NA. According to Neil Hurley, the government exaggerated the degree of dispersal. Hurley, "The Role of Accelerated Tax Amortization," p. 70.

15. Ibid., 75-82.

16. Ibid.

17. Remarks of various representatives on the Rains Amendment to H.R. 3871, July 11, 1951, 82nd Cong., 1st sess., *Congressional Record* 97:6:7978-88.

18. Ibid.; Senate Subcommittee on Armed Services, Subcommittee on Civil Defense, *Hearings on Operations and Policies of the Civil Defense Program,* Feb. 22, 26, March 3, 4, 8, 1955, Part I and Appendix (Washington: U.S. Govt. Printing Office, 1955), 33, 406.

19. Ibid.

20. Harry S Truman, "Statement by the President," Aug. 23, 1951, Processed Documents File, RG 304, NA.

21. Henry Parkman, "Nonmilitary Measures of National Defense," *Bulletin of Atomic Scientists* 9:7 (Sept. 1953): 259-60; Ralph E. Lapp, "Eight Years Later," ibid., 324-36. Much of this issue is devoted to dispersal and related issues of civil defense; *New York Times,* June 7, 1956, p. 12.

22. Claude Witze, "U.S. Will Spur Dispersion of Industry," *Aviation Week* 64:2 (Jan. 9, 1956): 26-27; Anthony Leviero, "U.S. Report Notes Civil Defense Lag," *New York Times,* Jan. 4, 1956, sect. 4, p. 11; *New York Times,* Feb. 2, 1956, p. 4; Hurley, "The Role of Accelerated Tax Amortization," 73, 85.

23. For the Senate debate on decentralization, see account of various senators speaking on H. R. 9852, June 1956, 48th Cong., 2nd sess., *Congressional Record* 102:8:10825-57.

24. Sen. Carl Mundt speaking on H. R. 9852, June 22, 1956, 48th Cong., 2nd sess., *Congressional Record* 102:8:108-54. The debate runs from pp. 10825 to 10857.

25. Various representatives speaking on H.R. 2486, June 28, 1956, 84th Cong., 2nd sess., *Congressional Record* 102:8:11283-94; remarks of various senators on dispersal, June 22, 1956, 84th Cong., 2nd sess., ibid., 102:8:10825-57.

26. Ibid.

27. For the Senate vote see *Congressional Record* 102:8:10855; and for the House vote see ibid., 11293-94.

28. Ann Markusen, Scott Campbell, Sabina Dietrich, and Peter Hall, *The Rise of the Gunbelt* (NY: Oxford Univ. Press, 1991).

29. Ibid.

30. Remarks of Rep. Thomas Lane on the "Textile Industry in New England," March 26, 1953, 84th Cong., 1st sess., *Congressional Record* 98:3:2982–84.

31. Remarks of Sen. Blair Moody and Sen. Burnett Maybank on "Supplementary Unemployment Compensation Benefits to Certain Unemployed Workers," Jan. 23, 1953, 83rd Cong., 2nd sess., *Congressional Record* 98:1:420–25.

32. Markusen et al., *Rise of the Gunbelt.*

33. Remarks of Rep. Thomas Lane on "Textile Unemployment in New England," 83rd Cong., 2nd sess., *Congressional Record* 98:5:5699–6400.

34. "Statement of Seymour Harris, Chairman of the Committee on the New England Textile Industry," in extension of the remarks of Rep. Edith N. Rogers, March 31, 1952, 83rd Cong., 2nd sess., *Congressional Record* 98:9:A2040–43.

35. "Statement of William F. Sullivan, president of the National Association of Cotton Manufacturers," quoted in extension of the remarks of Rep. Edith N. Rogers, March 20, 1952, 83rd cong., 2nd sess., *Congressional Record* 98:9:A2006–9.

36. "Statement of Solomon Barkin, Textile Workers Union of America," quoted in extension of the remarks of Rep. Thomas J. Lane, March 24, 1952, 83rd Cong., 1st sess., *Congressional Record* 98:9:2019–21.

37. Extension of the remarks of Rep. John F. Kennedy on "Conditions in the Textile Industry," April 1, 1952, 82nd Cong., 2nd sess., *Congressional Record:* 98:9:A2080–81.

38. John F. Kennedy, "New England and the South: The Struggle for Industry," *Atlantic Monthly* 193:4 (April 1954): 32–36.

39. Extension of the remarks of Rep. Herbert C. Bonner, on "Application of Defense Manpower Policy No. 4 to the Textile Industry," March 28, 1952, 82nd Cong., 2nd sess., *Congressional Record* 98:9:A1988–89.

40. Extension of the remarks of Rep. Thurmond Chatham on "The Distribution of Government Business," Feb. 11, 1952, 82nd Cong., 2nd sess., *Congressional Record* 98:8:A765.

41. Editorial from the *Raleigh News and Observer,* quoted in extension of the remarks of Rep. Carl T. Durham, March 26, 1952, 82nd Cong., 2nd sess., *Congressional Record* 98:8:A1899.

42. Debate over Defense Manpower Policy No. 4, June 20, 1952, 82nd Cong., 2nd sess., *Congressional Record,* 7720–30.

43. Ibid.

44. Ibid.

45. Remarks of Representative Mendel Rivers on H. R. 5969, July 29, 1953, 83rd Cong., 1st sess., *Congressional Record* 99:8:10345.

46. Remarks of Rep. John Shelley on "Manpower Policy," June 17, 1953, 83rd Cong., 1st sess., *Congressional Record* 99:6:7422–23.

47. Remarks of Rep. John Shelley on Defense Manpower Policy No. 4, June 26, 1953, 83rd Cong., 1st sess., *Congressional Record* 99:6:8180–82.

48. Remarks of Sen. William Knowland on H. R. 5969, July 22, 1953, 83rd Cong., 1st sess., *Congressional Record* 99:7:9504.

49. Remarks of Rep. Carl Perkins on H. R. 5969, July 22, 1953, 83rd Cong., 1st sess., *Congressional Record* 99:7:10342.

50. Hurley, "The Role of Tax Amortization," 64–65.

51. "Plant Dispersal Plan Scored," *New York Times,* March 13, 1958, p. 8, p. 14; "End of Plant Dispersal Asked," *New York Times,* April 4, 1958, p. 36; "Extension of the Defense

Production Act of 1950," Feb., 21, 1958, 85th Cong., 2nd sess., *Congressional Record* 104:2:2526; remarks of Rep. John Dingell on the "Industrial Dispersion Program," 85th Cong., 2nd sess., *Congressional Record* 104:5:6268–70.

52. Thomas J. Kerr, *Civil Defense in the U.S.: Bandaid for a Holocaust,* (Boulder, Colo.: Westview Press, 1983), 20–21, 35–38, 83–99.

53. Leonard Bridgman, comp. and ed., *Jane's All the World's Aircraft, 1956–57* (NY: McGraw-Hill), 313; *Jane's All the World's Aircraft, 1957–58,* 331; *Jane's Aircraft, 1962–63,* 401; Joint Committee on Printing, comp., 84th Cong., 2nd sess., *Official Congressional Directory* (Washington, D.C.: U.S. Govt. Printing Office, 1956), 227, 238.

54. *Jane's Aircraft, 1959–60,* 325; *Jane's Aircraft, 1952–53,* 218; *Jane's Aircraft, 1956–57,* 260; *Jane's Aircraft, 1952–53,* 208; *Jane's Aircraft, 1951–42,* 251c; *Jane's Aircraft, 1952–53,* 208; *Jane's Aircraft, 1957–58;* 315; Rand McNally, *Standard Mileage Guide,* 1987, p. 53; *Jane's All the World's Aircraft, 1956–57,* 297.

55. *Jane's Aircraft, 1961–62,* 244; *Jane's Aircraft, 1952–53,* 191.

56. *Jane's Aircraft, 1962–63,* 249, 406; *Jane's Aircraft, 1961–62,* 515; *Jane's Aircraft, 1959–60,* 152; *Jane's Aircraft, 1961–62,* 298, 488, 515.

57. *Jane's Aircraft, 1987–88,* 413–17, 425, 483–91, 511, 959, 961.

58. Markusen et al., *The Rise of the Gunbelt,* And more would occur in the future; witness the post-1961 moves of Bell Helicopter to Dallas; a Fairchild branch to San Antonio; a Grumman operation to St. Augustine, Fla.; several Sikorsky branches to Fort Rucker, Tallahassee, Alabama, and West Palm Beach, Fla.; a Piper branch to Vero Beach, Fla.; Morton Thiokol installations to Ogden and Brigham City, Utah, Huntsville, Ala., Marshall, Texas, and Shreveport, La.; and a Pratt and Whitney establishment to West Palm Beach.

59. "State's Bloc Asks U.S. Defense Jobs," *New York Times,* May 8, 1959, p. 7; "California Fears Industry Pirates," ibid., May 17, 1959, p. 80.

60. Jeffrey R. Crump, "Spatial and Temporal Patterns of Military Prime Contract Awards in the United States, 1941–1944 and 1951–1985," *Growth and Change,* forthcoming; Markusen et al., 1–34.

61. "House Sets Inquiry on Defense Outlay," *New York Times,* Jan. 16, 1959, p. 31.

62. John D. Morris, "More U.S. Work Sought for State," *New York Times,* Jan. 1, 1959, p. 8; Douglas Dales, "Joint Job Action for State Hailed," ibid., April 19, 1959, p. 60; "California Fears Industry Pirates," ibid., May 17, 1959, p. 80.

63. Ibid., 80.

64. Douglas Dales, "State Sets Drive for U.S. Contracts," *New York Times,* April 18, 1959, p. 1; Morris, "More U.S. Work Sought for State," p. 8; "Javits Finds Contract Drop in State Jobless Areas," *New York Times,* July 6, 1960.

65. "More Work for State"; "House Ends Emergency," *New York Times,* June 25, 1960; "State Contracts Rise: Javits Says Share of U.S. Defense Dollar Is Larger," ibid., Oct. 3, 1960, p. 33.

66. Richard E. Mooney, "Gates Approves Ex-Officers' Jobs," *New York Times,* July 8, 1959, p. 1; "Navy Held Lax on Cost Control," ibid., July 16, 1959, p. 16; "Sparkman Critical over Procurement," ibid., July 28, 1959, p. 15; John W. Finney, "Hearings Assess Atom War Effect," ibid., June 23, 1959, p. 13; C. P. Trussell, "Toll of 50 Million Pictured in an Atom Attack on U.S.," ibid., Aug. 31, 1959, p. 1; "Navy's View," ibid., Sept. 10, 1959, p. 52; "High Jobless Areas To Get Added Help," ibid., June 8, 1960, p. 34; "Aiding Business in Distress," ibid., Aug. 13, 1959, p. 38; "Pentagon Helps Small Business," ibid., Aug. 25, 1960, p. 39; "Sparkman Criticizes Pentagon over Report on Small Business," ibid., Aug. 26, 1960, p. 36; ibid., Nov. 3, 1960, p. 32; Jack Raymond, "President Says 'Munitons Lobby' Stirs His Concern," ibid., June 4, 1959, p. 1.

67. Eric Goldman, *The Crucial Decade and After: American, 1945–60* (NY: Vintage Books, 1960); Robert J. Donovan, *Conflict and Crisis: The Presidency of Harry S. Truman, 1945–1948* (NY: W. W. Norton, 1977); Godfrey Hodgson, *America in Our Time: From World War II to Nixon: What Happened and Why* (NY: Vintage Books, 1976); Norman L. Rosenberg and Emily S. Rosenberg, *In Our Times* (Englewood Cliffs; Prentice Hall, 1982); Paul A. Carter, *Another Part of the Fifties* (NY: Colombia Univ. Press, 1983); Howard Zinn, *Postwar America: 1945–1971* (Indianapolis: Bobbs-Merrill, 1973); James Gilbert, *Another Chance: Postwar America, 1945–1968* (NY: Alfred A. Knopf, 1981); William E. Leuchtenburg, *A Troubled Feast: American Society Since 1945* (Boston: Little, Brown, 1983). Gilbert is one of the few historians of the postwar era who even list the term "Sunbelt" in their indexes, although a few do discuss the military-industrial complex.

Index